KNOW
THE MOST FASCINATING
PEOPLE
OF THE BIBLE IN
30 DAYS

KNOW
THE MOST FASCINATING
PEOPLE
OF THE BIBLE IN
30 DAYS

J. STEPHEN LANG

Guideposts®

New York, New York

Know the Most Fascinating People of the Bible in 30 Days

ISBN-10: 0-8249-4886-6
ISBN-13: 978-0-8249-4886-3

Published by Guideposts
16 East 34th Street
New York, New York 10016
Guideposts.org

Distributed by Ideals Publications, a Guideposts company
2630 Elm Hill Pike, Suite 100
Nashville, TN 37214

Guideposts and *Ideals* are registered trademarks of Guideposts.

Acknowledgments

Every attempt has been made to credit the sources of copyrighted material used in this book. If any such acknowledgment has been inadvertently omitted or miscredited, receipt of such information would be appreciated.

All Scripture quotations are taken from *The Holy Bible, New International Version*. Copyright © 1973, 1978, 1984, 2011 by Biblica, Inc. Used by permission of Zondervan. All rights reserved worldwide. www.zondervan.com

Scripture quotations marked (ESV) are taken from the Holy Bible, English Standard Version, copyright © 2001 by Crossway Bibles, a division of Good News Publishers. Used by permission. All rights reserved.

Scripture quotations marked (KJV) are taken from *The King James Version of the Bible*.

Library of Congress Cataloging-in-Publication Data

Lang, J. Stephen.
  Know the most fascinating people of the Bible in 30 days / J. Stephen Lang.
     p. cm.
  Includes index.
  1. Bible—Biography. I. Title.
  BS571.L28 2011
  220.092'2—dc23

2011018850

Cover and interior design and typesetting by Cindy LaBreacht
Cover art left to right: "David Quits Jerusalem" by James Tissot, courtesy Jewish Museum, New York, NY; "Pilate Washing His Hands" by Matthias Stom, courtesy Musee du Louvre, Paris, France.
Indexing by Frances S. Lennie/Indexing Research

Printed and bound in the United States of America
10 9 8 7 6 5 4 3 2 1

CONTENTS

From Aaron to Zimri

Know the most fascinating people of the Bible in a mere thirty days? Impossible, you say?

Well, we will not make the rash promise that you will be an all-wise Bible scholar within one month. Some people study the Bible their entire lives and, late in life, stumble across things in it that they never noticed before. These people include not only the "pros"—professors, ministers, etc.—but also the many laypeople who immerse themselves in the book day after day, year after year. In a sense, no person ever knows the Bible completely. There is always more to discover, more to stimulate the mind, more words to hang our hearts upon, more to apply to one's life in this world.

But, though you may not be an MB (Master of the Bible) upon finishing this book, you will be familiar with its most intriguing characters—and, through them, the Bible's key themes and its most valuable life lessons. You will know it well enough that when you hear it quoted, and misquoted, and misconstrued in pop culture, you will have a sense of what the Bible *really* says, not what its critics (and sometimes even its friends) say that it says. You will also have a sense of how to apply its teachings to your own life day by day, hour by hour.

Most of all, you will have a sense of the Bible as a living thing, not some dry, dead document from centuries ago. You will know it not as dull ancient history, but as God's manual for life, for all people, in all times, in all situations. It is my hope that you will not find the Bible boring or intimidating, but a supremely riveting book.

I trust you will enjoy this thirty-day journey, on which you will get a closer look at some familiar names—such as Moses, Abraham, David and Paul—and be introduced to some new ones—such as the hero Zerubbabel, and Zimri, the traitor who murdered his king, took his place, reigned seven days, and then committed suicide by burning himself up inside his palace. What an utterly fascinating collection of people—and life lessons—the Bible is!

A Book of Characters—and Character

Pollsters point out an interesting contradiction: many people say they regard the Bible as the inspired word of God, but many of those same people are not familiar with it. Many can't name the four Gospels, the Ten Commandments, where the Sermon on the Mount is found, or other significant information that ought to be well-known to people who sincerely regard the Bible as divinely inspired. But are we really biblically illiterate? If we refer to a Judas or a Jezebel or a doubting Thomas, most people know what we mean. If we are somewhat vague on the Bible, we do at least seem familiar with some of its more colorful characters. This is not surprising: People are interesting, and it's no coincidence that one of the most popular magazines around is named *People*. While readers may be turned off at the thought of studying history or religious doctrine, the study of people intrigues us—in fact, it hardly seems like study at all.

The book you are holding in your hand is based on three assumptions:
1. Colorful people are a pleasure to read about.
2. The Bible is full of colorful, fascinating people.
3. You can best learn the key ideas and life lessons of the Bible by learning about these people.

The people are, of course, a motley crew. Some are admirable role models—for example, Abraham, regarded by both Jews and Christians as a shining example of deep faith in God. Of such people we need reminding. But some are less admirable, such as Abraham's grandson Jacob, who is presented in Genesis as a scheming, manipulative, stay-at-home mama's boy who deceives his blind father and dimwitted brother, and who spoils one of his twelve sons so shamelessly that the other sons sell the spoiled one into slavery. Yet there are admirable things about Jacob, such as his willingness to work hard for seven years in order to marry the woman he loves—although the seven years turn into fourteen when he finds himself hoodwinked by his wily father-in-law, a classic case of a schemer getting a dose of his own medicine. The Jacob saga in Genesis is just one of many stories that prove that the Bible is anything but boring.

One of the most appealing things about the Bible is that it presents people warts and all. Thus one of its most colorful characters, David, is shown as a valiant fighter, a tactful politician, a devoted friend, a gifted poet and musician, a man so intoxicated with God that at times he dances for joy. But David is also a lustful adulterer, a schemer, a liar, a man of violence, a father who seems utterly clueless about how to manage a houseful of unruly children—not to mention numerous wives and concubines. The term *dysfunctional family* could have been coined to describe David's brood. David is one of the great heroes of the Bible, but his life teaches as many lessons about how not to behave as it does about how to behave. This amazing honesty about people is probably one of the best indications we have that the Bible is history, not myth or legend. Saintly people like David and Solomon and Peter are shown doing great things—and also shameless things, things that a work of fiction would not have included. The Gospels record many stories that show Jesus' disciples in a bad light: their quarrels over which of them is most important, their cowardly flight after Jesus' arrest, the denial by chief disciple Peter that he even knew Jesus. If the Bible consisted of merely human documents, those embarrassing items would have been left out. They must have been included because they were true, and because God intended people to know just how human the disciples were. There is breathtaking honesty in the Bible.

As entertaining as these stories are, entertainment is not the reason they were recorded. The aim of the Bible's writers, all those centuries ago, must have been to put in writing what they believed God wanted written down: God's will, revealed in words to humankind. For many centuries, copyists faithfully passed on the words, believing that every new generation needed to be told the old but ever-living stories of God's dealings with the world and how God intended human beings to live rightly with each other. God meant the Bible to be a book not just about "them" and "then," but about "you" and "now." "The Bible is never about someone else," said an old preacher I once knew. "It's always about you—and God." There is no point in reading the stories about Paul, Abraham, Job, Solomon, Samson, Elijah and Peter unless we learn large, durable life lessons and then apply them to ourselves. The stories of these people can teach us how to live—and how *not* to live. Through these characters we can learn about character. The stories can also teach us this very valuable lesson: God accomplishes his purpose through imperfect people, and even though the Bible urges us to strive for perfection, again and again it shows God forgiving people when they fail. It shows people who, like us, were often depressed and distressed, who dealt with frets and dreads, setbacks and calamities, and who found their solace in God. We human beings sometimes hit rock bottom—and so did people in the Bible. Their stories give us light and hope in a world of darkness and despair.

The Bible is an ancient book, yet it differs from most other ancient writings in one important way: people still try to apply it to life today. Homer, Sophocles and Plato may have been inspired in some way, and *The Odyssey* does tell a rousing good story, but almost no one uses those old writings as a road map through life. But people have been doing just that with the Bible for centuries. Homer and Sophocles don't change lives, and neither do Shakespeare and Dante. But the Bible changes lives. Its devoted readers believe that in some hard-to-define way, it says what God wants it to say. They read it and try to apply it to life because they see in it a timeless quality that they don't find in the numerous "experts" spouting advice in books and on TV talk shows. They see its ancient insights as perennially fresh. They study it and consult it because they believe that Jesus and Paul and Moses and Isaiah and Solomon had a clear idea of what God intended for human beings. If those people did not understand what the will of God is, then who does? Put another way, if we can't find God in the Bible, where can we find him? More than any book ever written, the Bible is something we can hang our hearts on. It gives us the comfort of knowing that a living, loving God reveals the way we ought to live, instead of believing we are alone on an indifferent planet, forced to discern the truth for ourselves.

Here is a bold statement: *If you understand the Bible, you understand the world*. It doesn't make you an expert in every subject, just in the ones that truly matter. Even if you do not fully understand science, the Bible lets you know why the world exists, who made it and who sustains it. Even if your grasp of history and politics is shaky, the Bible has timeless insights into the nature of power and the way human beings abuse it. Even if you know little of psychology, the Bible reveals all you need to know about the human mind and heart—and much of what it reveals is in striking contrast to the shallow pop psychology you encounter in the media. A recent US president stated that "the Bible is pretty good about keeping your ego in check." He might have added, "The Bible reveals to us someone bigger and more reliable than our own egos." After hearing all the superficial hype in our pop culture, we encounter in the Bible a divine wellspring of wisdom so deep we can bathe in it.

The Bible also teaches us how to succeed in life—or, to put it another way, to be what we were meant to be. This won't necessarily mean becoming rich, attractive or famous, of course. Success in human terms often involves spiritual and moral failure. There are people who are losers by the world's standards but who are highly successful in the eyes of God. Jesus promised his followers that he came into the world "that they might have life, and that they might have it more abundantly" (John 10:10, KJV). The whole Bible has that same purpose. It shows the way to abundant life—something that makes worldly successes and accomplishments seem small by comparison. Through the Bible's characters we can see that abundant life can be found no matter what our condition.

In *Robinson Crusoe*—one of the world's classic novels—the title character, marooned on an island, has a Bible among his few worldly possessions. In this difficult situation, he records: "I daily read the Word of God and applied all the comforts of it to my present state. One morning, being very sad, I opened the Bible upon these words, 'I will never, never leave thee, nor forsake thee.'"

The book you are now holding is designed to help you do what Robinson Crusoe did: read the Word of God daily and apply it to your life. You probably have more distractions in your life than Crusoe did (and surely more comforts also), but each day for the next thirty days, set aside some time to read one chapter of this book. In doing so, you will read some of the most-studied and most-loved sections of the Bible, encounter its most intriguing characters, discover its most important themes, see where its events fit into history, gain some valuable insights into the culture of biblical times, and learn the take-home value of each day's reading. That last item is most important because, as already stated, the Bible is never about someone else—it is about you, and God, and you and God.

Features to Help You on the Journey

KEY TERMS FOR TODAY

These are important words and phrases that every reader of the Bible ought to know. Obviously these are terms illustrated by the characters in each chapter. When you finish the thirty-day journey, consider your time well spent if you can define all or most of these terms. Later, use these items as a handy way to refresh your memory about what you learned.

MEMORY VERSE

Don't feel pressured to memorize any or all of these, but they provide a helpful way to keep each chapter's lesson tucked away in your mind. Some of these will already be familiar, but we hope that after you finish each chapter, the familiar verses will be richer in meaning for you.

CHARACTERS AT LARGE

The main text in each chapter looks at the people as they are presented in the Bible. The Characters at Large boxes take a look at how some of those characters have been represented—and too often misrepresented—in movies, art, literature and other forms of pop culture. These boxes are not just to entertain you but also to help you separate the biblical truth from the popular distortions.

CHARACTER CLOSE-UPS

These are brief glimpses at some overlooked (and, in some cases, nameless) biblical characters who are worth getting to know.

CULTURAL INSIGHTS

Stories written thousands of years ago present us with a culture gap, and the Cultural Insights boxes help to bridge that gap, providing some historical and religious information to make the Bible passages clearer. These items include information on Israel's neighboring nations and their religions, as well as some revealing glimpses into the religious and social practices of Jews and Christians in biblical times. Part of the pleasure here is finding that, in spite of that centuries-long gap between biblical times and ours, history has a way of repeating itself.

DID-YOU-KNOW?

These are brief, factual odds and ends worth knowing—and, sometimes, worth applying to your daily life. We think you'll find these factoids both useful and enjoyable.

PUTTING THE WORD TO WORK

This book—and the time you spend on it—would be a failure if your reading did not lead you to apply each day's truths to your own life. Each chapter will conclude with five thought-provoking questions to guide you in applying the knowledge you've gained to your daily walk. After all, the Bible is never just about someone else—it is about you and God.

A WORD ABOUT JESUS: he is the most important and most fascinating person in the Bible. I covered his life and teachings—adequately, I hope—in my earlier book *Know the Words of Jesus in 30 Days*. In the present book, I focus on several Jesus episodes not covered in the earlier book and also devote three chapters to some of the titles used for Jesus—such as Son of Man, Son of God, Savior, Lord, Servant, Word, Prophet and others. The Jesus material in this volume is entirely new, not reprinted from the earlier book.

KNOW
THE MOST FASCINATING
PEOPLE
OF THE BIBLE IN
30 DAYS

Shout for Joy!
DAVID'S DANCE WITH GOD

Two words that might describe King David of Israel are *versatile* and *emotional*. He was versatile in the roles he played: shepherd, musician, songwriter, soldier, king, religious leader, husband (to many wives), father (to numerous children by different mothers), and—very important—sinner. A man who wore many hats, he also expressed every

conceivable emotion—and never halfheartedly—for the books of Samuel and Psalms overflow with his enduring and endearing expressions of joy, anguish, despair, elation, puzzlement, anger, repentance, bitterness and abandonment. No one in the Bible opened up his heart to us the way David did.

In *Know the Bible in 30 Days*, I surveyed the fascinating life of David chronologically. Here we will take a different approach, looking at David from the emotional angle, and in particular focusing on the element of joy he experienced in his long and tumultuous life.

KEY TERM FOR TODAY Joy

The Bible is not a joyless book, nor does it depict the life of faith as joyless. David, king of Israel, had his failings, yet he is the classic case of a man of faith who genuinely enjoyed the walk with God, and who encouraged others to shout, dance and sing to honor God.

THE LIVING ANTIDEPRESSANT

Saul's attendants said to him, "See, an evil spirit from God is tormenting you."

So Saul said to his attendants, "Find someone who plays well and bring him to me."

One of the servants answered, "I have seen a son of Jesse of Bethlehem who knows how to play the harp. He is a brave man and a warrior. He speaks well and is a fine-looking man. And the Lord is with him." (1 Samuel 16:15–18)

Slings—Low-tech but Lethal

Slings had been in use for thousands of years before David killed Goliath. A sling consisted of a leather pouch with two leather cords attached. The man wound one cord around his wrist and lower arm, and clasped the other cord with the hand of the same arm. A stone was placed in the pouch and whirled rapidly over the head. Then the man released his handheld cord, sending the stone flying. The typical stone used in a sling was fairly small—usually three inches or less in diameter—but if the man was well-practiced, stones hurled from a sling were lethal, moving at speeds of up to eighty miles per hour. They were a perfect example of a very low-tech but effective weapon, requiring no metal, only a skilled eye and hand.

In 1 Samuel, we read the story of the Israelites begging their leader, the prophet Samuel, to give them a king so they can be like other nations. Samuel is reluctant, but he anoints the handsome and charismatic Saul as king. Though Saul has some military successes, he does not fully obey the words of God spoken through Samuel, so God orders Samuel to anoint—secretly—someone else to be the next king. This is David, youngest son of Jesse of Bethlehem.

Saul had "an evil spirit" in his life; perhaps in our own day we would say he suffered from depression. His moodiness would worsen in time and would alienate many people, including his mentor, Samuel. But for a time he found some relief through the companionship of a young man recommended to him: David. The young man is described as one who is physically attractive, "speaks well," plays the harp, and—of great interest to a king always in need of good soldiers—a brave man as well, one whose youth spent as a shepherd gave him training in fighting off lions, wolves and other predators. David is not just a musician but a well-rounded man who will make a fine addition to Saul's court. And most importantly, his music lightened Saul's moods.

The fact that David speaks well is important: He knows how to use words; the Bible records not only his amazing life story, but also the seventy-three psalms that are said to be his. David spoke well not only to his own time, but also to many generations after, to the people who have read, recited and sung his psalms over the centuries. So great was his reputation as a poet-songwriter that 2 Samuel 23:1 refers to him as "Israel's singer of songs."

The Lord is "with" David, as he was with so many of the other great heroes of the Old Testament. And David always—even in his moments of despair, his dark-hearted, rock-bottom days—was aware of God's presence.

Saul was impressed with the young man: "Then Saul sent word to Jesse, saying, 'Allow David to remain in my service, for I am pleased with him'" (1 Samuel 16:22). Saul had found himself not a medicine but a walking, harp-playing antidepressant. And much more, as we see in 1 Samuel 17, where the spunky David does the unthinkable: he strides out to meet, one on one, the hulking giant warrior of the Philistines, Goliath. Saul initially protested; he loved David and didn't want to see his young aide sliced up and thrown to the vultures. But David insisted he was more experienced that his years would indicate: he had killed bears and lions attacking his flocks. But aside from spunk, he had something more, as he made clear to Goliath: "You come against me with sword and spear and javelin, but I come against you in the name of the Lord Almighty, the God of the armies of Israel, whom you have defied" (1 Samuel 17:45).

We all know the outcome of that fight. With his sling and one smooth stone, David felled Goliath and then beheaded him with his own sword. The deed made him famous. But, alas, it also made Saul extremely jealous; the rest of 1 Samuel is essentially the story of Saul's love-hate relationship with David. It is also the story of David's being mostly on the lam from the king, seeking refuge at times among the enemy Philistines, and even hiding out in a cave. Psalm 57 is David's cry for help to God while in the cave: "Have mercy on me, O God, have mercy on me, for in you my soul takes refuge. I will take refuge in the shadow of your wings until the disaster has passed" (Psalm 57:1).

CHARACTER CLOSE-UP Jesse, Father of David

Jesse's biggest claim to fame is being the father of the amazing David. In fact, most of the mentions of his name in the Bible are in the phrase "son of Jesse," applied to David. Jesse lived in or near Bethlehem, and was the grandson of Ruth and Boaz, whose story is told in the Book of Ruth. Ruth was from Moab, and on one occasion, when Saul was threatening David and his family, David sent his parents off to Moab for safekeeping.

Jesse had eight sons, David being the youngest. When the prophet Samuel came to Jesse's home with the intention of anointing the next king of Israel, Jesse did not bother to call David in from the field, on the assumption that the youngest son in the family certainly could not be a king. Obviously, God saw things differently.

Isaiah 11 contains an interesting prophecy: "There shall come forth a Rod from the stem of Jesse, and a Branch shall grow out of his roots. The Spirit of the Lord shall rest upon him." Christians believe this "shoot," meaning descendant, was Jesus. Artists liked to depict a Jesse tree, which shows the sleeping Jesse with a tree coming up from his loins—a literal family tree with the kings of Israel and, of course, Jesus. It was a favorite subject for stained-glass windows; many an old church has a "Jesse window."

David ruled Israel
c. 1010 BC–970 BC

David is in the depths, but he has not lost faith. Even though he is surrounded by "lions," something in his heart enables him to sing out to his Lord: "My heart is steadfast, O God, my heart is steadfast; I will sing and make music. Awake, my soul! Awake, harp and lyre! I will awaken the dawn" (Psalm 57:7–8). Later in the chapter we will look at more of David's "under-pressure" Psalms.

MOVED BY GOD

David . . . danced before the Lord with all his might. (2 Samuel 6:14)

You turned my wailing into dancing; you removed my sackcloth and clothed me with joy. (Psalm 30:11)

David "lived out loud." Nothing illustrates that better than the episode of David's dancing when the ark of the covenant was brought to Jerusalem.

The ark was the gold-covered chest that symbolized God's presence in Israel. It was constructed in the time of Moses and carried by the Israelites when they settled in Canaan. In 1 Samuel, when the ark was captured by the enemy Philistines, horrible things happened to them, so they returned it to Israel. The ark had no permanent home for many years, but in 2 Samuel we read the story of David's bringing the ark into his new capital city, Jerusalem, where it would remain for centuries.

We know Jerusalem as probably the most important city in the Bible, and even today it is considered a holy city by Jews, Christians and Muslims. But in David's day it was small and unimpressive. David's armies had captured it from the original inhabitants, the Jebusites. Although it lay within the territory of David's tribe, Judah, it had only recently been added to Israel, meaning it had no real connection to any tribe or family in Israel. David wisely saw it was a perfect choice to be Israel's capital city. He was also wise enough to see that the small city needed something to make it important in the Israelites' eyes, and that something was the ark, the visible sign of God's presence.

The ark was not exactly sneaked into the city. David made the bringing of the ark a national celebration. There was much to celebrate. David had lived for years as a fugitive from the jealous wrath of Saul. After Saul's death, David became king and—to the nation's great relief—defeated the troublesome Philistines. And so David "and the entire house of Israel brought up the ark of the Lord with shouts and the sound of trumpets" (2 Samuel 6:15). And David "danced before the Lord with all his might." He was not afraid to look foolish in public. He felt joy, and he released it. Although the Bible does not say so, we must assume that many of the other Israelites joined him in the dance. If this was a solemn occasion, it was also a festive one.

Dancing

The prevalent, modern form of dancing—men and women dancing as couples—is not mentioned in the Bible. Most dancing took the form of what we would call folk dancing, done in a group setting, with both men and women, though women are mentioned more often. The first mention of dancing is the spontaneous victory dance following the Egyptian troops being drowned in the Red Sea, in which Moses' sister Miriam "took a tambourine in her hand, and all the women followed her, with tambourines and dancing" (Exodus 15:20). Groups of women with their tambourines also danced to celebrate the military victories of Jephthah (Judges 11:34) and David (1 Samuel 18:7).

Joyous dancing could also be part of worshipping God, as evidenced by the story of David, who "danced before the Lord with all his might" in celebration of the ark of the covenant's being brought to Jerusalem (2 Samuel 6:14). Psalms—the Bible's book of praise songs—says, "Let them praise his name with dancing and make music to him with tambourine and harp" (Psalm 149:3). Jeremiah, who prophesied disaster for the wayward people, also foretold a better time ahead: "Then maidens will dance and be glad, young men and old as well" (Jeremiah 31:13). In Jesus' parable of the prodigal son, there is music and dancing to celebrate the long-lost son's return (Luke 15:25).

Judges 21:21–23 tells the peculiar story of the men of the tribe of Benjamin. Not having enough women to take as wives, they abduct a group of young women who have come to dance at a religious festival at Shiloh.

Was there erotic dancing in the Bible? Certainly, human nature being what it is. The first mention of dancing that was probably immoral is in the episode of the golden-calf idol: Moses comes down from Mount Sinai and is horrified to see the Israelites engaging in a sort of orgy, including dancing around the idol (Exodus 32:19). In 1 Kings 18, in the story of the prophet Elijah's confronting the horde of Baal prophets, the Baal men "danced around the altar they had made" (1 Kings 18:26). Given that Baal was a god of fertility, there was almost certainly a sexual element to these dances, as there often was in fertility religion.

By the way, the Hebrew word *mecholah*, translated "dance," literally means to whirl or move in a circle.

One who did not join in the festivities, or approve of David's ecstatic dancing, was his wife Michal, daughter of Saul. She had dearly loved David once, and had even saved him from being murdered by her father's men. But her father was gone, and David had taken other wives and concubines. Watching David joyously dancing in the streets, she "despised him in her heart." When David came to his own house, Michal cut him to the bone, scolding him for making a fool of himself in public. But David would not allow her to dampen his mood. He told her: "I will celebrate before the Lord" (2 Samuel 6:21).

David understood that a religion has to grab the heart if it is to give people pleasure and purpose in life. The ark, constructed by Moses and connected with the giving of the divine law on Mount Sinai, symbolized the high moral standards of Israel's religion. But David understood that the morality had to go hand in hand with a belief in a personal God, a God who not only had to be obeyed but also was a source of joy. God was not the Supreme Being, or Providence, or First Cause; he was a personality, someone who could be loved and enjoyed.

The verse from Psalm 30 is the one occasion that David mentions dancing in his Psalms. Here he is speaking figuratively, and refers to sorrow being turned by the Lord into joy. Perhaps when he wrote the psalm, he was thinking back to the joyous day when the ark was brought to Jerusalem—a day he and his people were so animated by their pleasure in the Lord that they could not keep still. David, a man of fizzing vitality, had a relationship with God that was just as vital.

JOY—IN LIGHT OF THE ALTERNATIVES

O Lord, how many are my foes! How many rise up against me! Many are saying of me, "God will not deliver him." But you are a shield around me, O Lord; you bestow glory on me and lift up my head. . . . I will not fear the tens of thousands drawn up against me on every side. (Psalm 3:1–3, 6)

Let all who take refuge in you be glad; let them ever sing for joy. Spread your protection over them, that those who love your name may rejoice in you. (Psalm 5:11)

The Lord is my strength and my shield; my heart trusts in him, and I am helped. My heart leaps for joy and I will give thanks to him in song. (Psalm 28:7)

Psalm 3 is the first of the psalms attributed to David; it is supposed to have been written when he was fleeing the rebellion of his son Absalom, which we deal with in detail in another chapter (Day 21). This is one of several psalms that David wrote in a sweat, the emotional man pouring out his fears—and his faith—to his God.

Note that this passage refers to God as a shield. David was an experienced military man, and in the midst of this rebellion, shields would have been much on his mind. But in this situation, he knew that his true defense was not any human shield but God himself. He refers to God several other times, as in Psalm 28, in which his awareness of God as his shield makes his heart leap for joy.

Psalm 5 is one of many psalms that opens with a desperate cry for help: "Give ear to my words, O Lord, consider my sighing. Listen to my cry for help, my King and my God." And yet, like the other psalms of lamentation, it ends not in despair or bitterness but in trust and joy: "Let all who take refuge in you be glad; let them ever sing for joy." It begins in tears, and it ends with singing. The life of faith has emotions painted in very rich colors.

Psalms like these make us aware of the role adversity plays in the life of faith. David had not exactly led a sheltered life. In spite of being king and being praised as a great military leader, his life was seldom without conflict, and like all great men, he made enemies—even in his own household. Adversity turns many people away from God— but turns others toward him. David was frequently in danger, frequently in fear for his very life. Yet being surrounded by foes called forth his faith. Backed into a corner, in a situation where his enemies were sure that his God had abandoned him, he could feel joy in his heart. The words "I will give thanks to him in song" were penned by one who knew great contrasts in life—the heights of fame and good fortune, the depths of his own sins and the fear of powerful enemies. David had some amazingly high highs and profoundly low lows; and the lows made him appreciate the highs all the more. David is the classic case of a man whose woes made him appreciate God.

RESTORING THE JOY

Have mercy on me, O God, according to your unfailing love; according to your great compassion blot out my transgressions. . . .

Let me hear joy and gladness; let the bones you have crushed rejoice. Restore to me the joy of your salvation and grant me a willing spirit, to sustain me. (Psalm 51:1, 11–12)

No man was more blessed than David. He had been chosen by God to be Israel's king. He had survived numerous attempts by the first king, Saul, to murder him. He had conquered Israel's numerous enemies and expanded his kingdom enormously. He had popped the cork on life's bottle.

And yet this working-class boy who had become king and seemingly had it all set his eyes on the most dangerous type of woman: another man's wife. We find in 2 Samuel 11–12 the sordid story of the king and Bathsheba. One late afternoon, David saw from his rooftop a woman bathing. He was infatuated, and he sent servants to find out who she was. Not only was she married, but, even worse, she was also the wife of one of his own devoted soldiers, Uriah. David didn't care. His lust overruled his brain and his morals; he slept with Bathsheba—and got her pregnant. Hoping to cover up his crime, he had Uriah brought to Jerusalem on the assumption that Uriah would sleep with his wife,

Tradition says that the prophet Nathan was the recorder of the history of David's court, which was later incorporated into the books of Samuel and Chronicles.

and that people would assume the child Bathsheba was carrying was her husband's. But Uriah, instead of playing the amorous husband, chose to play the steadfast soldier and did not visit his wife. So David decided to cover up his adultery with something worse: murder. He sent a message to his army commander Joab: in the next battle, send Uriah into the thick of the fighting and then draw back from him so he will be killed. Uriah was killed—and David rather quickly took Bathsheba as his own wife.

David seems to have forgotten, in his lust, that even if human eyes did not see his crimes, God did. God sent the prophet Nathan to tell David a parable about a rich man who had everything he wanted. But the rich man took the one lamb belonging to a poor man. David was aghast at such a story; a man who behaved in such a way deserved to die! Nathan uttered his famous words: "You are the man!" Because David had behaved shamefully, a curse of violence would rest on his house as long as he lived—and his child with Bathsheba would die.

Out of David's experience came one of the great poems of the Bible, and probably its greatest plea of repentance: Psalm 51. Like many of the psalms, it begins in despair—the words of someone who has bottomed out, who can do nothing but throw himself on the mercy of a compassionate God. In Psalm 51, David expresses a key sentiment of the Bible: When we sin, we not only harm our fellow man, but we also offend God, who is holy. God is pure, and his people are to be pure, so our failings are "soil" that separates us from God. David cries out for cleansing: "wash me, and I will be whiter than snow…. Create in

CHARACTER CLOSE-UP   ## Uriah

Uriah offers a striking contrast to David. As a Hittite foreigner in Israel's army, Uriah likely was a convert to Israel's religion. Instead of being born into the faith as David was, Uriah had made a conscious choice to convert. David was remiss in his duties as a king and a follower of God, but Uriah followed the path of duty, not willing to sleep in a soft bed while his men were encamped in the field. We can well imagine David was foaming-at-the-mouth angry, wondering how a man could be so dutiful and dedicated that he would pass up a chance to spend time with a wife as beautiful as Bathsheba. We can also imagine it was with a certain amount of vindictiveness that David sent the order (via Uriah himself) to Joab to place Uriah in the thick of the fighting: "So if he's such a dutiful soldier, then let him die a hero's death!"

Uriah's name, by the way, means "light of the Lord."

me a pure heart, O God, and renew a steadfast spirit within me" (Psalm 51:7, 10). Note the word *steadfast*: David, the man whose life has shown that God was with him and who would express his pleasure in God through dance and song, was anything but steadfast. Or, put another way, he seemed steadfast enough until he caught sight of Bathsheba. So he was begging God: give me back that spirit of total, unwavering commitment to you, Lord.

In the psalm, after the sorrow and the pleading, there is the hope that the joy in God will return again, that the relationship will be restored: "Let me hear joy and gladness . . . Restore to me the joy of your salvation." This is one of the great verses of the Bible. How often do we use the words *joy* and *salvation* in the same sentence? For David, the two were inseparable.

THE NAKED SOUL

O Lord, you have searched me and you know me. You know when I sit and when I rise; you perceive my thoughts from afar . . . Before a word is on my tongue you know it completely, O Lord. You hem me in—behind and before; you have laid your hand upon me.

You created my inmost being; you knit me together in my mother's womb. I praise you because I am fearfully and wonderfully made . . .

Search me, O God, and know my heart; test me and know my anxious thoughts. See if there is any offensive way in me, and lead me in the way everlasting. (Psalm 139:1–2, 4–5, 13–14, 23–24)

One thing that set apart the religion of the Bible from the other religions of ancient times is that the God of the Bible can read minds. The gods of the other religions are interested only in appearances, which means that if a person makes the right sacrifices in the temple—goes through the motions of religion—everything is fine. But this is not Israel's religion. God can see through hypocrisy, can see straight through to the heart. God's back is never turned, and no act or thought escapes his notice.

David knew this, but apparently forgot it when he lusted for Bathsheba, slept with her, and then tried to cover up his crime by having her husband killed in battle. What was David thinking? Was his lust so powerful that it could override his awareness of God's

DID YOU KNOW?

The Psalms use the word *shout* twenty times, usually in the phrase "shout for joy."

presence? Apparently so. But as we saw in Psalm 51, David threw himself on the wide mercies of God, asking for the restoration of the joy in belonging to God.

Psalm 139 is also one of the greatest of psalms. We don't know what the occasion was that prompted David to compose it, but it shows him in a very reflective mood. He is

The Psalms in the New Testament Period

Of the psalms in our Bible, seventy-three are labeled "of David." But many of the rabbis of Jesus' day had such a high opinion of David that some said he wrote *all* the psalms, which is a bit absurd, considering some of them refer to the Babylonian exile, hundreds of years after David died. Just as the great Moses was revered as the author of the Torah, the first five books of the Bible, so David was said to be the illustrious author of Psalms, which was eventually divided into five parts—or "books"—so as to make David as important as Moses. Teachers would refer to the Torah with "Moses says," and likewise would refer to Psalms with "David says."

aware that everything he does is in full view of God. God sees his every act, and hears his every word—even hears the words before David speaks them. David is hemmed in by God. There is no escaping him. God's hand is on him wherever he goes.

Is this a pleasant thought? It wasn't for Adam and Eve, who hid themselves from God after they disobeyed. And for all of us, at certain times, God's presence is not a pleasant thought. We all, at times, would prefer to live our lives without a busybody parent or teacher looking over our shoulders.

But David does not chafe at being hemmed in by God. The hand of God, after all, is a guiding hand. And that hand has been present from the very beginning, even when David was an unborn child in the womb. David, like every human being ever born, is "fearfully and wonderfully made." The human body is more than just a collection of organs and muscles, it is God's creation, and he watches over all of us. Being watched over is a cause for praise, not anxiety or fear.

"Search me, O God, and know my heart; test me and know my anxious thoughts. See if there is any offensive way in me, and lead me in the way everlasting." This great psalm, full of joy and praise for God's presence, ends with a petition: David wants to be clean, morally and spiritually, wants to be deserving of God's fellowship.

CREATION CELEBRATION

O Lord, our Lord, how majestic is your name in all the earth! You have set your glory above the heavens . . . When I consider your heavens, the work of your fingers, the moon and the stars, which you have set in place, what is man that you are mindful of him, the son of man that you care for him? (Psalm 8:1, 3–4)

The meadows are covered with flocks and the valleys are mantled with grain; they shout for joy and sing. (Psalm 65:13)

> The trees of the forest will sing, they will sing for joy before the Lord, for he comes to judge the earth. (1 Chronicles 16:33)

"Worship God, not nature" is one of the key messages of the Bible. The peoples of the surrounding nations literally did worship nature, regarding the sun, moon and stars as gods, believing that natural forces such as wind and rain were gods that required sacrifices. In the Genesis story, God—the only God—brings the world into being through the power of his word. At each stage of his creation, God announces it is "good." But his people are forbidden to worship nature: They may only worship the one who made it all. But that doesn't mean they can't take pleasure in contemplating the amazing world around them.

Certainly David did. Like most men in his time and place, David would have spent most of his life out of doors. As a young shepherd, he would have spent many nights not in a house but sleeping in the field with his flocks, which would give him time—and quiet—to contemplate the stars and the other works of God as well as time to fight off the bears and other predators attacking the flocks, proof that nature can be dangerous as well as beautiful. Even after becoming king and settling in Jerusalem, David was often

CHARACTERS AT LARGE ## David on Film

David is about as cinematic as a character can get, so naturally moviemakers have been attracted to his story. The earliest movies made about him, both from 1908, were *David and Goliath* and *Saul and David*—both short, silent and black-and-white, of course. But the standout among David movies is the 1951 movie *David and Bathsheba*, the only case in which a biblical movie was the top-grossing film in its year of release. It starred two attractive screen idols of the time: Gregory Peck and Susan Hayward. The screenwriter said he found David fascinating, because David did the things most people fantasize about doing—and got away with it. (That is hardly the case, however, since we see clearly in 2 Samuel that David's philandering and his spoiling of his children brought constant turmoil to his life.) The movie excuses the David–Bathsheba adultery: Bathsheba tells David she has been married seven months and has only spent six days with her husband and that it was an arranged marriage, so she barely knows him and did not marry for love.

A much less successful David movie was the 1985 film *King David*, starring another screen idol, Richard Gere, as David. Unlike the 1951 movie, this one depicts the sordid but fascinating story of Amnon, Tamar and Absalom, certainly one of the most intriguing episodes in David's history. *King David* stuck reasonably close to the Bible, except that at the movie's end David tells his son Solomon that God speaks to man through the heart, not through the prophets.

DID YOU KNOW?

The psalms labeled "of David" are these: 3–9, 11–32, 34–41, 51–65, 68–70, 86, 101, 103, 108–110, 122–124, 131, 133, 138–145. The Hebrew word *ledawid* in the Psalms can mean "of David" or "to David" or "about David."

outdoors, either on military campaigns or fleeing from the conspiracy of his treacherous son Absalom.

Psalm 8 is one of many psalms that celebrates God's creation. In this psalm, David is so in awe of the vastness of it all that he wonders how God even has time to contemplate man. And yet, as the later part of the psalm indicates, man is not just one more part of the created order, but the lord of it all, with dominion over the animals and birds—an idea going all the way back to Genesis, where Adam's dominion over the rest of creation is one aspect of being in "the image of God."

Psalm 65 tells us that the meadows and valleys "shout for joy and sing." The same sentiment is found in 1 Chronicles 16, the song David sang when the ark was brought to Jerusalem. David didn't literally mean that inanimate objects could shout and sing, of course, and yet it is figuratively true, for the whole creation itself "sings" the message that there is a loving Creator who made and sustains everything. David, so caught up in the pleasure in seeing God's hand everywhere, could easily imagine that mute nature would, if it could, sing out to the Lord.

When Jesus, a man from a small town brought up near the countryside, praised the beauty of the lilies of the field, he was very much in the tradition of his great ancestor, David.

THE ONE EVERYONE KNOWS

> The Lord is my shepherd, I shall not be in want. He makes me lie down in green pastures, he leads me beside quiet waters, he restores my soul. He guides me in paths of righteousness for his name's sake.
>
> Even though I walk through the valley of the shadow of death, I will fear no evil, for you are with me; your rod and your staff, they comfort me.
>
> You prepare a table before me in the presence of my enemies. You anoint my head with oil; my cup overflows.
>
> Surely goodness and love will follow me all the days of my life, and I will dwell in the house of the Lord forever. (Psalm 23)

Not so long ago, many people knew this brief and beautiful poem by heart, usually in the familiar words of the King James Version. Like many beloved passages in the Bible, it deserves a closer look now and then, for its very familiarity makes us miss much of the meaning.

"The Lord is my shepherd." This may not mean much to us, since most of us seldom see live sheep and have no clue what a shepherd's duties really are. David certainly did, for he was a shepherd himself, and knew there was much more to it than merely standing around in a pasture leaning on his staff. It required constant vigilance, for there were wolves, bears and even lions in the region in those days, and David's abilities as a soldier were honed in his days of fighting off the beasts that preyed on the flocks. A shepherd also had to go searching for sheep that wandered off and got themselves stuck in ravines. David, the former shepherd, knew God was *his* shepherd, protecting him from his many enemies and leading him back when he was lost.

One of the amazing things about the statement "the Lord is my shepherd" is that David, a vigorous, mettlesome man, was exactly the sort of man who—as history has proved countless times—came to think of himself as a god. He ruled a kingdom and expanded it greatly, quelling most of his enemies, surviving many threats. Such a man would usually have a high opinion of himself, someone in no need of a shepherd or Lord. But David was not that type of man. His hectic life had taught him that God, not David, was in charge of things.

The mention of "green pastures" reminds us that such pastures were not the norm in David's home turf. The area around Bethlehem had sparse vegetation, not wide fields of lush grass. In the psalm, David is speaking figuratively: God has blessed him abundantly, giving him "green pastures" instead of rocky soil with meager grass.

The Bible scholars tell us that "the valley of the shadow of death" really means "a dark valley," and they are probably right. But we can be thankful that most Bible versions have "valley of the shadow of death," for this verse has given great comfort to millions of readers, especially those facing the threat of death. As the books of Samuel clearly show, David, so richly blessed in many ways, lived much of his life in the "shadow of death," facing the wrath of Saul, the rebellion of his son Absalom, and many other enemies. Even in this situation, David tells us, we need "fear no evil," for God is with us. If God can see us through the "valley of the shadow of death," surely he can see us through the typical frets and dreads of everyday life.

With the mention of the rod and staff we face another culture gap: What do a rod and staff mean to people in the twenty-first century? For David they were tools of the shepherding trade, used to goad straying sheep onto the right path and, if needed, to discipline them. David had, on occasion (notably in his adultery with Bathsheba), strayed from the path, and God had

DID YOU KNOW?

The Old Testament often uses the expression "man of God" to mean the same as prophet. Moses, Elijah, Elisha and several unnamed prophets are addressed as "man of God." Chronicles and Nehemiah, some of the latest of the Old Testament books, also refer to "David the man of God."

David in Art and Literature

Inevitably a charismatic figure like David has generated a huge amount of art and literature. Probably the most famous statue on earth is Michelangelo's marble *David*, one of the most beautiful artworks ever—and also, technically, an incorrect one, since the young man is uncircumcised—something Michelangelo must have known was wrong. (He also painted David beheading Goliath on the Sistine Chapel.) Michelangelo was not the first nor the last artist to sculpt the young David, for artists have been intrigued by the David-Goliath story. Sculptors have shown David with the severed head of the giant (Donatello's famous bronze *David*) or in the muscle-flexing pose in which David is wielding his sling (Bernini's marble *David*, who looks as if he is about to move). The David and Goliath episode has fascinated painters as well; Caravaggio painted at least three young Davids.

The adult David has appealed not to sculptors but to painters, who have often depicted the scene where David, on his rooftop, sees Bathsheba bathing, or where the jealous Saul throws his spear at him, or the dramatic scene where the prophet Nathan confronts David with "You are the man!" In a more subdued vein, many paintings show David playing the harp. In fact, when a painting, stained-glass window or sculpture depicts a man with a crown playing a harp, inevitably that man is David.

Writers have had a field day with the David saga. John Dryden (1631-1700), who was England's poet laureate, wrote the long comical poem *Absalom and Achitophel*, based on the story in 2 Samuel 15 of Absalom, who rebels against his father David. Dryden connected the biblical events with a recent rebellion of the Duke of Monmouth against his father, England's King Charles II. In a more serious vein, Dryden's contemporary Abraham Cowley (1618–1667) wrote the epic poem *Davideis*, about the life of David. American author Joseph Heller, best known for his novel *Catch-22*, also wrote *God Knows* (1984), an amusing retelling of the story of King David. James Barrie, author of the famous play *Peter Pan*, also wrote the play *The Boy David* (1936). Tim Rice, who wrote the lyrics for *Jesus Christ Superstar* and *Joseph and the Amazing Technicolor Dreamcoat*, also wrote the lyrics for the less successful play *King David*.

The David saga has also proved to be a rich source for titles. The 2007 movie *In the Valley of Elah*, which dealt with the US war in Iraq, took its title from the site where David fought Goliath. An Edgar Allan Poe story is titled *Thou Art the Man*, the famous words Nathan spoke to David. William Faulkner wrote the novel *Absalom, Absalom*—the title taken from King David's lament over his wayward son Absalom (2 Samuel 18:33).

to discipline him. No one likes discipline, and yet, in the psalm, David says that God's rod and staff "comfort" him. He is happy knowing that his shepherd will do what is necessary to make him live rightly.

In the second part of the psalm, David seems to leave behind the shepherd images. But he is still focused on God's blessings. Despite his many enemies—both outside and inside Israel, and at times even in his own household—he is richly blessed with a full table and a cup that, according to the King James Version, "runneth over."

"I will dwell in the house of the Lord forever." What did David mean by "house of the Lord"? There was no temple in his day; the task of building one would fall to his son Solomon. Possibly "house of the Lord" simply means "in God's presence." Possibly he was also thinking of a house as the place that shuts out the predators and inclement weather that a flock must endure. For countless generations, readers have interpreted "house of the Lord" in one obvious way: it means heaven. And David, with his event-filled, turbulent, active, and—most importantly—God-intoxicated life, could not see his joyous relationship with the Lord ending at death. It had to continue, somewhere, in some way, forever.

PUTTING THE WORD TO WORK

1. Take a moment to reflect on David as a man of deep emotion. Think of your own life of faith. Do you feel you allow yourself to pour out your thoughts to God? To express emotion in a worship setting? How can you do more of this in your life?

2. People of faith have often disagreed on the subject of dancing, but in light of this chapter, think of times in your life when you felt moved—physically—by your awareness of God's presence. Have there been occasions when you were so emotionally moved you could not keep still?

3. Reflect on some of the psalms David composed while fleeing his enemies. Then think of people who, like David, have had their faith deepened by their adversities.

4. Psalm 139 speaks of being hemmed in by God—a thought that gave David pleasure. How does your knowing that all our thoughts are known to the Lord affect you?

5. If you can, make an effort to memorize Psalm 23. It is one of the great short chapters in the Bible and has given comfort to millions.

The Occasionally Shaken Rock

PETER

Today we look at a flawed but supremely lovable character, the Galilean fisherman named Simon, better known as Peter. Peter's character is captured well by artists thus: He is shown looking serene and saintly and authoritative—but usually with a rooster at his side, the symbol of his denying his Master three times before the rooster crowed. Among the twelve disciples, Peter was always first—first to rise to his Lord's defense and also first to act rashly and sometimes stupidly, prone to overestimate his faith and also prone to putting his foot in his mouth. Peter as presented in the Gospels and Acts ought to be proof positive that the New Testament authors were recording history, not sugarcoating the apostles or making them appear more than human.

> **MEMORY VERSE**
>
> You also, like living stones, are being built into a spiritual house to be a holy priesthood.—1 Peter 2:5

KEY TERM FOR TODAY Rock

Jesus bestowed the nickname "rock" on the disciple Simon Peter, and despite some notorious lapses and misunderstandings, Peter did in time prove himself an example of loyalty and zeal, one of the great evangelists and letter-writers of the New Testament.

"FOLLOW ME"

As Jesus was walking beside the Sea of Galilee, he saw two brothers, Simon called Peter and his brother Andrew. They were casting a net into the lake, for they were fishermen.

"Come, follow me," Jesus said, "and I will make you fishers of men." (Matthew 4:18–19)

Andrew, Simon Peter's brother, was one of the two who heard what John had said and who had followed Jesus. The first thing Andrew did was to find his brother Simon and tell him, "We have found the Messiah" (that is, the Christ). (John 1:40–41)

Some might see the two quotations above as an indication that the Gospels contradict each other. Not so. John, as was his habit, included some information that the other Gospels left out. Andrew, Peter's brother, had been a follower of John the Baptist; possibly Peter himself was too. Considering their attachment to John and his message of repentance, the brothers would have been men who took their faith seriously. Andrew believed John when he identified Jesus as the "lamb of God," and he took his brother to meet Jesus. The more familiar "fishers of men" episode from Matthew 4 probably occurred later. Jesus, already familiar with the two fisherman brothers and knowing them to be men of faith, called them to join his band of followers. They left their work immediately, but probably they had been giving much thought to Jesus already.

The next mention of Peter in Matthew's Gospel involves Peter's mother-in-law, who is sick with a fever. Jesus enters Peter's house in the village of Capernaum, touches the hand of the sick woman, and the fever leaves her. It is a minor healing compared to some of the more dramatic miracles—raising the dead, casting out demons—but we can imagine it had a profound effect on Peter, since he is the only one of the twelve disciples who, so far as we know, experienced Jesus' compassionate power in his own home.

The next mention of Peter in Matthew is important because it gives us our first revelation of Peter's character—bold, devoted to Jesus, yet prone to overestimating himself.

CHARACTER CLOSE-UP Andrew—in the Shadow of the Rock

Poor Andrew! He was Simon Peter's brother, but in the Gospels he cuts a much less impressive figure. The tight inner circle of the disciples, the ones closest to Jesus and present at some of the great events such as the Transfiguration, consisted of Peter, James and John—but not Andrew.

Still, Andrew is an important character, and we do know more about him than most of the other twelve disciples, some of whom are only names. John's Gospel tells us that Andrew had been a disciple of John the Baptist, and was present when John pointed to Jesus and identified him as the "lamb of God." Andrew immediately sought out Peter and told him, "We have found the Messiah" (John 1:40–41).

John's Gospel records that when some Greeks wanted to meet Jesus, it was Andrew who took them to him (John 12:20–22). This incident, plus the fact that Andrew's name is Greek (it means "manly"), suggests that Andrew (and probably Peter also) was bilingual, speaking both Aramaic and Greek.

Matthew 14:22–33 records the famous story in which Jesus walks on the Sea of Galilee while his disciples, in a boat, fear for their lives. Jesus tries to calm them: "Take courage! It is I. Don't be afraid." Peter appears to be heartened by Jesus' words—and, no doubt, by the sight of the Master walking on the troubled waters. He wants to be part of the miracle: "Lord, if it's you, tell me to come to you on the water." Jesus tells him, "Come." Peter is doing what Jesus told him to do: follow him. It is a bold act, and an act of deep faith—but his faith wavers. Once out of the boat, Peter lets the fear of the wind and water get to him, and he begins to sink: "Lord, save me!" Jesus reaches out his hand and caught him. "You of little faith, why did you doubt?"

Peter overestimated himself—and yet, remember, he alone among the disciples made the bold move, getting out of the boat on the troubled lake.

PETER'S "MESSIAH HIGH"

"But what about you?" [Jesus] asked. "Who do you say I am?"

Simon Peter answered, "You are the Christ, the Son of the living God."

Jesus replied, "Blessed are you, Simon son of Jonah, for this was not revealed to you by man, but by my Father in heaven . . .

Jesus turned and said to Peter, "Get behind me, Satan! You are a stumbling block to me; you do not have in mind the things of God, but the things of men." (Matthew 16:15–17, 23)

After spending months with Jesus, hearing him teach and watching him perform amazing miracles, the disciples must have formed an opinion of their Master. In Matthew 16, Jesus asks them: "Who do people say I am?" They replied, "Some say John the Baptist; others say Elijah; and still others, Jeremiah or one of the prophets." All the men referred to were dead, of course, but like many Jews, the disciples would have hoped that one of the great prophets of the past would return to earth. But then Jesus asked the disciples directly: "Who do you say I am?" Peter spoke the immortal words: "You are the Christ, the Son of the living God."

Christ had the same meaning as the Hebrew title *Messiah*: anointed one. The Messiah, the saving figure that all the Jews had prayed for, was here—so Peter believed. He also believed Jesus was "Son of the living God." The phrase "living God" was used several times in the Old Testament. The people of Israel believed their God was the only living God, in contrast to the "dead" gods, the idols of the pagans.

Peter saw what the people did not see: Jesus was not a prophet; he was the longed-for Messiah, and he was God himself in human form. Peter had to use familiar words—Messiah, Son of God. (Later, the disciple Thomas caught the full reality: "My Lord and my God.") When Jesus cast out demons from people, the demons, having spiritual insight that humans did not possess, recognized that Jesus was the "Holy One of God." Now Peter saw that reality also.

Jesus commends Peter's statement: "Blessed are you, Simon son of Jonah, for this was not revealed to you by man, but by my Father in heaven. And I tell you that you are Peter, and on this rock I will build my church" (Matthew 16:17, 18). The church would be founded on both the rocklike Peter and on his confession that Jesus was the Messiah and Son of God. In fact, "church" is not the best translation of the Greek word *ekklesia*, which means "assembly." Jesus was not talking about a building or a bureaucracy, but an assembly of people with a common purpose. In the Old Testament, Israel was God's *ekklesia*. In the New, the *ekklesia* would be followers of Jesus.

But Peter's "Messiah high" soon diminished. Jesus told the disciples about the suffering the Messiah would endure. Peter could not bear such talk: "Peter took him aside and began to rebuke him. 'Never, Lord!' he said. 'This shall never happen to you!'" (Matthew 16:22). Peter cannot conceive that the Messiah, the Son of God, would have to "suffer many things." Jesus had commended Peter, calling him "blessed," but now his tone is different: "Get behind me, Satan! You are a stumbling block to me; you do not have in mind the things of God, but the things of men."

How did Peter so quickly go from being "the rock" to "Satan"? Jesus didn't mean that Peter literally was Satan, of course. The word *Satan* in Hebrew meant "adversary." In opposing the route of suffering and humiliation that Jesus was destined to follow, Peter was setting himself up as an adversary. He was holding on to the Jewish ideas of the Messiah as a power figure, a conqueror who would lead an army and defeat Israel's enemies. But this wasn't God's way of doing things. Peter had much to learn. Peter and the others had to let go of their deceitful dreams of a political Messiah.

And yet, in this episode, Peter is supremely lovable. He is utterly devoted to Jesus, and so he cannot bear the thought of seeing his Master suffer in any way. Humanly speaking, what more could we expect of a disciple? Jesus was asking Peter to stretch himself, spiritually speaking, to try to see things as God saw them. Peter had been right in discerning that Jesus was Messiah and Son of God. What he could not see—yet—was that the Messiah would reach his goal not through conquest but through suffering.

> **DID YOU KNOW?**
>
> The name that Jesus actually bestowed on Peter was *Kepha*, Aramaic for "rock." In Greek it is *Petros*. The name Kepha, in the form *Cephas*, appears in John 1:41, 1 Corinthians 1:12, 3:22, 9:5 and 15:5, and Galatians 1:18 and 2:9. Paul, for whatever reason, usually referred to Peter by his Aramaic name.

> Peter replied, "Even if all fall away on account of you, I never will."
>
> "I tell you the truth," Jesus answered, "this very night, before the rooster crows, you will disown me three times." (Matthew 26:33–34)
>
> The Lord turned and looked straight at Peter. Then Peter remembered the word the Lord had spoken to him: "Before the rooster crows today, you will disown me three times." (Luke 22:61)

Here we have one of the great stories of the Bible, showing Peter at his best—and worst. No fiction writer could ever have created such a story.

It begins at the Last Supper. Jesus had been warning the disciples for weeks that he has a date with destiny in Jerusalem; yet they—so slow to understand—never fully accept this. During the supper, Jesus told them bluntly that they will all fall away from him.

Not Peter—or so "the rock" believed. Jesus saw the future more clearly: Peter will not only fall away, but will also deny three times that he even knows Jesus. Given Peter's bluntness and boldness, the other disciples might have agreed that if anyone stuck by Jesus, it would be Peter.

When they left the house in which the Last Supper was held, they went to the garden of Gethsemane. Jesus was in agony, and he took the inner circle—Peter, James and John—aside from the others and asked the three to keep watch while he prayed alone. He prayed to his Father that, if it was God's will, the ordeal ahead not take place. In the depths of such agony, he came and found the three disciples, his closest companions on earth, asleep: "Watch and pray so that you will not fall into temptation. The spirit is willing, but the body is weak" (Matthew 26:41).

Indeed, the flesh was weak. When Judas arrived with the arresting party and Jesus was taken, the disciples fled, just as Jesus had predicted. Peter, to his credit (he loved his Master and wanted to defend him) and blame (he chose violence), cut off the ear of one of the men in the party. But then he too fled.

But he could not stay in hiding. He followed the band at a distance—in fact, all the way into the courtyard of the high priest's house, the belly of the beast. He had reacted like a coward and then had corrected himself. But in the courtyard he would be tested further. When Peter was by the fire in the courtyard, it was likely the servants were discussing what had just occurred, no doubt making various statements about Jesus and the disciples. A servant girl thought she recognized Peter as being with Jesus. Peter denied it. Then another girl made the same accusation. Peter: "I don't know the man!" Peter's own voice betrayed him: He had the accent of a Galilean, so someone else said that Peter was surely among Jesus' followers. "Then he began to call down curses on himself and he swore to them, 'I don't know the man!' Immediately a rooster crowed. Then Peter remembered the word Jesus had spoken: 'Before the rooster crows, you will disown me three times.' And he went outside and wept bitterly" (Matthew 26:74–75).

Peter "wept bitterly." We can well imagine what was racing through his mind—not just the prediction of his own denials but also Jesus' stern warning: "Whoever acknowledges me before men, I will also acknowledge him before my Father in heaven. But whoever disowns me before men, I will disown him before my Father in heaven" (Matthew 10:32–33).

Luke 22:61 provides this important detail: "The Lord turned and looked straight at Peter. Then Peter remembered the word the Lord had spoken to him." Jesus would not have looked at Peter with hatred or shock; probably it was a look of sadness and disappointment. The look must have cut Peter to his heart. In denying his Master, he had so distanced himself from Jesus that he had not even spoken Jesus' name: "I don't know the man!"

But the beauty in the story is the weeping. Peter's tears were water for his soul, the "godly sorrow" which "brings repentance that leads to salvation" (2 Corinthians 7:10). Was Paul, who came to know Peter, thinking of him when he wrote those words? Certainly Peter's sorrow was far different from the sorrow of Judas, who saw no alternative but to end his own wretched life.

By the time the Gospels were written, there were already persecutions—either by governments or from the harassment of unbelieving neighbors. Peter's denial provides

CHARACTERS AT LARGE ## Peter in Art

In artworks, Peter is often depicted as an older man, gray haired and balding, while John is usually shown as young and beardless. The Bible says nothing whatsoever about what the disciples looked like, but John 21 hints that Peter will die long before the "other disciple" (John), and thus artists have assumed Peter is older. Also, John relates that Peter and the other disciple run to Jesus' empty tomb, but the other disciple gets there first—the younger man outrunning the older one (John 20:3–6).

In art, the crucifixion of Peter is a favorite subject, showing Peter—old and bald—being crucified upside down, based on an old legend that when Peter was about to be crucified as a Christian, he stated that he did not deserve to die in the same way as his Lord, and the Romans complied by crucifying him head downward.

not only an intriguing bit of sacred history but also a model for believers not to follow, as well as a reminder that there is repentance and forgiveness available for those who stumble. Peter is a reminder that anyone who ever breaks a promise—which is probably everyone who has ever lived and will live—can be forgiven. The rooster that is almost always featured in paintings of Peter is a reminder to us: We may have a high opinion of our abilities, and we may sorely disappoint ourselves and God, but, like Peter, our failings are a path to healing.

FROM FAILURE TO SHEPHERD

As soon as Simon Peter heard him say, "It is the Lord," he wrapped his outer garment around him (for he had taken it off) and jumped into the water. (John 21:7)

The third time he said to him, "Simon son of John, do you love me?" Peter was hurt because Jesus asked him the third time, "Do you love me?" He said, "Lord, you know all things; you know that I love you." Jesus said, "Feed my sheep." (John 21:17)

Where was Peter when Jesus was flogged and crucified? The Gospels don't tell us. But wherever he was, he was coping with the enormous grief of having denied his Master three times. Even if he had believed Jesus' prophecy of rising from the grave the third day after his death, he might not have looked forward to the event, given his denial.

John 20 tells of Mary Magdalene's going to the tomb on Easter morning and finding it empty. She ran to tell the news to Peter and the others. Peter and another disciple—tradition says it was John—ran to the tomb. The other disciple arrived first, saw the empty linen shroud, and believed in the Resurrection. It is not stated that Peter believed. But he did believe that very evening when Jesus appeared to the disciples and spoke the words, "Peace be with you," which must have brought indescribable peace to Peter's troubled soul. Jesus tells them they are to go out to the world and proclaim the Gospel.

John 21 records a later appearance of the risen Jesus to the disciples. Seven of them, Peter included, had been fishing at night on the Sea of Galilee but had caught nothing. Jesus, from the shore, told them to cast their net on the right side of their boat. They complied and dragged in a huge catch that they could barely manage to haul in. The unnamed disciple—again, probably John—recognized Jesus from the boat and said, "It is the Lord!" Impulsively and joyously, Peter jumped into the water and made for the shore. He and the others then enjoyed a breakfast with their Master.

But the delightful encounter turned painful. Jesus asked Peter, "Do you love me?" Peter replied, "Yes, Lord, you know I love you." This happened again—and then a third time. Peter was hurt and said, "Lord, you know all things." He knew Jesus could see into his heart and also remembered how Jesus had foretold his three denials.

Jesus asked Peter, "Do you truly love me more than these?" referring to the other disciples. He was reminding Peter that he had said, "Even if all fall away on account of you, I never will" (Matthew 26:33). At this point Peter did not protest that he lovesd Jesus more than the others did; he had to rely on what Jesus saw inside him. This is clearly an example for all to follow; boasting of our devotion is pointless if our hearts are not in accord.

Undoubtedly, Jesus' three-time questioning of Peter is to remind the reader that Peter, who three times denied knowing Jesus, is then given a position of leadership by the risen Jesus: The Good Shepherd commissions Peter to "feed my sheep." Jesus is not trying to keep Peter in a state of never-ending guilt. He is reminding him of his notorious failing, but, in the same breath, giving him the commission to "tend the flock" of the faithful. Peter will be important, but never can he forget his humanness.

Jesus adds a prophecy: "When you were younger you dressed yourself and went where you wanted; but when you are old you will stretch out your hands, and someone else will dress you and lead you where you do not want to go." The Gospel adds, "Jesus said this to indicate the kind of death by which Peter would glorify God" (John 21:18–19). Peter, who had said before his denials that he was willing to die for Jesus, would in the future be able to make that ultimate sacrifice. Thus he would be the faithful shepherd who, like his Master, lays down his life for the flock of the faithful. It is clear in John 21:19 that Peter's death has already occurred when the Gospel was written. The phrase "stretch out your hands" was commonly used among the early Christians to refer to crucifixion. Peter literally followed his Master to the cross.

But before he did so, the "rock" and the "shepherd" of Jesus' flock had much work to do on earth. He would, as Jesus prophesied, "strengthen the brothers" (Luke 22:32).

SPIRIT-FIRED PREACHER

"Let all Israel be assured of this: God has made this Jesus, whom you crucified, both Lord and Christ."

When the people heard this, they were cut to the heart and said to Peter and the other apostles, "Brothers, what shall we do?"

Peter replied, "Repent and be baptized, every one of you, in the name of Jesus Christ for the forgiveness of your sins. And you will receive the gift of the Holy Spirit." (Acts 2:36–38)

Acts 2 is one of the great chapters in the Bible; it tells the story of Pentecost. Following Jesus' ascension into heaven, the apostles were in Jerusalem at the time of the Jewish feast of Pentecost, a holy celebration that drew Jews from far and wide. The house in which the apostles met was shaken as if by a violent wind. Then the twelve "saw what seemed to be tongues of fire that separated and came to rest on each of them. All of them were filled with the Holy Spirit and began to speak in other tongues as the Spirit enabled them" (Acts 2:1–3). The Spirit had filled them for a reason: They were going to preach the message of Jesus to the diverse people assembled in the city.

At first the visitors did not know what to make of the apostles' sudden ability to speak other languages. Some onlookers mocked; perhaps these men had been drinking early in the day!

Peter replied with the first Christian sermon. No, the apostles were not drunk at nine in the morning. To the contrary, they were filled with the Spirit, fulfilling the Old Testament prophecy of Joel that God's Spirit would be poured out on many "in the last days." The "last days" had arrived, as witnessed by the doings of Jesus, a man who had done many great miracles—a man crucified by "you." Yet God had raised him to life again, and the apostles were witnesses of this. Men had crucified Jesus—but God had made Jesus both Lord and Messiah.

Acts emphasizes the diversity of the listeners. They are all either Jews or proselytes (Gentile converts to Judaism), yet they come from as far away as Rome, Parthia and Libya. Peter has addressed them as "men of Israel"—not Israel as a political unit, but the spiritual Israel, those who follow the true God. They are all devout; that is, they take their faith seriously and are not mere tourists in Jerusalem. Belief matters to them, so they are receptive to what Peter says.

Hearing Peter's sermon, the listeners were "cut to the heart and said to Peter and the other apostles, 'Brothers, what shall we do?'" Peter told them, "Repent and be baptized, every one of you, in the name of Jesus Christ for the forgiveness of your sins. And you will receive the gift of the Holy Spirit." The sermon lit a fire in men's hearts.

Jesus had foretold that after he returned to heaven, the disciples would perform even greater works than he had done (John 14:12). On Pentecost this happens, with three thousand converts at one time. Of the three thousand, some of them must have been "cut to the heart" because they themselves had been present at Jesus' trial and crucifixion and given their approval. Others may have watched and wondered if Jesus was guilty or not. But even those who had been favorable to Jesus would still have been "cut to the heart" by Peter's sermon, aware of what a tragedy it was for the Jews to have given their Messiah up to be crucified.

"Repent and be baptized." Inner change was to be accompanied by an outward sign. This baptism was something new, however, for it is "in the name of Jesus Christ." This is the first use of "Jesus Christ" in Acts. Peter, who had been the first to grasp that Jesus was the "Christ, the son of the living God," was now preaching "in the name of Jesus Christ."

HEAL THE SICK, RAISE THE DEAD

> He found a man named Aeneas, a paralytic who had been bedridden for eight years. "Aeneas," Peter said to him, "Jesus Christ heals you. Get up and take care of your mat." Immediately Aeneas got up. (Acts 9:33–34)

> Turning toward the dead woman, he said, "Tabitha, get up." She opened her eyes, and seeing Peter she sat up. He took her by the hand and helped her to her feet. Then he called the believers and the widows and presented her to them alive. (Acts 9:40–41)

Jesus had told his disciples "Heal the sick, raise the dead, cleanse those who have leprosy, drive out demons" (Matthew 10:8). They had seen him do all these things, but did they ever think they themselves could actually raise the dead?

In Acts 9, Peter is in Judea, but away from Jerusalem, visiting the dispersed Christians who had fled Jerusalem. Presumably Aeneas was among the Christians at the town of Lydda. The evangelist Philip had earlier passed through this region, so perhaps Aeneas was one of his converts. The Greek words describing Aeneas' condition may mean he had been bedridden for eight years, or since he had been eight years old. In either case, his was a serious affliction. Peter gave credit to Jesus Christ, not to himself. Not only was Aeneas healed immediately, but others also heard about the miracle and came to faith.

In the same chapter, we find an even greater miracle than a healing. In the seaside

---

CULTURAL INSIGHTS

Joppa

Joppa was already an ancient city when Peter went there; it existed as early as 1500 BC. It is mentioned several times in the Old Testament, most famously as the port from which the prophet Jonah tried to flee from God. Joppa—today called Jaffa—is the home of St. Peter's Church, which commemorates Peter's raising of Tabitha. The stained-glass windows in the church depict other episodes from the life of Peter, including the Transfiguration and Jesus' washing the disciples' feet. The original church was built by the Crusaders in the 1200s; in the 1800s Napoleon resided in the church for a while during his Palestinian military campaign.

town of Joppa lived a believer named Tabitha, "who was always doing good and helping the poor" (Acts 9:36). Tabitha became sick and then died, and her friends laid her out in an upstairs room. Having heard of Peter's healing of the paralyzed Aeneas, some of the Christians sent word to Peter: "Please come at once!"

When Peter arrived, the women were wailing—genuinely wailing, for in this time and place, mourners did not hold back their tears but let them flow freely. They had lost a dear friend and a woman of compassion, and they could not resist showing Peter some of the clothing Tabitha had made for them. Acts refers to the "believers and widows" present, which doesn't mean that some of the widows were not Christians ("believers"), only that Tabitha had a special concern for widows, and possibly her charity extended beyond the circle of Christians.

What followed resembles another biblical healing: Peter may have remembered when Jesus healed the daughter of Jairus. Jesus had sent the mourners out of the room and said to the dead child, *Talitha, kumi*—"little girl, get up." Peter would have spoken the same Aramaic words, with one small difference: *Tabitha, kumi*—"Tabitha, get up." She did so, and her friends were overjoyed. As with other healings, word of the miracle furthers the spread of the Gospel.

This story is pleasant to read because it brings into the foreground one of many, many women—mostly unnamed—whose deeds of kindness too often go unpraised. Tabitha "was always doing good and helping the poor." Her life had been one of those steady, decent lives that the history books, which focus on the "important" people, typically fail to record. While the memorable part of the story is the miracle that Peter performs, we can be glad that Acts records some details about Tabitha and her works of compassion.

ANGEL IN PRISON

The night before Herod was to bring him to trial, Peter was sleeping between two soldiers, bound with two chains, and sentries stood guard at the entrance. Suddenly an angel of the Lord appeared and a light shone in the cell. He struck Peter on the side and woke him up. "Quick, get up!" he said, and the chains fell off Peter's wrists. (Acts 12:6–7)

Acts 12 records a time of persecution, initiated by Herod Agrippa I, called simply "Herod" in Acts. We look at the character of this immoral ruler more closely in another chapter (see Day 18). Having executed the apostle James—the first of the twelve to be martyred for the faith—Herod saw that it pleased the Jews, so he planned further persecution, and he threw the chief among the apostles in prison. Peter was a natural choice: He was the boldest among the apostles, and he was also associated with the spread of the faith to the Gentiles.

Peter seemed to be in an impossible situation—not only in prison, but also chained between two guards. Herod must have heard of the earlier incident of the apostles' being miraculously released from prison, so he was taking no chance with Peter.

But things did not go as Herod planned. The believers in Jerusalem prayed for Peter, and their prayer was answered. On what Herod intended to be the last night of Peter's life, Peter was awakened by an angel. The mere fact that Peter was able to fall asleep under such circumstances—chained between two soldiers, knowing he would probably die the next day—is almost a miracle in itself, but Peter had put his fate in God's hands. In fact, Peter's sleep had been so sound that when the angel tapped him and told him to get up, Peter thought it was all a dream. Peter's chains fell off, and the angel escorted him out past the guards into the street and then disappeared as suddenly as he had appeared.

Peter realized this was not a dream, that he really was free. "Free" did not mean "out of danger," however, for he knew Herod's men would be searching frantically for him when it was discovered he was gone. Some men might have simply fled the city as fast as possible and hoped to stay in hiding a long time, but Peter went to a meeting place of the Christians—the home of John Mark and his mother Mary. The believers were at prayer at the time. A servant girl, Rhoda, went to answer Peter's knock and was so excited to hear his voice she forgot to open the door. The other believers thought she was hysterical. They had all been praying for Peter, yet obviously not expecting his actual release. Their reply to Rhoda—"It must be his angel"—reflects the common view of the time that each person had a guardian angel who could at times put on the appearance of the person he guarded. But Peter kept knocking, and when they let him in, he told the excited and astonished group of how he escaped. Peter then "left for another place," presumably far from Jerusalem.

The story ended happily for Peter and his friends, but unhappily for the poor guards, for when it was learned that Peter had escaped, Herod ordered their execution.

Peter had come through various trials, proving to be the "rock." His experience with persecution would serve him well years later, when he wrote his two epistles to people whose faith was under fire.

EPISTLES FROM BABYLON

To the elders among you, I appeal as a fellow elder, a witness of Christ's sufferings and one who also will share in the glory to be revealed. (1 Peter 5:1)

Say *epistle* and most Bible-readers immediately think Paul. Often overlooked are the two brief but highly readable epistles known as 1 and 2 Peter. Martin Luther, the great Reformation leader of the 1500s, thought well of 1 Peter, calling it one of the great books

Peter on Paul

"Our Lord's patience means salvation, just as our dear brother Paul also wrote you with the wisdom that God gave him. He writes the same way in all his letters, speaking in them of these matters. His letters contain some things that are hard to understand, which ignorant and unstable people distort, as they do the other Scriptures, to their own destruction" (2 Peter 3:15–16). This is the only case in the New Testament where one author refers to the writings of another. Acts shows some interaction between Paul and Peter, but here Peter is commenting on Paul's writings, which, Peter says, "contain some things that are hard to understand." True enough, but note that he classes Paul's writings as "Scripture." At this early date—before Peter's death in AD 64—Paul's writings were already so highly regarded they were considered Scripture, sacred writings inspired by God.

of the New Testament. Certainly it is one of the underappreciated gems of the Bible, not only richly readable but also delightful in showing the gentle side of Peter: Peter as an "elder statesman" among Christians, offering advice and consolation.

Tradition says Peter died in the horrible persecution of Christians in Rome, which began in AD 64 after emperor Nero blamed Christians for the great fire in Rome. Obviously Peter's two letters were written prior to this. However, he was probably in Rome when he wrote 1 Peter, because at the letter's end he sends greetings from "Babylon"—definitely not the ancient faraway city of Babylon, but a code name for Rome, which—like Babylon—was a pagan and immoral place. At this time there was no official persecution of Christians in Rome. Yet persecution was taking place, not only in Rome but also everywhere the faith spread. It came not from the government but from pagan neighbors.

The persecution theme comes out in the letter's opening: "Peter, an apostle of Jesus Christ, To God's elect, strangers in the world, scattered throughout Pontus, Galatia, Cappadocia, Asia and Bithynia" (1 Peter 1:1). The place names were locales in the region evangelized by Paul in Acts. But more important are the names Peter uses for Christians: They are the "elect," the "called" people, called out of a sinful world. In fact, they are "strangers in the world," not destined to be fully at home in it, and they are "scattered" everywhere. Acts shows how Paul was harassed and almost killed while spreading the Gospel, and now his many converts are also being harassed.

No one likes to suffer, but Peter assures them it can be endured. After all, they have the perfect example to

DID YOU KNOW?

Peter's actual birth name in Aramaic was not Simon but the Old Testament name *Simeon*. The name appears in the opening of 2 Peter.

follow, Jesus himself. Jesus was the "example," the *hupogrammos*, which was literally a tablet showing all the letters of the alphabet, giving the students a pattern to follow as they learned to write. "Christ suffered for you, leaving you an example, that you should follow in his steps" (1 Peter 1:21).

In fact, believers should "rejoice" in being able to suffer for Christ's sake (1 Peter 4:13). Peter could speak with authority on this subject, for in Acts he and the other disciples did indeed rejoice when they suffered in the name of Jesus (1 Peter 5:41). The theme of good people suffering is also found in 2 Peter, which reminds the faithful that God will in time deliver them, just as he delivered Lot from the immoral city of Sodom (2 Peter 2:7).

But there is more to the life of faith than suffering. There is a great "inheritance" awaiting them. Such a promise must have given great hope to the many Christians who were poor—or, even worse, slaves, with no hope at all for any kind of earthly inheritance. Life in this world of immorality and selfishness could often be unpleasant, but people of faith were, like Jesus himself, "rejected by men but chosen by God and precious to him" (2 Peter 2:4). Peter, the rock, told Christians they were "living stones," being built into a great spiritual temple for the Lord (2 Peter 2:5). Of course, the chief stone, the "capstone," is Jesus himself.

These persecuted ones might be treated as outcasts by their pagan neighbors, but God had a higher view of things: "You are a chosen people, a royal priesthood, a holy nation, a people belonging to God, that you may declare the praises of him who called you out of darkness into his wonderful light" (2 Peter 2:9).

Recall that Peter, along with James, John and Andrew, had questioned their Master about the end times and his return to earth. Time was passing and Christians were

---

CULTURAL INSIGHTS

"Christian"—a Slur?

"The disciples were called Christians first at Antioch" (Acts 11:26). Was it a compliment, a slur or merely a descriptive term? The fact that it occurs only three times in the New Testament, and that the usual terms used by the Christians themselves are "brothers," "disciples," "believers," "saints," and "followers of the Way" suggests it was a slur. In Acts 26:28, Agrippa asks (with a sneer, we sense) if Paul thinks he can persuade him to be a Christian. And consider 1 Peter 4:16: "If you suffer as a Christian, do not be ashamed, but praise God that you bear that name." It sounds like nonbelievers said "Christian" with a smirk. Outside the Bible, the Roman historians Tacitus and Suetonius both refer to "Christians" with undisguised disgust. If "Christian" was originally a derogatory term, it fits the historical pattern of a title of contempt, coined by the opposition, which comes to be accepted by the group itself.

beginning to wonder: Has Jesus forgotten his promise to return? In 2 Peter, the apostle addressed that nagging question: "With the Lord a day is like a thousand years, and a thousand years are like a day. The Lord is not slow in keeping his promise, as some understand slowness. He is patient with you, not wanting anyone to perish but everyone to come to repentance" (2 Peter 3:8–9). In the meantime, people of faith ought to live holy lives—a theme common to both letters. Regardless of what they may have to endure from the people around them, they can look forward to "a new heaven and a new earth, the home of righteousness" (2 Peter 3:13).

PUTTING THE WORD TO WORK

1. Think about Peter's ill-fated attempt to walk on the water. Can you think of times when you overestimated your own faith or abilities? What did you learn from your failures?

2. Put yourself in Peter's place when Jesus said to him, "Get behind me, Satan!" How do you think Peter reacted inwardly to this scolding?

3. Think of people you know (including yourself) who have, under pressure, denied their faith or passed up an opportunity to speak out for it. How did it affect their walk with God?

4. The episode of Peter's deliverance from prison shows that his friends had prayed for his release and then were shocked when the prayer was answered. Has this happened in your own life? What does this say about the nature of prayer?

5. Reflect on the words in 1 Peter about "rejoicing" when we suffer for belonging to Jesus. Do Peter's words take on a richer meaning when we are aware of what Peter himself endured?

Jacob, Joseph and Family

The last half of Genesis is the amazing story of the patriarch Jacob, a deceitful trickster who in turn is deceived by his scheming father-in-law—and later by his sons. Through his adversity, Jacob becomes a more mature man, and this is also true of his favorite son, Joseph, who goes from being a spoiled son to a slave to a prisoner to the right-hand man of the most powerful ruler on earth. This is the story of a blended family with many conflicts and woes, and dysfunctional though it seems, it is an inspiring tale full of fascinating people who run red with emotion.

> **MEMORY VERSE**
>
> **Endure hardship as discipline; God is treating you as sons. For what son is not disciplined by his father?—Hebrews 12:7**

KEY TERM FOR TODAY   ## Maturity

God uses adversity to shape us into spiritually mature people, as illustrated by the stories of Jacob and Joseph, flawed men whose hardships drew them closer to the Lord.

BROTHERLY LOVE—NOT!

The Lord said to her, "Two nations are in your womb, and two peoples from within you will be separated; one people will be stronger than the other, and the older will serve the younger." . . . The boys grew up. Esau became a skillful hunter, a man of the open country, while Jacob was a quiet man, staying among the tents. (Genesis 25:23, 27)

The patriarch Abraham had been promised by God that he would become the father of a great nation. His faith was severely tested by the long years of waiting as his beloved wife, Sarah, continued to be childless. There was great rejoicing when at long last their son Isaac was born. However, when Isaac married Rebekah, the same problem arose again: barrenness. Isaac prayed, and the couple did not have to wait nearly as long as Abraham and Sarah had.

Rebekah conceived, but it was, to put it mildly, a difficult pregnancy. She was carrying twins, and they "jostled within her," causing her such distress that she prayed to God for an explanation. The Lord's answer: The two sons within her would be the ancestors of two nations, "and the older will serve the younger." A question arises: How can we talk of "older" when discussing twins? Technically, one twin has to exit the womb first, and in ancient times people took birth order seriously, with many privileges going to the firstborn. Rebekah gave birth to twins, the first named Esau, the second Jacob—the Hebrew word meaning "grabber," for Jacob literally had hold of his brother's heel as he exited the womb. Rebekah took the Lord's words to heart. Esau, the "older" brother, was destined to serve Jacob, the "younger." And as if to emphasize the brothers' differences, Jacob was a smooth-skinned infant while Esau was hairy.

Their personalities were very different too. Esau was an outdoorsman, fond of hunting, and he pleased his father Isaac by bringing home game for him to eat. "Jacob was a quiet man, staying among the tents." He was his mother's favorite, and though it is tempting to peg Jacob with the label "Mama's boy," it would be wrong to think of Jacob as some milksop. Isaac, like his father Abraham was a nomad, a herder of sheep and goats. Jacob was no doubt learning the trade of keeping the flocks, while Esau was off on the hunt. In other words, Jacob was proving more useful to the family, but Isaac favored the woodsy Esau, who brought him venison to eat.

Genesis 25 records the brief but important episode of Esau coming in from the hunt, almost starving. Jacob, as it happened, was cooking some delicious-smelling stew. Esau, famished, asked for some stew. Jacob made an offer: some stew in exchange for Esau's birthright—that is, his inheritance rights as the older son. Esau—possibly thinking Jacob was joking, but who knows?—claimed he was about to die from hunger, so what good was his birthright then? So Esau sold his birthright, swearing to the deal. He ate and went his way, apparently not giving the deal any further thought.

Commentators have written much about this story. Was Jacob being cruel, denying food to his brother? Was he taking advantage of his hunger? Possibly. But Esau knew that a birthright was a serious matter: You don't sell your inheritance because you happen to be ravenously hungry. Sermons on this passage emphasize Esau's carnal nature, a materialistic man who gave no thought to the consequences of his actions, who was witless enough to sacrifice the long-term good (his inheritance) for a short-term good (lentil stew).

Whatever the deeper meaning of the episode, it shows Jacob's chief character trait coming to the fore, his selfish, manipulative, scheming nature, a man willing to take advantage of another person—his twin brother—to benefit himself.

Genesis 27 reveals that his scheming nature came from his mother. Isaac, having grown blind, feared he was near death and wanted to pronounce a blessing on Esau. He asked Esau to go hunting and bring him back some venison to eat. Rebekah overheard the conversation and concocted a way to turn the blessing to Jacob's advantage. She cooked some young goats from the flocks—after living with Isaac for many years, she seemed to know how to cook a dish that resembled venison enough to fool him. The plan was for Jacob to carry his father the food, pretend to be Esau, and receive the paternal blessing. (Alert readers notice that Esau and Isaac were one of a kind in their attitude toward food, for Isaac was fond of venison, which Esau supplied, and Esau stupidly sold his birthright for a pot of stew.)

DID YOU KNOW?

Esau's descendants became the nation known as Edom, which was frequently at war with Israel over the centuries.

Jacob hesitated. The deception of Isaac could have been perceived not only as stealing Esau's blessing, but also as mocking the old man's blindness. Jacob feared this mockery, if found out, would make Isaac curse him instead of blessing him (Genesis 27:12). Also, he was smooth-skinned while Esau was hairy, and certainly Isaac would touch him when bestowing his blessing. Rebecca thought of that too: Jacob would wear pieces of goatskin on his hands and the back of his neck to fool Isaac. Then she dressed him in Esau's "best clothes," which probably meant garments worn at times of celebration or sacrifices, garments belonging to the elder son.

When Jacob did as his mother suggested, the old man was surprised: How had Esau hunted down his game so quickly? Jacob's reply was, "The Lord your God gave me success." Jacob had actually taken God's name in vain in the deception. Isaac was still skeptical, so he asked Jacob, "Who are you?" Jacob seemed to be disguising his voice, and he was not quite successful. But when Isaac pulled him near and felt his hairy hands and neck and smelled Esau's garments, he was certain it was Esau. He pronounced a blessing—something the people of the time took very seriously, since it was like a prophecy that had to come true. Jacob, the younger son, had his older brother's birthright and blessing.

No sooner did Jacob leave—no doubt feeling very pleased with himself—than Esau returned. On discovering he had been deceived, the aged Isaac "trembled violently," becoming almost apoplectic. Esau was overcome with emotion too, crying out in his bitterness and rage. He knew the blessing bestowed on Jacob could not be retracted. He asked Isaac for a blessing on himself. Isaac complied, but it was a lesser blessing than he had bestowed on Jacob.

DID YOU KNOW?

When Michelangelo painted Jacob on the ceiling of the Sistine Chapel in Rome, he gave Jacob a furtive, suspicious look, an appropriate demeanor for this deceiver, who was often at risk for being caught up with—or being deceived by—someone else.

Not surprisingly, Esau nursed a grudge against Jacob. Thinking Isaac did not have long to live, Esau promised that once Isaac was buried, he would kill Jacob. Hearing of this, Rebekah sent Jacob far away, to her brother Laban.

According to Job 5:13, God "catches the wise in their craftiness." The words certainly apply to Rebekah and Jacob. Jacob and Rebekah's deception of the aged, blind Isaac got them what they wanted—his blessing on Jacob—but also brought its own punishment: Jacob's exile and separation from his mother, whom he never saw again. And he was about to learn some further lessons in deceit—very painful ones.

ANGELS AND LOVE—AND A GREAT COMEUPPANCE

He had a dream in which he saw a stairway resting on the earth, with its top reaching to heaven, and the angels of God were ascending and descending on it. . . . He was afraid and said, "How awesome is this place! This is none other than the house of God; this is the gate of heaven." (Genesis 28:17)

Jacob's destination was Haran, which had been Rebekah's home before she married Isaac. Jacob would find great satisfaction in Haran—and great frustration as well.

His journey there was eventful. He stopped to sleep and, resting his head on a stone, had an awesome dream: Angels were going to and from heaven on a stairway. He heard the voice of God: "I am the God of your father Abraham and the God of Isaac. I will give you and your descendants the land on which you are lying. . . . I am with you and will watch over you wherever you go, and I will bring you back to this land" (Genesis 28:13).

Consider Jacob's situation: having always lived at home, he had never been separated from his parents. Here he was, alone in the wilderness, and he heard the voice of God, the same God who promised to make a great nation of Abraham's descendants. He is also the God of Isaac—the father Jacob had so recently deceived. Yet God did not scold Jacob. He promised him land and descendants—and made an even greater promise: "I will be with you and will watch over you."

Up to this point, Jacob had never seen God or heard his voice. Perhaps he was not even aware that the place he was lying on was Bethel—the name means "house of God"—where his grandfather had built an altar to God many years before. But the formerly unreligious Jacob was changed by his experience. "Surely the Lord is in this place!" He was so awed by his experience that he set up a pillar on the site. The trickster, the mama's boy who had shown so little respect for his father and twin brother, had his mind turned to God.

Then Jacob had another life-changing experience: He fell in love. On reaching Haran, he encountered a beautiful young woman who was bringing sheep to a well to water them. She happened to be his own cousin, Rachel, daughter of his uncle Laban. "Then Jacob kissed Rachel and began to weep aloud" (Genesis 29:11). We mustn't read too much into the kiss. It may have been a romantic kiss, but it was customary to kiss

Kissing

"Then Jacob kissed Rachel and began to weep aloud" (Genesis 29:11). It's a touching episode, and one that stands out, because most of the kisses in the Bible were not of a romantic nature. People kissed idols of the gods they worshipped, kissed relatives or old friends, and, as in the infamous case of Judas Iscariot and Jesus, kissed their teachers. There was romantic kissing, as found in the Song of Solomon (1:2, 8:1), though even there it is only mentioned twice. Aside from this, Proverbs speaks of a woman kissing a man in public—but this is the immoral woman that the proverb condemns heartily (Proverbs 7:13).

The first kiss mentioned in the Bible is aged, blind Isaac asking his favorite son, Esau, to come and kiss him (Genesis 27:26). When feuding brothers Jacob and Esau reconcile, they weep and kiss (Genesis 33:4). Moses and his brother Aaron, when they first meet as adults, kiss (Exodus 4:27). And of course, the most famous friends in the Bible, David and Jonathan, kiss (1 Samuel 20:41). Later, David's scheming son Absalom, plotting to oust his father as king, initiated the "political kiss": "Whenever anyone approached him to bow down before him, Absalom would reach out his hand, take hold of him and kiss him" (2 Samuel 15:5). Absalom was pressing the flesh, the ancient version of political handshaking and backslapping to win support.

Among the early Christians, a "holy kiss" (probably a peck on the cheek) was common practice. Paul closed four of his letters with the instructions "Greet one another with a holy kiss" (see Romans 16:16), which in 1 Peter is called the "kiss of love" (1 Peter 5:14).

family members as a greeting, and, later, Jacob would kiss his uncle Laban when they met. Jacob had been on the road alone for many days and no doubt missed his family.

But as the story continues, we see that Jacob really was in love with Rachel. His uncle Laban was fond of him immediately, for at this point Laban had no sons of his own, so Jacob was to be his surrogate son, and, it would turn out, his son-in-law as well. Jacob was willing to work for his uncle. In fact, he was willing to work for him for seven years, his "wages" being the hand of the beautiful Rachel.

Jacob, for all his faults, is an emotional and loving man. Clearly he inherited the loving disposition from both parents, who had had such a lovely courtship; plus, his grandparents Abraham and Sarah were a devoted couple. Laban had lucked out. He would have been pleased to have Jacob as a son-in-law regardless, but as it was, he got seven years of service in the process.

"So Jacob served seven years to get Rachel, but they seemed like only a few days to him because of his love for her" (Genesis 29:20). Naturally he was an eager groom when the seven years were up. On his wedding night, he and his bride went to bed—she would have been veiled during the wedding—and in the morning he discovered he had spent the night not with Rachel but with her older sister Leah. "Leah had weak eyes, but Rachel was lovely in form, and beautiful" (Genesis 29:17). " Jacob, the deceiver, had gotten a taste of his own medicine. He confronted his uncle with the deception. Laban explained that it was the custom of the country for a family to marry off the older sister first. However, he was willing to give Rachel as Jacob's wife also—if Jacob was willing to work for him for another seven years.

Laban must have assumed—correctly—that Jacob had enough honor not to cast Leah aside. He would stay married to her, and then work still another seven years for Rachel. Laban had hit upon a crafty way to marry off the older, less attractive daughter. Jacob finally had his comeuppance for what he had done to Isaac. He had tricked his own father. Now his father-in-law had tricked him.

The morning after this incident must have been an ordeal for the sisters as well as for Jacob. We can only imagine what Rachel was thinking as she watched Leah and Jacob head for the bridal chamber. Leah could not have been too pleased either, being wedded and bedded only through deception.

CHARACTER CLOSE-UP ## Reluctant Polygamists

People often remark that the Bible condones polygamy. It does—barely. In fact, as we see in the stories in Genesis, it was *not* highly thought of. God's original intention was one man with one woman—made clear enough in the story of Adam and Eve. Likewise, Noah, the one righteous man who gives mankind a new start after the flood, has only one wife, and so do his three sons. Lamech, an evil, violent character, is the first polygamist, and Esau, Jacob's brother, has three wives.

But didn't Jacob have two wives and two concubines as well? He did, but it is clear in Genesis that he had one true love, Rachel, and was willing to work seven years to gain her hand—only to be deceived by his scapegrace father-in-law into marrying Rachel's older sister Leah. Out of a sense of honor, Jacob stayed married to Leah and then married Rachel as well. Later, at his wives' insistence, he fathered children with two concubines, his wives' maids. Jacob was, we might say, a reluctant polygamist. In a classic case of God using a bad situation to a good end, Jacob's relations with his two wives and two concubines resulted quickly in a very large family—a family that would become in time the twelve tribes of Israel.

It should be noted that Isaac, Jacob's father, had only one wife, whom he loved. Abraham, Jacob's grandfather, loved only his wife Sarah, and it was at her urging that Abraham fathered a child by Sarah's maid Hagar. All three patriarchs were monogamous and loving—as God intended men to be.

But God smiled on Leah. She began having children, while Rachel was barren. Leah was unloved, yet she had four sons in quick succession. By the standards of the day, a plain woman with several children was better off than a pretty woman with none. Although the Bible doesn't say, Jacob's affection for her had to have increased, given the desire of men for sons.

Rachel became unhappy. She begged Jacob to give her children. Jacob told her he was not God—and, as Leah had proved, Jacob was not sterile. So Rachel followed the path of Jacob's grandmother Sarah: She offered up her maid as Jacob's concubine. Any children born to the maid would be, legally, Rachel's. So Rachel's maid bore Jacob a son, and then another. Jealous, Leah—who had ceased giving birth—offered up her own maid for the same purpose; that maid bore Jacob another two sons. Then Leah herself gave Jacob two more sons and a daughter, Dinah. And finally, at long last, the barren Rachel gave birth to a son, Joseph, who became his father's favorite.

One result of bedding four women in the household was that Jacob rather quickly became head of a large family, much larger than would have been possible had there been only one woman. The strange events that brought about Jacob's marriage to two women and then the fathering of children with their maids, was a kind of genetic jumpstart to the "great nation" that God had promised Abraham. In the providence of God, all the children except for Dinah were sons who would be ancestors and heads of Israel's tribes. It is possible that his eleven sons and Dinah could have been born within eight years. God's promise to make a great nation of Jacob was happening in a dramatic way.

SEPARATIONS AND REPARATIONS

It was also called Mizpah, because he [Laban] said, "May the Lord keep watch between you and me when we are away from each other." (Genesis 31:49)

Then the man said, "Your name will no longer be Jacob, but Israel, because you have struggled with God and with men and have overcome." (Genesis 32:28)

Jacob and Laban, despite the ill will that Laban's deception must have caused, seemed to have gotten along reasonably well. Both had prospered by working together, but Jacob remembered God's promise of the land of Canaan. He determined to pack up his enormous household and move back there—and chose to do so behind Laban's back. Jacob's two wives, Leah and Rachel, apparently had no hesitation about leaving their father.

Jacob and his retinue left without telling Laban, who was away at a sheep-shearing. Furious on finding out, Laban pursued them for a week. In a dream, God told him to speak neither good nor ill to Jacob. "Ill" would be attacking or reproaching Jacob, while "good" would be trying to smooth-talk him into returning. Nonetheless, when Laban overtook the band, he scolded Jacob about carrying off his daughters and doing it stealthily. The old man lied and said if he had known they were leaving, they would have held a feast with mirth and music. He feigned affection and said that at least Jacob should have given him the chance to kiss his children and grandchildren good-bye.

The connection between the deceitful Jacob and the deceitful Laban ended at a place called Mizpah. The two men set up a stone marker on the spot. According to their agreement, Jacob would not take other wives or treat his wives badly, and neither he nor Laban would ever pass the monument with the intention of going to the other to do him harm. Laban pronounced what is called the Mizpah Benediction: "May the Lord keep watch between you and me when we are away from each other." Beautiful as the words are, in the context they were simply Laban's way of saying, "You contemptible sneak, I hope God keeps his eyes on you when I can't watch you!"

Jacob and his wives must have been pleased to see the last of the deceitful old man. But Jacob had slid from the frying pan to the fire. In Canaan, he ran the risk of running into the angry man he had deceived, his brother Esau. Back in Genesis 27:45, Rebekah had told Jacob she would send him word when Esau's anger cooled. There is no indication she ever sent such a message. For all Jacob knew, Esau still held a grudge.

But as Jacob journeyed on, "the angels of God met him" at a place called Mahanaim (Genesis 32:1–2). Esau, the great hunter, presumably was more of a fighter than Jacob. But God had given Jacob a heavenly message: The armies of the Lord were on Jacob's side.

Even so, Jacob was taking no chances. He sent messengers on ahead to Esau, calling himself "servant" and Esau "master." Messengers came back with a noncommittal message: Esau was on the way to meet Jacob—with four hundred men. It sounded threatening, but we have to remember that Esau, for his part, had no clue whether Jacob was coming in peace. Certainly he had no reason to trust him. Jacob, not wanting Esau to wipe out his entire family, divided the caravan up into two groups.

That night, Jacob was left alone, "and a man wrestled with him till daybreak." In this tense situation, he must have assumed at first that this attacker was Esau or one of Esau's men. But as they continued to wrestle, something about this man disturbed Jacob. He was not wrestling with a man but with God. Jacob was stubborn: He told the man he would not let him go without a blessing. The man blessed him and bestowed a name change: Jacob's new name would be *Israel*, meaning "struggles with God." Jacob had struggled with both man and God. "So Jacob called the place Peniel, saying, 'It is because I saw God face-to-face, and yet my life was spared'" (Genesis 32:30).

This episode has fascinated artists and preachers. Readers like to believe the episode symbolizes every believer struggling in prayer with God. But for Jacob the encounter was very real, for the heavenly wrestler had pulled his hip joint out of its socket. The limp would have reminded him, probably for the rest of Jacob's life, that the wrestling match had not been a dream. For the moment, the importance of the encounter was this: Having faced God himself and lived, what threat could Esau possibly hold?

The next day, Jacob's caravan encountered Esau. Jacob went forth and bowed to the ground seven times. It was a tense moment. "But Esau ran to meet Jacob and embraced him; he threw his arms around his neck and kissed him. And they wept." The past was past, the anger and hatred gone.

Esau would have to have been amazed at Jacob's having so many children in such a short time. To the ancient mind, so obsessed with fertility and seeing it as God's blessing, it would have been clear that God had smiled on Jacob. In fact, Jacob pressed Esau to accept a gift. Esau resisted, but Jacob insisted, for he thought that seeing Esau's face was like seeing the face of God—a forgiving face, as it turned out.

The peaceful, happy reconciliation would have impressed everyone present. Jacob or Rachel must have told Joseph of it when he grew older, and perhaps it lodged in his mind years later when he forgave his own brothers in a tearful reunion.

DREAMER IN THE FAMOUS FROCK

Now Israel loved Joseph more than any of his other sons, because he had been born to him in his old age; and he made a richly ornamented robe for him. When his brothers saw that their father loved him more than any of them, they hated him and could not speak a kind word to him. (Genesis 37:3–4)

Jacob had proved himself good at fathering children—twelve sons and a daughter. Fathering children and being a wise father are two different things, as Jacob proved in his favoring of Joseph.

It was inevitable he would adore Joseph, since he was the long-awaited son of Jacob's beloved Rachel, who later died giving birth to another son, Benjamin. With Rachel gone, Jacob must have seen her image in young Joseph. He gave Joseph a beautiful robe—a "coat of many colors," as the King James Version so memorably phrases it.

So the brothers were jealous, and their jealousy increased even more when Joseph reported having mysterious dreams. In one dream, the brothers were binding up sheaves

Cisterns

In a dry region like Israel, it was common to store rainwater in cisterns, which were in-ground storage reservoirs. In effect, they were enormous holes dug in the ground and lined with stone or plaster to prevent leakage. Cisterns might be as much as a hundred feet deep. The cistern Joseph's brothers cast him into was probably dry at the time. Centuries later, the prophet Jeremiah was punished by being thrown into a cistern with mud at the bottom.

of grain in the field—his sheaf stood upright, and the sheaves of his brothers bowed down to his! Then came a second dream: eleven stars—his brothers, obviously—were bowing down to him. The brothers hated him "for his dreams and for his words." Obviously they thought he should have kept the dreams to himself—and he could have. But in the mysterious workings of God, Joseph's dreams—and his brothers' reaction to them—would have a good effect in time. Jacob, considering his own dream of the stairway into heaven, must have given serious thought to his son's dreams.

An opportunity arose: The brothers were tending flocks far from home, and Joseph went to check on them. With Jacob far away, they could easily kill the dreamer, throw his body in a cistern, and tell Jacob an animal had killed him. Reuben, the oldest son, would not agree to this; as the eldest, he had a duty to look after his brothers, including Joseph. So he suggested throwing Joseph into a cistern without harming him

DID YOU KNOW?

Joseph's famous coat, or robe, is referred to by the Hebrew word *passim*—translated "of many colors" in the King James Version but probably means "richly ornamented" or "with long sleeves."

—while he planned all along to come back later and rescue Joseph. While Joseph was in the cistern, Judah, another older brother, had a better idea: Why abandon or kill him when they could make some money by selling him to some of the slave-trading caravans passing by? In an odd turn of events, Joseph's life was spared due to his brothers' greed.

So Joseph was carried off, probably in chains, to faraway Egypt. The brothers took Joseph's beautiful robe and dipped it in blood. They presented it to Jacob and, without telling any actual lies, let Jacob draw the conclusion that Joseph had been devoured by a wild beast. Jacob, the deceiver of his father, was now deceived by his own sons. In his blindness to his sons' feelings, it seems not to have occurred to him that they would have been jealous of the spoiled Joseph.

> The Lord was with Joseph and he prospered, and he lived in the house of his Egyptian master. (Genesis 39:2)

Joseph was purchased by a high official named Potiphar, who quickly learned that he was no ordinary slave. Joseph was intelligent and industrious, and before long he was made overseer of Potiphar's house.

Let's pause here to consider Joseph's character. We know he was Jacob's favorite, and we assume that he was spoiled, especially when we consider the fine robe Jacob gave him. But there was no doubt more to being the favorite than merely gifts. Joseph must have spent more time with Jacob than the other brothers did, and Jacob would have tried to imbue him with moral teaching. Given Jacob's past tendency to deceitfulness—and his dealings with the deceptive Laban—Jacob might have pressed on Joseph the importance of integrity and honesty. And besides that, Joseph's recent experience as a slave must have had a humbling effect. No longer could he count on special treatment from anyone like Jacob. He would have had to rely on his own resources—and on God. Some people bloom in adversity, and clearly Joseph was one of those people. Instead of stewing in hatred for his brothers or for God, he made the most of his situation.

So he made a deep impression on Potiphar—and, alas, on Potiphar's wife. Joseph was about to learn that the most dangerous type of woman is another man's wife. Joseph was not only competent but attractive as well. And so Potiphar's wife tried to coax him into bed. Many men would have yielded to the temptation; among the upper-class Egyptians of

---

CULTURAL INSIGHTS

Eunuchs

Potiphar is referred to by the Hebrew word *saris*, usually meaning "eunuch," but it can also mean "court official." So many high officials in ancient times were eunuchs that the word for eunuch came to be the generic word for "chamberlain."

Why were eunuchs so common as royal officials? It was assumed they could be trusted with the king's wives and concubines—and, just as important, that a man with no sexual drive would channel all his energy into serving his master dutifully. Also, since the ancient world placed such importance on a man having sons, there was no danger that any eunuch would seize the throne and try to establish his own dynasty.

Potiphar, since he was married, was almost certainly not a eunuch, although readers have noted that, if he was, that would explain his wife's amorous behavior toward Joseph.

---

the time, it was probably a common-enough occurrence. Joseph did not just push her away brusquely. He justified his refusal: It would be a betrayal of all the trust the master put in him. There was a deeper reason: It was a sin against God. But when Joseph persistently refused her advances, she turned on him and accused him of trying to rape her.

Potiphar could have had Joseph killed immediately for the seduction of his wife, but he did not, which suggests he might have had doubts about his wife's story. The fact that he didn't press for Joseph's execution hints that he hoped at some point to bring him out of prison and have him manage the household again.

So Joseph went to prison—and even there, God was with him, for Joseph's good qualities made him the right-hand man of the jailer. As it happened, two fellow prisoners were the chief butler and chief baker to the pharaoh. Each of them had had a disturbing dream. The butler dreamed of three vine branches that blossomed and put forth grapes, which he squeezed into the pharaoh's cup. Joseph, the man with dreams, also had the God-given power to interpret them. He told the butler the meaning: In three days he would be released from prison and be in the pharaoh's service once again. The baker dreamed of three baskets of baked goods on his head, and the birds were eating from them. Joseph's interpretation was far from pleasant: In three days the pharaoh would cut off the baker's head, and the birds would eat his flesh.

Three days later, both dreams came true. It was the pharaoh's birthday, and according to custom, he released one prisoner—the butler. The baker was executed. But the butler forgot his promise to Joseph to mention Joseph's plight. So poor Joseph spent another two years in prison. Meanwhile, the pharaoh himself was having dreams. In one dream, seven fat cows came out of the river but were then devoured by seven scrawny cows. In the other dream, seven plump ears of grain were devoured by seven thin ears. What did the dreams mean? His court soothsayers were stumped. Then his butler remembered the imprisoned Joseph. Joseph was brought in—a slave and prisoner, was being asked for help by the most powerful man on

CHARACTERS AT LARGE ## Joseph in Art and Literature

Joseph's story has been popular with artists, particularly the attempted seduction by Potiphar's wife. Novelists and poets have been drawn to the story as well, and the noted German novelist Thomas Mann wrote a four-novel series titled *Joseph and His Brothers*. Composer George Frideric Handel wrote an oratorio, *Joseph and His Brethren*. The story was the basis of the popular musical play *Joseph and the Amazing Technicolor Dreamcoat*—which never once mentions the name of God.

earth. Joseph revealed the meaning of the dreams: Egypt would have seven years of bumper crops, followed by seven years of severe famine. The fact that the pharaoh had dreamed the same thing twice assured that it was God himself who sent the dreams.

There was more: Joseph told Potiphar that coping with the coming famine would mean choosing a wise man to set up a system of storing food during the fat years so the country would not starve in the famine. The pharaoh agreed—and who better to do this than the dream interpreter himself? Very suddenly, the lowly prisoner was the pharaoh's right-hand man, clothed in finery with a gold chain around his neck, honored above anyone but the pharaoh himself.

Joseph was thirty when this happened. He had been seventeen when his own brothers sold him as a slave. In thirteen years he had learned wisdom and patience. He was capable of resisting temptation. He had become a man in the best sense. It is worth noting that before he interpreted Pharaoh's dream, Joseph assured the pharaoh that he himself could not do it, but that God would provide the interpretation. His experience had taught him to rely on God.

And he was destined to meet his brothers again. The famine that struck Egypt after seven years affected the whole region. In Canaan, Jacob's family was on the verge of starvation. Jacob heard grain could be brought in Egypt, so he sent ten of his sons there, holding back the youngest, Benjamin, son of his beloved Rachel.

So the brothers went to Joseph to purchase grain. They bowed down to him—little knowing that Joseph's long-ago dream had come true. They did not recognize him, for he had an Egyptian name, spoke Egyptian to his servants and was dressed in Egyptian garb, including the heavy eye makeup that both men and women wore. Joseph recognized his brothers and, unbeknownst to them, understood their language. Joseph had been tested by his hardships. He decided to test the brothers as well. Were they still the spiteful, jealous rogues who sold him as a slave, or had they matured? Were they maybe even *sorry* for what they did?

Speaking through an interpreter, he accused them of being spies from Canaan. They protested: no, they were honest men, all brothers. Joseph pretended not to believe them. He took one of them, Simeon, into custody. The brothers, speaking Hebrew to each other, wondered if they were being punished for what they had done to Joseph long ago. Joseph understood them. His brothers had changed; they had developed a moral sense. (In fact, this is the only case in Genesis of anyone expressing sorrow over their sins.)

After they left Egypt, they discovered the money they paid for the grain had been put back in their sacks. The famine in Canaan continued, and when the brothers went back to Egypt to buy more grain, Joseph treated them as honored guests—their feet washed, their animals fed, food set before them. This time they brought the youngest brother, Benjamin, with them, as Joseph had insisted. At dinner, to their surprise, the brothers were seated in birth order—which Joseph knew. Joseph also sent extra portions of food from his own table to Benjamin's. This was another way of testing them: If they showed resentment, he would conclude they had not changed much. But they passed the test.

There was one more test: He sent the brothers back to Canaan with their grain—but he had his servants hide his precious silver cup in the sack of Benjamin. Before they left Egypt the brothers were stopped, their bags searched. The cup was in Benjamin's sack.

The brothers returned as a group with Benjamin—that is, they did not abandon him to his fate after the cup was found in his sack. When they appeared before Joseph, he made it clear that only Benjamin would suffer for the crime, and the others would be allowed to go back to Canaan. The brothers were of course well aware of what would happen to the aged Jacob if they went back without Benjamin. Judah made an impassioned plea, tugging on Joseph's heartstrings by telling of Jacob's affection for the youngest son. Then Judah went further: He was willing to take Benjamin's punishment and to be imprisoned—or executed—in his place. This was Judah, the brother who, years earlier, had had the idea of selling Joseph into slavery.

To Joseph's great pleasure, his brothers had matured into decent, honest men. He sent his Egyptian servants from the room. To the brothers' great surprise, he spoke to them in their own language. "I am your brother Joseph, the one you sold into Egypt! And now, do not be distressed and do not be angry with yourselves for selling me here, because it was to save lives that God sent me ahead of you" (Genesis 45:4–5). God in his wisdom had used the brothers' jealousy of Joseph as a way of saving the entire family—and the future of Israel. What the brothers intended as evil had been turned by God into good (Genesis 50:20).

"And he kissed all his brothers and wept over them" (Genesis 45:14). We have to wonder if the brothers remembered, many years earlier, the tearful reunion of their father and their uncle Esau.

PUTTING THE WORD TO WORK

1. Jacob, a deceitful man, is deceived by his scheming father-in-law. Have there been times in your life when you were deceived or misled by people you trusted? Did this make you want to practice more honest living yourself?

2. Men, even moral men like Joseph, often face sexual temptation. Take a moment to pray for men in your family and circle of friends, asking God to give them a sense of priorities when they meet with temptation.

3. Despite many sordid instances in Jacob's life, his deep love for Rachel is admirable. Have you known people whose deep love for their spouse changed their character for the better?

4. Joseph, the spoiled child, seems to bloom in adversity. As you face obstacles and frustrations in your own life, try to think of Joseph and other biblical characters whose characters were improved by misfortune.

5. How does the ending of the Joseph story affect you? Are there people in your family that you need to forgive, or whose forgiveness you need to ask?

Maximized Compassion
SEVEN JESUS VIGNETTES

Most teachers are more inspiring in word than in deed, but Jesus taught compassion and his actions matched his teachings. In this chapter we will look at one of his most memorable parables about divine compassion, and also see that compassion in action as he encounters and heals the demon-possessed and lepers—and raises the dead.

We will also look at an episode in which his compassion engendered compassion in others—and an often-overlooked episode in which a man marching to his death can still show deep compassion for others.

KEY TERM FOR TODAY ## Compassion

In some of Jesus' parables, such as those of the prodigal son and the good Samaritan, he praises the quality of compassion. More importantly, he modeled it in his deeds.

HAPPY COMMOTION IN HEAVEN

"Suppose one of you has a hundred sheep and loses one of them. Does he not leave the ninety-nine in the open country and go after the lost sheep until he finds it? And when he finds it, he joyfully puts it on his shoulders and goes home. Then he calls his friends and neighbors together and says, 'Rejoice with me; I have found my lost sheep.' I tell you that in the same way there will be more rejoicing in heaven over one sinner who repents than over ninety-nine righteous persons who do not need to repent.

"Or suppose a woman has ten silver coins and loses one. Does she not light a lamp, sweep the house and search carefully until she finds it? And when she finds it, she calls her friends and neighbors together and says, 'Rejoice with me; I have found my lost coin.' In the same way, I tell you, there is rejoicing in the presence of the angels of God over one sinner who repents." (Luke 15:2–10)

Here is a case of a parable so familiar that we can easily miss some of the meaning. In taking a fresh look at it, first note the contrast: The outcasts are gathering around to hear Jesus, while the "respectable" Pharisees and teachers of the law are grumbling. Jesus' critics, who seem to be high on their own self-righteousness, are inevitably grumbling, testing Jesus with questions or plotting to trap him with his own words. It is impossible to learn from a teacher if we do not listen with an open mind and heart. "This man welcomes sinners and eats with them" is a statement that should have been followed not with grumbling but with "Praise God!" But they had snapped their minds shut. They were so in the habit of cold-shouldering sinners that they could not imagine reaching out to them. The snarling contempt they felt for sinners—and for the Man who reached out to them—is evident throughout the Gospels.

In the shepherd story, Jesus brings out a neglected teaching of the Old Testament: God seeking out the lost. In the Old Testament, God is shown as merciful and forgiving to those who repent. The same idea is found in many of Jesus' parables, notably that of the prodigal son. But here God is not just waiting to receive the sinner; he is seeking him out. This notion was not widely spoken of among the Jews, yet it is found in the Old Testament: "I will search for the lost and bring back the strays. I will bind up the injured and strengthen the weak" (Ezekiel 34:16). As so often happens in Jesus' teaching, he was not introducing new ideas but simply reminding them of neglected ideas in their own Scriptures.

Most of the pastureland in Galilee was not green. Little of it was verdant and level. It had sparse vegetation, meaning the sheep had to roam over a wide area to get enough food, and the land they roamed was full of ravines and gullies they could get trapped in. A shepherd looking for a sheep was practically entering a maze, and if he happened to find the sheep, he had the task of carrying it back over the rough terrain. A lost sheep will lie down helplessly and refuse to budge, even if prodded, so the shepherd may have to carry it home on his shoulders.

> **DID YOU KNOW?**
>
> The parable of the lost sheep was the inspiration for some of the earliest Christian art, depicting Jesus—as a young and beardless man—carrying a sheep over his shoulders. The image was found in some statues dating from the 200s and in drawings in the Roman catacombs. The shepherd-and-sheep image was used in art long before the cross was.

Flocks of sheep were often owned communally by a village; a lost sheep was not just the concern of one man but of many. Thus when the shepherd—God—finds the lost sheep and brings it back, there is widespread rejoicing in the village—in heaven. The idea that there is actual rejoicing in heaven over a repentant sinner is one that is too often overlooked. A repentant person causes a happy commotion in heaven.

The Pharisees could not comprehend the "rejoicing in heaven," since in their view, it pleased God when sinners perished. They conveniently overlooked the words of Ezekiel 18:23: "Do I take any pleasure in the death of the wicked? declares the Sovereign Lord. Rather, am I not pleased when they turn from their ways and live?"

In Matthew's Gospel, this parable follows Jesus' stern warnings about those who lead his "little ones" astray. In this context, Jesus is saying that when the foolish sheep go astray—either through their own folly or through the leading of a sinner—God is still eager to reclaim them. To the world at large, any particular sheep might be a loser, not worth any concern, but God does not see people that way. The deep compassion in this parable is that Jesus is encouraging us to be like God, going after the straying ones instead of judging them harshly. The lost sheep may indeed be getting what it deserves or what it has brought on itself, but "Why bother with that one?" is not the right response. The shepherd is patient with sheep because he understands something crucial: Yes, sheep do stupid things. That's the way they are, and the shepherd who is true to his calling will go after them. Likewise people do stupid and sinful things, but God shows compassion on them instead of abandoning them. The distressed and depressed are precious to God. When they are found, there is rejoicing in heaven.

The parable of the woman with the lost coin has the same theme, but with a different twist. In the first parable, the shepherd had a hundred sheep, meaning he was moderately well off. But in the second parable, the woman is poor, possessing only ten coins. So her hunt for the lost one is more frantic, more urgent. Losing a coin in a badly lighted house of Palestine would have involved lighting a lamp, even in daylight. Like the shepherd, the woman is ecstatic over finding what was lost. Jesus tells us that God and the angels also feel such ecstasy.

This is indeed, the Gospel, the "good news" the apostles spread: The Creator and Lord of the universe does not detest or scorn wayward human beings. He loves them and wants to save them.

A man in their synagogue who was possessed by an evil spirit cried out, "What do you want with us, Jesus of Nazareth? Have you come to destroy us? I know who you are—the Holy One of God!"

"Be quiet!" said Jesus sternly. "Come out of him!" The evil spirit shook the man violently and came out of him with a shriek.

The people were all so amazed that they asked each other, "What is this? A new teaching—and with authority! He even gives orders to evil spirits and they obey him." (Mark 1:22–27)

In Jesus' day, demons were called *mazzikin*, "those who harm." Jesus' contemporaries thought of demons as being on the side of Satan, but there were other beliefs about their existence. Many thought they were the evil descendants of "sons of God" who had mated with human women long ago (Genesis 6:1–8). Or they were believed to be the souls of evil people who had died.

Skeptics often say that in ancient times every illness, whether physical or mental, was believed to be caused by demons. This is not the case at all, for some of Jesus' healings are said to be a matter of casting out demons while others were not. The people of the Bible definitely had a stronger belief in demons than we do, but this does not mean they attributed every human affliction to demons.

People of the twenty-first century may be inclined to ask: Were the demons real? At a distance of two thousand years, we have no way of knowing whether some of the people possessed by demons might have been simply delusional—that is, they *thought* they were demon-possessed and so they acted like it, in which case the power of Jesus was in making the person believe that the demon had no power over him. In the case of a certain demon-possessed boy whose father begged Jesus for healing, the boy's symptoms seem to fit the symptoms of epilepsy, in which case the healing was not a matter of casting out a demon but of curing epilepsy—a great miracle in itself. (We will look at the story more closely later in this chapter.)

But we would be very unfair to the Bible—and to reality—if we ruled out the possibility of actual demon possession. There are far too many well-documented stories of demonic activity—and of people of faith casting out demons—for us to regard all demon possessions as fiction. One thing is certain: Jesus definitely meant for people to be free from the fear of demons.

This is the first recorded instance of Jesus expelling a demon. This happened in Capernaum in Galilee, the lakeside town that Jesus had made his home base when he moved from Nazareth.

Note the sequence of events here: Jesus has joined his fellow Jews in Sabbath worship in the synagogue, and he uses this as an occasion for teaching. The people are impressed: He teaches with obvious authority, not like the teachers of the law (called "scribes" in many translations), who constantly "footnoted" their teachings by referring to great teachers of the past. The people sense Jesus is a new sort of teacher. It turns out he is more different than they thought: He has the power to cast out demons.

In the Gospels, demon-possessed people often cry out in their agony. On this occasion in Capernaum the demon-possessed man's cry interrupts the synagogue service—a sign of his desperation, or perhaps the terror of the demons who sense the presence of an enemy. This is the first miracle recorded after Jesus' baptism, in which the Spirit descended on Jesus like a dove, and the voice of God commended Jesus as his "beloved son." The demons recognize that this Spirit-empowered man is out to destroy the kingdom of Satan. Long before humans are fully aware of who he is, the demons already see that he is the "Holy One of God." Jesus got the better of Satan in the temptation, and now he has the demons on the run.

The possessed man—or, rather, the demons—cry out to Jesus, "What do you want with us?" The "us" occurs in other confrontations with the demons, as if there were a kind of herd mentality among the forces of evil. Elsewhere it is mentioned that Mary Magdalene became a follower of Jesus after he drove seven demons from her (Luke 8:2). And of course there is the famous episode of the wild man who told Jesus, "My name is Legion, for we are many" (Mark 5:9).

Note that Jesus not only expelled the demons but also gagged them. True, they could see what the human observers could not: God's Holy One was at work on earth. But Jesus was not going to have his Messiah status proclaimed by the voices of demons.

The Old Testament refers to God numerous times as "the Holy One of Israel" or simply "the Holy One." Here in this episode the demon calls Jesus "the Holy One of God." It is worth noting that in the Synoptic Gospels, the demons perceive what humans do not—that Jesus is Son of God and the Holy One. "Son of God" is not spoken by men but by Satan and the demons—and by God himself. Only the supernatural perceive that Jesus is the "Holy One of God." Note that in Luke 1:35, Mary is told by the angel that her son will be "called holy, the Son of the Most High." God, the angels and the demons see that Jesus is the divine Son long before human beings accept it.

The people in the synagogue were correct: Something—Someone—entirely new had arrived on the scene.

A man in the crowd answered, "Teacher, I brought you my son, who is possessed by a spirit that has robbed him of speech. Whenever it seizes him, it throws him to the ground. He foams at the mouth, gnashes his teeth and becomes rigid. I asked your disciples to drive out the spirit, but they could not."

"O unbelieving generation," Jesus replied, "how long shall I stay with you? How long shall I put up with you? Bring the boy to me." So they brought him. When the spirit saw Jesus, it immediately threw the boy into a convulsion. He fell to the ground and rolled around, foaming at the mouth. Jesus asked the boy's father, "How long has he been like this?" "From childhood," he answered. "It has often thrown him into fire or water to kill him. But if you can do anything, take pity on us and help us."

"'If you can'?" said Jesus. "Everything is possible for him who believes." Immediately the boy's father exclaimed, "I do believe; help me overcome my unbelief!"

When Jesus saw that a crowd was running to the scene, he rebuked the evil spirit. "You deaf and mute spirit," he said, "I command you, come out of him and never enter him again." The spirit shrieked, convulsed him violently and came out (Mark 9:15–25).

This miracle follows a mountaintop experience, the Transfiguration. Jesus and the inner circle of disciples—Peter, James and John—have been on the mountain, where Jesus has been seen in a state of glory with Moses and Elijah. While they are absent, the other disciples have tried but failed to heal the boy.

Mountaintop experiences are fine in themselves, but it wasn't intended that Jesus and the three disciples would stay there. They had to return to the world of sin and sickness and demon possession. Jesus spent much more of his life at ground level than he did on mountaintops. He did not spend his life inside a temple or cathedral, for his mission was to the people in the streets and village lanes.

The crowd gathered there must have been on pins and needles: Would the renowned teacher and healer be able to do what his disciples could not? The disciples' failure reflected badly on the Master.

The miracle to some extent depended on the father's faith. The fact that the disciples had failed must have temporarily lessened his faith in them or in their Master. Coming face-to-face with Jesus boosted the little faith he had. The father's faith is uncertain, since he asks Jesus to help "if you can." Jesus assures him that anything is possible—to one who believes. The father, in what must have been a pitiful situation, says he does believe but asks for more faith: "I do believe; help me overcome my unbelief!"

"Moonstruck"

In Matthew's version of the story of the boy and his father we find the Greek word *seleniazetai* used to refer to a demon-possessed person. The word literally means "moonstruck," and our word *lunatic* originally meant the same thing (*luna* refers to the moon, of course). Modern versions use words and phrases like *epileptic* or *has seizures*, while the King James Version was actually closer to the Greek when it used "lunatick." Based on what Matthew 17 and Mark 9 tell us about the boy, he probably was an epileptic, but the ancient world knew nothing about the biological causes of epilepsy, so it was attributed to demons or to the power of the moon.

(The King James Version is more familiar: "I believe; help thou my unbelief.") Jesus responds, "All things are possible for him who believes." The power and willingness of God are never in doubt, only the faith of fickle human beings.

In a sense, Jesus brings the boy back from the dead. By his word he drives the demon out, and after an extremely violent convulsion, the boy appears dead, but Jesus takes him by the hand and raises him up. In effect, a new life has begun for the boy and his father. He is no longer in the grip of his affliction.

One important point of the story is the failure of the disciples to perform a healing. Jesus' servants on earth frequently disappoint us, but that is no call to lose faith in him.

10 PERCENT GRATEFUL

As he was going into a village, ten men who had leprosy met him. They stood at a distance and called out in a loud voice, "Jesus, Master, have pity on us!"

When he saw them, he said, "Go, show yourselves to the priests." And as they went, they were cleansed.

One of them, when he saw he was healed, came back, praising God in a loud voice. He threw himself at Jesus' feet and thanked him—and he was a Samaritan. Jesus asked, "Were not all ten cleansed? Where are the other nine? Was no one found to return and give praise to God except this foreigner?"

Then he said to him, "Rise and go; your faith has made you well" (Luke 17:11–19).

On several occasions Jesus healed people with leprosy, and at times he touched them—a shocking thing to do, since leprosy was contagious. Lepers were required by Jewish law to live apart from healthy people, and to announce their presence by calling out "Unclean, unclean!" Here, however, Jesus heals from a distance—not because he is unwilling to be near lepers, but because the lepers themselves follow the custom and keep their distance. They ask for "mercy"—which may mean charity, a healing or both.

The curious thing about the healing is that Jesus does not tell the lepers he will heal them or that he has healed them. He simply says, "Go, show yourselves to the priests"—something that Jewish law required when a leper believed himself to be cured; a priest validated that the person was indeed "clean." The men do not question his instructions but simply obey, and on their way, they discover they are healed. In a sense, Jesus' order to "show yourselves to the priests" is a test of the lepers' faith—and they pass the test. When he speaks the words, they are still lepers, but as they make their way to the priests, in faith, following Jesus' command, they find themselves healed. They can live again and be part of the community of man instead of existing as despised outcasts who watch themselves literally rot away. Although they do not all turn back to thank Jesus, their trust that they will be cured is commendable.

Presumably nine of them continued on their way to the priests—not wrong in itself, since they were carrying out Jesus' command. But the tenth leper turns around and goes back to Jesus, his feet animated by gratitude. He praises God "in a loud voice" and throws himself at Jesus' feet, thanking him.

Luke begins the story by giving the geographical detail that Jesus is on the border between the provinces of Galilee (where he grew up) and Samaria. The Jews of Galilee detested the Samaritans, and vice versa. But as the Gospels show, Jesus had compassion on Samaritans, and in one of his most famous parables, the man of compassion is not a Jew but a Samaritan.

In this story of the ten lepers, the one who returns to thank Jesus is a Samaritan. He is referred to in the original Greek as *allogenes*, "foreigner" or literally "another race."

CULTURAL INSIGHTS

Leprosy, or Something Like It

Dermatology was not exactly an advanced science in ancient times, and when the Bible refers to leprosy, it could be referring to any number of skin diseases. Some of these were contagious, some not, but the general rule was to quarantine the person, since true leprosy—Hansen's disease—really is contagious and also incurable, causing the poor person to literally rot away. In the case of diseases that were not true leprosy—conditions we would probably describe today as psoriasis or seborrhea or dermatitis—the ailment often passed in time and the person could live a normal life. The Old Testament records the miraculous healing of the leper Naaman, a Syrian, by the prophet Elisha. Most people who had real leprosy were not so fortunate, which is why Jesus' healing of several lepers so impressed people.

This is one of many stories in Luke's Gospel in which the outsider, the outcast, shows more human decency than others. The other nine lepers were presumably Jews, and were Jewish enough to obey Jesus' instructions to show themselves to the priests—but what about gratitude? The nine lepers were playing by the rules, yet clearly the one whose behavior is most commendable is this Samaritan, who bursts out in heartfelt gratitude to God and to Jesus.

When the Samaritan saw he was healed, he saw more than a change of his skin: His eyes were opened to the reality of having encountered the power of God. The leper "turns back" to Jesus, implying not only a physical change but a spiritual one as well. He falls at Jesus' feet in worship and awe.

Jesus' words "Your faith has made you well" can also mean "brought you salvation." The man's faith in Jesus brought him not only physical healing but spiritual wholeness also.

Reader, take note: This is the only place in the Bible where a person thanks Jesus.

"GET UP AND WALK"

Now there is in Jerusalem near the Sheep Gate a pool, which in Aramaic is called Bethesda and which is surrounded by five covered colonnades. Here a great number of disabled people used to lie—the blind, the lame, the paralyzed. One who was there had been an invalid for thirty-eight years.

When Jesus saw him lying there and learned that he had been in this condition for a long time, he asked him, "Do you want to get well?"

"Sir," the invalid replied, "I have no one to help me into the pool when the water is stirred. While I am trying to get in, someone else goes down ahead of me."

Then Jesus said to him, "Get up! Pick up your mat and walk." At once the man was cured; he picked up his mat and walked. The day on which this took place was a Sabbath . . . The man went away and told the Jews that it was Jesus who had made him well. So, because Jesus was doing these things on the Sabbath, the Jews persecuted him.

Jesus said to them, "My Father is always at his work to this very day, and I, too, am working" (John 5:1–9, 15–17).

The man in this story is a truly pathetic creature. He has been an invalid for thirty-eight years and he wants desperately to be healed, yet he has no one to help him into the pool whose waters were believed to have healing power. Presumably the man would have been a beggar.

Jesus asks him, "Do you want to get well?"—literally "Do you want to be made whole?" The Greek word translated "well" is *hygies*, the root of our word *hygiene*. It could refer to being made physically healthy but could encompass what we would call mental or spiritual health also.

After all these years as an invalid, the man is healed by the mere word of Jesus. He picks up his mat, his pallet, which by the strict Jews' definition is a piece of furniture, and thus not to be moved on a Sabbath. He and Jesus both, despite the strictest ideas about the Sabbath, "labor" on the day of rest. But Jesus informs the leaders that God himself created the Sabbath and is not bound by his own rules: "My Father is always at his work to this very day, and I, too, am working." The Genesis account of creation says God "rested" on the seventh day—not that he was tired, or needed rest, but simply that he ceased or paused from his initial work of creation. But as Jesus says, God is always working in his world, even on the Sabbath, and Jesus is performing works of kindness every day, just as God does. The Sabbath law was intended to give mankind a day of rest and worship, not to inhibit good deeds, and certainly not to prevent a crippled man from picking up his pallet and walking away with it. The Son is going to do the will of God, regardless of what day of the week it is, or what foolish manmade regulations have been imposed on people. Legalism had curdled their common sense, and their human decency.

The story of compassion ends on a sour note: "The Jews tried all the harder to kill him; not only was he breaking the Sabbath, but he was even calling God his own Father, making himself equal with God" (John 5:17). In a sense Jesus' ministry was an illustration of the adage "No good deed goes unpunished." All too often his deeds of compassion provoked snarling contempt from those who made up the religious establishment. But he would not be deterred by the narrow-minded and narrow-hearted.

FUNERAL INTERRUPTED

Jesus went to a town called Nain, and his disciples and a large crowd went along with him. As he approached the town gate, a dead person was being carried out—the only son of his mother, and she was a widow. And a large crowd from the town was with her.

When the Lord saw her, his heart went out to her and he said, "Don't cry." Then he went up and touched the coffin, and those carrying it stood still. He said, "Young man, I say to you, get up!"

The dead man sat up and began to talk, and Jesus gave him back to his mother (Luke 7:11–15).

Jesus' heart went out to this woman, a widow whose only son was being carried out for burial. If you have read the Bible often, you have surely noticed it expresses a great concern for widows. Jesus' compassion for this nameless widow is very much in the mainstream of

Jewish thought. He would have been aware that a woman with no husband and no son was without a male protector—in that time and place, a highly undesirable situation.

But of course, Jesus does more than feel sympathy. With a word, he raises the young man to life again. In this miracle, Jesus has gone beyond his miracle of raising the dead daughter of Jairus. On that occasion, the child had just died, meaning it was possible she was only comatose until Jesus came to her. But here it is obvious the young man is truly dead, since they are carrying him out for burial.

Note that one reaction of the people is, "A great prophet has appeared among us." They would have recalled the Old Testament story of the great Elijah bringing a dead child back to life (1 Kings 17:23). They are correct that Jesus is a great prophet. But they are more correct in saying, "God has come to help his people."

> **DID YOU KNOW?**
>
> The story of the widow of Nain refers to her son's coffin, but this probably did not refer to an actual coffin but to an open bier—that is, the man's body was being carried on a sort of pallet or board that would have been lowered into the grave.

This story is found only in Luke's Gospel, and it is noteworthy that here he refers to Jesus as "the Lord" for the first time. It is very appropriate in this story because Jesus is demonstrating he is the Lord of life. Also noteworthy is the fact that he takes the initiative in this miracle. He is surrounded by a large crowd of followers, and the funeral procession is also composed of a large crowd, yet no one asks Jesus to do anything. The raising of the young man to life is his spontaneous reaction to the situation, not to a request from anyone.

Jesus touched the man's bier; technically, according to the Law of Moses, this rendered Jesus unclean. But as we see so often in the Gospels, Jesus did not allow religious legalism to stand in the way of a miracle of compassion. The people of Nain "were all filled with awe and praised God. 'A great prophet has appeared among us,' they said. 'God has come to help his people'" (Luke 7:16).

WONDERFUL, WASTEFUL LOVE

Jesus arrived at Bethany, where Lazarus lived, whom Jesus had raised from the dead. Here a dinner was given in Jesus' honor. Martha served, while Lazarus was among those reclining at the table with him.

Then Mary took about a pint of pure nard, an expensive perfume; she poured it on Jesus' feet and wiped his feet with her hair. And the house was filled with the fragrance of the perfume.

But one of his disciples, Judas Iscariot, who was later to betray him, objected, "Why wasn't this perfume sold and the money given to the poor? It was worth a year's wages." He did not say this because he cared about the poor but because he was a thief; as keeper of the money bag, he used to help himself to what was put into it.

"Leave her alone," Jesus replied. "It was intended that she should save this perfume for the day of my burial. You will always have the poor among you, but you will not always have me" (John 12:1–8).

The theme of this beautiful story might be stated as, "Love is extravagant." It takes place after one of the great miracles of the Bible: Jesus' raising his friend Lazarus to life. Understandably, Lazarus' sisters, Martha and Mary, who were devoted to Jesus even before the great miracle, host a dinner in Jesus' honor. We can well imagine what the two sisters, as well as their guests, experienced at seeing their brother, once dead, sharing a dinner with the man who brought him back to life.

It was custom for a host to wash his guests' feet—or, more accurately, to have a servant do it. Lazarus' sister Mary went beyond the usual custom: She wiped Jesus' feet not with water but with a jar of very expensive perfume, and then wiped his feet not with a towel but with her own hair. It was also a custom—regarded as somewhat extravagant—for a host to sprinkle an honored guest with a few drops of perfume. Mary had, in effect, combined two customs in a dramatic way.

"And the house was filled with the fragrance of the perfume." It is hard for us in the twenty-first century to fully appreciate how much people in ancient times valued perfume. Household sanitation was not up to our modern standards, to put it mildly, and if any of us were sent back to Jesus' day, we would probably be put off by the scents—humans who very seldom washed themselves all over, animals and animal waste nearby, decaying food, plus the impossibility of filtering or recirculating the air in any building. People of those times valued perfume and incense much more than we do, for they provided some relief from the usual smells of life. When Mary anointed Jesus' feet with the perfume, she was not only showing her devotion and gratitude to him, but also, in a sense, sharing it with the entire party, for all of them could enjoy the pleasant scent for a while.

The spoiler at the feast was, alas, one of Jesus' own disciples—the worst of them, that is. Judas, who in a few days would arrange to betray his master, objected to Mary's act of love: "Why wasn't this perfume sold and the money given to the poor? It was worth a year's wages." Judas' objection by itself seems rational enough: Viewed from an economic standpoint, Mary's act really was wasteful. When many people lived at or below the poverty line, wasn't it foolish—maybe even immoral—to spend a year's wages on something that did nothing more than scent the house for a few hours?

John's Gospel gives us some information about Judas that the other Gospels do not: "He did not say this because he cared about the poor but because he was a thief; as keeper of the money bag, he used to help himself to what was put into it." His protest against Mary is hypocritical: He cares nothing for the poor, but obviously he wants the others present to think of him as compassionate—more compassionate than the "wasteful" Mary.

Jesus, of course, saw into Judas' soul—and, more importantly, into Mary's. From the standpoint of financial calculation, Mary was wasteful. From the divine standpoint, she was brimming over with love and gratitude and had to express her emotions in a tangible way. Acting out of compassion himself, Jesus says, "Leave her alone." He will not have Judas spoil the moment. Jesus, of course, had great compassion for the poor himself, but he understood that there are occasions when the heart must focus on the individual at hand.

Jesus says, "It was intended that she should save this perfume for the day of my burial." He was referring to the custom of using an entire jar of perfume to anoint a body before burial. His words make it clear that he knew that in a few days he would indeed be buried. Mary did not know this, of course; she poured out the perfume on Jesus because of the love he had shown her family—love giving back to love.

DAUGHTERS OF JERUSALEM

A large number of people followed him, including women who mourned and wailed for him.

Jesus turned and said to them, "Daughters of Jerusalem, do not weep for me; weep for yourselves and for your children. For the time will come when you will say, 'Blessed are the barren women, the wombs that never bore and the breasts that never nursed!' Then 'they will say to the mountains, "Fall on us!" and to the hills, "Cover us!"' For if men do these things when the tree is green, what will happen when it is dry?" (Luke 23:27–31).

This episode occurs as Jesus is on his way to be crucified. A large crowd was following him, and we can be certain that more people turned out for his crucifixion than for his entry into Jerusalem on a donkey—alas, people would turn out in droves to see a criminal executed. But the lamenting of the women is a reminder that not all the people of Jerusalem were against Jesus—quite the contrary. The women raise the death wail over Jesus, while Jesus raises his own lament over the city that welcomed him one day and shouted for his death less than a week later.

Jesus on the way to the cross tells the women of Jerusalem, "Do not weep"—words he had also said to the widow of Nain and the household of Jairus, cases where someone was dead but raised again. Here again, a resurrection was about to take place.

Why did he tell the women "weep for yourselves"? Jesus saw clearly enough that the Romans would, in the not-too-distant future, decide to clamp down on the rebellious Jews, storm Jerusalem and destroy the Jews' temple. The women of the city would soon have something of greater concern to weep over than the death of a wandering teacher from Galilee. There is another message hidden in his words: Women of Jerusalem, if this is the suffering that comes upon a truly innocent man, imagine what fate awaits this city at large. The Romans will burn up the "green tree" (Jesus) and even more so the "dry" (the rotten religious establishment in Jerusalem). The Roman concept of justice had been shown, in the trial of Jesus, to be a sham, so imagine the cruelty they could bring to bear on a Jewish revolt. Another likely meaning: If God allows the fully innocent Jesus to suffer, imagine what suffering is in store for the sinful city that rejected him. Pilate had assented to Jesus' crucifixion as a political threat, even though he knew Jesus was innocent—so surely an even worse fate awaited the Jews who really were a threat to Roman authority.

Consider that when Jesus spoke these words he was already in agonizing pain, having been scourged, a punishment that for many men was itself fatal. The crown of thorns was pressed down upon his head, and he knew that shortly he would be facing an excruciating execution. But even in his agony he is still able to respond in sympathy and compassion to others.

DID YOU KNOW?

Among Roman Catholics, Jesus' speaking to the women of Jerusalem is the eighth of the fourteen Stations of the Cross—stages of Jesus' journey from being condemned to death to being laid in the tomb. Christian pilgrims to Israel can actually walk "the way of the cross" in Jerusalem, as they have done for centuries, but many Catholic churches have set up "stations" within the church so that people can reenact the route as a devotional exercise.

PUTTING THE WORD TO WORK

1. Think of some "lost sheep" you know. What are ways you can reach out to them to let them know someone cares—and that God cares?

2. Consider the man with the demon-possessed son, the man who believed but asked Jesus to help him overcome his unbelief. When you feel your own faith faltering, make it a point to do as this man did and ask for more and deeper faith.

3. Reflect on the story of Jesus healing the crippled man and then being criticized for healing on the Sabbath. Have there been times in your life when you broke the rules in order to do an act of kindness?

4. In the story of the ten lepers, only one turned back to thank Jesus. Keeping that story in mind, make it a point today and in the future not to miss an opportunity to express gratitude.

5. Jesus' act of bringing the man of Nain back to life is remarkable because of its spontaneity—he performs the miracle without being asked. What were times in your own life when a stranger did you an act of kindness without being asked? How did you respond?

Wisdom, Limited
SOLOMON, JOB AND COMPANY

The topic today is wisdom, which is highly praised in the Bible—but also shown to have its limits. The Bible praises wise people but recognizes that wisdom can lead to conceit and pride and—as the story of Job shows—can fail to provide comfort to the suffering.

MEMORY VERSE

Better a poor but wise youth than an old but foolish king who no longer knows how to take warning.—Ecclesiastes 4:13

KEY TERM FOR TODAY ## Wisdom

Wisdom in the Bible doesn't refer to learned knowledge but to understanding, perceptiveness and insight. It always has a practical value. The Bible praises human wisdom highly but also recognizes its limits in understanding the ways of God.

SOLOMON: WISE BEGINNING

Solomon showed his love for the Lord by walking according to the statutes of his father David. . . .

"Give your servant a discerning heart to govern your people and to distinguish between right and wrong. For who is able to govern this great people of yours?"

The Lord was pleased that Solomon had asked for this. (1 Kings 3:9–10)

In the Bible, the gold standard for wisdom is Solomon, richly blessed in so many ways. Tradition credits Solomon with writing that great treasury of wisdom, Proverbs—and also that great treasury of doubts about wisdom, Ecclesiastes. In his long life, Solomon learned to value wisdom, and also to question its worth.

Solomon grew up in a violent household, with his oldest brother, Amnon, raping his sister Tamar and later murdered by his brother Absalom. Solomon's mother was Bathsheba, a married woman when Solomon's father, King David, lusted for her, seduced her and then arranged for her husband to be killed in battle. The first son born to David and Bathsheba died, but later Bathsheba gave birth to Solomon, and when David was near death, he selected Solomon to succeed him. This was contested by Solomon's oldest surviving brother, Adonijah, and a rebellion ensued, resulting in Adonijah's death. Much blood had flowed during Solomon's early life, so it was appropriate that his own name meant "peace" and that peace became the byword of his forty-year reign.

Early in his reign, Solomon had a dream in which God asked him what he desired. Solomon's reply was memorable: "Give your servant a discerning heart to govern your people and to distinguish between right and wrong. For who is able to govern this great people of yours?" Not surprisingly, "the Lord was pleased that Solomon had asked for this" (1 Kings 3:9–10). Most men would have asked for long life, for riches or for the defeat of their enemies. Solomon asked for wisdom. So God blessed him with wisdom, and also riches and long life and peace in the kingdom. But the blessings were conditional: They would continue so long as Solomon was faithful.

Then follows a famous story of Solomon's wisdom at work. Two prostitutes come before the king, both claiming a certain infant as their own. Solomon renders his famous verdict: Take a sword and divide the child in half. The real mother of the child intervenes. She is willing to give the child to the other woman rather than see it killed. Thus the real mother makes herself known. Solomon had indeed been blessed with wisdom, and word of his judgment spread to all Israel and far beyond (1 Kings 3:16–28).

One who heard of Solomon's wisdom was the queen of Sheba, an area in Arabia noted for its spices and other luxury items. Her visit to the king is recorded in 1 Kings 10, where it is stated that she "came to test him with hard questions." Not surprisingly, "Solomon answered all her questions; nothing was too hard for the king to explain to her." The queen

CHARACTERS AT LARGE Solomon the Magician

There are probably more legends told about Solomon than about any Old Testament figure. Some of them are connected with the king's famous wisdom and his knowledge of bird and animal life. Solomon's wide knowledge was often extended to the world of magic, so that he was said to have power over demons and angels, birds and beasts, wind and water. In some legends he could fly on a magic carpet anywhere he wished. Animal figures carved on Solomon's throne would magically assist the king when he wished to seat himself. The legends are colorful and amusing, but they are a distraction from the Bible's serious picture of Solomon as a man whose appetite for fame, sophistication and women led him astray spiritually.

DID YOU KNOW?

Solomon reigned in Jerusalem forty years, probably 970 BC–931 BC.

was deeply impressed—not only with Solomon's mental abilities, but also with his lavish court and the splendid temple he had built for the Lord. She was "overwhelmed" —or, as the literal Hebrew has it, "there was no more breath in her." Israel had not long ago been a scattered confederation of tribes. Now it was a large and peaceful kingdom, and its wise king lived in luxury. It would have seemed to the queen that Solomon's God was clearly on his side.

DWELLING IN PEACE

He ruled over all the kingdoms west of the River, from Tiphsah to Gaza, and had peace on all sides. During Solomon's lifetime Judah and Israel, from Dan to Beersheba, lived in safety, each man under his own vine and fig tree (1 Kings 4:24–25).

Israel's first two kings, Saul and David, had been men of the sword—not by choice, but because Israel was surrounded by expansive enemies. David had bequeathed to his son a very large kingdom—not huge by world standards, but larger than Israel was before or since. And, happily, most of the neighboring nations were quiet during Solomon's reign. Things would change radically after his death, which is why 1 Kings speaks so glowingly of his peaceful reign.

Solomon was not a man of war like his father was, but he had no illusions about peace: It had to be maintained through strength and military readiness. Whereas David's army had relied on its sturdy foot soldiers (infantry), Solomon's more professional army relied on mounted soldiers and charioteers. Solomon "had fourteen hundred chariots and twelve thousand horses, which he kept in the chariot cities and also with him in Jerusalem" (1 Kings 10:26). These "chariot cities" were military posts in various locales around Israel. Solomon knew that his nation, situated between Egypt on the south and Assyria in the north, and smaller than either, could become easy prey unless the country showed itself ready for war.

"During Solomon's lifetime Judah and Israel, from Dan to Beersheba, lived in safety, each man under his own vine and fig tree" (1 Kings 4:25). The phrase "his own vine and fig tree" has been quoted for centuries to refer to domestic peace and security. Not only was the country safe from invaders, but technology had also made a useful leap: The Philistines' monopoly on ironworking had been broken, and every Israelite farmer benefited from having iron tools. Israel's population expanded from about five hundred thousand under Saul to one million under Solomon.

DID YOU KNOW?

Solomon had an alternate name, Jedidiah, which means "beloved of the Lord."

But there was more to the reign than peace and security.

> The Lord became angry with Solomon because his heart had turned away from the Lord, the God of Israel, who had appeared to him twice. Although he had forbidden Solomon to follow other gods, Solomon did not keep the Lord's command. (1 Kings 11:9–10)

The author of 1 Kings clearly admired Solomon, and he records in loving detail the wealth of the king. Peacetime is good for trading (war is, after all, a terrible waste of human and material resources), and Israel even had a port on the Red Sea, and also a fleet of ships trading with countries far to the east. The king lived so lavishly that there were no silver vessels at his table, only gold ones (1 Kings 10:21). And as a sign of his devotion to God, he built the awesome temple, Israel's first, and Solomon's beautiful prayer at the temple's dedication is recorded in 1 Kings 8:22–53.

Alas, Solomon built more than one temple. He built houses of worship for his many foreign wives—seven hundred wives, according to 1 Kings 11:3. These marriages—though the word *marriage* seems oddly inappropriate when the wives number in the hundreds—were primarily political ones, matters of the king of Israel cementing political alliances with the kings of other nations. Most famously, Solomon had married

---

CULTURAL INSIGHTS

Harems

You won't find the word *harem* in most Bibles, but the institution definitely existed in Israel. David had numerous concubines, Solomon even more—three hundred, according to 1 Kings 11:3. Concubines were essentially pleasure servants, living in their own quarters in the king's palace, doing a certain amount of domestic work but mostly being available for the king's indulgence. They were strictly for the king's use only, which explains why, in the rebellion of Absalom against David, he slept with David's concubines—they were royal property, and in effect Absalom had made himself king by sleeping with them. (Note that David made them live as widows afterward. He provided for them, but never touched them again, nor did any other man.)

Solomon's enormous harem raises a question: Why would any man, no matter his physical appetites, need three hundred concubines? The obvious answer is that no man would, but that is beside the point. A large harem was a sign of prestige, and one aim was to impress foreign kings, who also had large harems. Solomon's wealth reflected well on Israel. It was a sign of God's blessing but, as 1 Kings 11 relates, possessing a huge harem had its spiritual downside.

---

a daughter of the pharaoh of Egypt—a sign that Israel had arrived politically, for the pharaoh would not have married his daughter to just anyone. But the foreign women had their own gods, and instead of them accommodating Israel's faith and worship, Solomon accommodated his women. So Jerusalem, the site of the Lord's only temple, also had places of worship devoted to the gods of the pagans. There was even worship of Chemosh, the Ammonites' god, which often included sacrifice of infants. The temples Solomon built for his wives would have housed pagan priests and their retinues, and these would lure some of the Israelites away from worshipping God. Solomon—the man who built the Lord's temple—sowed the seeds for idol worship.

Solomon's wisdom had deserted him—and not just in the area of religion. To support such a lavish court—not to mention the temples and priests of his women—Solomon became a notorious taxer-and-spender. In fact, Samuel's prophecy of the burdens a king would impose on Israel came true under Solomon (1 Samuel 8:10–18). Many in Israel were full of anger and resentment. One of Solomon's officials was Jeroboam, an overseer of the forced-labor gangs involved in government construction projects. One day a prophet named Ahijah met Jeroboam on the road and did a peculiar thing: He tore his new cloak into twelve pieces and gave ten of them to Jeroboam. This symbolized the division of Israel. It would split into two kingdoms, one with ten tribes, the other with two. This would occur because Solomon had abandoned the sole worship of God and condoned worship of his wives' gods.

Solomon's last act recorded in 1 Kings is his attempt to kill Jeroboam, but Jeroboam went into exile in Egypt (1 Kings 11:40). The stage was set for the division of the kingdom disaster that would occur under Solomon's son Rehoboam.

THE WISDOM OF SOLOMON—AND MANY, MANY OTHERS

Kings detest wrongdoing, for a throne is established through righteousness. (Proverbs 16:12)

As we have seen, Solomon certainly qualifies as one of the most fascinating people in the Bible. His life story teaches some valuable lessons, showing that a man richly blessed by the Lord can make very bad choices. But Solomon's greatest legacy to the world is not found in his biography in Kings and Chronicles, but in the two books attributed to him, Proverbs and Ecclesiastes—two books with differences that complement each other in some amazing ways.

Solomon inherited a large kingdom and managed to enlarge it peacefully even further, thus fulfilling one human fantasy—political power. He had a harem even larger than his father's, fulfilling another fantasy. But he also had a reputation for being a really smart man—yet another fantasy. In some ways this is the greatest goal, for while a person's political achievements will not endure—nor will his harem—his wise sayings can influence countless generations.

Solomon "spoke three thousand proverbs" (1 Kings 4:32). Many of these are, we assume, written down in Proverbs. Solomon didn't necessarily create them all, of course. No doubt a lot of good plain folk wisdom made its way into Proverbs. God didn't reveal his wisdom or bestow good sense merely on kings. In fact, some of the common-sense sayings in Proverbs had to have come from folk sources, for Solomon's sheltered court life effectively shut him off from the life of ordinary people. Proverbs is about the ordinary decencies in life. It is not designed to appeal to humankind's heroic streak or the drive to do astonishing things. It is about ordinary life—something Solomon probably knew very little about, but that didn't blind him to the accumulated wisdom of many nameless ancestors.

Proverbs takes on a personal tone, addressing itself to "my son" or "my sons" twenty-seven times. Ironically, one person who definitely paid no heed to his father's wisdom was Solomon's real son, the stupid and tactless Rehoboam. Perhaps Solomon was painfully aware of this and felt the need to impart his wisdom to other "sons" of his own time and in later generations. If Rehoboam did not listen to his father's teachings, millions of other people have.

It is not surprising that a wealthy king like Solomon would have much to say about wealth and poverty. In fact, one of the key teachings of the book is that virtue, diligence and hard work lead to prosperity, while sin and laziness lead to poverty. In fact, people have criticized the book for teaching a "prosperity gospel," but actually the different sayings show great diversity in how they see wealth and poverty. True, some proverbs present wealth as a reward from God: "The blessing of the Lord brings wealth, and he adds no trouble to it" (Proverbs 10:22). "Humility and the fear of the Lord bring wealth and honor and life" (Proverbs 22:4). But others teach that the poor may be better off than the rich: "A good name is more desirable than great riches; to be esteemed is better than silver or gold" (Proverbs 22:1). "Better a poor man whose walk is blameless than a rich man whose ways are perverse" (Proverbs 28:6).

Some sayings teach that there is a level playing field: "Rich and poor have this in common: The Lord is the Maker of them all" (Proverbs 22:2). Other sayings teach a sensible moderation: "Do not wear yourself out to get rich; have the wisdom to show restraint" (Proverbs 23:4). "Give me neither poverty nor riches, but give me only my daily bread" (Proverbs 30:8). And some sayings teach the joy of immaterial things: "There is deceit in the hearts of those who plot evil, but joy for those who promote peace" (Proverbs 12:20). "A man finds joy in giving an apt reply—and how good is a timely word!" (Proverbs 15:23). "A cheerful look brings joy to the heart, and good news gives health to the bones" (Proverbs 15:30).

Money is not the only topic, of course. Parenting is an important one, which is why parents throughout the centuries have turned to the book. This is ironic—Solomon, having grown up in one of the most dysfunctional households in history and having no experience with monogamous marriage, compiled a book filled with sayings about the proper rearing of children. With so many wives and concubines, did Solomon even know the names of all his children? Yet the many sayings on parenting are excellent, which we can attribute to Solomon's compiling earlier proverbs or to his learning from his own experience of how *not* to raise children. Given how his foolish son Rehoboam turned out, we can assume Solomon was not very strict with parenting, yet Proverbs is full of verses urging parents to practice tough love, such as 13:24: "He who spares the rod hates his son, but he who loves him is careful to discipline him."

Solomon, led astray spiritually by his foreign women, had a lot to say about the loose woman who leads so many men astray. Here he may have been writing from his own experience! The loose woman in Proverbs 2:16–19, Proverbs 5:1–23 and Proverbs 7:1–27 may refer to a sexual temptress, but also there might be a second meaning: She is the way of self-indulgence and wickedness, in contrast to the way of wisdom that the book promotes. In fact, the book speaks of wisdom as a woman, calling men to follow her: "To you, O men, I call out; I raise my voice to all mankind. You who are simple, gain prudence; you who are foolish, gain understanding. . . . Choose my instruction instead of silver, knowledge rather than choice gold, for wisdom is more precious than rubies, and nothing you desire can compare with her" (Proverbs 8:4–5, 10–11). Perhaps Solomon, with all his women, realized late in life that wisdom was the one "woman" he had forsaken, to his great shame.

And perhaps he realized that pursuing wisdom had not fully satisfied him—that is one of the key themes in Ecclesiastes.

"ADULT" BOOK—IN THE BEST SENSE

I applied myself to the understanding of wisdom, and also of madness and folly, but I learned that this, too, is a chasing after the wind. For with much wisdom comes much sorrow; the more knowledge, the more grief. (Ecclesiastes 1:17–18)

Much of Ecclesiastes is an illustration of one of the great sayings of Jesus: "What good is it for a man to gain the whole world, yet forfeit his soul?" (Mark 8:36). The answer of Ecclesiastes is: No good at all!

One of the key words in Ecclesiastes is the Hebrew *hebel*, meaning literally "vapor" or "breath." It occurs thirty-five times in the book, always referring to something transient or insubstantial. In many English versions it is translated as "vanity," meaning something pointless or futile. Ecclesiastes opens by saying that "all" (or "everything") is vanity, useless and meaningless, and the announcer of this deep insight is "the son of David, king in Jerusalem"—that is, Solomon. Here he is Solomon the Disillusioned. He achieved amazing things: built houses, planted gardens, owned slaves and livestock, heaped up silver and gold, was entertained by his singers and concubines. "Yet when I surveyed all that my hands had done and what I had toiled to achieve, everything was meaningless, a chasing after the wind" (Ecclesiastes 2:11).

Possessions do not bring lasting pleasure—but neither does wisdom. Wise men die the same as fools do. Even worse, "with much wisdom comes much sorrow; the more knowledge, the more grief" (Ecclesiastes 1:18). Having said again and again in Proverbs that wisdom was to be pursued at all costs, in Ecclesiastes Solomon admits that it may not lead to lasting happiness. Part of wisdom is realizing wisdom's limitations.

In a sense, Ecclesiastes is the perfect complement to Proverbs, the book that places a high value on being a decent human being, not an earth-shaker. Solomon had it all. He had popped the cork on life's bottle but found no satisfaction. Ecclesiastes is an "adult" book, written by a reflective man who now sees how foolish the desires and plans of his youth were. The youth sees the goals in life as material pleasures, in doing things other people notice. The adult sees value in hard and steady work, in bringing children into the world and passing worthwhile values on to them. Proverbs and Ecclesiastes both applaud the steady, quiet, decent lives that go unnoticed in the history books. Although Ecclesiastes questions whether work is truly fulfilling, it finally comes down on the positive side. Disciplined work is a good thing, even if it is not man's ultimate source of satisfaction. We have to wonder if perhaps Solomon might have stopped to

---

CULTURAL INSIGHTS

Translating *Hebel*

The Hebrew *hebel*, used many times in Ecclesiastes, means "vapor," something insubstantial and impermanent. When Jerome translated the Bible into Latin around AD 400, he used the Latin word *vanitas*. Many English versions have used "vanity" not in the sense of conceit or pride but in the old sense of futility and pointlessness—things done "in vain." The Geneva Bible of 1560 translated Ecclesiastes 1:2 with the now-familiar words, "Vanity of vanities, all is vanity," the wording later used in the King James Version. Some contemporary versions have dropped "vanity" in the interest of clarity. For example:

"Meaningless! Meaningless! Utterly meaningless!" (New International Version)
"Absolute futility! Everything is futile." (Christian Standard Bible)
"Smoke, nothing but smoke." (*The Message*)

---

chat with some of the carpenters and masons who built his houses, finding such men simple, perhaps, but possessing something that a "success" like himself did not possess: "A man can do nothing better than to eat and drink and find satisfaction in his work" (Ecclesiastes 2:24). "The sleep of a laborer is sweet, whether he eats little or much, but the abundance of a rich man permits him no sleep" (Ecclesiastes 5:12). You don't have to be rich—or smart, or famous—to live a rich life.

In the next section we will look at the story of Job and the difficulty wisdom has in explaining human suffering. The author of Ecclesiastes is in a different position than Job: He isn't suffering. In fact, things are great—good health, success, no problems to speak of. Job wants to understand his suffering. The author of Ecclesiastes wants to understand why his own success doesn't bring more satisfaction. It is worth noting that Solomon's father, David, who faced adversity and struggle throughout his life, also found great joy in life (think back to Day 1), while Solomon, who had a peaceful kingdom handed to him, could announce, "All is vanity!" David could contrast his pleasures with his pains; Solomon could not. In a sense, Solomon was the victim of his own good fortune.

Like Job, Ecclesiastes does not bring closure to the question of life's meaning. Both books leave us, spiritually speaking, in suspense; we have to trust God and accept what he sends us, good and bad. The core issue—finding meaning in life—is not resolved for them but resolved perfectly for the Christian: "We know that in all things God works for the good of those who love him" (Romans 8:28).

JOB AND "FRIENDS": WISDOM MEETS REALITY

If only you would be altogether silent! For you, that would be wisdom! (Job 13:5)

Do you listen in on God's council? Do you limit wisdom to yourself? (Job 15:8)

One of the great books of the Bible, and in all the world's literature, is Job, with its appealing story of a good man who suffers terribly, having no clue what brought on his calamities. Among his sufferings are the "explanations" of his wife and three closest friends. Their "wisdom" is part of Job's torment.

At the beginning of the book we are told that Job is "blameless"—not meaning perfect or sinless, but complete or whole. He has no inconsistencies in his character. He loves God and God loves him, and he is wealthy, with several children. Satan makes a bet with God: Let all these blessings disappear and Job will not be so faithful. Satan's cynicism about Job's piety is typical of what many non-religious people believe about people of faith.

Alas for Job! One disaster follows another: He loses all his livestock and wealth, and his children are all killed. Job does not turn on God, so Satan tests him further, afflicting his body with loathsome sores. Job is a physical and emotional wreck, his head shaved, sitting in an ash heap. His wife has an explanation: God is not good, so curse him and die. Job cannot accept this: "You are talking like a foolish woman. Shall we accept good from God, and not trouble?" (Job 2:10).

Job's three friends, Eliphaz, Bildad and Zophar, arrive to comfort him. They are men of wisdom. In fact, Job's story is set in "the East," considered to be the home of all wisdom. The three friends come up with much more eloquent explanations for Job's calamities than Job's wife could devise. In doing so, they add to Job's misery.

The three friends agree with Job that Job's wife's explanation was wrong: Certainly God is not evil or unjust. God can only do good to man—assuming the men are good, that is. Eliphaz has it all figured out: "As I have observed, those who plow evil and those who sow trouble reap it" (Job 4:8). Therefore, "Blessed is the man whom God corrects; so do not despise the discipline of the Almighty" (Job 5:17). Job cannot accept this; there is no meaning or purpose in what he is suffering: "Let me alone; my days have no meaning" (Job 7:16).

Bildad, also wise in his own eyes, defends God's fairness: "Does God pervert justice? Does the Almighty pervert what is right?" (Job 8:3). Obviously the answer is no. Therefore, "if you will look to God and plead with the Almighty, if you are pure and upright, even now he will rouse himself on your behalf and restore you to your rightful place" (Job 8:5). Job's reply: "I am blameless" (Job 9:21).

Zophar thinks he can see into Job's soul—and so does God: "Surely he recognizes deceitful men; and when he sees evil, does he not take note?" (Job 11:11). Therefore, Job, "if you devote your heart to him and stretch out your hands to him, if you put away the sin that is in your hand and allow no evil to dwell in your tent" (Job 11:13). Job's reply: "I desire to speak to the Almighty and to argue my case with God. You, however, smear me with lies; you are worthless physicians, all of you!" Zophar presses the issue further: "The mirth of the wicked is brief, the joy of the godless lasts but a moment" (Job 20:5). Job disagrees: sometimes the wicked get their deserts in this world, sometimes not: "Why do the wicked live on, growing old and increasing in power?" (Job 21:7).

In the course of the book, the three friends state their case eloquently. These are men who know how to use words, and they are also men who are convinced of their own intelligence. The more they talk, the less Job trusts human wisdom. He lashes out with sarcasm: "Doubtless you are the people, and wisdom will die with you!" (Job 12:2). "If only you would be altogether silent! For you, that would be wisdom" (Job 13:5). "Do you listen in on God's council? Do you limit wisdom to yourself?" (Job 15:8). "What advice you have offered to one without wisdom! And what great insight you have displayed!" (Job 26:3). In his first speech to Job, Eliphaz had stated that God "catches the wise in their craftiness, and the schemes of the wily are swept away" (Job 5:13). The more Job listened, the more he must have been tempted to say "Amen" to that statement.

We might say that Job's three friends are ideologues. They are locked into an ideology: They believe in a righteous God who punishes sin and rewards virtue. And they are right—*up to a point*. In fact, all their statements about sin and suffering are right—*up to a point*. But reality is more complicated, as Job has figured out. Sometimes good people suffer and bad people get away with murder. Why? Human wisdom can't answer that.

Job's suffering is proof that there is no science, no laws that ensure that virtuous living will always lead to success. The Old Testament's constant emphasis on behaving well and expecting to be rewarded may have helped people choose the right path. But any fool could see that sometimes good people suffer while wicked people succeed. The book raises the possibility that calamities may have some other purpose than just punishment.

Eliphaz, Bildad and Zophar are not being made fun of. They are stating what most people at the time believed. Their problem is that everything is black and white for them. They fell prey to the theologian's occupational hazard: not allowing for mystery. Worse, they did not conceive of the idea of serving God strictly for love.

Job's friends arrived with the purpose of comforting him. They began as loving, compassionate friends, but they end up talking like overly confident philosophers or

CHARACTER CLOSE-UP ## The Job Prophet

A companion book to Job is the Book of Habakkuk, in which the perplexed prophet Habakkuk dares to ask God why he would use the evil Babylonians to punish the Jews. Why should the bad be punished by those who are even worse? The prophet was looking at evil on the international level, something that people of faith have done throughout history—and something that we do even more now, since we know what is happening everywhere in this "global village." Obviously the only answer to man's puzzlement is to live by faith, as Habakkuk says in a verse quoted by Paul centuries later: "The righteous will live by his faith" (Habakkuk 2:4, quoted in Romans 1:17 and Galatians 3:11).

Habakkuk, unlike Job, is not concerned with his personal calamities but with the calamities that come upon the whole nation. But like Job, Habakkuk's answer is the awesomeness of God: "The Lord is in his holy temple; let all the earth be silent before" (Habakkuk 2:20). Like some of the lament psalms, it begins in anxiety but ends in joy and trust: "Yet I will rejoice in the Lord, I will be joyful in God my Savior" (Habakkuk 3:18).

professors. They seem more concerned about their own airtight explanations than about Job's condition. They seem more devoted to their wisdom than to Job. Intelligence overrides love. Wisdom is worthless if it cannot console.

Finally, Job's only true friend is God. Job had prayed that God himself might appear to discuss what had happened. God does appear, speaking from a "whirlwind." But there is no discussion or debate—or explanation. Instead, in chapters 38 through 41, in breathtaking poetry, God speaks of the wonders of the vast creation. Compared with the divine task of running the entire universe, human wisdom seems small: "Who endowed the heart with wisdom or gave understanding to the mind? Who has the wisdom to count the clouds? Who can tip over the water jars of the heavens? . . . Does the hawk take flight by your wisdom and spread his wings toward the south?" (Job 38:36–37, 39:26). God's long speech to Job makes the point that the moral order is like the order of nature: too complex to be understood by man. The deepest wisdom is to realize wisdom's limitations.

In speaking to Job, God says not a word about guilt or innocence, suffering or its meaning. The upshot of what he says to Job is this: I show loving concern for every living thing in the world, so can't you trust me to do the right thing concerning you?

At the end, Job "repents in dust and ashes" because he sees that even his genuine integrity makes no claim on God. God doesn't owe him an explanation—or earthly possessions. What God gives any of us is a gift. If Job has any answer, it is the phrase, "Thy will be done." Knowing God is in charge is the deepest wisdom we can aspire to. The story of Job is not about understanding God; it is about faith.

SMART GUY AT THE END OF HIS ROPE

> Now David had been told, "Ahithophel is among the conspirators with Absalom." So David prayed, "O Lord, turn Ahithophel's counsel into foolishness." (2 Samuel 15:31)

We turn from Job and Solomon to some lesser-known but interesting Bible characters, all of them reputed to be wise. One took his wisdom way, way too seriously.

No king ever lacked for people to give him advice, although advisors who were genuinely wise were hard to come by. One man who made a deep impression on all who knew him was David's counselor Ahithophel. "Now in those days the advice Ahithophel gave was like that of one who inquires of God" (2 Samuel 16:23). In short, Ahithophel was regarded as the pinnacle of human wisdom.

Unfortunately for David, this wise counselor deserted him and threw in his lot with David's rebellious son Absalom, who intended to reign in David's place. Why did

Ahithophel change sides? Probably he thought the young, handsome, affable Absalom was the likely winner in the contest. Many of the Israelites would have noted Ahithophel's switch and concluded that the wise man knew what the outcome would be. Power seemed to be shifting from the older generation to the young one.

David was of course disheartened that his former counselor had deserted him. So David prayed: "O Lord, turn Ahithophel's counsel into foolishness" (2 Samuel 15:31). The prayer would be answered but not without David doing some scheming of his own. David sent another advisor, Hushai, over to Absalom's side. Hushai greeted Absalom as king. Absalom was suspicious, but Hushai assured him he was completely loyal to "the one chosen by the Lord." He was referring to David, of course, but the vain Absalom decided Hushai was indeed on his side. All the time, Hushai was a mole for David, keeping him informed of Absalom's plans. Ahithophel, David's trusted advisor, had proved treacherous—now Absalom was getting a dose of his own medicine, taking Hushai into his circle.

Even so, Absalom's rebellion gained such strength that David and his court fled Jerusalem. Ahithophel gave Absalom this bit of worldly advice: Sleep with the women of David's harem. Absalom did—not in the privacy of a bedroom, but on the palace roof, with people watching (2 Samuel 16:21–22). The whole incident is quite disgusting, but in fact Ahithophel's advice was wise: To possess the king's women was, in effect, to become king.

This was the last time Ahithophel's advice would be followed. In the next chapter, both Hushai and Ahithophel gave their advice on what Absalom's next move should be. Absalom, not knowing Hushai was still devoted to David, chose to follow Hushai's counsel. It would lead to the end of his rebellion and his own death.

"When Ahithophel saw that his advice had not been followed, he saddled his donkey and set out for his house in his hometown. He put his house in order and then hanged himself" (2 Samuel 17:23). It is a sad ending to the story of an ambitious, wise but treacherous man. For all his wisdom, Ahithophel was lacking

> **DID YOU KNOW?**
>
> Ahithophel's suicide is one of seven mentioned in the Bible.

in another desirable trait, loyalty. Had he remained loyal to David, Absalom's rebellion might never have progressed so far, and much bloodshed could have been avoided.

DAVID AND TWO WISE WOMEN

Joab sent someone to Tekoa and had a wise woman brought from there. (2 Samuel 14:2)

A wise woman called from the city, "Listen! Listen! Tell Joab to come here so I can speak to him." (2 Samuel 20:16)

Wisdom in the Bible is usually associated with men, but there were many examples of wise women—and, no doubt, many unnamed mothers, wives and sisters who exercised a good influence on men.

The long, colorful saga of King David includes the story of his treacherous wise man Ahithophel but also two stories about wise women. Both are unnamed, though very important.

Prior to Absalom's rebellion against his father, he had fallen from grace by murdering his half-brother Amnon, who had raped and discarded Absalom's sister Tamar. David was in a terrible situation, emotionally speaking, having to keep Absalom at a distance but very much wanting to be near his favorite son. Joab, David's faithful military man, "knew that the king's heart longed for Absalom" (2 Samuel 14:1). So Joab arranged an elaborate ruse to get David to bring Absalom back. Joab sent for a "wise woman" from the town of Tekoa. She dressed and acted the part of a woman in mourning, a widow with two sons, one of whom had just killed the other. Her whole clan demanded that she hand over the other son for execution. Technically, this would be justice—executing a murderer. But for this poor woman, it would be the extinguishing of "the only burning coal I have left." She would be alone in the world, and she and her late husband would have no descendants.

David was touched by the story. He told her to go home, with his order that the living son would be spared. "Not one hair of your son's head will fall to the ground." This was the moment the woman—and Joab—had been waiting for. David had come down on the side of mercy. Now the woman told him to apply it to his own situation. Justice demanded the killing of her son, but mercy allowed for letting him live. Justice demanded Absalom's exile, but mercy allowed for calling him back. The woman was full of practical wisdom: "Like water spilled on the ground, which cannot be recovered, so we must die. But God does not take away life; instead, he devises ways so that a banished person may not remain estranged from him."

CULTURAL INSIGHTS

Goel or King?

In the story of the wise woman of Tekoa, David was being asked to judge in a murder case (although a fictional one), something King Saul was never asked to do. A change had occurred from Israel's former custom of the *goel*—the family's blood avenger, who was to find and kill the murderer. Saul, as king, had been primarily the commander-in-chief of Israel's army. David filled that role also, but as the story shows, he was taking on the role of judge, with his royal decrees overriding the tradition of the *goel*. The assumption was that the king, God's anointed servant, would possess the wisdom to judge such cases.

The king was no fool: He could see that Joab had put the woman up to this. He confronted her with her ruse, but he was not angry with her or Joab. And so he recalled Absalom from exile.

Another wise woman in the David story is found in 2 Samuel 20, the account of another rebellion against David, the revolt of the troublemaking Sheba. Joab, David's faithful military commander, had pursued Sheba to the town of Abel Beth Maacah. Like all ancient cities, this one had walls and could literally lock itself up, but in going after Sheba, Joab and his men built siege ramps and also attempted to batter down the walls.

Enter the wise woman of the city. She called out to Joab: "Long ago they used to say, 'Get your answer at Abel,' and that settled it." In other words, the people of the town had a reputation for practical wisdom. She continued: "We are the peaceful and faithful in Israel. You are trying to destroy a city that is a mother in Israel. Why do you want to swallow up the Lord's inheritance?" Why, indeed? Why was an entire city suffering because the rebel Sheba happened to be holed up in it? Joab wisely agreed. So he made a deal: Hand over Sheba, and the troops would withdraw. "The woman said to Joab, 'His head will be thrown to you from the wall.'" It was a gruesome end to a rebellion that, had this woman not intervened, might have led to much more bloodshed with many innocent lives lost. The woman was—despite the grisly end of Sheba—a peacemaker.

In reading of these two wise women, we ought to remember that in ancient times, there were no college degrees, no certification of wisdom or intelligence, and most women received no schooling at all. These two women were regarded as wise based on their experience with family members and neighbors—people who had learned that these women made sense when they spoke, that they possessed common sense, which is in fact so rare it should not be called common. Kings and philosophers might idle away their time in useless speculation, but in the real world are countless wise women and men, grounded in reality, using the minds God gave them to benefit themselves and their neighbors.

PUTTING THE WORD TO WORK

1. Solomon's youthful prayer for wisdom is impressive—and worth imitating. Take a moment and pray for wisdom.

2. Reflect on Solomon's spending on military matters and on his palaces and temples. Do you think he was making wise choices?

3. Ecclesiastes is sometimes called "cynical" in its view of wisdom. Do you think it is? Do you find truly wise people to be cynical or satisfied with life? Why?

4. Job's three "wise" friends gave him no consolation. Keep this in mind next time a loved one is hurting, and resist the temptation to explain the hurt.

5. Reflect on the wise woman in the last section of the chapter. Does she remind you of any people you have known, people who intervened in a situation using sound common sense?

Caesars and Friends

"Doing as the Romans do" is, in the Bible, not a good thing, for most of the Romans depicted here are not attractive characters, especially the higher-ranking ones. In this chapter we will take a close look at one of the best-known figures in the Bible, Pontius Pilate, and at three Roman emperors who played important roles in the New Testament, in spite of their being mostly offstage. One of those emperors was probably the model for the Beast in the Book of Revelation.

You won't find any worthy role models among these men of high rank and low principles, but you need to know about them in order to truly understand the world in which Christianity took root. And in looking at what the Roman rulers of the day were like, we will take an in-depth look at one of the most famous and controversial passages in the Bible, the "powers that be" passages from Romans, in which Paul counseled Christians to obey government authority.

KEY TERM FOR TODAY Benefactor

Jesus and the early Christians had no illusions about secular rulers, for they understood that rulers not only wish to dominate, but also to be praised and admired and called "Benefactors" by those they oppressed.

THE FIRST EMPEROR

In those days Caesar Augustus issued a decree that a census should be taken of the entire Roman world. (Luke 2:1)

Caesar was originally just the family name of the famous Julius, and even though he was assassinated by a group of high-ranking Romans, his name still had such an aura of importance that the first emperor, Augustus, and all later emperors were officially titled Caesar. When people of that time referred simply to Caesar, it meant the current emperor, whoever that was. Luke is careful in his Gospel to state the full name of the emperor (Augustus in 2:1, Tiberius in 3:1).

Luke 2:1 connects the birth of Jesus in Bethlehem to a census ordered by Caesar Augustus. Unwittingly, the Roman emperor set events in motion that would result in Jesus being born in Bethlehem, Joseph's ancestral home. The ruler of the pagan Roman empire is, without his consent or knowledge, an agent in the birth of the Messiah in Bethlehem, which the Jewish prophets foretold.

Augustus' actual name was Octavian, and he was the great-nephew (and legally adopted son) of Julius Caesar. A period of civil war followed Julius Caesar's assassination in 44 BC, but Octavian, only eighteen at the time of Caesar's assassination, eventually emerged as sole ruler of the Roman empire in 27 BC, when the Roman Senate conferred on him the title *Augustus*, Latin for "honorable." For the first time in two hundred years the doors of the temple of the Roman god Janus were shut, symbolizing that the empire was at peace. Although critics mocked the *Pax Romana* ("Roman peace") and claimed it was rooted in violence and oppression (which was true), there was relative order throughout the empire, and it was into this relatively benign empire that Jesus was born.

Because Augustus brought some stability and security to the empire after a period of civil war, he was often referred to as "savior" and "god" in inscriptions on statues and buildings. Luke intended his readers to catch the irony: The real savior and divine one was not Augustus at all, and the peace he would bring would not be the peace the Romans made at the point of a sword. Augustus had officially been declared, in 42 BC, "son of god," the "god" being the late Julius Caesar. (The Romans were not shrewd enough to ask the question "If Julius Caesar was a god, how did he end up being assassinated?") The name Augustus was borne as a title by all the later emperors, who were, in theory, "sons of god." The Romans described themselves as rulers of the world, a very pretentious notion, and what they ruled was petty compared with the eventual rule of the Messiah over all the earth.

What sort of man was Augustus? Compared with many of the later emperors, he was relatively decent, but historians today are aware that much of what was written about him during his lifetime was propaganda, not fact. Some high-profile authors, such as the poets Virgil, Horace and Ovid, praised him to the skies—and were well rewarded for it. Augustus was what we might call a practical politician: He wasn't moral himself, but he saw the value of his subjects being docile and decent, so he enacted a number of laws that we would call pro-family and pro-morality. He even exiled his promiscuous daughter, Julia, to a remote island—though whether such punishments did much to reduce the wild, duty-free sex of the upper classes is doubtful. Historians such as Tacitus looked back on his reign as a kind of golden age, but this was wishful thinking more than fact. (Even the cynical, worldly Romans could fantasize about the good old days.) However, it is to Augustus' credit that though he insisted his great-uncle Julius had been

DID YOU KNOW?

The more devout Jews would not even touch a coin that had the Roman emperor's image on it. The Jews were allowed to mint their own coins, the main purpose of which was to pay the temple tax.

divine and built temples to honor him, he discouraged his subjects from regarding him as divine. Later emperors would take their divinity seriously—and as a result would persecute Christians who would acknowledge only one Lord.

Augustus built and repaired many temples to the Roman gods, and he claimed the god Apollo as his special patron—but this was all civil religion, done for show. If Augustus had any religion at all, it was astrology, something the Romans had received from the Greeks, and in a sense astrology was the most common belief system in the empire. (See page 264 for more about astrology.) On several occasions the Roman emperors were disturbed by the influence of astrologers—*mathematici*—on the people, and these might be banished for a while, but inevitably they returned, for the people demanded their services.

Aside from ordering the census that took Joseph and Mary to Bethlehem, Augustus had another connection to the region where Jesus would live: The emperor had been Herod the Great's sponsor and was responsible for his being king of the Jews. Herod showed his gratitude to the emperor by rebuilding the ancient city of Samaria in a lavish way and renaming it Sebaste, which was the Greek equivalent of Augustus. Naturally the city had a temple dedicated to the divinity of Augustus. Herod also built the new port city of Caesarea, a locale that figures in many episodes in the Book of Acts. As if he had not honored Augustus enough, Herod built another temple to the emperor on the site that would later be called Caesarea Philippi. And he instituted games, held every four years, in honor of Augustus.

When Herod died in 4 BC, a Jewish delegation went to Rome to beg Augustus to remove the area from the rule of Herod's loathsome family, but Augustus honored Herod's will, which divided up the territory among three sons. The son Archelaus inherited Judea and Samaria, and he continued his father's lavish building projects, but the Jews hated him and complained so loudly to Rome that the emperor exiled him in AD 6 and used this as an excuse to convert Judea and

DID YOU KNOW?

Latin, the language of the Romans, had no letter *K*, but used the letter *C* for the *K* sound (and never for the *S* sound). Thus the Romans pronounced "Caesar" as "Kaesar." In the Greek New Testament, the word is *Kaisar*. Obviously this evolved, over the centuries, into the term *Kaiser* for the German emperors.

Samaria into Roman provinces. The first Roman governor, Coponius, assumed office, residing in Herod's palaces in Caesarea and Jerusalem. He and his successors, including Pontius Pilate, collected taxes for the empire and had the power of capital punishment.

Pilate had a notice prepared and fastened to the cross. It read: Jesus of Nazareth, the King of the Jews. Many of the Jews read this sign, for the place where Jesus was crucified was near the city, and the sign was written in Aramaic, Latin and Greek.

The chief priests of the Jews protested to Pilate, "Do not write 'The King of the Jews,' but that this man claimed to be king of the Jews." Pilate answered, "What I have written, I have written." (John 19:19–22)

In my book *Know the Words of Jesus in 30 Days*, I cover the fateful encounter between Jesus and the Roman governor Pontius Pilate, an encounter in which Pilate sensed that Jesus was quite harmless, yet which ended with Pilate's caving in to pressure from the crowd and ordering Jesus crucified. Pilate cracked under the threat that he might be reported to the emperor, Tiberius, for having released a possible revolutionary. The Jerusalem mob, egged on by the corrupt and unspiritual priests, taunted Pilate: "If you release him, you are no friend of Caesar." If they thought this would push Pilate over the edge, they were correct.

Having covered that encounter in the other book, let's consider what followed. The Gospels refer to a notice fastened on Jesus' cross. This was the *titulus*, a plaque made of wood or gypsum, in which the crucified man's offense was written in large red or black letters, the wording often being deliberately sarcastic in nature. In John's Gospel, Pilate clearly detests the Jewish priests, whom he has taunted by referring to Jesus as "king of the Jews." Though he has grudgingly caved in to their demand to crucify Jesus, he still can't resist taunting them. Normally one of Pilate's aides would have written out the *titulus*, but it's possible that Pilate wrote it with his own hand. Either way, the words were those he chose with a view to irking the Jewish authorities. The placard mocks the Jews, implying that Jesus really *is* the king. Pilate had asked Jesus, "What is truth?" and ironically ends up putting the truth on the placard. The Romans had a certain respect for things that were put in writing, so Pilate had no intention of altering the *titulus* once it was written.

John's Gospel records that the message was written in three languages: Latin, Greek and Aramaic, meaning any of the locals would have been able to understand it. Latin was the Romans' main language, Aramaic the main language of the people in Judea, and Greek the second language of both groups, as well as the common language in that part of the Roman empire.

What did the *titulus* actually say? The Latin would have read: IESUS NAZARENUS REX IUDAEORUM. In the countless artworks showing the crucifixion, the plaque above Jesus' head usually has not the whole Latin inscription but the abbreviation INRI.

Why did Pilate add "of Nazareth" to the inscription? Partly because Jesus was a common name in those days, and "of Nazareth" made the name more specific. But it is almost certain he had another motivation: "Jesus of Nazareth" was intended to remind the snobbish Jerusalem Jews that their "king" was from a small town in Galilee. Pilate, the sophisticated, worldly Roman official, could not resist mocking the leaders of the Jews. And this was perfectly in keeping with what we know of his character from secular historians.

> Pilate was prefect of the Roman province of Judea AD 26–36.

Pilate was the protégé of the unscrupulous and ambitious Sejanus, advisor to the emperor Tiberius, and notoriously anti-Jewish. When Pilate first came to Judea in AD 26, he had his soldiers smuggle Roman military standards, bearing the emperor's image, into Jerusalem at night. The Jews, as Pilate well knew, had a horror of any kind of graven image, since it implied worship of someone beside God. The Jews begged Pilate to remove the standards, and after he refused, they stood around his home in Caesarea for five days in silent protest. Pilate had the crowd surrounded by soldiers with drawn swords, ready to kill them if they continued to protest. The Jews bared their necks, willing to die rather than tolerate the imperial images. Pilate was amazed and had the standards removed. The memory of this incident must have stuck in his craw, for it would not be until his encounter with Jesus that he would cave into the Jews again.

> **DID YOU KNOW?**
>
> Jewish tombstones in Rome sometimes had their inscriptions in Greek, Latin and Hebrew (or Aramaic).

The Jews protested because Pilate used money from the temple treasury to build an aqueduct—something useful, but something the Jews saw as a profane use of sacred money. Pilate had backed down once before, but not this time: he had his soldiers move among the protesters and cudgel them to death. The reference in Luke 13:1 to Pilate mingling people's blood with their sacrifices may refer to this incident, since some of the people would have had their offering animals with them at the time of the cudgeling.

> **DID YOU KNOW?**
>
> The Gospels refer to Pilate with the Greek word *hegemon*, meaning "leader" but usually translated "governor." In fact, his actual title was *prefect*, because a building unearthed at Caesarea had an inscription referring to Pilate as *praefectus Iudeae*, prefect of Judea.

Some time after Pilate's fateful encounter with Jesus, the Jewish ruler Herod Agrippa I wrote to the Roman emperor Caligula, complaining about Pilate, describing him as "inflexible by nature and cruel because of stubbornness." He accused Pilate of "graft, insults, robberies, assaults, wanton abuse, constant executions without trial, unending grievous cruelty." Even allowing for some exaggeration, what we know from this and other non-biblical sources of information about Pilate is almost all bad. Still, it is likely that the meeting of Pilate and Jesus as reported in the Gospels is probably true, since Pilate was not so much on the side of Jesus as he was opposed to be bullied by the Jewish priests, whom he despised. He might have felt some sympathy for Jesus, a common working man who seemed decent and harmless enough, and who certainly seemed a more appealing specimen of humanity than the effete, corrupt priests.

Mel Gibson's popular but controversial 2004 film *The Passion of the Christ* was criticized for its extreme (but realistic) violence. Some Christians criticized it for another reason: it makes Pilate a sympathetic character, doubtful and indecisive about Jesus' fate, in contrast to the cruel Jewish priests who are unrelenting in their efforts to destroy Jesus. Critics

CHARACTER CLOSE-UP ## Pilate's Wife

Matthew's Gospel records an interesting detail that the other Gospels omit: While Jesus was on trial before Pilate, Pilate's wife sent her husband a curious message: "Have nothing to do with that righteous man, for I have suffered much because of him today in a dream" (Matthew 27:19, ESV). The Gospel says nothing else about this incident, leaving us to wonder what sort of woman this was—and why her husband chose to ignore her words. Pilate might have had the usual pagan superstitions. Although he had no use for the Jews or their religion, something about Jesus might have unsettled him, notably his reticence. We also cannot underestimate the effect his wife's dream had on him. The Romans, like most people in ancient times, took dreams seriously. Every Roman governor would have been aware of Julius Caesar's wife Calpurnia having a dream warning him of the assassination conspiracy. Caesar disregarded his wife's dream and was stabbed to death.

In her message to Pilate, his wife referred to Jesus as *dikaio*, "righteous one." What did she mean? It is certainly possible that her dream had its origin in God himself. But it is also possible that during the days leading up to Jesus' arrest and trial, she had heard things about the teacher from Nazareth. Roman women were notoriously changeable about religious matters. Some changed religions as easily as others changed clothes, and we have no idea what religion Pilate's wife had, if any, or whether her religious nature had any substance to it. Nonetheless, what she said to Pilate was quite true: Jesus really was a righteous man, and Pilate was very much in the wrong for not releasing him.

Because of Pilate's wife's dream, many stories circulated about both her and her husband. History does not record her name, although some very old traditions call her Claudia, or Procula, or Claudia Procula. In some legends, she becomes a Christian; in others both she and her husband do. The Coptic church, which has existed in Egypt for almost two thousand years, regards Pilate and his wife as Christian saints. We have no way of knowing if the man who sent Jesus to the cross finally found salvation, but it is a pleasant thought.

said that Gibson's film seemed to shift all the blame from Pilate to the priests. But that accusation doesn't hold water. If Pilate really did believe—as the movie makes clear, and as the Gospels suggest—that having Jesus crucified was wrong, then his final assent to the crucifixion makes him *more* responsible, not less. His caving in to pressure is a horrible thing, and his washing of his hands is hardly a moral act, since it is obviously just an evasion of his own responsibility. You might say that Gibson's sympathetic Pilate is more of a sinner than some of the crueler Pilates seen in other films. Gibson's Pilate is a decent man who, at a crucial moment, doesn't have the courage to keep something horrible from happening.

Rome finally heard enough complaints about Pilate, so that he was called before the emperor, and he vanishes from history, some stories saying he committed suicide, some

CULTURAL INSIGHTS

Friendship in the Roman Empire

John 19 relates that when Pilate was about to pass judgment on Jesus, the Jerusalem mob issued a verbal threat: If Pilate released Jesus, he was "no friend of Caesar." The phrase "friend of Caesar" reveals a lot about how the ancient Greeks and Romans viewed friendship. Strictly speaking, little genuine friendship existed among them. Rather, there was a self-serving, cynical quality to the relationships. A person hoping to move up the social ladder would attach himself as "friend" to someone higher up, regarding that person more as patron than as familiar friend—someone who could offer him social and political benefits. In turn, the one higher up the ladder would expect slavish groveling from the one who was lower, the vile waited on by the servile. To be one of the coveted "Friends of Caesar" was to live in expectation of favors from the emperor—in return for servile flattery and corrupt practices.

Even among social equals, men were friends mostly to cement political and business connections. So there was a cold, calculating quality to most so-called friendships among the pagans, and to read the history of the Greeks and Romans is to be appalled at how easily "friends" could turn on each other, never being able to fully rely on a friend when the chips were down. Of course, what was true of them has been, sadly, true of many friendships throughout history.

Contrast the worldly title "friend of Caesar," with the patriarch Abraham, who was a "friend of God" (James 2:23), one whom God dearly loved. Also, God spoke to Moses face-to-face, "as a friend" (Exodus 33:11). Someone seeking a friend in high places could do much better than being a "friend of Caesar."

that he was executed. (It was common for Roman officials condemned to execution to take their lives themselves.) Some people believed that both he and his wife became Christians, a belief no doubt based on Matthew's account of Pilate's wife referring to Jesus as an "innocent man" (Matthew 27:19). While it is pleasant to think that the man who condemned Jesus to death later became a Christian himself, given what we know of Pilate, it is unlikely. But who can say?

THE STUTTERING CAESAR

"These men who have caused trouble all over the world have now come here . . . They are all defying Caesar's decrees, saying that there is another king, one called Jesus." When they heard this, the crowd and the city officials were thrown into turmoil. (Acts 17:6–8)

The verses above are from the story of the missionaries Paul and Silas carrying the Gospel to the Greek city of Thessalonica. Following their usual custom, they took their message to the Jewish synagogue, where they made some converts among the Jews and among the Gentile God-fearers. But, also following the usual pattern, they aroused the ire of some of the Jews, who, with the aid of some local riffraff, got the city in an uproar, so that Paul and Silas were compelled to flee the city by night.

If the verses above sound vaguely familiar, compare them to John 19:13–14: "'Shall I crucify your king?' Pilate asked. 'We have no king but Caesar,' the chief priests answered." The irate Jews of Thessalonica were, for the moment, pretending to be loyal subjects of the Roman emperor, and claiming that Paul and Silas were proclaiming a rival king, Jesus. The Jews of Thessalonica were doing just what the Jewish priests had done at Jesus' trial: rattle Roman officials by suggesting that a revolution was in the making, something the Romans could not abide. In both instances there was no threat at all, of course.

> **Claudius reigned AD 41–54.**

The Caesar referred to in Acts 17 was the emperor Claudius. Much of the action in Acts takes place during his reign, though he is mentioned by name and deed only once: "[Paul] met a Jew named Aquila, a native of Pontus, who had recently come from Italy with his wife Priscilla, because Claudius had ordered all the Jews to leave Rome." (Acts 18:2) This may be referring to the same incident reported by the gossipy Roman historian Suetonius: "As the Jews in Rome were indulging in constant riots at the instigation of Chrestus, Claudius banished them from Rome." This Chrestus was probably a misspelling by Suetonius of Christus, and what lay behind this was controversy among the Jews of Rome caused by the preaching of the gospel. At any rate, Claudius expelling the Jews from Rome resulted in Aquila and Priscilla being in Corinth, where they became the close friends of Paul, another example of an imperial decree affecting the spread of Christianity in a positive way.

Claudius was the uncle of the insane emperor Caligula, the man who disgustingly put into practice his maxim that "I can do anything I want, to anybody." When Caligula was, to the great relief of everyone, finally assassinated in AD 41, the aging, stuttering, weak-kneed gambler Claudius (who was found hiding behind a curtain) was made emperor. Claudius' own mother had often referred to him as a "monster" and "fool," and though he could at times appear dignified, when under stress he slobbered uncontrollably. Though he was an improvement over Caligula—most anyone would have been—he was depraved and corrupt, and the notorious promiscuity of his young wife Messalina gave the Romans much to snicker about. He eventually had her killed, but he himself was killed (with poisonous mushrooms) by his wife Agrippina, who put her son Nero on the throne. Agrippina was in fact Claudius' niece, and it was illegal to marry her—so Claudius changed the law. Claudius' life has become fairly well known, thanks to the popular novel *I, Claudius* by Robert Graves and the British TV miniseries based on it. His story helps us understand why so many people in the empire were drawn to Christianity.

Although Claudius was an immoral man, he had the advantage of having a predecessor and successor who were much worse. Probably the most favorable thing to be said about him is that during his reign, from AD 41 to 54, Christianity spread widely, with no

---

CULTURAL INSIGHTS

"Benefactors"

In Luke's account of the Last Supper, he records Jesus saying to the disciples, "The kings of the Gentiles lord it over them; and those who exercise authority over them call themselves Benefactors" (Luke 22:25). Throughout history, even the worst tyrants have liked to pose as men's benefactors, one of the great lies of humanity. Even a vile, immoral Roman emperor like Nero could be referred to in official inscriptions as *euergetes* (benefactor) and *soter* (savior). The worst dictators of history, and today, may be known as thugs to those outside their own borders, but inside they wish to be perceived as caring and protective. Like Nero, they wish not only to be feared but also to be loved as well. The oppressor and exploiter not only must satisfy his urge to dominate but also must pass himself off as doing it for the good of those beneath him—in other words, playing God by being in charge and claiming to dispense good things. In his words at the Last Supper, Jesus was reminding the disciples that the only true Benefactor is God. And, ironically, immoral rulers like Nero, calling themselves Benefactors, have often persecuted the real benefactors in their societies, the decent people of faith whose names were never carved in marble on public buildings.

interference from the Roman authorities. And while Claudius and his court were wasting themselves in gluttony, gambling and promiscuity, thousands of people's lives were being transformed by an enduring and endearing faith that would long outlive the empire.

APPEALING TO THE UNAPPEALING

Paul made his defense: "I have done nothing wrong against the law of the Jews or against the temple or against Caesar . . . I have not done any wrong to the Jews, as you yourself know very well. If, however, I am guilty of doing anything deserving death, I do not refuse to die. But if the charges brought against me by these Jews are not true, no one has the right to hand me over to them. I appeal to Caesar!"

After Festus had conferred with his council, he declared: "You have appealed to Caesar. To Caesar you will go!" . . .

Agrippa said to Festus, "This man could have been set free if he had not appealed to Caesar" (Acts 25:8, 10–12; 26:32).

This calls for wisdom. If anyone has insight, let him calculate the number of the beast, for it is man's number. His number is 666 (Revelation 13:18).

One of the great villains in Christian history is mentioned—though not by name—in the Bible. This was the Roman emperor Nero, referred to as Caesar in Acts 25:11–12.

One of the privileges of being a Roman citizen was the right to have one's case tried before Caesar, that is, the Roman emperor. As a Roman citizen, Paul availed himself of this privilege, one of his motivations being that he could witness to his faith in Rome, the busy center of a vast empire. Thus one of the greatest men in history would be brought face-to-face with one of the worst—a seasoned and saintly Christian missionary on trial before an effete, spoiled, depraved aristocrat still in his twenties.

As a moral man of faith, Paul would have had no illusions about the Roman emperor. As we have already seen, no emperor in Paul's lifetime had been a paragon of morality—quite the opposite, in fact. At age sixteen, in AD 54, Nero had become emperor because his scheming, unscrupulous mother Agrippina had killed her half-senile husband, the emperor Claudius, with poisonous mushrooms. Afterward she systematically eliminated anyone who might be her son's rival for the throne. It became clear that Nero had inherited her ruthlessness, for in time he had her murdered. Traditionally, human beings have regarded matricide—killing one's own mother—as one of the most horrible crimes imaginable. (A man does not kill the very person who gave him life.) But they were not horrified at the death of Agrippina, which tells us a lot about the esteem felt for her.

However, in the early part of Nero's reign he seemed to be on the right path, guided in his policies by his former tutor, the philosopher Seneca, who put an end to the frequent executions and treason trials of Claudius' reign. (It is worth remembering that Paul wrote his Letter to the Romans, in which he told Christians to be subject to "the powers that be," probably in AD 57 or 58, a time when Nero was not yet widely hated. We will look at that passage later in this chapter.) For a few years Seneca and other officials governed the empire reasonably well, while Nero pursued frivolous pleasures. While he did not scandalize the jaded Romans much by murdering his treacherous

Nero reigned AD 54–68.

mother, taking the sensuous Poppaea away from her first husband, or going through a mock marriage with the boy Sporus, he did offend the Romans by performing in the arenas as a charioteer or lyre player. Such behavior was seen as contemptible in a ruler, and Nero grew paranoid as he became aware that the Romans detested him.

Regarding the reign of Nero, the Roman historian Tacitus wrote, "Roman morals had long become impure, but never was there so favorable an environment for debauchery as among this filthy crowd. Here every form of immorality competed for attention, and no chastity, modesty, or vestige of decency could survive."

In July 64 a great fire engulfed much of Rome, and many people blamed the fire on the emperor, knowing he had long wanted to rebuild much of the city for his own vanity. According to Tacitus, "Nero fabricated scapegoats—and punished with every refinement the notoriously depraved Christians. Their originator, Christ, had been executed in Tiberius' reign by the governor of Judea, Pontius Pilate. But in spite of this temporary setback the deadly superstition had broken out afresh, not only in Judea (where the mischief had started) but even in Rome. All degraded and shameful practices collect and flourish in the capital. First, Nero had self-acknowledged Christians arrested. Then, on their information, large numbers of others were condemned—not so much for incendiarism [starting fires] as for their anti-social tendencies. Their deaths were made farcical. Dressed in wild animals' skins, they were torn to pieces by dogs, or crucified, or made into torches to be ignited after dark. Despite their guilt as Christians, and the ruthless punishment it deserved, the victims were pitied. For it was felt that they were being sacrificed to one man's brutality rather than to the national interest." Suetonius wrote that in Nero's reign, "punishments were inflicted on the Christians, a sect professing a new and mischievous religious belief."

DID YOU KNOW?

Possibly the best novel with biblical characters is *Quo Vadis*, by Polish author Henryk Sienkiewicz, who won the Nobel Prize for literature. This classic deals with a decadent Roman Empire and how it reacts with the new religion of Christianity. The effeminate, snobbish Emperor Nero is a key character, and so are Peter and Paul, both of whom are executed by Nero—Paul by beheading, Peter by being crucified (upside down, since he claimed he did not deserve to die in the same manner as his master Jesus).

Clearly Tacitus and Suetonius had no love for this new sect, though they weren't precise about just what the Christians did that was depraved and deadly and mischievous. Tacitus lamented the Romans' immorality—with good reason—but he knew so little about the Christians that he was not even aware that the Christians taught and practiced a high morality, and that Christians believed everyone—even a lowly slave—was precious to God. But Tacitus was at least aware that the cruel persecution provoked pity among some of the Romans, who felt drawn to a faith that would enable people to face death courageously and nobly, even forgiving their executioners. As one early theologian wrote, "the blood of the martyrs is the seed of the church." The depraved emperor could kill Christians, yet he could not kill the faith. Some of the later emperors would make Nero's persecution of Christians seem small by comparison, yet the faith continued to spread.

At the time Paul appealed to Caesar, this great persecution lay about eight years in the future. We don't know what happened at his trial before Caesar, since the Book of Acts ends with Paul living under house arrest in Rome, free to witness his faith. Although Paul had appealed to Caesar, Nero often had another official handle the appeals, so even if Paul was tried, he did not necessarily meet Nero face-to-face. According to some old traditions, Paul was eventually tried and released, and continued as a missionary in the empire, but both he and Peter were among those who perished during Nero's persecution in AD 64. As a Roman citizen, Paul would not have had to endure the horrors that Tacitus described; he would have been executed quickly, probably by beheading by sword.

Nero did not long outlive the victims of his persecution. The Romans hated the Christians, but they hated Nero as well, and several revolts broke out. In AD 68, seeing that the latest revolt was going to be successful, the vile man cut his own throat, mourned by no one. He was thirty years old. For many years the name "Nero" still evoked horror among Christians, and there were rumors that he had not really died, but was still alive somewhere, eager to launch another bloody persecution.

Nero certainly deserves the infamy that has been heaped on his name. Raised in an atmosphere of court intrigue, where people murdered their own relatives and engaged in every sort of vice, Nero typified the empire he ruled over, an empire where power and status seemed to be all that mattered. He is a classic case of the old maxim that "power corrupts."

Regarding Nero in the Book of Revelation: the apostle John probably wrote Revelation sometime around AD 95, a time when many Christians, including John, were being persecuted by the emperor Domitian, who required all people in his empire to honor him as a god. Revelation 13 contains the famous passage about the Beast who possesses great political power and persecutes the saints. "If anyone has insight, let him calculate the number of the beast, for it is man's number. His number is 666" (Revelation 13:18). Who was John referring to here? Could it have been Domitian, his own persecutor? A future Roman emperor? (There were several who were even worse than Domitian.) Or someone centuries in the future? Much ink has been spilled over determining who, or what, the Beast of Revelation is, and every generation of Christians has found people to pin the number 666 on—and no wonder, for in every period, somewhere on earth, there has been persecution of Christians. One very old theory, though, is that John had in mind the belief of many Christians of his day that Nero was still alive—or that he had died but come back to life again. Somehow—by assigning a numeral value to each letter—the letters in Nero's names and titles could be arranged to add up to 666. But then, throughout history clever people have found ways to make just about any famous person's name fit the 666. The most likely explanation is that 666 is intended to represent incompleteness, based on the fact that in the Bible, seven is a "good" number, while six is a "bad" number because it falls short of seven. If John's original readers knew whom he was referring to, the identity of the 666 man was soon forgotten, for by AD 180 the theologian Irenaeus lamented that no one knew who he was. Perhaps the one thing that we can be certain about is that the early Christians, including the author of Revelation, thought of the evil Nero as the template for government-imposed persecution of believers.

PAUL'S AUTHORITY PASSAGE

Everyone must submit himself to the governing authorities, for there is no authority except that which God has established. The authorities that exist have been established by God. Consequently, he who rebels against the authority is rebelling against what God has instituted, and those who do so will bring judgment on themselves. For rulers hold no terror for those who do right, but for those who do wrong. Do you want to be free from fear of the one in authority? Then do what is right and he will commend you. For he is God's servant to do you good . . . . Give everyone what you owe him: If you owe taxes, pay taxes; if revenue, then revenue; if respect, then respect; if honor, then honor (Romans 13:1–4, 7).

Whether he was conscious of it or not, Paul was echoing the words of Jesus: "Render to Caesar what is Caesar's." Jesus' enemies had tried to make him look like an anti-Roman rebel by asking him if it was right to pay taxes to Caesar. His answer was yes, but we must also render to God what is God's. Caesar has a legitimate claim on citizens' taxes, but we owe our ultimate loyalty to God.

When Paul wrote the Letter to the Romans, the vile Nero was emperor, but at that time he had largely left the government in the hands of his advisors, who were much wiser men than he. So when Paul told Christians to respect government authorities, the imperial government that almost all Christians lived under was relatively benign. Ironically, in a few years Nero would launch the first official persecution of Christians, blaming the great fire of Rome on them and executing and torturing many of them. Some of the later emperors would do much worse, but then, even more severe and systematic persecutions would take place in the twentieth century. Believers have debated this question: Would Paul have told Christians to submit to the government in Nazi Germany? In Communist Russia? In Communist China? In Muslim Sudan? What if those governments told Christians to betray each other to the authorities? To turn over copies of the Bible? To renounce their faith?

Paul's passage on government in Romans 13 is not the only New Testament passage dealing with obedience to authority. Acts 5 shows a situation in which obedience to earthly powers has its limits, for when Peter and the other apostles were told to stop preaching the gospel, they replied: "We must obey God rather than men!" (Acts 5:29). Rendering to God what is his due must, in such cases, require disobeying man.

The New Testament on the whole counsels believers to be good citizens, to obey the state—to render to Caesar what is Caesar's, as Jesus said. At the same time it is clear that the state can be a persecutor—and a long history of such persecution resulted in the Christian tradition of looking at kings and other rulers with a skeptical eye. Even after the Roman empire became Christian—officially, anyway—and every emperor was regarded as protector of the church, the church never regarded any emperor as divine, although the Romans as pagans did, and so did the Egyptians with their pharaohs. The Christian tradition, firmly rooted in both Old and New Testaments, was to regard governments as a necessity. They keep order in society and restrain crime and deserve respect for doing so. Certainly Paul himself took advantage of the well-maintained Roman roads and the safe sea routes as he spread the gospel. But three centuries later, the great theologian Augustine summed up the skeptical Christian view with his famous question "What are kingdoms, but great robberies?" A government, he said, consisted of a gang of thieves, who had achieved legitimacy over time, and who, unlike other thieves, could act with impunity. It is worth noting that when Augustine wrote these words, he was living in a Roman empire that was officially Christian. Yet he was realist enough to know that no government, not even one that pays lip service to faith, is perfect. Yet, like Paul, he knew that all governments, even bad ones, play a useful role in keeping down crime and disorder.

In concluding this chapter, it is worth noting that the Roman government during the New Testament period was, all things considered, not too bad. Certainly there were more brutal and oppressive regimes in other times and places—such as the Assyrians in the Old Testament period. And for all their brutality, the Romans could not hold a candle to some of the totalitarian horrors of the last century. The urge to dominate and oppress our fellow man lives in us like a dark disease. This is why the Bible tells us to put our ultimate faith in God, not in any human individual or institution. When Jesus taught "the kingdom of God," he knew his listeners, in whatever time and place they lived, would lend him their ears, for they could not have found any real satisfaction in any earthly kingdom. The kingdom of the corrupt and immoral Caesars is long gone, but the kingdom inaugurated by Jesus and his disciples—"nobodies," by imperial standards—goes on and on.

PUTTING THE WORD TO WORK

1. Having read about the Caesars mentioned in the Bible, how do you respond? Can you imagine yourself living a decent life under them? Respecting their authority?

2. How do you react to today's Memory Verse? Do you think Jesus was being cynical or realistic? Keep in mind that in the following verse he told his disciples that they must strive to be *servants*, not rulers.

3. After reading the section on Nero, how do you interpret the 666 passage in the Book of Revelation?

4. Does the information on the Roman emperors and Pilate affect your understanding of Paul's "authority" passage from Romans 13?

5. Having read about persecution of people of faith centuries ago, take a few moments to pray for those who are being persecuted now. Pray also for people who face the dilemma of having to disobey man in order to obey God.

Women Who Dared

L ike strength and intelligence, boldness is a neutral quality, not necessarily either good or bad. In the pages of the Bible we meet with some very bold women who used their assertiveness for bad purposes, the classic cases being the Bible's wickedest queen, Jezebel, and her wicked daughter Athaliah, whom we

MEMORY VERSE

When I called, you answered me; you made me bold and stouthearted. —Psalm 138:3

deal with in other chapters. But boldness can be a fine quality in the right circumstances and for the right purposes. In this chapter we will look at a diverse group of women from various time periods, all of them bold for the right reasons.

KEY TERM FOR TODAY ## Boldness

Although courage and boldness are usually considered "manly" virtues, the Bible is full of stories of women who acted with boldness and determination.

IN-LAW AS OUTLAW

Judah was told, "Your daughter-in-law Tamar is guilty of prostitution, and as a result she is now pregnant." Judah said, "Bring her out and have her burned to death!" (Genesis 38:24)

Chapter 1 of Matthew's Gospel is the genealogy of Jesus and traces his descent all the way back to the patriarch Abraham. Most people don't read the genealogy very closely, mostly because it is a long list of *begats*—Abraham begat (was the father of) Isaac, Isaac begat Jacob, etc. While this "begat list" contains mostly men's names, four women are mentioned in it, all of them outsiders—either foreigners or women of shady repute. Matthew's Gospel is often called the Jewish Gospel because he so often quotes the Old Testament and saw Jesus as the Jewish Messiah, and yet Matthew goes out of his way to show that Jesus was sent to save not just the Jews but all people. And so Jesus' genealogy does not include the four women that Jews thought of as the "mothers of Israel": Sarah, wife of Abraham; Rebekah, wife of Isaac; and Rachel and Leah, the wives of Jacob. Instead, Matthew gives us the names of four outsiders: a prostitute, Rahab; an adulteress,

Bathsheba; a foreigner, Ruth; and a woman who deceived and seduced her own father-in-law, Tamar. Jesus was fully human, and like all human beings, he had ancestors who were far from perfect.

Let's look at the first woman mentioned in the genealogy: Tamar. Matthew 1:3 tells us that Judah was the father of Perez and Zerah, whose mother was Tamar. Matthew's Jewish readers would have recognized those names immediately and realized right away that Matthew's genealogy of the Messiah included some sordid elements.

The sordid but oddly inspiring story is found in Genesis 38. Judah, one of the twelve sons of Jacob, had separated from his father and brothers and lived among the Canaanites and married a Canaanite woman. While this sounds innocent enough to us, it was far from innocent, for the Canaanites were notoriously immoral, and a Canaanite wife would often lead her husband into idol worship. We don't know if Judah's wife corrupted him, but we are told she gave birth to three sons: Er, Onan and Shelah.

Judah married Er off to a woman named Tamar. "But Er, Judah's firstborn, was wicked in the Lord's sight; so the Lord put him to death" (Genesis 38:7). Tamar, at a very young age, had become a widow. But the ancient Hebrews had a custom, a way of dealing with such circumstances. If a man died before he had fathered children, his brother would sleep with the widow, and any children they conceived would be considered the children of the man who died. Judah ordered Onan to fulfill this duty, but Onan "knew that the offspring would not be his; so whenever he lay with his brother's wife, he spilled his semen on the ground to keep from producing offspring for his brother" (Genesis 38:9). (Obviously the Bible authors could be very blunt about sexual matters.) Because Onan had refused to fulfill his brotherly duty, he too died.

CULTURAL INSIGHTS

Levir

"If brothers are living together and one of them dies without a son, his widow must not marry outside the family. Her husband's brother shall take her and marry her and fulfill the duty of a brother-in-law to her. The first son she bears shall carry on the name of the dead brother so that his name will not be blotted out from Israel" (Deuteronomy 25:5–6). This law is called the levirate law, the word *levir* meaning "brother-in-law." At the time of Judah and Tamar, the law had not yet been given to Israel, but as the story shows, the custom already existed long before it was written down.

What if the brother-in-law had no desire to father children with the wife of his dead brother? In that event, he had to acknowledge it publicly, and the widow would spit in his face. In short, it was considered a supreme disgrace not to fulfill his duty.

The Hebrew Midwives

The Book of Genesis ends with Jacob and his sons living comfortably in Egypt. But Exodus opens with a dramatic change: Jacob's descendants, the Hebrews, have been made slaves by the Egyptians, but because the Hebrews are so numerous, Egypt's pharaoh fears they might eventually rebel violently. And so the pharaoh "said to the Hebrew midwives, whose names were Shiphrah and Puah, 'When you help the Hebrew women in childbirth and observe them on the delivery stool, if it is a boy, kill him; but if it is a girl, let her live'" (Exodus 1:15–16). The two midwives, however, "feared God," so they refused to follow the command. When he summoned them and demanded to know why they had disobeyed, they told a blatant lie: "Hebrew women are not like Egyptian women; they are vigorous and give birth before the midwives arrive." Because they had not carried out the pharaoh's horrible command, God blessed these two women.

Alert readers might ask: Was Pharaoh really gullible enough to believe this rather obvious lie about Hebrew women? The likely answer is yes. Throughout history, people have shown themselves capable of believing nearly anything about different ethnic groups. In the New Testament period, supposedly sophisticated writers like Cicero and Seneca showed themselves laughably gullible, believing the most ridiculous things about Jews. Pharaoh thought of the Hebrew slaves as being more like animals than human beings, so he probably did believe they gave birth in a way different from Egyptian women.

Of course, the real point of this story is that two very humble women—midwives in a nation of slaves—stood up to the Egyptian pharaoh, the mightiest man on earth. To their great credit, they feared God more than they feared any earthly power.

In effect, Tamar had been widowed twice. She was living, as was the custom, in her husband's father's household, but Judah told her to go back to her parents and said that when his youngest son, Shelah, came of age, she could marry him. But Genesis tells us what was really on Judah's mind: He feared Shelah, too, would die, since Tamar clearly seemed to be "bad luck"—in spite of the fact that Judah's two dead sons had brought about their own fate.

To be a childless widow was a great tragedy in ancient times. It was even worse for someone in Tamar's situation, for she was young and healthy, capable of bearing many children, and already she was consigned to the ranks of lonely widows. It was as close to a living death as could be imagined.

Tamar did as Judah told her, living under her own father's roof again. At some point, Judah's wife died, and he mourned for her. Shelah had grown up, but it was clear Judah wasn't going to let him anywhere near Tamar. The young widow had had much time to reflect on her lot and decided to take matters into her own hands. Casting off her widow's garb, she dressed like a prostitute and stationed herself by a road where she knew Judah would pass by. Like two businessmen, they dickered over the price: Judah would pay her with a kid goat for her services. Not having the goat with him, he gave Tamar, as a pledge, his staff and his personal seal, a signet that would be used in putting his stamp on legal documents.

As Tamar hoped, she became pregnant. In effect, she had kept the bloodline alive by conceiving a child with her father-in-law. Sordid as this sounds to us, the whole act was for the purpose of conceiving a child, and after Judah was gone, Tamar donned her widow's garb again. In a few months, Judah was told that Tamar was pregnant. Knowing she was unmarried, and hearing that she was guilty of prostitution, he ordered that she suffer the penalty: death by burning. Legally, Tamar was part of Judah's household, and as head of the household, he had to impose punishment on her. But Tamar sent Judah's seal and staff back to him, saying that she was pregnant by their owner—Judah himself. Judah realized it was he, not Tamar, who had done wrong, for he had not kept his promise and allowed Tamar to bear children by his son Shelah. In due time, Tamar gave birth to twins, Perez and Zerah. From Perez descended Israel's greatest king, David, and, in time, the Messiah, Jesus.

Tamar does not strike us as a paragon of morality—what sort of woman dresses as a prostitute and then deceives and sleeps with her own father-in-law? But Genesis makes it clear that Tamar was not acting out of lust or malice. Like any woman in ancient times, she wanted to bear children, yet Judah was not fulfilling his duty by giving her his son Shelah. In this world that was dominated by men, Tamar had taken a bold step, and in doing so not only achieved her goal—children—but also became the mother of the line that would produce the royal family of Israel.

CULTURAL INSIGHTS

Lying for the Right Reason

The Bible places a lot of emphasis on honesty and integrity, and one of the Ten Commandments specifically forbids bearing false witness against someone in court (Exodus 20:16). We might well ask why the commandment didn't simply forbid all lying. The answer may be found in the stories of the Hebrew midwives and Rahab, where in both cases lies were told to protect innocent lives. The midwives lied to the pharaoh to cover the fact that they had disobeyed his order to kill Hebrew infants. Rahab lied to the men of Jericho in order to protect the Hebrew spies. Obviously these lies were told under duress, and they shouldn't make us believe that lying ought to be done on a regular basis.

Keep in mind that Tamar knew all the facts in the story, but Judah did not. Her first husband, Er, had died because he was so wicked. And his brother Onan had died because he had not fulfilled his brotherly duty. Judah feared giving his remaining son, Shelah, to Tamar because he believed Tamar to be under some kind of curse, but in fact it was his own sons who were in the wrong, not Tamar.

The Judah-Tamar story is a classic example of why we should try to read the Bible straight through instead of in bits and pieces. The story is found in Genesis 38, and it seems to interrupt the story of Judah's brother, Joseph. But in fact, its place in Genesis is deliberate, for Genesis 39 tells the story of the attempted seduction of Joseph by the wife of Potiphar. Joseph resists the advances of his boss's wife, while Judah is easily seduced by a roadside prostitute.

MADAM JERICHO

Then Joshua son of Nun secretly sent two spies from Shittim. "Go, look over the land," he said, "especially Jericho." So they went and entered the house of a prostitute named Rahab and stayed there. (Joshua 2:1)

In the first section, we met the Bible's first prostitute—or, to be precise, we met Tamar, who was willing on one fateful occasion to play the role of a prostitute. The next prostitute to be mentioned is the proverbial "prostitute with a heart of gold," Rahab of Jericho. In between Tamar and Rahab came the law of Moses, which specifically prohibits any Israelite from acting as a prostitute and from contributing the wages of a prostitute to the Lord's service.

Is the Bible indecisive about whether or not prostitution is really a bad thing? Not at all. As already noted, Tamar was not a prostitute by trade but merely posing as one on one occasion. Rahab is a different matter. She clearly did make a living as a prostitute, but remember that her home was Jericho, a city in Canaan. The Canaanites did not have the divine law that God had given to Israel, and like most ancient cultures, the Canaanites pretty much took prostitution for granted. Yet despite the lax morality that Rahab had grown up in, she showed that she possessed some basic human decency and was capable of great kindness—and great courage as well.

In Joshua 2, the Israelites are preparing to conquer Canaan, the land God had promised them. Joshua, leader of the Israelites after the death of Moses, sends spies to scope out the walled city of Jericho. The spies stayed at the home of Rahab—a wise choice, for, after all, it was a normal thing to see strange men coming and going from the house of a prostitute. But even so, the king of Jericho heard there were Israelite spies in the city, and he demanded Rahab turn them over. Rahab lied. The men had indeed come to her house, but she did not know who they were, and they left before dusk, when the city gates were shut. There is something slightly impish about Rahab's words: "I don't know which way they went. Go after them quickly. You may catch up with them." She is doing a "they went that-away." Taking her at her word, the Jericho elders took to the road in hot pursuit of the spies. In fact, the spies were still at Rahab's—on the roof, hidden among stacks of flax, the fiber used in making linen—an interesting bit of feminine camouflage.

Obviously Rahab was putting herself in danger, since she almost certainly would have been killed if it was found out she had sheltered the Israelite spies. Why was she taking the Israelites' side? News of what the Israelites had done had reached her ears—or, more precisely, she had heard of the great miracles God had done for Israel: "We have heard how the Lord dried up the water of the Red Sea for you when you came out of Egypt, and what you did to Sihon and Og, the two kings of the Amorites east of the Jordan, whom you completely destroyed. When we heard of it, our hearts melted and everyone's courage failed because of you, for the Lord your God is God in heaven above and on the earth below" (Joshua 2:10–11). Note her last words: God is not just up there somewhere but is very active on earth, doing great things for his people. Rahab was, spiritually speaking, far in advance of the Egyptian pharaoh, who had witnessed many miracles but still resisted Israel's God. In fact, she was spiritually in advance of many of the Israelites, who were blessed by so many of God's miracles but who continually complained against Moses. Rahab was a sensible woman: God was clearly on the side of the Israelites, and far better to join that side than to resist. In fact, she was not the only person in the vicinity who understood the power of God, for other people were "melting in fear" of Israel.

So Rahab asked a favor: Since she had shown kindness to the Israelite spies, she wanted kindness in return. When the Israelites captured Jericho, would they please spare her life, as well as the lives of her parents and other family members? Rahab's concern is touching. Here is a worldly woman, a woman who has been around, yet she is not concerned just for her own skin but for her parents, brothers and sisters, and all those in their households.

The Israelite spies gladly agreed. Since the city gates had been shut up for the night, they escaped the city by being let down the city walls by a rope. Odd as it may seem to us, Rahab's house was in fact built into the city's stone walls. Rahab told them not to take the main road—that is where the pursuers were—but to head for the hills and hide out for three days. Clearly Rahab was very street smart. Dealing with many men who passed through, she had a good idea of how long the Jericho pursuers would be gone.

The spies told her that when the Israelites attacked the city, Rahab should tie a scarlet cord to her window, so that everyone in her household would be spared. She kept her word—she did not give the spies away—and when the city was taken by the Israelites, they kept their word and spared her household.

Rahab may not have had a clue about the effect her words had on the Israelite spies. Who better than a prostitute to keep up with local gossip, to know what rumors were floating about? And from her customers Rahab had learned that much was being said about these Israelites and the divine power that seemed to be favoring them. Taking her words to heart, the spies reported back to Joshua: "The Lord has surely given the whole land into our hands; all the people are melting in fear because of us" (Joshua 2:24).

What follows is the famous story of the walls of Jericho tumbling down (see page 409). The Israelites spared Rahab's household and in time she came to live among the Israelites—no longer an outsider but part of the community (Joshua 6:25). And according to Matthew 1:5, she married the Israelite named Salmon, and their son was Boaz, who married Ruth, whom we will meet shortly. And so Rahab—a prostitute and a foreigner—is listed among the ancestors of Jesus.

Rahab is mentioned two other times in the New Testament: "Was not even Rahab the prostitute considered righteous for what she did when she gave lodging to the spies and sent them off in a different direction?" (James 2:25). This is part of James' famous passage in which he discusses the importance of faith resulting in good works. Note that he specifically refers to Rahab "the prostitute." He is not commending her profession but is pointing out that even a bad girl can do good things at times. Because of her act of courage and bravery in sheltering the Israelite spies, Rahab went from being part of the immoral Canaanite culture to being incorporated into Israel, the community

---

CULTURAL INSIGHTS ## Rahab the "Innkeeper"?

Was Rahab really a prostitute? Probably. Yet experts in ancient languages tell us there is another possibility. The Hebrew word usually translated "prostitute" might, in some contexts, mean "innkeeper." Put another way, many ancient establishments could serve both purposes—inn and brothel. Men passing through a strange town might seek lodging for the night and sexual pleasure as well, and in many cases both could be had under the same roof. Some modern versions of the Bible have footnotes stating that "innkeeper" is an alternative translation for "prostitute" in the story of Rahab.

of faith. Thus she is included in the Faith Hall of Fame in Hebrews 11: "By faith the prostitute Rahab, because she welcomed the spies, was not killed with those who were disobedient" (Hebrews 11:31).

"A MOTHER IN ISRAEL"

> Deborah, a prophetess, the wife of Lappidoth, was leading Israel at that time. She held court under the Palm of Deborah between Ramah and Bethel in the hill country of Ephraim, and the Israelites came to her to have their disputes decided. (Judges 4:4–5)

> Village life in Israel ceased, ceased until I, Deborah, arose, arose a mother in Israel. (Judges 5:7)

In some ways the Book of Judges is a guy story, telling of the exploits of the military leaders who helped deliver Israel from its enemies. Its heroes are well-known figures like Samson, Gideon and Jephthah. But the first real power player in the Book of Judges is the amazing Deborah.

Bible scholars like to point out that "Judges" is an inappropriate title for the book, because the military leaders in the book weren't judges in our sense—they were fighting men, men who brought justice by fighting off Israel's oppressors. But Deborah was different: She really was a judge, someone who settled legal disputes, holding court not in a building but "under the Palm of Deborah." We are told nothing about her background, but she must have been considered an exceptionally wise woman, since it was rare for a woman to serve as judge.

But Deborah was more than a judge. She was also an amazing encourager, a kind of national cheerleader for Israel. The nation was being oppressed by Jabin, a Canaanite king who, with his army and its nine hundred iron chariots, tormented Israel for twenty years. Deborah summoned a man named Barak, telling him it was the Lord's will for him to lead a large Israelite army against the Canaanites. Barak told her he would, but only if she herself would go with the army. Deborah agreed—but because Barak had shown some hesitancy, Deborah assured him that the honor of getting rid of the Canaanite general Sisera would not go to Barak but to a woman.

Barak led an army of ten thousand men, yet what seemed to give him courage was that Deborah was there. This must have been a truly amazing and charismatic woman. When Barak faced the Canaanite army with its hundreds of chariots, Deborah encour-

---

DID YOU KNOW?

Deborah is one of the few women in the Bible referred to as a prophetess, meaning the Israelites believed that she spoke on behalf of God.

---

aged him: The Lord had revealed that he would defeat the Canaanites that day. And indeed, the battle went in the Israelites' favor, aided by the flash-flooding of the nearby river, so that the Canaanites' sole survivor, the general Sisera, had to flee on foot.

If he thought he had been spared, he was mistaken. He had gotten away from Barak's army, and he found shelter in what he thought was a safe place—a tent where there was only one person, a woman. This was Jael, who invited him in, offering him milk and a place to rest from the battle. Sisera asked her to stand guard at the door of her tent, so if anyone was looking for him she could send them away. It never occurred to him that a mere woman might herself be dangerous. When Sisera lay sleeping, Jael took a tent peg and drove it into his skull. Barak arrived, and Jael showed him what she had done. As Deborah had prophesied, the honor of getting rid of Sisera had fallen to a woman.

Let us admit that this story—like so many stories in Judges—disturbs and disgusts us. These were violent times, and often Judges seems to glory in the bloodshed. But we have to beware of judging the Old Testament by New Testament standards. Jesus' preaching of nonviolence and turning the other cheek was far in the future. In the time of Judges, Israel was fighting for its life, surrounded by cruel and violent nations, and it had to fight back with violence of its own. Jael had killed one man, Sisera, but this was a man who had led the Canaanite army and caused many deaths in Israel. Had she let him escape, he would have gone on to do more harm.

Jael's bravery is celebrated in Judges 5, known as the "Song of Deborah," the victory song over the Canaanites. Though she had acted deceitfully and treacherously, giving shelter to a man and then killing him as he slept, her acts are praised in the song. Deborah even praises herself, one who rose up as a "mother in Israel," giving leadership at a time of foreign oppression. Like a mother, she can scold when necessary. She upbraids the tribes of Reuben and Dan for sitting by their campfires, not joining the other tribes in the battle. She also praises the "willing volunteers among the people."

CHARACTERS AT LARGE ## Deborah in Art and Music

In paintings, Deborah is often shown as an elderly and somewhat stern woman. George Frideric Handel wrote an oratorio about her, and the composer Ildebrando Pizzetti wrote the opera *Deborah and Jael*.

Women rulers throughout history have sometimes been compared to the great Deborah, and this was especially true of England's Queen Elizabeth I, who was many times referred to as "a new Deborah, Judge and Restorer of Israel." The queens Jezebel and Athaliah were wicked women, so Deborah was the Old Testament's most admirable role model as a female power figure.

"Then the land had peace forty years" (Judges 5:31). The defeat of the enemy marks the last time that the original Canaanite inhabitants of the area mount a large-scale attack on Israel. Afterward, the attacks come from the nations on Israel's borders. So the bravery of Deborah, Barak and Jael had helped eliminate the enemies within Israel's borders. Under Deborah, the Israelites finally corrected the situation that is lamented in the opening chapters of Judges, the troublesome existence of the original pagan inhabitants of Canaan, who were corrupting the Israelites through intermarriage. It would be fair to say that Deborah helped to bring about, at long last, the conquest of Canaan, something begun centuries earlier under Joshua.

SWEETENING THE BITTER

"I've been told all about what you have done for your mother-in-law since the death of your husband—how you left your father and mother and your homeland and came to live with a people you did not know before. May the Lord repay you for what you have done. May you be richly rewarded by the Lord, the God of Israel, under whose wings you have come to take refuge." (Ruth 2:11–12)

It is pleasant to turn from the violent story of Deborah, Jael and Barak to an exceptionally peaceful story set in the same time period, the story of Ruth, where we will see an entirely different type of courage at work in a woman.

Though it is set in the time of the judges, the enemy in the Book of Ruth is not any foreign army but, we might say, life itself, which is full of hardships. When the book opens, the hardship is a famine, a common occurrence in ancient times when long-term food storage was almost impossible. To escape the famine, an Israelite man named Elimelech took his wife, Naomi, and their two sons and settled in the land of Moab. In time the two sons married women of Moab, named Ruth and Orpah. The two sons died, as did Elimelech, leaving a household composed of three childless widows. To understand how bad the situation was, we have to recall that in ancient times a woman did not just go and find a job. Other than working as servants—or more often, as slaves—a woman had no career prospects. Most women could not imagine living in any household without a man. This is one of the many reasons that all women wanted children, especially sons, for when a woman became widowed she typically went to live in the household of one of her sons. For a woman, being left to one's own resources meant essentially no resources at all.

Hearing that Israel was no longer in a famine state, Naomi decided to return there. Her two daughters-in-law were devoted to her, and they offered to go with her. Naomi was touched by this, but she insisted that the women stay in Moab, their homeland; hopefully

Harvest and Gleaning

In biblical days, grain was cut with wooden sickles with bits of sharp flint embedded in the blades. Binders came behind the reapers and bound the stalks of grain into sheaves. These were taken to a level area, the threshing floor, where sleds—large wooden boards with knobs of stone or metal on the bottoms—pulled by oxen were dragged over the grain to loosen the kernels and break up the stalks. Alternatively, the threshing might be done by beating the stalks with flails. Then there was winnowing, using pitchforks or shovels to toss the grain into the air to let the wind blow the chaff away. Sieves were used to sort out the remaining chaff. Then the sifted grain was placed in large earthenware pots. Threshing floors were communal places, and if the harvest had been good, there was an air of celebration—hard work, but with a kind of party atmosphere.

What about people too poor to own their own farmland? "When you are harvesting in your field and you overlook a sheaf, do not go back to get it. Leave it for the alien, the fatherless and the widow, so that the Lord your God may bless you in all the work of your hands" (Deuteronomy 24:19). This law lies behind the story of Ruth gleaning in the fields of Boaz. The same group of laws also mandates that the pickers of grapes and olives also leave something behind for the poor. The Law of Moses is often thought of as being a long list of "don'ts," but as these gleaning laws show, there was also a place for compassion.

they would in time find new husbands. Orpah agreed to do this, but Ruth would not. She must have sensed that Naomi had become bitter in all her adversity, and she insisted on going to live with her in Israel. In one of the most touching passages in the Bible, Ruth told Naomi, "Don't urge me to leave you or to turn back from you. Where you go I will go, and where you stay I will stay. Your people will be my people and your God my God" (Ruth 1:16). She was willing to share Naomi's fate—and, even more important, she was willing to share her faith as well. Having grown up in Moab with its lax morality and fertility gods, Ruth was transferring her allegiance to Naomi's God, the God of Israel.

And so they settled in Naomi's hometown, Bethlehem, where the locals found Naomi changed. Naomi, whose name means "pleasant," had become Mara, meaning "bitter." She had left Bethlehem at a time of famine, yet inwardly she was "full," for then she had a husband and sons. Now, though the famine was past, she was "empty." She was angry and bitter toward God for bringing calamity on her. We might almost say she was a female Job. Her grief seemed unremitting, and she had a grudge against life.

Pause for a moment to consider Ruth's situation: She made the choice to stay with a mother-in-law who was growing increasingly bitter. It is not a choice most people would make, especially since it involved uprooting herself from her own homeland. Somehow she must have sensed that what little pleasure Naomi got from life was in knowing that, whatever else had befallen her, Ruth had not abandoned her. It would not be too much of a stretch to say that Naomi at this time was not a pleasure to live with, and at times she must have tried Ruth's patience, so Ruth's devotion to her is all the more remarkable.

The two women were reduced to gleaning in the barley fields, meaning they were allowed to gather up the little that was left after the harvesters had done their work. Impressed with Ruth's devotion and hard work was a man named Boaz, who overlooked Ruth's foreign birth and ordered his farm workers not to harass her in any way.

In a way, the Book of Ruth is a love story, but a most unusual one, for we are told that Boaz is not attracted by Ruth's physical appearance but by her compassionate nature. While Judges emphasizes heroism in battle, the story of Ruth is about how decent human beings respond to pain and loss in their own lives and the lives of others. In their quiet, everyday way, Ruth and Boaz are heroes of the best sort. History, focusing on battles and politics, often fails to record the kindness of people who lead steady and decent lives, so we can be thankful for the quiet story of Ruth being included in the Bible.

In time Boaz married Ruth, and she bore him a son. By the custom of the time, Naomi took the infant son onto her lap, and from that time on he was regarded as her own son, so the aging widow had become, in effect, a mother. The boy's name was Obed, and he was father of Jesse, who became the father of David, Israel's greatest king. And so Ruth became one of the four women named in the family tree of Jesus.

A TALE OF TWO WIVES

His name was Nabal and his wife's name was Abigail. She was an intelligent and beautiful woman, but her husband, a Calebite, was surly and mean in his dealings. (1 Samuel 25:3)

David sent messengers to Ish-Bosheth son of Saul, demanding, "Give me my wife Michal, whom I betrothed to myself for the price of a hundred Philistine foreskins." (2 Samuel 3:14)

David was not lacking in courage, and, as it turned out, he married two different women who, at times, could show great courage.

The first of these was also his first wife, Michal, daughter of Saul, Israel's first king. The young and spunky David impressed all Israel with his slaying of Goliath, and in time Saul's appreciation for David turned into life-threatening jealousy, which we explore more closely in another chapter (Day 17). Michal had fallen in love with David, and the bride price Saul required from David was a hundred foreskins from the Philistines—in other words, David had to kill a hundred Philistine soldiers and bring back the proof. David ended up bringing back *two* hundred of them, evidence of both his valor and his love for Michal. This thwarted Saul's plan, which was that David would probably be killed in trying to obtain the bride price.

Michal, alas, was put in the uncomfortable position of having a father who was trying to kill her husband. Knowing Saul's men were after David, she talked David into fleeing through an upstairs window. Saul, of course, was furious, just as he was furious at his son Jonathan, who had also acted to save the life of David. Jonathan and Michal both lived in a time when a father's word was law, but they were not about to join their father in persecuting an enemy who in fact was his most valiant warrior.

Having helped her husband escape, Michal was not to see him for many years, because David was for a long time on the lam, fleeing the wrath of Saul. Out of spite for David, Saul gave his daughter to be the wife of another man, Palti.

In the meantime, David was not lacking for female companionship. He took another wife, Ahinoam. And in his years as a fugitive, he encountered a very remarkable woman named Abigail, who had the bad luck to be married to an extremely surly man named Nabal. David and the band of men who had gathered around him were in effect outlaws, so they had to live off the charity of people they encountered. They sent a message to Nabal, asking to join in the sheep-shearing on his farm. Nabal apparently regarded this as a veiled threat: allow David's men to join in the sheep-shearing feast, or, perhaps, have the men steal whatever he would not give them freely. So he hurled insults at the messengers; just who was this David anyway?

Abigail, described as both beautiful and intelligent, was also resourceful and courageous. Hearing how her husband had responded to David's request, she packed up some bread, meat, wine and cakes and went to David, asking him to please overlook her stupid, surly husband, whose very name, *Nabal*, meant "fool." Like many people who encountered David, she was convinced that God was on his side and probably understood that in time he would be king in Israel.

Abigail returned home. The next morning, she told Nabal what she had done for David. The news so horrified Nabal that he "became like a stone," and ten days later he died. Relieved to be rid of such a husband, Abigail presented herself to David and he married her.

Thus far in the story, David and Michal, separated from each other, both have spouses and presumably have found some happiness while parted. But after the death of Saul, there was a brief period when it wasn't clear who would be king—David, the obvious choice, or Saul's son Ish-Bosheth. To make his claim to the throne of Israel valid, David insisted that Michal return to live with him as his wife.

We sense a certain coldness in this negotiation: David seems to be acting not out of love but out of political concern. In being married to Michal, Saul's daughter, David is part of the royal family as Saul's son-in-law.

At any rate, Ish-Bosheth sent Michal back to David. "Her husband, however, went with her, weeping behind her" (2 Samuel 3:16). Poor Palti! The Bible tells us nothing about him except that, obviously, he was an emotional man very attached to his wife. Abner, the rough commander of the army, barked at Palti and told him to go back home, and thus he disappears from the story, his personal life falling victim to the power politics of the day.

We aren't told whether Michal was as devoted to Palti as he was to her. But certainly her being restored as David's wife did not make for happiness in that household. At the time she returned to David, he already had six wives, with a son by each. Michal had fallen in love with David when they were both young, but by the time this incident occurred, he had married other wives who bore him children. The bloom is off the rose in this marriage. If Michal had any privileged position—as David's first wife and as the daughter of Saul—she was outranked by the later wives who bore David sons.

The coolness in the relationship is evident in the last episode in which Michal appears. David, a man of rich emotion, danced with joy in the street when the ark of the covenant, the symbol of God's commitment, was brought to Jerusalem. At the time of this spiritual high, Michal mocked him for his vulgar display in the street. David responded with cutting words of his own: God had chosen him, not her father, to be king over Israel. "And Michal daughter of Saul had no children to the day of her death" (2 Samuel 6:23). The verse implies that David never touched Michal again.

While TV shows and movies often get us to laugh at marital squabbles, there is in fact nothing at all funny in a marriage going sour. In fact, it is a tragedy, especially in cases like this, where Michal and David had loved each other deeply, and Michal had stood up to her wrathful father in order to save David's skin. Despite Michal's cattiness toward David when the ark was brought to Jerusalem, she strikes us as more of a victim than a villain—a woman whose personal life was tied up with the politics of the time. We can admire her courage in saving David's life and lament the effect the David-Saul rivalry had on her life.

PUTTING THE WORD TO WORK

1. Of the women in this chapter, which do you most admire? Which do you think is the best role model for women today?

2. Reflect on the lies told by the Hebrew midwives and by Rahab. Have you been in situations where you felt you had to lie to prevent great harm from being done?

3. Ruth is, among other things, a role model of someone willing to share the life of a bitter person. Make a special point today of trying to reach out to someone you know who is lonely or bitter.

4. Deborah, a "mother to Israel," must have been an imposing presence. Think of women you have known who have had a powerful and positive effect on people around them.

5. The David–Michal story is a classic case of a loving marriage that went sour. Take a moment to pray for married couples you know, especially for those whose love has cooled over time.

Long Life, Many Roles
THE APOSTLE JOHN

John the apostle is mostly remembered as the author of the Gospel that bears his name, but Gospel writer was one of several hats he wore. He also wrote three epistles and, in his old age, the Book of Revelation. He was also one of three men making up the inner circle of disciples closest to Jesus, and in Acts he and Peter are the most prominent among the original twelve apostles. He is an underappreciated character, a "son of thunder" (so Jesus called him) who wrote down the frightening images of the wrath of God in Revelation but also the "disciple who Jesus loved," who wrote tenderly of God's love.

KEY TERM FOR TODAY ## Love

John, the "son of thunder," full of ambition and fire, was also the "disciple whom Jesus loved," and in his writings he showed he had learned much about the nature of self-giving love modeled by Jesus.

DIM DISCIPLES

James and John, the sons of Zebedee, came to him. "Teacher," they said, "we want you to do for us whatever we ask." "What do you want me to do for you?" he asked. They replied, "Let one of us sit at your right and the other at your left in your glory." "You don't know what you are asking," Jesus said. "Can you drink the cup I drink or be baptized with the baptism I am baptized with?" "We can," they answered. Jesus said to them, "You will drink the cup I drink and be baptized with the baptism I am baptized with." (Mark 10:35–39)

Three of the Gospels record that the brothers James and John were Galilean fishermen, following the trade of their father, Zebedee, and that while they were at work, Jesus called the two to join his band of twelve disciples. Mark's Gospel provides an additional detail: Jesus gave them "the name Boanerges, which means Sons of Thunder" (Mark 3:17). This has led to some speculation that the two might have been Zealots, patriotic Jews who opposed the rule of the Romans and sometimes resorted to violence. This might or might not be true, but it certainly is true that the two brothers could at times urge bold action on the part of Jesus, which inevitably led to Jesus urging them to grow up and simmer down. In Luke 9, the two are appalled at the surliness of some Samaritan villagers who do not want Jesus among them: "When the disciples James and John saw this, they asked, 'Lord, do you want us to call fire down from heaven to destroy them?'" (Luke 9:54). No, he did not. He told the two that he came to earth to save men's lives, not destroy them. On another occasion John saw a man—not part of their band—who was driving out demons in Jesus' name, so he told him to stop; Jesus informed him that "whoever is not against us is for us" (Mark 9:40). The fellowship of faith was wider than John thought it was.

The two brothers, along with Peter, formed an intimate inner circle. These three disciples were closest to Jesus—present at some events the others did not witness, such as the Transfiguration and the healing of Jairus' daughter, but most famously in the garden of Gethsemane, when Jesus agonized over his approaching death. James and John were human, of course, and this closeness to their master led them to arrogance, which is evident in the Mark 10 quote that opens this section.

The Gospels make it clear that Jesus' disciples were amazingly slow to understand him and his mission. In spite of his clear teaching that the kingdom of God was a spiritual reality, not an earthly one, they seemed to hold on to the old view that God's Messiah would usher in a kingdom of material benefits. James and John clearly held on to such hopes.

This episode immediately follows Jesus telling the disciples on the way to Jerusalem that he will be arrested and condemned to death by the Jewish authorities and then handed over to the Gentiles for execution. This humiliation and agony will be followed by his Resurrection on the third day. Did James and John hear only the last part, concerning the Resurrection, and fail to comprehend the intense suffering that would come first? Several times Jesus had made it clear to the disciples that he would in Jerusalem be humiliated and condemned to death, but his words had fallen on deaf ears.

The brothers ask to sit at Jesus' right and left hand —the places of honor—in the heavenly banquet. To be seated by the host meant you would be the first to drink from his cup. But Jesus makes it clear that this cup is not what they expect. Were the disciples willing to drink even if it was a bitter drink, a cup of sorrow?

Jesus speaks of the baptism he has to undergo, and he means not baptism in water but in suffering. It is probably this that Paul had in mind when he wrote Romans 6:3–4: "Don't you know that all of us who were baptized into Christ Jesus were baptized into his death? We were therefore buried with him through baptism into death in order that, just as Christ was raised from the dead through the glory of the Father, we too may live a new life." The way to new life is through suffering.

It is probably not a coincidence that in the same place Jesus refers to his baptism and to the cup he must drink, both having to do with suffering and death. Although baptism was a symbol of repentance, cleansing and new life, it was also a symbol of the death of the person's former life. Likewise the cup taken at communion is a symbol of the spilling of the blood of the innocent Jesus. Communion and baptism are both about suffering and dying.

The two brothers respond to Jesus' challenge with "We can." They seemed stirred by the challenge. We might attribute their response to the uninformed arrogance of youth. They are full of the enthusiasm of their inexperience. But later, when they see Jesus arrested, they flee, like the other disciples.

Jesus can only point the way to glory by what he himself will endure. If they are as stouthearted as they think they are, then they are truly his disciples. If they think they are privileged characters because of the things they have witnessed before—the raising to life of Jairus' daughter, the Transfiguration—they should be clear in their minds that privilege entails sacrifice.

Shortly before this, Peter had made his statement to Jesus about the disciples giving up so much to follow him. Given that Peter, James and John were the most important among the twelve, we can almost sense some jockeying for position here, with the two brothers wanting positions in the kingdom more important than Peter's. This rivalry is evident in Mark 10:41: "When the ten heard about this, they became indignant with James and John." At this point, Jesus' followers still had to learn that ambition had to give way to the ideal of being servants, as Jesus himself was.

James and John had asked for places of honor in Jesus' kingdom. They would get what they asked for, but through the route of self-giving and sacrifice.

LEANING ON THE LORD

When Jesus saw his mother there, and the disciple whom he loved standing nearby, he said to his mother, "Dear woman, here is your son." (John 19:26)

Throughout the Gospels, John, like the other disciples, constantly misunderstands his Master's mission on earth, in spite of John, James and Peter being closer to Jesus than the others. But of course, the Gospels do not record every detail of Jesus' life, and it is fairly clear in John's Gospel that John himself was "the disciple whom Jesus loved," a phrase that occurs several times in the Gospel. Jesus must have seen something—some great potential, something very lovable—in the ambitious "son of thunder."

How do we know this beloved disciple was John? Strictly speaking, we don't. John is never mentioned by name in the Gospel of John. However, the Gospel does make it clear that "the disciple whom Jesus loved" is also the one who "bears witness to these things" (John 21:20, 24)—that is, the author of the Gospel. And John 21:2 refers to the disciples who were present at the final encounter with Jesus: Peter, Thomas, Nathanael, two unnamed disciples, and "the sons of Zebedee," meaning James and John. Among these, one is the "disciple whom Jesus loved," and the very old tradition that it was John is almost certainly correct.

This disciple "leaned against Jesus" at the Last Supper, meaning he was reclining at Jesus' side, a place of honor. After Jesus' arrest, all the disciples fled in panic—but Peter "and another disciple" followed Jesus and his captors, and the "other disciple" got them admitted to the high priest's courtyard, where they could monitor what was happening. The Gospel doesn't identify "the other disciple" with "the disciple whom Jesus loved," but they are almost certainly the same. It is interesting that this disciple was "known to the high priest" (John 18:16). We would not expect a Galilean fisherman like John to have friends in high places. But it is possible that his father, Zebedee, might have been a priest, since most priests did not live permanently in Jerusalem but went there twice yearly for a week of service and then back to their normal occupations, which could have included being head of a fishing business. Zebedee might have maintained a home-away-from-home in Jerusalem, and this might have been the room for the meal where the "beloved disciple" leaned on Jesus' breast, since there was a custom that if the host himself was absent, his son sat to the right of the guest of honor.

John's is the only Gospel to mention that Jesus' mother was present at the crucifixion, and that he commended her into the care of "the disciple whom he loved"—the only disciple present at the cross. There must have already been a close emotional bond between Mary and this disciple, because "from that time on, this disciple took her into his home" (John 19:27).

John, like the other disciples, had fled when they saw their Master arrested—as Jesus had predicted they would. John and James had boasted that they could "drink the cup" of suffering that Jesus himself would drink—and they had failed the test. And yet we see that John could not stay in hiding, just looking to save his own skin. He and Peter mustered enough courage to follow the arrested Jesus. Obviously John was putting himself at risk entering the high priest's yard if the priest knew him. Love had overcome cowardice. John had fled, but he couldn't tear himself away from the cross, and he was able to share his agony with Jesus' own mother.

NEW LIFE

> She [Mary Magdalene] came running to Simon Peter and the other disciple, the one Jesus loved, and said, "They have taken the Lord out of the tomb, and we don't know where they have put him!"
>
> Peter and the other disciple started for the tomb . . . . Finally the other disciple, who had reached the tomb first, also went inside. He saw and believed. (John 20:2–3, 8)
>
> Afterward Jesus appeared again to his disciples, by the Sea of Tiberias . . . . The disciple whom Jesus loved said to Peter, "It is the Lord!" (John 21:1, 7)
>
> This is the disciple who testifies to these things and who wrote them down. We know that his testimony is true. (John 21:20–24)

John 20 records the story of Mary Magdalene's going to Jesus' tomb on Easter morning and finding it empty. Mary ran to report this to Peter "and the other disciple, the one Jesus loved." The tomb was empty—news that animated the feet of the two disciples who ran to the tomb, though the "other disciple" outran Peter and looked inside. "He saw and believed" (John 20:1–8). In a sense, the beloved disciple was the first Christian, the first person to believe in Jesus' Resurrection. Later in the same chapter, he and the others—except Thomas—would be visited by the risen Jesus. Thomas, the infamous doubter, would finally come to faith when he saw Jesus himself. John believed on less evidence: the empty tomb.

John 21 records the later episode of a group of disciples encountering Jesus again by the lake. These were "Simon Peter, Thomas (called Didymus), Nathanael from Cana in Galilee, the sons of Zebedee, and two other disciples were together" (John 21:2). Jesus had

> **DID YOU KNOW?**
>
> John's is the only Gospel to refer to the Sea of Galilee as the Sea of Tiberias, as the Romans called it. Herod had renamed the sea to flatter the Roman emperor Tiberius. The body of water is today called *Bahr Tabariyeh*.

made a fire on the lakeshore and the disciples were in a boat. Appropriately, it was the "disciple whom Jesus loved" who was first to recognize him. The Gospels, especially John's, hint that Jesus' resurrected body was like his earthly body and yet, in some mysterious way, also different. The bond of love between Jesus and John opened John's eyes to his Master.

John 21:24 says, "We know his testimony is true," with "his" referring to the beloved disciple. Who is "we"? An old tradition says that John wrote his Gospel on behalf of, and with the approval of, the other apostles, and they are the "we" here. But more likely "we" refers to the followers of the beloved disciple, who committed his memories to writing in this Gospel. Later in the chapter we will look at the distinctive features of John's compelling Gospel. For now, we turn to Acts, where Peter and John form an amazing power team among the first Christians.

BEAUTIFUL GATE, BEAUTIFUL DEED

When they [the priests] saw the courage of Peter and John and realized that they were unschooled, ordinary men, they were astonished and they took note that these men had been with Jesus. . . .

They called them in again and commanded them not to speak or teach at all in the name of Jesus. But Peter and John replied, "Judge for yourselves whether it is right in God's sight to obey you rather than God. For we cannot help speaking about what we have seen and heard." (Acts 4:13, 18–20)

In the early part of Acts, Peter is the dominant one among the twelve apostles, and Acts 2 records the stirring sermon he preached on the day of Pentecost, a sermon that led many to turn to the faith. He preaches an equally stirring sermon in Acts 3, following the remarkable episode of healing.

We have seen already in John's Gospel that Peter and John were special, and though John's brother James was also part of the inner circle of the disciples, James (probably the elder brother, given that his name was usually mentioned first) has taken a back seat to his younger brother. In the list of apostles in Acts 1:13, Peter is mentioned first, John second, James third. Considering that Peter and John were the only two disciples to follow after the arrested Jesus, we can understand their prominence. They had shown great courage. In Acts 3, they show power also, and as their Master had foretold, they were capable of working miracles, just as he had done.

Going to the temple in Jerusalem to pray, Peter and John encounter a beggar—a man crippled from birth, accustomed to sitting at "the temple gate called Beautiful." He was begging for money—he got much more. "Peter said, 'Silver or gold I do not have, but what I have I give you. In the name of Jesus Christ of Nazareth, walk.'" His healing was immediate. Right away he was "walking and jumping," which naturally drew a crowd. Not one to pass up an opportunity, Peter attributed the healing to the power of Christ—and he preached a fine sermon. He spoke of the horrible act of crucifying God's Messiah. But there was a way to escape the wrath of God: "Repent, then, and turn to

God, so that your sins may be wiped out, that times of refreshing may come from the Lord" (Acts 3:19).

The sermon turned many listeners to the faith—five thousand, in fact, making even more converts than Peter's fiery sermon at Pentecost. But this drew the attention of the Jewish authorities in Jerusalem. The priests' guards seized Peter and John and threw them in jail. This is a familiar pattern in Acts: The apostles are persecuted, but the faith continues to spread.

The priests Annas and Caiaphas—both of whom had questioned Jesus—are both involved in the interrogation the next morning. Peter and John face what Jesus himself faced, a questioning of what authority they possess. And like Jesus, they are being persecuted for performing a healing. Peter and John claim to have done the miracle through the power of Jesus, whom they believe had been raised from the dead. There was no denying the miracle. And the healed man is present. What a contrast—the ill temper of the priests and the unfettered giddiness of a former cripple who literally leaped for joy.

When the priests "saw the courage of Peter and John and realized that they were unschooled, ordinary men, they were astonished and they took note that these men had

CHARACTERS AT LARGE

James of Spain

The apostle James has for centuries been connected with the city of Santiago de Compostela in northwestern Spain. Tradition says that in AD 813, shepherds guided by a star found the grave of James in an old Roman cemetery. The legend went that James had evangelized the country before his martyrdom in Jerusalem in AD 44, and after his death his body was taken to Spain. Shortly after the finding of the supposed grave, a church was built on the site, and then a grander church and finally a town grew up around it. Santiago (Spanish for "St. James") became one of the three great pilgrimage destinations for Christians (Rome and Jerusalem being the other two). The fine cathedral was completed in 1211.

Naturally the Spanish took James to be one of their patron saints, and during the Middle Ages, when the Spanish Christians gradually drove out the Muslim Moors who had invaded the country, people claimed to see visions of James on a white steed, urging on the Christian soldiers. James was referred to as *Santiago Matamoros*, "St. James the Moor-Slayer," and though his connection with Spain is pure legend, there is no doubt that the belief that Spain held the remains of Jesus' first martyred apostle played a key role in the Christian reconquest of Spain. Because of the Spaniards' affection for the site, there are cities and provinces named Santiago in several Spanish-speaking countries, including Cuba, Chile and the Dominican Republic.

been with Jesus" (Acts 4:13). The apostles are regarded as *agrammatoi*—literally "without letters,"—but they are not illiterate by any means, since most Jewish boys learned to read and write in the synagogue schools. The priests and Sadducees regard them as uneducated since they have no training as rabbis. Yet clearly they speak with authority, as Jesus himself did. The snobbery of the elite was something Jesus himself had faced: "The Jews were amazed and asked, 'How did this man get such learning without having studied?'" (John 7:15). The two Galilean fishermen were unlettered in the eyes of the snobbish priests but wise in the ways of God.

These unlettered men were bold as well. The priests "commanded them not to speak or teach at all in the name of Jesus. But Peter and John replied, 'Judge for yourselves whether it is right in God's sight to obey you rather than God'" (Acts 4:18–19). The gospel could not be restrained: "We cannot help speaking about what we have seen and heard" (Acts 4:20).

Recall that Jesus had given John and James the nickname "sons of thunder." John was being true to his name. Also recall him and James assuring Jesus that they had the courage to "drink the cup" of suffering along with him. Persecution had indeed come, and John was proving himself able.

So was his brother. James does not play a prominent role in Acts, but he does hold one great distinction: He is the first of the apostles to die as a martyr. The Jewish ruler Herod Agrippa I had James, the brother of John, put to death "with the sword" (Acts 12:2), hoping it would please the Jewish authorities—and it did. Why James? Probably Herod was testing the waters. He would have heard that Peter, John and James had been close to Jesus, and that Peter and John were speaking out boldly. By executing James, John's brother, Herod was determining how the apostles would react—with violence, perhaps, giving him an excuse to brand them all as trouble-makers and have them killed. But the apostles did not react violently to James' death, though, no doubt, it was a great blow to them. Since it led to no reprisals, and since it seemed to please the Jewish authorities, Herod threw the most prominent apostle, Peter, in jail, a story we look at more closely in another chapter.

Recall at the beginning of this chapter that James and John had asked Jesus for places of honor in his kingdom. James got what he asked for—and not through selfish ambition but through the same sacrificial love that Jesus had shown.

James was gone, Peter and John had been thrown in jail, and Peter had been jailed yet again. But the gospel continued to spread. In fact, it spread to Samaria. John had undergone a great change: In Luke 9, he and James had wanted to call down fire from heaven on a Samaritan village that gave them a chilly reception. In Acts 8, Peter and John preach the gospel to Samaritans; in effect, John was calling down fire from heaven on Samaritans but in a very different way from Luke 9.

A GOSPEL LIKE NO OTHER

These are written that you may believe that Jesus is the Christ, the Son of God, and that by believing you may have life in his name. (John 20:31)

We saw that John is a prominent character in the early chapters of Acts. The last mention of him is in Acts 8, which reports him and Peter preaching to the Samaritans. The Bible tells us nothing else about John until many years later, when the elderly John is in exile during the persecution of the Roman emperor Domitian. (More about that later in this chapter.) In between Acts and Revelation, tradition says John was associated with the great city of Ephesus, which had been evangelized by Paul and came to have a large Christian community. The tradition says that John wrote his Gospel while in Ephesus.

John is unique among the Gospels and is one of the most unique books ever written. Bible scholars refer to the other three Gospels as the Synoptics—*syn*, "together," and *optikon*, "see," for they see and report many of the same events, often in the same order. John does his own thing, with his Gospel reporting deeds and sayings that the others omit. Tradition says his Gospel was the last of the four to be written down, and he wrote with the assumption that the other three were already familiar, so there was no need to cover the same ground.

John's uniqueness is obvious at the very beginning. Where Matthew begins with a genealogy of Jesus, John begins with "In the beginning . . ." and identifies Jesus as the divine "Word" of God. With the first chapter, John refers to Jesus not only as Word but also as Lamb of God, Son of God, Messiah/Christ, King of Israel, and Son of Man. Yet this divine figure was also "made flesh," and no Gospel emphasizes more than John that Jesus was fully human. Only John tells us that "Jesus wept."

Jesus is "the Word," and the Greek word John uses is *Logos*, a term used by Greek and Roman philosophers. (We will look at this title more closely in another chapter.) John uses Word/Logos as a hook to Gentile readers, especially those influenced by Greek thought. However, it is clear that the Gospel was intended for

> **DID YOU KNOW?**
>
> One reason John may have kept his own name out of his Gospel is that he devotes a lot of space to another John, the Baptist, and may have wanted to avoid confusion.

Jews as well as Gentiles, because John goes out of his way to show that Jesus is the longed-for Messiah, the Son of God, and that Judaism has been superseded. John shares with Matthew the aim of showing that Jesus is far superior to Moses and the Law: "The law was given through Moses; grace and truth came through Jesus Christ" (John 1:17).

John's Gospel—
Every Word—On-screen

The year 2003 saw something radically new released in theaters: a movie in which an entire book of the Bible was presented on screen. This was *The Gospel of John*, directed by Philip Saville and starring Henry Ian Cusick, and it included every word of the Gospel, either narrated or spoken by the actors. The movie presented characters and incidents seldom seen in movies about Jesus—the washing of the feet, the woman at the well, Nicodemus, the healing of the invalid at the pool. The movie assumes that "the disciple that Jesus loved" was John, which is the traditional view.

The movie's timing was, alas, not good, for many people passed it by, knowing that Mel Gibson's much-anticipated *The Passion of the Christ* would be released in spring 2004.

The Gospel has been accused of being anti-Semitic because John frequently refers to "the Jews" in a disparaging way. But "the Jews" does not mean *all* Jews, but the main Jewish authorities in Jerusalem, most of whom opposed Jesus. They are ensnared in their own spiritual pride. For them, their deep knowledge of the Law enables them to look down on others: "This mob that knows nothing of the law—there is a curse on them" (John 7:49).

John says more than the other Gospels about the world and its opposition to the truth. In John the conflict is cosmic: God and Christ vs. the world, which is under the power of Satan. In this conflict, every person has to choose one side or the other. "This is the verdict: Light has come into the world, but men loved darkness instead of light because their deeds were evil" (John 3:19). "In this world you will have trouble. But take heart! I have overcome the world" (John 16:33).

John records fewer miracles than the Synoptics—curiously, he never shows Jesus casting out demons—nor does he record parables. But in chapter 11, he does record the greatest of Jesus' miracles, the raising of his friend Lazarus. He records some oft-quoted dialogues between Jesus and individuals such as Nicodemus ("You must be born again," in chapter 3) and the Samaritan woman (chapter 4). And of course, John is the source of what may be the most-quoted Bible verse of all, 3:16, which in the familiar King James Version is "For God so loved the world, that he gave his only begotten Son, that whosoever believeth in him should not perish, but have everlasting life."

One striking feature of John's Gospel is the presence of several "I am" speeches of Jesus, in which he identifies himself as the light of the world, the good shepherd, the resurrection and the life, the bread of life, and others. Also, Jesus often prefaces his sayings with *Amen, amen*— "Truly, truly"—indicating he is saying something of profound importance.

Like the other Gospels, John devotes a lot of space to Jesus' arrest, trial and crucifixion, and he includes some unique items, such as the dialogue between Jesus and Pilate and some sayings from the cross that the other Gospels did not include. John also records the encounters of the risen Jesus with Mary Magdalene and doubting Thomas.

Earlier in this chapter we looked at the reasons John's name became attached to this Gospel, and also his being identified as the "disciple whom Jesus loved." While it is impossible to be a hundred percent certain, the tradition associating John with this Gospel is very old, and probably reliable. However, in the 1800s and early 1900s, scholars were very skeptical about this tradition and thought that John was written very late, possibly as late as AD 200, and thus far removed from the time of Jesus and with very little historical basis. But we know now this is not the case. Archaeologists unearthed the pool with the five porticos mentioned in John 5:2 and the Stone Pavement mentioned in John 19:13. The author was clearly someone who was familiar with the locales Jesus and the disciples knew. Numerous other details point to their origin in a firsthand witness. Scholars now think John—though definitely later than the other three Gospels—contains the authentic memoirs of the apostle John and is solidly grounded in history. In fact, the oldest New Testament fragment we possess is a small scrap of John 18, dated AD 150 at the latest, but probably a good bit earlier. The tradition that John wrote circa AD 90, when he was an old man with a lifetime to reflect on Jesus, is probably sound.

An early sect called the Alogi denied the authority of John's Gospel on the grounds that it contradicted the other three. Happily, their view did not prevail. John does not contradict but supplements the others, and it is probably safe to say that John is the most loved of the four Gospels.

LOVE LETTERS

This is how we know what love is: Jesus Christ laid down his life for us. And we ought to lay down our lives for our brothers. (1 John 3:16)

Whoever does not love does not know God, because God is love. (1 John 4:8)

"God is love." Those familiar words are found twice in the Bible, in 1 John 4:8 and 16. By themselves, the words are pretty meaningless—after all, "love" has numerous meanings, many of them selfish. The word used in 1 John is *agape*—unselfish love—and in case John's readers weren't sure about just what agape entailed, the letter makes it plain: Real love is about giving up oneself for others, just as Jesus did. If people do not know that kind of love, they really do not know God.

The theme of agape binds the Gospel of John together with the three short letters known as 1, 2 and 3 John. The similarities of the writings are evident in English as well as the original Greek. Agape is a key theme. John's Gospel speaks of love thirty-nine times (Matthew has eleven mentions, Mark six, Luke thirteen), and 1 John, short as it is, mentions love twenty-six times. Given the tradition that John the apostle wrote the Gospel that bears his name, he almost certainly wrote the three "love letters," although they, like the Gospel, never mention his name. The writer calls himself "the elder" at the beginning of 2 and 3 John, and no one has ever identified this elder as anyone else but the apostle John.

But far more important than the authorship are the ideas in the letters. The main idea is that real love, the kind Jesus modeled for the world, is a matter of deeds, not talk: "Dear children, let us not love with words or tongue but with actions and in truth" (1 John 3:18). In the Gospels, Jesus stated that the two greatest commandments were to love God and to love our neighbor as ourselves. In 1 John, the two ideas are merged: To truly love God, we have to love our neighbor. The other human beings we share this world with are a kind of test. If we can't bring ourselves to love them, we can't love God either. "Anyone who does not love his brother, whom he has seen, cannot love God, whom he has not seen" (1 John 3:20). This strikes many readers as wrong: can't we love God, who is holy, beautiful, and perfect, and not love human beings, who are frustratingly difficult to get along with? 1 John clearly says that there's no way. Jesus loved human beings not because they were lovable, but in spite of all their failings. We must do the same. "If anyone says, 'I love God,' yet hates his brother, he is a liar" (1 John 3:20).

In John's Gospel, Jesus gives his disciples a "new commandment": they are to love one another, as he had loved them, and the greatest love of all is when someone lays down his life for his friends (John 13:34 and 15:13). The letter takes these simple-to-grasp but difficult-to-practice thoughts and reiterates them, looks at them from different angles, almost seems to wear them out by restating them. The repetition has a purpose: to drive home the point that the life of faith involves real love, self-giving love, love that is made evident in deeds.

The idea of spiritual rebirth, so important in the Gospel, is also prominent in 1 John. The Gospel emphasizes being "born again," and the letter again and again speaks of being "born of God" (1 John 2:29, 3:9, 4:7 and 5:1). Being "born of God" is, like love, more than a matter of words—deeds are essential.

Like the Gospel, 1 John says much about the world, which is hostile to people of faith. That idea ties the Gospel and the letters to another writing of John, a radically different one, Revelation.

> I heard what sounded like a great multitude, like the roar of rushing waters and like loud peals of thunder, shouting: "Hallelujah! For our Lord God Almighty reigns." (Revelation 19:6)

> They will make war against the Lamb, but the Lamb will overcome them because he is Lord of lords and King of kings—and with him will be his called, chosen and faithful followers. (Revelation 17:14)

We come full circle: from John the disciple, dubbed by Jesus a "son of thunder," to the last book of the Bible, a book that mentions thunder, symbolizing divine power, ten times. But John is no longer a thunderous young man; he is a seasoned, elderly saint in exile, waiting on God's justice.

In Revelation, John identifies himself by name. He also gives his location: Patmos, a bleak island in the Mediterranean Sea. Tradition says he was exiled there by the Roman emperor Domitian, who had launched an empire-wide persecution of Christians. Earlier Roman emperors had been called divine, but Domitian took the title seriously and insisted that all residents of the empire officially state that he was Lord and God. Many Christians refused, and suffered for their faith. Revelation is a book of a persecuted man, aware that many of his fellow believers are paying the ultimate price for their faith. He is "John, your brother and companion in the suffering and kingdom and patient endurance that are ours in Jesus" (Revelation 1:9). John, unlike Job's friends, is not

---

CULTURAL INSIGHTS

The Language Difference

Experts in the Greek New Testament say that Revelation was written by someone who probably spoke Aramaic as his first language and knew Greek, but not very well. In other words, Revelation is written in exactly the kind of Greek we would expect a Galilean fisherman like John to use.

However, the Gospel and letters of John are in very different Greek—correct, simple but often eloquent, the writing of someone who was very at home in the language. Could Revelation have been written by the same person? Probably the best answer is that it was the same mind but a different writer. Revelation may well have been written down by John himself while he was in exile on the island of Patmos. In the Gospels and the letters he probably employed a scribe—someone more skilled in the language than himself.

---

an outsider trying to explain suffering; he is suffering himself. He offers no explanation. Instead, he provides something even better: hope.

In my book *Know the Bible in 30 Days* I cover Revelation and try to explain this powerful but often puzzling book. I will not cover the same ground here, for my focus is not on the book itself but the elderly John. His persecutor, the emperor Domitian, was assassinated in AD 96, so John wrote down his vision in that year or earlier. Thus more than sixty years separate Revelation from John's time with Jesus, so John was at least in his eighties, possibly in his nineties when he wrote the book. He had had a lifetime to reflect on Jesus and his teaching, much time to mull over the many sayings about love—and also much time to recall his own youthful impulsiveness, when he and his brother asked Jesus to send fire from heaven to destroy some surly Samaritans. By the time he wrote Revelation, that youthful hotheadedness and vengefulness were gone. He is willing to suffer for his Lord, as so many Christians were doing, and he is not seeking vengeance on the persecutors. "The world," as Jesus had told the disciples, is hostile to the life of faith. The saints must endure, relying not on vengeance but on the justice of God.

John sees horrible things in his visions: good people suffering, a loathsome "beast" that dazzles the world and leads most people astray. But God is in control, and what triumphs over the powers of evil is . . . a lamb. Obviously this is Christ, the Jesus whom John the Baptist had called "the lamb of God, who takes away the sins of the world" (John 1:29). The wicked powers are finally defeated, and the saints sing, "Worthy is the Lamb, who was slain, to receive power and wealth and wisdom and strength and honor and glory and praise!" (Revelation 5:12). And while Revelation has puzzled many readers who sit comfortably in their homes, it has also provided great comfort to the ones suffering persecution. John, the brother in suffering, asks the persecuted to fix their minds on the Lamb of God.

Recall that at the beginning of this chapter the brothers James and John had asked for places of honor in Jesus' kingdom. They got what they asked for, and in the way Jesus modeled for them: through self-sacrificing love and service.

PUTTING THE WORD TO WORK

1. James and John told Jesus they would share in his sufferings but fled when he was arrested. What were some times in your own life when you overestimated yourself?

2. Why do you think John chose not to mention himself by name in his own Gospel? Do you think this adds to or takes away from the Gospel's authenticity?

3. John and Peter spoke the gospel boldly and were even willing to defy the Jewish authorities. Think of people you have known who were willing to take risks in order to do what God wanted them to do. And thank God for such people.

4. Mull over 1 John 3:20 ("If anyone says, 'I love God,' yet hates his brother, he is a liar"). Think of some relationships in your own life that need mending and then take steps to do so.

5. Reflect on the image, common to John's Gospel and Revelation, of Jesus as the Lamb of God. How do you react to the prophecy that the evil powers of the world will ultimately be conquered by one who is meek and self-sacrificing?

Three Faith-Walkers
NOAH, ABRAHAM, ENOCH

What does it mean to walk with God? In this chapter we will look at three people from Genesis, two of them (Noah and Abraham) very well known, one (Enoch) less so. All three walked with God, serving as role models of deep faith.

KEY TERM FOR TODAY Walking with God

The life of faith involves commitment to and relationship with God. The great saints of the Bible "walked with God" in trust and obedience.

THE BIBLE'S FIRST SAINT

Enoch walked with God; then he was no more, because God took him away. (Genesis 5:21–24)

Genesis begins with man in loving fellowship with God. The fellowship is broken by man's disobedience, and for several chapters we see humans growing more and more distant from God. The distancing begins in Eden: "The man and his wife heard the sound of the Lord God as he was walking in the garden in the cool of the day, and they hid from the Lord God among the trees of the garden" (Genesis 3:8). Presumably Adam and Eve had been comfortable walking with God before, but once they disobeyed, the fellowship was broken, and they hid themselves. Later humans showed no inclination to draw near to God. Cain, Adam and Eve's first child, murdered his younger brother, Abel. Genesis 5 gives us numerous "begats," with the names of Adam's descendants who, though they lived to phenomenal ages, were no closer to God than prior generations.

But standing out in the long genealogy is Enoch: "When Enoch had lived sixty-five years, he became the father of Methuselah. And after he became the father of Methuselah, Enoch walked with God three hundred years and had other sons and daughters. Altogether, Enoch lived 365 years. Enoch walked with God; then he was no more, because God took him away" (Genesis 5:21–24). Most people are familiar with the name Methuselah, since he was the longest-lived, surviving to the age of 969. Unfortunately, they forget his more important father, for Enoch, unlike the other people named in Genesis 5, "walked with God." This can only mean that he had a close relationship with God, that his behavior pleased God. In fact, he so pleased him that "God took him away."

Over the centuries, Enoch has held a great fascination for people. No doubt this is because of the aura of mystery around the words "he was no more, because God took him away." To heaven? Presumably. Certainly the author of the Letter to the Hebrews thought so. God took Enoch to heaven without his having to experience death. He "pleased God." This makes him one of only two men in the Bible who are taken without having to die, the other being the great prophet Elijah, who was taken to heaven in a fiery chariot (2 Kings 2).

If you have read the Old Testament closely, you know that the ancient Israelites were slow to come around to a belief in heaven. Enoch's and Elijah's miraculous departures from this world at least gave a hint that there was something more than life, death and burial. Note that Enoch lived "only" 365 years on the earth, while his son Methuselah, the oldest man ever, lived 969 years. Other men mentioned in this part of Genesis likewise lived to extreme ages. Clearly Enoch got the greater reward. Who wouldn't choose walking with God over 969 years of walking on earth?

In the Letter to the Hebrews, Enoch is included in the Faith Hall of Fame: "By faith Enoch was taken from this life, so that he did not experience death; he could not be found, because God had taken him away. For before he was taken, he was commended

CHARACTERS AT LARGE ## Enoch in the New Testament

The brief Letter of Jude in the New Testament quotes a prophecy, which it attributes to Enoch. This puzzles readers, since Genesis says nothing about Enoch's being a prophet. Jude verses 14–15 quote from a book called 1 Enoch, written in the period between the Old and New Testaments. The Enoch of Genesis did not write it, of course, but the book claims to contain divine revelations that Enoch wrote down, including prophecies of the end of time. Neither Jews nor Christians have ever accepted it as inspired Scripture, and it certainly has no direct connection with Enoch. But it is an example of the kind of literature that was often written under the name of some biblical character. Since Enoch had been taken into heaven, it was assumed he had special insights into the divine plan for mankind, and so several books were written with his name attached—1, 2 and 3 Enoch and several others.

Revelation 11 refers to two witnesses of the end times, two men who will prophesy but will be slain during the great Tribulation. One common interpretation of this passage is that the two witnesses were Enoch and Elijah, who had been taken to heaven instead of dying, but who will be martyred after their return to earth.

as one who pleased God" (Hebrews 11:5). Enoch had broken the pattern, established by Adam and Eve, of disobeying and displeasing God. He is the Bible's first hint that something more is in store for saints than life in this world.

GOD'S LIFEBOAT

> The Lord was grieved that he had made man on the earth, and his heart was filled with pain. . . . Noah was a righteous man, blameless among the people of his time, and he walked with God. (Genesis 6:6, 9)

Noah is one of the best-known men in the Bible, yet he is also one of the least known, because people tend to neglect the important aspects of his character and his story and focus on distracting questions like "Did the flood actually cover the whole earth?" and "How could he have taken all those animals into the ark?" Noah's real importance in the Bible is that he, like his ancestor Enoch, walked with God, a moral man in a frighteningly immoral world.

Noah's story begins in Genesis 5:29. He is the son of Lamech, who bestows on his son the name "Noah" because it means "comfort": "He will comfort us in the labor and painful toil of our hands caused by the ground the Lord has cursed." Lamech harks back to the curse on nature caused by Adam's sin. His naming of Noah is a prophecy, or at least a hope, that he will be comfort in the sense of giving the world a new beginning.

Lamech must have been a man of deep faith—or at least an optimist—for the world around him gave no hint that man would ever be any better than he was: "The Lord saw how great man's wickedness on the earth had become, and that every inclination of the thoughts of his heart was only evil all the time. The Lord was grieved that he had made man on the earth, and his heart was filled with pain" (Genesis 6:5–6). Here, and in many other places in the Bible, we see that God is not some far-off force or supreme being. He is a present personality, and he can feel pleasure and pain. What human beings do to each other gives him grief.

Man has obeyed the divine mandate to be fruitful and multiply, but the result has been an increase in wickedness. Because of this, God has decreed that man's normal age will be a hundred and twenty (Genesis 6:3). He is not so much limiting life as limiting wickedness. Men were living to amazing ages (think of Methuselah) and instead of growing in love and kindness, they were growing more skilled in wickedness.

DID YOU KNOW?

One bizarre explanation of Enoch's disappearance is that he was abducted by aliens. People who believe this also believe that Noah was righteous because he had alien ancestry, and the great flood was caused by aliens wanting to rid the earth of wicked humans and repopulate it with Noah's descendants. Some claim that the giants and "men of renown" of Genesis 6:1–4 were the offspring of evil aliens, not good ones.

In many ancient religions and mythologies, the distant past is often thought of as a golden age. Clearly this is not the case in the Bible. From Adam on, things have degenerated morally and spiritually. It is revealing that in Genesis 6:1–2 and 6:4, the giants and heroes of the distant past are presented as evil, not good. The heroic age that most ancient religions and myths regarded so highly, full of mighty men to honor, is not depicted that way in the Bible. In God's view, the violent, promiscuous, egotistical men that the ancient Greeks and Romans regarded as children of gods are not heroes; they are wicked. Genesis 6:4 refers to the *nephilim*, often translated "giants," but probably meaning "fallen ones" or "those who fall upon others." If the latter is correct, they are attackers, men of violence, human predators. Critics of the Bible often point to Joshua and Judges and the violence in those books, but on the whole violence is not praised in the Bible, and not at all in Genesis, where Cain is the first murderer and God destroys the earth in Noah's day.

"God saw how corrupt the earth had become, for all the people on earth had corrupted their ways" (Genesis 6:12). The verb translated "corrupt" can also mean "destroy." Instead of walking with God, as Noah did, the people walked the path of destruction. God had created all things and called them "good." Man seemed bent on corrupting and destroying.

The earth had grown so wicked that God would destroy his own creation—but not totally. "Noah found favor in the eyes of the Lord," for he was "a righteous man, blameless among the people of his time, and he walked with God" (Genesis 6:8–9). "Blameless" here does not mean perfectly sinless, but more something like whole or complete. Noah was a man of integrity and decency—an amazing feat in any age, but especially in the depraved world he lived in. Here we see a familiar theme of the Bible: The whole group deserves God's harsh judgment, but one man (or sometimes a few) stands out for his righteousness and is saved.

Critics of the Bible point out that the story of a great flood is almost universal, that the Noah saga is just one of many. But the Noah story is radically different because the God of the Bible is different. Gods of other nations were notoriously capricious, often angry with man for no reason. This was not true of God. If he was angry, there was a purpose. This is what makes the Noah story so distinct from the many other flood stories told around the world. God floods the world because people have grown so corrupt, but he saves a righteous man to make a new beginning for mankind.

The means of salvation is familiar: the famous ark. The measurements for it are given in Genesis 6:15, in cubits (the Hebrew cubit was about eighteen inches). The ark was about 440 feet long, seventy-five feet wide, and forty-four feet high, and scientists and engineers have observed that the proportions were perfect, for it would have been difficult to capsize and would have righted itself even when tossed by giant waves. In terms of volume, the ark could have held the equivalent of more than five hundred railroad cattle cars. Preachers have not ignored the fact that the ark had only one door—thus one way to be saved.

The ark is interesting in itself, and over the years many people have designed scale models of it, and it certainly has held a fascination for artists. But to focus on the physical aspects is to miss this point: Noah, in the middle of land, was constructing an enormous wooden lifeboat. The Letter to the Hebrews commends his deep faith: "By faith Noah, when warned about things not yet seen . . ." (Hebrews 11:7). Unlike Adam

---

CULTURAL INSIGHTS

Ararat

Mount Ararat, in what is now Turkey, is an extinct volcano, seventeen thousand feet in height. Genesis says Noah's ark came to rest "on the mountains of Ararat," meaning not necessarily Ararat itself but somewhere in the vicinity. It is interesting that the Bible, so focused on the land of Israel, would locate the resting place of the ark on faraway Ararat.

People have long wondered if Noah's ark, or parts of it, might still exist. In 1887, a bishop from India scaled lofty Mount Ararat. The bishop claimed he came upon a ship nine hundred feet long and one hundred feet high, but Turkish authorities blocked his efforts to explore further. In 1955 a Frenchman, Fernand Navarra, brought back pieces of timber from the mountain, found in a glacier at an elevation of thirteen thousand feet. Scientists who tested the wood said it was indeed old—maybe a thousand years old, but certainly not old enough to date back to Noah.

In 1916, two Russian pilots claimed they saw Noah's ark from the air, and the next year Czar Nicholas II sent two expeditions with more than 150 people to find it. Because of the Russian Revolution, the photographs never reached him.

In the 1970s, many people got excited at the "discovery" of Noah's ark on Ararat. An enormous wooden boat roughly matching the description in Genesis was there, high on the mountain. When examined closely, however, it was found to be about a thousand years old.

Noah in Popular Culture

For the world at large, the moral part of the Noah story has been mostly forgotten. Artists and filmmakers have enjoyed depicting the building of the ark and showing the parade of animals entering it. It is no wonder that a chain of pet stores is named Noah's Ark. In dramas written in the Middle Ages, Noah was depicted as a henpecked husband, lashed by the tongue of his shrewish wife, who thinks him a fool for building the ark. In Jewish legend, more than a hundred different names are given for the wife, who is unnamed in Genesis. In the Koran, the wife is named Waila, and she tries to persuade people that her husband is out of his mind.

Noah has been portrayed in numerous movies, notably in 1966: *The Bible . . . In the Beginning*, in which John Huston, in addition to directing and narrating the film, played an appealing Noah.

and Eve, he heeded God. No doubt this led to intense ridicule while the building took place. As a moral man in an immoral world, Noah would probably have been a figure of fun already, but certainly the enormous boat he and his three sons constructed was a subject of mockery.

Yet Noah persisted. In 2 Peter 2:5 we are told that Noah was a "preacher of righteousness." No one, it seems, responded. Perhaps, in his centuries of life, he had preached to many but to no avail. During the long construction project, people had ample time to repent of their wickedness. None did. God established a covenant—his agreement—with Noah, just as later he would establish another covenant with the righteous Abraham.

Thanks to that agreement, Noah and his family survived. Noah obeyed God fully. Four times it is said that Noah did all God commanded him. This sets him apart from Adam and Eve, obviously. In fact, he is given a much heavier task than them, since they were asked only to avoid eating the fruit of one tree. Morally, Noah was a giant of a man, nothing like the *nephilim* and heroes of other religions.

"The Lord then said to Noah, 'Go into the ark, you and your whole family, because I have found you righteous in this generation'" (Genesis 7:1). The "you" here is singular, not plural. We know nothing about the moral or spiritual state of his wife, sons or daughters-in-law. Noah alone is described as righteous. Some scholars note that in this verse, "Go into the ark" would more accurately be "Come into the ark." The difference is revealing. If "come" is correct, God is telling Noah that he will be with them in the ark.

The Hebrew word translated "flood" is not the usual word for a typical flood, but a word denoting a deluge of epic proportions. In the New Testament the Greek word *kataklusmos* is used, and again, this is not the Greek word for a normal flood. Much ink has been spilled over whether the entire world was flooded or not, but to debate this is to miss the point. It is interesting to note, however, that the flood is not just a matter of rain but also of "the springs of the great deep" opening up. Water was coming from both above and below.

What did the family ponder while in the ark? Doubtless they regretted the loss of many family members, friends and acquaintances. Doubtless their belief in God was deepened, since it was proved beyond all doubt that God's communication to Noah had been real.

After one hundred fifty days the waters began to subside. "The ark came to rest on the mountains of Ararat" (Genesis 8:4). The ark "rested," as if for five months it had been at work—which in fact it had, since it was saving human and animal life.

The family was in the ark a total of three hundred seventy-one days, including the period on Ararat spent waiting for the waters to recede. Two and a half months after coming to a rest there, they could see the tops of nearby mountains.

Genesis 8 has the story of Noah sending out birds—a raven and a dove—for the purpose of discerning if there was any dry land to speak of. The dove at first returned, having found no place to alight. A week later the dove went out again but returned with an olive leaf in its beak, a sign the waters were receding. A week later the dove did not return at all—a sign that it was making its home on dry land somewhere.

CHARACTER CLOSE-UP   The Naked-and-Drunk Episode

The Bible is a warts-and-all book, not afraid to show that even great saints can do bad things. This is true even of the "blameless" Noah, for Genesis 9:2–27 records the rather sordid story of Noah planting a vineyard, becoming drunk with his wine and lying uncovered in his tent. One of his three sons, Ham, saw what had happened and told his two brothers, Shem and Japheth. Wanting to spare their father embarrassment, Shem and Japheth took a garment and, walking backwards, draped it over Noah. When he awoke from his drunken stupor, he realized what had happened. Shem and Japheth had done right:They had shown respect for their father, despite his making himself look ridiculous. Ham, however, had behaved badly. Seeing his father naked and drunk was an incitement to mock his authority. He would have done well to tell no one what he saw. Presumably all three sons had been obedient to their father throughout the building of the ark and the long period inside it. But here in the "cleansed" new world, parental authority is already breaking down. Noah pronounced a curse on his disobedient son.

It is interesting that though the Bible has, overall, a positive opinion of wine, the first mention of it is this story of drunkenness and dissipation. Wine itself is not condemned but drunkenness is.

Noah was blameless but clearly not perfect. Adam's sin has not been obliterated by the flood, for the best man of all is still flawed.

Noah and his family could begin life again on earth. This second beginning for man was radically different from the first, for this was no Eden. They would have seen no animal life outside but plenty of dead bodies, including humans. The landscape would have been ugly at first. Morally, however, it was clean.

Considering what they had been through, Noah was grateful to his God. "Then Noah built an altar to the Lord and, taking some of all the clean animals and clean birds, he sacrificed burnt offerings on it" (Genesis 8:20). This is the first mention of an altar in the Bible, and the second mention of sacrifice. God's command before the flood was to take seven of every "clean" animal into the ark, and some of these were used in the sacrifices. Obviously the sacrifice required faith on Noah's part, because the food supplies taken into the ark would not last forever, and there certainly were no food supplies in the barren, dead landscape. It was an act of devotion, and it pleased God. Noah was not only expressing thanks for his preservation but also showing faith that God would continue to care for him. Appropriately, God promised never again to flood the world.

In a way, Noah is like a new Adam. But in one respect he is very different: His faith has already been tested, and he has been fully obedient to God.

God also gave a stern warning: "I will demand an accounting for the life of his fellow man. Whoever sheds the blood of man, by man shall his blood be shed; for in the image of God has God made man" (Genesis 9:5–6). This reminds us that before the flood, the earth was filled with violence. Presumably people knew then that it was wrong, but it must have been taken for granted. Now God specifies that if you shed blood, your own blood will be shed. The principle here is not vengeance but justice. God intends that the new earth be less violent and corrupt than the old.

In the New Testament, Noah is praised as a man of deep faith and righteousness, and his story is a reminder that God will always preserve his righteous ones.

HEEDING THE CALL OF GOD

When Abram was ninety-nine years old, the Lord appeared to him and said, "I am God Almighty; walk before me and be blameless." (Genesis 17:1)

By faith Abraham, when called to go to a place he would later receive as his inheritance, obeyed and went, even though he did not know where he was going. (Hebrews 11:8)

Abraham is the first real personality in the Bible, the first person whose character is revealed deeply over many chapters. We get insights into the characters of Adam, Eve, Cain, Noah and others, and we learn great moral lessons from them, but we know so little about them that they do not seem to be three-dimensional, flesh-and-blood human beings. Abraham's character is richly revealed, and he is the first person for whom we have a general idea of the dates when he lived.

Until Genesis 12, where the story of Abraham begins, we see mankind getting further and further alienated from God. Enoch and Noah stand out as good men who walked with God, but they are isolated individuals in a sinful world. Beginning with Abraham, we see a movement back to God, beginning with one righteous man who is promised he will be the ancestor of a great nation.

The man originally named Abram was a native of Ur, in what is today Iraq. When he was seventy-five years old, something amazing happened: "The Lord had said to Abram, 'Leave your country, your people and your father's household and go to the land I will show you. I will make you into a great nation and I will bless you'" (Genesis 12:1–2). People in ancient times took separation from their families very seriously. Yet Abram does not seem to have hesitated at all in obeying God's command. He severs his ties with his old way of life and relies entirely on God's promises of many blessings.

Following the Lord's command to settle in Canaan, Abram would have headed a caravan covering perhaps fifteen miles per day, with all their possessions loaded onto donkeys. They would have passed through Damascus, known as the "city of donkeys." Camels were not domesticated at this point. Along the way, he and his family would likely have pitched in with other caravans on the same route, for protection against bandits.

Abram took with him his beloved wife, Sarai, and his nephew Lot. Abram and Sarai were a devoted couple, but they had no children, and since Lot's father was dead by this time, he seems to have been a surrogate son for Abram. Lot, as we shall see, plays a major role in the story of Abram.

On reaching Canaan, the land God had promised to him and his descendants, Abram showed his devotion to God by building an altar. As in the days of Noah, the relation between God and his people is a personal relationship. There are no priests, no institutional religion. No middleman is needed, and when sacrifices are offered, the patriarchs themselves do the act instead of requiring a priest.

Soon after reaching Canaan, a famine occurs, so Abram and his household must go to Egypt for food. Already his faith is being tested. Is he sure God meant him to settle in Canaan, which is subject to famines? Yet his survival in Egypt is a sign that God is still watching him.

In the 1600s, as many English were preparing to settle in America, their pastors would often preach sermons on Genesis 12, the story of Abraham leaving his homeland to seek a new life in another country where God's promises would be fulfilled.

Ur, Very Real

The biblical city of Ur was thought by many people to be fictional until it was actually excavated in 1854. Further excavations in the 1920s show that the city was already old by Abraham's time. The people of ancient Ur worshipped many gods, particularly the moon, so Abraham had grown up in an atmosphere of idolatry. The typical house of that time was made of brick and built in a kind of beehive shape, and each home would have had a shrine housing a statue of the family's favorite god.

The site of Ur is in what is today Iraq.

After their return to Canaan, Abram and Lot both become prosperous, wealthy with livestock and money. A problem arises: The two men's herdsmen are quarreling over grazing rights. Abram wisely decides to divide up the land with his nephew, generously giving Lot his choice of land. Lot chooses the land on the east, which is green and fertile. From a material standpoint, Lot makes a wise choice, choosing land that was "like the garden of the Lord," meaning Eden. From a moral standpoint, he is going to live among wicked heathen, for the people of nearby Sodom are notoriously evil. At first Lot lives in tents near the city, but in time he lives in the city itself, a choice he would come to regret.

Abram separated from his surrogate son—but now he receives assurance from God that the land around him will belong to his countless descendants. As an aging man with a barren wife, Abram had to have deep faith to keep harking to God's voice.

In the meantime, he has to come to Lot's rescue. A coalition of kings from the east make war on Sodom and the surrounding cities; Lot and his family and goods are captured. Loyal to his nephew, Abram and three hundred eighteen of his servants make a night raid on the conquerors and free Lot and his family.

What follows is his meeting with one of the mystery men of the Bible, Melchizedek, who is both a priest and a king. He is said to be king of Salem, which is

DID YOU KNOW?

The visit of the three men to Abraham in Genesis 18 has often been called the "Old Testament Trinity," since Genesis refers to the three visitors collectively as "the Lord."

probably the original name of Jerusalem. He is also priest of God Most High, the same God Abram serves. This in itself is remarkable, for Melchizedek was a Canaanite, and we would expect him to be priest of the Canaanite fertility god Baal, yet he served Abram's God. He blessed Abram, and Abram gave him a tithe—one-tenth—of his goods. The encounter with Melchizedek takes up only a few verses in Genesis 14, yet for Jews and Christians the episode has deep meaning. The belief developed that Melchizedek was an eternal priest who had no beginning or end, unlike the priests of

Israel, who died and had to be replaced. The Letter to the Hebrews says that Christ in heaven is the eternal high priest in the manner of Melchizedek.

The priest-king had blessed Abram, but Abram was still childless. God reassured Abram: He would surely have a son, and his descendants would be as numerous as the stars. Then follows one of the great verses of the Bible: "Abram believed the Lord, and he credited it to him as righteousness" (Genesis 15:6). The key word is "believed." In Hebrew it is *aman*, with the same root as the word *amen*. To believe is more than intellectual, since the Hebrew word contains the idea of establishing and confirming. The person who believes commits himself to God. Abram said yes to God. He had been in Canaan ten years, and he still has no children—yet he continues to have faith.

Abram trusts God's promise of children. But the mother is not identified. The stage is set for the episode of Genesis 16. Sarai, Abram's beautiful but barren wife, does not have the patience to wait on God. Her plan: Let Abram conceive a child with her Egyptian maid, Hagar. It sounds peculiar to us, but more than once in the Old Testament we encounter this custom: A barren wife allows her husband to conceive a child with a concubine, and then the wife adopts it as her own.

Abram had more faith than his wife did—but he gave in to her plan. This was a foolish mistake, as foolish as when Adam listened to Eve. Hagar did conceive, and began to despise Sarai. Hagar was a mere slave, a piece of property, but she had conceived the child of the rich master, so it is not surprising she looked down on the aging Sarai. Though the plan had been hers, Sarai complained loudly to Abram—and drove Hagar away.

CULTURAL INSIGHTS

Circumcision in Ancient Times

Circumcision in most ancient cultures was done either at puberty or just before marriage. Clearly it had a connection to a boy becoming a man, reaching sexual maturity. For Abraham, it was not a sexual symbol but a sign that the child was in a covenant relationship with God from birth. Only Abraham's descendants, the Israelites, attached any spiritual meaning to circumcision.

Apparently most of the surrounding nations practiced circumcision, for only the warlike Philistines are regularly referred to as "the uncircumcised." In the New Testament period, Jews were in frequent contact with Romans and Greeks, who mocked circumcision and considered it mutilation. If pagan men wanted to become full converts to the Jewish religion, they had to undergo circumcision—at a time of no anesthesia. Understandably, few made that choice. Although most of the first Christians were Jews, it was soon decided that Gentiles who became Christians would not have to be circumcised.

The Way

In the New Testament, the word *Christian* appears only three times—twice in Acts, once in 1 Peter. Much more often the Christians referred to themselves as brothers and disciples. But five times in Acts they are referred to as people who follow "the Way." The Greek word translated "way" literally means "road" or "path," but it could be used figuratively as in English. The meaning in Acts is that the Christians were following "the Way"—to life, to salvation, to God. Paul on one occasion called himself a "follower of the Way, which they [the Jews] call a sect" (Acts 24:14). For Paul and his fellow believers, their faith was no mere sect but the path to salvation, having God as guide and companion in this world and the next. Faith is not a matter of saying yes to a creed or idea but one of an ongoing relationship with God.

Poor Hagar, a pregnant woman driven into the wilderness! God took pity on her and told her to return to her mistress, and that she would bear a son who would have many descendants. She gave birth, and the son was named Ishmael—but, not surprisingly, Sarai did not adopt the child as her own.

Ishmael means "God hears." God does not hear just the important people, like Abram, but even hears a slave. Hagar is a minor character in the story, but God clearly has her welfare in mind.

In Genesis 17, God again speaks to Abram, telling him, "Walk before me and be blameless." He makes a covenant—a binding agreement—with Abram, just as he had made with the righteous Noah. The sign of the covenant is circumcision, and Abram is to circumcise every male in his household. As another sign of this new order of things, Abram's name is changed to Abraham and Sarai's to Sarah. In effect, they are new people. Then God again promises a son—but this time he is specific: Sarah will bear the son, despite her being ninety years old and Abraham a hundred. Before this occurs, we read the unsettling story of Sodom.

While Abraham sat in the opening of his tent, three visitors appeared from nowhere. In the custom of the time, Abraham received them hospitably and offered them food and drink. The three "men," collectively, are "the Lord." The Lord promises Abraham that he will pass that way again in a year—and Sarah will have a son by then. Sarah, in her tent, laughs. She does not have as much faith as her husband.

The three men leave—two going on to Sodom, one remaining behind to talk with Abraham. He tells Abraham that Sodom's wickedness has become too great, that the city will be destroyed. For the first time in the Bible, a man intercedes with God. Abraham asks, "Will you sweep away the righteous with the wicked? What if there are fifty righteous people in the city?" (Genesis 18:23). The Lord assures him that if there are fifty righteous people, the city will not be destroyed. Abraham goes further: What about forty-five people? Forty? Ten? The Lord assures him he will not destroy Sodom if ten righteous people are there.

Clearly there were not ten. Yet Abraham's pleading was not in vain. The two other visitors—angels—went on to Sodom, where they were invited by Lot to stay in his home. The rest of the sordid story is familiar: That night, the men of the city surround Lot's house and demand Lot bring out the visitors so that they may "know" them—that is, have sex with them. The men try to force their way into the house, but the two angelic visitors strike the men with blindness. They tell Lot the city is about to be destroyed. Lot begs his two sons-in-law, presumably local men, to flee with him, but they think he is jesting. Lot himself lingers. The angels practically have to drag him, his wife and his two unmarried daughters from the doomed city. The angels warn the family to flee and not look back. Lot's wife—she must have been deeply attached to the place—disobeys, looks back and is turned into a pillar of salt. In the early morning, Abraham looks off in the distance and sees smoke rising from the destruction of Sodom. Due to his pleading with the Lord, Lot had been spared.

Then what the Lord had foretold came true. At the age of one hundred, Abraham finally had a son, whom he named Isaac, meaning "laughter." Alas, the joyous event did not lead to peace in the household, for the older son, Ishmael, mocked the newborn, and Sarah insisted that Abraham send Ishmael and Hagar away for good. The incident does not show Sarah in a good light. She was willing to drive away the woman who had served her faithfully for many years. Out in the wilderness, Hagar and Ishmael nearly died of thirst, but God took pity on Hagar again and brought her to a well. Ishmael was not the "child of the promise" that Isaac was, yet God watched over him anyway.

What follows is one of the most disturbing stories in the entire Bible. God decides to test Abraham's faith. God tells him, "Take your son, your only son, Isaac, whom you love, and go to the region of Moriah. Sacrifice him there as a burnt offering" (Genesis 22:2). We can only imagine what went through Abraham's mind. The child he and his wife had longed for, the child of the promise—*sacrifice him*?

Child sacrifice was taken for granted in that time and place. There was, strictly speaking, nothing remarkable about God commanding Abraham to sacrifice Isaac—except that it would nullify all the promises God had made to Abraham. And yet, since God had, to everyone's great amazement, given Abraham and Sarah a son in their old age, could he not provide another? Miraculous things had happened, and other miracles might be in store.

Whatever Abraham thought or felt, he obeyed God fully. He took two servants with him on the three-day journey to Moriah, and set about piling up wood for the sacrifice. Isaac wondered: There was an altar with fire and wood, but where was the animal to be sacrificed? Abraham answered: "God will provide." He bound the boy and was about to plunge the knife into him. "But the angel of the Lord called out to him from heaven, 'Abraham! Abraham! . . . Do not lay a hand on the boy . . . Do not do anything to him. Now I know that you fear God, because you have not withheld from me your son, your only son" (Genesis 22:11–12).

One of the blessings Abraham receives for his obedience is the promise that his descendants will be as numerous as the stars. In being willing to offer up his only son, he will have countless sons.

Abraham clearly deserves his reputation as a man of deepest faith, a man who walked with God in total obedience. Heeding the call of God, he had left his homeland, settled among strangers, interceded to save his nephew Lot from a doomed city, and—against all odds—continued to believe God's promise of a son, long past his wife's childbearing years. So committed was he to his God that he was willing to offer up the one thing he loved most in the world. Abraham's story sets the pattern for the Christian life: breaking from a former way of life, enduring testing, emerging purified. In a sense, each Christian is a little Abraham.

In closing this chapter, it is worth noting that Genesis 22:2 is the first mention of love in the Bible, when God tells Abraham to take the son he loves and sacrifice him. It is appropriate that this first mention of love refers to the love of father for son, given that one of the great themes of the Bible is love of the heavenly Father for his children. Appropriately, in the Gospels the first mention of love is at the baptism of Jesus, where God refers to his "beloved Son." Hebrews 11 commends the faith of Abraham in being willing to offer up his "only begotten son." God, a Father himself, was also willing to offer up his "only begotten son."

PUTTING THE WORD TO WORK

1. Reflect on the verse in Genesis 6 that says God's "heart was filled with pain" over human behavior. How does it affect your own life to know that what you do can cause God pain?

2. Noah continuously obeyed God's commands, despite the mockery of the people around him. Keep the example of Noah in mind the next time you are tempted to follow the crowd and stray from the right path.

3. How do you react to the story of Noah's drunkenness? Do you think people of faith can grow closer to God after episodes of stumbling?

4. Put yourself in Abraham's place and imagine the long delay in God's fulfilling his promises. How do you think he coped? What kept his faith strengthened?

5. Try to think of people you have known who had deep faith like Abraham and were willing to sacrifice something dear to them.

Paul as Parent/Pastor

The theme of this chapter is tough love, as exemplified by a man who had no biological children but many, many spiritual children in many locales. Paul is remembered as the great missionary and evangelist of the Book of Acts, where he is shown boldly presenting the gospel to unbelievers.

> **MEMORY VERSE**
>
> I speak as to my children—
> open wide your hearts also.
> —2 Corinthians 6:13

But in his letters he is Paul the pastor, writing to converts, speaking sometimes lovingly and sometimes sternly, playing the often-thankless role of spiritual father. In so doing, he bequeathed to the world some of its most inspired writings, which have guided and consoled people of faith for two thousand years.

KEY TERM FOR TODAY ## Overseer

Paul as pastor was the gold standard of the *episkopos*, the "overseer," spiritual guide and guardian of his many converts, who were scattered across the Roman empire.

PAUL, APPALLED

You foolish Galatians! Who has bewitched you? (Galatians 3:1)

There is neither Jew nor Greek, slave nor free, male nor female, for you are all one in Christ Jesus. (Galatians 3:28)

To get acquainted with Paul in his role as spiritual father, let's consider two very different letters, Galatians and Philippians. In both he was writing to people who had been converted to the faith through his preaching. In both he was stern *and* loving, yet in Galatians the sternness seems to dominate. It is the least warm of all his letters, something that is clear at its very beginning. In his other letters, Paul opens with a warm and effusive greeting: "To all in Rome who are loved by God and called to be saints" (Romans 1:7). "To the saints in Ephesus, the faithful in Christ Jesus" (Ephesians 1:1). The greeting in Galatians is abrupt and businesslike: "To the churches in Galatia." And Galatians does not have Paul's customary "I thank God for you." Paul cuts to the chase, for his honor as an apostle has been impugned by his critics and, worse, the Galatian Christians are at risk from the Judaizers, Jewish Christians who wanted to impose circumcision and other Jewish laws on the Christians.

"I am astonished that you are so quickly deserting the one who called you by the grace of Christ and are turning to a different gospel—which is really no gospel at all" (Galatians 1:6–7). "Some people" are throwing the Galatians into confusion, and that is the main reason for the letter. The troublemakers had not only cast doubts on Paul's calling as an apostle but also introduced something new, the belief in Christians putting themselves under the Jewish law—or at least being circumcised. For Paul, this was a "different gospel." But there was only one true gospel.

Since his apostleship has been put in doubt, Paul deals with that criticism in his greeting itself: "Paul, an apostle—sent not from men nor by man, but by Jesus Christ and God the Father." In his days as a persecutor of Christians, Paul tried to please men—his fellow Jews, particularly the priests in Jerusalem. He is now aware that such behavior was not pleasing God! Now his enemies say his gospel is for the purpose of pleasing men. On the contrary, he is a "slave" of Christ, not a man striving to please or impress others.

Chapter 3 lets loose his anger: "You foolish Galatians! Who has bewitched you?" In his translation of this passage, J. B. Phillips uses "idiots," and it is probably a good choice, for Paul is very riled up at these people. They are idiots because they have already put their faith in Jesus and have received the Holy Spirit into their hearts, so what more do they need? Why are they letting themselves be bewitched into legalism? Paul mentions that the Galatians had witnessed miracles. What else did they need to prove that God was at work among them? What could circumcision possibly provide?

Paul speaks about the great Old Testament hero Abraham, the man the Jews regarded as both their spiritual and physical father. For the Jews, Abraham was the role model of circumcision; for Paul, he is the role model of faith in God. The real children of Abraham are the people who have faith. Abraham is referred to as *pistos*, "the believer" or "the man of faith," a favorite title for him among Greek-speaking Jews. Paul contrasts "those of faith" (Galatians 3:7) with "those of the deeds of the law" (Galatians 3:10).

Later in the letter, Paul lashes out against "those agitators." He wishes "they would go the whole way and emasculate themselves!" (Galatians 5:12). Among the pagans, some of the devotees of the wild cults, like that of the goddess Cybele, literally did castrate themselves. Paul is being sarcastic: If the Christians are going to mutilate their adult bodies by circumcision, why not go the whole way and undergo castration? Paul understood the mind of the legalist: it wants some physical proof of its devotion. But such physical proof does not save us: "What counts is a new creation" (Galatians 6:15). If we are not made new on the inside, what is outside makes no difference.

In Galatians 3:24, Paul refers to the Jewish law as *paidagogos*, literally "boy leader," the servant or slave who led a boy to and from school. (It is the root of the word *pedagogue*.) In finding salvation in Christ, people are now of age and no longer need the *paidagogos*. "Now that faith has come, we are no longer under the supervision of the law" (Galatians 3:25). Paul may have had in mind the ceremony of the Roman boy putting aside his childhood clothes and putting on the *toga virilis*, the ordinary garb of an adult man. Also, some of his readers would have been familiar with the mystery religions, where initiation into the cult actually involved putting on a special cloak.

"There is neither Jew nor Greek, slave nor free, male nor female, for you are all one in Christ Jesus" (Galatians 3:28). This is the climax, the spiritual high point, of the letter. Spiritually, there was a level playing field. Any person, whatever their background, could find salvation in Christ, and there was no need to turn back to the Jewish law.

"Now that you know God—or rather are known by God—how is it that you are turning back to those weak and miserable principles? Do you wish to be enslaved by them all over again?" (Galatians 4:9). In their former lives as pagans, the Galatians had been playing at religion, going through the motions of meaningless rituals. Now

---

CULTURAL INSIGHTS

The Circumcision Group

In Acts and Paul's letters, we find constant references to the "circumcision group." These were Christians who insisted that Christian men be circumcised. The response of Paul and the other apostles was: No! Circumcision was regarded with horror by most Gentiles, who thought of it as mutilation, and to require it would have kept many Gentile men from becoming Christian. But more important was the simple fact that Christianity was not just a new and improved sect of the Jewish religion. It was something entirely new, and there was no need to impose circumcision—or any Jewish rules—on Christians.

People reading the New Testament today may wonder what this issue has to do with the life of faith now. Plenty. Paul was aware that the same legalistic mentality that wanted to impose circumcision on Christians would also impose other meaningless rules, such as food restrictions, which Paul also condemned. Paul never ceased to emphasize that the key thing in the life of faith was the inner transformation. Rules about external matters—circumcision, food, rituals—had no place in the Christian life.

that they have found real salvation, how can they think of turning back to those "weak and miserable principles" of their old religions? And how could they become obsessed with "observing special days and months and seasons and years"? (Galatians 4:10). The "special days" are probably the Jewish holidays, including the Sabbath. These days have no place in the lives of Christians. Legalism, whether from Jewish or pagan sources, is not what saves people.

After all this scolding, we sense Paul smiling, remembering better days: "What has happened to all your joy? I can testify that, if you could have done so, you would have torn out your eyes and given them to me. Have I now become your enemy by telling you the truth?" (Galatians 4:15–16). This is the only part of Galatians in which he pays the readers a compliment. They were once grateful to him for preaching the message of salvation. Now he fears he may become their enemy by speaking the truth. "My dear children . . . how I wish I could be with you now and change my tone, because I am perplexed about you!" (Galatians 4:19–20). There is deep love here. Paul is in agony over these people. They are Christians but not mature ones. Like any loving parent, Paul feels the need to scold—and to embrace.

Paul launches into one of the great chapters of the Bible, chapter 5, in which the key word is freedom: "It is for freedom that Christ has set us free. Stand firm, then, and do not let yourselves be burdened again by a yoke of slavery" (Galatians 5:1). The Galatians must choose: freedom under Christ, or slavery under legalism. There is no compromise. The Judaizers seem to have had a cafeteria approach to Judaism: The religion would include circumcision, observance of Jewish holidays, etc. Paul says no. Letting in a little legalism is a slippery slope.

But like any parent, he understands that the "children" may abuse their freedom. "Do not use your freedom to indulge the sinful nature; rather, serve one another in love" (Galatians 5:13). The Christian's freedom is not to live wildly and selfishly, but to live a life of love. Freedom should not lead to immoral "acts of the sinful nature." He makes no bones about such behavior: "I warn you, as I did before, that those who live like this will not inherit the kingdom of God" (Galatians 5:22). Rather, their lives ought to exhibit "the fruit of the Spirit," which is "love, joy, peace, patience, kindness, goodness, faithfulness, gentleness and self-control" (Galatians 5:27–28). The law of Christ is the love for others. And to put ourselves under the protective authority of God is to be free.

PAUL, APPEALING

I thank my God every time I remember you . . . . I long for all of you with the affection of Christ Jesus. (Philippians 1:3, 7–8)

We now turn to a much warmer letter, Philippians. Here Paul is mellow, the loving father in a relaxed mood—even though he was writing from prison! After greeting "the saints in Christ Jesus at Philippi," he adds his familiar "I thank my God every time I remember you"—a note of joy at the beginning of this letter that was conceived in joy and is a joy to read.

Paul is confident that these people, his spiritual children, will continue to grow in the faith. God had begun a "good work" in them and would see it through. "It is right for me to feel this way about all of you, since I have you in my heart . . . God can testify how I long for all of you with the affection of Christ Jesus" (Philippians 1:7–8). "The affection of Christ Jesus" is a memorable phrase. Paul had no conception of religion as a joyless, loveless thing.

Paul is pleased with these people, and he urges them to continue making him proud: "Whatever happens, conduct yourselves in a manner worthy of the gospel of Christ" (Philippians 1:27). He reminds them that even when he is absent, as he is now, he hears things about them. Then a somber note enters the letter: "It has been granted to you on behalf of Christ not only to believe on him, but also to suffer for him" (Philippians 1:29). Paul is himself in prison when he writes the letter, so when he counsels the people to be prepared to suffer for Jesus, he has already led the way himself.

In the next chapter, Paul the father tells his children to play well with others—to make his "joy complete by being like-minded, having the same love, being one in spirit and purpose" (Philippians 2:2). They ought always to act out of consideration for others, not out of selfishness. In thinking more of others and less of themselves, they will show the attitude of Jesus, who "made himself nothing, taking the very nature of a servant, being made in human likeness" (Philippians 2:7). If they are "in" Christ, they need to behave like Christ—a humble servant to the death. Jesus did not stand on his dignity as the Son of God. He "emptied himself" out for mankind. Jesus was "in very nature God" but took on the "very nature of a servant." The one who would be called Lord was willing to lower himself as low as a slave, even suffering the cruel punishment used on slaves. Jesus not only lowered himself by becoming a human; he also became the lowest form of human. The sequel to this degradation is that God exalted Jesus as Lord. The basic Christian creed "Jesus is Lord" is here amplified—yes, he is Lord, but he had to go the route of humiliation to get there. The same will be true of Christians.

Again, Paul praises the Philippians' obedience to his teaching—even when he is locked up in prison! In continuing to follow him, they will "become blameless and pure, children of God without fault in a crooked and depraved generation, in which you shine like stars in the universe" (Philippians 2:15). Philippi, part of the Roman empire, had its share of pagan immorality, but Paul's spiritual children could maintain their own integrity and "shine like stars" in a dark world.

Paul, the Family Man

The great apostle, unmarried and childless, was in fact very much a family man. Aside from constantly referring to fellow Christians as "brothers"—a common usage at the time—he could refer to them with other family metaphors as well:

Husband and wife: "I am jealous for you with a godly jealousy. I promised you to one husband, to Christ, so that I might present you as a pure virgin to him." (2 Corinthians 11:2)

Mother: "We were gentle among you, like a mother caring for her little children." (1 Thessalonians 2:7)

"My dear children, for whom I am again in the pains of childbirth until Christ is formed in you. . . ." (Galatians 4:19)

Father: "Even though you have ten thousand guardians in Christ, you do not have many fathers, for in Christ Jesus I became your father through the gospel." (1 Corinthians 4:15)

"I am sending to you Timothy, my son whom I love, who is faithful in the Lord." (1 Corinthians 4:17)

In prison for his faith, Paul could hold himself up as a moral example: "Join with others in following my example, brothers, and take note of those who live according to the pattern we gave you" (Philippians 3:17). "Imitate me" may sound conceited, but Paul has nothing to hide, nothing to be ashamed of. Rather than a sign of conceit, it is a sign of his willingness to have his behavior scrutinized. In fact, throughout his ministry, Paul lived an amazingly public life, and this kept him on his toes, morally speaking. He urged other pastors to live this way.

Despite all the compliments paid to the Philippian brothers and sisters, the fellowship there was not perfect. In chapter 3, Paul deals with the same issue he dealt with in Galatians: the Judaizers who were trying to impose circumcision and other Jewish rules on the Christians. As always, Paul takes a firm stand against these people. At the end of the letter, he deals with a quarrel that has arisen: "I plead with Euodia and I plead with Syntyche to agree with each other in the Lord." These sisters in the faith have been a help to him in the past, and he wants them to settle their quarrel and act like members of one spiritual family, people "whose names are in the book of life" (Philippians 4:2).

Like any good father, Paul wants his children to aim high in life, to have ideals: "Brothers, whatever is true, whatever is noble, whatever is right, whatever is pure, whatever is lovely, whatever is admirable—if anything is excellent or praiseworthy—think about such things" (Philippians 4:8). In an immoral and cynical world, the brothers were told to set their minds on the heights.

He ends the letter on a note of gratitude. The Philippians had shared in his troubles. In chapter 4 verse 14 , the word is *thlipsis*, usually translated "troubles," but it actually has a stronger meaning: "tribulation." Paul's present imprisonment is just one part of the great tribulation that people of faith must undergo. These generous people had on two occasions sent him money to provide for his needs. Such generosity is all the more remarkable because Paul had established the Philippian church on his second mission but had not visited it since. However, while he was evangelizing Thessalonica, the Philippians had sent him money, and he accepted—which is interesting because Paul generally did not accept financial remuneration. He must have accepted the Philippians' gift because of his warm relationship with them.

Clearly, Philippians is a love letter from Dad, Paul at his warmest, the spiritual father full of praise for exceptionally well-behaved and high-minded children.

NO ELEGANCE, NO ELOQUENCE

When I came to you, brothers, I did not come with eloquence or superior wisdom as I proclaimed to you the testimony about God. (1 Corinthians 2:1)

You yourselves know that these hands of mine have supplied my own needs and the needs of my companions. (Acts 20:34)

It would horrify the noted Greek and Roman authors of Paul's day to know that their own writings have fallen by the wayside while millions of people continue to read the writings of Paul. It would not surprise Paul, however. He understood that his letters were not literature but writing, with a purpose. He made no claim to be an eloquent author or speaker, and he understood that the pagan authors and speakers swayed their audiences with their smooth ability with words. Paul had no interest in this: He was a man with a mission from God, and the important thing was the gospel, not his ability to woo with words.

In the opening chapter of 1 Corinthians, Paul states that he preached "not with words of human wisdom, lest the cross of Christ be emptied of its power." In fact, he was aware that his message was "foolishness" to most people, "but to us who are being saved it is the power of God" (1 Corinthians 1:17–18). The pagans looked for eloquence and philosophical wisdom in speeches and writings, "but to those whom God has called, both Jews and Greeks,

> **DID YOU KNOW?**
>
> The goat-hair cloth of Paul's native province, Cilicia, was known to the Romans as *cilicium*. The goat-hair cloth and tanned goatskins Paul worked with as a tentmaker were from the goats of the mountains of Cilicia.

Stoics

Acts 17 mentions two schools of philosophy, the Stoics and the Epicureans. The Stoics and Paul shared some common ground, for the Stoics took morality and duty seriously, and many of them believed in one God, although he was more of a force than a person. Stoics emphasized being content and tranquil no matter what happened, and Paul shared that sentiment. The Stoics believed in an afterlife, though they saw it as more of an absorption into a world soul than as a heaven where individuals enjoyed endless fellowship with God.

For the educated Greeks and Romans of Paul's day, Stoicism was close to being "what everyone believes," if *everyone* means "the smart people." It gave them the satisfaction of having high ideals, of being rational and seeking after the truth—and also the satisfaction of not taking the various gods seriously.

Stoicism is probably one of the best philosophies human minds ever concocted, but it lacked the appeal of a warm, personal relationship with a loving father. Also, Stoicism had little or no effect on people's morals, and some of the great Stoic writers like Cicero and Seneca admitted that their ideas and ideals had little real influence on how people lived. But there is no doubt that the Stoicism in the air was for many people a preparation for hearing the gospel.

Christ the power of God and the wisdom of God" (1 Corinthians 1:24). No wonder that most of the people considered wise by the standards of the time did not accept the gospel.

Acts 17 records the famous story of Paul visiting Athens, considered the intellectual capital of the world in that day. Acts is honest in recording that Paul made few converts there. The Athenians placed more emphasis on cleverness and eloquence than on truth, and for them Paul was a "babbler." These were shallow people, with a city full of idols that disturbed Paul, probably because he understood that the Athenians revered the beauty of the statues more than they honored any god. Acts notes that the Athenians enjoyed discussing "the latest ideas," so they might have been, in theory, open to the gospel. But they had too high an opinion of their own intelligence to accept Paul and his simple teaching about a man crucified and resurrected. Having grown up in Tarsus, a city that also had a reputation for sophistication and learning, Paul could not have been surprised at his lack of success in worldly, shallow, snobbish Athens.

The Athenians had heard too many ideas to have much enthusiasm for any. Philosophies and religions were entertainment for them, so Paul was out of place in this city, for his own faith was a matter of life and death. Even the Romans criticized the Greeks for their habit of playing with philosophy and religion, enjoying discussion but never taking anything too seriously.

Though he was highly intelligent and could write Greek very well—and even quote pagan poets, as he did in Athens—Paul had a mistrust of elegance and eloquence. He was aware of the human tendency to turn religion into a matter of prettiness and fine words, just as he was aware of how sophisticates and intellectuals seldom humbled themselves and admitted the need for the salvation he preached.

This man who emphasized directness and simplicity in his preaching also lived simply. And he provided for his own needs financially, plying his trade as tentmaker, a trade he shared with his dear friends Priscilla and Aquila. Our phrase "tentmaker ministry"

CULTURAL INSIGHTS

Tarsus, Home of Paul

At one point in Acts, Paul refers to himself as "a Jew, from Tarsus in Cilicia, a citizen of no ordinary city" (Acts 21:39). Indeed, Tarsus was very proud of itself, often referred to as "first, greatest, and most beautiful." It had culture and learning, it was prosperous thanks to its linen industry and the fertile farmlands nearby, and its riverfront port kept it in touch with a wider world.

The birthplace of one of the greatest men of the Bible was in the region called Cilicia, which is today in southern Turkey. The city was already many centuries old when Saul, who later became Paul, was born there, and legend says its founders included the Greek heroes Perseus and Hercules. It existed at least as early as the ninth century BC. It became thoroughly Greek in culture during the reign of Antiochus IV, who also settled a large numbers of Jews in Tarsus to foster commerce, and Paul's ancestors were probably among these. In 67 BC, it was made part of the Roman Empire, and it hosted such notables as Julius Caesar, Mark Antony and Cleopatra. Mark Antony granted Roman citizenship to its people, and Paul was to make good use of that citizenship.

A great academy was established there and became a center of Greek philosophy, and one of its notables, Athenodorus, was the teacher of the emperor Augustus. Along with Athens and Alexandria, it was considered one of the intellectual centers of the empire. As a devout Jew, Paul would not have been educated in pagan philosophy, but there is no doubt that an intelligent child growing up in Tarsus would be familiar with it. The city was a center of worship for the Persian god Mithra—a cult very popular with Roman soldiers—and the Greek demigod Hercules; these were but two of the many "lords" that the pagans honored. Religiously and intellectually, Tarsus was a more diverse city than the towns known to Jesus and his disciples. It was a perfect place for the man known as the apostle to the Gentiles to have grown up. As a Jew living in a predominantly pagan city, he understood from childhood the difficulty of living a moral life in an immoral world, a world that often showered contempt on people of faith.

refs to someone who works in ministry (pastoring a church, or as a missionary) but also has a full-time job during the week. Paul was the original tentmaker minister, of course, and 1 Corinthians indicates that his fellow missionary Barnabas also worked for a living (1 Corinthians 9:6). But apparently the pattern emerged quickly among the Christians that someone who gave himself full-time to the ministry of a congregation had the right to be supported by those he served, and Paul defends this principle heartily: "If we have sown spiritual seed among you, is it too much if we reap a material harvest from you?" (1 Corinthians 9:11). Paul states that by right he could be supported financially by the people he ministers to—yet he chooses not to.

Apparently some of his critics cast doubt on his being a real apostle because he did not accept support. In other words, he was seen as an amateur, as a tentmaker who was merely moonlighting as an evangelist. In 1 Corinthians 9:15 he makes it clear that in speaking of his waiving the right to financial support, he is not dropping a hint that he wants support now. In providing for his own financial needs, Paul not only was not a burden on the believers but also set the model for tentmaker ministry, which is still common today. Aside from being a role model for ministers, he was a role model of selflessness in general.

Paul was wise enough to perceive the obvious danger in a minister being supported by his flock: He might be tempted to water down his message, to avoid offending people. Paul, making his own living, was in no danger of this, and so he could state the truth boldly—sometimes harshly—to his spiritual children.

KEEPING FAITH IN SIN CITY

I am not writing this to shame you, but to warn you, as my dear children.
(1 Corinthians 4:14)

Do you not know that your bodies are members of Christ himself?
(1 Corinthians 6:15)

If the Roman empire had a Sin City, it was probably Corinth, a city in Greece with a deserved reputation for immorality in all its forms. No wonder Paul wrote two of his longest letters to the church there, for the believers in Corinth were swimming in a sea of vile behavior. The church in Rome also received a letter from Paul, and Rome was also a den of iniquity. But when Paul wrote his letter there, he had never visited the city, whereas the church in Corinth was one he founded himself, and he had spent many months there, so he was familiar with its members, and with the diverse temptations believers faced in this cosmopolitan, duty-free-sex locale.

Not surprisingly, Paul had to deal with sexual morals. Corinth was home to a famous—or infamous—temple to the goddess Aphrodite, although *brothel* would be more accurate, since the priestesses were nothing but prostitutes. Corinth was also home to the cult of the goddess Cotys, whose worship was a nocturnal orgy that even the Romans found a bit much. The verb *Korinthiazesthai*, "to Corinth," meant to forni-

cate. A *Korinthiases* was a whoremonger. "To live like a Corinthian" meant to live a life of depravity, and a "Corinthian girl" was a prostitute. How could one live a moral life in such a place—and for that matter, how do we explain so many Corinthians being attracted to Christianity in the first place? The attraction was obvious enough: In an immoral environment, some people will seek out an alternative. Corinth, like the other cities Paul evangelized, had a Jewish synagogue, and many pagans were drawn to the Jews' high standards of morality, so the pagans Paul preached to in the synagogue were already receptive to his teachings on sex.

In fact, a problem had arisen among the believers: Some were teaching that it was better to have no sex at all, even to the point of swearing off marriage. We gather from 1 Corinthians 7 that some married couples were even swearing off sex with each other. Paul, unmarried and celibate himself, was a realist about the sexual urge: "Since there is so much immorality, each man should have his own wife, and each woman her own husband" (1 Corinthians 7:2). And husbands and wives should fulfill their "marital duty" toward each other. Paul understood that a husband or wife denying sex to the other could lead to infidelity, which could be easily had in a place like Corinth. The smutty songs sung in the street, the pornographic sculptures and paintings, the anything-goes atmosphere made for a sex-saturated society—so the sensible thing for Christians was to marry a fellow believer and enjoy each other fully.

Paul's idea was shocking in its day: Married couples could have sex on demand with each other. This was against the Jewish notion of having it seldom, and mostly for pregnancy, and the pagan idea that a man dare not let his wife start enjoying—and demanding—sex. (Pagans thought that women, not men, were sexually insatiable.) Paul leveled the playing field. A married woman could enjoy sex, and it was fine—even good. A married couple owed each other sex—to withhold it was unkind and ungenerous. And Paul definitely could not abide the double standard of the pagans: fidelity on the part of wives, but husbands free to sleep with whomever they chose. The attraction of Paul's teaching for women is obvious enough.

Essentially, Paul's teaching on marriage was the "one flesh" theme of Genesis, which Jesus quoted approvingly.

Was Paul married?

"Now to the unmarried and the widows I say: It is good for them to stay unmarried, as I am" (1 Corinthians 7:8). During his long and world-changing ministry, Paul was single, and he recommended the single state for those rare individuals who could endure it. But was Paul ever married? Most Jewish men married—although, notably, Jesus did not, nor did John the Baptist. Paul was trained in Jerusalem under the famous rabbi Gamaliel, and it's quite possible he was training to be a rabbi himself, and unmarried rabbis were unheard of. It is possible Paul had been married and widowed, though he never mentions being married in his letters, nor does he mention having children. One thing we do know for sure is that Paul counted many as his spiritual children.

A person's highest obligation is to God—but the second highest is to the spouse. This was much more than using marriage as merely an approved means to create more children. A Roman wife took a backseat to her own children and to her husband's parents. But in the Christian view, husband and wife were equal partners, and fidelity was expected of both.

It is ironic that Paul is sometimes considered "anti-woman," for his teaching on marriage definitely raised the status of wives. A Christian woman could expect her Christian husband to sleep in his own bed—something no pagan woman could reasonably expect. After two thousand years of Paul's teaching setting the standard for marriage, we forget how new and shocking it was in his own day.

For people with an exceptional amount of self-control, Paul offered another option: celibacy. Paul's passage on recommending celibacy was written to a society where finding the right mate was not an option for many people. Many marriages were arranged and loveless, and cohabiting—becoming "tentmates," as it was called—was often mere exploitation. A married man could have it both ways, having a neglected wife, a mistress (or several), and recourse to male and female prostitutes. In this situation, a wife was expected to keep quiet and accept her fate. But among the Christians, there was no stigma if a woman remained single. Paul opened up the possibility that women might not marry at all yet still find happiness. Men and women could do something beside regard each other as providers and breeders. A Christian woman had a great amount of freedom to come and go as she pleased if she was not tied to husband and children. Single women among the Christians were among the most active and charitable members.

But note that Paul also condemned false teachers who were "forbidding to marry" (1 Timothy 4:3). Clearly Paul the celibate did not regard marriage as a bad thing—in fact, for most people, then as now, it was the best choice, given human beings' sexual nature. "Better to marry than to burn with passion" (1 Corinthians 7:9).

Elsewhere in 1 Corinthians, Paul makes it clear that the church has to have higher standards than the sex-saturated society around it: "I have written you in my letter not to associate with sexually immoral people" (1 Corinthians 5:9). He goes on to say that he is referring to immoral people *within the church*. In fact, avoiding all association with immoral people would involve leaving the world! But the faith fellowship has to take a strong stand for morality. What we do with our bodies matters. "Do you not know that your body is a temple of the Holy Spirit, who is in you, whom you have received from God? You are not your own; you were bought at a price. Therefore honor God with your body" (1 Corinthians 5:19–20).

LOVE VS. THE WORLD

Now about food sacrificed to idols: We know that we all possess knowledge. Knowledge puffs up, but love builds up. (1 Corinthians 8:1)

If I have the gift of prophecy and can fathom all mysteries and all knowledge, and if I have a faith that can move mountains, but have not love, I am nothing. (1 Corinthians 13:2)

Chapter 8 of 1 Corinthians puzzles many readers, for it covers what many people regard as a dead issue: eating meat that had been sacrificed to the pagan gods. The issue isn't dead, for the matter of knowledge vs. love is very much alive.

Among the pagans, the meat for sale in most butcher shops had first been offered up as a sacrifice in a pagan temple. The priests normally sold what was left over to butchers. In normal social life, any meal would involve such meat. This was true in people's homes, but even more true in the various banqueting halls that were attached to pagan temples. To the Jew or Christian, the meat had already been tainted by being "given" to a false god. In fact, some of the recent pagan converts to Christianity might have had scruples also, associating meat-eating with their former way of life. The controversy in Corinth was that some Christians had no problem with eating "pagan" meat, while others did.

Paul's solution: If a "weak" brother is scandalized by a brother participating in a pagan banquet, the brother should think twice about it. Paul is showing an amazing amount of fair-mindedness here: mentally, he is on the side of the "strong" Christians who have no qualms about food of any kind. But he can see the point of the "weak" brothers too. Love for the spiritual family requires us to consider others' feelings.

DID YOU KNOW?

In the margin of 1 Corinthians 13, translator William Tyndale printed the note, "A little love is better than much knowledge."

The knowledgeable among the Christians did not fuss over such matters and were obviously looking down on those who did. Paul agrees with the knowledgeable ones:

The pagan gods don't even exist, so what difference does it make if the meat was offered to them? But for Paul, knowledge is not the only thing; love of others is much more important. Paul appreciates the diversity of spiritual gifts among Christians, but he isn't going to see the fellowship divided between the "smart" and "not smart."

Appropriately, in the same letter is Paul's great chapter on agape. One reason he wrote chapter 13 was that pagans had no notion of love that was done for its own sake. Male friendship existed mainly for business and politics, family love helped strengthen the family, self-sacrifice in war helped create a military machine, hospitality made trade and travel run smoother. As Jesus said, even the pagans love their "friends," but he calls people to love even their enemies, and love those who cannot repay them.

In describing self-giving love, Paul does not use adjectives—though the translations do. Rather, he uses verbs: agape acts kindly, does not act jealously, does not act brutally, does not boast, does not get full of itself. Agape is not just feeling. It acts positively, and avoids acting negatively. Real love is love in action.

"If I speak in the tongues of men and of angels, but have not love, I am only a resounding gong or a clanging cymbal . . . . If I give all I possess to the poor and surrender

CHARACTER CLOSE-UP Ephesian Farewell

Acts 20:17–30 is one of the great episodes in Paul's life—and in the whole Bible. Headed for Jerusalem, where he knows great troubles are in store, he summons the leaders of the church in Ephesus. The meeting is both pastoral and personal. He tells them to be on their guard against false teachers in the future. They are "savage wolves," and the church leaders must be faithful shepherds of the flock. In the three years Paul lived among them, he had set the example of a faithful *episkopos*—an overseer not afraid to speak the truth, not requiring financial support, always more willing to give than to receive.

On the personal level, Paul knew that "prison and hardships are facing me." Worse, "I know that none of you among whom I have gone about preaching the kingdom will ever see me again." Paul and his friends knelt down and prayed. "They all wept as they embraced him and kissed him. What grieved them most was his statement that they would never see his face again. Then they accompanied him to the ship."

Anyone who thinks the Bible is unemotional—or anti-emotional—needs to read this great passage, for we see that Paul and his brothers in the faith loved each other deeply. These men from Ephesus were grieved to see their faithful friend depart, especially since he seemed certain they would never meet again. "They all wept as they embraced him and kissed him." Though there is no romance in the New Testament, it runs rich with the emotion of brotherly love, love that grows from people sharing in common faith and values, even in the sharing of hardship.

my body to the flames, but have not love, I gain nothing" (1 Corinthians 13:1, 3). One of the most appealing things in this great chapter is that Paul speaks in the first person—he realizes that if he, Paul, is not loving, nothing else he has done matters. He must have, at times, felt he was unloving or he could not have written this way.

In emphasizing love—not just in 1 Corinthians, but in all his writings—Paul never ceased to remind believers: Live in peace with each other, pursue harmony. "I fear that there may be quarreling, jealousy, outbursts of anger, factions, slander, gossip, arrogance and disorder" (2 Corinthians 12:20). He had good reason to fear, for Christians—being human—constantly quarreled. People often think of Paul as antisex, which is not accurate, as we saw earlier; anti-quarreling would be more accurate. Paul saw himself as father to a large spiritual family, and a family needs to remember its kinship and live in peace. He was painfully aware of his own quarrelsome nature—Paul would never back down in an argument—so he warned his protégé Timothy that "the Lord's servant"— that is, an *episkopos*, a "pastor"—"must not quarrel" (2 Timothy 2:24).

For Paul and for the many people touched by his ministry, the real enemies were not fellow believers but the hostile world outside, an environment that often treated people of faith as "the scum of the earth, the refuse of the world" (1 Corinthians 4:13). Paul's spiritual children could not leave the world, but they could set their sights on a higher one. If they could not change the world, they could certainly change themselves: "Do not conform any longer to the pattern of this world, but be transformed by the renewing of your mind" (Romans 12:2).

PUTTING THE WORD TO WORK

1. After reading this chapter, what do you think of Paul as "overseer" of his converts? Did his concept of them as his spiritual children affect his work?

2. Take a minute to reflect on people you've known—pastors, Sunday-school teachers, family friends—who have showed a deep concern for your spiritual growth. Thank God for sending these people into your life.

3. Who are some childless people you have known who did as Paul did, creating their own "spiritual families"? In what ways did they influence the people in those families?

4. Having read the section on Paul's teaching on sex and marriage, what do you think of the common accusation that Paul is anti-woman? Did this section give you some new insights into the nature of marriage?

5. Reflect on Paul's words about agape, and on the importance of peace with fellow believers. Today, try to reconcile with any fellow believer you've disagreed with.

"My Servant Moses"

It is not surprising that one of the most popular movies ever made, *The Ten Commandments*, is about one of the greatest men of the Bible, the amazing Moses. Born a slave, reared in the court of the most powerful ruler in the world, then a fugitive, called by God from a burning bush, witness to some of the most astounding miracles, reluctant leader of a ragtag herd

MEMORY VERSE

The Lord would speak to Moses face to face, as a man speaks with his friend. —Exodus 33:11

of ex-slaves who were often on the verge of killing him—his story is, to put it mildly, an adventure worthy of an epic movie.

In this chapter, though we won't ignore the adventure part of the story, we will focus more on the one great relationship, the one great love, in Moses' life—his walk with God, a relationship so unique that Moses was said to be "face-to-face" with God.

KEY TERM FOR TODAY ## Man of God

More than any other Old Testament figure, Moses was the humble man of God, a reluctant but committed leader who was privileged to see God in a unique way.

A MOST UNPROMISING BEGINNING

Moses, when he had grown up, refused to be known as the son of Pharaoh's daughter. (Hebrews 11:24)

The Book of Genesis ends happily: Joseph, after being sold into slavery by his own brothers, rises to the post of right-hand man to Egypt's pharaoh, and during a time of famine his father and brothers settle in Egypt. With Joseph as their sponsor they are given pleasant land in Egypt to dwell in. The twelve sons of Jacob have large families, and the whole clan—known as Hebrews as well as Israelites—increases tremendously.

Then something happened: "A new king, who did not know about Joseph, came to power in Egypt" (Exodus 1:8). A new dynasty had taken over, and a new dynasty is always insecure. The new pharaoh looked at how numerous the Hebrews were and worried: What if these resident aliens turned against us and toppled the government?

The Egyptians had always been somewhat uncomfortable with foreigners; they tolerated them but never fully accepted them. So the new pharaoh made a swift political change: The Hebrews in Egypt would be forced to do slave labor. Yet the Hebrews continued to multiply.

Pharaoh called in the Hebrew midwives and gave them a horrible order: When a male Hebrew child is born, kill it. But "the midwives feared God," and they would not obey the order.

So Pharaoh did openly what the midwives would not do quietly. He ordered that Hebrew infant sons be drowned in the mighty Nile—Egypt's river of life but for the Hebrews a river of death. The Egyptians would have regarded these child murders as sacrifices to the river god.

The Hebrew women did not all hand over their newborns to the Egyptians. One woman hid her son in a papyrus basket coated with pitch, floating it in the river while the son's sister kept an eye on it. As it happened, Pharaoh's daughter and her servants came to bathe in the river. Hearing the infant cry, she took pity on it, even though she recognized it as a Hebrew child. The sister nearby fetched a woman—the baby's own mother—to be a wet nurse. But in time the son went to live at the Egyptian court, officially the son of Pharaoh's daughter.

Contrary to the movie *The Ten Commandments*, the son, Moses, was well aware that he was a Hebrew, the child of slaves. We have to wonder what sort of divided mind or heart he had growing up as a pampered prince in the Egyptian court, being waited on hand and foot, with a slave at each elbow—and yet dimly aware that his biological kin toiled as

CULTURAL INSIGHTS

Bulrushes

Most Bible translations say that the infant Moses was hidden in a basket made of "bulrushes." This refers to the papyrus plant, which was common in the Nile and is still common today in lakes and rivers worldwide. The name papyrus is the source of our word *paper*, because the stalks of the papyrus plants were used by the Egyptians to make a flat surface for writing on.

It is interesting that Moses was kept alive in a papyrus basket, because such baskets were often used as the coffins for Egyptian infants. It is also interesting that the Hebrew text of Exodus refers to the basket with the word *teba*, translated "ark" in the story of Noah. In both cases the *teba* was a lifeboat.

slaves making bricks for the pharaohs' massive building projects. The Bible passes over his youth in complete silence. But we know from the history of Egypt that he would have been taught that the pharaoh was a god, the son of the sun god Ra, and that he was even responsible for the annual Nile floods that irrigated Egypt's farmlands and made them fertile. He would have been taught that slaves, who went barefoot and spoke only when spoken to, were nonpersons, mere property.

And yet he felt a connection to these people. When he was grown, he saw an Egyptian foreman abusing one of the Hebrew slaves—"his people." He struck the Egyptian and whether it was intentional or not, killed him. He then hid his body in the sand. The following day, when he tried to separate two quarreling Hebrew men, they were irate: Did he mean to kill them as he had killed the Egyptian the day before?

Two things stand out in this episode. First, Moses tried the way of violence to end slavery. He literally struck a blow for freedom. But it would become clear to him over time that the way of violent revolution was not God's way. God would free the people in his own way and in his own time. But the other aspect of the story that was an omen of things to come is the ingratitude of the two quarreling Hebrews. They had heard of his killing the abusive Egyptian, but instead of thanking him or praising him, their reaction was, "Who do you think you are?" This would happen again and again throughout his life.

HOLY GROUND

During that long period, the king of Egypt died. The Israelites groaned in their slavery and cried out, and their cry for help because of their slavery went up to God. (Exodus 2:23)

Moses, raised as a prince, suddenly became a criminal on the lam. He fled east to the wilderness, to Midian. The Midianites were relatives of the Hebrews, both groups being descendants of Abraham. Moses met some Midianite shepherd girls at a well and was welcomed into the home by their father, Jethro, a priest of God. Moses married one of his daughters, had two sons by her, and settled into a peaceful life of tending flocks of sheep and goats.

We aren't told how long this went on. However long it was, the time would have been a humbling experience for Moses, an "Egyptian" prince trained to give orders and have them obeyed, now a tender of flocks in a desolate wilderness. Moses was grown at the time he murdered the Egyptian overseer, and eighty when he confronted Pharaoh, so it is safe to say many decades had passed in Midian, possibly fifty years or more. In short, he spent more of his life as a shepherd than he did as a prince.

Sometime during this period, Egypt's Pharaoh died. A regime change was always a time of hope for conquered people, and so the Hebrew slaves hoped and prayed that the new pharaoh might change their lot. The Hebrews "groaned," and God heard their groaning.

Moses was tending flocks near the mountain called both Sinai and Horeb. He saw a bush on fire—not an unusual sight in itself, because in the desert heat, some of the shrubs with their oily stems would catch fire spontaneously. But this bush burned without being consumed. Moses heard a voice calling his name from the bush. The voice told him to take off his sandals, for he was standing on "holy ground." Moses, raised in the court, understood what this meant: Taking off one's shoes meant taking on the aspect of a slave, who normally went barefoot. Moses was humbling himself before this God, who identified himself as the God of Abraham, Isaac and Jacob, the Hebrews' ancestors. "Moses hid his face, because he was afraid to look at God" (Exodus 3:6).

God said he had heard the groaning of his oppressed people, and that he intended to deliver them. And it would be Moses who would lead them out. Moses protested. Who was he to lead the people from Egypt? God gave one of the great assurances of the Bible: "I will be with you."

Such an assurance should have been enough, but Moses was still reluctant. How could he lead the Hebrews, for he was "slow of speech and tongue"? God answered: "Who gave man his mouth? Who makes him deaf or mute? Who gives him sight or makes him blind? Is it not I, the Lord?" Moses still protested: "Lord, send someone else" (Exodus 4:11). No, Moses was God's choice. But God would give Moses an aide, his own older brother, Aaron, who could speak well.

We pause here to wonder: Why was Moses so reluctant? There were many possible reasons. Having murdered an Egyptian, he would have assumed that he was not exactly welcome back in Egypt. He might even be killed if he went back. And perhaps he had settled into his quiet family life in Midian and given up all thoughts of Egypt and his Hebrew kin so far away. Perhaps he had gotten rusty in the Egyptian language he had learned at court—hence his protest of being "slow in speech." None of this mattered: He was God's choice. And his conversation at the burning bush set a pattern: So often in the Bible, the best man for the job is the reluctant one, the one who is not ambitious or self-seeking.

Moses asked Jethro permission to take his wife and sons back to visit the family in Egypt. He did not tell Jethro his true purpose in going back, and later, when he realized how hard the struggle with Pharaoh was going to be, he sent the family back to Midian for safety. It is worth noting that Moses was humble enough to ask his father-in-law's permission to leave. The former prince of Egypt had learned humility through his various adventures.

WHO RULES NATURE?

> The Lord said to Moses, "See, I have made you like God to Pharaoh, and your brother Aaron will be your prophet." (Exodus 7:1)

Although we aren't a hundred percent sure, the hated pharaoh whose death is recorded in Exodus 2:23 was probably Seti I, who died in 1290 BC. When a hated ruler died, conquered peoples would naturally hope for a more compassionate successor—or for a deliverer. In a sense the people were poised for the miracles of God and Moses.

Back in Egypt, Moses with his brother, Aaron, reported God's commissioning of Moses to the Hebrews, and the elders, the leaders among them, were overjoyed. The joy would soon fade, however. The new pharaoh was probably Rameses II, an egomaniac who was even more of a monument-builder than his predecessor was. (Archaeologists know Rameses as "the great chiseler" because he would have his own name carved on monuments that were in fact images of his predecessors.) The vain Rameses was not moved by Moses' insistence that the Hebrews' God had ordered, "Let my people go." At first, Moses was not asking for liberation; he was asking permission for the Hebrews to journey to the wilderness for a brief religious festival. Pharaoh took this as

CHARACTERS AT LARGE Moses and America

When Europeans began to settle in North America in the 1600s, they often referred to it as the Promised Land, a place where they could be free from the tyranny and religious persecution of Europe. When the American colonies decided to break free from Britain in 1776, Founding Father Benjamin Franklin proposed that the new nation's national seal should show Moses leading his people through the Red Sea. Thomas Jefferson suggested another image from the Moses story: Israel being led by the pillar of cloud and fire through the wilderness.

In the 1800s, the antislavery movement in America often appealed to the story of Moses and the Exodus. Though abolitionists admitted that the Bible did not actually prohibit slavery, they held up the story of Moses and the Israelites as a clear example that God did not intend his creatures to live as slaves. When Abraham Lincoln issued the Emancipation Proclamation in 1863, he noted the words of Exodus 6:5 (KJV): "I [God] have also heard the groaning of the children of Israel, whom the Egyptians keep in bondage." Lincoln knew his Bible—and he also knew that one of the great spiritual songs of the slaves was "Go Down, Moses," with its refrain, "Tell old Pharaoh to let my people go." Thousands of years after Moses, his story gave hope to slaves and those who worked to free them.

A site on the Red Sea shore is called "Pharaoh's Bath," and an old tradition says it was where the Israelites crossed over. The sulfurous smell in the area supposedly comes from the corpses of the drowned Egyptians.

a flimsy excuse to take useful slaves away from their work. No, the slaves could not go into the wilderness to worship their God. They would continue to toil at making bricks—in fact, the work would be harder, for from now on they would have to make bricks without the useful straw used as a binder in the bricks. Moses had not delivered the people—in fact, their work had grown more demanding.

Moses and Aaron went back to Pharaoh. The mighty king had not been swayed with words, so perhaps a miracle would turn him. Aaron lay his staff on the floor and it turned into a snake. Pharaoh was not impressed. His own magicians could do the same trick. But Aaron's snake ate up theirs! Still, Pharaoh was unmoved; his heart was hardened. The man who thought he was a god was not easily convinced.

In Exodus 7 begins the story of the ten horrible plagues God sent on Egypt. The first was directed at the "divine" river Nile, which was worshipped as a god—understandably so, since this rainless land relied on its waters for irrigation. The Nile waters turned to blood at Moses' command. Fish died and the water stank and was undrinkable. The people were terrified, but Pharaoh was not. Nor was he moved by the second plague,

---

CULTURAL INSIGHTS

Which Sea and Which Sinai?

Most Bibles say that God parted the "Red Sea" for the Israelites. The Hebrew text says it was the *Yam Suph*, literally "the Sea of Reeds," and this was almost certainly not the large body of water that we call the Red Sea today. There is a great deal of speculation about just where the *Yam Suph* was—possibly a marshy area that is today called Lake Timsah. The fact is, Egypt's shoreline has changed greatly over the course of four thousand years, and there is no way to be certain where the great miracle occurred. The main point of Exodus is that it happened.

Likewise there is no certainty about Mount Sinai. A mountain in Egypt called Jebel Musa—Arabic for "mount of Moses"—has a long tradition of being the mountain where Moses met God, and in fact, director Cecil B. DeMille chose to film part of *The Ten Commandments* at Jebel Musa. But several other sites have been proposed as the "real" Sinai. Interestingly, Jewish rabbis have shown no interest in the location of Sinai. In their interpretation, the Law had been given "in the wilderness," meaning it was not tied to any locale but valid for the whole world. There is some merit to that interpretation: The point of the Moses story is not that we know where the mountain is, but that we believe God and Moses met there.

How Many Slaves?

Exodus 12:37 says there were six hundred thousand men on foot, plus women and children. This has led to some skepticism: how could the desert support millions of people, and why didn't they leave archaeological evidence? The usual estimate is that total group would have been 2.5 million—which would have been half the population of Egypt in that period. The Hebrew word usually translated "thousand" is *elef*. Elsewhere, however, *elef* is translated as "tribe" or "clan" or "group." (In Judges, Gideon laments that his clan—*elef*— is the weakest in Manasseh.) Exodus might be saying "six hundred extended families." This helps explain why Pharaoh sent six hundred charioteers against the group. No one would have been fool enough to send six hundred charioteers against 2.5 million people—or, for that matter, six hundred thousand people.

the loathsome invasion of frogs. The third plague was of *kinnim*—usually translated as "gnats," but possibly meaning ticks or other annoying insects. Whatever they were, Pharaoh did not budge. But the fourth plague, flies, was worse, bringing all outdoor work to a halt. Pharaoh relented temporarily. He said the Hebrews could go. But when the Lord removed the flies, Pharaoh changed his mind.

More plagues followed: a disease killing the livestock of Egypt but not of the Hebrews. Then both men and beasts were affected by boils. Then came hail—an amazing phenomenon in a land that rarely received rain, much less hail. The hail damaged the crops. And then something worse followed: clouds of locusts, voracious grasshoppers that devoured every plant in sight. Egypt was an amazingly fertile land, but the hail and the locusts made the fertility null. At this point, Pharaoh cracked, admitted he was wrong, and at the command of God a strong west wind drove the locusts out—and Pharaoh changed his mind again.

The ninth plague, total darkness over the land, was a slap at Egypt's mighty sun god, Ra. Pharaoh almost caved in, but did not. Instead he told Moses to leave the court and never come back lest he die. One mighty miracle after another, each showing the powerlessness of Egypt's pathetic gods, had terrified the people but not Pharaoh.

The tenth plague finally broke Pharaoh. All the firstborn died—but not among the Hebrews, for Moses had them mark their doorposts with lamb's blood, and the Lord's angel of death passed over their homes but struck the Egyptians. Moses ordered his people to dress themselves to leave Egypt and eat a meal together to commemorate the night of deliverance. Even today Jews continue to celebrate the event known as Passover.

And so the thousands of Hebrew slaves left Egypt—to the great relief of the Egyptians, who were glad to see them go. The common people of Egypt readily acknowledged what

Pharaoh would not: the Hebrews' God had tremendous power, and the gods of Egypt could do nothing against him.

But of course, Pharaoh changed his mind once more. After a few days had passed, the king realized he could not let so many useful slaves disappear into the desert. So off went his troops on their chariots, finding the Hebrews trapped with their backs to the water. It was not coincidence that the people had encamped by the water, but it was the planning of God, so that he could show the people once and for all that he was in control of things, and that even the feared Egyptian army with its chariots was nothing to fear.

Naturally the Hebrews were horrified to see the chariots approach. Moses had liberated them, only to lead them out into the desert to be cut down by Pharaoh's troops. After all the miracles they had witnessed, the Hebrews' hearts were as hard as Pharaoh's, unwilling to trust in God's power. But another miracle was in store: God parted the waters, and the Hebrews passed through. When the Egyptians tried to pass through, the waters closed in over them.

The story is familiar, of course. Often overlooked is the detail that God drove back the waters with a "strong east wind." Throughout the Bible, the east wind, blowing in off the desert, is always a bad thing—a hot, withering wind that people dread. And yet here it was what saved the Hebrews from destruction. God was clearly not just the Creator but the Controller of all nature.

FACING GOD—AND INGRATES

The Lord said to Moses, "I will rain down bread from heaven for you." (Exodus 16:4)

Israel camped there in the desert in front of the mountain. Then Moses went up to God. (Exodus 19:2–3)

People often remember the stubborn Pharaoh as the villain of the Moses' story. But a closer reading of the story shows that Moses' real enemy was not Pharaoh; it was ingratitude. The Hebrew slaves who had been freed from the world's mightiest nation through the power of God never ceased to grumble. Just a short time after watching Pharaoh's mighty army drown in the sea, the people complained. Yes, they were slaves in Egypt, but they had plenty to eat, and now they were in a wilderness where they would starve.

They did not. Throughout the long years in the wilderness God kept them supplied with a daily ration of manna, the "bread from heaven." Scientists argue over just what this was: perhaps a genuine miracle food that God literally did rain down from heaven—or was it a sweet-tasting secretion, from insects, on desert plants, still found in the Middle East? Whatever it was, it sustained the people for forty years. Lack of water was a continuous problem, for they were in an almost rainless region with few springs or oases, yet God continued to provide the people with water, sometimes from a most unlikely source: rocks. (Some of the porous rocks in the region actually do hold water—in which case the miracle lay in directing the Israelites to the right rocks.) The Hebrew ingrates continued to witness one miracle after another, yet they never ceased to doubt or to grumble, and on more than one occasion they were ready to stone Moses.

As the journey continued, Moses was reunited with his Midianite wife and their children. On greeting his father-in-law, Jethro, Moses bowed down to the ground and kissed him. Having confronted Pharaoh and been the witness to God's might, Moses was humble enough to bow down to his own father-in-law.

But the great humbling experience was to come on Sinai, the mountain where Moses had first encountered God in the burning bush. With the Hebrews camped at the foot of the mountain, Moses went to the top to meet God. There God made an agreement with the people: "If you obey me fully and keep my covenant, then out of all nations you will be my treasured possession. Although the whole earth is mine, you will be for me a kingdom of priests and a holy nation" (Exodus 19:5–6). The Hebrew word *kohen*, "priest," meant someone who had the right of access to the king or to God. The whole nation was a kingdom of priests. This kingdom would abide by the Law that God delivered to Moses on Sinai.

The Sinai episode marks Israel's birth as a spiritual nation. It would be not just a nation as a political unit, but a people bound together by a moral framework. God's covenant with Israel was conditional: If they disobey, they will bring disaster on themselves. Obey and thrive, or disobey and suffer. Much of the Old Testament is the story of how they most often disobeyed.

Exodus chapters 20 through 31 contain some of the laws God gave to Moses, beginning with the famous Ten Commandments, which God himself wrote on stone tablets. Other laws in this section deal with setting up Israel's priesthood, and its first high priest would be Moses' own brother, Aaron. Perhaps the greatest sign of Moses' humility was his willingness to share authority with his brother. Logically, Moses was the Israelites' king, military chieftain and high priest, and certainly he played the role of intercessor for Israel many times. But in the wisdom of God, authority was shared.

Little did Moses know that while he was on Sinai with God, the ungrateful Israelites were running wild at the foot of the mountain. When Moses stayed away, they lost faith in him and coaxed Aaron into making them an idol to worship, the famous golden calf. The story is full of irony: One of the Ten Commandments specifically prohibited making any idols. More ironically, Aaron, the man who would be Israel's first priest, was the maker of a calf idol, symbolic of the pagan fertility gods. (Although most translations have "calf," the Hebrew word here actually means "young bull," which in pagan religion was always a fertility symbol. Worship of such an idol usually resembled an orgy.)

We can only imagine what Moses experienced on the mountain. What was it like to be with God? Whatever it was like, descending the mountain was both a literal and figurative letdown, for Moses saw the people—God's chosen people—running amok and bowing down before a false god. He was angry—and so was God, who let Moses know he was willing to destroy the people and begin anew, making a great nation starting with Moses himself. Certainly it was a tempting proposal. Perhaps it was even a test of Moses' humility. If it was, Moses passed: He begged God to forgive the people—and, not for the last time, God relented in answer to Moses' prayer.

But Moses' own anger had not subsided. He was so furious he broke the stone tablets of the Law. He took the calf idol, ground it into dust and made the people drink it. The message was clear: What kind of god was it that could be smashed, pulverized and poured into drinking water? Alas, the calf idol would not be the last idol the Israelites made for themselves. When would they ever learn that the only true God was the invisible one who delivered them from the Egyptians and gave them food in the wilderness?

Pause for a moment to reflect on the truthfulness of the Bible: One reason that even skeptics think the Exodus story is true is that it is so radically different from other nations' founding epics. The human tendency is to emphasize the grandeur and heroism and glories of the past—but Exodus is no such thing. No other nation proclaimed that

---

CULTURAL INSIGHTS ## The Living God

The Bible often refers to God as "the living God." This image lies behind the Second of the Ten Commandments: "You shall not make for yourself an idol in the form of anything in heaven above or on the earth beneath or in the waters below." (Exodus 20:4) The key idea here is that God is beyond and above anything that human beings can see with their eyes. The ban on images was a constant reminder that God was not "like" anything in the universe. One reason the Bible often refers to God as "the living God" is to contrast him with the "dead" gods, the lifeless idols.

Some might see an inconsistency in having no visual images of God, yet constantly speaking of God's eyes, ears, hands, mouth, feet, etc. Apparently in revealing himself to mankind, God understands that people could only imagine a personal God as being in some way like themselves. There was no likelihood of their entering into a personal relationship with an abstract God—a "force." The God who communed with Moses face-to-face was most definitely a Person, a Being with mind, heart and personality—Someone so great that no visual image could do him justice.

it had originated as a race of slaves, and certainly no other nation would have admitted to requiring forty years to get from one locale to another. The Israelites are fickle and ungrateful, and the true hero in the story is God. While Moses is on the mountain receiving the handwritten words of God, the people are at the foot of the mountain staging a pagan orgy.

The Lord ordered Moses to set up a tent of meeting, a place inside the Israelite encampment that symbolized God's presence. Moses would enter the tent to commune with God. "The Lord would speak to Moses face to face, as a man speaks with his friend" (Exodus 33:11). Indeed, the Lord told Moses, "I know you by name and you have found favor with me." How had he found favor with God? Moses possessed one of the great God-pleasing qualities: humility. Throughout both Old and New Testaments, pride is condemned and humility praised. Moses had been raised as a prince in Egypt, yet he identified with his ancestors and kin, who were mere slaves, and he knew firsthand what it was like to sweat at hard labor. Tending his father-in-law's flocks in the wilderness, he must have had much time to think, to reflect on the creature comforts he had known in Egypt, to see how unimportant they were. And then there were the ungrateful Israelites themselves—if he had any tendency to become egotistical, these unruly ingrates would cut him down to size quickly enough.

Moses the humble was privileged to speak face-to-face with God as a friend. Moses made a request: "Now show me your glory." God gave him what he asked, in his own way: "I will cause all my goodness to pass in front of you, and I will proclaim my name, the Lord, in your presence. But you cannot see my face, for no one may see me and live" (Exodus 33:18–20). What, in fact, did Moses see or experience? The passage goes on to say that Moses saw the "back" of God, though not his face. Perhaps the meaning is that God is something far too amazing for the human mind to take in completely. Yet Moses saw more of God than any other man in the Old Testament.

At times his closeness to God made him literally glow. According to Exodus 34, "when Moses came down from Mount Sinai with the two tablets of the Testimony in

his hands, he was not aware that his face was radiant because he had spoken with the Lord." The Israelites, even his own brother, Aaron, were afraid—understandably so—and so Moses put a veil over his face. Again, this is Moses the humble. We can easily imagine a vain man parading around the camp, eager to impress the Israelites with this evidence of his closeness to God. But a vain man like that would not have been God's choice to lead the Israelites.

Perhaps the reason Moses glowed is that he saw what should have been obvious to all the other Israelites: They had a gracious, loving and powerful God looking after them. What more could they ask for? Several times in the Moses saga, and later in the Old Testament, God is referred to as "the Lord, the Lord, the compassionate and gracious God, slow to anger, abounding in love and faithfulness, maintaining love to thousands, and forgiving wickedness, rebellion and sin" (Exodus 34:6–7). Moses had no doubts that this was what God was like. He saw God clearly, while the Israelites were blinded by their doubts and complaints—by the recurring wish that they could return to Egypt, preferring the security and stability of slavery to freedom and the privilege of being God's people.

REBELLIONS AND RELEASE

> Remember this and never forget how you provoked the Lord your God to anger in the desert. From the day you left Egypt until you arrived here, you have been rebellious against the Lord. (Deuteronomy 9:7)

> Since then, no prophet has risen in Israel like Moses, whom the Lord knew face to face . . . No one has ever shown the mighty power or performed the awesome deeds that Moses did in the sight of all Israel. (Deuteronomy 34:12)

What Moses endured from the Israelites is, in a sense, part of the story of the human race: ingratitude to God. In fact, it is a kind of extended version of Genesis 3, in which Adam and Eve rebel against God, not satisfied with what he has given them.

Moses had to endure rebellion from within his own family. Aaron, his older brother, who had stood by him when he confronted Egypt's Pharaoh, was the man who made the golden calf for the Israelites—and, when Moses confronted him over it, made the flimsy excuse that the gold he melted down just happened to come out in the form of a calf idol (Exodus 32:24). After that, Aaron was more reliable—but not always. At one point both Aaron and Miriam began to complain: "Has the Lord spoken only through Moses? . . . Hasn't he also spoken through us?" The answer to those questions is: no. God spoke only through Moses, and the two seemed to have gotten swollen heads, being close kin to a great leader. Clearly there was great danger in having Moses' leadership questioned by members of his own family. Miriam was punished with leprosy. Moses, as always the compassionate intercessor, prayed that the Lord would heal her, and the Lord assured Moses the leprosy was only temporary.

More dangerous rebellions sprang up. A man named Korah led one, while Dathan and Abiram led another, both groups questioning Moses' fitness to rule over the people. God showed his approval of Moses by destroying both groups of rebels.

But the worst rebellion of all is the one that resulted in the Israelites spending forty years in the wilderness. Let's pause here to note a geographical fact: The distance from Egypt to Canaan, the Israelites' destination, is not far. Granted, a huge group of people traveling on foot in a desert cannot make good time. But *forty years*? This long period was not a matter of slowness but a matter of lack of faith. As they came close to Canaan—the Promised Land—Moses sent scouts out to the land they were about to enter. The scouts, as recorded in Numbers 13, were impressed with the fertility of the land. It was, as God had told them, a land of "milk and honey." But it was also full of fortified cities, and the people of the land were huge—compared to them, the Israelites were "grasshoppers." So the Israelites lost heart. Though one of the scouts, Caleb, assured them they could enter Canaan and conquer it—after all, wasn't God on their side?—the other scouts insisted they could not triumph over the "giants" who lived there.

So the familiar grumbling began again. Why hadn't they died in Egypt, or in the wilderness? Wouldn't it be better to choose a new leader and head back to Egypt? Their complaints angered God, who threatened to strike them with a plague. But again Moses interceded. And again God relented—but not totally. These grumbling doubters, who had witnessed the plagues in Egypt, the parting of the sea, and the provision of food and water in the wilderness, would never enter the land they had been promised. Only the two faithful and optimistic scouts, Caleb and Joshua, would enter. And so a journey from Egypt to Canaan turned into forty years.

And what about Moses himself? One of the saddest parts of the Moses saga is that the great man himself did not enter Canaan. According to Numbers 20, God ordered Moses to speak to a rock, which would bring forth water for the thirsty people. Moses did not speak to the rock but struck it—though it gave water anyway. But God told Moses that because he had not obeyed him fully in the matter, he would not enter Canaan.

> **DID YOU KNOW?**
>
> The mountain from which Moses viewed Canaan is called both Mount Nebo and Pisgah. Both are popular names for churches, especially in the South.

Poor Moses! In this episode, we are tempted to think God was unfair to this great and humble man, the man called the "servant" of God so many times in the Bible. After all he had been through, did he not deserve to complete his great assignment on earth, and lead the people to their destination?

The Bible does not answer all our questions. It does tell us that Moses did at least see the land of Canaan. Looking down from Mount Nebo, Moses got a panoramic view of the land God had promised to Israel. Moses then died, at the age of a hundred and twenty, and was buried—by God himself, so that no one ever knew where his grave was. The Israelites mourned for their leader for thirty days. The fact that his gravesite is unknown is a good thing: Instead of honoring the location, future generations would honor his memory.

We may well mourn for Moses ourselves, since his story does not seem to end happily and is not wrapped up in the way a good fiction writer would end a story. This is one of the many indications that the Bible is giving us history, not legend, for a fiction writer would have given Moses a more satisfying end. But in fact, Moses had a more satisfying life than any of the Israelites who would go on to enter Canaan. Moses was, for most of his life, a homeless man—run out of Egypt, separated from his in-laws in Midian, wandering through a desolate wilderness for forty years. And yet, far more than any of the Israelites, he was often face-to-face with God—a friend, and a far more reliable one than any of the Israelites, including his own brother and sister. The years in the wilderness had been no picnic, from a material point of view. Spiritually, they were incredible, though the ungrateful complainers did not realize it. A ragtag band of ex-slaves had been called to be God's people, handed down a law code from God himself, led by a man who was not a power-hungry egotist but a humble man of God.

In Hebrews 11, the great chapter known as the Faith Hall of Fame, Moses is praised because, among other things, "when he had grown up, refused to be known as the son of Pharaoh's daughter" (Hebrews 11:24). Though he was born the son of slaves, he was raised a child of comfort and privilege—and he chose to side with the poor and oppressed instead of with wealth and power. Had he kept his place in the Egyptian court, he would have lived in splendor, died attended by numerous slaves, and been mummified and buried in a magnificent tomb—and probably forgotten. Siding with slaves—and with God—he has never been forgotten. The great man is referred to thirty-five times in the Bible as the "servant" of God. Israel's greatest leader was a servant. Perhaps Jesus had Moses in mind when he told his disciples, "whoever wants to become great among you must be your servant" (Matthew 20:26).

PUTTING THE WORD TO WORK

1. What do you make of Moses' "holy ground" episode on Mount Sinai? Can you recall times in your own life when you felt God's presence in a unique way?

2. Like many great leaders of the Bible, Moses initially resisted the call of God. Try to think of people you have known who were reluctant leaders. How do they compare with ambitious people who eagerly seek power and recognition?

3. Try to imagine yourself in Moses' place as he came down the mountain and found the people worshipping the calf idol. Can you see yourself doing as he did, asking God to show mercy on the people?

4. The Israelites, freed from slavery by God's miracles, were constantly tempted to return to Egypt. What were times in your own life when you felt yourself moving on to greater spiritual freedom but tempted to fall back into your former condition?

5. How do you react to Moses being denied entry to the Promised Land? Does it seem unfair of God? Or had Moses already "arrived," spiritually speaking, in living in such closeness to God?

Traitors, High and Low

One of the great tragedies in any life is to be betrayed, to find that someone we believed to be on our side is in fact our enemy. And one of the great themes of the New Testament is that God himself, walking the earth as Jesus of Nazareth, experienced just that, learning that his religion's highest officials—and, worse, one of his own friends—were traitors.

MEMORY VERSE

You killed the author of life, but God raised him from the dead.—Acts 3:15

This is a "villain chapter," but along the way we will get a look at two fainthearted admirers of Jesus who, in the end, turned out to be more heroic than villainous.

KEY TERM FOR TODAY ## Traitor

Jesus was the victim of the treachery of one of his own disciples and of the religious leaders of his people.

ROME'S PRIESTS

Caiaphas, who was high priest that year, spoke up, "You know nothing at all! You do not realize that it is better for you that one man die for the people than that the whole nation perish." (John 11:49–50)

The Jewish priests of the Bible are a mixed bag—some decent and saintly men, but many materialistic and corrupt ones as well. In the New Testament, all the priests with the exception of John the Baptist's father, Zechariah, are a sorry lot, unspiritual men going through the motions of rituals. In the case of the chief priests of Jerusalem, they grew wealthy and powerful from their position, which they were determined to hold on to at any cost, even if it meant executing a traveling prophet from Nazareth.

Jesus had no illusions about the priests. He watched devout people come from far and wide to make contributions to the temple, and he knew those contributions allowed the priests to live lives of luxury. He also knew the history of the family that controlled the priesthood.

From 66 BC, when the Romans were in control of the region, the high priests were appointed and removed by the Romans, and clearly they were not going to appoint anyone who was not an eager supporter of Roman policy. The Romans insisted on having a priest who would try to stamp out any anti-Roman rebellions. Any prophet, rebel or would-be Messiah would have to be disposed of, with the approval and collaboration of the Jews' highest religious official. The high priestly robes were not kept in the temple precincts but in the Romans' Antonia Fortress. The high priest could not dress for the right occasions without the Romans' permission.

From AD 6 to 15 the high priest was Annas, who was as pro-Roman as could be. However, the Roman governor Gratus, Pilate's predecessor, was such a greedy man that he decided to increase his wealth by auctioning off the high priesthood to the highest bidder. So in a very short time, there were five high priests—Annas was deposed, followed by three others who were deposed (including one of his sons), and then his son-in-law Caiaphas. In Jewish eyes a high priest served for life, so even though Annas was removed from office by the Romans, many Jews seemed to regard him as the *real* high priest. At the time Jesus and his disciples entered Jerusalem for the Passover celebration, the high priest was technically Caiaphas, Annas' son-in-law, but as we see in the Gospels, Caiaphas deferred to his father-in-law, the power behind the throne.

Caiaphas held office from AD 18 to 36, meaning he was already in office when Pilate became governor in 26. Unlike his predecessor, Pilate never felt the need to remove the high priest from office, which tells us he felt very comfortable with Caiaphas, a reliably pro-Roman man. With members of the Herod family as political puppets, and pliable allies like Caiaphas controlling the priesthood, the Romans had Judea well in hand.

When Jesus and his disciples entered Jerusalem on the day we now call Palm Sunday, he had already warned them what would occur: The chief priests would have him put to death. Despite this gloomy prophecy, he entered the city triumphantly, with admirers and well-wishers laying down palm branches in his path and shouting, "Hosanna to the Son of David." The priests, so the Gospels tell us, were "indignant" at this. Though they lived in luxury and looked down on the common people, they were jealous of any star the people admired, and they were eager to paint any such person as a potential troublemaker.

All the Gospels record the event called the "cleansing of the temple." To understand that event, a little background on Jewish customs is in order. Jewish pilgrims to Jerusalem at Passover time had to pay the annual half-shekel temple tax, and it could not be paid in foreign coins. So money changers set up stalls in Jerusalem,

DID YOU KNOW?

The Gospels have been accused of deliberately making the Jewish priests look bad, but in fact Jewish writers then and later agree that Caiaphas and his family were utterly worldly and corrupt.

exchanging non-Palestinian coins for local ones and, of course, making a commission on each exchange. Also, visitors needed the local coins for purchasing sacrificial animals. Pilgrims could bring their own sacrifices with them, but most people ended up buying from the approved livestock sold in the temple courts. Price gouging for the sacrifices was typical, and the poor were affected most. Some of the more pious Jews pressured the money changers to keep costs down, since the poor could hardly afford it.

The family of Annas, according to Jewish chroniclers, benefited from all the selling. In fact, the animal market was referred to as "the bazaar of the sons of Annas." When Jesus entered the temple area and began overturning the money changers' tables, Annas and Caiaphas would not have taken Jesus' action there lightly. It may be that the reason no one intervened in Jesus' action was that the priests knew that the people detested their price gouging and would have approved Jesus' action. The priests could not have been pleased that Jesus spoke out against the "den of thieves," for Annas and his family were the chief thieves.

John 11 records a meeting of the Sanhedrin, the Jews' ruling council. The priests and other leaders were disturbed: Jesus had a reputation for performing miracles, and the people loved him. "If we let him go on like this, everyone will believe in him, and then the Romans will come and take away both our place and our nation" (John 11:48). Note the repetition of *our*. These selfish, decadent men had no concern whatever for the people at large, and it meant nothing to them that Jesus had healed people of their diseases and cast out demons. The priests thought of the magnificent Jerusalem temple as "our" temple—not God's temple, not the Jews' temple, but their family property, their source of income and prestige.

Caiaphas, presiding over the Sanhedrin, put the matter bluntly: Jesus had to die. Better that one man perish than the whole nation. He wasn't being completely honest: He had no concern for the nation except that its people were his source of income.

Without meaning to, Caiaphas spoke a profound truth: Jesus would indeed "die for the people," but not in the way the priest would have understood.

In the following days, with Jerusalem packed with Passover visitors, Jesus taught the people many things, and the priests and other leaders sensed Jesus was directing his parables at them. But how would they get rid of him, a popular figure, since arresting him openly might instigate a riot?

Enter the arch-traitor of history, one of Jesus' own band of disciples, Judas Iscariot. Just as the priests were willing to sell out their people and their religion to the Romans, Judas was willing to sell out his Master.

THE MYSTERIOUS MOTIVE

> Jesus replied, "Have I not chosen you, the Twelve? Yet one of you is a devil!" (John 6:70)

> Jesus asked him, "Judas, are you betraying the Son of Man with a kiss?" (Luke 22:48)

The Bible does not explain Judas Iscariot—much to our frustration. It does tell us that Satan "entered into" Judas, and in John 6, Jesus says Judas "is" a devil—meaning his horrible deed is attributed to the power of darkness. Yet Jesus also says that he "chose" Judas—and would he have chosen a man he knew was certain to be a traitor?

The Gospels tell us almost nothing about Judas, up to the final week in Jerusalem. One incident that is very revealing of his character is the anointing at Bethany, covered in Day 4. To summarize that event, Mary, the sister of Lazarus, anointed Jesus' feet with costly perfume, and Judas sneered that this was an extravagant "waste," given that the price of the perfume would have been better used to aid the poor. But, "he did not say this because he cared about the poor but because he was a thief; as keeper of the money bag, he used to help himself to what was put into it" (John 12:6).

Had he done this from the very beginning? Surely not. Since he was entrusted with the money, he must have been trustworthy and scrupulous—at first. Although it may be risky to try to read the mind of a man who lived two thousand years ago, here are some tentative suggestions about the traitor: Judas seems to have been an ambitious character, and the line between ambition and covetousness is thin. Probably Judas expected the Jewish Messiah of popular belief and hoped to share in his reign—as, clearly, did James and John and the others, though Judas more so than the rest. Jesus' awareness of this misplaced ambition in his close followers was a severe test of his patience. Judas and the others may have hoped for some vengeance when John the Baptist was beheaded, and perhaps his disappointment began that early. Likewise he may have been grieved at Jesus not responding to the Pharisees' demand for a sign, and at Jesus' occasional withdrawing to avoid danger. No doubt the worst disappointment at all was the growing number of references to his own death and shame. Judas had expected to sign on with a winner, and he was convinced Jesus was a loser. He revealed his true colors when Mary anointed Jesus with the expensive perfume, and Judas, posing as a friend of the poor, had protested against the waste.

Mired in disappointment and stinging from the scolding Jesus gave him over the anointing, Judas undoubtedly came to hate Jesus, and the wisest course would have been to simply abandon his master and return home. Instead he continued in his office of treasurer, lining his own pockets, not so much out of greed as out of spite, and then looking for an opportunity to destroy the man who had so utterly disappointed him—destroy him, or finally force him to be the Messiah he had hoped for.

Remember that early in the story of Jesus, Satan tempted him to take on the dominion of all the kingdoms of the world. The temptation of political power was the temptation to be the kind of Messiah that so many Jews expected—including his own disciples. Immediately after Peter was praised for declaring Jesus is "the Christ, the Son of the living God," Peter then made it clear he wouldn't hear of Jesus suffering and dying—and Jesus responded harshly by referring to him as "Satan." The old temptation was back: be the power-wielding political Messiah, not the suffering Messiah that was in the divine plan. When we are told that "Satan entered into Judas Iscariot" (Luke 22:3), we can probably assume that Judas had the same idea that Peter had: Jesus was the political Messiah they all expected, and at this point Judas was either highly disappointed, or he hoped that by staging a confrontation with the priests and Romans, Jesus would be forced to out himself as the Messiah. If Jesus was that kind of Messiah, good, and if not, he deserved to die for misleading his disciples—so Judas may have reasoned, and possibly the other disciples also.

Conveniently, Judas Iscariot, one of the twelve men on earth closest to Jesus, came to hate him at the same time as the Jewish leaders did. So Judas presented himself and solved their problem, also giving them the hope that Jesus' own disciples were forsaking him. If Judas expected to be honored by them for his service, he was disappointed there also, for the priests treated him as a common informer and a contemptible traitor, which he was. They would have seen it as beneath their dignity to show too high regard for

---

CULTURAL INSIGHTS

Iscariot

Both Judas and his father, Simon, are referred to as "Iscariot." Most commentators think this meant they were from a village named Kerioth, but in fact no one is sure that a Kerioth even existed. There are other possibilities. One connects the name with the Sicarii, the Jewish terrorists who stealthily assassinated Romans or pro-Roman Jews. Since Judas' father was also Iscariot, that would mean Judas was a second-generation terrorist, someone who had been reared in anti-Roman sentiment and eagerly hoped for a Messiah to boot out the Romans.

But another possibility connects the name Iscariot with the old tradition of Judas being shown as a redhead. It is possible Iscariot is derived from the Aramaic words *sakray, sekara* and *iskara*, referring to someone with a ruddy complexion. Since another of Jesus' disciples was named Judas, it is conceivable that Judas Iscariot meant "the redheaded Judas."

Giving a Common Name a Bad Name

Judas was a common name in the New Testament period, and there were five men in the Bible named Judas besides the notorious Iscariot: one of Jesus' brothers (Matthew 13:55); one of the twelve disciples, designated "son of James" (Luke 6:16, John 14:22); a Galilean rebel (Acts 5:37); the owner of the house where Paul stayed (Acts 9:11); and a prophet also called Barsabbas (Acts 15:22). Judas was the Greek form of the Hebrew name Judah, the name of one of Jacob's twelve sons.

The brief Letter of Jude in the New Testament was probably written by Jesus' brother Judas. For obvious reasons it became a custom to refer to him as Jude, not Judas. Likewise the disciple/apostle Judas—the good one—also came to be referred to as Jude, famously known in Catholic circles as St. Jude.

such a man. The thirty pieces of silver—the price of a slave—showed contempt for both the betrayer and the betrayed. It is also possible, in the twisted minds of the priests, that in their view they were literally buying a slave—someone less than human—to hand over for killing. The fact that Jesus was "bought" by money for the temple treasury is ironic, for this was money used to purchase sacrifices. So the priests saw him, from the economic standpoint, not as the Son of God or even as a human being but as a lowly slave—or even lower, as an ox or lamb destined to be slaughtered.

And so Judas watched for an opportunity to betray the man he supposedly loved and admired. What did Jesus know of his schemes? In Luke's Gospel, Jesus sends Peter and John to make the arrangements for the supper. Jesus clearly knew already of Judas' plotting, and by keeping arrangements out of his hands, and out of his hearing as well, he ensured that Judas would not interrupt the Last Supper with a band of armed men.

At the Supper, Jesus pronounced a "woe" on the traitor—better that that man had never been born! The "woe" was both a prophecy and a final warning—Judas still could have changed his mind and not gone through with the betrayal. But he did so, leaving the Supper, and the other disciples were so clueless about his character that none of them suspected he was the traitor Jesus spoke of. Was this a matter of their own dullness—or would we be correct in assuming that Judas had turned into such a skilled hypocrite that only Jesus could read his emotions?

Judas probably led the group of soldiers first to the house where the Supper had been held, but Jesus and the disciples were already gone. He knew Jesus had gone often to the garden of Gethsemane to pray. In leading the group there, Judas would have been out front, so as to give the illusion that he came to warn Jesus and the other disciples of the pending arrest.

"Going at once to Jesus, Judas said, 'Greetings, Rabbi!' and kissed him" (Matthew 26:49). Some of the other disciples had called Jesus "Lord," but Jesus was clearly not Judas' Lord, only a rabbi. Jesus greets Judas as "friend"—not the usual Greek word *philos*, but *hetairos*, meaning "close companion" or "comrade." The traitor was more than just a casual friend. Six times the Gospels identify Judas as "one of the Twelve," emphasizing that he was one of the men closest to Jesus. The deepest cut is not from some distant enemy but from one's dear companion. Judas must have loved and admired Jesus in the past. What went through his mind, and the mind of Jesus, when he planted his hypocritical kiss upon the cheek of his master?

WHO IS ON TRIAL?

When Jesus said this, one of the officials nearby struck him in the face. "Is this the way you answer the high priest?" he demanded. (John 18:22)

They spit in his face and struck him with their fists. (Matthew 26:67)

As already stated, Caiaphas was high priest the entire time Pilate was Roman governor, so the two had a cozy arrangement worked out. When Pilate went to bed that night, he would no doubt have known something was afoot, and that he might be expected to judge a case the following morning. He probably did not lose any sleep over the matter, because at Passover season he had about five hundred Roman soldiers in the city, living in the Antonia Fortress. The priests had their temple police, but these were probably unarmed and untrained, and the group that arrested Jesus in Gethsemane must have included some of Pilate's troops. In fact, John 18:12 says the leader of the band was a chiliarch, one of six officers attached to each Roman legion.

The members of the Sanhedrin were probably not awakened out of a sound sleep but rather were prepared for the possible arrest of Jesus that night, given the deal made with Judas. No doubt some of them, certainly Caiaphas, were looking forward to calling Jesus on the carpet, away from his disciples and the crowd.

DID YOU KNOW?

Caiaphas and Annas appear in one of the world's greatest poems, Dante's *Divine Comedy*. In the Inferno (hell), the two are crucified naked on the ground, while the other condemned hypocrites, wearing cloaks of lead, walk over them for eternity.

One important detail that John supplies is that Jesus was taken to Annas before meeting with Caiaphas and the Sanhedrin. As we already noted, Annas had lost his post as high priest, but most Jews still regarded him as the elder statesman in Jerusalem, and he probably had as much, or more, clout than his son-in-law, Caiaphas. Annas wanted to know about Jesus' disciples and teachings. Jesus replied that he had nothing to hide—he had taught openly. The priest could ask the public, for people knew Jesus' teachings. At this point one of them struck Jesus in the face for such "insolence." Jesus responded, "If I spoke the truth, why did you strike me?" (John 18:23).

Annas sent Jesus along to Caiaphas and the Sanhedrin. "The chief priests and the whole Sanhedrin were looking for false evidence against Jesus so that they could put him to death" (Matthew 26:59). Pause here to consider that Caiaphas' actual name was Joseph. We can imagine what went through Jesus' mind when standing before him. During his childhood, Jesus had stood in a relationship of affection and respect with a righteous man named Joseph. Here was the closest thing the Jews had to an earthly spiritual father, the high priest. He was no father to Jesus, but at this moment his mortal enemy.

False witnesses came forward, and the lie that got the council's attention was that Jesus had supposedly said he would destroy the temple—and rebuild it in three days. Caiaphas asked Jesus if this was so. Jesus remained silent. The high priest became more insistent: The high priest said to him, "I charge you under oath by the living God: Tell us if you are the Christ, the Son of God" (Matthew 26:63).

After months of playing down his identity and telling his disciples not to tell people he was the Messiah, Jesus finally spoke the open truth: "Yes, it is as you say . . . But I say to all of you: In the future you will see the Son of Man sitting at the right hand of the Mighty One and coming on the clouds of heaven" (Matthew 26:64).

For Caiaphas, this was enough: Jesus had uttered "blasphemy." Technically, he had not: Claiming to be the Christ, the Messiah, was not blasphemy—if he really *was* the Messiah, that is. As a symbol of his horror and disgust, Caiaphas tore his priestly robe.

CULTURAL INSIGHTS

Kangaroo Court?

Some historians doubt the Gospels' account of Jesus' trial before the Sanhedrin because, they say, it does not conform to the normal way the council heard cases. This is true—but in fact, the Gospels are not reporting a formal trial, but an informal gathering at Caiaphas' house. Technically the Sanhedrin was not supposed to meet at night, nor on Sabbaths or holy days, or their eves, nor could it convene—officially— anywhere except the Sanhedrin chamber in the temple. Technically, the group at Caiaphas' house did not pronounce the death sentence but only that he was "worthy of death." When the Gospels say that "all the Council" condemned Jesus, it doesn't literally mean all seventy-one members but that those who were present definitely expressed the general will of the Sanhedrin, for it had been determined days before that Jesus had to die. Joseph of Arimathea, secretly an admirer of Jesus, was one council member who did not approve of the others' action.

The council members pronounced that Jesus was "worthy of death." At this point, these dignified men, the highest-ranking officials in the Jewish religion, began acting like barbarians—or children: "They spit in his face and struck him with their fists" (Matthew 26:67).

A trial is supposed to reveal the truth. This one certainly did. The man from Nazareth was an innocent, harmless man. The priest and his minions were the scum of the earth, with no sense of justice or compassion. They could not even conduct themselves as dignified adults.

LET THE ROMANS DO IT

Pilate announced to the chief priests and the crowd, "I find no basis for a charge against this man." . . . The chief priests and the teachers of the law were standing there, vehemently accusing him. (Luke 23:4,10)

They shouted, "Take him away! Take him away! Crucify him!" "Shall I crucify your king?" Pilate asked. "We have no king but Caesar," the chief priests answered. (John 19:15)

For Israel there was never any clear line between the religious and the political. The priests envied Jesus' popularity with the people and saw him as a blasphemer, but they may have genuinely believed that he was holding back himself and his followers, pretending to be peaceful and waiting for the Romans to let their guard down. Jesus' one act of violence—driving out the money changers—was directed against the temple itself. Obviously this was not a man the priests could tolerate. Also, the priests would have known of the incident of Peter cutting off the ear of Malchus, the high priest's servant. When they handed Jesus over to Pilate, they may have genuinely believed he was a violent threat.

Pilate certainly knew better. Not a Jew himself, he took a more objective view of things, and his worldly wisdom, his street smarts, made him aware that these priests were all abuzz over nothing, jealous of a wandering teacher who was no real threat to anyone.

Pilate must have seen some humor in these proceedings. These Jewish leaders, who supposedly represented a religion of high moral standards, were trying to get him to execute an innocent carpenter—yet they were so fussy about their religious rules that they would not set foot in Pilate's headquarters, the praetorium, at Passover time because it would render them unclean. Weren't their priorities a bit odd?

Yet the cynical, worldly Pilate had his weak points, and Caiaphas certainly knew them. He knew presenting Jesus as a false Messiah would not get Pilate's attention. So he had to present Jesus as a political threat to Rome. Caiaphas would have been well aware that Pilate's political mentor, Sejanus, had either fallen from power already or was under suspicion as a traitor. From the priest's point of view, the timing was superb, for Pilate was not going to let it be thought he was not totally loyal to Rome. The priests wanted Pilate to think that Jesus' statements about destroying the temple might lead fanatical followers to become violent. And if Pilate did not aid them in destroying this potential troublemaker, then Pilate was "no friend of Caesar."

One loophole Pilate tried to exploit was the custom of the governor releasing a Jewish prisoner at Passover time. One prisoner who really was a troublemaker and a threat to Rome was Barabbas, one of the Zealots who had committed a murder and tried to start an insurrection. The Gospels refer to Barabbas with the Greek word *lestes*, usually translated "robber," but "marauder" or "terrorist" would be more accurate. These men waged small-scale guerrilla war on Roman soldiers and officials, or sometimes on whoever happened to be passing by. Mark's Gospel refers to Barabbas as *stasiastes*, a rioter, which could refer to any kind of troublemaker or rebel. The Gospels give no indication whether Barabbas had been tried yet or found guilty. He was clearly just the sort of man that a Roman official like Pilate would want to get rid of, and the sooner the better. Perhaps there was no sure evidence he was guilty, otherwise Pilate would not have even considered releasing him. But whatever his legal status, he was the darling of the crowd on this occasion—a violent criminal released while an innocent man was condemned. A few days earlier, crowds had shouted approvingly as Jesus entered the city—now they shouted to have him die. The city had welcomed him in and was now expelling him.

It is interesting that the priests' original plan was to get rid of Jesus as quietly as possible, but once the crowd was part of the drama, they were willing to shift tactics and use the crowd. Noted for their contempt for the mob, the priests were only too willing to use it.

In one of his sermons in Acts, Peter had some harsh words for the people of Jerusalem: "You disowned the Holy and Righteous One and asked that a murderer be released to you. You killed the author of life, but God raised him from the dead" (Acts 3:14–15). They released a murderer and murdered an innocent man—two crimes. They killed the author of life. So much for human justice. And so much for the holiness of the priests, who had engineered the murder of the Holy and Righteous One that God sent.

"Give us Barabbas!"—these are some of the most disturbing words in the Gospels. Equally disturbing: "We have no king but Caesar!" With those words, the Jerusalem priests had committed blasphemy, for no true Jew acknowledged any king but God. The priests were traitors to both their religion and their nation.

Condemned as a blasphemer, Jesus should have been stoned to death, as stipulated in the Law of Moses. The priests were pleased to hand over Jesus to the Romans, for crucifixion was considered an even more degrading punishment than stoning. Also, by having the Romans do the dirty work, the priests were trying to shift the responsibility. They knew Jesus had many admirers, and they assumed those admirers would blame the Romans for getting rid of Jesus.

Once Pilate condemned Jesus, the priests do not vanish from the story. Dying on the cross, Jesus had to endure their mockery: "He saved others, he cannot save himself." As far as they were concerned, his death settled the matter: The false "Son of God" had clearly been abandoned by God.

But things were not quite settled. They remembered that the impostor had spoken of coming back from the dead. So they convinced Pilate to give them some soldiers to guard the tomb, knowing the disciples would not dare try to steal the body with Roman soldiers present.

God had other plans. Come Sunday morning, the tomb was empty, and the frightened guards knew it was not the disciples who had done the deed. They reported what happened to the priests, who bribed them to spread the story that the disciples came and stole the body while the guards were asleep. The bribe to the soldiers means that a miracle has obviously occurred but the priests would not believe it. They had "hardened their hearts" the way Pharaoh did—no miracle, no matter how great, will convince the spiritually blind person.

In concluding this section, let's consider the brief interchange between Jesus and Pilate. The governor made it clear to Jesus that he had the power to release him. But Jesus answered, "You would have no power over me if it were not given to you from above. Therefore the one who handed me over to you is guilty of a greater sin" (John 19:11). Some think he was referring to Judas, but in fact he was referring to Caiaphas, the high

CHARACTERS AT LARGE Barabbas on Film

In several movies about Jesus, Barabbas appears as a character, not just in the scenes involving Jesus' trial, but earlier, where Barabbas is shown as a Zealot, with his way of violence and revolution contrasted with Jesus' way of peace and forgiveness of enemies. Barabbas as a Zealot is prominent in the 1961 movie *King of Kings* and the popular 1977 TV mini-series *Jesus of Nazareth*.

Barabbas was the title of a 1962 movie starring Anthony Quinn as the violent, callous man who, after his release, becomes a gladiator and, later, a Christian, dying on a cross. Interestingly, in *Jesus of Nazareth*, Quinn played the role of Caiaphas.

priest. Pilate, Judas, so many others—all had behaved disgracefully. But it was the highest official in the religion who had done worst. Instead of welcoming his religion's Messiah, he condemned him.

And what about Judas? The other villain in the story had done something Caiaphas did not do: suffered remorse. Having seen Jesus condemned, Judas had a change of heart. He was "seized with remorse," having betrayed "innocent blood." He returned the money to the callous priests, who had no interest in Judas' change. "What is that to us?" they said. Perhaps he was hoping the priests would grant him absolution, thanking him for turning over a false Messiah and blasphemer, thus putting his mind at rest. But what did the priests care about the stricken conscience of some weasel turncoat?

Unlike Peter, who had denied Jesus, wept bitterly and then become a faithful follower again, Judas could not live with his conscience. He threw the money into the temple and hanged himself. True to form, the legalistic priests would not put this blood money back into the temple treasury, so they used it to buy a burial ground for foreigners.

TWO, LATE

Even after Jesus had done all these miraculous signs in their presence, they still would not believe in him. . . . Yet at the same time many even among the leaders believed in him. But because of the Pharisees they would not confess their faith for fear they would be put out of the synagogue; they loved praise from men more than praise from God. (John 12:37, 42–43)

Joseph of Arimathea asked Pilate for the body of Jesus. Now Joseph was a disciple of Jesus, but secretly because he feared the Jews. With Pilate's permission, he came and took the body away. (John 19:38)

John's Gospel reminds us that not all the establishment Jews condemned Jesus. A handful were on his side—though peer pressure kept them from taking his side openly.

Two of these were Nicodemus and Joseph of Arimathea. You remember that Nicodemus appears in John 3, the famous "born again" chapter in which the respected Nicodemus visits Jesus at night. He admires Jesus and regards him as a teacher sent from God—and yet he visits him under cover of dark, not wanting his friends in the Jewish establishment to know he is too cozy with the controversial teacher from Nazareth. Jesus told him that "you must be born again"—each person, even a respected leader among the Jews, had to start off fresh with God, experiencing a spiritual rebirth.

Nicodemus appears later in John, when the Jewish leaders are discussing the fact that the mob may be fond of Jesus, but none of the Jewish leaders are. Nicodemus raises a feeble defense of Jesus: "Does our law condemn anyone without first hearing him to find out what he is doing?" (John 7:51). He is not willing to take Jesus' side openly—yet.

All four Gospels speak of Joseph of Arimathea, a rich Jew who was a "good and upright man" but also a member of the Sanhedrin. He was a disciple of Jesus—but secretly, "because he feared the Jews." Peer pressure had held both him and Nicodemus back while Jesus was alive. Where were they during his trial, and why hadn't they spoken up for him sooner? It is tempting to judge the men harshly—until we recall that all of Jesus' disciples had fled when he was arrested. In a sense, every disciple, not just Judas, had betrayed Jesus.

But we have to applaud Joseph for what happened afterward. With Jesus dead, it would have been easier—and wiser—never to admit to anyone that he had believed in Jesus. But he took a bold step: He went to Pilate and asked to have Jesus' body, to give it a proper burial in his own tomb. Obviously this act would become known to the Sanhedrin members, who would have been horrified that Joseph would give an honorable burial to a condemned blasphemer. No doubt at this point Joseph was utterly disgusted with the Sanhedrin, particularly Caiaphas, who had proved himself an utterly unworthy high priest, unfit to enter the temple's most holy place.

CULTURAL INSIGHTS

Joseph's "New" Tomb

John 19:41 says this was a new tomb, meaning no one had been buried in it before. While this sounds strange to us, it was not unusual in ancient times to open up old tombs, gather up the bones and place them in a stone "bone box," and thus free up tomb space for new burials. But this tomb had never been used before, a significant detail for two reasons. One is that no human being had ever been buried in it—the burial place of the Son of God, the Messiah, was his alone. The other reason the newness of the tomb is important is that it would contain no other bodies or bones, so that when it was found empty the following Sunday, there was no chance of possibly confusing it with some other tomb nearby.

The tomb probably had a low opening about a yard high, so a person had to stoop to enter. The fact that it was a new tomb meant it probably had only one burial chamber. The loculus was a large, deep pigeonhole, about two feet in width and height, maybe seven feet deep, receiving the corpse headfirst. Another layout involved a low stone bench on which the corpse was laid. Or there could be a sort of trough for the body. Most likely it was an arcosolium, a semicircular niche about a yard up from the floor, with a bench or trough at the bottom. Such a rock tomb would have the opening sealed by a large circular stone—a wheel, in effect—that was rolled across the opening, with a kind of track cut into the ground for the stone to move in.

Joseph and the Shroud of Turin

The shroud in which Joseph wrapped Jesus is, tradition says, housed in the cathedral of Turin, Italy. In 1988, small segments of the famous Shroud of Turin were scientifically tested (by carbon-14 dating), and it was announced that the shroud could not have been produced earlier than the year 1200, and *Time* magazine claimed that the matter was closed, that the shroud was indeed a fake. But the matter is far from settled, for it was later found that the segments that had been tested were not from the original shroud itself but from patches that had been stitched on due to the shroud's having been through several fires. Many people around the world are still convinced that the shroud, with its amazing image that is neither paint nor dye, is the actual burial cloth of Christ.

Aside from upsetting the Sanhedrin, burying Jesus might have made Joseph suspicious in the eyes of Pilate, and in the event of any future revolt, Pilate would have Joseph marked as a person of interest. Then again, Joseph was not known to be a disciple of Jesus, so Pilate may have seen him as just a pious Jew doing an act of kindness to an executed man. Though Pilate does not impress us as a man with a tender conscience, it might have stuck in his craw that Jesus really was innocent, and certainly Pilate would have remembered his wife's dream about the innocence of Jesus.

Joseph had not risked anything while Jesus was alive. Now he was taking a great risk. In a sense, he was the first person to be deeply moved by the events of Jesus' Passion: a good man, God's man, treated like the scum of the earth. The story has attracted people from all cultures and all times, and even some atheists and agnostics admit they are moved by the story of Jesus' trial and death. Jesus had foretold that when he was "lifted up," he would draw all men to him (John 12:32).

Joseph was the first to be drawn. So he, along with Nicodemus, took the body. Though he was rich, Joseph provided a no-frills burial—no washing and no anointing, though this was due to having to hurry before sundown. Ordinarily the Jews would have washed the body—which in Jesus' case would have been caked with blood and perspiration—anointed it with oil and clothed it. Jesus was wrapped only in a *sindon*, a linen cloth that would have been like a sheet or large towel.

When John recorded Joseph's burial of Jesus, he had in mind many of his fellow Jews, who were harboring some admiration for Jesus of Nazareth but not yet willing to out themselves as true disciples. John must have hoped and prayed that such people would follow the example of Joseph and Nicodemus. Certainly the people John was writing for knew something that Joseph and Nicodemus did not know when they buried Jesus: He would not be needing the tomb for long.

PUTTING THE WORD TO WORK

1. How do you react to the information about the Jewish high priests being appointed by the Roman government? Does this help you understand the Gospels better?

2. Picture yourself in the meeting between the priests and Judas. What would you say to them in Jesus' defense?

3. Reflect on the fact that the same Jerusalem crowd that had hailed Jesus on Palm Sunday later asked Pilate to release the violent Barabbas. What does this tell you about the psychology of crowds? Do the people always make wise choices?

4. Every religion in every time has had ministers who were unworthy, and Caiaphas is not unique. Take a moment to pray for ministers you know, thanking God for the ones who are faithful in their calling.

5. Reflect on Joseph and Nicodemus deciding late in the game to out themselves for Jesus. Make a promise to yourself not to be this kind of person, but to speak out at the right time to defend an unpopular person or cause.

Saints Elsewhere

One theme of the Bible could be stated as "home is where God is." The Old Testament devotes a lot of attention to the land of Canaan, the Promised Land, promised by God to Abraham and his descendants—and yet, those descendants, the Israelites, have spent relatively little time there. Often they have been strangers and exiles in other lands, the victims of wars and conquests. And while they never ceased to think of the homeland, Israel, they learned that God could be served and worshipped everywhere.

> **MEMORY VERSE**
>
> You are no longer strangers and aliens, but you are fellow citizens with the saints and members of the household of God.—Ephesians 2:19 (ESV)

In this chapter we look at Old Testament heroes who were exiles in Babylonia and Persia, people who remained true to their faith in a foreign land and did what they could to aid their fellow believers.

KEY TERM FOR TODAY ## Strangers

An important theme throughout the Bible is that God's people are strangers and exiles in the world, a theme that is very obvious in the stories of the Jewish exiles in Babylon and Persia.

ANOTHER JOSEPH

To these four young men God gave knowledge and understanding of all kinds of literature and learning. And Daniel could understand visions and dreams of all kinds. (Daniel 1:17)

In another chapter (Day 3) we look at the amazing career of Joseph, son of Jacob, a young man sold into slavery by his jealous brothers but who, in the workings of God, became second-in-command to the Pharaoh of Egypt. Joseph was the prototype of the foreigner who is faithful to God and prospers in a strange land. But Joseph was an individual, sold as a slave. Here we are looking at people who were taken away with thousands of others, victims of conquest and deportation, settled in a foreign land on the assumption that they would soon adapt to the new land and its gods and morals, and many did.

One who did not become a pagan was the famous Daniel, who was young and intelligent, and, in the eyes of the Babylonian conquerors, the perfect sort of man to be trained for the empire's government service. Daniel and three friends were trained in the language and literature of Babylonia—or to be precise, trained in the Aramaic language, which the empire used widely. In receiving this training they were ahead of the curve, for in time most Jews would cease speaking Hebrew and speak Aramaic.

The four young men were to receive three years of training and then would "stand before the king" by serving as advisors and aides. Part of their training involved eating what the king ate, but apparently some of the food was non-kosher, so Daniel and his friends resolved not to defile themselves with the food. This irritated the eunuchs who had charge of the men's training, but it turned out that the men fared very well on a simple diet.

They were very bright men: "To these four young men God gave knowledge and understanding of all kinds of literature and learning. And Daniel could understand

visions and dreams of all kinds" (Daniel 1:17). Daniel possessed the dream-interpreting ability of Joseph, and, also like Joseph, he could interpret dreams that mystified the king's own court soothsayers.

Daniel 2 records the troubling dream of one of the great names in ancient times, the mighty Nebuchadnezzar of Babylon. The king summoned his magicians and gave them a stern warning: "This is what I have firmly decided: If you do not tell me what my dream was and interpret it, I will have you cut into pieces and your houses turned into piles of rubble. But if you tell me the

dream and explain it, you will receive from me gifts and rewards and great honor. So tell me the dream and interpret it for me" (Daniel 2:5–6). Not surprisingly, the men were terrified; the king decided that since they would not—or could not—interpret the dream, he would have them all killed. This "massacre of the wise men" would have included Daniel and his friends, but Daniel knew he could interpret the dream. Daniel had the gift of interpretation—the Aramaic word *peshar* means "to untie" or "loose." Daniel had the power to unravel the puzzling dreams of Nebuchadnezzar. Daniel offered up a prayer of thanksgiving to God, who could remove or install kings, and who gave the wise their wisdom.

Standing before the king, Daniel assured him that no human mind could decipher the king's dream—but that the God of heaven could. Then Daniel did something amazing:

He told the king exactly what he had dreamed, and what it meant. In the king's dream, a statue of a man had a head of gold, chest and arms of silver, belly and thighs of bronze, legs of iron, and feet made of iron mixed with clay. Then a great stone "cut by no human hand" struck the statue and destroyed it. "But the rock that struck the statue became a huge mountain and filled the whole earth" (Daniel 1:35).

The head of gold was Nebuchadnezzar himself, ruler over the Babylonian empire. The other parts of the body were later empires, each inferior to the one before it, the weakest being the last, the clay mingled with iron. The great stone represented God's kingdom, which would last forever. Note the difference: A statue is by definition a manmade object, and this one was destroyed by a rock "cut by no human hand." What God makes will outlast what human rulers make. Keep in mind that the original readers of Daniel, who were Jews, would have been horrified at any kind of idol or statue, since the Ten Commandments prohibit any graven image. In the eyes of Daniel and his fellow Jews, any statue of any god or human ruler deserved to be destroyed.

For centuries, readers have debated the prophecy of the statue: If the gold head was the Babylonian empire, then the silver arms and chest were, say, Persia, and the bronze belly and thighs were . . . who knows? To fuss over the interpretation is to miss the point: Every political system, even "golden" Babylon, will eventually end. Governments and nations are temporary, while God—the rock in the dream—endures. Daniel had lived in Judah under one king, was deported to Babylon to live under a foreign king, and, later in the story, would serve yet another foreign king. The one constant in his life was God.

But back to Nebuchadnezzar. Believing Daniel's interpretation to be true, the king kept his word and showered Daniel with high honors, making him ruler of a province and promoting his three friends as well.

Regrettably, Daniel's interpretation of the king's dream did not seem to sink in, for some time later the king had a huge golden statue of himself set up on the plain. A grand dedication service was held with music and pomp. All people were ordered to bow down to it. But later, some of the king's counselors informed him that Daniel's three friends had not obeyed the order. The punishment was drastic: They were cast into a fiery furnace. The three informed the king that God would deliver them—and even if he did not, they still would not worship the king's gods or bow down to his image. The king was furious. He ordered the furnace heated even more, and the men were bound and thrown in. But God protected them, and when the Babylonians looked into the furnace, they saw the three walking about—and also, a mysterious fourth man who looked "like a son of the gods" (Daniel 3:25). Awed by this miraculous deliverance, the king had the men released from the furnace and decreed that no one be allowed to mock the God that had saved the men.

You will be driven away from people and will live with the wild animals; you will eat grass like cattle and be drenched with the dew of heaven. Seven times will pass by for you until you acknowledge that the Most High is sovereign over the kingdoms of men and gives them to anyone he wishes. (Daniel 4:25)

Soon the king would call upon Daniel again to interpret a dream. He had dreamed of an enormous tree, so tall that its top reached to heaven. It also provided shade and fruit in abundance. But a "holy one" from heaven ordered that the tree be chopped down, leaving behind a stump. Daniel understood the dream all too well. The tree was the king, whose greatness was known everywhere. He would lose his mind and for a long period live as a madman, but in time would return to his throne. Interestingly, Daniel told the king that the dream was not necessarily a prophecy but a warning: If he began to rule righteously and showed mercy to the oppressed, perhaps he could continue on his throne.

But he did not heed the warning. A year later, walking on his palace roof and admiring his many buildings, the vain and arrogant monarch lost his mind. For a time he lived like an animal, eating grass like an ox, with his hair and nails growing long and grotesque. But as Daniel foretold, the king in time regained his reason and his throne, recognizing that it is God who is truly in charge of things.

The Book of Daniel does not record Nebuchadnezzar's death. History tells us he died in 562 BC. Daniel 5 speaks of King Belshazzar, a name that delighted skeptics about the Bible, because historians had never found any evidence such a man existed, so it was believed Daniel's story was pure fiction. But in 1854 archaeologists uncovered a text that

CHARACTERS AT LARGE ## Nebuchadnezzar in Art and Music

It would grieve the breathtakingly proud Nebuchadnezzar to know that the most familiar image of him was the work of English artist-poet William Blake, who gave the world the picture of the mad king on all fours, his eyes wild, his hair long and shaggy, and his nails like bird claws. The king's insanity is also featured in Giuseppe Verdi's great opera *Nabuco*, which chronicles the Jews' exile in Babylon. The king's dream of the statue with the gold head has been featured in many artworks, which sometimes show the great stone about to smash the statue. It is ironic that one of the most powerful rulers of history is today remembered not so much as a conqueror and builder, but as the insane man in the Book of Daniel.

Daniel, Dead and Buried

Susa, the old Persian capital, had the supposed tomb of Daniel. The Koran, the Muslims' holy book, makes no mention of Daniel, and when the Muslims conquered Persia, they didn't hesitate to carry off all the treasure from the tomb of Daniel. They broke up the silver coffin and carried off the mummified corpse. They removed the corpse's signet ring, which showed a man between two lions. Oddly, the Muslims later came to revere Daniel, and there is still a tomb of Daniel in the city.

said that Belshazzar did indeed exist, that he was the son of the last king of Babylon, Nabonidus, who was often away on military campaigns and left his son to rule in his place. The Bible refer to Belshazzar as "son" of Nebuchadnezzar, and it appears "son" here means "descendant," for Belshazzar's mother was a daughter of Nebuchadnezzar.

As Daniel says, Belshazzar was ruling in Babylon when the mighty empire fell to an even mightier one, the Persians. The king was warned, for at a grand banquet at which they were using some of the Jews' temple vessels for drinking mugs, a disembodied hand appeared on the wall, frightening Belshazzar so much that his knees knocked together. The hand wrote the words *Mene, Mene, Tekel, Parsin*. Daniel was sent for and asked what the words meant. Simply put, the king's reign was at an end, and the Babylonians, who had conquered so many people, would be conquered by another power, the Persians.

The detail that Belshazzar and his guests were drinking from the Jews' temple vessels is important: Those vessels had been plundered from Jerusalem when Nebuchadnezzar's armies destroyed the temple. Under the Persians, the Jews would be allowed to take these items back to Jerusalem.

Daniel, born a Jew in the nation of Judah, had been deported against his will to Babylon and trained to serve the Babylonian king. Now another government was in charge, but Daniel would continue in government service because "he was trustworthy and neither corrupt nor negligent" (Daniel 6:4).

The Persians were relatively tolerant of the religions of the people they conquered, and in theory Daniel and his friends could have continued to practice their religion with no interference. Yet human nature being what it is, an outsider or foreigner is often at a disadvantage, and some of the counselors to the king of Persia had it in for Daniel. Finding nothing in his job performance to fault him, they persuaded the king that for a period of thirty days, no man in the empire could offer up any petition to anyone except the king himself—so no one could pray to any god. (The Persians, like most ancient empires, regarded their rulers as divine.) The king wasn't permanently outlawing all religions, of course, but was temporarily requiring the people of his vast empire to acknowledge him as a great power. Like most rulers, his vanity was monumental.

Daniel disobeyed the rule, continuing to pray to God three times per day, as was his custom. So, despite his high office in the empire, he was punished by being thrown into a den of lions. The kings kept these not as pets or for zoo displays, but to turn loose on the royal hunting preserves, bolstering the kings' image as lion hunters. We all know how this story turned out: The lions did no harm to Daniel at all, for his God was with him.

As far as we know, Daniel never returned to his homeland, yet he served God faithfully, no matter what earthly ruler was on the throne. Daniel, like so many people of faith, gave his real allegiance to the kingdom of God: "His kingdom is an eternal kingdom; his dominion endures from generation to generation" (Daniel 4:3).

A QUEEN IN GOD'S GOOD TIME

If you remain silent at this time, relief and deliverance for the Jews will arise from another place, but you and your father's family will perish. And who knows but that you have come to royal position for such a time as this? (Esther 4:14)

Esther is unique among the Old Testament books in that all the action takes place in Persia—specifically, in the capital city of Persia, one of the great cities of ancient times. At that time the Persian empire was one of the largest and most diverse the world had ever known, stretching from India on the east to the edge of Greece on the west, and including all the other empires that had at one time dominated or harassed Israel—Egypt, Assyria, Babylonia.

> **DID YOU KNOW?**
>
> Esther and the Song of Solomon are the only two books of the Bible that do not mention God.

At the opening of the Book of Esther, the ruler of this vast domain is Ahasuerus—probably the ruler that secular historians know as Xerxes, who reigned from 486 to 424 BC. He was already an experienced administrator when he came to the throne, having held power as crown prince for twelve years, being the successor his father handpicked over several older brothers. In other words, he was not a man to be trifled with or stymied. What would stymie him, to his great consternation, was his wife.

The king had held a great feast for his court, entertaining them lavishly over several weeks. The golden vessels the men drank from symbolized the power and wealth the king held. When the king was somewhat drunk, he told his officials to summon the queen, who was hosting her own banquet for the women. He wanted her to come and "display her beauty" to his guests. She refused. The king was, of course, furious. His counselors were alarmed: If the king's wife could defy her husband, might not other women become equally defiant? So the king decided to put his wife away and find another.

Chapter 2 of Esther is in effect the story of a beauty pageant, for the king of Persia decided to bring all the beautiful girls of the empire to the capital, where they would be put through a beauty regimen, the winner becoming the new queen. Among the young women was Hadassah, a Jewish orphan under the care of her older cousin, Mordecai. The king was attracted to the girl "more than to any of the other women, and she won his favor and approval more than any of the other virgins. So he set a royal crown on her head and made her queen" (Esther 2:17).

When she married the king, Hadassah was going by her other name, Esther—Hadassah being a Hebrew name meaning "myrtle." Following Mordecai's advice, she did not reveal her ethnic background to the king. In time it would turn out to be very important.

Another person who was promoted highly was a totally different character altogether. This was Haman, who became the king's right-hand man and expected to be treated as such. All people were supposed to bow down to him. One man did not: Mordecai. We are not told why, but we are told that Haman was furious, and because he knew Mordecai was a Jew, he burned with hatred, not just for one individual but for all the Jews. The human heart is a curious thing: Here was a man with amazing power and prestige, a success by worldly standards, someone who should have been supremely happy. But he became obsessed with destroying all Jews, just because one Jew had shown him no respect.

Since he had great influence with the king, he informed him that "there is a certain people dispersed and scattered among the peoples in all the provinces of your kingdom whose customs are different from those of all other people and who do not obey the king's laws; it is not in the king's best interest to tolerate them" (Esther 3:8). If this argument was not persuasive enough, Haman also agreed to pay the king ten thousand talents of silver, a huge sum. For Haman this was an investment—he would conceivably profit from the Jews' goods once they were destroyed. The order for the destruction of the Jews was thorough, making sure to mention "young and old, women and children."

When Mordecai learned of the decree, he was horrified. He put on sackcloth—what we would call burlap—as a sign of his distress, and throughout the empire other Jews did the same. Esther herself was in no danger, since she had kept her Jewishness a secret. Yet she was horrified to learn of what Haman had done. Mordecai sent her a message: Did she think that she would necessarily escape this ethnic purge just because she lived in the palace? But his message was also hopeful: "Who knows but that you have come to royal position for such a time as this?" A Jewish girl had become wife of the king, and now the Jews faced destruction. Wasn't it clear enough that God was behind all this?

Esther had to act—but how? We might imagine that the queen could see the king any time she liked, but this was not the case in ancient Persia. The only way to see the king was to be summoned—barging in unsummoned would result in death. So Esther did the obvious thing. She made herself attractive by putting on her royal garb and went to stand near the throne room. Pleased to see her, the king allowed her to speak. She had a request: Would the king and Haman join her at a feast?

Haman—who at this point did not know the queen was a Jew—was elated at being asked to dine with the king and queen. His joy was spoiled, however, at the sight of Mordecai, who would not bow down to him. Haman ordered that a high gallows be built to hang Mordecai.

But God was watching over Mordecai. Sometime earlier, Mordecai had learned of two members of the court plotting to murder the king. He revealed the plot and saved the king's life. But the king had neglected to reward him for this good deed at the time. On a night when he could not sleep, the king had the chronicles of the kingdom brought in and read aloud, and he realized Mordecai had gone unrewarded. As it happened, the next day Haman headed to the king with his request to hang Mordecai. The king informed him that Mordecai was long overdue for recognition. Haman was given the honor—or, to him, the punishment—of leading the beaming Mordecai through the streets, shouting, "This is what is done for the man the king delights to honor!" (Esther 6:11).

Worse was in store for Haman. At the feast Esther held for him and the king, she revealed that she was herself a Jew, and she made the king understand what a diabolical

---

CULTURAL INSIGHTS

Purim

The Jewish holiday of Purim is based on the Book of Esther, commemorating the deliverance of the Jews from the fiendish plot of Haman. The book itself states that the Jews "observe the fourteenth of the month of Adar as a day of joy and feasting, a day for giving presents to each other" (Esther 9:19). On Purim, the entire book is read aloud, and the people often used noisemakers to drown out Haman's name whenever it is mentioned. The day is surely the most secular of Jewish holidays, with a great deal of drinking, and also eating the fruit pies known as "Haman's hats."

Esther on Film

Given its exotic setting in Persia and a story involving plots and violence, the Book of Esther seems a natural for movies. Joan Collins, of all people, played the virtuous queen in the 1960 movie *Esther and the King*, which, to put it mildly, takes great liberties with the biblical story. (For example, Vashti, the first queen, is shown as a promiscuous minx, having an affair with Haman, among many others.) More recently, the 2006 movie *One Night with the King* stuck much closer to the Bible, with the British actor John Rhys-Davies as a very appealing Mordecai. Interestingly, both movies mention God many times, even though the Book of Esther does not.

Director Cecil B. DeMille, famous for *The Ten Commandments*, intended to make an epic film of the story but never got around to it. We can only imagine what the story would have been like with the DeMille touch.

plot Haman had hatched. Haman ended up being hanged on the gallows he had built to hang Mordecai. Esther had put herself at great risk: How could she know for sure that her husband might not condemn her along with the other Jews? Some women in her place might have stayed quiet, preferring to retain the secure place as queen regardless of what happened to all the other Jews. Esther was not only beautiful but also brave.

But the royal decree for the destruction of the Jews could not be revoked—such were the laws of the Persians. However, the king could issue another decree: the Jews could arm and defend themselves against their destroyers. And so, on the day that had been determined for the destruction of the Jews in the empire, many thousands of Persians perished.

In a final twist—in a very twist-filled story—Mordecai became second-in-command to the king, taking the place of Haman. Mordecai was "preeminent among the Jews, and held in high esteem by his many fellow Jews, because he worked for the good of his people and spoke up for the welfare of all the Jews" (Esther 10:3).

The story was and is very popular with Jews—less so with Christians, who are disturbed by the book's vengeful spirit, which celebrates the Jews turning on their enemies in such a bloodthirsty fashion. Jesus' teaching about mercy and love for one's enemies makes us uncomfortable with the story. Perhaps to appreciate it we have to put ourselves in the place of the Jews of that day, a conquered people, settled against their will in a foreign country, trying to live peacefully and make no trouble, yet facing persecution that is totally uncalled for. Whatever we may think of the violence in the book, Esther and Mordecai are admirable characters, decent people who make the best of things in a foreign court filled with ambitious schemers.

SWAPPING COMFORT FOR CONFRONTATION

I answered the king, "If it pleases the king and if your servant has found favor in his sight, let him send me to the city in Judah where my fathers are buried so that I can rebuild it." . . . And because the gracious hand of my God was upon me, the king granted my requests. (Nehemiah 2:5, 8)

One of the Bible's most neglected books and neglected characters is Nehemiah. This is unfortunate, because he is a fascinating, multifaceted character, and the story is appealing, although many readers are put off by the long "list" sections that seem to clutter both Nehemiah and Ezra.

In examining Daniel and Esther, we looked at exiled Jews living in Persia, and sometimes facing persecution or even extermination. In fact, the Bible's view of Persia is on the whole favorable, one reason being that the Persian emperor Cyrus decreed in 539 BC that the Jews living in exile could return to their homeland. In other words, he was undoing the deportation that had been done under the Babylonian king Nebuchadnezzar. And while the Babylonians had destroyed the temple in Jerusalem, Cyrus decreed that the Jews could rebuild it. Encouraged by the preaching of the prophet Haggai, the Jews completed the temple in 515 BC. Technically, the Jews in Jerusalem were part of the Persian empire and had to pay taxes to it, but the Persians had a lenient policy toward conquered people and allowed them a certain amount of self-rule. It wasn't the same as total independence, but it was close.

In 458 BC, a priest and scribe named Ezra left exile and came to Jerusalem. Ezra and people who thought like him were certain that the Babylonian exile—and in fact, all the calamities that had befallen the Jews—were the result of the people's not keeping the Law of Moses faithfully. We get the impression that, while Israel's kings ruled, the Law was mainly the concern of the priests and the upper classes, and that the common people had little knowledge of it. Being an observant Jew had mostly meant participating in the holy day festivals and making occasional sacrifices. But after the return from the exile, obeying the Law meant being conscious of it—and of God—through every moment of the day. The Law became an ordered way of life—and where it was silent, principles could be deduced from it to cover every conceivable situation. With this zeal for the Law, the Jews who remained behind in Babylon could be just as faithful as those who returned, at least on a day-to-day basis, even though they were too far away to visit the temple or make regular sacrifices.

Even so, all Jews, no matter where they lived, took an interest in the welfare of Jerusalem, which they regarded as a holy city. One who was deeply concerned was Nehemiah, who held the post of cupbearer to the Persian King Artaxerxes, who ruled from 464 to 424 BC. The king was favorable to the Jews—in fact, he wanted to keep them happy because Egypt, which was part of his empire, was often rebellious, and he wanted to keep the Jews in Judea on his side, given their nearness to Egypt.

"Cupbearer" may not sound important, but in fact it was, for this official would have been at the king's side constantly, tasting his wine and food (for poison). He was not only a servant but a counselor and confidant as well, someone the king trusted completely. Nehemiah was, in short, a highly placed man, one who might have been perfectly content to live in peace and security at the court. But his brother took a long journey from Jerusalem to bring him some distressing news: Jerusalem's city walls were in shambles, and in ancient times a wall-less city was easy prey for bandits and conquerors.

Nehemiah was distressed at the news. Like all devout Jews, he had a heart for Jerusalem. He shared Ezra's assessment of things: The Jews' calamities were due to their being unfaithful to the Law of Moses. They had been punished with exile, but God had been merciful and allowed some to return to the homeland. But the situation with the city's security had to be remedied. Catching the king in a receptive mood, Nehemiah made a request: let him leave the comfort and security of the palace and journey to Jerusalem to get the city back in shape. The king granted the request.

As it turned out, the condition of the city walls would be the least of Nehemiah's problems. Two of the local officials, Sanballat and Tobiah, were about to oppose him at every turn. Sensing hostility, Nehemiah rode out by himself at night to inspect the walls, which were indeed in a sad state. Apparently Nehemiah had a certain amount of

---

CULTURAL INSIGHTS

Nehemiah the Eunuch?

In ancient Persia, the royal cupbearer was almost always a eunuch. Was Nehemiah? We can't be absolutely sure, because so many royal officials were eunuchs that often the same word meant both "eunuch" and "chamberlain."

One hint that Nehemiah was a eunuch is that four times in his book he uses the phrase "Remember me, O my God." For Jewish men of his time, a man lived on through his descendants, who would visit his grave and honor his memory. A eunuch, with no children, would have to rely on God to perpetuate his memory. However, another explanation of these "remember me" verses is that Nehemiah wrote his book as a reply to the scurrilous rumors circulated by his enemies. (Since his book is still read and discussed, obviously God did answer his prayer to be remembered.)

If Nehemiah had been a eunuch, this would explain his enemies' plot to try to lure him into the temple. Eunuchs were not allowed inside the temple itself, and if he had gone there, he would have violated the temple and lost face with the Jews.

charisma, for when he told the Jewish leaders, "Let us start rebuilding," they joined in enthusiastically.

Rebuilding the walls involved enduring some heckling from Sanballat and Tobiah, who sneered that the "feeble" Jews were building a wall that even a fox could tear down. The workers became discouraged, fearing violence. Nehemiah had a knack for encouraging the weakhearted: "Don't be afraid of them. Remember the Lord, who is great and awesome, and fight for your brothers, your sons and your daughters, your wives and your homes" (Nehemiah 4:14). To ensure that the work continued, he had each worker keep a sword strapped to his side, ever ready for an attack. At night they slept in their day clothes, never knowing if they would need to rise up and fight. These were blue-collar workers, not trained soldiers, but they had to play the role of a very alert militia under the circumstances.

But Nehemiah was more than a civil engineer. He was a moral engineer as well, painfully aware that many of the wealthy Jews had turned into loan sharks, reducing some of their poorer brothers to poverty. Property was being mortgaged, and some of the bankrupt people had to sell themselves into slavery, with their property garnished. Nehemiah reminded them that the Law of Moses prohibited charging interest to fellow Israelites. Nehemiah gave the people a severe scolding and ordered them to return what they had seized (Nehemiah 5:1–13).

He was himself a generous man. As a Persian official he could have lived luxuriously, but he chose not to. The normal human practice is to profit from one's position of power. He did not—nor was he too high and mighty to stoop to physical labor himself. And at times he had paid to release the Jews who, bankrupt, had sold themselves into slavery.

Remember that Nehemiah had had a cushy job in Persia. Most Jews who were sitting pretty in the Persian empire chose to stay there and prosper, and even though he clearly intended to return to Persia, and did, he ran some obvious risks in taking on the task of rebuilding Jerusalem.

> **DID YOU KNOW?**
>
> The Persian emperor was referred to as "king of kings," a title that, centuries later, Christians would apply to both God and Christ.

Among those risks were plots against his life. Sanballat sent him a message, requesting a meeting, but Nehemiah knew they meant him harm, so he sent a message saying he was too busy with his work. Later, he got another message, saying there were rumors he was plotting to be made king and lead a Jewish rebellion against Persia, and that he has even encouraged prophets to praise him. This message from Sanballat was sent unsealed—meaning he wanted the bearers to read it and spread the rumor far and wide. As a servant of the Persian king, Nehemiah well knew that the Persians punished treason with either beheading or crucifixion. But he sent a message back to Sanballat: All these rumors and accusations were nonsense.

Later, Tobiah and Sanballat bribed a Jew named Shemaiah to try to lure Nehemiah into the temple at night, where he would be murdered. Or perhaps what was intended was that Nehemiah would flee for safety to the Holy Place in the temple, the inner sanctuary where only the priests were allowed, and had he done so, this would have discredited him before the Jews. Nehemiah would not fall for this ploy, and he had no intention of showing fear of these schemers.

Just how serious the plots were is hard to discern. Whether they succeeded or not, one key aim was to intimidate Nehemiah. The plotters must have hoped he would give up and simply return to Persia. They may have thought a royal cupbearer would be a soft man, easily discouraged, but he proved them wrong.

DEDICATION AND BACKSLIDING

> They read from the Book of the Law of God, making it clear and giving the meaning so that the people could understand what was being read. Then Nehemiah the governor, Ezra the priest and scribe, and the Levites who were instructing the people said to them all, "This day is sacred to the Lord your God. Do not mourn or weep. . . . Go and enjoy choice food and sweet drinks, and send some to those who have nothing prepared. . . . for the joy of the Lord is your strength." (Nehemiah 8:8–10)

Nehemiah's zeal bore fruit, for the city walls were completed in October of 445 BC. The project was done in a little over seven weeks. The Jews attributed the work to God.

With the walls rebuilt, the people could live securely and begin to function again as a faith community. The priest and scribe Ezra mounted a platform and read publicly from the Law of Moses. This led to weeping, for the Law made the people aware of how far out of line they were morally and spiritually. Nehemiah and Ezra told them not to weep, for this was to be a day of joy, a celebration of a community of faith. They celebrated the Feast of Booths, a joyous holiday that had been neglected for centuries. But several days later they made a group confession of their sins, and also the sins of their fathers, which had resulted in the Babylonian exile. The leaders signed their names to a covenant, swearing they would act differently from their wayward ancestors.

Things seemed to be going well, so Nehemiah returned to Persia, having spent twelve busy and productive years in Jerusalem. When he returned years later in a follow-up visit, he found the people had violated the covenant at every turn. Men were marrying pagan wives, transacting business on the Sabbath, and otherwise behaving as if they were not the people of God.

The buyers and sellers were doing business on the Sabbath just as on any other day. Nehemiah brought this to a halt by shutting the city gates on the Sabbath. But the greedy merchants worked around this by setting up their shops just outside the walls. Nehemiah threatened to lay hands on them.

Nehemiah was horrified that the Jews had continued to intermarry with foreigners. In our day, we are taught to value tolerance and diversity, so we have a hard time appreciating Nehemiah's point of view. He was painfully aware that Jewish men were often led into worshipping their foreign wives' gods. Amazingly, the grandson of the Jewish high priest had married a daughter of the trouble-making Sanballat. On top of that, the other great troublemaker, Tobiah, even had his own quarters in the temple complex. Nehemiah, a man with a temper, threw Tobiah's belongings out. He took decisive action with the ones who had married foreign wives also: "I rebuked them and called curses down on them. I beat some of the men and pulled out their hair. I made them take an oath in God's name and said: 'You are not to give your daughters in marriage to their sons, nor are you to take their daughters in marriage for your sons or for yourselves'" (Nehemiah 13:25).

Nehemiah was obviously a man of action and a man of deep conviction. If some of his acts seem a bit extreme, keep in mind that on one famous occasion, Jesus drove the moneychangers out of the temple. Nehemiah took the Law and the temple seriously, and he wanted the people to live as children of God. And in fact, the reforms that took place under Ezra and Nehemiah did eventually sink in. Four centuries later, in the New Testament period, the Jews were guilty of many sins—after all, they were human—but they did take the Law seriously, and few of them were guilty of worshipping foreign gods. Jesus and the apostles would take things a step further, going beyond the Law to a deeper form of spirituality.

Presumably Nehemiah returned to Persia and died there—probably comfortable and happy enough, but aware that he was a foreigner, an exile. The same is true of Daniel and Esther. Like them, most of the exiled Jews did not return to the homeland, but lived on in Babylonia and Persia. Later, when Alexander the Great's Greek empire conquered Persia, many Jews settled in Greek cities and, still later, many would be further scattered throughout the Roman empire. The Jews who did not live in Israel became known as the Diaspora—a word that means "dispersion" or "scattering"—and Diaspora Jews far outnumbered those in Israel, even today. Christians early on adopted the belief in themselves as the "new Diaspora," God's people scattered across the world. They inherited from the Jews the knowledge that the real holy land is not a place on the map but wherever people live in fellowship with God. Thus 1 Peter is addressed to "God's elect, strangers in the world, scattered . . ."

PUTTING THE WORD TO WORK

1. Given the opportunity, Daniel was a witness for God in the Babylonian court, willing to attribute his skills to the Lord. Have you known people who served faithfully in environments where their faith might have been a handicap?

2. Although Daniel had enemies, no one could find fault with his work habits, for he was conscientious and diligent. Take a moment to consider your own work habits, and remind yourself that, as a person of faith, how you do your work reflects on your faith.

3. What do you find appealing about the story of Esther and Mordecai? Even though the book does not mention God, do you think the events make it clear that God is at work?

4. Try to imagine doing what Nehemiah did: giving up a position as trusted aide to a mighty ruler and traveling a thousand miles to help rebuild a city in ruins. Have you known people who gave up comfortable situations to engage in charitable endeavors?

5. Having read the chapter, reread the Memory Verse. Meditate for a moment on Paul's phrase "fellow citizens with the saints."

Faces of Jesus
LORD, SON OF GOD, SAVIOR

Today we will focus on the one who is without a doubt the most fascinating person in the Bible: Jesus. While we have already looked at some of his healings, today we will look at three of the titles the first Christians applied to Jesus: Lord, Son of God, and Savior. All three titles emphasize Jesus' divine nature, yet, as we shall see, it was Jesus' humility and obedience to God that opened the first believers' eyes to his divinity.

> **MEMORY VERSE**
>
> We have seen and testify that the Father has sent his Son to be the Savior of the world.—1 John 4:14

KEY TERM FOR TODAY **The Right Hand of God**

The New Testament uses this phrase often to express the belief in Jesus' divine nature. The Old and New Testaments both refer to God as *Lord* and *Savior*, and the New applies the same titles to Jesus.

THE FIRST—AND SHORTEST—CREED

With great power the apostles continued to testify to the resurrection of the Lord Jesus, and much grace was upon them all. (Acts 4:33)

If you confess with your mouth, "Jesus is Lord," and believe in your heart that God raised him from the dead, you will be saved. (Romans 10:9)

Could you summarize your basic spiritual beliefs in three words? Some of the early Christians could. The oldest and briefest statement of Christian belief is "Jesus is Lord"; in the original Greek, it is *Kurios Iesous*, found in Romans 10:9 and 1 Corinthians 12:3. Though brief, it was rich with meaning, for it acknowledged that Jesus was the divine being to whom the person was attached, and presumably Jesus had total claim on the person's life. Because Jesus was Lord, Christians could pray directly to him as they could pray to God. We think that the habit of praying to the Father "in the name of Jesus" is rooted in the Bible, and indeed it is, but in fact there are examples of prayer directly to Jesus himself, such as in 2 Corinthians 12:8 and 1 Thessalonians 3:12.

In the very first Christian sermon, given in Jerusalem on the Day of Pentecost, the apostle Peter announced that "God has made this Jesus, whom you crucified, both Lord and Christ" (Acts 2:36). Here was one of the beauties of the Christian message: The man who suffered the most degrading form of execution, a method used on slaves and terrorists, had been raised from the dead and declared by God to be Lord and Messiah, the Christ. It is no coincidence that Peter uses "Lord" before "Christ," because he sees the first title as more important than the second.

In Philippians 2, Paul quotes from what may well be the oldest Christian hymn. Paul uses it in the context of reminding Christians to exercise humility and to serve each other—a frequent theme in Jesus' own teaching. In referring to such humility, Paul presents Jesus himself as the supreme example: "Being in very nature God, [he] did not consider equality with God something to be grasped, but made himself nothing, taking the very nature of a servant, being made in human likeness. And being found in appearance as a man, he humbled himself and became obedient to death—even death on a cross!" And what was the fruit of this divine humility? "Therefore God exalted him to the highest place and gave him the name that is above every name, that at the name of Jesus every knee should bow, in heaven and on earth and under the earth, and every tongue confess that Jesus Christ is Lord" (Philippians 2:6–11). Readers often miss the fact that "the name above every name" is the title "Lord." Why is it above every name? Because it is the name of God himself. Jesus is not just one of the many semi-divine godlings of Greek and Roman mythology, he is sharing the name and status of God himself. Thus the risen Jesus could tell his disciples, "All authority in heaven and on earth has been given to me" (Matthew 28:18).

How was this message "Jesus is Lord" perceived by those the apostles preached to? As used by non-Jews, *kurios*—or "lord"—could have both a secular meaning and a religious one. A *kurios* was one who exercised authority and was entitled to respect and obedience. One's *kurios* was the master or boss. (One did not necessarily love this *kurios*, of course. The *kurios* was simply a power that had to be respected—or else you would suffer the consequences.) In the religious realm, most of the diverse religions of the Roman empire referred to their god as *Kurios* (or *Kuria*, if referring to a goddess). The god that the worshipper devoted himself to, would, of course, be *the* Lord. Paul, growing up in the primarily pagan city of Tarsus, was aware of the many lords whom people worshipped: "Even if there are so-called gods, whether in heaven or on earth (as indeed there are many 'gods' and many 'lords'), yet for us there is but one God, the Father, from whom all things came and for whom we live; and there is but one Lord, Jesus Christ, through whom all things came and through whom we live" (1 Corinthians 8:5–6).

The secular and religious uses of "Lord" merged in addressing the Roman emperors. At first the Romans resisted the idea of rulers as being divine, but as time passed they realized that having people across the empire pay homage to the emperor's supposed divinity was a useful way of uniting diverse peoples. So temples were built to honor the divinity of past emperors but, later, also to celebrate the reigning one. Some of those emperors mocked, in private, the ridiculous idea that they were divine. The Roman poets like Ovid and Virgil helped perpetuate the myth that the emperors had gods and goddesses among their ancestors. Thus, when a resident of the empire addressed the emperor, he was expected to call him *Kurios Kaisar*, "Lord Caesar," and to acknowledge both his political power and his divinity. *Kurios Kaisar* was almost the same as *Theos Kaisar*, "Caesar is God." In their vanity and egotism, the Romans liked to think that the ruler of a vast empire must possess some divine power (an idea proved foolish when several of the emperors were assassinated).

The Jews, of course, acknowledged only one *Kurios*, God, also known as Yahweh. *Kurios* was the Greek equivalent of the Hebrew word *Adonai* (which, as in Greek, could refer to either God or to a human master). The Jews shared with other religions the custom of calling their god "Lord" instead of by his name. In fact, they had over the centuries felt that the name of God—Yahweh—was so majestic and exalted that they almost ceased to use it. In fact, when they read the Scriptures aloud, they would not pronounce the sacred name Yahweh but would say *Adonai*, Hebrew for "Lord." When the Old Testament was translated from Hebrew into Greek, *Yahweh* and *Adonai* were both rendered "Lord"—at times creating an awkward situation, because the Hebrew text sometimes referred to *Yahweh Adonai*—in Greek, *Kurios Kurios*, although the Jews would have understood what it meant.

At the risk of complicating matters, let us recall that Jesus and his disciples and listeners spoke to each other in Aramaic. The disciples would have addressed him by the Aramaic word *Mar*, "Lord," or *Mari*, "my Lord"—but this had no religious meaning, and certainly did not equate Jesus with God. In calling Jesus *Mar*, the disciples were acknowledging him as their master, their rabbi. In the custom of that place and time, using the term twice would have indicated great respect—*Mari, Mari*—"Lord, Lord." This is reflected in a statement of Jesus himself: "Not everyone who says to me, 'Lord, Lord,' will enter the kingdom of heaven, but only he who does the will of my Father who is in heaven" (Matthew 7:21). Put another way, one who calls Jesus "Lord" or "Master" ought to act accordingly and do as the Master says.

When did the disciples realize that their *Mar*, their Master, was something more than just an ordinary human teacher? Obviously with the passage of time,

> **DID YOU KNOW?**
>
> The phrase "Lord Jesus" or "Lord Jesus Christ" is used ninety-nine times in the New Testament.

hearing him teach on his authority, watching him heal the sick and even raise the dead and still a storm, they knew that divine power was at work. "They were terrified and asked each other, 'Who is this? Even the wind and the waves obey him!'" (Mark 4:41) Even more important is that Jesus took on one of the prerogatives of God, forgiving sins: "The other guests began to say among themselves, 'Who is this who even forgives sins?'" (Luke 7:49). Yet, while the disciples were growing more aware of what their Master was like, in the many instances in the Gospels that Jesus is addressed as *Kurios*, "Lord," it is simply a title of respect. On the lips of the disciples it means "Master"; on the lips of others, such as those who ask for healing, it is more like "Sir."

But from the Resurrection on, something changes. The risen Jesus is regarded as a divine being—which he was all along, even if the people could not see it clearly. Jesus after the Resurrection is not just "Lord," but "the Lord," the divine one, which formerly Jews used only to refer to God himself. The Gospels only refer to "Lord Jesus" in two passages, both of them referring to the risen Jesus: "After the Lord Jesus had spoken to them, he was taken up into heaven and he sat at the right hand of God" (Mark 16:19). "When they entered [the empty tomb], they did not find the body of the Lord Jesus" (Luke 24:3). Calling Jesus *Kurios Christos*, "Lord Christ," would inevitably upset many Jews, who could not accept anyone but God being the Lord—not to mention the fact that most Jews would not accept Jesus as the Christ, the Messiah. And yet most of the first Christians were Jews who not only accepted Jesus as the long-awaited Messiah but also saw him as the divine Lord.

One result of the first Christians honoring Jesus as Lord is that they applied most of the Old Testament references to "the Lord" to Jesus. The passage from Philippians 2 quoted above, which speaks of every knee bowing and every tongue confessing to Christ, was clearly modeled on the words of God in Isaiah 45:23: "Before me every knee will bow; by me every tongue will swear." Also, all the titles that the Old Testament uses for God—Lord, King, Savior, Redeemer and others—were applied to Jesus, with the single exception of Father, which was never applied to Jesus because he himself had referred to God as Father. And the Last Judgment, which the Old Testament prophets called "the day of the Lord," has in the New Testament become "the day of the Lord Jesus" (2 Corinthians 1:14). The apostles' preaching was referred to as "the word of the Lord," with Lord referring to Jesus, just as the Old Testament prophets described their preaching as "the word of the Lord," with "Lord" referring to God.

As the apostles spread the gospel, they frequently proclaimed that Jesus is at "the right hand of God." This is the same idea as Jesus as Lord. The phrase occurs twenty-one times in the New Testament, often quoting Psalm 110:1: "The Lord says to my Lord: 'Sit at my right hand until I make your enemies a footstool for your feet.'" In the original Hebrew, it would be, "Yahweh says to my Lord," with "Lord" referring to the king of Israel. When translated into Greek, *Yahweh* became *Kurios*, creating the awkward sentence, "Kurios says to my Kurios," although Greek-speaking Jews would have understood that the first *Kurios* was God. At any rate, the first Christians quoted this verse frequently as a prophecy of "the Lord" (God) elevating "my Lord" (the risen Jesus) to heaven.

At the end of 1 Corinthians, Paul shifts from his usual Greek to Aramaic and uses the term *Maranatha*—which can mean either "Our Lord comes" or "Our Lord, come." Either way, it expresses the hope of the early Christians for the swift return of their *Mar* (Lord) to earth. It also expresses their desire for his spiritual presence among them at that moment. Appropriately, the last book of the Bible ends with "Come, Lord Jesus" (Revelation 22:20).

LORD VS. CAESAR

While the message of Jesus as Lord and Christ was spreading—causing controversy and hostility, but also leading to many conversions—the old emperor cult of *Kurios Kaisar* still existed. Some of the emperors were taking their divinity seriously. Hoping the silly emperor cult would lend some stability to the empire, they required all people to publicly confess *Kurios Kaisar*, "Caesar is Lord," and also offer a sacrifice on the emperor's behalf. There was one further demand on the Christians: They also had to curse Christ. Perhaps a few Christians might have been willing to go through the "Caesar is Lord" ritual, knowing the whole act was meaningless if they honored Jesus in their hearts. But cursing Christ publicly was another matter. The situation is reflected in 1 Corinthians 12:3: "I tell you that no one who is speaking by the Spirit of God says, 'Jesus be cursed,' and no one can say, 'Jesus is Lord,' except by the Holy Spirit." Paul was reminding Christians that some of them had to make hard choices: If they genuinely regarded Jesus as Lord, they had better be willing to say so under duress. Thus martyrdom was the fate for many who accepted only Jesus as Lord. The Christians remembered Jesus saying that they should give to Caesar what is Caesar's and to God what is God's. Caesar had asked for what he was not due—worship—and so the Christians could not comply.

In the inevitable battle for lordship—Christ or Caesar?—Caesar won in the short term (many Christians died) but Christ won in the long term (the faith continued to spread and long outlived the Roman empire). While the persecutions were under way, some of the Roman judges marveled at the Christians' stubbornness: What harm was there in going through the motions of calling Caesar "Lord" and cursing Christ? For the Christians the answer was, "all the harm in the world." Like the author of Revelation, they saw Christ not as just one Lord among many—the hodgepodge of religions in the empire—but as the King of Kings and Lord of Lords, the ultimate authority, far greater than Caesar. "Even if there are so-called gods, whether in heaven or on earth (as indeed there are many 'gods' and many 'lords'), yet for us there is but one God, the Father, from whom all things came and for whom we live; and there is but one Lord, Jesus Christ, through whom all things came and through whom we live" (1 Corinthians 8:5–6).

SONSHIP: OBEDIENCE TO THE NTH DEGREE

The beginning of the gospel about Jesus Christ, the Son of God. (Mark 1:1)

When the centurion, who stood there in front of Jesus, heard his cry and saw how he died, he said, "Surely this man was the Son of God!" (Mark 15:39)

If anyone acknowledges that Jesus is the Son of God, God lives in him and he in God. (1 John 4:15)

The first Christians used "Lord" more often than "Son of God" to speak of Jesus' divinity. This was probably a wise choice, since "son of God" could have been misconstrued by the Greeks and Romans who believed their promiscuous gods had numerous half-divine sons walking around on the earth. Magicians were sometimes called "sons of God," and their sleight-of-hand tricks might convince the gullible that the magic had a divine source. In the various mystery cults that were scattered around the empire, people initiated into the cult became the "sons" and "daughters" of the god. Also, there was the lingering Middle Eastern idea of the king being the son of a god, such as the Egyptian pharaoh being the son of the sun god Ra, and the equally ridiculous legend that the gods Venus and Mars were both ancestors of the Roman emperors. (Considering how promiscuous and war-loving the emperors were, Venus and Mars would have been suitable ancestors!)

The idea of a god as father of a ruler is even present in the Old Testament, where God is the spiritual (but not physical) father of Israel's King David (2 Samuel 7:14): "I will be his father, and he will be my son." This passage makes it clear that God chooses David, and that David must obey God or be punished. As always in the Bible, a true son is one who obeys his father completely. David was not a total success in that area, nor were any of the later kings of Israel. Naturally the Jews were only too aware what miserable failures most of their kings were, but then, the spiritual backslidings of the kings were mirrored in the people as a whole. It is not surprising that the "royal Psalms," those in which God refers to the king as "son," were regarded as prophecies of the Messiah (Psalms 2, 72, 89). God's special "son" was clearly not any of the wayward kings of Israel but someone yet to come, the Messiah, an ideal king who would obey God fully.

In a few passages, all Israel is spoken of as God's "son," such as Hosea 11:1—"When Israel was a child, I loved him, and out of Egypt I called my son"—and Exodus 4:22—"This is what the Lord says: Israel is my firstborn son." Here and elsewhere in the Old Testament is the belief that the "son," Israel collectively, has been chosen by God for a special mission on earth (Isaiah 30:1, 63:16, Jeremiah 3:22). For the Old Testament authors, being God's son has nothing to do with divine conception as in the pagan myths or with the presence of amazing powers (also in the myths). Rather, it comes from being chosen by God for participation in a divine mission, and the position of sonship hinged on being totally obedient. Israel and Israel's kings failed in their mission as God's sons. We see this in the Book of Malachi, in which God addresses Israel: "'A son honors his father, and a servant his master. If I am a father, where is the honor due me? If I am a master, where is the respect due me?' says the Lord Almighty" (Malachi 1:6).

As the Son of God, Jesus in some sense identified with all of Israel. The fact that Jesus chose twelve disciples indicated he was initiating a new Israel, a spiritual one based not on physical descent from the twelve sons of Jacob but on joining a new spiritual family, a family that began with his twelve closest followers. Part of the hostility of the Jewish leaders to Jesus and his followers is that Jesus, not all Israel, was seen as the Son of God. In Acts, Paul, after his conversion, begins to preach that Jesus is the Son of God, and soon the Jews are plotting to kill him (Acts 9:20, 23).

But Jesus was certainly not seen as the Son of God during the early part of his ministry. In a famous episode, Jesus asked his disciples, "Who do you say I am?" Simon Peter answered, "You are the Christ, the Son of the living God" (Matthew 16:15–16). It is interesting that when Peter states his belief that Jesus is "the Son of the living

---

CULTURAL INSIGHTS ## "Sons" and "Children" in John's Writings

"For God so loved the world that he gave his one and only Son, that whoever believes in him shall not perish but have eternal life." So runs one of the most-quoted Bible verses, John 3:16, although most people like the more familiar phrase "only begotten Son" found in the King James Version. John here uses the Greek term *monogenes*, which means both "only" and "beloved" when referring to a child. The same term is found in 1 John 4:9: "This is how God showed his love among us: He sent his one and only Son into the world that we might live through him." In both verses, John is affirming that Jesus is a very special only child from God's point of view. He is in a unique relationship with the Father. Through faith, people may be adopted by God: "to those who believed in his name, he gave the right to become children of God" (John 1:12). John, unlike some of the other New Testament authors, does not refer to believers as "sons of God," but as "children of God." There is no real difference, of course, but John is careful to use *Son* only to refer to Jesus, who, as John emphasizes, was present with the Father from all eternity.

Baptism and Sonship

We see in Acts that "Jesus is the Son of God" was one of the earliest summaries of Christian belief. This is evident in the episode of the evangelist Philip in his encounter with the Ethiopian eunuch: "As they traveled along the road, they came to some water and the eunuch said, 'Look, here is water. Why shouldn't I be baptized?' Philip said, 'If you believe with all your heart, you may.' The eunuch answered, 'I believe that Jesus Christ is the Son of God'" (Acts 8:36–37).

Note that the statement "Jesus is the Son of God" is connected with the act of baptism—and remember that it was at his own baptism that Jesus was called "my beloved Son" by God. Baptism seems the appropriate occasion to confess Jesus as Son of God. As baptism symbolizes a new spiritual life, so affirming that Jesus is God's Son indicates that we have a new spiritual insight into Jesus—like Peter, "flesh and blood" did not reveal Jesus as the Son to us, but God revealed it. This idea is seen in Paul's statement to the Christians in Corinth: "From now on we regard no one from a worldly point of view. Though we once regarded Christ in this way, we do so no longer" (2 Corinthians 5:16).

God," Jesus responds by saying that "flesh and blood" had not revealed this to Peter, but the Father had (Matthew 16:16–17).

What flesh and blood do not see, spiritual beings see clearly. In his temptation of Jesus, Satan begins his overtures by saying, "If you are the Son of God, then . . ." Clearly Satan knows Jesus is the Son, though he is tempting him to act in a way unworthy of the Son. In fact, the temptation story shows Satan with one concept of "Son of God" and Jesus with a radically different concept. Satan has the worldly, pagan view—if Jesus is this kind of Son of God, he will perform marvelous deeds that will dazzle people (turn stones into bread, throw himself from a pinnacle of the temple), or he will wield great political power. But Jesus has his own view of what being Son of God means: it entails total obedience to God, which will involve getting real with human beings, coming into contact with lepers, the crippled and the demon-possessed, taking constant criticism from his own religion's leaders, enduring the constant complaining of his disciples. Indeed, the disciples themselves at times showed that they saw miracles as evidence of Jesus being the Son of God, as in the episode where Jesus walked on the water: "Then those who were in the boat worshiped him, saying, 'Truly you are the Son of God'" (Matthew 14:33). Note that on this occasion, Jesus did not commend the disciples for calling him "Son of God." Later, in Matthew 16, when Peter called Jesus "Son of the living God," Jesus knew that Peter, at least, understood the real meaning of "Son of God"—one fully obedient to God, not a worker of wonders.

While human beings are mostly blind to Jesus' true nature, the demons see who Jesus is, as shown in their reaction to him: "What do you want with us, Son of God?" (Matthew 8:29). "Whenever the evil spirits saw him, they fell down before him and cried out, 'You are the Son of God'" (Mark 3:11). It is one of the great ironies in the Gospels that Jesus' enemies accuse him of driving out demons through the power of Beelzebub, the prince of demons, when in fact Jesus is operating through the power of God, which the demons themselves see all too clearly.

But of course God also knows who his Son is, as he affirms by speaking at Jesus' baptism: "A voice from heaven said, 'This is my Son, whom I love; with him I am well pleased'" (Matthew 3:17). The divine voice was heard again at the Transfiguration, when three of the disciples witnessed Jesus speaking with the long-dead Moses and Elijah: "A bright cloud enveloped them, and a voice from the cloud said, 'This is my Son, whom I love; with him I am well pleased. Listen to him!'" (Matthew 17:5). God is pleased because his Son and he are in complete unity. What God wants, Jesus wants. The prophets and apostles were God's servants, carrying out his mission in the world, but in some unique way Jesus was the Son, with his will totally in harmony with God's.

A few human beings would use the term "Son of God" in a mocking way. At his trial, "the high priest said to him, 'I charge you under oath by the living God: Tell us if you are the Christ, the Son of God'" (Matthew 26:63). This is not a honest inquiry—the corrupt priest Caiaphas is trying to goad Jesus into saying he is God's Son, with the priest knowing this will make Jesus guilty of blasphemy. When Jesus is dying on the cross, the mockers have a field day: "Come down from the cross, if you are the Son of God! . . . He trusts in God. Let God rescue him now if he wants him, for he said, 'I am the Son of God'" (Matthew 27:40, 43). These taunts were among the many sorrows of the crucifixion. The irony was that in dying on the cross, Jesus was being obedient to God's will—thus proving he really was the Son of God.

Jesus' death impressed someone else in a radically different way: "When the centurion, who stood there in front of Jesus, heard his cry and saw how he died, he said, 'Surely this man was the Son of God!'" (Mark 15:39). Mark's Gospel opens with the declaration that it is the good news about "Jesus Christ, the Son of God." In a sense the centurion's words are the climax of the crucifixion episode. The centurion had no doubt witnessed men crucified before and had heard them calling down curses on their tormentors. But Jesus had not done this. He had in fact asked his Father to forgive them. This was extraordinary, even superhuman behavior. The centurion, who was probably a pagan, not a Jew, saw what the priests and other Jewish leaders did not see, that the crucified man was somehow divine—God's Son.

After Jesus' resurrection, all Christians honored him as Son of God: "If anyone acknowledges that Jesus is the Son of God, God lives in him and he in God" (1 John 4:15).

The Son and the Theologians

We see in the Book of Acts that Christians periodically held councils to discuss issues that were dividing believers. Beginning in the 300s, several major councils met to discuss the question, "In what way is Jesus the Son of God?" In AD 325 the Roman emperor Constantine, who had become a Christian, called a council at the city of Nicaea, in what is now Turkey. Several items were on the agenda, but the chief one was the issue of Jesus' Sonship. Specifically, a teacher named Arius taught that Jesus possessed a divine nature "like" the nature of God, while his opponents said Jesus had the same nature as God. The argument hung on one Greek letter, the *i*, called *iota*. Arius and his followers said the Son was *homoiousios*—"of like nature"—while his opponents said the Son was *homoousios*—"of the same nature." Arius' teaching was condemned by the council, and for many years after the Arian version of Christianity was a rival to the non-Arian—a huge division hanging on one letter.

Officially, most Christian churches today subscribe to the view of the Council of Nicaea, that the Son was "of the same nature" as the Father. Unofficially, of course, most Christians would be totally baffled by this theological hair-splitting. The theologians of centuries ago seemed to enjoy this sort of thing, however, and many of the early councils continued to define—or so they thought—the Son's nature.

Does it sound like they were complicating things unnecessarily? It seems so. When Christianity spread to the Gentile world, many of the converts were people who had dabbled in Greek and Roman philosophy and had made a kind of intellectual game out of debating and defining. Unfortunately, some of them carried this mentality over into Christianity, and made the simple faith of the New Testament into something complex and intimidating. We can safely assume that Jesus and the apostles would have told the theologians to place more emphasis on living their faith than on debating it.

Christians saw something in the phrase "Son of God" that no other people did: God's Son could actually suffer and die. "We were reconciled to him through the death of his Son" (Romans 5:10). The pagans could not have imagined a son of the gods dying, much less redeeming mankind by his death. Nor could one's death enable other human beings to be adopted as sons and daughters of God: "To all who received him, to those who believed in his name, he gave the right to become children of God" (John 1:12).

Some people have argued that Jesus did not really see himself as Son of God. They base this on the fact that Jesus usually referred to himself as "Son of Man." In fact it is quite clear in the Gospels that Jesus knew he was God's Son. Consider the story of Jesus' healing the paralyzed man, whose friends had dug a hole through the roof of a house so as to lower the paralyzed man down to Jesus. "When Jesus saw their faith, he said to the paralytic, 'Son, your sins are forgiven.' Now some teachers of the law were sitting there, thinking to themselves, 'Why does this fellow talk like that? He's blaspheming! Who can forgive sins but God alone?'" (Mark 2:5–7). The teachers of the law were correct: It would have been blasphemous for any normal human being to claim to forgive someone's sins. But the answer to their question "Who can forgive sins but God alone?" was "God's Son." The teachers understood that Jesus was identifying himself with God.

YESHUA SAVES

Today in the town of David a Savior has been born to you; he is Christ the Lord. (Luke 2:11)

Grow in the grace and knowledge of our Lord and Savior Jesus Christ. (2 Peter 3:18)

We have seen and testify that the Father has sent his Son to be the Savior of the world. (1 John 4:14)

The Old Testament frequently uses the title "Savior" for God, although it also applies the name to human deliverers. The Jews of Jesus' day definitely expected the Messiah to be a Savior, although they conceived of this salvation as political and material, not spiritual. There was no conception of saving people's souls.

This was also true in the pagan world, where gods and heroes were often referred to as saviors—saving from disease, natural disasters, etc. Asklepios, the Greek god of healing, was often called Savior. Also, rulers liked to present themselves to the world as saviors, keeping their people from harm, maintaining order, punishing criminals. Since many rulers, including the Roman emperors, were supposedly divine, it was not uncommon for people to pray to their rulers for healing, and temples built to honor the emperor's divinity were there to encourage just such absurd ideas.

Obviously these uses of Savior were totally "this-worldly," but many of the religious cults in the Roman empire had a definite otherworldly goal, and in each of these a god—such as Mithra or Isis—was called Savior, and though the god might bestow blessings in this life, his main benefit was to ensure the devotees' salvation in the afterlife. The popularity of such cults was, for many people, a preparation for belief in the true Savior, Jesus.

The Greek word *soter*, meaning "savior," is from the root word *sozein*, meaning "to save" or, more narrowly, "to heal." Clearly the many people whom Jesus healed from their diseases or freed from the oppression of demons thought of him as their Savior, at least in the sense of being healed. But in fact the Gospels only record two instances of Jesus being called Savior—one in the prediction of his birth by the angel Gabriel (Luke 2), and another in Jesus' encounter with the Samaritan woman (John 4). In his ministry among his fellow Jews, Jesus was never called Savior, although certainly he had much to say about salvation. In fact, he clearly defined himself as Savior: "It is not the healthy who need a doctor, but the sick. I have not come to call the righteous, but sinners" (Mark 2:17).

We see in Acts and in the epistles that the first Christians saw Jesus as the Savior from sin. Jesus' contemporaries would have called him by his Aramaic name, *Yeshua*, a form of the Old Testament Hebrew name *Yehoshua*, which we normally print as *Joshua*. The name means "Yah [God] saves," as is made clear in Matthew 1:21: "She [Mary] will give birth to a son, and you are to give him the name Jesus, because he will save his people from their sins." People in ancient times never chose a name because it sounded nice but because of its meaning. Many ancient names were theophoric ("god-bearing"), meaning they incorporated the name of a god—for example, the Egyptian name Rameses means "the god Ra is his father." Yeshua means "Yah saves," and in fact "Jesus saves" in Aramaic would be *Yeshua Yeshua*. In Greek it is *Iesous Soter*, and the fact that the title is redundant in Aramaic but not in Greek may explain why referring to Jesus as Savior was more common among speakers of Greek.

Pause a moment to reflect on Matthew 1:21: "He will save his people from their sins." Jesus is not going to be the one who saves the Jews from Roman political oppression, although when he reaches adulthood Satan will tempt him to do so. He is not to be the this-worldly Savior, the *Soter*, in the sense that either the Jews or pagans had expected. He will save people from sin and bring them into loving fellowship with God. For the New Testament, this is what salvation really means. It is thanks to the first Christians that the word "Savior" has a spiritual, not material or political meaning.

We see in the preaching of the early Christians how the meaning in Jesus' name became part of the proclamation: "Salvation is found in no one else, for there is no other name under heaven given to men by which we must be saved" (Acts 4:12). We also see that the first Christians baptized converts "in the name of Jesus" (Acts 2:38, 8:46, 10:48, 1 Corinthians 1:13–15). Those first Christians, aware of the meaning of Jesus' name, understood something that we often miss: The theme of the whole Bible is salvation, and Jesus' name means "God saves." In a literal sense, Jesus is the theme of the Bible.

Jesus was more than the Savior from sins. He saves us from the fear of death. According to Paul, "the last enemy to be destroyed is death" (1 Corinthians 15:26). Paul also refers to "the appearing of our Savior, Christ Jesus, who has destroyed death and has brought life and immortality to light through the gospel" (2 Timothy 1:10). While the various false cults across the empire promised their followers immortality, Jesus actually delivered it. Jesus' own Resurrection from death is the sign that

> **DID YOU KNOW?**
>
> Soteriology is the branch of theology dealing with salvation. The Greek word for Savior is *Soter*.

his followers will experience death but be raised at last. Contrast the Christians' belief in Jesus' victory over death with the Greek and Roman belief that the healing god, Asklepios, was destroyed by the head god, Zeus, for daring to bring people back from the dead. Zeus begrudged man eternal life, but Jesus and his Father did not.

In John 4:42 the Samaritans refer to Jesus as the "Savior of the world." John's original readers would have been familiar with that title, since it was used by the Roman emperors. The emperors were, of course, far from being saviors of the world. They did not rule the entire world, and as for saving, the millions of people oppressed by their taxation and their military presence—not to mention the trickle-down effect of Roman morals—hardly thought of the emperors as saviors. But the title fit Jesus perfectly, for he was not an earthly ruler but "the Lamb of God, who takes away the sin of the world" (John 1:29).

Jesus had come to earth to save people from their sins, and one important message of the New Testament is that this mission was accomplished. But we also see the idea that the Savior will return to earth again, as in Philippians 3:20: "Our citizenship is in heaven. And we eagerly await a Savior from there, the Lord Jesus Christ." We have salvation now, but in the full sense it will be completed at the Second Coming.

One closing thought: The first Christians saw Jesus as a great moral teacher and chose to write down his words and pass them on. But the New Testament makes it clear that Jesus the teacher is secondary to Jesus the Savior. The need for salvation is greater than the need for wise words. If the New Testament authors had only seen Jesus as teacher, not Savior, the faith would not have spread, and Jesus might only be a footnote in textbooks on philosophy and world religions. The human race needs wise and profound teachers, and Jesus was one of them, but it has a more pressing need for a Savior.

PUTTING THE WORD TO WORK

1. When you pray today, pause to reflect on the meaning of "Lord," on the reality that God is the Master you serve. See if this doesn't affect what—and whom—you pray for.

2. Many early Christians faced persecution because some of the Roman emperors demanded to be called "Lord." Pray for faithful people in the world today who are persecuted because they give their ultimate loyalty to God.

3. Imagine yourself in the place of the centurion who watched Jesus die and then proclaimed, "Surely this was the Son of God." What is there about Jesus on the cross that would have given this impression?

4. The New Testament teaches that those who put their faith in Jesus as Son of God are themselves the sons and daughters of God. In what ways does being a child of God influence your actions, words and thoughts?

5. Yeshua, Jesus' name in his native language, means "God saves." As you go through the day, consider the meaning of this name for your own life.

Boldness and Badness

ELIJAH, ELISHA AND THE WORST RULERS EVER

Heroes look most heroic when contrasted with villains. In this chapter we will look at two of the Bible's great heroes—the prophets Elijah and Elisha—standing up to two of the vilest villains, Ahab and Jezebel. The two heroes were men of amazing courage and zeal, willing to play the role of solitary men of God, speaking truth to corrupt political power. Politically and numerically they were weak, but spiritually they were stronger than all their adversaries.

> **MEMORY VERSE**
>
> Never be lacking in zeal, but keep your spiritual fervor, serving the Lord.
> —Romans 12:11

KEY TERM FOR TODAY   ## Zeal

God's people sometimes show great courage for the truth, even at great risk and against formidable odds. Such zeal comes through deep faith that God is truly in control of things.

SETTING THE STANDARD FOR BADNESS

Ahab son of Omri did more evil in the eyes of the Lord than any of those before him. (1 Kings 16:30)

Elijah the Tishbite, from Tishbe in Gilead, said to Ahab, "As the Lord, the God of Israel, lives, whom I serve, there will be neither dew nor rain in the next few years except at my word." (1 Kings 17:1)

Most of the kings of Israel were real rogues, so truly despicable that they give monarchy a bad name. The competition for Baddest King is fierce, but probably the prize would go to Ahab, a tyrant who seems to have gotten his ideas about royal power from his foreign-born wife.

Let's pause a moment to consider the Bible's view of kings in general: They stink. There are some noble and notable exceptions (Josiah and Hezekiah), but most kings in the Bible—likewise for all of human history—are a pretty rotten bunch. The reason is obvious: Give a human being a lot of power, and given the selfishness of human nature, chances are he will abuse it. It is a testimony to human stupidity that monarchy proves time and again to be a failure, yet for thousands of years

people keep setting up kings who tyrannize them. No form of government is perfect, since human beings aren't, yet monarchy has to be one of the worst—and yet it has continued, sadly and destructively.

Ancient Israel was not originally a monarchy. Its true king was God, who raised up leaders like Moses, Joshua and the various military heroes described in the Book of Judges. Israel was more a confederacy of tribes than a real nation, and for this reason it had trouble defending itself against the more powerful and king-led nations around it. So the people of Israel began agitating for a king to rally around. The saintly and wise leader Samuel delivered a speech to the Israelites, telling them just exactly what they could expect from a king—and it was not a pretty picture he painted. Samuel's speech, found in 1 Samuel 8:10–18, is a reminder that oppressive, tax-hungry government is nothing new. At any rate, God did give in to the nation's request for a king, and as he and Samuel foretold, it was a request the nation would regret for many generations.

Now, on to Ahab. By the time he came to rule, Israel had already split into two nations, Israel in the north and Judah in the south—a split caused by the arrogance and stupidity of an earlier king, Rehoboam. (More about him in another chapter.) Both kingdoms faced the age-old challenge of keeping out foreign enemies, and by the time Ahab became king, Israel was doing well. It was so stable and prosperous that foreign nations referred to Israel as "the house of Omri"—Omri being Ahab's father. Omri was apparently a successful politician—successful and powerful, but not good. Though he built the capital city of Samaria and gained an international reputation during his twelve-year reign, the Bible dismisses his worldly achievements with the words "Omri did what was evil in the sight of the Lord" (1 Kings 16:25). Specifically, Omri worshipped false gods, neglected the true God, and passed on his bad habits to his son.

But in worldly terms, Omri made Israel a prominent player on the world stage. With power comes sophistication, the desire to hobnob with the other kings, even if those kings were pagans who engaged in disgusting rituals such as child sacrifice. One piece of evidence of Omri's high political standing and cosmopolitanism is the fact that his son Ahab married the daughter of the king of Sidon, a thriving and immoral commercial city. That daughter was one of the baddest of the Bible's bad girls, the infamous Jezebel. Her father, Eth-Baal, was not only king of Sidon but also priest of the god Baal, as you might

Ravens

These large, shaggy black birds are members of the crow family, and like other members of that family they are highly intelligent and can even be taught to speak a few words. Their first appearance in the Bible is in the story of Noah and the ark, with Noah sending forth a raven over the flooded earth to see if the bird would return. In the story of Elijah in the wilderness, the ravens brought the prophet food every morning and evening (1 Kings 17:6). Based on this story, ravens have often been used as symbols of God's care for his people. Elijah's being fed by the ravens has been a popular subject in artworks. In the classic novel *Robinson Crusoe*, the narrator, shipwrecked alone on an island, records that "I had been fed even by a miracle, even as great as that of feeding Elijah by ravens."

guess from his name. Her father brought her up as an aristocrat and as a devoted follower of Baal, and Baal worship was not exactly solemn and chaste. Baal was a god of fertility, so worship of him often involved what we call ritual prostitution—sex with male or female prostitutes in the name of "good religion." If worshippers performed their duty, then, so they believed, their crops would grow, their women would bear children, etc. And if none of this happened, well, at least they enjoyed the worship service. Baal worship horrified devout people in Israel, who saw such religion for what it was: an excuse for promiscuity. But it was an attractive religion, one that seemed sophisticated and chic, and many Israelites were tempted to forsake their true God and to follow Baal. The Baal cult had been the original religion of Canaan before the Israelites settled there. Now, centuries later, there was a real danger of the land reverting back to Baal worship—with the backing of Israel's royal family.

When Jezebel married Ahab, she had every intention of making the Baal cult Israel's national religion. She was fortunate to have a real pushover for a husband. No doubt he was impressed with the prosperity of Jezebel's homeland, Sidon, and he probably assumed that the god of such a place must be very powerful. In a sense he was repeating Solomon's sin of being led into idolatry by a pagan wife. Inevitably there had to be a showdown between God and Baal.

God's man at this crucial point in history was the prophet Elijah, called simply "Elijah the Tishbite." His name is peculiar, for most men were identified as "X, son of Z" (no one had last names in those days). Elijah is "the Tishbite," meaning he came from the village of Tishbe, and there is no mention of his father. In 1 Kings 17:1, Elijah appears, suddenly and mysteriously, before Ahab with a dire prophecy: "As the Lord, the God of Israel, lives, whom I serve, there will be neither dew nor rain in the next few years except at my word." Drought was a serious thing, and as Elijah foretold, Israel literally starved for water for many months.

The prophet himself did not lack for provision. He lived by the Cherith Brook, got his water there, and was brought food by ravens, not the last time that God would miraculously provide for his prophet. When the brook dried up, he was commanded by God to live with a widow in the village of Zarephath. The poor woman could barely provide enough food for herself

Ahab reigned as king of Israel 874–853 BC. Ahaziah, his son, reigned 853–852 BC. Joram, also his son, reigned 852–841 BC. Jezebel died in 841 BC, when Jehu led the revolt that exterminated Ahab's dynasty.

and her son to eat, much less Elijah, but God again looked after Elijah, the woman and the son by miraculously multiplying the oil and flour the woman used in cooking. When the woman's son died, Elijah restored him to life. The raising of the widow's son to life is a tender contrast to the more fiery side of Elijah's nature that is shown later in the story.

The miracles occur in Zarephath, which was not in Israel but belonged to Sidon, Jezebel's home. The widow of Zarephath, a pagan, praises the God of Israel, while Israel's own king and queen are promoting the Baal cult.

Because of Ahab's and Jezebel's evil, Israel suffered a disastrous drought, though God saw that his prophet was provided for. God decided to send rain—and in a way the Israelites would never forget.

CULTURAL INSIGHTS

Loveless Fertility Religion

Israel's prophets often spoke of the worship of pagan gods as "fornication" or "adultery." Literally, it often was, for the worship of Baal, Asherah, and other nature gods was more like an orgy than what we think of as a worship service. But it was like fornication in another respect: It was a shallow, no-strings, temporary relation between a human being and a non-sentient being, an idol. In fact, there was no relation, period, because the idol was not real, just as in fornication the other party was not seen as human.

Marriage involves relation, exclusive commitment, plumbing the depths of one person. Promiscuity is about variety, skimming the surface of another person. The relationship of God and Israel was supposed to be like marriage—"till death do us part." A pagan really had no sense of commitment to one god; every god was there to provide some good or service in exchange for sacrifice—pray and sacrifice to the fertility gods during planting season, pray to the storm god during drought, etc.

> While Jezebel was killing off the Lord's prophets, Obadiah had taken a hundred prophets and hidden them in two caves. (1 Kings 18:4)

> "Now summon the people from all over Israel to meet me on Mount Carmel. And bring the four hundred and fifty prophets of Baal and the four hundred prophets of Asherah, who eat at Jezebel's table." (1 Kings 18:19)

Ahab, under his wife's influence, had built a temple to Baal in the capital city, Samaria. The long drought did not have the effect of turning Ahab back to the true God. On the contrary, we see in 1 Kings 18:4 that Jezebel had continued her pro-Baal, anti-God policy by killing some of the Lord's prophets. A showdown had to take place. God told Elijah to present himself to Ahab. Elijah encountered Obadiah, the manager of Ahab's household and a devout man who had risked his master's wrath by hiding some of the Lord's prophets in a cave. Obadiah was pleased to see Elijah, but unnerved when Elijah told him to arrange a meeting between himself and Ahab. Obadiah had shown great courage in protecting the Lord's prophets, but he knew Elijah's reputation for appearing and disappearing quickly, and he feared that if he announced Elijah to Ahab, Elijah would disappear suddenly. Elijah assured the frightened man that he would not disappear but would meet with the wicked king.

Obadiah had been happy to see Elijah. Ahab was not. "When he saw Elijah, he said to him, 'Is that you, you troubler of Israel?'" (1 Kings 18:17). Here we have a classic case of the politician who wants to set himself above the people and not be accountable to anyone. He tags Elijah as the "troubler of Israel," when in fact Elijah is doing the will of God by pointing out that trouble already exists, and it is of Ahab's making. If the king was doing his job as God intended, no prophet would be needed to correct him. To an evil, corrupt politician, anyone who points out his crimes is a "troubler." The long drought was the result not of any malice on Elijah's part but of Ahab's idol worship and desertion of God.

Elijah sets up a meeting: He, the zealous prophet of God, will meet four hundred fifty prophets of Baal on Mount Carmel. "All Israel" is invited to watch.

Elijah chose Carmel for a reason. It had been a place where God was worshipped—an altar to him had been there, but it was torn down. Under Ahab and Jezebel the mountain was a center of Baal rites. For the Baalists, the site would have symbolized Baal's triumph over God. And yet the long drought that Elijah had prophesied was a great blow to the Baal cult, for the Baalists believed that Baal sent fertility—and rain.

> **DID YOU KNOW?**
>
> The Arab name for Mount Carmel is *Jebel Mar Elyas*, "mountain of the great Elijah."

With the Baal prophets and the people assembled on the mountain, Elijah posed the great question: "How long will you waver between two opinions? If the Lord is God, follow him; but if Baal is God, follow him" (1 Kings 18:21). The people said nothing. Elijah ordered bulls brought in for sacrifice. Elijah would call on God, and the four hundred fifty Baal prophets would call on Baal, to set the sacrifice on fire.

The Baal prophets put on a show; in fact, that is what the typical worship ritual of this fertility religion consisted of—a show involving music and frenzied dancing of a highly erotic nature. The Baal prophets kept up their act for hours, dancing and calling out to Baal. They even gashed their own skin, thinking the blood would draw Baal's attention. Elijah mocked the foolish commotion—perhaps, he said, Baal was asleep or away on a journey—or even relieving himself. In this tense situation, Elijah is more than just anti-idolatry; he is pro-monotheism. The great showdown is not about which god to worship, but about there being only one God. Baal is not weak or impotent—he simply doesn't exist. It is time for the Israelites to grow up, to realize there is only one God, and though he rules over nature, he is not identified with forces of nature.

Elijah rebuilt the altar to God, made up of twelve stones symbolizing the twelve tribes of Israel. Then what followed was direct and simple, involving no frenzied dancing or cutting of his own flesh: "Elijah stepped forward and prayed: 'O Lord, God of Abraham, Isaac and Israel, let it be known today that you are God in Israel and that I am your servant and have done all these things at your command. Answer me, O Lord, answer me, so these people will know that you, O Lord, are God, and that you are turning their hearts back again.'" His prayer was heard. Fire—lightning, probably—fell

CULTURAL INSIGHTS ## The High God

Historically, most people on earth have been polytheists, believing in more than one god. However, historians and anthropologists have observed that most cultures believe in an invisible "high god," usually thought of as a Father and Creator, who is usually not represented by idols. For the Canaanites, the original inhabitants of Israel, this high god was El—the name simply means "god." But as is true of so many religions, this divine father, El, was generally ignored, and the people's worship instead focused on personified forces of nature. Baal, El's son, was the god of rain and fertility and was much more important than El. In the showdown on Mount Carmel, the Baal prophets would have been calling out to *Baal Shamem*, "lord of the heavens."

from heaven and consumed the sacrifice. The people responded wisely: "They fell prostrate and cried, 'The Lord—he is God! The Lord—he is God!'" (1 King 18:39). Not surprisingly, they took the Baal prophets and killed them.

Atop Carmel, Elijah's servant sighted a cloud "as small as a man's hand" in the distance. Not only had God consumed the sacrifice on Carmel, but the long drought was also at an end. Clearly God—not the nonexistent Baal—was in control of things. The sky grew black with rain clouds, and Ahab headed back in his chariot to his palace in Jezreel. Elijah, on foot, outran him.

GOD'S WHISPER

He came to a broom tree, sat down under it and prayed that he might die. "I have had enough, Lord," he said. "Take my life". . . .

After the earthquake came a fire, but the Lord was not in the fire. And after the fire came a gentle whisper. (1 Kings 19:4, 12)

Elijah's feat of outrunning Ahab's chariot amazes us. Perhaps it amazed Elijah himself, a man who was energized by the Lord and was witness to an awesome miracle: the apparent defeat of the false god's worshippers. But this spiritual high was followed by a rock-bottom low.

Ahab had witnessed the Carmel episode. Jezebel had not. When Ahab told her what happened, she did not repent or relent. She sent Elijah a message: "May the gods deal with me, be it ever so severely, if by this time tomorrow I do not make your life like that of one of them" (1 Kings 19:2)—a clear reference to the Baal prophets who had been killed at Carmel.

Jezebel had a perverse nature. The obvious reaction to what happened on Carmel would have been repentance—or at least the acknowledgement that Israel's God was superior to Baal. Instead, she resolved to kill Elijah, or at least drive him from Israel. Didn't it occur to her that the same God who manifested himself on Mount Carmel might not take kindly to his faithful prophet being persecuted? Jezebel is a classic case of sticking by a fantasy and ignoring the facts. An astonishing miracle witnessed by many could not break the stubbornness of her proud heart.

The queen's stubbornness led to Elijah's dejection, for he must have hoped and assumed that the Carmel episode would bring an end to paganism in Israel. So Elijah fled to the wilderness. He sat under a tree and prayed to God to end his life. Not for the first time in his life, he awoke to find food and water nearby. Refreshed—physically, at least—he journeyed many days to the mountain of God, called Horeb or Sinai, the same place where God had given Moses the law. There he lodged in a cave.

God came to him, and in a dramatic way. A tree-shattering wind passed by—"but the Lord was not in the wind." Then an earthquake shook the mountain—"but the Lord was not in the earthquake." Then came a fire—"but the Lord was not in the fire." Then came "a gentle whisper"—or, in the familiar words of the King James Version, "a still, small voice." The voice gave Elijah courage: no, Elijah was not the only man in Israel who remained true to God. In fact, there were seven thousand people who had not bowed down to Baal.

God's power on Horeb had been manifested through the wind, the earthquake, the fire and then the "still small voice." Elijah knew God was on his side, that God was in control of the forces of nature but could also gently speak to him as a friend. Yet, even so, he needed assurance that there were other human beings on the same side. Elijah, the classic "lone wolf," seems like a tough-minded, steel-hearted man who can take the position of "me and God against the world"—yet even he needed companionship.

As confirmation that he has not left his great prophet alone in the world, God sends Elijah to find the man who will become his bosom friend, protégé and successor as prophet, Elisha. Elijah is not all alone in the world, for God can raise up another prophet—and provide a friend for the friendless.

"Elijah went from there and found Elisha son of Shaphat" (1 Kings 19:19). Elisha was at work—plowing, in fact. Elijah threw his cloak over him, a sign of adopting him, spiritually speaking. Elisha had of course already heard of the mighty prophet. He knew his life had been changed forever. He took the twelve oxen he was plowing with and sacrificed them. The sacrifice is in fact a feast for his family and neighbors—he is celebrating his "ordination." After the sacrifice, he destroys his farm implements, putting his old life behind him.

Despite this affiliation of two great men, when we next meet Elijah he is back in his familiar role: the solitary prophet confronting a wicked ruler.

WHO RULES?

Ahab said to Naboth, "Let me have your vineyard to use for a vegetable garden, since it is close to my palace. In exchange I will give you a better vineyard or, if you prefer, I will pay you whatever it is worth." (1 Kings 21:2)

There was never a man like Ahab, who sold himself to do evil in the eyes of the Lord, urged on by Jezebel his wife. (1 Kings 21:25)

Jezebel intended to change Israel's religion—and also to change its concept of kingship. In her homeland, kings were autocrats. If a king wanted to seize your property, it happened. This wasn't true of Israel, where God was still considered the true king, and

The Jezebel Artifact

In 1964, archaeologists discovered a stone seal believed to be Jezebel's that may contain part of her name. The seal shows a sphinx figure with a lion's body and a woman's head, and also shows a winged sun disk. A king always possessed a royal seal, but queens usually did not, and if this seal is truly Jezebel's, it backs up the Bible's image of her as a true power player in her own right, not just the wife of a king.

the earthly king had limited power. Jezebel learned that Ahab was sulking because he wanted the vineyard of a man named Naboth. He had gone about it the right way: He made Naboth a generous offer for the vineyard, but Naboth turned it down, claiming he had no desire to sell his family land. A family's land was sacred and was almost never sold to an outsider, and no king had the right to confiscate any citizen's property. So Ahab sulked and refused to eat.

Jezebel's and Ahab's fathers had something in common: They had not inherited their thrones but usurped them. Jezebel's father, Eth-Baal, had seized power in Sidon at the same time as Omri, Ahab's father, in Israel. The two men must have admired each other's spunk, and their mutual admiration was sealed in a political alliance. Jezebel shared this "if you want something, take it" mentality.

Jezebel was appalled at Ahab's wimpy behavior: "Is this how you act as king over Israel? Get up and eat! Cheer up. I'll get you the vineyard of Naboth." She hatched one of the nastiest plans recorded in the Bible: Ahab would order a gathering of the notables in the town, and when they were all together, two hired thugs would publicly accuse Naboth of cursing God and the king. Naboth was stoned to death, and Ahab took possession of his land.

This barbaric, tyrannical behavior (call it "judicial murder") did not go unnoticed by the prophet Elijah. The God of the Bible is above the king and can call him on the carpet anytime he steps out of line. In Jezebel's religion, the gods are basically there to rubber-stamp whatever the rulers decide. In Israel, kings were answerable to God for their sins, and kings had to respect individuals and their private property. This true prophet of God confronted Ahab right in Naboth's vineyard and made a horrifying prediction: Dogs would lick up Ahab's blood. And Jezebel? She too would be devoured by dogs. (A tidbit worth remembering: dogs in those days weren't beloved household pets but rather nasty scavengers of the streets. *Dog* was also a slang term for prostitute.)

DID YOU KNOW?

In the story of Ahab's death, one printing of the King James Version had, in 1 Kings 22:38, "the dogs liked his blood" instead of "licked his blood."

Elijah in Jewish Tradition

Because of his zeal for the Lord, and because he had been taken into heaven without dying, Elijah became a much-loved character among the Jews. Also, it was believed he would return to earth in the end times, as foretold in Malachi 4:5: "See, I will send you the prophet Elijah before that great and dreadful day of the Lord comes." In the New Testament, Jesus was thought by some to be Elijah returned to earth.

When the disciples James and John asked Jesus if they should send fire down from heaven on a village that rejected them (Luke 9:54), they no doubt had in mind Elijah's miracle in 2 Kings 1:10–12.

The account of Jesus' crucifixion suggests that the Jews of that time thought of Elijah as a kind of guardian angel who could provide help in time of need, which explains why when Jesus agonized—"*Eloi, eloi, lamasabachthani*?"—this was misinterpreted as a cry for help from Elijah. (The words were in fact the Hebrew for "My God, my God, why have you forsaken me?")

Jews today still have the custom of setting out a cup of wine at the seder, the meal that marks the beginning of the Passover celebration. After Elijah's cup is filled, the home's door is open to let him in. Some wealthy families have expensive wine cups especially made for Elijah. Also, an empty chair is reserved for Elijah at the Jewish circumcision ceremony.

But apparently the vile king did possess a small shred of conscience. According to 1 Kings 21:27–29, Ahab was so moved by Elijah's warning that he performed the usual acts of despair and repentance: He tore his royal clothes, put on sackcloth (something like burlap—and about as comfortable), and fasted. The Lord took notice of it, and told Elijah that the king's acts of humility had delayed judgment on his dynasty.

Ahab's mood of repentance didn't last long. And no wonder, since, like all kings of those days, he had his official court prophets who were nowhere near as moral or truthful as Elijah was. Basically the court prophets were bootlicking yes men who would never dream of telling the king he was on a disastrous course. So naturally the king detested a faithful prophet named Micaiah.

Ahab contemplated going to war against the king of Aram. Ahab's ally was the saintly Jehoshaphat, king of Judah. Ahab asked his court prophets their opinion. One of the yes men prophesied in a dramatic way: "Zedekiah son of Kenaanah had made iron horns and he declared, 'This is what the Lord says: "With these you will gore the Arameans until they are destroyed"'" (1 Kings 22:11). Jehoshaphat was skeptical. Was there a genuine prophet of God who would speak the truth? Reluctantly, Ahab had Micaiah brought in. Mockingly, Micaiah foretold victory against the Arameans. Ahab knew he was being sarcastic and ordered him to speak the truth: Ahab's court prophets were all liars, and the battle against Aram would end in disaster. The surly Ahab went off to battle after ordering Micaiah to be thrown in prison, with bread and water rations. Micaiah predicted correctly that Ahab would not come back alive.

There is a hint in the story that Ahab just may have believed Micaiah's words, for 1 Kings tells us that Ahab went into battle in disguise, not in his royal robes. (Another possibility: He was a coward.) The disguise failed, for Ahab was fatally wounded by an arrow—fired at random, ironically enough. You get the impression from the story that Ahab had just enough religion to put some stock in the words of real prophets like Micaiah and Elijah, and so he held onto the vain hope that his disguise would keep him safe from the divine wrath. It did keep him from being fired upon by the enemy's archers—but not from the "random" arrow that killed him. (If you read the Bible with the eye of faith, you hardly believe there was anything random about the arrow.) The bleeding king was carried in his chariot back to Samaria, where, as Elijah predicted, Ahab's blood was licked up by the dogs (1 Kings 22:29–40). The narrative adds the colorful—and disgusting—fact that "the prostitutes washed themselves in it."

GOD'S CHARIOTS

Elijah said to Elisha, "Tell me, what can I do for you before I am taken from you?" "Let me inherit a double portion of your spirit." Elisha replied. . . .

Elisha saw this and cried out, "My father! My father! The chariots and horsemen of Israel!" And Elisha saw him no more. (2 Kings 2:9, 12)

Elijah's prophecy had come true. Ahab—the promoter of idol worship, the man with no respect for the property rights of the people he ruled over—had died violently, his blood licked up by dogs. But politically, nothing had changed. Jezebel still lived, and Ahaziah, son of Ahab and Jezebel, ruled as king.

He did not rule for long. After a serious fall in his palace in Samaria, he sent messengers to get a divine word about whether he would survive or not. The messengers did not inquire of God but of Baal. Elijah met the messengers of the king and gave them a word from God: Ahaziah would not recover; he would die. Ahaziah, like his parents, relied on a false god, Baal.

Angry, Ahaziah sent fifty soldiers to capture the prophet. They did not succeed: God sent fire from heaven—probably lightning—to destroy the men. This happened a second time, and then a third. Ahaziah died, as Elijah had foretold.

The king's men had learned a hard lesson: Elijah's God was more powerful than any human forces.

Hairy and Bald

Was there a distinctive "look" to Israel's prophets? Possibly, for some. Consider 2 Kings 1:8, in which the king sends troops to capture Elijah, who is described as "a man with a garment of hair" in most versions, but "a hairy man" in the King James Version. Elijah may have been a man with abundant body hair, but the modern versions are probably correct, and his hair mantle might have been part of his garb as a prophet.

Later, we are told that Elisha is taunted by some youths: "Go on up, you baldhead!" As punishment, they are mauled by two she-bears who come out of the woods. The story seems horribly cruel: forty-two boys mauled because they made fun of a man's baldness? It is possible that Elisha was not naturally bald, but that he shaved part of his head in keeping with the look of the "sons of the prophets," the religious fraternity he associated with. In making fun of Elisha's distinctive "cut," the youths were in effect mocking God's prophets.

What follows this episode is one of the most colorful scenes in the Bible: Elijah's departure from this world. Elijah and Elisha were "walking along and talking together, suddenly a chariot of fire and horses of fire appeared and separated the two of them, and Elijah went up to heaven in a whirlwind. Elisha saw this and cried out, "My father! My father! The chariots and horsemen of Israel!" And Elisha saw him no more" (2 Kings 2:11–12). As a sign of grief at losing his master and friend, Elisha "took hold of his own clothes and tore them apart."

Elisha's words to the departing Elijah are revealing: "The chariots of Israel and its horsemen" are not material assets but the power of God. Recall that after the episode on Carmel, Elijah outran Ahab's chariots. Recall also that when Ahaziah sent troops to capture the prophet, they were destroyed by fire. Elijah and Elisha were servants of a power mightier than any human forces.

In leaving this world, Elijah had thrown down his mantle on Elisha. It was more than a mere article of clothing; it was a sign of the prophet's power and charisma. Just before being taken to heaven, Elijah had struck the waters of the Jordan River with the mantle, and the waters had parted. After his departure, Elisha performed the same miracle.

In the Bible, no mention is ever made of Elijah's parents, wife or children. His "son" is clearly Elisha, who as the "firstborn" and only child receives a "double portion" of Elijah's inheritance—not worldly goods but his "spirit." He received what he had asked for from his friend, a "double portion" of his spirit.

The men were similar in many ways, different in others. Elijah was the lone wolf, the brave soul who by himself confronted Ahab and the prophets of Baal. Elisha, by contrast, associated himself with the "sons of the prophets," groups of men in Israel who lived in communities and pursued a religious life. After Elijah's dramatic departure into heaven, the "sons of the prophets" went out to meet Elisha and acknowledged him as their master. These men were fortunate to have Elisha among them at times, for he performed several miracles for them, including purifying some poisonous stew and, like Elijah, multiplying food for them.

Elisha's most famous miracle involved the healing of an outsider, not a fellow Israelite. Naaman, commander of the armies of Syria, suffered from leprosy. As it happened, on one of the Syrians' raids into Israel, they had captured a young Israelite girl, who became a slave in Naaman's household. The girl told her masters about Elisha, the powerful prophet in Israel. Taking a huge sum of silver and gold, Naaman went to Israel, willing to pay Elisha for a miracle. Instead of meeting him in person, Elisha sent a message: Wash seven times in the Jordan River, and he would be cured. Naaman was irked by the message. No doubt he had heard of some of the dramatic miracles of Elijah and Elisha and expected something similar. What would immersion in the Jordan—more a creek than a river—possibly accomplish? But his servant convinced him to do as the prophet said. Naaman did so "and his flesh was restored and became clean like that of a young boy" (2 Kings 5:14). God, who could speak through a "still, small voice," could perform quiet yet amazing miracles.

Naaman praised Israel's God and offered to reward Elisha handsomely. The prophet would accept nothing. But Elisha's servant, Gehazi, thought his master foolish for turning

CHARACTERS AT LARGE — Jezebel in Pop Culture

In one of his Top 40 hits, Rod Stewart sang about a "mean old Jezebel" with her "red lips, hair and fingernails." Whether or not they had ever read the Bible, listeners were expected to know that a Jezebel was a wicked woman—and, incidentally, one who went overboard with her makeup. The original Jezebel was indeed a "painted woman," and her name passed into common usage as "the worst kind of woman." Throughout history, her name has again and again been used to refer to any famous bad woman, particularly one with any political clout.

Interestingly, the Bible says nothing about Jezebel's personal sexual morals. For all we know, she may have been a faithful wife, but her promotion of the Baal cult tells us she was tolerant of sexual looseness. Even so, people associate her name with sexual immorality, and throughout history any famous woman with a "reputation" was likely to be called a Jezebel. In the 1500s, the famous Mary Queen of Scots, who conspired in the murder of her husband and then quickly married another man, was called a Jezebel. So was her cousin, Queen Mary I of England, who tried to turn England from a Protestant country back into a Catholic one —and executed a lot of Protestants in the process, leading to her nickname, "Bloody Mary."

down money. He ran after Naaman and told him a lie: Elisha just had some guests arrive, so would Naaman please supply him with some silver? Naaman did so, and Gehazi went home, having profited from his master's miracle. Elisha knew precisely what had happened. He questioned Gehazi, but Gehazi denied any wrongdoing. For his presumption and deception, he was punished with—appropriately—leprosy. Though this strikes us as harsh, it reminds us that in the Bible, miracles are gracious acts of God, not deeds done for material reward.

The story of Naaman is another case of a pagan, someone from outside Israel, praising God, while Israel's rulers promote the cult of Baal.

DRESSED FIT TO KILL

[Jezebel] painted her eyes and adorned her head and looked out of the window. And as Jehu entered the gate, she said, "Is it peace, you Zimri, murderer of your master?" (2 Kings 9:30–31, ESV)

Thus far in the story, two bad kings—Ahab and Ahaziah—have both died. The wicked queen, Jezebel, was still very much alive, although hanging over her was Elijah's prophecy that she would be devoured by dogs. But Elijah, her archenemy, was gone. As the years passed, she must have come to believe she would die safely in her bed. She continued to promote her false religion in Israel while her son Joram reigned. But Jezebel would indeed come to the end Elijah foretold.

In a separate chapter we look at the revolt of Jehu against Ahab's wicked dynasty. That revolt was set in motion when Elisha arranged for the anointing of Jehu as king over Israel. Jehu, a violent man, would take divine vengeance on Ahab's violent family.

After killing Jezebel's son Joram in a surprise attack, Jehu headed to the royal palace at Jezreel. Awaiting him was the queen, who already knew a revolt was in motion. Jezebel "painted her eyes," arranged her hair and looked out of a window. Did she hope to seduce Jehu—or awe him with her regal bearing? Possibly. But most likely she knew the game was up, and she intended to die like a queen. "As Jehu entered the gate, she asked, 'Have you come in peace, Zimri, you murderer of your master?'" Zimri was an earlier king of Israel who had reigned only seven days after killing the previous king. (Zimri committed suicide by burning down his palace around him.) Jezebel was taunting Jehu by reminding him that men who kill the king and steal the throne will likely meet a sad end themselves. Perhaps she remembered that her own father and father-in-law had been usurpers. No ruler on any throne was truly secure.

Jehu ordered the palace eunuchs to throw Jezebel down from the palace window. "So they threw her down, and some of her blood spattered the wall and the horses as they trampled her underfoot." Oddly, at this point Jehu remembered that Jezebel was "a king's daughter," so he ordered the men to bury her. "But when they went out to bury her, they found nothing except her skull, her feet and her hands." As Elijah had predicted, she had been eaten by the dogs of the street. The king's daughter had not exactly been given a royal burial. And, ironically, she, a power-hungry woman, had died at the hands of eunuchs—men who were literally impotent.

In 2 Kings 13 we read of Joash, king of Israel and grandson of Jehu, going to visit the dying Elisha. Since Elisha had helped bring his family to power in Israel, Joash greeted the old man reverently: "My father! My father! The chariots and horsemen of Israel!" These were the same words Elisha spoke to the departing Elijah. In spite of his family's violent nature and ability as military men, the king recognized that the true power in Israel was not found in swords, spears, chariots or warhorses, but in its faithful men of God.

PUTTING THE WORD TO WORK

1. Ahab ruled a kingdom that was economically prosperous but spiritually poor. What is true for a nation can be true for individuals as well. Can you think of people you've known who were successful by worldly standards yet poor spiritually?

2. After the high of the Carmel episode, Elijah fell into deep dejection, believing he was alone in his faith, and then God guided him to Elisha. Can you recall times when God also sent someone into your life that shared your beliefs and values?

3. Ahab called Elijah the "troubler of Israel," the typical reaction of power figures who have their misdeeds pointed out. Have you known people who were as bold as Elijah in pointing out abuses of power? What motivated them?

4. Reflect on the miracle of Elisha healing Naaman's leprosy and his refusal to accept payment. Make a resolution to do someone a kindness without accepting any reward or recompense.

5. Jezebel and Ahab both come to violent ends. These stories disturb us, but we have to remember the violence they themselves perpetrated. Reflect for a moment on these two corrupt rulers, considering the opportunities they had to change direction and walk the moral path.

Three Men with a Message

Today we will look at three of the most important men in the Bible, three men about whom we actually know very little, the Gospel writers Matthew, Mark and Luke. It is appropriate that we know little about them, for the story they wrote down for the ages was not about them but about the man they knew to be the Son of God, the long-awaited Messiah, the bringer of salvation. Yet they were not mere instruments of God's inspiration; they

> **MEMORY VERSE**
>
> Day after day, in the temple courts and from house to house, they never stopped teaching and proclaiming the good news that Jesus is the Christ. —Acts 5:42

were individuals with distinct personalities of their own, personalities that came through clearly in the way they presented the Jesus story. They are worth getting to know.

Traditionally, the authors of the Gospels are known as the Evangelists, those who report the *euangelion*, the "good news" about Jesus. In a sense they are the most effective evangelists in history, for while living evangelists may preach to hundreds and even thousands in their lifetimes, the Evangelists of the Bible wrote down words that have touched many millions.

We know more about John, writer of the fourth Gospel, and for that reason—and because his Gospel is so different from the others—we will look at him and his writings in another chapter (Day 8).

KEY TERM FOR TODAY ## Gospel

Our word *gospel* is derived from the Old English word *godspell*, "good news," which is the meaning of the Greek word *euangelion*. Matthew, Mark and Luke were men from different backgrounds, yet they shared the commitment to publishing the good news about Jesus as the Son of God and Savior of the world.

MATTHEW: TAXMAN TURNED WRITER

Matthew is probably the most quoted of the four Gospels, meaning it is one of the most-quoted books ever written. This is appropriate, for Matthew presents Jesus as a wise, profound teacher as well as Messiah and Son of God. Matthew is the most Jewish of the Gospels. He quotes the Old Testament more often than the other Gospels and presents Jesus as the fulfillment of the Old Testament prophecies. Matthew cites the Old Testament forty-one times, more than any of the other Gospels, and of these forty-one citations, thirty-seven are introduced with the formula "that it might be fulfilled."

Matthew mentions the Law and the Pharisees more than the other Gospels. It was one of his purposes to show that Jesus was the new lawgiver, a greater one than Moses. Jesus taught a higher righteousness than the Old Testament Law and emphasized that his followers must be more righteous than the legalistic and hypocritical Pharisees.

Ironically, though Matthew's Gospel was directed at Jews, it is Gentiles—the wise men, or Magi—who are first to acknowledge Jesus as Messiah. These foreigners come from afar to worship Jesus, but Herod, the king of the Jews, tries to kill him. Matthew frequently shows the Gentiles being more enthusiastic for Christ than the Jews. The Jews were the first invited but also first to refuse the offer.

One indication of Matthew's Jewishness is his extensive use of the Greek word *idou*—"behold!" or "lo!"—which appears fifty-three times in his Gospel, compared to ten in Mark's and nine in John's. Most modern translations do not bother to translate the word, although the King James Version does. Essentially it is to draw attention to what follows, as in Matthew 8:1–2: "Great crowds followed him, and, behold, a leper came to him." In our modern idiom we could render this as, "Large crowds followed him and—get this!—a leper came to him." "Listen closely!" or "Pay attention!" are other possible translations. The equivalent word (and purpose) occurs many times in the Old Testament. "Behold" reminds us that long before the Bible stories were written

---

CULTURAL INSIGHTS

Capernaum

The Gospels show Jesus constantly on the move as he preached and healed, and yet he also had a base in Galilee—not his hometown of Nazareth, which rejected him, but the town of Capernaum (Matthew 4:13), on the northwest shore of the Sea of Galilee. Jesus did many miracles there, including the healing of the centurion's servant and of the paralyzed man whose friends lowered him through a hole they cut in the roof of a house. It was in Capernaum that he called the tax collector Matthew to be his disciple. Even so, Jesus considered the town unrepentant in spite of his miracles there, and he predicted the complete ruin of the place (Matthew 11:23). The prophecy came true, for the town has completely disappeared. The site known as Tell Hum today may be where Capernaum was situated, but no one is certain. Thankfully, though the city itself disappeared, the miracles done there lived on in memory, and one of its most despised citizens, Matthew, gave the world a small book that has never ceased to inspire.

down, they were passed on by word of mouth, and even after being written, the stories were often read aloud. Probably more people learned the Bible by hearing it read than by reading it themselves.

Only Matthew uses the word *ekklesia*, usually translated "church," although the word definitely did not refer to a building or to any kind of organizational bureaucracy. It meant "assembly," a gathering called together by some high official. The fellowship of Christian believers is God's "assembly," replacing Israel, the disobedient "assembly" of the Old Testament. Another indication of Matthew's Jewish background is that he uses "righteous" or "righteousness" twenty-nine times, compared to twice in Mark, eight times in Luke and three times in John.

In Matthew, Jesus is Messiah and Lord, but also the great teacher. But in Matthew, Jesus' disciples always address him as "Lord," never as "teacher" or "rabbi," where Mark has them call him "rabbi" and Luke has "teacher." The Gospel contains five large blocks of Jesus' teaching, and within them are some of the most-quoted passages of the Bible:

The Sermon on the Mount (chapters 5–7)
Duties of leaders (10)
Parables of the kingdom (13)
Greatness and forgiveness (18)
The Second Coming (24–25)

A very old tradition says that Matthew wrote down the *logia*—the "words" or "sayings" of Jesus—and *logia* probably referred to these five blocks of teachings. The Sermon on the Mount is, of course, one of the greatest passages in the Bible, and probably the most quoted, particularly its opening section, the Beatitudes. Although Luke records much of the same material, Matthew's version is most quoted, and there is a power and profundity in the sermon that even skeptics and atheists admire. Matthew also includes some great parables not found elsewhere, such as the ten maidens, the talents, and the touching and disturbing parable of the Last Judgment (the "sheep and goats") in chapter 25.

Though Jesus is the divine Teacher in Matthew, the idea of Jesus as king is more important than in the other Gospels, and thus Matthew uses "Son of David" more than the others. The Gospel opens with "the lineage of Jesus Christ, the Son of David." The title "Son of David" had little meaning for Gentiles, but for Matthew's primarily Jewish readers, it was important that Jesus was a descendant of David, as their Messiah was expected to be. The Sermon on the Mount also shows Jesus' kingly quality in his repeated "But I say to you."

Gospel Writers in Art

An old tradition connects the four Evangelists with these symbols: a man (Matthew), a lion (Mark), an ox (Luke) and an eagle (John). Centuries ago some imaginative Christian fancied that the four Gospels were symbolized in the prophet Ezekiel's vision of the "living creatures" with four faces—man, lion, ox and eagle (Ezekiel 1:10). Through the ages, Christian artists have often depicted the four Evangelists with these mascots nearby. Due to their importance in recording the story of Jesus, the Evangelists are among the most painted and sculpted men in history.

Matthew uses the phrase "kingdom of heaven"—or literally "kingdom of the heavens"—instead of "kingdom of God," a sign of respect for his primarily Jewish readers, who often respectfully spoke of "heaven" instead of "God." No other New Testament book uses "kingdom of heaven." Matthew uses "heaven" seventy-three times, more than the other three Gospels together.

In a sense Matthew is a very public Gospel. Matthew mentions forty times the "multitudes" (and sometimes "great multitudes") who gather to hear Jesus. And more than the other Gospels, Jesus tells his followers they will be persecuted. At the time when Matthew wrote, the persecution of Christians by the Jews made him recall Jesus' many prophecies of the persecution that was inevitable.

Who wrote this Gospel? A very old tradition says the writer was Matthew, the tax collector of Capernaum, whose calling by Jesus is recorded in Matthew 9:9. The Gospels make it clear that Jews despised tax collectors, since tax collectors were the greedy, corrupt flunkies of the Romans and of Herod. Jesus' band of twelve disciples included one called Simon the Zealot, and the Zealots were known for their hatred of Roman collaborators, sometimes committing violence against them. Thus Jesus' closest followers were, to put it mildly, a diverse group.

The calling of Matthew follows the healing of the paralytic man, an episode in which Jesus shocked some people by telling the paralyzed man that his sins were forgiven. Obviously this leads into his hobnobbing with "sinners," such as the tax collector Matthew, and Jesus' statement that he has come to heal the sick.

As hated as the tax collectors were in Jesus' day, things had been worse in the past. In the days of Julius Caesar, taxation in Judea and other provinces was handled by a *societas publicanorum*, wealthy Romans who practically bled the provinces dry with oppressive taxation, but Caesar did away with their system and considerably reduced taxes on the Jews. Nonetheless, taxes were not exactly light in Jesus' day.

The tax collectors, the *publicani*, were probably the most hated of Roman officials because to the average citizen they were the most visible and most burdensome. Roman soldiers were disliked, of course, but the average Jew's actual encounters with them were rare, and we see in the Gospels and Acts that relations with soldiers could be cordial at times. The fact that "prostitutes and tax collectors" seem to have been a stock phrase tells us that they were considered the scum of the earth. And yet John the Baptist did not tell tax collectors to quit their jobs but to do them honestly. Even bureaucrats in the hire of a foreign power could find salvation—something Jesus and John understood even if their contemporaries did not.

Living in the town of Capernaum where Jesus spent so much time, Matthew would definitely have encountered Jesus before being called by him. No doubt Matthew, snubbed and despised by the respectable Pharisees and scribes, knew that they also detested Jesus. The sinner and the sinless had, oddly, common enemies. Clearly Jesus saw something in Matthew that other Jews did not. The Jews who despised Matthew as just another self-serving, materialistic Roman flunky could never have imagined his name would be known worldwide as author of the story of the Messiah. Of course, there were probably Jews who consorted with tax collectors for less noble motives than Jesus did. Being on the side of such a potentially dangerous neighbor made sense. If you live under the thumb of tyranny and its flunkies, it might be wise to cozy up to the flunkies or become one yourself.

Given his profession of tax collecting, Matthew no doubt had an orderly mind that helped him organize the many words and deeds of Jesus into his well-planned Gospel. Although Matthew was an eyewitness of much of what he recorded, he clearly used Mark's Gospel (based on the memories of Matthew's fellow disciple, Peter) as his basis, but included the five great blocks of Jesus' teachings mentioned above, as well as the many quotations of Old Testament prophecies that Jesus fulfilled. Matthew's Gospel was probably written down sometime in the mid- or late AD 60s.

MARK: COHORT OF THE GREAT

Two of the Gospels—Matthew and John—are attributed to two of Jesus' twelve disciples, those who would have been eyewitnesses of the events they report. Mark was not one of the twelve, so why did the early Christians regard his version of the story trustworthy? A very old tradition connects Mark with the most famous disciple of all, Peter. According to Papias, a noted bishop who wrote in the second century: "When Mark became Peter's interpreter, he wrote down accurately, although not in order, all that he remembered of what the Lord had said or done. Mark was careful not to omit or falsify anything of what he heard." If what Papias writes is true, we could almost refer to the second Gospel as "The Gospel According to Peter, as Told to Mark."

As the recorder of the memories of Peter, Mark has a "you are there" quality that is a delight to read. Mark often uses what is called the historic-present verb tense—for example, "he says to them" instead of "he said to them." We don't notice this in translation because the translators often "correct" Mark's Greek by using the past tense, as Matthew and Luke did when they reported the same events. This is probably unfortunate, for the present tense does give Mark's Gospel directness, as if the story is unfolding before us instead of being something in the distant past. Rather than having a "once upon a time" quality, Mark's Gospel has a "breaking news" feel.

All four Gospels present Jesus as fully human, but Mark emphasizes the humanness in little details, as seen in the different ways the Gospels report the same events. Mark 6:3 has "Isn't this the carpenter?" while Matthew 13:5 has "Isn't this the carpenter's son?" It is as if Matthew can't quite bring himself to refer to Jesus, the Son of God, as a mere carpenter. Mark also emphasizes Jesus' humanness by referring to his emotional reaction to events: "He looked around at them in anger and, deeply distressed at their stubborn hearts, said . . ." (Mark 3:5). "He was amazed at their lack of faith" (Mark 6:6). "He sighed deeply" (Mark 8:12). In reporting these events, Matthew and Luke omit the sighs, the anger, the amazement.

Many of the details remind us we are reading an account based on eyewitness testimony. Compare Mark 9:36—"He took a little child and had him stand among them. Taking him in his arms, he said . . ."—with Matthew 18:2—"He called a little child and had him stand among them." Compare Mark 4:37–38—"A furious squall came up, and the waves broke over the boat, so that it was nearly swamped. Jesus was in the stern, sleeping on a cushion"—with Matthew 8:24: "Without warning, a furious storm came up on the lake, so that the waves swept over the boat. But Jesus was sleeping."

Mark at times gives the exact words of Jesus in Aramaic. But since he is writing for people who knew no Aramaic, he almost always explains it. "He took her by the hand and said to her, '*Talitha koum!*' (which means, 'Little girl, I say to you, get up!')" (Mark 5:41). "You say that if a man says to his father or mother: 'Whatever help you might otherwise have received from me is *Corban*' (that is, a gift devoted to God)" (Mark 7:11). "He looked up to heaven and with a deep sigh said to him, '*Ephphatha!*' (which means, 'Be opened!')" (Mark 7:34). "*Abba*, Father, everything is possible for you" (Mark 14:36).

As noted earlier, Matthew, writing his Gospel for Jews, quotes the Old Testament frequently. By contrast, Mark, writing for Gentiles, directly quotes the Old Testament only once, in Mark 1:2–3. And, appropriately, he omits Jesus' prohibition of preaching to Samaritans and Gentiles. Since he is writing for Gentiles, he often explains Jewish customs and geography: "The Pharisees and all the Jews do not eat unless they give their hands a ceremonial washing, holding to the tradition of the elders. When they come from the marketplace they do not eat unless they wash. And they observe many other traditions, such as the washing of cups, pitchers and kettles" (Mark 7:3–4). He adds the details that the Mount of Olives was "opposite the temple" (Mark 13:3) and that on the first day of the Feast of Unleavened Bread, "it was customary to sacrifice the Passover lamb" (Mark 14:12).

Mark's first readers were probably not totally new to the Christian message. Since he speaks of John the Baptist and the Holy Spirit without explaining them, he was apparently writing to Gentiles who already had some knowledge of the basics of Christianity.

CHARACTERS AT LARGE ## Mark, Here and There

Mark is connected with two cities: Alexandria, Egypt, and Venice, Italy. Given the nearness of Alexandria to Jerusalem, the tradition that Mark took the gospel to Alexandria is very probable. More doubtful is the connection with Venice. In fact, the city of Venice did not exist in Mark's day; it was not founded until the fifth century. However, an old tradition says Mark preached the gospel in the region that eventually was home to Italy. His name is connected with Venice's beautiful cathedral and the nearby plaza, because in AD 828 some Venetian sailors managed to steal the body of Mark from Alexandria, which at that point was a Muslim city. However, the Muslims did not want the body taken, and the Venetians craftily smuggled it out by hiding it under carcasses of pork, which no Muslim would dare touch. Mosaics in the cathedral proudly depict the story of procuring Mark's body. We have no way of knowing if the body in the cathedral is actually the Mark of the New Testament, but thanks to the power of Venice to draw tourists from all over the world, the Basilica di San Marco—St. Mark's Basilica— and Piazza San Marco—St. Mark's Square—are certainly the most-visited places in the world connected with any of the four Gospel writers.

The Roman Catholic and Eastern Orthodox churches celebrate April 25 as the Feast of St. Mark. Because of his connection with Alexandria, Mark is especially honored by the Coptic church, the native church of Egypt.

Although Mark wrote his Gospel in Greek, the Romans' primary language was Latin, and Mark uses some occasional Latinisms. For example, in Mark 12:42, in the story of a poor widow putting two small coins in the offering box, Mark refers in Greek to the coins as two *lepta* and then notes that these are equal to a *quadrans*, a Roman copper coin. Very likely he was writing for people who spoke Latin as their first language and Greek as their second, which was true of many people in the Roman empire.

We know that Peter went to Rome and that he was probably martyred in the persecutions under Emperor Nero around AD 66, so Mark probably wrote his Gospel before then. It is certain that Mark was the first of the four Gospels to be written down, probably in the early AD 60s.

Because Matthew and Luke report most of the events in Mark, and also add many stories of their own, they are read and quoted more often than Mark, and Mark is the most neglected of the Gospels. Despite this neglect, Bible translators estimate that Mark is probably the most translated book of the Bible, with versions in more than a thousand different languages and dialects. Because Mark's Gospel is so simple, direct and full of action, new believers are often urged to read Mark before they read the other Gospels.

Mark is the only Gospel that actually titles itself *euangelion*, "good news." Mark does not include the genealogies of Jesus that are found in Matthew and Luke, but in fact Mark does open with a minigenealogy: Verse 1 announces the good news of Jesus, "the Son of God." The genealogy would have bored Gentile readers, so Mark cuts to the chase, announcing on the first page that the story he is about to unfold concerns the Son of God.

Mark also sees Jesus as the Christ, the Messiah, but one of the key ideas of Mark's Gospel is the "messianic secret": Jesus knows he is the real Messiah, but he tries to keep this from the public, referring to himself as the "Son of Man." If people believed he was the Messiah, they could not accept his suffering and death as part of God's plan.

Who was Mark anyway? He does not appear in the Gospels, but he is mentioned several times in Acts and the Epistles. Acts 12:12 says that the home of "Mary, the mother of John, also called Mark" was a gathering place for the first Christians. (Jews, especially those who moved in Gentile circles, often had both a Jewish and Gentile name, the most familiar case being Saul/Paul. John was a Jewish name, Mark a Gentile one.) Mark would have heard the stories of Jesus told not only by Peter but by the other apostles as well. Later, the missionary pair Barnabas and Paul took Mark along as a helper (Acts 13:5), Mark and Barnabas being cousins. However, at some point Mark left the mission and returned to Jerusalem (Mark 13:13), and when Paul and Barnabas planned another missionary journey, Paul refused to take Mark, the "deserter," along. (Mark 15:37) Why did such a close and effective missionary team split up? Paul may have seen Mark as unstable or insufficiently committed. Certainly the missionary life was demanding, and the mission field was no place for someone who was halfhearted. Then again, there is much about Mark we do not know. Did he have health problems? It is also possible that he resented the way his cousin Barnabas seemed to be playing second fiddle to Paul. Whatever the case, Paul did not see him as a suitable fellow traveler while Barnabas—who, after all, was a relative—did. Acts does not assign blame here—there is no "bad guy" in the story, not Paul, nor Barnabas, nor Mark. The "sharp disagreement" had a pleasant outcome; instead of one missionary team of Paul, Barnabas and Mark, there were now two—Paul and Silas, and Barnabas and Mark. In considering this dispute, remember that it was Barnabas who vouched for Paul and was his "sponsor" for Paul's acceptance by the Jerusalem Christians. Paul would never have forgotten this kindness, of course, and it must have made the parting more bitter for him. Luke, who wrote Acts and was an admirer and close friend of Paul, could have told the story in such a way to put Paul in a better light than Barnabas, but he did not.

We should be glad Acts includes the story of Paul and Barnabas disagreeing about Mark. Acts has been accused of sugarcoating the story of the early Christians, but if that were the case Acts could have simply omitted this incident and said that Paul and Barnabas chose different mission partners and went on their way amicably. But Acts told the truth. These early missionaries were heroes and saints—but they were human beings. (We will look more closely at Barnabas in another chapter, Day 22.)

If there was some bad feeling between Paul and Mark, the two must have reconciled, for Paul refers to Mark favorably in Colossians 4:10, and in Philemon 24 he calls him a "fellow worker." And in 2 Timothy, Paul's final letter, he says, "Get Mark and bring him with you, because he is helpful to me in my ministry." But the warmest reference to Mark is in 1 Peter 5:13, which refers to "my son Mark." What a privileged character Mark was, a companion of great men like Peter, Paul and Barnabas.

Does Mark himself make an appearance in his own Gospel? Possibly. Consider Mark 14:51–52 (ESV): "A young man followed him [Jesus], with nothing but a linen cloth about his body. And they seized him, but he left the linen cloth and ran away naked." These two verses, which appear after Jesus' arrest in the garden of Gethsemane, have fascinated readers for centuries. Who would have known about this incident but the young man himself? So either he—whoever he was—told it to Mark or, more likely, it was Mark himself. Matthew

> **DID YOU KNOW?**
>
> More than half the sentences in Mark's Gospel begin with the Greek word *kai*, which means "and," although most English translations do not translate all the "ands." Bible scholars say Mark's frequent use of *and* indicates that his primary language was Aramaic and that he was not totally at home with writing his Gospel in Greek. When Matthew and Luke draw on Mark's material, they often polish and correct it, since they were more adept at writing Greek.

and Luke chose not to include the incident in their Gospels, perhaps not seeing its significance. It may be Mark's sly way of saying, "I was actually present when Jesus was betrayed and arrested."

Mark's was probably the earliest of the four Gospels, and is certainly the shortest, but it is a small book that has left a big footprint.

LUKE: HISTORIAN WITH STYLE

A noted biblical scholar of the 1800s referred to Luke's Gospel as "the most beautiful book ever written." It is definitely one of the most appealing books in the Bible, coming from the pen of a very gifted writer.

Luke's Gospel is unique in many ways. It is the only Gospel addressed to an individual, a certain Theophilus, whom Luke calls "most excellent," meaning he was probably a man of wealth and influence. (Theophilus was a common enough name, so Luke may have addressed it to an individual with that name, although the actual meaning of the name—"one who loves God"—gave it a wider application.) Luke definitely did not write his Gospel and his other book, Acts, for one person alone. He clearly wrote for a wide Gentile audience of people interested in the new Christian faith that was spreading across the Roman empire. Luke writes excellent Greek, and though he was not a witness of the events he records, he emphasizes that his Gospel draws on the testimony of witnesses. Reading aloud in a group was a common pastime for both Romans and Jews, so though the Gospel and Acts are addressed to an individual, Theophilus, Luke wrote it on the usual assumption that it would be read out loud.

Unlike the other Gospels, Luke takes pains to relate the events to the chronology of the time, referring to the reigns of Roman emperors Augustus and Tiberius (Luke 2:1, 3:1). His mention of historical figures not only helps us fix dates for the life of Jesus but also sets the stage for Jesus' encounters with some of the people later in the story. One thing worth noting about all the names of officials that Luke supplies is that as high and mighty as they were in their own lifetimes, they are now long forgotten—mere footnotes in the story of a Jewish carpenter who was far beneath them in social status. Who would remember Pontius Pilate or Caiaphas if they were not connected with the story of Jesus, the man they condemned to death?

Like Matthew, Luke used much of the material found in Mark's Gospel. He did some minor editing of Mark's stories, improving the storytelling. For example, in Luke 8:22–25, which tells of Jesus stilling the storm on the lake, he mentions that Jesus had fallen asleep in the boat before describing the storm striking; Mark first tells of the storm, and then mentions that Jesus had fallen asleep. The story is the same, of course, but from the standpoint of keeping the reader interested, Luke is the better writer.

While Matthew quotes the Old Testament many times to show that Jesus was the fulfillment of prophecies, Luke seldom does, for he knows this would not interest Gentile readers. So Luke avoids most Semitic (Hebrew and Aramaic) words, except *amen*. As one example of how he reported events differently from Matthew, consider this:

Luke 6:31: "Do to others as you would have them do to you."

Matthew 7:12: "Do to others what you would have them do to you, for this sums up the Law and the Prophets."

Luke apparently did not think his readers needed to read this reference to the Law and Prophets. Some other examples of his de-Semitizing: Instead of *rabbi*, he uses *kurios*—"lord"—or *epistates*—"teacher." Instead of *Golgotha*, he uses *Kranion*. Instead of *grammateus*—"scribe"—he sometimes substitutes *nomikos*—"lawyer."

Luke mentions the Holy Spirit more often than Matthew and Mark. Several times he uses the phrase "filled with the Spirit," which is not found in the other Gospels; he describes several people as "filled," including Jesus, John the Baptist, John's parents, Simeon and, in Acts, the apostles. In each case, the Spirit enables the person to speak out boldly. The miraculous conception of Jesus is said to be the work of the Spirit. Luke also mentions prayer more than the other Gospels, and Jesus is depicted

---

CULTURAL INSIGHTS

Books vs. Scrolls

Scholars have wondered why the early Christians preferred the codex—the early form of book—to the traditional scroll. Part of it may have been economy: Most early Christians were poor folk, and the codex—which used both sides of the material, while scrolls used only one—was more economical. The codex also traveled better, so it was easier for missionaries to carry. And a codex could be "paged" while scrolls could not. To both Jews and pagans, the codex seemed a shocking innovation, something new-fangled and trendy. But the Christians were on the cutting edge: The codex in time replaced the scroll—as proved by what you are now holding in your hand.

The earliest Christian writings were more often in codex form than on traditional scrolls. Archaeologists have found that this is less true of Luke's Gospel and the other book by Luke, Acts. Why so? It seems likely that Luke's two books, which may have originally been one, were intended for public consumption in the form of outreach to pagans who wanted to know more about the new religion. For this reason, Luke and Acts may have been copied more often on scrolls because copyists knew that pagans still preferred scrolls to the new codex form.

as praying often. Given the role of prayer in Acts, Luke wants us to see that frequent and fervent prayer is a way of following Jesus.

All the Gospels emphasize concern for the poor and the perils of being attached to worldly possessions, but the emphasis is stronger in Luke, which is why he is often called the Gospel of the Poor. The note of divine love for the poor is sounded near the beginning in the Song of Mary. The first persons to see the newborn Jesus are not the wealthy Magi but mere shepherds. Luke alone tells the parable of the rich man and the beggar Lazarus.

Luke uses *Savior* or *salvation* eight times. Mark and Matthew use neither word. The fact that Savior became a common title for Jesus is in part due to the words of the angel in Luke. Luke's Gospel contains the well-loved story of Jesus' birth in a stable, followed by the visit of the shepherds. And Luke alone tells of Jesus' visit to the temple as a child. The details about Jesus' infancy and childhood are the basis of an old tradition that Luke knew Jesus' mother personally. And just as Luke supplies many details about the beginning of Jesus' life, he is also the only Gospel writer to describe Jesus' ascension to heaven, which is also detailed in Acts, and to refer to "Christ the Lord" (Luke 2:11). In fact, Luke's infancy narrative is a kind of preview of the whole story, presenting Jesus as Savior, Messiah and Lord.

The great poet Dante referred to Luke as *scriba mansuetudinis Christi*, the faithful recorder of Christ's lovingkindness. We have Luke to thank for recording such beautiful parables of compassion as the good Samaritan and the prodigal son, and for the story of Jesus on the cross forgiving his enemies and promising paradise to the penitent thief. No wonder Luke has been called the Gospel of Great Pardons.

Curiously, although Luke did not write his Gospel for Jews, he is obsessed with Jerusalem and its temple, which may be the reason that in his telling, Jesus' last temptation takes place on the pinnacle of the temple. The Gospel begins and ends in Jerusalem, with Zechariah, John the Baptist's father, in the temple at the beginning. As a boy, Jesus speaks his first recorded words in the temple. The Gospel ends with the disciples "continually at the temple, praising God." Given Luke's obvious affection for the temple, he was probably a proselyte or a God-fearer, that is, a Gentile who attached himself to the Jewish religion. Many of the proselytes and God-fearers were more devout and fonder of the temple than the Jews themselves were.

In Luke's Gospel, the baptism of Jesus is followed by Jesus' genealogy, going all the way back to "Adam, the son of God." Note that at his baptism Jesus has just been called God's "beloved son." Luke's genealogy is unique, for no one ever referred to Adam as "son of God," nor did any genealogy include such a phrase. Luke is telling us that, great as it is to be descended from the famous Abraham and David, Jesus is ultimately the son of God. Luke's genealogy seems to de-emphasize Abraham and David and emphasize Jesus as, like Adam, the son of God, not the Messiah who would be a descendant of Abraham and David—even though Luke elsewhere emphasizes that role. Among other purposes, Luke's genealogy broadens the appeal of the Gospel to all people, not just the Jews, the descendants of Abraham. Also, note that Luke's mention of Adam is immediately followed by the temptation story—how appropriate!

Luke's is the Gospel of Women, telling us much more about Mary than the other Gospels do, and also introducing such characters as Elizabeth, the mother of John the Baptist; the prophetess Anna; and the widow of Nain. Matthew's Gospel mentions that several women gave their financial support to Jesus and the disciples, but Luke actually names them. Luke alone reports the incident of the Jerusalemite women who wept for Jesus as he made his way to Golgotha.

Luke is the only Gospel to speak of the large band of seventy disciples, which has led to speculation that he himself was one of this group or, more likely, he knew some members of this group. As the twelve disciples symbolized the heads of the twelve tribes of Israel, the seventy were the new form of the seventy elders of Israel appointed to assist Moses and mentioned in Numbers 11:16.

In Jewish tradition, seventy was a "good" number. The Sanhedrin had seventy members. According to tradition, seventy people translated the Septuagint, the Greek version of the Old Testament. Also, the rabbis spoke of the seventy nations of the world, based on Genesis 10, the list of the descendants of Noah, a list with seventy names. Some said the seventy bulls sacrificed at the Feast of Tabernacles symbolized the heathen nations. Considering that Jesus would be condemned to death by the seventy-member Sanhedrin, it is appropriate that he would gather to himself seventy devoted disciples, men who would proclaim the kingdom instead of trying to destroy it.

Luke's introductory reference to "many" other attempts to tell the Jesus story suggests to us that the book was not written early. He certainly was familiar with Mark and Matthew, and so his Gospel is later than theirs, and we can probably date it in the late AD 60s. His is also the longest Gospel—19,404 words in the original Greek.

LUKE AND PAUL

We know from Acts that Luke was a friend and companion of Paul, and Paul in one of his letters refers to Luke as the "beloved physician" (Colossians 4:14). While one Gospel writer, Matthew, collected taxes, which made him well-off but hated, Luke had a much more respectable profession—although medicine was unscientific enough in those days that many people regarded doctors as charlatans, and no doubt many of them were. Luke's name in Greek is Loukas, likely a short form of Loukios, which is the Latin name Lucius. Tradition says Luke was Greek, but we don't know this for certain. The fact that he wrote Greek well and seemed to direct the Gospel and Acts toward Gentiles does not prove he was Greek. Luke is mentioned in Colossians 4:14 in a passage referring to Paul's friends who are "not of the circumcision," meaning not Jewish nor proselytes, so Luke was almost certainly a Gentile, though just as certainly a God-fearer.

Whether Luke was Greek or not, he most certainly was an eyewitness to many of the events in Acts, as seen in the "we" passages, the portions of the book in which Luke writes in the first-person plural: "we" did such-and-such. The "we" passages are Acts 16:10–17, 20:5–15, 21:18, and 27:1–28:16. All the "we" sections focus on the activity of Paul, so he and Luke were apparently fellow missionaries. The fact that Luke was an eyewitness to these events adds a nice touch of authenticity to Acts. When William Tyndale made the first translation from Greek into English in the 1520s, he gave Acts this title: "The Acts of the Apostles, written by St. Luke Evangelist which was present at the doings of them."

It is a good thing that Acts was written by a Gentile, someone who understood the Greek and Roman mentality. Luke was wise enough to see that in Roman eyes, Christianity began with a serious handicap: Its founder had been a felon, executed by a Roman official for sedition. Worse, as Christianity spread, it seemed to create disorder, something the Romans could not abide. But the Gospels, including Luke's, show that Jesus' trial was a gross miscarriage of justice, that the Roman governor Pilate knew Jesus was no political radical, and that even Herod declared Jesus not guilty. In Acts, Luke tells of one highly placed Roman official, Sergius Paulus, giving the faith an ear and converting to it, while in Philippi the civil magistrates offer a formal apology to Paul and Silas for beating them. Here and elsewhere in Acts, the hubbub over Christianity is not a matter of the Christians stirring up trouble, but of hostile Jews and troublemaking pagans. And Acts ends with Paul living peacefully under house arrest in Rome, spreading his faith under the noses of Roman soldiers. Luke, as a close friend of Paul, knew that Paul hated riots and violence as much as the next person, and that Paul never intended to stir up trouble. Yet trouble followed Paul wherever he went. In a sense, a large part of Acts is Luke's defense of Paul, a decent man who preached salvation and yet was regarded as an agitator.

Luke clearly admired Paul, and the affection was mutual. In Paul's last writing, 2 Timothy, he bids the world and his friends farewell. Probably he was writing from prison in Rome, during the persecution unleashed on the Christians by Emperor Nero in AD 64. The letter contains the sad note that "only Luke is with me." Others, including the disloyal Demas, who was "in love with this present world," had deserted him. The impression is that Luke was with Paul by choice, not as a fellow prisoner. In visiting a man who was in disgrace with the Roman authorities, Luke was risking his own reputation and safety, but he was also putting into practice the great compassion modeled by the Jesus of his Gospel.

One question that has puzzled many readers of the New Testament is: Why does Acts end with Paul's house arrest in Rome? One possible answer is that by this point, Luke had accomplished his purpose, which was to show Paul, after his many travels, taking the gospel to Rome, the center of the empire. However, some of Paul's letters date from later than this, meaning that Paul must have been released from his confinement in Rome and gone on to do further missionary work—so why didn't Luke record those later adventures? And since Paul was released from this first imprisonment in Rome, why didn't Luke record his trial before Nero? Simply put, we don't know. Luke was still alive when Paul wrote 2 Timothy, and he may well have intended to write a further history of Paul and the other apostles but simply never got around to it. He may have died a natural death—or, like so many of his fellow believers, he may have died as a martyr. But rather than feel disappointed that he did not write more about the spread of the faith, we can be thankful that he wrote as much as he did, bequeathing to the world not only his beautiful Gospel but Acts as well.

PUTTING THE WORD TO WORK

1. Matthew, as a tax collector, would have been despised by most of his fellow Jews, yet, ironically, this hated man wrote one of the greatest and most influential books of all time. Who are some people in your own life who have had amazing turnarounds in life? What caused the changes?

2. Though they were telling the same story, Matthew, Mark and Luke tailored the telling to fit their different audiences. What are ways that you can make the sharing of your own faith more effective?

3. In Acts, Luke did not omit the story of Paul and Barnabas disagreeing about Mark. Does this truthfulness increase your respect for the historic value of the Bible?

4. If you can, buy or borrow a copy of *Gospel Parallels*, a reference book showing the similar passages of Matthew, Mark and Luke side by side. Note the different ways they report the same events and sayings.

5. Matthew, Mark and Luke wrote their Gospels on the assumption that they would most likely be read aloud and in a group setting. The next time you read from one of the Gospels, read it aloud, even if you're alone. Do you find there is a certain "live" quality in this that is missing when you read silently?

Might-Have-Beens and Wayward Sons

The Bible, like all of human history, is full of stories of might-have-beens, people who did great things but turned out to be disappointments in the end. The classic case is Saul, Israel's first king, but other might-have-beens in the Saul story are the wayward sons of Saul's mentor, Samuel. In fact, the theme of this chapter is not only disappointment but also fathers and sons.

> **MEMORY VERSE**
>
> **It is better to take refuge in the Lord than to trust in man. —Psalm 118:8**

KEY TERM FOR TODAY ## Disappointment

Saul, Israel's first king, was a great and charismatic man with enormous potential, but like many gifted people, he let petty emotions rule him and proved a failure to God and others.

THE BOY AT THE SHRINE

The boy Samuel grew up in the presence of the Lord. (1 Samuel 2:21)

The two books of Samuel were originally one book, named for the man who is the main character in the early chapters, the man who played a pivotal role in making a king for Israel. His story opens in a touching way: His barren mother has gone with her husband to pray at the town of Shiloh, which in that period was the center of Israel's worship, since the ark of the covenant, the gold-covered chest that symbolized God's presence, was kept there.

The woman, Hannah, was the wife of Elkanah—but not the only wife, for there was another, Peninnah. Hannah had no children, but Peninnah did. We don't know all the circumstances of this arrangement, but it's quite possible that Elkanah had married Hannah, lived with her childless for years, and then taken the second wife in the hope she would bear children, which she did. It is clear that Peninnah mocked Hannah's barrenness. Elkanah, a man of sensitivity, doted on poor Hannah, reminding her that his own love for her counted for something. Contrast his kind treatment of Hannah with Jacob's surly reply to Rachel when she begged for children: "Jacob became angry with her and said, 'Am I in the place of God, who has kept you from having children?'" (Genesis 30:2). But like all women in ancient times, Hannah desperately wanted children.

On the annual visit to Shiloh, Hannah prayed in the house of the Lord. If God gave her a son, she would dedicate him to lifelong service for the Lord. The priest, named Eli, saw Hannah praying—or rather, he saw her mouth moving but did not hear her words, though people in ancient times almost always prayed aloud. Eli assumed she must have been intoxicated, so he gave her a sound scolding—being drunk in the house of the Lord was shameful! But Hannah assured him she was not drunk, only distraught and desperate. Eli relented. He told her to go in peace, with his hope that God would answer her prayer. The next time she saw Eli, she had the son, whom she had named Samuel. Like Sarah and Rachel in Genesis, the barren woman had conceived at long last. Chapter 2 contains Hannah's heartfelt song of thanks for the God who does amazing things.

Hannah did not forget her vow. God had given her a son, and in time she gave the son to the service of the Lord, at the shrine at Shiloh. As it turned out, Samuel found a second father in Eli, the priest. Eli's sons were called "sons of Belial," though most modern versions have "worthless sons." Eli was a good man, but his sons "did not know the Lord." Eli's sons were literally growing fat from the meat that people offered at Shiloh as sacrifices. An act of devotion on the part of the people had turned into an excuse for Eli's sons to eat well.

Samuel, however, had been dedicated to God from his birth. At a young age he went to live with Eli at Shiloh, but Hannah was not grieved, for God blessed her further, giving her three more sons and two daughters.

ELI'S REAL SON

Eli's sons were wicked men; they had no regard for the Lord. (1 Samuel 2:12)

The Lord was with Samuel as he grew up, and he let none of his words fall to the ground. And all Israel from Dan to Beersheba recognized that Samuel was attested as a prophet of the Lord. The Lord continued to appear at Shiloh, and there he revealed himself to Samuel through his word. (1 Samuel 3:19–21)

As the story continues, we learn that Eli's sons were not only shameless about filling their own bellies with people's sacrifices but were also sleeping with the women who were

The God Dagon

The Philistines' god Dagon figures in the Book of Judges. Mighty Samson, as his last act, manages to demolish the imposing temple of Dagon, along with several thousand Philistines. In 1 Samuel, the ark of God wreaks havoc in another temple of Dagon. The statue of Dagon falls facedown—the posture of a slave before a master. The head and hands being broken off symbolize impotence—Dagon can neither think nor act.

It used to be assumed that statues of Dagon showed him as a kind of merman—human from the waist up but fish-shaped from the waist down—because his name was thought to derive from the root *dag*, "fish." In fact, his name probably meant "grain," and he was a god of fertility of the fields. Two Canaanite locales are referred to as *Beth Dagon*, meaning "house of Dagon."

attached to the shrine at Shiloh. Eli gave his sons a thorough dressing-down, reminding them that they were not only sinning against man but against God as well. But they paid him no heed. Yet "the boy Samuel continued to grow in stature and in favor with the Lord and with men" (1 Samuel 2:26). Eli's sons were "sons of Belial," but Samuel was the good "son," and God provided for him.

We have no idea why Eli's sons were so bad. Sometimes decent people make poor parents, and the impression 1 Samuel gives us is that he must have been too lenient with them in their younger days. A prophet—here called "a man of God"—came to Eli with a dire prediction: Eli's family could have been priests in Israel forever, but because of his sons' behavior, the family would be entirely snuffed out. The sign that his words were true was that both sons would die on the same day.

Eli was a priest and thus of the tribe of Levi. Samuel was from the tribe of Ephraim, yet he was brought up to serve in the Shiloh sanctuary just as if he had been born a Levite. Eli's sons were Levites but were reprobates. This was one of many instances in the Bible where God showed a willingness to think outside the box. If a boy from Ephraim was a more worthy minister than the priests from Levi, so be it. This is not the first instance of a consecrated priest having unworthy sons. The tradition began early, with Aaron's sons Nadab and Abihu (see Day 23.)

In contrast to inheriting the priesthood, Samuel was called by God. In the past God had called Abraham, Moses, Gideon and Samson. Samuel was already serving in the temple, but this in itself meant nothing, for Eli's sons were also serving there.

Samuel's call came in the early morning, for the temple lamp, which normally would have been put out at daybreak, was still burning. God called Samuel's name, and Samuel, thinking it was Eli, went to him. Eli told him it was not he who had called. Three times God called to Samuel in the night, and Samuel understood. The word from the Lord was the same dire word the prophet had uttered earlier: Eli's line would be cut off. When Samuel came to tell him what God had said, Eli already knew the message was not good. The man who did not rear his own sons properly knew he had failed and would pay the price. Rather than feeling anger or bitterness or despair, Eli accepted the divine verdict: "Samuel told him everything, hiding nothing from him. Then Eli said, 'He is the Lord; let him do what is good in his eyes'" (1 Samuel 3:18).

Though "the word of the Lord was rare in those days," Samuel was now clearly a prophet as well as a priest. The word soon got out all over Israel that a new prophet had arisen. "The Lord was with Samuel as he grew up, and he let none of his words fall to the ground" (1 Samuel 3:19). As with other great figures, God was "with" Samuel.

Israel's chief enemies in those days were the brutal Philistines, who lived in cities on the coast and were constantly invading and looting Israel. In 1 Samuel 4, we read that they captured the ark of the covenant—an ironic twist to the story, since the Israelites had brought the ark to the battle front in the hope it would be a blessing to them. Israel lost thirty thousand men in the battle—including Eli's two sons, Hophni and Phinehas. A man came from the battle to tell Eli what had happened. The ninety-eight-year-old Eli literally fell off his chair and dropped stone-dead when he heard the news that his sons were dead and the ark had been captured. He had led Israel—but not his sons—for forty years.

Eli and both his sons were dead, and yet his daughter-in-law, the wife of Phinehas, was giving birth. The birth brought her no joy—her husband and her revered father-in-law were both dead, and the ark had been captured. She named the newborn Ichabod, meaning "no glory," for it seemed the glory of God had departed from Israel.

However, chapters 5 and 6 of 1 Samuel show that the ark brought the Philistines no end of trouble. When they placed it in the temple of their god Dagon, it caused Dagon's statue to fall down, and later it caused a great plague among them, so eventually they returned it. The ark, a sign of God's presence, was back, and Israel had Samuel, a worthy man, as its leader. While the sinful Hophni and Phinehas were bearers of the ark, the ark brought no aid to Israel. With both of them dead, things changed. Eli's corrupt house was no longer in charge of Israel's political or spiritual affairs.

"LIKE THE OTHER NATIONS"

All the elders of Israel gathered together and came to Samuel at Ramah. They said to him, "You are old, and your sons do not walk in your ways; now appoint a king to lead us, such as all the other nations have." (1 Samuel 8:4–5)

[Kish] had a son named Saul, an impressive young man without equal among the Israelites—a head taller than any of the others. (1 Samuel 9:20)

In the Book of Judges, most of the "judges" were really military leaders, not judges in the usual sense. But Samuel was indeed a real judge, setting up a kind of judicial circuit in Israel. He made a profound impression on Israel, as prophet, priest and judge, but what had happened to Eli happened to him as well: The good man had worthless sons. His two sons, Joel and Abijah, acting as judges, became notorious for taking bribes and perverting justice. Whatever his merits as a leader and as a man of God, Samuel seems to have been a failure as a parent. Or maybe it would be more accurate to say that his sons had minds of their own and were not interested in following their saintly father's example. Samuel was aging, and Israel wanted a good man as their leader. Clearly his sons did not qualify.

In fact, Israel wanted what the other nations had: a king, a permanent leader. Clearly they had forgotten one of the key teachings of the Law of Moses: Israel was supposed to be different from the other nations, for Israel was holy, a people committed to God. Israel's true king was God, as Samuel understood, so he was deeply distressed by the Israelites' request.

But God told Samuel to give the people what they asked for—their request was in keeping with their rejection of God himself, from the very time he brought them out of Egypt. But Samuel was also ordered to tell the people what having a king would entail. His warning, found in 1 Samuel 8:10–18, is one of the Bible's key passages on the subject of politics. A king, Samuel says, is a "taker"—one who not only will oppress the people with taxes but also will take the men to be his soldiers and the women to serve in his palace. A king will live well, while the people live under oppression. Samuel must have remembered how Eli's greedy sons had kept the choice cuts of meat and fat from the people's sacrifices.

The people did not listen to the warning, so they continued to press Samuel to make them a king. The story has already told us that Samuel's sons were greedy for gain, which might explain why Samuel's warning about a king's greed fell on deaf ears. If the people heeded Samuel's warning and decided not to have a king, would they have been any better off under Samuel's greedy, corrupt sons?

As it turned out, Israel's first king was not a greedy man. Later kings would follow the tax-and-spend pattern that Samuel spoke of, but the first king was not an economic oppressor. And yet, sadly, he was a great disappointment to both God and Samuel.

The man was Saul, from the tribe of Benjamin. His family was well-off, and he was tall and handsome. The Bible seldom mentions people's physical appearance, so Saul must have been quite impressive for the Bible to

DID YOU KNOW?

America's Founding Fathers, working to gain independence from Britain, often referred to the story of Samuel's reluctance to give Israel a king. Thomas Paine, author of the influential tract *Common Sense*, wrote that the Bible made it clear that "the Almighty hath entered his protest against monarchical government."

mention it. His encounter with Samuel occurred in a curious way: Some of his father's donkeys were lost, and he and a servant went looking for them. Being near the home of the seer Samuel, they went to him to ask his aid in finding the donkeys. Samuel had been told by the Lord of Saul's coming.

Saul was, despite his wealth and physical attractiveness, a humble man. He was taken aback by Samuel telling him he was to be Israel's king. Unlike the ambitious and unscrupulous Abimelech in Judges, who tried to make himself king, Saul did not seek out the kingship—always a good sign. So Samuel made him king, signified by anointing—pouring scented oil on Saul's head, marking him for the service of God. Previously, anointing had been done only for Israel's priests. From then on, the king was also to be God's "anointed one." The fact that Saul kept this anointing to himself is amazing. How many men could resist shouting, "I've just been made king!"?

Later, in a public ceremony, Samuel presented Saul to the Israelites, while reminding the people of the rights and duties of the kingship. Instead of strutting and swaggering, Saul kept a low profile. The tall man seemed to impress the Israelites, except for some worthless "sons of Belial" who had doubts. But Saul "held his peace." He had self-control—but not always, as the story would show.

SAUL IN RASH MODE

Your kingdom will not endure; the Lord has sought out a man after his own heart and appointed him leader of his people, because you have not kept the Lord's command." (1 Samuel 13:14)

To obey is better than sacrifice, and to heed is better than the fat of rams. (1 Samuel 15:22)

The new king was not to lead a life of luxury in a palace. On the contrary, he went right to work on the most important aspect of his kingship, leading Israel into battle. One of Israel's cities was besieged by the vicious Ammonites. Saul, coming in from plowing in the fields, heard what happened and sprang into action. He rallied the Israelites to defend the city, and they defeated the Ammonites. Some of the Israelites remembered the "worthless men" who had scoffed at Saul earlier and had not joined the battle. They claimed these men should be put to death, but Saul showed compassion. Saul's victory over the Ammonites sealed his reputation, assuring the Israelites that God had sent them the right man. Israel "rejoiced."

This is followed by a sad story: Samuel delivered his farewell address to Israel. "Here I stand. Testify against me in the presence of the Lord and his anointed. Whose ox have I taken? Whose donkey have I taken? Whom have I cheated? Whom have I oppressed? From whose hand have I accepted a bribe to make me shut my eyes? If I have done any of these, I will make it right" (1 Samuel 12:3). The people assured him that he had never done them wrong. Samuel told them they had done wrong to ask for a king, yet God had honored their request—with conditions. If they obeyed and served God, all would be well, but if not, disaster would follow.

In some ancient cultures, the leader was both priest and king, both the religious head and the political. This was not true in Israel, where the functions were divided, according to what political scientists might call "separation of powers." In the wisdom of God, no one man in Israel could hold too much power, for the king was, in theory, at least, subject to being called on the carpet by a priest or prophet from God.

Saul's first failure was to take for himself the role of priest. Trying to rally the Israelites for another battle, Saul waited for Samuel to come and offer a sacrifice. Samuel delayed, and after a week Saul gave up hope and offered the sacrifice himself. Immediately Samuel appeared, horrified at what Saul had done. This rashness and impatience, Samuel said, would cost Saul his kingdom, eventually.

This revelation must have cut Saul to his heart—his beloved mentor had given up on him. But despite Samuel's prophecy that Saul's dynasty would not endure, Saul took heart from the bravery of his son Jonathan. Eli and Samuel had worthless sons who would not succeed them, but Saul had a son who seemed made to be king. Jonathan's first adventure is told in 1 Samuel 14, in which Jonathan and his aide enter the Philistine camp and create a panic, which the other Israelites see from a distance, causing a rally among the Israelites. Jonathan was not only a brave and crafty soldier but a man of deep faith as well, for in sizing up the forces of the Philistines, he told his aide, "Nothing can hinder the Lord from saving, whether by many or by few" (1 Samuel 14:6). With God on his side, the word "outnumbered" had no real meaning. As the battle showed, the act of the brave and faithful fired the hearts of those with less courage and faith.

The sad follow-up to the victory sparked by Jonathan's raid is that Saul made a foolish vow: No Israelite could touch food until the defeat was total. Anyone who disobeyed would be killed. Jonathan knew of this vow but nonetheless ate some wild honey he found in the forest. Like the other warriors, he was about to faint from exhaustion. When Saul discovered what happened, he intended to keep his vow and kill Jonathan. But Saul's men would not hear of it: Jonathan's bold action had helped save Israel.

> **DID YOU KNOW?**
>
> Among people of the ancient Middle East, the Philistines stood out for being clean-shaven. They were also known for their feathered helmets.

Thus far, the handsome, brave, charismatic Saul had committed two rash acts: making sacrifices instead of waiting for Samuel, and almost killing his own son. He was a good but unstable man, and the Bible commends him for taking into his service any military man with abilities. And certainly he had not become the luxury-loving, tax-and-spend king that Samuel warned the people about. But clearly he was not the man for the job. God had someone better in mind.

Samuel had not completely given up on Saul yet. But Saul was to disappoint him again. The Israelites had to face another enemy, the barbarous Amalekites. Before going into battle, Saul received clear instructions from Samuel: After defeating the Amalekites, put everyone and everything to death, even the livestock. This strikes us as incredibly cruel, but the writer of 1 Samuel saw it differently: A defensive war was not to be an excuse for plundering the enemy and making off with his goods.

After the battle, Samuel arrived, greatly disturbed: Saul had not destroyed the Amalekites' livestock or their king, Agag, who was in his custody. Why, Samuel asked, had Saul disobeyed the clear command of God? Saul excused himself: The livestock could be used for sacrifices to God. "Samuel replied: 'Does the Lord delight in burnt offerings and sacrifices as much as in obeying the voice of the Lord? To obey is better than sacrifice, and to heed is better than the fat of rams'" (1 Samuel 15:22). Saul made another excuse: He was only bowing to the will of the people. Impatience and caving in to the crowd—these were not the traits of a wise ruler.

Saul begged Samuel for forgiveness, but it was too late. It was not Samuel's rejection but God's. Yet Samuel was not completely heartless. "Saul replied, 'I have sinned. But please honor me before the elders of my people and before Israel; come back with me, so that I may worship the Lord your God.' So Samuel went back with Saul, and Saul worshiped the Lord" (1 Samuel 15:30–31). Samuel was still willing to treat Saul with respect publicly, even though he knew God had another king in the waiting.

But privately, Samuel was in mourning. Samuel's own biological sons were worthless men, just as the sons of Samuel's mentor, Eli, had been worthless. God had given Eli a surrogate son, a "heart son," Samuel, and God had given Samuel a heart son, Saul, but like his biological sons, Saul was not obedient to God.

JONATHAN'S EMOTIONAL TUG OF WAR

Jonathan made a covenant with David because he loved him as himself. (1 Samuel 18:3)

Saul listened to Jonathan and took this oath: "As surely as the Lord lives, David will not be put to death." (1 Samuel 19:6)

In this book an entire chapter is devoted to Saul's rival and successor, David, the "man after God's own heart," a man with many flaws of his own. Here we will focus on his rivalry with Saul, his mentor, friend, father-in-law—and worst enemy.

The story of David's anointing as king is told in 1 Samuel 16, a touching story in which the sons of Jesse of Bethlehem are presented to Samuel and, to the family's great surprise, the one God chooses as king is the youngest, David. The story contains one of the great verses of the Bible: "The Lord does not look at the things man looks at. Man looks at the outward appearance, but the Lord looks at the heart" (1 Samuel 16:7). David is not as tall or impressive as his older brothers, yet he is right "in the heart."

As we see in another chapter (Day 1), David entered Saul's service, for the sad king's melancholy was eased by David's playing on the lyre. David made an even deeper impression when he defeated, one on one, the Philistines' hulking warrior Goliath. Saul, who should have been delighted to have such a spunky young man in his service, became consumed with envy, as he realized David, not he, was the people's hero.

Complicating matters further was one of the great friendships in history, between Jonathan and David. Jonathan had already proved himself as a bold and intelligent soldier, and he was drawn to David. "Jonathan became one in spirit with David . . . And Jonathan made a covenant with David because he loved him as himself" (1 Samuel 18:1, 3). At this point David was no longer living with his father's family but in Saul's household, though his battle skills often kept him, and Jonathan, in the field against Israel's enemies. Unofficially he was part of Saul's family. Soon he would be part of it officially, for Saul's daughter Michal was in love with David and wanted to marry him. Saul agreed to this, but he wanted David to supply a grotesque bride-price: a hundred foreskins from the uncircumcised Philistines. This meant David had to kill a hundred Philistines—raising the likelihood, as Saul hoped, of David dying in battle. David and his men did more than was asked: They returned to Saul with *two* hundred Philistine foreskins.

So Saul had a new son-in-law. His daughter was in love with David, his son was David's bosom friend, and the people loved David. Saul, who had the word of Samuel that God had rejected him, was a profoundly unhappy man. The public must have believed things were going well for him: He was king, he was keeping Israel's enemies at bay, his son was a valiant warrior, and his daughter was married to the greatest warrior of all. Things were sunny on the outside, but Saul was raining on the inside, for he knew his grip on the kingdom was not secure, and he knew his best soldier was also his chief rival, not only on the battlefield but in the affections of his own son and daughter too.

Saul had hoped David would die in his effort to bring home a hundred Philistine foreskins. This would not be his last attempt to destroy David. Fortunately for David, Jonathan—now David's brother-in-law as well as his best friend—kept his eyes and ears open for Saul's plots. "Jonathan spoke well of David to Saul his father and said to him, 'Let not the king do wrong to his servant David; he has not wronged you, and what he has done has benefited you greatly. He took his life in his hands when he killed the Philistine. The Lord won a great victory for all Israel, and you saw it and were glad. Why then would you do wrong to an innocent man like David by killing him for no reason?' Saul listened to Jonathan and took this oath: 'As surely as the Lord lives, David will not be put to death.' So Jonathan called David and told him the whole conversation. He brought him to Saul, and David was with Saul as before" (1 Samuel 19:4–7).

Not for long. Saul's oaths and repentances proved to be short-lived. His resentment of David boiled over into anger toward Jonathan as well, and naturally he tried to turn Jonathan against David. Saul assured him that as long as David lived, Jonathan's own succession to the kingship would be in doubt. Saul became so angry he hurled his spear at Jonathan. For the second time Saul came close to killing his own son.

David, the best fighting man in Israel, had to go into hiding for a long time. Jonathan went to him "and helped him find strength in God" (1 Samuel 23:16). Jonathan made his intentions clear: David would eventually be king, and Jonathan would be content

CHARACTER CLOSE-UP ## How Old Was Saul?

The "mystery verse" of the Old Testament is 1 Samuel 13:1, which tells how old Saul was when he became king and how long he reigned—but the numbers are missing in the original Hebrew. Some translations supply a likely number, some do not. When Saul died, he had a son, Ishbosheth, who was forty, so Saul was at least sixty, perhaps even older. At the time of Saul's death, David was thirty.

The actual dates of Saul's reign—probably about 1030–1010 BC—are not important, but the difference between Saul's and David's ages is. Saul was definitely old enough to be David's father, perhaps even his grandfather, and the difference in their ages would have weighed heavily on Saul, who saw himself fading both physically and in the people's esteem, while the young and vigorous David was clearly the rising star in Israel, so well-regarded that many of the Philistines assumed that David, not Saul, was king of Israel. It is probably safe to say that people over forty read the story of Saul and David in a different light than younger people. Saul was a flawed man, yet it is not difficult to muster sympathy for him. Human nature being what it is, it is remarkable that Saul, in his calmer moments, could refer to David as "my son," since he knew David had already replaced him as Israel's hero.

Saul vs. David

Despite Saul's obvious flaws, artists and writers have been fascinated by him and his rivalry with David, so he has often been depicted sympathetically. Voltaire, the noted French author who was so contemptuous of Christianity, wrote the play *Saul* (1763), in which Samuel and David, the men of God, look bad, while Saul and the Amalekite King Agag are the heroes. The 1660 painting *Saul and David*, by Rembrandt, shows a melancholy Saul who holds a spear and wears a turban topped with a crown. The very Jewish-looking David plucks a harp, absorbed in his music. George Frideric Handel wrote the oratorio *Saul*, containing a famous "Dead March." English poet Robert Browning's long poem "Saul," published in 1855, is the meditation of the young harpist David, called in to soothe the mind of the tormented king. Poet Laurence Housman wrote *The Kingmaker*, a play about Samuel, Saul and David. James Barrie, author of the famous play *Peter Pan*, also wrote the play *The Boy David* (1936). Like *Peter Pan*, it celebrates boyish innocence, but it is also sympathetic to the adult Saul, who was once a boy himself. In movies dealing with David, Saul is usually an important character. In the 1960 movie *David and Goliath*, Orson Welles played Saul and was billed above the two actors playing the title characters. In the 1949 Cecil B. DeMille film *Samson and Delilah*, Saul as a boy is a servant to the strongman Samson—not probable, given the chronology, but since Samson and Saul both fought the Philistines, the movie has us believe that Samson passed the torch to the boy before he died.

to be second-in-command. As far as Jonathan was concerned, there was no rivalry with his dearest friend. The rivalry was only in the mind of the tormented Saul.

"The two of them made a covenant before the Lord" (1 Samuel 23:18). With these words the story of the friendship ends. David and Jonathan would never meet again. Jonathan had proved himself a model son, a brave fighter and a loyal friend. David owed his life to Jonathan, who had walked a thin line in showing himself loyal to both his father and his friend.

RUNNING FROM THE MESSIAH

[David] said to his men, "The Lord forbid that I should do such a thing to my master, the Lord's anointed, or lift my hand against him; for he is the anointed of the Lord." (1 Samuel 24:6)

The Hebrew word *Messiah* means "anointed one." The later chapters of 1 Samuel are the story of David on the lam from the man he continually referred to as "the Lord's anointed one," his father-in-law, Saul.

David fled to Nob, one of the sacred sites in Israel, and the priest there, Ahimelech, gave the famished David some bread to eat. He gave something even more important— a weapon, the very sword of Goliath that David had used to behead the giant. Word reached Saul that the priests at Nob had aided David, and Saul was furious. He already knew that David and Jonathan had made a covenant with each other, and now it seemed Israel's priests were on David's side. He summoned Ahimelech, who assured Saul that there was no more loyal man in Israel than David. Saul would not relent. He ordered his men to murder all the priests of Nob. His men flatly refused, but one of them, Doeg, a foreigner, carried out Saul's order, killing eighty-five men. Saul went even further and had the whole town massacred.

Naturally the word of the massacre of Nob alienated even more people in Israel. Nonetheless, when David was staying in the town of Keilah, the town was more than willing to hand him over to Saul—an episode of supreme treachery and ingratitude, for just before this, David and his companions had delivered Keilah from the Philistines. David and his men fled and hid out in the wilderness again. The people of nearby Ziph went to Saul and told him David was hiding in the vicinity, so again David had to flee.

As it happened, Saul ventured into a cave—the very cave where David and his men were hiding out. David's men were ecstatic: Wasn't this a clear case of God delivering David's worst enemy right into his hands? But David would not lay a hand on Saul. Stealthily, he cut off a piece of Saul's robe and later, when Saul had left the cave without knowing David had been close enough to touch him, David held up the piece of cloth as evidence that he had spared Saul's life. The episode is both exciting and touching, for David addresses Saul as "my father," and Saul, touched by David's mercy, addresses him as "my son." David had done something that, by human standards, was unthinkable: He let his sworn enemy escape alive.

Saul had relented—or so it seemed. But David did not trust him completely and did not go back with him. At some point, we aren't told how long, Saul went hunting for David again. Saul and some of his men were camped out in the wilderness, and David and his soldier Abishai crept into the camp by night. Saul's spear was stuck in the ground, and Abishai urged David to kill Saul with his own spear. David would not hear of it: He would not touch the Lord's own anointed king. But he did take Saul's spear and water jar, and later he displayed the spear and jar to show Saul that he had been close enough to kill him but had not. Again, Saul was deeply touched and called David "my son." Saul, at these moments, could see that David was a better man than he was.

But David had learned from hard experience not to trust Saul's mellow moods. Also, the Israelites had shown themselves willing to tell Saul of David's whereabouts. So David chose to hide out in the last place Saul would find him: among the Philistines. Naturally the Philistines were pleased at this, for they knew David was a formidable warrior, and

Dead Hero Worship

The ancient Greeks, like many other ancient peoples, offered sacrifices not only to gods but also to dead heroes—kings, warriors and seers who were regarded as being able to bring benefits to those who honored them, including foretelling the future. Israel was prohibited from such activity by the Law of Moses, which allowed for no attempt to contact the dead, but clearly the belief that it could be done—and that the dead could see the future—was a common one, as seen in the incident of Saul and the ghost of Samuel.

they believed that by serving on their side—or so they thought—David would be forever hated in Israel. They had not reckoned with David's craftiness.

David asked Achish, the Philistine king, for a country town for him and his two wives and six hundred men to live in, and Achish gave him Ziklag. David's band was in the Philistine country a year and four months, during which time the men raided the Amalekites and others, killing the inhabitants and carrying off the livestock and other goods. David's actions were favorable to Israel, since he was eliminating tribes that were a constant menace, but at the same time he was approved by Achish, who believed David was in fact raiding Israelite towns. Achish was taking comfort in thinking that David's raids were making him Public Enemy Number One to Israel, when in fact David was endearing himself forever to the Israelites.

The inevitable happened: Achish called on David and his men to go fight against Saul's army. In this dilemma, David told Achish, "Then you will see for yourself what your servant can do" (1 Samuel 28:2). But in chapter 29, the Philistine lords who had massed their troops to fight Saul were suspicious of David's loyalty. Achish was sure David was trustworthy, but the other Philistines were not. "He must not go with us into battle, or he will turn against us during the fighting. How better could he regain his master's favor than by taking the heads of our own men?" (1 Samuel 29:5). Achish told David of their decision but David protested: Had he not proved himself loyal to Achish? Achish agreed that he had but sent David on his way—to David's great relief, no doubt. Of all his hair's-breadth escapes, perhaps this was the most amazing. He would not have to go into battle against Saul and Jonathan.

It proved to be a fatal battle for both men. Before the battle, the distraught Saul sought some kind of encouragement from anywhere—even the world of the dead. Samuel had died, and poor Saul hoped his former mentor would give him a word of comfort. So Saul consulted a medium—or "witch," as the older translations have it. He approached the woman in disguise—understandably, since Saul himself had ordered all the mediums and other occultists out of Israel. Saul ordered her to call up the spirit of Samuel. To her own great surprise, she did. Samuel's shade had no word of comfort: On the contrary, the next day's battle would result in Saul himself entering the realm of the dead. The medium, not lacking in compassion, insisted that Saul eat some veal and bread that she quickly prepared.

Saul's sad end is told in the last chapter of 1 Samuel. Fighting on Mount Gilboa, Jonathan and two other sons of Saul were killed. Saul himself was wounded by the Philistine archers, and knowing how the Philistines would abuse him if they found him alive, he told his armor-bearer to run him through with his sword. The man would not, so Saul fell on his own sword. When the Philistines found him, they cut off his head and fastened his body to the walls of one of their cities. Hearing of this atrocity, the Israelites took down the bodies of Saul and his sons and gave them a respectable burial.

The Philistines were ecstatic over their victory. Israel mourned, and no one more deeply than David, whose lament for Saul and Jonathan is found in 2 Samuel 1: "Your glory, O Israel, lies slain on your heights. How the mighty have fallen!… Saul and Jonathan—in life they were loved and gracious, and in death they were not parted.… How the mighty have fallen! The weapons of war have perished!" (1 Samuel 1:19, 23, 27). David's lament suggests Saul and Jonathan were united in purpose—though certainly they were divided in their attitude toward David. But now that they are both dead, David remembers them as both being valiant warriors serving the same nation and the same God.

In time, David became king over Israel, as Samuel had foretold, and David showed great kindness to Mephibosheth, the son of Jonathan. David, who had faults of his own, proved a better king than the unstable, envious Saul. His loyalty to Saul was unwavering, whereas Saul's moods were frighteningly changeable, and his admiration and love for David always gave way to jealousy and malice. What a pity that his calm, sane moments, when he called David "my son," did not last.

PUTTING THE WORD TO WORK

1. How do you react to the story of Hannah, childless for so long, dedicating her son to the Lord's service? Do you think it's appropriate for every person of faith to dedicate children to God?

2. Eli, with two rogues for sons, unofficially adopted Samuel. Can you think of cases where people of faith found surrogate children outside their own families?

3. Samuel was disappointed in his own sons and in his surrogate son, Saul, yet he continued to pray for Saul. Keep Samuel in mind the next time you are tempted to give up praying for someone.

4. What impresses you about Jonathan? Have you known people like him, people who tried to make peace between quarreling members of their families?

5. Hunted relentlessly by Saul, David still continued to treat him with mercy and respect. Say a special prayer to God—for yourself and for all people—for extra patience and forgiveness in dealing with enemies.

A Herd of Herods

The New Testament presents us with a family that puts the "nasty" in "dynasty," Herod the Great and his descendants, a clan that in many ways typifies politics as it has been played out through history. These eager collaborators with the Roman empire were, from the birth of Jesus on, a constant menace to the community of faith, and also a striking contrast to it—worldly pomp and power coming face to face with another sort of power altogether.

KEY TERM FOR TODAY

Pomp

The Greek word *phantasias* is translated as "pomp," which could be the byword of the worldly, unscrupulous Herod family—and, in the Bible's view, of most politics. The New Testament is a study in the contrast between the pomp and show of worldly power versus the simplicity and spiritual power of God's people.

HEROD: SURVIVOR LEAVING FEW SURVIVORS

After Jesus was born in Bethlehem in Judea, during the time of King Herod, Magi from the east came to Jerusalem and asked, "Where is the one who has been born king of the Jews? We saw his star in the east and have come to worship him." When King Herod heard this he was disturbed, and all Jerusalem with him. (Matthew 2:1–3)

King Herod—"Herod the Great"—is a minor character in the Bible but a major one in the world that Jesus was born into. Luke's story of Jesus' birth mentions only Herod's name, but Matthew's account gives us more details about the paranoid king's reaction to hearing that a group of foreign visitors has come to pay respects to a new "king of the Jews." It is worth going beyond the Bible and getting to know Herod better so as to understand the New Testament world—and to contrast this worldly, corrupt king of the Jews with the heavenly king who was born in Bethlehem.

Herod is the classic case of a political survivor. However, "survivor" is not a name that could be applied to people close to him, since he had the habit of killing any wives, children, in-laws and anyone else who made him feel threatened—and practically everyone did. He was a survivor, an opportunist, a master politician who passed on much of his political savvy to his sons (the ones he did not execute), and he and they had

important roles to play in the Bible, since their lives happened to intersect with some working-class nobodies known as Jesus of Nazareth and his disciples.

Herod was known in his time as "king of the Jews"—but he was not a Jew, and the Jews never forgot this. He was an Idumean, a descendant of the Edomites, who in the Old Testament were often at war with Israel. In the period between the Old and New Testaments, the Jewish family known as the Hasmoneans conquered the Idumeans and forced them to accept the Jewish religion, which required the men to be circumcised. The Jews were always pleased to have foreigners convert to their faith, but being ruled by one of those foreigners was another matter. In fact, the Law of Moses forbade it: "Be sure to appoint over you the king the Lord your God chooses. He must be from among your own brothers. Do not place a foreigner over you, one who is not a brother Israelite" (Deuteronomy 17:15). Aside from the fact that the law originated with God himself, it was also sound politically: A foreigner might be tempted to sell out the nation to an outside force—precisely what happened under Herod. But the law in Deuteronomy wasn't going to stand in Herod's way, for he happened to have the backing of a rather imposing power known as Rome.

The connections between Herod's family and the power of Rome are fascinating but so complex that historians can barely keep all the names straight. Suffice it to say that the family had a knack for siding with whoever seemed to be in power, or rising to power. Herod's father had hobnobbed with the mighty Roman general Pompey, who conquered Jerusalem, and the great Julius Caesar—and wisely sided with Caesar when Caesar seemed to be the rising star. Caesar made Herod's father ruler of Judea and Herod ruler of Galilee. Among Herod's friends—although the word "friend" suggests an affection that these political alliances did not really possess—were the famous Mark Antony and Augustus Caesar. After a period of invasion and political turmoil in his region, Herod went to Rome, and Anthony and Augustus made him king of Judea as well as ruler of Galilee. When Antony and Augustus parted ways, Herod wisely sided with the triumphant Augustus, and gained some new territory, including Samaria, as his reward.

True love and politics don't sit well together, and an opportunist cannot afford to form lifetime attachments. Herod did have one true love in his life, the beautiful

Mariamne, who happened to be of the famous Hasmonean family that had ruled the Jews for a century. We can assume that Herod's attraction to her was not only romantic, for he was marrying into a Jewish family that had supplied legitimate kings of the Jews. Herod owed his title "king of the Jews" to the Roman Senate—and to the Roman army. By marrying Mariamne—one of his ten wives, by the way—he hoped to make himself acceptable to the Jews.

He failed but not for lack of effort. He decided that, publicly, he had to play the part of a true Jew, meaning conforming outwardly to the Jewish religion—and lavishing attention and funds on the center of the religion, the temple in Jerusalem. The temple that existed when he came to power was the second temple, not the first magnificent one built by Solomon, which the Babylonians had destroyed. Herod did not tear down the second temple, but he added and renovated on such a lavish scale that it was essentially a new building, such a thing of beauty that travelers went out of their way to see it. To non-Jews, it was "Herod's temple"; to Jews, it was merely "the temple." They were proud of the building, but they still detested Herod. They loved the gift, but not the giver. While lavishing attention on the temple, Herod had actually helped to lessen the people's respect for the priests. He detested both the Pharisees and Sadducees, and during his reign the high priests he appointed were of neither party but were nominal Jews steeped in Greek culture and philosophy. Naturally this further lowered the prestige of the priesthood among devout Jews.

They had reason to detest him. They suspected his heart wasn't Jewish, nor were his morals. They were correct. Political opportunists seldom have any spiritual core in them. Herod lavished attention on the temple to win the favor of the Jews, not the approval of God. And the Jews knew that Herod had also built a temple to his benefactor, the emperor Augustus—not in Jerusalem, of course, but in the new coastal city named, appropriately, Caesarea. They knew he had dotted the landscape with imposing fortresses, fearing, with good reason, that his subjects might at any time revolt against his—and Rome's—power. (His Jerusalem fortress, the Antonia, was named to flatter another Roman mentor, Mark Antony.) The Jews also knew that Herod, who loved Greek and Roman culture, built hippodromes and amphitheaters where athletes competed nude and where dramas about the promiscuous gods and goddesses were acted. In Jerusalem itself, Herod's magnificent palace was a constant and painful reminder of this Roman puppet's presence. In fairness, however, let it be noted that Herod did approve some large tax cuts during his reign, though it is doubtful they gained him much goodwill.

> **DID YOU KNOW?**
>
> In 2007, archaeologists found a red sandstone sarcophagus that was probably Herod the Great's tomb. Jewish rebels, who naturally hated the whole Herod family, vandalized the tomb centuries ago.

"The Great" Man in Art and Legend

As the first villain in the story of Jesus, Herod has often been depicted in art and literature. The slaughter of the infants of Bethlehem has been the subject of countless paintings, a kind of artistic monument to an unscrupulous politician. In the Middle Ages, Herod was often a character in plays connected with the Christmas story, usually shown as a ranting tyrant. "Acting Herod" on stage came to mean a scenery-chewing role as a villain, and in Shakespeare's *Hamlet* there is a reference to a hammy actor who can "out-Herod Herod."

Herod has been depicted in many movies dealing with the life of Jesus. In the 1961 movie *King of Kings*, Herod, played by Claude Rains, hears that the slaughter of the infants has been carried out—and he dies immediately afterward. (This may be pure fiction, but it is true that Herod did die shortly after the birth of Jesus.) In the popular 1977 TV movie *Jesus of Nazareth*, Herod, played by Peter Ustinov, hears rumors of a Messiah and laughs them off, confident that "great Caesar" has nothing to fear from any Messiah.

Herod had no respect for the earlier kings of the Jews. He and a few close aides secretly broke into the tombs of David and Solomon, hearing there were great treasures within. They proceeded to carry off some of the goods, but when two of his guards ventured into the chamber where the actual bodies were buried, a flame shot out and killed the guards. Herod, frightened out of his wits, later set up a monument at the tomb to atone for his act of desecration.

Herod had one foot in the Roman world, one in the Jewish—but his heart was all Roman, which is why the Romans kept him on his throne as their willing puppet, and why he sent his sons to Rome to be schooled. It is one of the great ironies of history that the temple made so magnificent by Herod, the puppet and devotee of the Romans, would be destroyed, in AD 70, by the Romans.

Of course, the Romans had no illusions about Herod. They knew he was utterly unethical—like so many successful Roman bureaucrats. Shortly before he died, Herod pressured Augustus to approve the execution of his own son. Augustus gave his approval, smirking that it is "better to be Herod's pig than his son." (It must be admitted that the son had plotted against Herod's life—making him not only a bad son but also, in Roman eyes, a traitor.) This son, who was executed just a few days before Herod's own death in 4 BC, was not the first of his relatives to die by Herod's order. Several wives, sons and in-laws were all dispatched; all that was needed was suspicion that they were plotting against him—and they often were. The sons of his beloved Mariamne detested him. In fact, everyone connected with her family did, which is why Herod succeeded in exterminating the renowned Hasmonean dynasty. His love for Mariamne was, it appears, a dangerous love, because she learned to her horror that, when Herod was abroad, he left an order that if anything happened to him, she was to be killed. His excuse for this: He loved her so much he could not bear to think of her being another man's wife.

Herod is not remembered today for his connections with the Hasmonean family or for his being the intimate of Julius Caesar, Mark Antony and Augustus. He is remembered for an incident that, at the time, went unnoticed by most of the world. This probably occurred in the last two years of his life, when this man who had been handsome and athletic in his prime was growing physically and mentally sick due to what we would today call hardening of the arteries. Herod was in Jerusalem and he received some visitors from the east, probably from the Parthian Empire. The visitors were Magi, practitioners of the old Zoroastrian religion and of astrology, and their study of the stars told them that a "king of the Jews" had been born somewhere in Herod's lands. Herod's counselors told the Magi that, based on Old Testament prophecies, this king would have been born in the small town of Bethlehem.

This visit horrified Herod. He had been notoriously paranoid, with good reason, his entire life, and he had learned that in the nasty world of politics, the best way to deal with opposition was to kill it. The last thing he needed were foreign visitors bringing expensive gifts to some "king of the Jews." The Magi were Parthians, and Romans never trusted the Parthians anyway. Who knew what they might have been plotting?

But Herod concealed his horror from the Magi. He sent them on their way, asking them a small favor: When you find the new "king," let me know where he is, so I can pay my respects to him also. Whether the Magi were duped by this is not certain. They surely must have heard rumors about what an unscrupulous, murderous tyrant Herod was. At any rate, after they bowed down before the newborn Jesus and presented him their famous gifts—gold, frankincense and myrrh—they were warned by God in a dream not to return to Herod.

Herod was furious. The Magi could have led him directly to the new "king." Since they didn't, he did the obvious thing: He ordered the killing of all the infant boys in Bethlehem. A man who could order the killing of his own children had no qualms about slaughtering the children of an unimportant village like Bethlehem. The dirty deed has been immortalized in a thousand paintings titled *The Massacre of the Innocents*, and some Christians regard the slain infants as the first Christian martyrs. Thanks to this bit of paranoid brutality, Herod will be remembered for all time—not to his credit. From a political point of view, Herod did the wise thing by trying to eliminate a potential rival. From any other point of view, it was a horror. And ultimately it was a failure, since God had warned Joseph and Mary to flee Bethlehem. When Jesus grew to adulthood, Galilee was ruled by Herod's vile son, Herod Antipas, who would execute the prophet John the Baptist and mock Jesus before sending him to Pontius Pilate. Jesus would be crucified because the Romans saw him as an upstart "king of the Jews"—a case of Herod's paranoia resurfacing after many years. Later, Jesus' apostles would suffer persecution under Herod's grandson, Herod Agrippa. There seemed to be no getting away from this family of political schemers. But Jesus and the apostles have fared better in the judgment of history than any of the Herod clan has.

Herod was a highly intelligent, highly cultured man. Born into other circumstances, he might have been a poet or a gentleman farmer on some country estate. But he was born into a family of political predators and married into another, during an age in which rulers were killed, not voted, out of office. It was a cruel world of epic brutality, and those who were not cruel—and cunning—did not survive. Being a "good" politician meant holding on to one's position, and whatever was required to do so was excusable. Reading a history of the times makes one appreciate the working-class "king of the Jews" that Herod tried to destroy, a king that made it clear that his kingdom was "not of this world." Reading about those times might even make us appreciate contemporary politics, with our politicians insulting and slandering one another but not murdering their rivals or slaughtering newborns.

One of the many fortresses Herod built was not far from Bethlehem. The round Herodium was constructed on a manmade hill. Herod was buried there in a spectacular funeral, though it is doubtful anyone actually regretted his passing.

One closing thought: History remembers this vile man as "the Great." That should remind us that God and the world have vastly different conceptions of what greatness is.

THOSE GIFTED MEN FROM THE EAST

When they saw the star, they were overjoyed. On coming to the house, they saw the child with his mother Mary, and they bowed down and worshiped him. Then they opened their treasures and presented him with gifts of gold and of incense and of myrrh. And having been warned in a dream not to go back to Herod, they returned to their country by another route. (Matthew 2:10–12)

Matthew's Gospel grounds the story of Jesus' birth in real history, for we know he was born while Herod was still king, and we know Herod died in 4 BC. (It is through a curious miscalculation centuries ago that AD 1, thought to be the year of Jesus' birth, was off by a few years. Jesus was born sometime between 6 and 4 BC.) Herod, as the previous section indicated, was a very real man with a very vivid history, a man known from many ancient writings. The other men involved in Matthew's story of Jesus' birth

Astrology

If "religion" could be defined as "belief system," then the most widely held religion at the time of Jesus' birth was astrology. Its roots were ancient, going back thousands of years to Mesopotamia (Babylon and Assyria, the region that is today Iraq). In Mesopotamia, as in most places in ancient times, the sun, moon and planets were regarded as gods, and their movements in the heavens were believed to cause effects on earth.

Around the fourth century BC, the Greeks absorbed astrology from Mesopotamia and added their own beliefs, such as identifying the planets with their own gods. While the Mesopotamians had focused on how the heavenly bodies influenced the king and the nation, the Greeks shifted the emphasis to the individual. They believed that the position of the bodies at the precise moment of a person's birth determined that person's destiny. The time of birth was the decisive moment when the new life was receptive to the powerful influences raining down from the gods in the sky. This was the belief not just of the common people but of philosophers like Plato as well.

The Romans absorbed Greek astrology just as they absorbed Greek art and literature (and, unfortunately, morals). At the time of Jesus' birth, the Roman Empire was home to hundreds of religions and philosophies, not to mention thousands of gods, but uniting all these belief systems was an unshakable belief that human destiny was somehow linked to the stars. One group who held out against this was the Jews, who were prohibited by the Law of Moses from regarding the stars and planets as divine, although some Jews did dabble in astrology on the sly. (See Leviticus 19:26, 31.) For the Jews, human destiny was in the hands of God, and the heavenly bodies were not gods at all. Just as important, people had free will and could choose their path in life, with no influence from distant stars and planets. Christianity, true to its Jewish roots, had no place for astrology, and as the new religion spread, belief in astrology waned.

are also fascinating characters, but we know almost nothing certain about them. That lack of fact has not stopped people from speculating, sometimes wildly, about who the wise men—or Magi—were.

Matthew tells us that after the birth of Jesus there came "wise men" from the East. The original Greek text refers to *magi*, though the King James Version's "wise men" definitely has a hold on people's affections, and certainly there is a lot of truth in the familiar Christmas sentiment, "Wise men still seek him." However, "wise men" is not a good translation. The Magi may have been wise, but what they really were was astrologers, men who studied the stars not from the scientific point of view but in the belief that the movements of the stars and planets had meaning for what was happening on earth. They were from "the East"—which is quite vague, but probably refers to Babylonia or Persia, both regions known for their interest in astrology. Both regions were then part of what was called the Parthian Empire, on Rome's eastern border and frequently at war with Rome.

As residents of the Parthian Empire, which was a rival to Rome, these men's presence would have disturbed Herod, particularly since they were seeking out a rival "king of the Jews." Men from a hostile foreign power were paying their respects to a rival king of the Jews—a situation that did not bode well for Herod and his cozy relations with Rome.

Religiously, the Magi were likely priests of the ancient creed known as Zoroastrianism. They believed in one god, which gave them something in common with the Jews. And they would have been familiar with the Jews' religion too, since, as recounted in the Old Testament, the Babylonians conquered the Jews and carried many of the people off to Babylon, which was later part of the Persian Empire. The books of Ezra and Nehemiah tell of Jewish exiles returning to their homeland—but most did not, staying on in Babylon and Persia. So in spite of the Jews and their God being "foreign," they would have been of great interest to these priests and astrologers. So would the many Jewish prophecies of a great king, the Messiah.

What made the Magi think the "king of the Jews" had been born? Matthew's Gospel has them telling Herod that they saw the new king's star "when it rose." People have been debating for centuries just what the "star of Bethlehem" was. Note that in Matthew, the Magi saw "his star when it rose," but the people in Judea did *not* see it—thus the star of Bethlehem was clearly not a comet or nova, as some have supposed. What the magi saw was not "public," as is clear in Herod's reaction to their visit. They "saw the star," but the locals didn't—meaning the magi were aware of an astronomical event that the average person would not notice. Without getting too terribly technical, here is one of the most plausible theories of what occurred: The "star" was the phenomenon of the planet Jupiter (taken by astrologers as the sign of the birth of a king) in the zodiac sign Aries (associated with Judea). The Magi would have interpreted this as a sign of a great king of the Jews, possibly the Messiah, being born. They would have set out for Judea with valuable gifts fit for a king. For safety they would have traveled with a merchant caravan. One astronomical authority of today thinks the conjunction of Jupiter occurred in April of 6 BC. While this "natural" explanation of what guided the Magi to Judea makes sense, one part of the story is plainly miraculous: "The star they had seen in the east went ahead of them until it stopped over the place where the child was" (Matthew 2:9). The Magi had journeyed to Judea because of an astronomical alignment, but what guided them to the very location of the newborn Jesus was plainly a miracle of God.

The account in Matthew tells us of the Magi first paying their respects to Herod, on the assumption his own astrologers were expecting the birth of the Messiah. They were not, but they did tell Herod and the visitors that the Messiah would be born in Judea, which was exactly the case. So the Magi journeyed to Bethlehem, found the infant Jesus with Mary and Joseph, and left the three famous gifts: gold, frankincense and myrrh. They left the country without reporting back to Herod, and they vanished from the story. All else that we know about them—even that there were three wise men—is pure speculation.

They are, of course, a vital part of the story. They are three foreigners, non-Jews, paying homage to the "king of the Jews"—while the reigning king of the Jews tries to kill the newborn. As happens so often in the Gospels, the outsiders are more receptive to the Messiah than the Jews are.

We would be assuming too much if we said that the Magi were devout, saintly men, sort of "pre-Christian Christians." They may or may not have been. All we know is that they were astrologers, and that they felt some compulsion to pay their respects to a newborn Jewish king. While Herod committed acts of violence, and most of the world totally ignored Jesus' birth, the Magi bowed down in reverence.

CHARACTERS AT LARGE ## Magi, Wise Men, Etc.

The Bible never says there were three Magi, and that assumption is based on the three costly gifts—gold, frankincense and myrrh. People assumed not only that there were three men but also various other things about them. They were often depicted as kings and as having three different complexions, the idea being that descendants of the sons of Noah, the ancestors of the races, are seeking the Messiah, symbolizing that the whole human race wanted to honor Jesus. A story written in the sixth century named the Magi as Gaspar, Melchior and Balthasar, and to this day many people assume those were their names. The names are mentioned in a wide variety of stories, novels and other works, including the novel and movie *Ben-Hur*, and the famous Christmas opera *Amahl and the Night Visitors*.

In the 300s, Helena, mother of the Roman emperor Constantine, supposedly found the Magi's tombs and sent the relics to Constantinople. At some point the relics made their way to Milan and then later to Cologne, where they became the foundation of the magnificent cathedral there. The bones were placed in a magnificent gold casket encrusted with jewels, and has been on view for eight hundred years. Appropriately, atop the spire of Cologne's cathedral is not a cross but a gold star.

Numerous towns in Iran and Iraq claim to have the birthplace or tombs or homes of the Magi. When the Italian traveler Marco Polo trekked through the region in the 1200s, he was shown what was reputed to be the tombs of the Magi.

A CHIP OFF HIS GRANDFATHER'S BLOCK

King Herod arrested some who belonged to the church, intending to persecute them. He had James, the brother of John, put to death with the sword. When he saw that this pleased the Jews, he proceeded to seize Peter also. . . .

Herod, wearing his royal robes, sat on his throne and delivered a public address to the people. They shouted, "This is the voice of a god, not of a man." Immediately, because Herod did not give praise to God, an angel of the Lord struck him down, and he was eaten by worms and died. But the word of God continued to increase and spread. (Acts 12:1–3, 21–24)

On Herod the Great's death in 4 BC, his domains were divided up among three sons. One of these was Herod Antipas, remembered for executing John the Baptist, and we will look at him closely in another chapter. Herod's son Archelaus inherited half his father's kingdom and Herod intended that he should have the title "king" as well, but the Romans nixed this. Archelaus, like his father, embarked on lavish building projects during his nine-year rule, but, like his father, he was deeply hated by the Jews. In AD 6 a delegation of Jews went to Rome to plead for Archelaus' removal. Rome complied by sacking Archelaus and making Judea, Samaria and Idumea into a Roman province, under the rule of a Roman governor. Thus the high-handed autocrat Archelaus was responsible for the political situation that existed in the time of Jesus.

Several Roman governors held office in the province, the only famous one being Pontius Pilate, who ruled from AD 26 to 36. All the Roman governors were resented by the Jews, of course, and the Herod family had plenty of men waiting in the wings, hoping the Romans might change course again and replace the Roman governor with another Herod. One of the men waiting was Herod Agrippa, grandson of Herod the Great and nephew of Herod Antipas. Herod Agrippa went to Rome for a while and became a friend of the future emperor Caligula. He was heard to remark that Caligula should be emperor, so the current emperor, Tiberius, put him in prison, where he stayed until Tiberius' death. Caligula, as emperor, released him and gave him a gold chain equal in weight to the chain he wore in prison. He also gave him the title "king," with dominion over the former territories of his uncles Herod and Philip. He happened to be in Rome when the insane Caligula was assassinated, and he quickly cozied up to the new emperor, Claudius, who confirmed his rule as king—and added Judea and Samaria, making him ruler over a territory almost as large as that of his grandfather. He had come to power not through any merit of his own but by being a close friend of an insane emperor—and by being available at a time when the Jews had complained so loudly about Pilate and Herod Antipas that both men were removed from office. Connections and timing are important in politics.

So is backstabbing. Hoping to get Pilate booted from office, Herod Agrippa had sent a letter to the emperor, accusing Pilate of "graft, insults, robberies, assaults, wanton abuse, constant executions without trial, unending grievous cruelty." Corrupt politicians often bring about the removal of other corrupt politicians.

Herod Agrippa was as corrupt and worldly as his famous grandfather had been. But while the Jews had detested Herod the Great, they loved Herod Agrippa. They were grateful that Herod Agrippa had been part of the Jewish delegation that managed to talk the mad Caligula, who believed himself a god, out of setting up a statue of himself in the Jewish temple. (Herod's motive here was not religious but political; he knew that a statue of a Roman emperor in the temple would provoke a Jewish revolt against Rome, possibly leading to his own downfall.) In fact, for all their faults, the Herods were seen as better rulers in the region than the Roman governors were, since they were more sensitive to Jewish interests.

The Jews, as we see in Acts 12, liked Herod Agrippa for another reason: He persecuted the Christians. He was an utterly unspiritual man, yet he was willing to act the part of the devout Jew in public, and he saw that most of the Jews, especially the Pharisees, were against the new sect. We read in Acts that for the first time one of Jesus' disciples, James, was martyred, beheaded by Herod Agrippa's order. Finding that this pleased the Jews, the king had Peter put in chains, and Peter would have suffered the same fate as James had not an angel delivered him from prison. The king was so furious that Peter escaped his clutches that he had the poor guards executed. It is interesting that the arrest of Peter coincided with the Feast of Unleavened Bread. Had Peter not been released miraculously from prison, he would have been martyred at the time of one of the great Jewish feasts—just as his Master had been. Herod's plan to make an execution a part of a holy day says a lot about his character.

But the faith was spreading, and no corrupt, hypocritical king was going to stop it, any more than the king's evil grandfather had been able to destroy the newborn Jesus.

Acts 12 begins with a story of persecution but ends with the death of the persecutor. His death is interesting because it is recorded not only in the Bible but in the writings of the Jewish historian Josephus as well. Herod had gone to the port city of Caesarea for an official audience, and he was wearing, Acts says, "royal robes." Josephus records that the robes were made of woven silver, and that the people gathered together saw the awesome sight of the morning sun reflecting off Herod's silver raiment. The people—most of whom would have been pagans, not Jews—were awestruck.

Some of the people in the crowd called out to Herod, "Be gracious to us! Before now we regarded you as a man, but now we see that you are beyond mortal nature." (Contrast this with Acts 10: Peter's reaction to Cornelius' bow was, "Get up, I too am a man.") Herod did not rebuke or correct the people who called him a god. It was the mark of a good politician that he put on a good show for the public.

His "divinity" was short-lived: He was suddenly struck down and died shortly thereafter—a divine punishment for his acting godlike (Acts 12:21–23). Josephus adds an interesting detail: At the moment before Herod was struck down, he saw an owl. At that moment he may have recalled a prophecy he had heard a decade earlier when he served a spell in prison: A fellow prisoner told Herod that if he ever saw an owl again, it would be an omen of his death. The omen proved true. Herod died at the age of fifty-four.

The time was August of AD 44. The Book of Acts omits an important detail from the story: Herod was in Caesarea because of games being held to honor the emperor Claudius. It is appropriate that this eager collaborator with the Romans would have died at an event intended to bring glory to the emperor.

The most important words in Acts 12 are the last verse: "But the word of God continued to increase and spread." An apostle had been executed and another apostle had been jailed, but despite these setbacks, the faith was growing.

A SPARROW AMONG PEACOCKS

The next day Agrippa and Bernice came with great pomp and entered the audience room with the high-ranking military officers and the prominent men of the city. At the command of Festus, Paul was brought in. (Acts 25:23)

Throughout the New Testament, there is no getting away from the Herod family. First, Herod the Great murdered the infants of Bethlehem in an effort to kill the newborn Jesus. Second, his son Herod Antipas executed the great prophet John the Baptist and mocked the arrested Jesus. Third, Herod Agrippa I executed the Apostle James and jailed Peter. And fourth, the great Paul was put on trial before yet another Herod, Herod Agrippa II, called simply Agrippa in Acts 25.

In the last section we looked at the dramatic death of Herod Agrippa I, in AD 44. After his death, government of the region was again in the hands of Roman rulers. Herod Agrippa's son was seventeen at the time of his father's death. Like most members of his family, he had been brought up in Rome and learned at a young age to cozy up to power, specifically Roman power. Being friends with the emperor Claudius served him well, for Claudius gave him some territories to rule, and later Nero gave him even more, but he never ruled a territory nearly as large as his father had. He would be a mere footnote in the history books, except for two things: his relations with his sister Bernice and his encounter with the Apostle Paul.

It was widely believed that Agrippa and Bernice had an incestuous relationship. The Romans, as immoral as they were, claimed to be shocked by such behavior, but the shock did not lead to the brother and sister being ostracized. Yet the Roman historians of this period did not hide their disapproval of such immorality.

Acts 25 is part of the story of Paul's trial after his being arrested and almost lynched in Jerusalem. He had been taken, in Roman custody, from Jerusalem to Caesarea, where the corrupt Roman governor Felix knew he was innocent but kept him in prison, hoping for a bribe. The next governor, Festus, was more conscientious and hoped to give Paul a fair trial. Agrippa and Bernice had to stop in Caesarea to pay their respects to the new governor, and since they were Jews and had a better understanding of Jewish religious matters than Festus himself did, he asked them to be present while Paul stated his case.

Since this was an official state visit, it was conducted with great solemnity. The original Greek text uses an interesting word to refer to the arrival of Agrippa and Bernice in the hall where Paul was to be tried: They came with great *phantasias*, sometimes translated "display" but usually "pomp." Indeed, "pomp" could be the byword for the entire Herod tribe, considering the time and money Herod the Great lavished on building his palaces, forts and amphitheaters—and, of course, the temple in Jerusalem. The other Herods were also lavish builders, but Herod Agrippa I had died on a notoriously pompous occasion, when his stunning silver robe in the morning sun convinced a pagan audience that he was a god, not a man.

Acts 25 gives us the striking contrast of a sparrow among peacocks: A prisoner—Paul, a man bearing scars from having been stoned and flogged, probably in ragged clothing and bound with chains—was defending himself before a wealthy, worldly brother and sister who were, in all likelihood, engaging in behavior that most societies throughout history have condemned as immoral. Paul would have been well aware that Agrippa's father had executed the Apostle James and thrown the other apostles in prison. Like all "Very Important People," Agrippa and Bernice entered not alone but attended by "the high-ranking military officers and the prominent men of the city"—a parade of worldly vanity, a normal part of the politics of shiny surfaces. Agrippa, Bernice and the others would have been horrified to think that their place in history hinged not on their own glory but on their brief encounter with a Jewish prisoner in shackles.

Defending himself before this worldly assemblage, Paul at one point addressed Agrippa, hoping the Jewish king might be sympathetic. Supposedly Agrippa was knowledgeable in Jewish matters, including the Scriptures. But his Jewishness was all for show, a matter of him being a more effective ruler by making his subjects think he was devout, when he was anything but. For him, Jewish teachings were mostly a matter of idle curiosity, a hobby, and a matter of public relations. Paul's question—"King Agrippa, do you believe the prophets? I know you do"—was wasted on this worldly king. Agrippa did not really "believe" anything, except whatever would maintain his power and status.

Agrippa's reply was probably delivered with a bit of a sneer: "Do you think that in such a short time you can persuade me to be a Christian?" Agrippa was reminding Paul to keep his distance. True, they were both Jews and supposedly revered the same Scriptures. But a man with power and authority was not going to take such matters seriously. Answering Paul this way was Agrippa's way of siding not with Paul but with the Roman governor, Festus, who had accused Paul of having gone mad with his study of religion. Agrippa did not say, "Paul, I think Festus is right—this religious stuff has unhinged your mind." But he implied the same. Agrippa had no intention of letting Festus think he approached religion the same way this itinerant preacher did. Note that he never answered Paul's question directly. He did not say he believed the prophets, or that he did not. What he really believed in was what Festus did—power and worldly success.

Did Paul in fact hope to convert the Jewish king? Probably not—and yet, Paul would have remembered that he himself had at one time seemed an unlikely candidate to conversion. History is full of unexpected turnarounds, and the Roman empire now had thousands of new Christians.

The encounter was revealing: *phantasias*, "display" and "pomp," vs. the simplicity and saintliness of the solitary apostle in chains. The pomp seemed to have the upper hand, and always does, yet the Bible holds up the goal of living a life rooted in God, not in material things.

PUTTING THE WORD TO WORK

1. Read all of chapter 2 of Matthew. The words will be familiar from their being read so often at Christmas, but try to read them fresh—maybe use a different translation—and focus on the character of King Herod.

2. Compare Herod with the wise men or Magi. All would have been men of high social standing, yet the Magi were willing to travel far to bow down to someone they considered truly great, while Herod saw the newborn Jesus as a rival and threat.

3. The word *phantasias*, translated "pomp" in Acts 25, is the root of our word "fantasy." Keep this in mind as you try to memorize today's Memory Verse from 1 John.

4. Overall, what is your opinion of the Herod family? Do you think that without meaning to, they played a positive role in the growth of Christianity, since their lives provided such a contrast with the teachings and lives of the first Christians?

5. Having read this chapter, try to watch the evening news and keep an eye out for the "pomp" and "display" element in politics. The Bible tells us to honor and pray for political leaders, yet it also tells us to be "wise as serpents" while we live in this world. Keep in mind that no individual, and no party, is totally free from the political requirement to put on a good show.

Kings Serving the King

In earlier chapters we have looked at some of the kings of Israel. Some were decent but disappointing (Saul, Solomon), many were downright wicked (Ahab). David, though a flawed man, was a model king in many ways, and his devotion to the Lord led to the Lord's promise that David's dynasty would endure. But most of his successors were disgraceful,

hardly fit to be called "the Lord's anointed" rulers, since anointing was the sign that the king was dedicated to the service of God. In this chapter we will look at a few gems among the pebbles—but we'll begin with the sad story of one of the pebbles.

KEY TERM FOR TODAY Anointed Kings

A handful of Old Testament kings were worthy of the title "the Lord's anointed," and the contrast with the wicked rulers is truly striking. Being the Lord's anointed meant seeking to serve God's people, never forgetting that all kings must answer to the greatest King.

DIVIDED THEY (WILL) FALL

The young men who had grown up with [Rehoboam] replied, "Tell these people who have said to you, 'Your father put a heavy yoke on us, but make our yoke lighter'—tell them, 'My little finger is thicker than my father's waist.'" (1 Kings 12:10)

We looked at the glorious reign of wise King Solomon, David's son, in an earlier chapter—glorious in that he made Israel a strong and peaceful country, and built a temple to the Lord that would symbolize for centuries the glory of Israel's God. Less glorious is the fact that his many building projects meant that Solomon was the prototype of the tax-and-spend politician, and while the country enjoyed peace and stability, many people grumbled against the policy of forcing adult male Israelites to work as forced laborers at times. Solomon's court, with its huge harem, was expensive to support, and the Bible renders a harsh judgment on Solomon building shrines for the gods of his pagan wives.

A man with such power was bound to make enemies. One was Jeroboam, a competent and industrious head of the forced-labor crews. One day on the road Jeroboam encountered a prophet named Ahijah, who was wearing a new cloak. Ahijah tore his cloak and gave part of it to Jeroboam, with this message: Because Solomon had not stayed faithful to the Lord, Solomon's kingdom would be divided after his death. The appearance of this prophet is noteworthy, because no prophet is mentioned in the account of Solomon's reign. In fact, in his younger days Solomon received revelations directly from God, but as he grew older and his heart turned away from God, these communications ceased. So God had revealed to Ahijah that Solomon's son would not rule the same large kingdom that Solomon had.

The son's name was Rehoboam, whose Hebrew name means "may the people expand." It would turn out to be an inappropriate name. After Solomon's death, Rehoboam met with the elders of Israel. They voiced their complaints about Solomon's tax-and-spend and forced-labor policies and let Rehoboam know that they were hoping for change. Rehoboam told them to come back in three days and he would respond to their request. The court's older counselors gave him wise advice: Give the people what they wanted and they would serve him faithfully. But the younger men of the court were on the side of arrogance, as was Rehoboam himself. So the stupid, tactless Rehoboam met again with Israel's leaders and gave them an unpleasant message: "My father made your yoke heavy; I will make it even heavier. My father scourged you with whips; I will scourge you with scorpions" (1 Kings 12:14). What could the foolish man have been thinking? Did he think the people could be bullied so easy? So the leaders of the ten northern tribes of Israel split, no longer regarding Rehoboam as their king. Jeroboam—who had been living in Egypt and hiding from the wrath of Solomon, who no doubt had heard of Ahijah's prophecy—became the king over the ten northern tribes. Brainless Rehoboam was left as king over only two tribes, Judah and Benjamin. His kingdom went by the name Judah, while the ten northern tribes continued to be called Israel.

Ironic, isn't it, that Solomon, known for his wisdom found in the Book of Proverbs, should have had such a foolish son? One of Solomon's proverbs ran this way: "A wise servant will rule over a disgraceful son, and will share the inheritance as one of the brothers" (Proverbs 17:2). Note how this applies perfectly to Jeroboam and Rehoboam. Through his stupidity and stubbornness, Rehoboam did indeed lose a huge part of his inheritance to the "wise servant," Jeroboam.

> **DID YOU KNOW?**
>
> Rehoboam ruled over Judah from 930 BC–913 BC. Jeroboam ruled over Israel from 930 BC–910 BC.

Psalm 72, ascribed to Solomon, speaks of a king far different from Solomon's son: "Endow the king with your justice, O God, the royal son with your righteousness. He will judge your people in righteousness, your afflicted ones with justice." Clearly Rehoboam was not that kind of king. Far from treating the afflicted ones with justice, he wanted to afflict them further.

The worst aspect of the division of the kingdom was that the large independent domain David and Solomon ruled no longer existed. Separated, Judah and Israel would inevitably become the prey or puppets of the bigger empires nearby. In the uninformed arrogance of youth, Rehoboam had done a horrible thing. In his rashness he planned to make war on the northern tribes to force them to accept his rule, but a prophet named Shemaiah spoke a word from the Lord: Rehoboam must not make war on his brother Israelites, for it was God's will that the kingdom be divided. While a united kingdom had been God's original plan, it was not his will that the unity be maintained by force.

Jeroboam is a slightly more admirable character, a hardworking official who did not inherit the throne as Rehoboam did, but rose to the rank of king after being called to the task by a prophet. But 1 Kings judges him harshly for building two temples, one at Dan in northern Israel, another at Bethel in southern Israel. Since Judah and Israel were no longer united, Jeroboam did not want the people of Israel journeying to Jerusalem, in Judah, to worship in the temple there. Again and again in 1 and 2 Kings, Jeroboam is criticized for setting up golden bull idols at these sanctuaries. It is almost certain that the king did not intend these statues at Dan and Bethel to symbolize Baal, the

CULTURAL INSIGHTS

Egypt, Haven for Rebels

"Solomon tried to kill Jeroboam, but Jeroboam fled to Egypt, to Shishak the king, and stayed there until Solomon's death" (1 Kings 11:40). Shishak, founder of a new dynasty of Egyptian kings, began rule around 945 BC, while Solomon was still on the throne. Shishak must have continued on outwardly friendly terms with Solomon, but he gladly took in the potential rebel Jeroboam, hoping that after Solomon's death Jeroboam might head a rebellion against Solomon's dynasty, which is precisely what happened. Not surprisingly, "in the fifth year of King Rehoboam, Shishak king of Egypt attacked Jerusalem" (1 Kings 14:25). Already the neighboring empires were taking advantage of the division of Solomon's kingdom. Shishak's armies carried off much of the gold from Jerusalem's temple—Solomon's golden age had literally come to an end.

Canaanite fertility god, but since the calf was a familiar Baal symbol, it was inevitable that in time the simple folk would not make the distinction and would assume the king had given his official approval to the worship of Baal.

So far the picture of the two divided kingdoms is not impressive, nor are its kings. Rehoboam strikes us as arrogant and selfish, not remotely interested in serving God or God's people, and Jeroboam seems like just another political opportunist. Even worse rulers would follow, but, thankfully, some worthy ones as well.

SOME LIGHT IN THE GLOOM

Asa did what was right in the eyes of the Lord, as his father David had done. (1 Kings 15:11)

Rehoboam was not only tactless and stupid but also tolerant of the fertility cults of Canaan, which sometimes involved child sacrifice. Perhaps this is not surprising, given that his mother was a foreigner, an Ammonite, one of many pagan wives Solomon married to seal a political alliance. Rehoboam's inglorious reign lasted seventeen years. His son Abijah (or Abijam, in some translations) was no better than his father, and he reigned only three years.

David's descendants were proving themselves a sorry lot—but a change came with Abijah's son, Asa. His name, appropriately, means "healer," and his reign was a time of spiritual healing in the land. Asa insisted that the country be faithful to God alone, so he tore down the pagan shrines, a religious housecleaning that was long overdue. While the temple had been stripped of many of its treasures in the reign of his grandfather Rehoboam, Asa refurnished the temple with vessels of gold and silver.

"He commanded Judah to seek the Lord, the God of their fathers, and to obey his laws and commands" (2 Chronicles 14:4). In setting the country back on the right course, Asa had to take a strict line with his own grandmother Maacah, who was devoted to the worship of the goddess Asherah. Maacah is referred to by the Hebrew word *gebira*, translated "queen mother," but literally "powerful woman." Asa could not remove her from being his grandmother, of course, but he could remove her pagan influence over the nation.

Asa is presented not only as a zealous religious reformer but also as a man of action, for he had to resist the encroachments of Israel's king, Baasha. Ramah, a town where Baasha tried to build fortifications, was only five miles north of Jerusalem, so this posed a

> **DID YOU KNOW?**
>
> David is called Asa's "father." In the context this means "ancestor," but it is also fatherhood in a spiritual sense, for he is a true son of David by being committed to the Lord.

real threat to Judah. A kind of "cold war" existed, with Judah and Israel suspicious of each other and spending extravagantly to build fortresses in case the other attacked. Asa's standing army was enormous: "Asa had an army of three hundred thousand men from Judah, equipped with large shields and with spears, and two hundred and eighty thousand from Benjamin, armed with small shields and with bows. All these were brave fighting men."

Despite this formidable army, Judah was attacked by a much larger army from Ethiopia (or Cush, in some translations), the land to the south of Egypt. With the two very unequal armies facing each other, the devout Asa realized that deliverance had to come from the Lord, not from human forces. "Then Asa called to the Lord his God and said, "Lord, there is no one like you to help the powerless against the mighty. Help us, O Lord our God, for we rely on our God; do not let man prevail against you'" (2 Chronicles 14:11). His prayer was answered, and they drove the Ethiopians out of their land.

Some time after this divine victory, a prophet named Azariah spoke to Asa: "Listen to me, Asa and all Judah and Benjamin. The Lord is with you when you are with him. If you seek him, he will be found by you, but if you forsake him, he will forsake you. . . . But as for you, be strong and do not give up, for your work will be rewarded" (2 Chronicles 15:2, 7). Asa took these inspiring words to heart and ordered a holy day of celebration in Jerusalem. Among those attending were faithful people from the northern tribes of Israel, who saw Asa as a more worthy king to serve than their own.

Asa was an admirable king, but not a perfect one. Facing a threat from Baasha, king of Israel, Asa stripped some of the treasures from the temple and from his own palace and sent them to the king of Aram (or Syria, in some translations). These were a bribe, for Asa wanted the king of Aram to break off his alliance with Baasha. The bribe worked, for the king of Aram sent his armies to harass Israel, and Baasha ceased

---

CULTURAL INSIGHTS

Ancient Medicine

In his old age, Asa suffered from some mysterious disease in his feet, but instead of relying on God, he relied on physicians. The Hebrew word translated "physicians" here is literally "healers." We must not assume these were doctors in any real sense of the word—"witch doctors" or "medicine men" would be closer to the truth. In effect, Asa was resorting to magic to cure his ailment, and the Law of Moses condemned such practices. Considering that the practice of medicine in those times was a mishmash of astrology, vile potions and poultices, and bizarre spells, a person was more likely to die from the doctors than from disease. If a person was healed, it was more likely in spite of than because of these charlatans.

Shrine Prostitutes

Much of pagan worship resembled an orgy more than a church service, for in ancient times people connected sex with the fertility of their crops and herds. In 1 Kings 14:24 we find the Bible's first mention of the "male shrine prostitutes," men who, on the pretext of serving their pagan gods, would have relations with both men and women. The Old Testament refers to such practices as "abominations," and part of Asa's spiritual housecleaning was his expelling of these men from Judah.

to menace Judah. Politically, what Asa had done was understandable. Spiritually, it was disgraceful, a fact pointed out by the prophet Hanani, who reminded Asa of the time when the Lord had helped Judah defeat the Ethiopians. At that time Asa had relied on God, but now he had changed, and God knew it, for, as Hanani said, "the eyes of the Lord range throughout the earth to strengthen those whose hearts are fully committed to him" (2 Chronicles 16:9). Because he had failed to rely on God, he would continue to face the threat of wars. Asa was so irked by the prophet's words that he had him put in stocks in prison. It is interesting that after Asa threw Hanani in prison, he also oppressed some of the people. When the king begins to persecute God's prophets, he has no qualms about oppressing others.

Despite these failings, Asa had made a deep impression on the people, so much so that his funeral was a lavish one, his corpse being covered with spices and perfumes, and a fire lit in his honor.

CHIP OFF THE OLD BLOCK

In everything [Jehoshaphat] walked in the ways of his father Asa and did not stray from them; he did what was right in the eyes of the Lord. (1 Kings 22:43)

His heart was courageous in the ways of the Lord. (2 Chronicles 17:6, ESV)

Among Asa's many blessings was having a son who was a worthy successor. In the list of the many disgraceful kings of Judah and Israel, Jehoshaphat was one who "did what was right in the eyes of the Lord." Like his father, he continued in the work of cleansing the land of pagan practices, though such reforms were never truly permanent, since the people were constantly tempted to build new shrines to the pagan gods.

In his zeal for the Lord, Jehoshaphat was the first king to institute a religious-education program for the nation, sending out his officials to teach people from the Book of the Law of the Lord (2 Chronicles 17:7–9). Among the teachers were priests and Levites, which was a sign that these staff members of the temple were being given tasks other than merely administering the sacrifices. If the people were going to serve God fully, they had to be familiar with the Law of Moses, a Law the people were constantly tempted to neglect.

Jehoshaphat had a concern not only for religion and education but for justice as well—which is appropriate, since the Hebrew name Jehoshaphat means "the Lord judges." "He appointed judges in the land, in each of the fortified cities of Judah. He told them, 'Consider carefully what you do, because you are not judging for man but for the Lord, who is with you whenever you give a verdict. Now let the fear of the Lord be upon you. Judge carefully, for with the Lord our God there is no injustice or partiality or bribery'" (2 Chronicles 19:6–7). For Jehoshaphat, as for all the worthy kings of the Bible, religion was more than rituals and sacred writings; religion had to bear fruit in seeing that people were treated fairly.

Like his father, Jehoshaphat pursued the policy of peace through strength and maintaining a large army. But, also like his father, on one occasion his army faced a much larger force, a coalition of Judah's violent neighbors. Faced with this threat, the king did the obvious thing: He turned to God. He proclaimed a nationwide fast, and standing in front of the Jerusalem temple with the people listening, he prayed: "We have no power to face this vast army that is attacking us. We do not know what to do, but our eyes are upon you" (2 Chronicles 20:12). That is a reasonably good summary of faith: not knowing what to do, we turn our eyes to God. After the king's prayer, the Lord spoke through a prophet named Jahaziel: "Do not be afraid or discouraged because of this vast army. For the battle is not yours, but God's" (2 Chronicles 20:15). The prophet's name is appropriate, for it means "God gives vision." Stirred by his words, instead of marching out to meet the enemy with fear or with faith in their own might, the people march out with singing, proclaiming their devotion to the Almighty God. As the prophet had foretold, Judah was victorious in the battle. "And the kingdom of Jehoshaphat was at peace, for his God had given him rest on every side" (2 Chronicles 20:30).

Like the story of his father Asa, the story of Jehoshaphat is not all rosy. In fact, 2 Chronicles chooses to end the story of his reign with an episode showing that even the best kings could do foolish things. The king had made an alliance with the king of Israel, Ahaziah, son of the wicked Ahab, who was wicked himself. Ahaziah and Jehoshaphat agreed to join together to build a fleet of trading ships, which would, they hoped, sail as far away as Tarshish—the region we today call Spain. But a prophet named Eliezer brought the word of the Lord to Jehoshaphat: He had done wrong in making an alliance with the wicked Ahaziah, and as a punishment, the ships would never serve their purpose, for all would be wrecked. To have a fleet of ships would have meant taking the nation to the level of glory it had under Solomon, but it was not to be.

Jehoshaphat's greatest error was allying himself with the dynasty of Ahab. It was probably done in the hope of keeping the two nations united against their enemies, but it was a stupid move morally, especially since it was clear that God was on his side as long as he walked the right path.

Still, Jehoshaphat was a great man and the son of a great man. He did not pass on his greatness or goodness to the next king, however, for his oldest son, Jehoram, who succeeded him on the throne, killed all his brothers, no doubt to make sure there would be no rivals. And while his father had entered into a naval alliance with the dynasty of Ahab, Jehoram did something much worse, marrying the wicked daughter of Ahab. Later in this chapter we will see what ensued from that tragic marriage.

HEADS WILL ROLL

Jehu said, "Come with me and see my zeal for the Lord." (2 Kings 10:16)

Here we look at one of the most fascinating and most violent men of the Old Testament, Jehu. Like all the good kings of Israel and Judah, Jehu was one who heeded the words of the Lord's prophets.

In an earlier chapter we looked at the sordid story of what was undoubtedly the wickedest royal couple in the Bible, Ahab and Jezebel. The fiery prophet Elijah had predicted doom for the two and for their whole vile dynasty as well. Initiating the events that led to the extinction of Ahab's dynasty was the prophet Elisha, who sent a fellow prophet off to the town of Ramoth–Gilead, where part of Israel's army was encamped. The prophet was to take a flask of oil and anoint Jehu, one of the commanders, as king over Israel, with the task of ridding the land of the violent and corrupt Ahab family. The anointing was done in secret, but Jehu's fellow soldiers wanted to know what happened. What did the prophet—they refer to him as a "madman"—want? Jehu did not regard him as a madman, and when he revealed what happened, neither did the other soldiers, for they immediately hailed Jehu as their new king. These hardened military men had little use for the prophets and their sometimes peculiar behavior. Even so, they accepted what had happened, perhaps because they were already aware of Jehu's leadership potential.

Elisha was reviving the old practice of the Lord's prophet anointing Israel's king, symbolizing that the king was God's choice, not simply the descendant of a previous king. The rotten kings who preceded Jehu had either inherited the throne or usurped it. In Jehu's case, it was a gift from God.

This is the first mention of anointing a king since Solomon. Presumably the others were anointed, but

DID YOU KNOW?

The Baal temple where the slaughter occurred was no doubt the one Ahab built, so the setting is appropriate.

Picturing the King

What did the kings of Judah and Israel look like? Despite all their digging in the Middle East, archaeologists have found only one item that might show an image of a king made during his life. The British Museum in London has an obelisk from the reign of Shalmaneser III, king of Assyria. Carved on it is the image of Jehu (or his representative), shown kissing the crown before Shalmaneser. Considering what a take-charge person Jehu is in 2 Kings, it is curious to see him in this servile posture.

Ironically, the obelisk refers to Jehu as "son of Omri"—ironic because Omri was the father of Ahab, and far from being a "son of Omri," Jehu exterminated Omri's dynasty. Probably the Assyrians just assumed that Omri's dynasty still ruled Israel.

2 Kings emphasizes that Jehu was not just another of the many ambitious usurpers in Israel's gory history; he is the chosen one of God.

The overthrow of Ahab's dynasty involved speed and secrecy. Jehu drove his chariot to Jezreel, where Israel's king, Jehoram, was recuperating from some war wounds. As it happened, he was hosting Ahaziah, the king of Judah. A watchman from the fort saw a chariot approaching at breakneck speed. Wondering how the war was faring in Ramoth–Gilead, the king sent a fast messenger out to meet Jehu, asking him, "Do you come in peace?"—meaning, "Good news or bad news from the front?" Rather than answering, Jehu told the messenger, "Fall in behind me." The same thing happened to a second and third messenger from the king. Jehu apparently had an air of authority about him.

Anxious to know why his messengers weren't returning, King Jehoram himself went out to meet the hard-driving Jehu, asking, "Do you come in peace?" Jehu then revealed his intention: There was no point in speaking of peace when the whole land had been polluted by the wickedness of the king's family. The king realized a rebellion was taking place, but he had no time to reflect on it, for Jehu killed him with an arrow. Fleeing, King Ahaziah was also killed by Jehu's men. Ahaziah was the son of Ahab's daughter Athaliah, so already two kings descended from Ahab were dead. Shortly afterward, Ahab's wicked wife, Jezebel, would also be dead, an episode told in another chapter (Day 15).

The butchery was just beginning. Ahab had seventy "sons"—which can mean "descendants," although it actually is possible he had seventy sons, since he would have had numerous wives and concubines. Whatever the degree of kinship, the seventy lived in Israel's capital city, Samaria. Jehu sent the royal officials there a message: Choose the most worthy among the seventy sons, make him king, and then fight for him. These officials were soft courtiers, not fighting men, and they weren't about to fight against Jehu, especially after hearing how he had already killed two kings. They sent him a message: They would gladly do whatever he commanded. He replied by telling them to send the "heads" of the seventy sons—meaning, figuratively, the leaders among them. But the officials took the message literally: They beheaded the seventy sons and laid the heads in two piles at the city gates.

Jehu made a smart political move: By giving him what he asked for, the chief men of Samaria had involved themselves in the political revolution, so there was no turning back. He told the city elders, "You are innocent"—he alone was responsible for the rebellion. But this was a bit of political theater, and the elders knew they were far from innocent. The two piles of severed heads would have made a macabre sight, as Jehu intended. Who would dare oppose him now?

Many readers are put off by this fascinating but grim narrative. Anyone with the tiniest amount of spiritual sensitivity must pause to ask: Why did the great prophet Elisha regard the violent Jehu as the Lord's anointed? The answer is found in the next episode, Jehu's extermination of the Baal cult. So far his actions had seemed like a political revolution, not a religious one. So like the king he had assassinated, Jehu claimed to be a devotee of the god Baal, and he ordered a solemn assembly at the Baal temple, with all the pagan priests and prophets gathered there. When all the worshippers were inside, Jehu had eighty soldiers cut down the entire congregation. He had a political motive as well as a religious one: Baal worship had been associated with Ahab and Jezebel, and though he had exterminated their entire families, he had to go after the Baal cult, for it would have included the people most loyal to Ahab and Jezebel. "So Jehu destroyed Baal worship in Israel" (2 Kings 10:28).

One of Jehu's supporters in his revolution was a devout man named Jehonadab, who eagerly climbed into Jehu's chariot when Jehu told him, "Come with me and see my zeal for the Lord" (2 Kings 10:16). In this very violent age, zeal for the Lord sometimes required drastic measures.

Because of his zeal for the Lord, Jehu's dynasty ruled Israel from 842 BC to 745 BC, the longest-reigning regime in Israel.

ONE PURGE LEADS TO ANOTHER

> When Athaliah the mother of Ahaziah saw that her son was dead, she proceeded to destroy the whole royal family of the house of Judah. (2 Chronicles 22:10)

We turn from the story of Jehu to a tale of two women, one courageous and saintly, the other bold and wicked. Sadly, their story is almost as violent as Jehu's.

Jehu's purge of Ahab's wicked family was not complete, for there was one survivor, and he could not touch her, for she was safe inside her palace in Jerusalem. This was Athaliah, daughter of Ahab and mother of Ahaziah, the king of Judah who had been killed by Jehu. She heard the news of what Jehu had done to her entire family, and she took swift and horrible action, killing off Judah's entire royal family—or so she thought.

God had promised that the dynasty of David would last—and of course the promises of God carry more weight than the violent acts of a reigning queen. God was at work in the palace through a woman named Jehosheba, who managed to have Ahaziah's infant son, Joash, hidden away in a bedroom in the temple complex—not a room for sleeping, but a room or large closet where bedding mats were stored. We are not told precisely how they were able to keep the child hidden for six years, although he was not living under the same roof as Athaliah. We have to applaud the amazing courage of Jehosheba, for defying the strong-willed Athaliah would almost certainly have brought the death penalty. She not only preserved the precious life of an innocent child but also preserved the dynasty of David.

Jehosheba was not the only one who had set her hopes on Joash's future. So did her husband, the priest Jehoiada. They both knew it would have been foolish to try to make an infant king over Israel. They waited until he reached age seven, and then staged a swift coup. Arming the temple guards with shields and spears that had belonged to David, he had them station themselves around the temple while young Joash was brought out. In front of the temple he was crowned and anointed, with the people proclaiming, "Long live the king!" Hearing the noise and realizing what had happened, Athaliah tore her clothes in agony and screamed, "Treason! Treason!" The guards put her to death with the sword, along with her followers. "All the people of the land were rejoicing and blowing trumpets" (2 Kings 11:14). Though engineered by Jehoiada and Jehosheba, the revolt clearly had some grassroots support. The "people of the land" were purer in their religion than sophisticates like Athaliah. After getting rid of her, Jehoiada institutes a covenant between the people and the young king. Athaliah had had nothing but contempt for the people.

Like her father, Ahab, Athaliah had been an avid follower of the god Baal. After she was executed, the people of Jerusalem went to the temple of Baal and demolished it, along with its idols and altars. "All the people of the land rejoiced. And the city was quiet, because Athaliah had been slain with the sword at the palace" (2 Kings 11:20).

Thanks to two revolutions—one in Israel under Jehu, the other in Judah under Jehoiada—the evil dynasty of Ahab had been exterminated along with, for the time being, the worship of Baal.

And the young king, Joash, was fortunate—not only for having survived the bloody purge by his grandmother Athaliah, but also because he had a spiritual father, the priest Jehoiada, to guide him as he ruled Judah. (The name Joash is spelled Jehoash in some versions.) Jehoash's father, who had been murdered by Jehu's men, was an evil character, and it was better having Jehoash's character shaped by Jehoiada than by his actual father.

So Jehoash began as a good king. When he was in his twenties he was disturbed to find that money that people had contributed to the temple was not being used for needed repairs; apparently some of the priests were lining their own pockets with it! To ensure honesty, Jehoiada the priest set up a chest—which was kept locked—with a hole bored in the top so people could put their offerings in it. Periodically it was unlocked, with the money taken to pay the carpenters and other workers on the temple.

Jehoash was the first king of Judah since Solomon who is mentioned as being anointed. Everything we are told about him in 2 Kings is positive—except that, oddly, two of his own servants assassinated him. Why? The answer is found in the longer account of his reign in 2 Chronicles. Jehoash's mentor and surrogate father, Jehoiada the priest, died at the ripe age of one hundred thirty and was given a high honor: burial among Judah's kings. Once the saintly Jehoiada was no longer on the scene, Jehoash changed dramatically, giving his approval to idol worship. He wasn't yet free from the influence of Jehoiada, however, because Jehoiada's son Zechariah was a prophet, and he spoke out boldly against Jehoash's slide into idolatry: "Because you have forsaken the Lord, he has forsaken you." Like so many prophets, Zechariah learned that speaking truth to power carried a fatal risk. By order of the king, Zechariah was stoned to death in the temple courtyard. "King Joash did not remember the kindness Zechariah's father Jehoiada had shown him but killed his son, who said as he lay dying, 'May the Lord see this and call you to account'" (2 Chronicles 24:22). The Lord did see, for Jehoash was wounded in a battle with the Arameans, and while he lay in bed, recovering from his wounds, his servants conspired against him and killed him for what he had done to the prophet Zechariah. He was not buried in the tombs of the kings, while his mentor Jehoiada was.

We should be grateful that the Bible, with its breathtaking honesty, presents its characters "warts and all." Like the other people we have looked at in this chapter, Jehoash was a mix of good and bad. But, like all other kings, Jehoash was human.

THE GOLD STANDARD OF REFORM

Neither before nor after Josiah was there a king like him who turned to the Lord as he did—with all his heart and with all his soul and with all his strength, in accordance with all the Law of Moses. (2 Kings 23:25)

The good kings we have looked at so far were all reformers, committed to getting the nation back on track, spiritually speaking. But the last and best of the reformers was the great Josiah.

Like the last king we looked at, Jehoash, Josiah did not have a promising beginning, for his father was an evil man and his grandfather was even worse. Josiah's grandfather was the notorious Manasseh, whose fifty-five-year reign was filled with idolatry and corruption unparalleled in Judah's history. Amon, his son, reigned only two years before being murdered by his servants. They spared his eight-year-old son, Josiah, who apparently had not inherited the awful qualities of the previous two kings. After the assassination of the wicked Amon, the court must have decided that the wise course was to bring the boy-king Josiah up as a godly man and hope he could turn the nation around.

> **DID YOU KNOW?**
>
> It is interesting that the prophetess Huldah is consulted, and not the prophets Jeremiah or Zephaniah, who were both active in Jerusalem at that time. Clearly Huldah was held in very high esteem.

The timing was excellent, for Judah was at peace during most of Josiah's reign. Assyria, the aggressive empire that had conquered the northern kingdom of Israel in 722 BC, was in a weak state and was no threat to Judah for many years. With no foreign enemies to fret over, Josiah could turn his attention to domestic—and spiritual—matters.

Like the other good kings, Josiah had a soft spot for the temple and ordered repairs on it. During the repairs the high priest, Hilkiah, found something amazing in the temple: the Book of the Law. Of course, Judah and Israel had had the Law since the days of Moses but apparently it was not widely read or copied. This helps explain, of course, why both nations so often slipped into idolatry and immorality, for most people were barely familiar with the writings of Moses.

The Book of the Law was read aloud to the king. Realizing how far Judah was from being obedient to the words of God, Josiah tore his clothes in agony. He sent his officials to the prophetess Huldah to inquire what all this might mean. Her reply was threatening—and hopeful. She told them that because the nation had been so unfaithful to the Lord, disaster was approaching, but because of the penitence Josiah had shown when he heard the Law read, the disaster would not take place in his lifetime.

Taking courage from this, Josiah summoned the people to the temple, where he swore to abide by the commands in the Book of the Law, and all the people joined him in this. Naturally the first item on the agenda was to remove the Baal idols and other pagan symbols that had been set up in—of all places—the temple of the Lord. As a symbol of utter detestation, these items were burned to ash and scattered. Like the reformist kings before him, Josiah expelled the male shrine prostitutes from the land, along with the astrologers and spiritualists, and he removed other pagan relics from Jerusalem. In fact, 2 Kings 23 is an amazingly long list of just how thoroughly paganized the nation had become. Whatever reforms had been done under previous righteous kings had to be done all over. Paganism, like a weed, always seemed to come back again.

Along with all this destruction came constructive things—such as reinstituting the great holy festival, the Passover. Israel, the northern kingdom, had been conquered by the Assyrians and no longer really existed as an independent entity, yet many faithful Israelites still lived in the region, so Josiah invited the tribes of the north to join in celebrating the Passover. He worked to reunite Judah with what was left of the northern tribes. His worthless ancestor Rehoboam had been specifically told by God, speaking through a prophet, not to make war on the northern tribes to force them to remain as part of the kingdom. Wooing them back and treating them as spiritual brothers was another matter.

The Passover was the perfect way to celebrate the reform, for it was a celebration of freedom from slavery to a foreign power. Josiah's grandfather and father had eagerly bowed down to foreign gods, but Josiah purged the country of pagan worship, at a time when no major foreign power was threatening the country. Reinstituting the Passover was both a political and religious act, for it reminded the people of their past, when God delivered them miraculously from an oppressor. All religions need regular rituals and celebrations to keep people's minds focused on the divine. Josiah had not only thrown out the old pagan rituals but also filled in the religious gap with rituals focused on the true God. A "housecleaning" was not enough; good rituals had to replace the bad ones.

It would be pleasant to report that this zealous reformer-king died peacefully at a ripe old age, but he did not. Most of his reign had been peaceful, but in his last years a power struggle developed between the mighty empires of Assyria, Babylonia and Egypt. In 609 BC, at a site called Megiddo, Josiah died in battle against the Egyptians. Judah lamented the death of its saintly king, and among the mourners was the prophet Jeremiah (2 Chronicles 35:25).

In concluding this chapter about earthly kings, we need to recall that a key theme of the Bible is that the

DID YOU KNOW?

The Book of the Law found during Josiah's reign was probably the Book of Deuteronomy. The reform he instituted is sometimes called the "Deuteronomic reform."

real King—the wholly good and all-powerful Ruler of all things—should be our object of worship, for all human rulers, even the cream of the crop, have their failings. The best of the kings in the Bible were those who kept their position in perspective and understood that all earthly kings are answerable to the great King.

PUTTING THE WORD TO WORK

1. Asa's name means "healer," and in a sense all the reforming kings in this chapter were healers. Who are some political healers you have known, either personally or through the news and history?

2. Reflect on Azariah's words to Asa: "The Lord is with you when you are with him." In what ways are you aware of yourself striving to be "with" God?

3. How do you react to the story of Jehu's bloody purge of Ahab's large family? Despite the violence, what qualities of Jehu can you find to admire?

4. Which of the kings do you find most appealing? Why?

5. Reflect on the important role the prophets played in the lives of the kings in this chapter. Then take a moment to pray for politicians, asking God to provide them with wise and discerning counselors.

Paul the Contented

T hanks to Acts and his many letters, Paul is one of the best-known personalities of the Bible, a man of fizzing vitality, a man who spoke of the life of faith as a "fight" and a "race," yet who also spoke of "contentment" and "peace." His hectic, event-filled

MEMORY VERSE

Godliness with contentment
is great gain.—1 Timothy 6:6

life taught him many lessons, including this one: Our life in God is bigger than our present circumstances.

In Paul's day, the Stoic philosophers praised *autarkeia*, contentment, but emphasized it as self-reliance, self-sufficiency and not having to rely on external circumstances for happiness. Paul had a knack for taking a Greek or Roman concept and putting a distinctive Christian spin on it. He knew that relying solely on oneself was nonsense. Who on earth can be completely independent and self-reliant? For the Christian, contentment is found not through relying on oneself but on a loving Father. Paul learned that he could do everything because he relied not on his own strength but on God's.

KEY TERM FOR TODAY   ## Contentment

For Paul, contentment isn't just being resigned to what is. It is confidence in God's providing for us. Ultimately, if we have God, we have everything.

RESTLESS SOUL OF SAUL

We all fell to the ground, and I heard a voice saying to me in Aramaic, "Saul, Saul, why do you persecute me? It is hard for you to kick against the goads." (Acts 26:14)

If anyone else thinks he has reasons to put confidence in the flesh, I have more: circumcised on the eighth day, of the people of Israel, of the tribe of Benjamin, a Hebrew of Hebrews; in regard to the law, a Pharisee. (Philippians 3:4–5)

Paul was most assuredly *not* content in his pre-Christian days. When we first encounter him in Acts, he is witnessing the martyrdom-by-stoning of the Christian Stephen—and approving of it (Acts 8:1). When we next meet him, in Acts 9, Paul is "breathing threats and murder" against the Christians, and he is authorized by the Jews' high priest to journey to Damascus to arrest Christians and bring them back to Jerusalem. Many Christians had fled Jerusalem in the wake of the persecution that followed the stoning of Stephen. But Saul wasn't content just to drive them away from Jerusalem; he actively went after them in other lands. In fact, it was he, not the high priest, who took the initiative in launching this mission.

Acts 9, one of the great chapters in the Bible, tells us things did not go as planned. On the road to Damascus, he saw a light from heaven. Falling to the ground, he heard a voice, speaking his Jewish name: "Saul, Saul, why are you persecuting me?" It was the voice of Jesus, informing Saul that it was he that Saul was persecuting—that is, in persecuting Christians, Saul was persecuting Jesus himself, for Christians were Christ's body on earth. Saul, blinded, was told go on to Damascus, where a Christian named Ananias restored Saul's sight and addressed the former persecutor as "brother." In a short time, Saul was preaching the message that Jesus was the Son of God. There soon followed a plot—the first of many—of the Jews to kill Saul, whom they now saw as an arch-traitor. He had to be sneaked out of the city by night in a basket lowered from the city walls.

Saul's conversion is one of the pivotal points of the Bible—and of world history, in fact, for it is hard to imagine Christianity without Paul. We have to wonder: What happened to Saul, inwardly? He gives us many clues in his letters. He had been raised a strict believer in the Jewish Law, a Pharisee, trained in Jerusalem under the famous teacher Gamaliel. He was, as he says in Philippians 3:5, a "Hebrew of Hebrews." In short, by Jewish standards, he was a model man. But his adherence to the Law had not

---

CULTURAL INSIGHTS

The Philippian Punishments

Acts 16 tells the colorful tale of the missionaries Paul and Silas in Philippi. Branded as troublemakers, the two were beaten severely and then put into stocks in the inner cell of the jail. The beating was probably done with rods, so this was not the same punishment that Jesus received—a flogging with metal-studded whips, which often proved fatal. However, beating with rods, always done on the person's bare back, often caused profuse bleeding. The stocks weren't meant just to immobilize a prisoner but also to cause him pain, as they forced the person's legs far apart. In the jail's inner cell, the men were probably in total darkness as well as physical discomfort. Obviously a situation like this was a severe test of Paul's contentment, but, amazingly, "about midnight Paul and Silas were praying and singing hymns to God, and the other prisoners were listening to them" (Acts 16:25). This—and an earthquake that shook the jail to its foundation—resulted in the conversion of their jailer.

DID YOU KNOW?

The great theologian Augustine referred to Paul as a "great lion of God." Novelist Taylor Caldwell's popular 1970 novel *Great Lion of God* told the story of Paul.

brought him inner peace. He took out his frustration on a new sect, the followers of Jesus. But somewhere along the way he perceived that these people had something. He watched Stephen die while asking God to forgive those who stoned him. In speaking of his conversion, Paul recalled that the voice of Jesus had said to him, "It is hard for you to kick against the goads." A goad was a cattle prod, a pointed stick used to direct livestock. Paul had been goaded toward faith by hearing Stephen's eloquent defense of it, followed by his martyrdom. There seemed to be a *living* faith among these people, while Saul's own religion seemed to be nothing more than a huge mass of rules to be kept. So the great change that occurred in Saul was his perception that the life of faith was a matter of relationships—of seeing God as loving Father, acknowledging Christ as Lord, of seeing fellow believers as brothers.

In finding new brothers and sisters among the Christians, Paul alienated many of his fellow Jews, and throughout his long career as an evangelist and missionary, his worst enemies were not pagans but other Jews, who regarded him as the worst sort of traitor and blasphemer. Paul never found peace or contentment under the Jewish law, which is why he was so dead set against the Judaizers, who wanted to force the pagan-born Christians to be circumcised, to observe the Jewish holy days, etc. He was now beyond the law, and so were they. Paul learned to put up with his Jewish enemies' convulsive outrage and constant harassment—including many attempts on his life—and to rest content in the grace of God. Perhaps one reason he could cope with Jewish hostility was that he never forgot his own career as a persecutor—the "chief of sinners" who had so wrongly persecuted the saints. It had taken the voice of Jesus himself to change Paul. He had to learn patience as he faced constant rejection by his fellow Jews.

IRON MAN PAUL

Five times I received from the Jews the forty lashes minus one. Three times I was beaten with rods, once I was stoned, three times I was shipwrecked, I spent a night and a day in the open sea, I have been constantly on the move. I have been in danger from rivers, in danger from bandits, in danger from my own countrymen, in danger from Gentiles; in danger in the city, in danger in the country, in danger at sea; and in danger from false brothers. (2 Corinthians 11:24–26)

In Acts, we see a familiar pattern in Paul's preaching of the gospel: He and his missionary partner (first Barnabas, then Silas) enter a town, visit its synagogue, preach that

Paul's Appearance in Art

The Bible says little about people's physical appearance, and so it tells us nothing about what one of its greatest heroes, Paul, looked like. However, a very old piece of writing known as the Acts of Paul does describe him, and though this writing may be pure legend, it is conceivable its description of him was based on fact. According to the Acts of Paul, the great apostle was "a man small in size, with meeting eyebrows, with a rather large nose, bald-headed, bow-legged, strongly built, full of grace, for at times he looked like a man, and at times he had the face of an angel." Over the centuries artists seemed to have worked from this description, because Paul is almost always shown as bald.

What is missing from this description are the "marks of Jesus" Paul spoke of in Galatians 6:17, the scars and wounds from his having been stoned, whipped, ship-wrecked and imprisoned. Outwardly, Paul was probably a wreck. Inwardly, he was strikingly beautiful.

Jesus is the Son of God and the long-awaited Jewish Messiah, and make converts—and enemies. The pattern began early, for shortly after his conversion, Paul began preaching the gospel in Damascus—leading to a plot against his life, from which his fellow believers helped him escape. Later, when he went to Jerusalem and met Jesus' original apostles, he also made many friends—and enemies. The apostles took him in, but he was regarded as a pariah by the priestly establishment—not surprising, since he had been in the past a loyal servant of the high priest and persecutor of Christians. So again Paul had to manage an escape from a difficult situation.

And yet, as we see in this passage from 2 Corinthians 11, Paul did not always escape danger. The stoning he refers to is recounted in Acts 14: Some Jewish enemies "stoned Paul and dragged him outside the city, thinking he was dead." Paul had suffered nearly the same fate as the martyr Stephen, the man whose stoning he had approved. But Paul recovered, which tells us this spiritually tough man must have been physically tough also.

Pause for a moment to consider Paul's upbringing: Trained to be a rabbi in his youth, he was destined for a life that was physically undemanding. He learned the trade of tentmaking—manual labor but hardly strenuous. He probably had expected a rather soft life, with most of his exercise being mental, engaging in spirited debates with like-minded Jews. Instead, he became a globetrotting missionary, not traveling in luxury and seldom enjoying comforts of any kind. Strictly speaking, once his missionary life began, Paul never had a home, nor did he ever know the comforts of a wife and children. And the people of his own ethnic group and religion, the Jews, mostly despised him and wanted him dead.

In Galatians 6:17, Paul refers to the stigmata, the marks of Jesus on his body. These were the scars from his various tribulations. Just as animals and slaves were often branded, so Paul had been "branded," marking him as belonging to Christ.

Enduring such things, most people would have become distressed and depressed and abandoned their faith, wondering why they served a God who would permit them to endure such travails. Paul's faith did not decrease; it grew. "We are hard pressed on every side, but not crushed; perplexed, but not in despair; persecuted, but not abandoned; struck down, but not destroyed. . . . Therefore we do not lose heart. Though outwardly we are wasting away, yet inwardly we are being renewed day by day" (2 Corinthians 4:8–19, 16).

One tribulation not mentioned in the list in 2 Corinthians 11 was prison. Paul was imprisoned more than once, a fate he shared with many missionaries over the centuries. He wrote some of his great letters from prison, including his most joyous letter, Philippians. With chains on his wrists, and probably his feet as well, Paul could write his classic passage on contentment: "I have learned to be content whatever the circumstances. I know what it is to be in need, and I know what it is to have plenty. I have learned the secret of being content in any and every situation, whether well fed or hungry, whether living in plenty or in want" (Philippians 4:11–12). And what is the secret of this contentment? "I can do everything through him who gives me strength" (Philippians 4:13). In the same letter, Paul assured his readers that "the peace of God, which transcends all understanding, will guard your hearts and your minds in Christ Jesus" (Philippians 4:7).

CULTURAL INSIGHTS

Salvation by Works

While it is true that the Jews in the New Testament period practiced a legalistic religion, the Jews did not actually believe in salvation by works. They believed they were saved by being Jews, which meant that only apostate Jews were excluded from heaven. The purpose in keeping the commandments was not to score points with God and earn heaven, but to show him gratitude for being Israel's Savior. This was essentially the same idea that Paul took over for Christianity—the idea that behaving well is a matter not of rules but of our love and gratitude to God. Paul, like Jesus, understood how any faith could degenerate into a ledger-book religion, with God keeping score of our good and bad deeds—and how people could practice religion for the eyes of their fellow men, not out of gratitude to God. Where Paul parted company with his fellow Jews—and earned their intense hostility—was in affirming that the Jewish Law no longer was needed in the life of faith.

It is worth noting that Paul wrote that he *learned* contentment—it did not come to him easily, and he was certainly not a contented person by nature. Struggles with adversity—and with himself—were his school of contentment.

THE "WHEW!" PASSAGE

When I want to do good, evil is right there with me. . . . What a wretched man I am! Who will rescue me from this body of death? (Romans 7:21, 24)

The Letter to the Romans is Paul's longest letter and his most important. It differs from his other letters in that he was writing to a church he had not established himself, in a city he had never visited, and so the readers were mostly strangers. Nonetheless, they were fellow Christians, spiritually his brothers and sisters, and so in some parts of the letter he writes in a very personal tone, opening up to his readers, particularly in chapter 7, verses 13–25, a passage that might be summed up in these words: To be ourselves, we have to be at war with ourselves.

As noted earlier, Paul in his pre-Christian days had found no inner peace in obeying the Jewish Law. In Romans, as in his other letters, he emphasizes to his readers that they need to guard against legalism and to beware of teachers who try to reimpose the Jewish rules. But in 7:13–25, he observes that even as a Christian his life of faith has its frustrations. Why? He wants to do the right thing—and often does not. In spite of becoming part of the body of Christ, and in spite of having the Holy Spirit within us, we do bad things. Sin is no longer our master and yet we are not free from it—not by a long shot!

Paul was struggling with a universal problem: having high ideals but unable to live up to them. The Roman poet Ovid had one of his characters say, "I see what is better and approve of it—but I follow what is worse." And Jesus famously said, "The spirit is willing, but the body is weak" (Matthew 26:41). Whether Jews or Gentiles, man aspires to be good, but like Paul, declares himself "wretched." The gap between man's aspiration and actual behavior is the stuff of comedy—such as our standard jokes about people breaking their New Year's resolutions. But ultimately it is tragedy, because the person with conscience, like Paul, finds himself wretched, unable on his own to match his life with his ideals.

The solution is not more aspiration or more rule-keeping, but Christ. Our reliance on Christ is a great spiritual release, a loud "Whew!" Dwelling on our failures to live up to our ideals makes us wretched. Dwelling on our relationship to Christ brings release, peace, contentment.

"Christ Jesus came into the world to save sinners—of whom I am the worst" (1 Timothy 1:15). Paul also refers to himself as the "worst" of sinners in the next verse. Was Paul engaging in a bit of play-acting, hoping that Timothy would be thinking,

"Oh no, Paul, you're not a sinner, you're a great man!"? No, Paul was not play-acting. He really was aware of his own failings—and of the divine solution to them. Paul was heeding the words of Jesus: "Why do you look at the speck of sawdust in your brother's eye and pay no attention to the plank in your own eye?" (Matthew 7:3). The fact is, we can't see into someone else's soul—but we can see into our own, and that is where our critiques have to focus.

Paul was eminently self-aware. He wasn't comparing his sin to Herod's or Nero's or anyone else's. He was just considering himself in light of God's nature. He was the "worst" sinner in the sense of "the worst that I really, deeply know." Back in Genesis, Adam and Eve had been evasive when caught in sin: Adam blamed it on the woman God had given him. Eve blamed the serpent. Paul understood spiritual maturity: You take an objective look at yourself and make no excuses. You regret your failings—and you thank God for providing a Savior. Frustration and regret over our flaws, then contentment and gratitude to God—this is the heart of Paul's Gospel.

PARADISE AND THORNS

> I know a man in Christ who . . . was caught up to paradise. He heard inexpressible things, things that man is not permitted to tell. . . . To keep me from becoming conceited because of these surpassingly great revelations, there was given me a thorn in my flesh, a messenger of Satan, to torment me. (2 Corinthians 12:2, 4, 7)

The two letters to the Corinthians are the most personal of Paul's writings, which is natural, since he had not only founded the church in Corinth but also lived there for many months. He bares his soul to these people, many of whom were old friends. In 2 Corinthians 12, he begins telling of the mystical experience of "a man," but later in the passage he refers to "me," so we know this experience is his own. Fourteen years earlier he had been "caught up to the third heaven." He is unsure whether he was "in the body or out of the body"—perhaps he was experiencing a vision or perhaps he was actually transported into heaven for a spell. Whichever it was, he "heard inexpressible things, things that man is not permitted to tell." Paul, the spiritual dynamo, the missionary and evangelist on fire for the Lord, had a brief glimpse of heaven, of what awaited him after death. Fourteen years later, he still remembers it vividly and fondly. It is a privilege that would have led many men to conceit.

Vigorous, mettlesome men like Paul are often conceited, and certainly his glimpse of paradise would have caused most men to boast. But something restrained him: a "thorn in the flesh" caused him great torment. Three times he pleaded with God to remove the thorn. But the Lord did not remove it. Rather, the Lord replied, "My grace is sufficient for you, for my power is made perfect in weakness." Paul's thorn reminded him that he

Roman Roads

Paul endured many hardships in his missionary travels, but he was fortunate in one respect: The Roman Empire had well-maintained roads that made travel relatively easy.

At the Roman Empire's peak in the second century AD, its main roads covered fifty thousand miles. Most were originally built for military use, and were constructed by the soldiers themselves, aided by slaves and prisoners of war. The Romans knew how to use concrete, mixing lime with volcanic ash. Land was leveled down to the bedrock, and then concrete filler and smooth paving stones were put down. In many areas these wide roads even had shoulders and drainage ditches.

Along the main roads were *mansiones*, "lodging places," spaced about every twenty-five miles. About every ten miles were relay stations with postings of horses, mainly for the use of imperial couriers. Though the Romans built the roads primarily for their troops and couriers, countless civilian travelers—including Paul—made good use of them. The gospel owed its spread not just to the zeal of missionaries but also, ironically, to a transport system designed to spread war and conquest.

was still grounded in the present world. He couldn't forget the vision any more than he could forget the thorn. The thorn will not last forever but the paradise will. The thorn was his reminder that human weaknesses are no obstacle to the life of faith. They make us see that our contentment is rooted in reliance on the Lord. And so, "I delight in weaknesses, in insults, in hardships, in persecutions, in difficulties. For when I am weak, then I am strong" (2 Corinthians 12:10).

Readers have wondered for two thousand years what Paul's "thorn" was. A physical ailment, perhaps, since Paul mentions the thorn as "in the flesh"? Paul was tough as nails physically, but even the toughest bodies are prone to occasional sickness. Given what Paul often said about the sinful nature of the flesh, people have speculated that Paul, unmarried and celibate, might have coped with sexual temptation. There would have been temptations aplenty in "sin cities" like Corinth, and we are probably safe in assuming that a man of Paul's amazing vitality might have had a strong sex drive, though he managed to keep it in check because of his dedication to his mission. But the thorn could have been his own ambitious nature, his desire to appear important. Or possibly the thorn was the ongoing hostility of the Jews, his own people, to the spread of the gospel.

It is all for the best that we don't know what the thorn was, for this passage gives hope to all people that their afflictions, whatever they might be, can cause great pain but also greater reliance on God.

There is neither Jew nor Greek, slave nor free, male nor female, for you are all one in Christ Jesus. (Galatians 3:28)

Slaves, obey your earthly masters with respect and fear, and with sincerity of heart, just as you would obey Christ. (Ephesians 6:5)

Paul's hardships had, amazingly, taught him to be content, to rest in the conviction that God was bigger than our present circumstances, no matter how difficult. That conviction affected his attitude toward an institution that was highly visible in his day, slavery.

In the past century, Christianity has been harshly criticized for its history of condoning slavery, and Paul in particular has come under fire because in more than one of his letters he told Christian slaves to obey their masters and serve willingly. It strikes people as odd, to say the least, that Paul, the man who wrote about freedom so glowingly, would accept the situation of one human being owning another. To understand why Paul wrote as he did, we need to take a close look at his faith and the world he inhabited.

First, Jesus provided no guidance to Christians on this issue. Jesus never once referred to slavery, and it is not mentioned in the Gospels. This is partly because it was relatively rare in the towns and villages Jesus visited. It was very much a feature of urban life in the Roman empire, however, so it is appropriate that Paul refers to himself as a slave of Christ and often speaks of slavery in both the literal and figurative senses. Growing up in the large city of Tarsus, Paul would have seen slaves everywhere.

DID YOU KNOW?

One overlooked New Testament verse referring to slavery is Revelation 18:13, where slaves, "the souls of men," are among the goods merchandised by the wicked city of Babylon. While the verse doesn't directly condemn slavery, it makes it clear that the buying and selling of human beings as if they were mere things is wrong.

Slavery goes back thousands of years. It was practiced in ancient Babylon, Assyria, Egypt, China and India— but it was the Greeks and Romans who created societies based on large-scale slavery. In the Roman empire, even small-scale farmers owned a slave or two. Slaves were considered such a necessity for free men that people even owned slaves when they could not afford them. The rich delighted in being overstaffed as a sign of their wealth. Social standing was measured by the number of slaves one owned.

Some slaves, such as those who became tutors to the master's children, were often treated well—almost like members of the family. But most slaves were treated like beasts. Greeks and Romans kept their farm slaves chained because many of them had been enemy soldiers, the booty of war. Pretty female slaves were used for sex, the less pretty ones for work. (Some slave boys were also used as sexual playthings by the masters.) In a way female slaves' lives were worse than male slaves, for some of their work—spinning wool—might continue well past sunset. The Roman historian Tacitus, often seen as a good example of an enlightened thinker for the period, excused the killing of slaves by saying "there were plenty more." Technically, he was correct: during certain periods, slaves outnumbered free men in Greece and Rome.

Among the Greeks and Romans, no one seriously questioned slavery. The noted philosopher Plato owned slaves and believed slaves were fated by their mental capacities to do menial work so their superiors could do nothing. Other philosophers, including Aristotle, agreed.

Compared to pagans, the Jews were more humane toward slaves, and the Law contained frequent reminders that the Israelites were to remember their own slavery and Egypt, and were not to treat their own slaves harshly. Death was the penalty for killing a slave, and a slave who suffered the loss of a limb or eye was to be freed. Slaves were not to be separated from their families. One Jewish sect, the Essenes, rejected slavery completely. But on the whole, almost everyone in the world in which Christianity was spreading accepted slavery.

Now, back to Paul. Why didn't he speak out openly against slavery? One obvious reason was that Christians were a small minority at this time and came mostly from the lower classes. Had Paul and the other apostles been seen by the Romans as slave agitators, they almost certainly would have been killed, at no benefit to the slaves. The Romans were notorious for ruthless suppression of slave revolts, as seen in the story of Spartacus, a story ending with mass crucifixion of the rebels. The empire could not conceive of a world without slavery, and had they sensed that Christians were attacking slavery, they would have done everything possible to exterminate them.

CULTURAL INSIGHTS

"Sons of God"

Paul's idea of Christians as "sons of God" was based on the Roman view of the family, in which a father could disinherit his biological children at will and adopt whomever he wished as his legal children. Several of the Roman emperors did so, having no legitimate, surviving or worthy sons of their own to rule after them. Being a faithful Jew, Paul also understood that a true son or daughter was one who obeyed their father and acted as he did (that is, showing love, mercy, forgiveness). To be a child of God, we have to obey God and be like God.

CULTURAL INSIGHTS

Christians and Abolition

Anti-Christian writers like to quote passages in which Paul told slaves to obey their masters—but they neglect to quote verses where Paul said slaves and masters are equal before God. In fact, as Christianity spread, many ministers encouraged masters to free their slaves in their wills. The great medieval saints all spoke out against slavery. Where it continued was in territories where Muslims and Christians came into conflict and sold each other. Christians were, alas, willing to sell other Christians as slaves—to Muslims. (Although Muhammad taught that slaves should be treated decently, the fact that he himself owned, bought, sold and captured slaves has ensured that Muslims never have questioned the institution of slavery.)

But slavery slowly died out in Europe, and when it emerged again in the New World, most of the popes protested. It is a blot on Christian history that it was tolerated in the United States until the Civil War brought it to an end, but it must be remembered that the most fervent abolitionists in America were Christians.

In Paul's writings, as in the rest of the New Testament, the emphasis is always on changing the individual, not a social structure. Paul told believers to remain in the same state they were in before their conversion—if they were married, stay married; if a slave, remain a slave, etc. Change of the heart was the important thing. It is to the Christians' credit that in their fellowships, the social barriers between slave and master were broken down, and in many churches, slaves were respected leaders. In fact, we see in the brief Letter to Philemon that Paul sent the runaway slave Onesimus back to his master—and reminded both that they were Christians and should treat teach other as dear brothers.

"Were you a slave when you were called? Don't let it trouble you—although if you can gain your freedom, do so. For he who was a slave when he was called by the Lord is the Lord's freedman; similarly, he who was a free man when he was called is Christ's slave" (1 Corinthians 7:21–22). This is a jarring passage: Paul tells the Christian slave "Don't let it trouble you." But how could it *not* trouble someone to be in the condition of slavery? The answer, of course, lies in Paul's notion of contentment. Outwardly, the slave was property, legally owned by someone else and forced to obey commands. Inwardly, the person belonged to Christ. In fact, every person in Christ is free, spiritually speaking—and every person in Christ is called on to serve Christ fully. Every believer, whether he is free or in slavery, is the servant of Christ.

Why were so many slaves drawn to Christianity? For one thing, it promised them a level playing field— unequal in the eyes of men, slaves were equal in the

WHEN AND WHERE

Paul's last letter, 2 Timothy, was written from Rome, probably in AD 66 or 67. Paul died as a martyr shortly afterward.

eyes of the Lord. In more than one letter, Paul emphasized that the barriers that divided people—Jew and Gentile, slave and free—did not exist in the brotherhood of faith. Another attraction of the faith was the promise of a better world after this one. "You know that you will receive an inheritance from the Lord as a reward" (Colossians 3:24). These words must have heartened the slaves in the congregation, for slaves had no inheritance at all in this life.

Slaves had no recognized families per se, so no family tombs to visit, and thus no eternal life in the pagan scheme of things—but Christianity promised them heaven. Family life was not an option for slaves. Even slaves in the most committed of monogamous relationships could not marry, and masters had no qualms about separating slave families. A slave was a *filius neminis*, "son of no one," and could make no claim on a man as father or on siblings, even if he knew who they were. But as Christians, slaves were part of a loving spiritual family. Imagine the emotions welling up in a slave the first time any human being addressed him as "brother" and the first time he heard he could call God "Father."

CHARACTER CLOSE-UP — Paul, the Urbanite

The parables and teachings of Jesus are full of images from country and small-town life—lilies of the field, mustard seeds, a sower, weeds choking out crops, mulberry trees, a hen with her chicks, a fisherman's net, vineyards, wells, shepherds, houses made of dried mud, sparrows, fig trees, a village wedding, foxes. Jesus grew up in Nazareth, a small town set in the hills and fields of Galilee, and his words reflect his upbringing.

Paul, on the other hand, grew up in the large cosmopolitan city of Tarsus, and though his extensive travels took him over vast tracts of the Roman Empire's countryside, his writings show that he had the mind of a city-dweller. Though on one occasion he could refer to God's people as a "flock" (Acts 20:28–29), and at times he spoke of "sowing" in a spiritual sense (1 Corinthians 9:11, 15:36, Galatians 6:7), more often Paul used urban images, such as the training and competitiveness of athletes (Philippians 3:14, Colossians 2:18, 1 Timothy 4:7, 2 Timothy 2:5), to fighting and racing (Galatians 5:7, 2 Timothy 4:7), to being Christ's "ambassadors" (2 Corinthians 5:20, Ephesians 6:20), and "citizen," referring not only to his own Roman citizenship but also to the believers' spiritual citizenship in heaven (Ephesians 2:19, Philippians 3:20). And although slavery existed in the country as well as in cities, it was much more a feature of urban life, and Paul speaks often of slavery, not only literal bondage but also of himself as a "slave" of Christ, and of people in spiritual slavery to sin. In the providence of God, the faith was spread to the cities of the Roman Empire through the acts and writings of one who spoke the language of city folk.

Critics of Paul never forget that Paul told slaves to obey their earthly masters—but they do often forget that Paul had some demands for the masters also: "Masters, . . . do not threaten [your slaves], since you know that he who is both their Master and yours is in heaven, and there is no favoritism with him" (Ephesians 6:9). "Masters, provide your slaves with what is right and fair, because you know that you also have a Master in heaven" (Colossians 4:1). Paul, who began many of his letters by referring to himself as a "slave" of Christ, never forgot that the only way to true spiritual freedom was in committing one's life to the loving Master. To put oneself under the protective authority of God is to be free.

GOODBYE, WORLD

The time has come for my departure. I have fought the good fight, I have finished the race, I have kept the faith . . . Do your best to come to me quickly . . . Do your best to get here before winter. (2 Timothy 4:6–7, 9, 21)

Paul's last letter is 2 Timothy, and like some earlier letters, it was written from prison. There is a difference this time: Paul knows his life is near its end. Inevitably this is a sad letter, yet also one overflowing with confidence and faith.

Paul probably was writing from Rome, in prison—again—for preaching the faith. The Roman imprisonment described at the end of Acts ended happily, for Paul was released and went on to spread the gospel further. But this later imprisonment ended, tradition says, with Paul's martyrdom under the vile emperor Nero.

In this situation, Paul's chief concern is not for himself but for the continuance of the faith. He counsels Timothy, his protégé and spiritual son, to take seriously his role as a pastor: "Preach the Word; be prepared in season and out of season; correct, rebuke and encourage—with great patience and careful instruction" (2 Timothy 4:2). Paul fears that in times to come, pastors will not preach the truth but will tell people what they wish to hear.

But under the circumstances, Paul can't help but think of his own situation. Terrible things have happened, not just the abuse of the Jews hostile to his message but also something worse: abandonment by fellow Christians. "Everyone in the province of Asia has deserted me, including Phygelus and Hermogenes" (2 Timothy 1:15). On the other hand, he commends Onesiphorus "because he often refreshed me and was not ashamed of my chains. On the contrary, when he was in Rome, he searched hard for me until he found me" (2 Timothy 1:16–17). Showing love and concern to a Roman prisoner took true loyalty.

Later in the letter he laments that "at my first defense, no one came to my support, but everyone deserted me. May it not be held against them" (2 Timothy 4:16). Paul is forgiving in the same way as Jesus and Stephen—but with a difference, for the harm done here is not by the enemies but by fainthearted friends. This "first defense" may refer to his trial at the end of the first Roman imprisonment, but more likely this is something more recent, the hearing of his recent case. But even in this situation, Paul was not without comfort: "The Lord stood at my side and gave me strength" (2 Timothy 4:17).

In the same passage Paul tells Timothy to "get Mark and bring him with you, because he is helpful to me in my ministry" (2 Timothy 4:11). Recall that in Acts, Paul and his missionary partner Barnabas had parted company because they disagreed about continuing to work with Mark. But the old disagreement is long past. Mark is helpful to him now.

Alexander the metal-worker had done Paul some great harm, but Paul leaves it up to the Lord to exact vengeance. Nonetheless, he warns Timothy to watch out for this troublemake (2 Timothy 4:14–15). Paul is admonishing Timothy to be wise as a serpent (watch out for Alexander) but innocent as a dove (do Alexander no harm and wait for God's justice).

Perhaps the most touching thing about this last chapter in Paul's last letter is that twice Paul tells Timothy, "Do your best to come to me quickly . . . Do your best to get here before winter" (2 Timothy 4:9, 21). Paul is human, and at this moment he feels lonely. Luke was with him in Rome—"with" in the sense of being nearby, but not living in the prison, of course. Luke must have been a great comfort, yet Paul desperately wanted to see Timothy. Paul had taken great comfort in the Lord's presence, but like any human being, he needed human companionship.

"Get here before winter" refers to the difficulty of winter sea travel in the Mediterranean. Paul fears that if he doesn't see Timothy before winter sets in, he will not see him at all. Clearly he expects his trial, and probably death, very soon. The memories of those who had deserted him had not made him bitter, but clearly he had not forgotten. He is anxious to see the face of someone who had always been faithful to him, someone who would continue preaching the faith after he was gone.

Prison, loneliness, memories of friends who had proven fickle and unfaithful… Paul had much to think on. The contentment he had spoken of must have been hard to come by in this situation. Yet he had no doubts he had "fought the good fight," taking the mature view of life, that pleasure is more than the avoidance of pain, that struggle and hardship have their own rewards, making us appreciate loyal friends and simple pleasures, not to mention drawing us closer to God. Paul knew that you don't have to be rich to live rich, for few men who ever lived had a richer life. Having fought the fight and run the race, Paul is confident that "the Lord will rescue me from every evil attack and will bring me safely to his heavenly kingdom" (2 Timothy 4:18).

PUTTING THE WORD TO WORK

1. Think of people you've known who have had dramatic conversion experiences like Paul's. Did they exhibit the same dynamism as Paul?

2. Reflect on the various hardships Paul endured—stoning, beatings, prison, shipwrecks. Have you known people who experienced great hardship but have maintained their faith in God?

3. Consider Paul's "thorn in the flesh." What are some difficulties in your own life that have drawn you closer to God?

4. Reflect on the section dealing with slavery, and consider: If slaves in the first century AD could find contentment in God, can't you?

5. In 2 Timothy, Paul reflects on both loyal and disloyal friends. Take a moment to do as he did, thanking God for your loyal ones and letting go of any bitterness toward the disloyal.

Lusting for Power

In an earlier chapter we looked at Israel's first two kings, Saul and David, and how neither of them sought out the kingship but were chosen by God. Despite their failings, both men were exemplary kings compared to most rulers in the Bible, most of whom were motivated by pride, greed and ambition more than by the desire to serve and protect their people.

KEY TERM FOR TODAY ## Domination

The urge to dominate others lives in human beings like a dark disease, and in this chapter we look at the Bible's first dominator, who was also the first king, and some other proud and domineering characters.

THE FIRST KING—ALAS!

> Cush was the father of Nimrod, who grew to be a mighty warrior on the earth. He was a mighty hunter before the Lord; that is why it is said, "Like Nimrod, a mighty hunter before the Lord." (Genesis 10:8–9)

The first king mentioned in the Bible is the mighty Nimrod, who is said to be the founder of several of the great cities of ancient times, including Nineveh, the chief city of Assyria, and Babylon. Nimrod had a reputation not only as an empire builder but also as a "mighty hunter before the Lord." What exactly was the connection between hunting beasts and ruling one's fellow man?

First, ancient people did not have a sentimental or environmental view of wild animals. There was no concept of endangered species because the most endangered species on earth was man himself, who had only low-tech weapons (knives, clubs, spears, arrows) to protect himself. Beasts were a real threat to man, and a man who could subdue them was honored.

The king as an avid hunter is, as Genesis shows, a very old tradition. The tradition continued even into the 1800s, with European kings taking great pride as huntsmen, and people would have no respect for a king who did not hunt. In ancient times in the Middle East, a king was expected to hunt and kill lions—the human king showing his dominance over the king of beasts. The Old Testament, by contrast, shows little admiration for hunters, and those who kill beasts—such as Samson and David—are admired not as hunters but as acting in

self-defense or in defense of their flocks. The few hunters depicted in the Bible—Nimrod and Esau, for example—are not admirable characters. Presumably a hunter would be a protector but perhaps someone who could subdue his fellow man as well. A man skilled in archery and spearing could kill men as well as animals.

The Bible does not actually say Nimrod was cruel or tyrannical, and yet the empires he founded, Assyria and Babylon, were notoriously cruel, not only invading and looting the smaller nations around them, but also in their public artworks depicting the torture and killing of their enemies. The cities named in Genesis as being founded by Nimrod were the urban centers of the pagan empires that would harass, plunder and eventually conquer Israel. In fact, one of those cities, Calah, still bears the name Nimrud. The prophet Micah referred to oppressive Assyria as "the land of Nimrod" (Micah 5:6).

Nimrod was the son of Cush, the son of Ham, the son whom Noah had cursed for his act of disrespect. The curse on him said he would be a "servant of servants." Clearly

CHARACTERS AT LARGE # Nimrod in Legend and Art

Despite being a very minor character in Genesis, Nimrod has been the subject of many legends. In Jewish tradition, he was not only the first tyrant and the builder of Babel, but a giant as well. Throughout history, any tyrannical ruler might be referred to as a "Nimrod." The 1966 movie *The Bible: In the Beginning* followed this tradition and showed Nimrod as the builder of Babel. At the top of the tower, he shoots an arrow high into the heavens, as if, in his arrogance, he is shooting God. In Dante's great poem *The Divine Comedy*, Nimrod is in hell, condemned eternally to speak in a language that no one understands, his punishment for what occurred at Babel. John Milton, in his epic *Paradise Lost*, says that Nimrod's "game" became men, not beasts.

On a lighter note, in the 1830s a popular American play, *Lion of the West,* had as its main character Nimrod T. Wildfire, a rugged frontier hunter based on the famous Davy Crockett. On the 1960s TV series *The Wild Wild West*, the heroes' gadget-laden railroad car was named the "Nimrod."

Nimrod, Ham's descendant, did not see himself as a cursed servant of servants but rather as a dominator of his fellow man. Nimrod's name may mean "let us rebel," a sign that Cush destined his son for domination.

Genesis says Nimrod ruled over the land of Shinar, another name for Babylon. Genesis 11 is set in Shinar, where the craft of brickmaking emerged, and in time the people of Shinar decided to show just how skilled they were as builders: "They said, 'Come, let us build ourselves a city, with a tower that reaches to the heavens, so that we may make a name for ourselves and not be scattered over the face of the whole earth'" (Genesis 11:5).

Humankind had gone beyond the stage of mere survival. They had learned to make bricks instead of relying on finding stones. Civilization had developed—not a bad thing in itself, except that as man's abilities grew, so did his ambition and conceit. The key term in the story is "let us make a name for ourselves." We already know that Nimrod gloried in his reputation as a mighty hunter. The people of Shinar wanted fame and glory also. They got it but not in the way they hoped. Seeing this high tower for what it was, a sign of man's vanity and ambition, God "confused the tongues" of the builders. They had all been speaking the same language, but suddenly they spoke differently. Instead of being united as a powerful empire, they were "scattered." The location was called Babel, and the tower of Babel, which was to have been a kind of monument to the power of Nimrod's empire, became a symbol of what happens when human beings strive too far.

Too many people united in a single purpose inevitably turn to conquest and plunder—as Nimrod's descendants in Babylon would prove. Even speaking different languages, humans have oppressed each other.

ISRAEL'S WOULD-BE KING

All the citizens of Shechem and Beth Millo gathered beside the great tree at the pillar in Shechem to crown Abimelech king. (Judges 9:6)

In the Book of Judges, the various "judges" are not men dressed in black robes in a courtroom but rather military leaders, men chosen by God at particular times to deliver Israel from its enemies. One of those leaders was the great Gideon, covered in another chapter (Day 28). Like many great men, Gideon did not have great children, and one of them became one of the great villains in Judges.

This was Abimelech, whose name in Hebrew means "the father is king." The name is curious, because in fact Gideon himself was humble enough to turn down the kingship: "The Israelites said to Gideon, 'Rule over us—you, your son and your grandson—because you have saved us out of the hand of Midian.' But Gideon told them, 'I will not rule over you, nor will my son rule over you. The Lord will rule over you'" (Judges 8:22–23). Like Samuel, as we saw in the previous chapter, Gideon seemed to understand that having a monarchy—especially one in which the crown passed from father to son—was an invitation to tyranny and oppression, and Israel was to be different from other nations, relying not on a human dynasty but on God himself. The "judges" were liberators that God raised up for a particular crisis. Their position was not permanent, and certainly their sons did not inherit any rights or privileges.

But Judges 9 shows what happens after Gideon's death. While the people had at one time offered him the kingship, once he was dead they forgot not only that he was a military liberator but also that he was a man devoted to God—and to stamping out worship of the false god Baal. So the Israelites fell into Baal worship once again.

Abimelech was not concerned about this idolatry—in fact, this egotistical adventurer seems to have made an idol of himself, and he saw his father's reputation as a path to power. Gideon, amazingly, had seventy sons—by different wives and concubines, obviously. Abimelech was the son of Gideon by a Canaanite concubine, and his mother's kin lived in the old pagan city of Shechem. Abimelech convinced them he would make a fine king—after all, wasn't he a son of the famous warrior Gideon? And he was better than Gideon's other sons, for Abimelech had Shechemite blood as well. So the men of Shechem took money from the temple of Baal, and gave it to Abimelech to hire "reckless adventurers, who became his followers." Consider the irony: Israel was supposed to be God's holy nation, but Israel's first king owed his position to a gang of thugs, hired by money taken from the treasury of the temple of a pagan god.

Then Abimelech did what many would-be kings have done throughout history: exterminate the competition. He and his bloodthirsty band proceeded to murder the other sons of Gideon—except one, Jotham, who managed to escape.

Speaking from a mountaintop, Jotham addressed the Shechemites and told a curious parable: The trees decide to make one tree a king, yet the useful trees—the olive with its fruit and oil, the fig with its fruits—prefer to do what they are good at, producing good things for mankind. But the thorn bush is more than willing to rule as king. Jotham's parable makes an obvious enough point: The man who makes himself king isn't necessarily the most deserving—usually the contrary. The best men have other things to do with their time—honorable things—than to conquer and dominate. Note that the thorn bush is of no use at all—it doesn't provide shade in a hot country and is even dangerous when it catches fire. So the typical king is either useless or dangerous.

And yet Jotham's parable had no effect, for Abimelech ruled Israel for three years. But he learned the hard way that a man who seizes power inevitably encounters another man who desires that power. Abimelech's rival was Gaal, who won the confidence of the people of Shechem and tried to turn them against Abimelech. Gaal's sales pitch

Millstones

Grain has to be ground into flour, and probably the oldest method was pounding it with mortar and pestle, but thousands of years ago mankind invented milling, which involved two circular stones, one on top of the other, with the upper stone turned by handles so that the rough surfaces of the two stones would grind the grain into fine flour. Bread was made on a daily basis, and the sound of millstones grinding was a familiar one in any household.

A home mill was portable, yet the two stones were heavy, each one heavy enough to crack a person's skull. The story of Abimelech says that it was the upper millstone that the woman dropped on Abimelech's head. The upper would have had wooden handles on it, so it would have been easier to maneuver than the lower stone. The great irony in the story is that a millstone, something we would call a kitchen appliance, was used to dispatch the ruthless adventurer Abimelech.

was that he was a true Canaanite, not a half-Canaanite like Abimelech. In effect, Abimelech was getting a taste of his own political medicine. In reaching out to his Canaanite "brothers," he set himself up to be toppled by someone who was pure Canaanite.

Gaal and his followers met Abimelech and his men in battle, and Abimelech triumphed. Abimelech was so vexed by the fickleness of the Shechemites that he burned the city and scattered salt on the soil so it would never produce crops again. The survivors remaining in the city took shelter in the central stronghold, which was presumably under the protection of Baal. They assumed Abimelech, who owed his kingship to money taken from the Baal temple, would not shed blood on a sacred spot, and indeed he did not. Instead, he and his men piled tree branches around the tower and set it on fire, killing everyone inside.

This violent, arrogant man came to a violent end, which is not surprising, yet his end came in a way that was both surprising and humiliating. Besieging the city of Thebez, Abimelech learned that its people had all gathered in a defensive tower. He planned to use the same tactic he used at Shechem, setting the tower on fire, but a woman inside the tower dropped a millstone on his head. Abimelech, fatally wounded but still conscious, ordered his armor-bearer to run him through with his sword, so that no one could say that a woman had killed him.

Abimelech paid for his bloody crime of murdering his seventy half-brothers, and likewise the people of Shechem had paid for their crime of making this brutal man king over Israel. Yet what stands out in the story is not the violence of the times but Jotham's parable about kingship. So often, the men who seek power are the people who will abuse it. The first man to want to rule as king over Israel is a thoroughly despicable, self-seeking character, a sign of what monarchy would involve in future days.

BEAUTIFULLY VIOLENT

In all Israel there was not a man so highly praised for his handsome appearance as Absalom. From the top of his head to the sole of his foot there was no blemish in him. (2 Samuel 14:25)

In ancient times, one sign of a man's success was that he could afford to maintain more than one wife, so he would add another wife or concubine to his household. As the Bible consistently shows, this might have satisfied the man's physical appetites but it made for frequent strife in the home. Nowhere is this more evident than in the saga of David and his painfully dysfunctional family.

David's oldest son—an important position in ancient times—was Amnon, who was much loved by his father. He also inherited his father's lustful nature, and regrettably his lust centered on his own beautiful half-sister Tamar. Amnon's longing for her prompted his friend Jonadab to propose a ploy: pretend to be sick and have Tamar play nurse. When Tamar went to Amnon to prepare him some cakes, he tried to seduce her, and when she resisted, he raped her.

Even worse, once his lust was satisfied, he immediately hated her, sending her out of his sight. Poor Tamar went to live in the household of her full brother, Absalom. David was very angry with Amnon, but did nothing about the outrage. David, except in the famous episode of his adultery with Bathsheba, was in fact a very patient and cautious man, one willing to engage in watchful waiting, as he proved over a long period in his relations with Saul. This policy stood him well in politics, but it was a disaster in managing his children.

Absalom was a rare young man: Besides being strikingly handsome, he had the ability to do long-range planning instead of acting on impulse. He hated Amnon for what he had done, but he kept his feelings to himself for two full years. Catching Amnon off-guard—drunk at a sheep-shearing festival—Absalom struck him down.

The killing of Amnon was done two years after the rape of Tamar—revenge served up cold. This tells us a lot about Absalom's character. We might understand and forgive his killing of Amnon immediately after the Tamar incident—he would have been a man caught up in passion. But he was willing to nurse his hatred for a long time, a period when men of mellower temperament might be tempted to forgive and forget. In a way, his long period of stewing in his hate corresponds to Amnon's long period of lusting for his half-sister. Both brothers could be categorized as obsessive.

Amnon had been the oldest son and thus heir to the throne. He was dead and the second son, Kileab, had died of natural causes. And given what we learn about Absalom in 2 Samuel, it's quite possible that his murder of Amnon was not only to avenge Tamar's humiliation but also to put Absalom in the position of heir to the throne.

For the time being he had to flee the country, taking refuge with his grandfather, the king of Geshur. Absalom may have had a high opinion of himself because both parents were royalty. This was not true of his two older brothers. Absalom's mother was Maacah, daughter of the king of Geshur, and while he was out of favor with David, he lived with his grandfather in Geshur. It appears living at court made him lust for royal power. If David had banished him to some backwater, he might have eventually come back to David, repentant and compliant, but life at court whet his appetite for power.

David was a man of deep emotion. He had adored Amnon, but instead of hating Absalom for killing Amnon, he shifted all his love for Amnon onto Absalom, so in the three years of Absalom's exile, David loved him all the more.

Joab, David's chief military man, knew how deep this love ran, so he arranged for a wise woman to present herself to David and try to get him to recall Absalom from exile. (See Day 5 for more about Joab and the wise woman.) So Joab returned—but not completely, for though he was allowed back in Jerusalem, he was not admitted to the king's presence. Absalom was not the type of man to be satisfied with half a loaf. Absalom repeatedly summoned Joab to intercede for him again, so that David would receive him. Joab would not come, so Absalom had Joab's barley field burned. Absalom told the irate Joab that he might as well have stayed in Geshur, since he was back in Jerusalem but still wouldn't be received by his father. So Joab, knowing he was dealing with a dangerous character, arranged for David and Absalom to be reconciled. But the stage was set for Joab to take vengeance on Absalom sometime in the future.

Absalom and David kissed and made up—or so it seemed. Absalom had been separated from his father for five years, and while David's love for his son grew, Absalom seems to have nursed only resentment toward his father. David seemed to be doting on him again, and yet his murder of his own brother was like a cloud following him around. Who knew if David, who had many other sons, might choose to disinherit him? Or perhaps, after David's death, Israel's tribes would not be willing to serve under Absalom, a man who had murdered his eldest brother.

Not being the type of man to take a wait-and-see attitude toward this matter, Absalom decided to act quickly while he was young and attractive. He chose to press the flesh, endearing himself to the people of Israel by shaking hands and kissing people as they journeyed toward Jerusalem. If people had complaints—and most people do,

Beautiful People

The Bible seldom refers to people's appearance except in unusual cases like Sarah, Saul, David and Absalom. In the first mention of Saul, it is said he was "an impressive young man without equal among the Israelites—a head taller than any of the others" (1 Samuel 9:2). But David, Saul's son-in-law, rival and (it would turn out) successor as king, was also good-looking, and so was David's son and rival Absalom. The careers of Saul, David and Absalom all point to the factor of a leader being physically attractive. In Saul's case, his being tall and handsome was somewhat canceled out by his melancholy streak, something no leader can afford to have.

The people mentioned as being physically attractive are: Sarah, Rebecca, Rachel, Joseph (in Genesis), Saul, David, Absalom, Abigail, Bathsheba, Tamar (Absalom's daughter), Abishag, Adonijah, Job's daughters and Daniel and his three friends. Suffice it to say that the Bible shows much more concern for inner than outer beauty, and Absalom is certainly the classic case of an attractive exterior concealing an ugly soul. "Charm is deceptive, and beauty is fleeting" (Proverbs 31:30). The New Testament does not once refer to any individual's physical appearance. In 1 Peter 3:3, the apostle told Christian women not to focus on their outward appearance but on their inner beauty, "which is of great worth in God's sight." Peter was speaking to women, but certainly his words apply to men as well.

regardless of how good the political situation might be—Absalom would present himself as the right man to bring justice to the land. Needless to say, the people were immensely pleased at having the king's own handsome, warmhearted son greeting them and claiming to take an interest in their affairs. Aside from his seeming warmth, Absalom also impressed people with his chariot and his entourage of fifty men. "And so he stole the hearts of the men of Israel" (2 Samuel 15:6).

As a politician, David was a master of what we would now call public relations. To his regret, Absalom inherited this skill. But whereas David had never been willing to rebel against his king Saul, "the Lord's anointed," Absalom had no such scruples about rebelling against the king—his own father. Absalom lied and said he was going to Hebron to worship God. David had moved the capital from Hebron to Jerusalem, which the people of Hebron probably resented. Hebron was regarded as a sacred place, having long associations with the patriarchs, and Jerusalem had only recently become part of Israel, and it was considered sacred only because David had moved the ark there. Although our familiarity with the Bible makes us think of Jerusalem as being the holy city of the Bible, it certainly was not thought of that way at this time. Hebron had tradition on its side. And there, to the sounds of trumpets, Absalom had himself proclaimed king of Israel.

> Joab was told, "The king is weeping and mourning for Absalom." And for the whole army the victory that day was turned into mourning, because on that day the troops heard it said, "The king is grieving for his son." (2 Samuel 19:1–2)

The revolt against David took place with surprising speed. Everything seemed to be going so well under David, yet there must have been resentment underneath. No matter how good and prosperous the times may be, there will inevitably be some discontented people whose resentments can be stirred up. One obvious lesson of the story is that not even the best of rulers ought to take his popularity for granted.

In a way history was repeating itself: David, when he was young and handsome, was a charismatic figure who attracted those who had some grievances against Saul. Now David is aging, and Absalom is the young pretty boy, nursing people's grievances. But the differences are notable too: David had grown up working-class and had proved his mettle as a shepherd and as the spunky slayer of Goliath. Absalom had nothing going for him but his looks and the politician's knack for backslapping and urging people to complain about the status quo.

Although David was far from perfect, he had delivered Israel from its many enemies. Absalom's rebellion proved there were plenty of people with grievances, but what is

---

CULTURAL INSIGHTS

Hebron

Twenty miles southwest of Jerusalem, Hebron is one of the oldest cities in the world. It is also one of the first cities mentioned in the Bible, and Abraham lived there for a while and built an altar to the Lord. Nearby was the Cave of Machpelah, where Abraham buried his beloved wife Sarah, and where he was eventually buried himself. Isaac and Jacob also lived in Hebron for a time. When the Israelites under Joshua conquered Canaan, Hebron was given as an inheritance to the faithful Caleb. David was anointed king at Hebron and lived there seven years before moving his capital to Jerusalem. Absalom made an astute move in having himself proclaimed king at this historic locale.

Because of its association with Abraham, Hebron has long been sacred to both Jews and Muslims. The supposed Cave of Machpelah, with the tombs of Abraham and Sarah, Isaac and Rebekah, and Jacob and Leah, is now inside the Muslim fortress known as the Haram. The reputed tomb of Joseph is also in the Haram. The Arabic name for the city is *Khalil Ar-Rahman*, "friend of God," the designation for Ibrahim (the Muslim name for Abraham). Muslims consider it one of their four sacred cities. After the Crusaders captured the city in 1099, it was called St. Abraham for many years.

---

most significant about this rebellion, and later the rebellion of Sheba, is that the Israelites were proving themselves terrible ingrates. They had asked for a king who would fight their battles and give them security by keeping the enemies at bay—and David had done that. While David was a poor manager of his own family, he was a sterling politician and commander-in-chief—and, in retrospect, not the taxer-and-spender that his son Solomon would be.

Being on the lam was nothing new to David, since he had spent much of his young adulthood fleeing the wrath of the jealous Saul. The difference this time was that he was fleeing from his own son. David had no wish to subject the innocent people of Jerusalem to a long siege, so he and his aides fled the city hurriedly. He may have hoped, in the open country, to rally more people to his cause—which proved to be the case—and certainly he trusted in his own background as a military man whose element was open space, and he definitely had more experience than the spoiled Absalom.

Unpleasant as it was to be fleeing from his own beloved son, David would learn he did not lack for friends. His soldier Ittai, from the Philistine city of Gath, offered to follow him wherever he went. David insisted he go back home, for clearly there was danger in a foreigner taking David's sign in this unstable time, but Ittai insisted he would stay by David's side no matter what happened.

The priest Zadok was also loyal to David, and since it was David who brought the ark of the covenant into Jerusalem, Zadok chose to follow David out, along with the ark, but David insisted that the ark be returned to the city. He apparently did not attach any superstitious meaning to the ark, did not see it as any assurance of God's presence with him. If God had abandoned him, having the ark with him would be no help.

As David and his entourage continued on their flight from Jerusalem, well-wishers brought them food and supplies. Absalom may have thought that all the men of Israel were on his side, but he was mistaken. David had built up a lot of goodwill over the years, and he learned that the incumbent can have an advantage.

Back in Jerusalem, Absalom proved he was not only ambitious but also lustful—and perverse. On the rooftop of his father's palace, with people watching, he made love to his father's concubines. There was more to this than mere vulgarity. The concubines were for royal use only. Perverse as it may seem to us, by being intimate with these women, Absalom was making it clear that he really was the king.

But David's cause was not lost yet. When his own wise counselor Ahithophel abandoned him to serve as advisor to Absalom, David turned the tables on them by having one of his loyal followers, Hushai, infiltrate Absalom's entourage and give him bad advice. (See Day 5 for more about the brief but eventful career of Ahithophel.) And

David still had a huge military following, and though he was a seasoned fighting man himself, they would not let their king go into battle himself. In the forest of Ephraim, which was more like a thick jungle than a forest, thousands of Absalom's followers fell, and it seemed the cause was lost. David had insisted that his troops "deal gently with the young man Absalom." If they did so, it was not for Absalom's own sake but for David's, for David's soldiers saw Absalom for the treacherous, scheming, unscrupulous rogue that he was. What would "dealing gently" with him mean? If they spared his life, could David ever trust him again? Could they? If he ever became king, wouldn't he likely take revenge on David's loyal supporters?

The strikingly handsome young man met a very unattractive end. Riding his mule through the forest, he got his head caught in the branches of an oak. The mule rode on, leaving Absalom dangling in midair. One of Joab's men saw him and reported it. Joab wondered why the man did not seize the opportunity and kill Absalom, but the man knew of David's order to "deal gently" with Absalom and would not harm him. Joab, whose barley field Absalom had burned, and who knew there would only be more trouble if Absalom survived, had no such qualms. He took three javelins and thrust them into Absalom's heart. Knowing the rogue did not deserve an honorable burial, Joab had his men throw Absalom into a pit in the forest, covering his body with stones.

The rebellion led by a conceited, ungrateful, scheming scoundrel had come to an end. Absalom's followers melted away quickly after his death. This suggests their resentments, whatever they were, did not run too deep. They were, in a real sense, a fan club, and with the star gone, they had nothing to rally around. We can well imagine that if David had been killed and Absalom truly became king, his star power might not have lasted long.

The one man who took no joy in this was David: "The king was shaken. He went up to the room over the gateway and wept. As he went, he said: 'O my son Absalom! My son, my son Absalom! If only I had died instead of you—O Absalom, my son, my son!'" (2 Samuel 18:33).

David's extravagant grief almost cost him the loyalty of his subjects. His army did what it was supposed to do—put down a serious rebellion—yet David's grief made the victory a hollow one for them, and they returned to Jerusalem under a cloud instead of elated, slinking back in like victims, not victors. The kingdom had been saved, yet David's own private emotion threatened to break it apart. The situation gave a hint that, well-loved as David was, holding the throne was not a sure thing, that any king could very well lose the kingdom.

> **DID YOU KNOW?**
>
> William Faulkner (1897–1962), the Nobel Prize-winning American author, wrote a novel with a biblical title, *Absalom, Absalom*, taken from King David's lament over his wayward son Absalom (2 Samuel 18:33).

Joab, the tough-minded soldier, was disgusted and did not hesitate to say so to his king: "Today you have humiliated all your men, who have just saved your life and the lives of your sons and daughters and the lives of your wives and concubines. You love those who hate you and hate those who love you. You have made it clear today that the commanders and their men mean nothing to you. I see that you would be pleased if Absalom were alive today and all of us were dead" (2 Samuel 19:5–6).

Joab was right, and David knew it. The king composed himself and returned to Jerusalem, where he was welcomed warmly. But there was still more rebellion to come out of David's household.

YET ANOTHER HANDSOME ROGUE

Now Adonijah, whose mother was Haggith, put himself forward and said, "I will be king." So he got chariots and horses ready, with fifty men to run ahead of him. (His father had never interfered with him by asking, "Why do you behave as you do?" He was also very handsome and was born next after Absalom.) (1 Kings 1:5–6)

The key phrase in the above verse is "put himself forward." Adonijah, son of David, did not wait to be called upon by God or designated by his father as heir to the throne of Israel. He chose himself, and, like Absalom, he had a chariot and "fifty men to run ahead of him." And, also like Absalom, he had led a spoiled youth, for David—good king, but bad father—had never said to him, "Why do you behave as you do?"

Adonijah was handsome and spoiled—and David, for all his failings as a father, was wise enough to see that such a man should not be king. The kingship in Israel was still a new thing, and no precedent had been established that the heir to the throne was necessarily the king's oldest son. Presumably the king could designate the son he thought most fit to rule. And so David had settled the crown on Solomon, who would prove to be—in most ways, at least—a good choice.

Whether David's choice of Solomon had been made public is not known. Adonijah, as spoiled and arrogant as his brother Absalom had been, didn't seem to know about it or care. But though he had a few highly placed followers, including the priest Abiathar and, more importantly, David's faithful old military commander Joab, he did not have the large following that Absalom had assembled years before. While Adonijah's followers were already starting to call him king and holding a feast in his honor, David had Solomon anointed king. News of this reached the Adonijah party, and Adonijah's following immediately melted away. Fearing the wrath of his brother Solomon, Adonijah went to the high altar in Jerusalem and held to it, hoping Solomon would not execute him in a holy place. Solomon sent word to Adonijah: If he behaved himself, no harm would come to him.

David had grown old, and in his old age could not keep warm, so an attractive young woman, Abishag, had been brought in as a literal bed-warmer, sleeping in the king's bed but not having relations with him. But technically, Abishag was the king's concubine, meaning no man but the king was ever supposed to touch her. After David's death, Adonijah asked Solomon a favor: Could he please have Abishag? In fact, he phrased his request as a kind of insult. He was the presumed heir to the throne, but this had been denied him, so could he at least have the king's concubine as a kind of consolation prize? Solomon saw through the request. Adonijah was never going to live quietly on the sideline but would always regard himself as the rightful ruler, and sleeping with David's concubine was a sign of his ambition to be king. Also, Adonijah still had Joab and Abiathar on his side.

So Solomon, whose reign was mostly peaceful, began it with bloodshed. He had Adonijah killed, which strikes us as horrible, and yet it undoubtedly prevented further rebellion and bloodshed. Solomon sent the priest Abiathar into exile.

And what about Joab? Before dying, David had made Solomon promise to execute Joab. Why, given how faithfully Joab had served David so many years, particularly in ending the rebellion of Absalom? Joab was in fact related to David, being the son of Zeuiah, David's half-sister. He first appears as a fighter for David in David's struggle with Ishbosheth, Saul's son, for the throne of Israel. David saw plenty of potential in Joab, and after Joab was first to enter the fortress of Mount Zion, David made him commander of his army. Joab also led the valiant fight against the Ammonites. It was Joab who obeyed David's horrible order to put Uriah the Hittite, husband of Bathsheba, in the thick of fighting so he would be killed. Joab was the intermediary between David and the estranged Absalom, and Joab led the fight against the rebellious Absalom, killing him himself and then snapping the grief-stricken David out of his mourning.

Strangely, David replaced Joab as military commander with Amasa, who, ironically, had been leader of Absalom's rebel forces. This seems bizarre but was politically wise: David understood that forgiving the rebels and keeping them close at hand was better than killing or exiling them all, thus sowing the seeds of more rebellion. But Joab got his vengeance by killing Amasa—stabbing him in the belly while kissing him, a vile act of treachery. Taking Amasa's place, Joab put down the revolt of Sheba, further proof of his loyalty to David.

In short, Joab was an extremely violent man—in an age that took violence for granted—but a man who had proved his loyalty to David. Yet David must have understood that it was not appropriate to let this violent and often treacherous man die peacefully of old age. Also, Joab had taken the side of Adonijah, when David's own choice as successor was Solomon. Joab had sided with Adonijah and then supposedly abandoned him. Could Joab ever be trusted by Solomon? Joab sought safety by grabbing hold of the altar—and to his surprise and horror, Solomon's man killed him there. The right of sanctuary, the right to be left alone in a sacred place, did not extend to murderers, as Joab found out. This very violent man came to a violent end.

We began this chapter looking at Nimrod, a "mighty hunter" and also the founder of ancient empires known for their violence and cruelty. We have looked at three would-be kings—Abimelech, Absalom and Adonijah—men whose ambition was rooted in their own vanity, not in any desire to be noble public servants. Their stories—and the stories of most of the kings in the Bible—are an illustration of Jotham's parable of the trees, with the most useful and productive trees wishing to go about their business and not dominate others, while the useless thorn bush wishes to reign. This is the Bible's cynical—no, realistic—view of politics and power.

PUTTING THE WORD TO WORK

1. How did you react to learning that the first king mentioned in the Bible, Nimrod, was a builder of oppressive empires? Does this seem to be a warning of how the Bible will view earthly rulers?

2. Have you known people like Abimelech, people who tried to use their parents' good reputations to advance themselves? Were they successful, or were they found out eventually?

3. Saul, David and Absalom are all described as physically attractive, yet in Absalom's case it was his only real merit. Reflecting on his story for a moment, make a resolution to take the God's-eye view of things, assessing people by their deeds and not by their appearance.

4. How do you react to the death of Absalom and David's mourning? Do you sympathize more with the emotional David or with Joab, who saw future troubles if Absalom was allowed to live? Are people like Joab sometimes necessary in such situations?

5. David's later years are a kind of object lesson in what indulgent parenting leads to. Take a moment to pray for parents you know—and for yourself, if you have children at home—asking God to endow them with the tough love that is often required.

Apostles and Yokefellows

The apostle Paul is very much the star in Acts, but many other fascinating people are found in its pages, most of whom crossed paths with Paul at some point.

In Philippians 4:3, Paul addresses himself to Syzygus—which may be a man's name, or it may be a term of affection. The word means "yokefellow," and in this context it would have meant a fellow laborer for the faith. In this chapter we will take a look at several dynamic, Spirit-filled yokefellows.

MEMORY VERSE

He [Barnabas] was a good man, full of the Holy Spirit and faith, and a great number of people were brought to the Lord.—Acts 11:24

KEY TERM FOR TODAY ## Yokefellow

Paul uses this term to refer to his fellow laborers for the faith.

DYING TO WITNESS

Stephen, a man full of God's grace and power, did great wonders and miraculous signs among the people. (Acts 6:8)

Stephen, full of the Holy Spirit, looked up to heaven and saw the glory of God, and Jesus standing at the right hand of God. (Acts 7:55)

In another chapter (Day 2) we look at the first part of Acts, including Peter's fiery sermon on the day of Pentecost. Many people came to put their faith in Christ and, as Jesus predicted, the apostles suffered persecution from the Jewish leaders in Jerusalem. Acts 1 through 5 gives the impression that these first Christians were, though harassed, united. Acts 6 shows that this unity was not total. There was already a certain division between Greek-speaking Jews and Aramaic-speaking Jews. As people from both groups converted to Christianity, the old division continued. Acts 6 says that the Greek-speaking Christians felt they were being neglected in the charitable distributions from the fellowship. The apostles—all of them Aramaic speakers—understood that they did not have time to attend to such matters themselves, so they appointed seven men of good reputation, all of them, judging from their names, Greek speakers. The last of the seven men listed, Nicolaus, is referred to as a "proselyte," so at this early stage an important man in the fellowship is one who was not born a Jew.

Note that the apostles did not choose the seven men. The people did, and the apostles gave their stamp of approval by the laying on of hands, which in the Old Testament had indicated blessing. Although the seven men are often referred to as the first "deacons" in Christianity, the Greek word *diakonos* is not used to refer to them. At this early stage of Christianity, it is really not appropriate to use such terms, since all the people in the fellowship were servants of Christ.

Why were seven chosen? Each synagogue had seven elders. In effect, the Christian community was becoming a new synagogue.

Though Acts 6 makes it sound as if these seven men were in charge of the charitable work among the Greek-speaking Christians, it is clear that they did more than that, especially since Stephen and Philip appeared to both be eloquent preachers. Given the division between the Aramaic- and Greek-speaking Christians, the seven men must have been regarded as the leaders among the Greek speakers.

Most prominent of the seven was Stephen, "a man full of God's grace and power." Not only had he performed miracles, but he also proved to be a skilled debater when he was confronted by Jewish opponents. Among these opponents were Jews from Cilicia, the home province of the man who would become the major figure in Acts, Paul. Though Acts does not tell us of Paul and Stephen debating each other or even meeting face-to-face, it is very likely.

Stephen had such wisdom that his critics could not beat him in debate. So they did to him what had been done to Jesus not so long before: accused him of blasphemy and dragged him before the Sanhedrin, the Jewish ruling council. They claimed he had blasphemed against Moses and against the temple—and that he claimed Jesus would destroy the temple. It was all lies, of course. Jesus, at his trial, had been accused of wanting to destroy the temple.

Any perceived threat to the temple would rile up not only the priests but also the working class of Jerusalem, for to a large degree they catered to the tourist trade in Jerusalem, the many people—both believers and sightseers—who came to see the magnificent temple. Stephen was perceived as a commercial threat, the same as Paul in Ephesus, when the devotees of the goddess Artemis were alarmed at people converting to Christianity. Also, Acts 6:7 says that some of the priests had converted to Christianity, and this would have disturbed the ones who had not.

"All who were sitting in the Sanhedrin looked intently at Stephen, and they saw that his face was like the face of an angel" (Acts 6:15). What did this mean? We are so familiar with the mild, almost lifeless look of angels in paintings that we forget that the angels in the Bible are often intimidating to the people they encounter, awesome in demeanor. Stephen probably did not look mild in this situation—he was "full of grace and power." There was something otherworldly in Stephen's look, a hard-to-define quality that deeply impressed his fellow believers but disturbed and provoked his opponents. We have to wonder, since Saul, the future Paul, was present on this occasion, just how he reacted to Stephen's angelic look.

Acts 7, one of the great chapters of the Bible, contains Stephen's defense of himself—or, more accurately, of his faith. Stephen's accusers said he had spoken out against the laws handed down by Moses. In his speech, Stephen goes back much further than Moses to Abraham, a man from faraway Mesopotamia. Though Abraham settled awhile in the promised land, Canaan, in fact he moved about constantly throughout his life. He was a "friend of God," and the man regarded as both physical and spiritual ancestor of the Jews, yet he was a man on the move, not tied to the land—or to a temple. Within three generations, Abraham's descendants are in another faraway land, Egypt. God gave his laws to Moses not in Jerusalem but in the wilderness, in a period when no temple existed, and the Hebrews worshipped in a tent, the Tabernacle. Stephen's point is that God and the faith are not tied to Jerusalem or to the temple. For all their supposed reverence for Moses and the Law, the Jews conveniently forgot that Moses never set foot in Jerusalem or worshipped in a temple. Moses is not really the issue for the priests—the temple is. Although Stephen lived in Jerusalem and presumably worshipped often at the temple, as any devout Jew would, he was familiar with Israel's history and knew that God exists everywhere and can be worshipped and served everywhere. Beautiful as the temple was, God was too big to be contained in it.

> ## DID YOU KNOW?
> Over the centuries, many Christians have died for the faith, and many have repeated Stephen's words, "Lord Jesus, receive my spirit" (Acts 7:59).

The high priest who presided over the Sanhedrin may have been Caiaphas, the same man who condemned Jesus. If so, Caiaphas must have sensed history repeating itself, facing another man that he saw as a threat to the temple and priesthood. Jesus had not in fact been convicted of disparaging the temple, but perhaps Stephen could.

And indeed he would, for he concluded his speech with some very harsh words: "You stiff-necked people, with uncircumcised hearts and ears! You are just like your fathers: You always resist the Holy Spirit!" He accused them of persecuting God's prophets—including Jesus. They had persecuted the prophets who foretold the Messiah—and murdered the Messiah himself.

And now they would murder the Messiah's spokesman. The mob who heard his speech had snapped their minds shut, and they were seized by convulsive outrage.

Stephen, who must have understood what fate awaited him, saw a vision: Jesus at the right hand of God in heaven. He saw glory—and a mob dragged him out of the city and stoned him. His last words were, "Lord, do not hold this sin against them."

Stephen had a vision of where God was—not in the temple, but in heaven, which was not up there but in another dimension. The Holy Place was not in the temple, but where God is.

The first Christian had died for his faith. He seemed amazingly calm during his ordeal. The people who killed him behaved like manic children, plugging their ears and shouting to drown out the truths he spoke. The rituals in the temple were solemn and dignified, but this mob behaved like delinquent children or beasts.

Acts says that Stephen "fell asleep," a familiar image in the New Testament. The saints' deaths are not permanent, only temporary.

"On that day a great persecution broke out against the church at Jerusalem, and all except the apostles were scattered throughout Judea and Samaria." (Acts 8:1) God uses adversity to good advantage: believers were "scattered," giving them opportunity to spread the faith far beyond Jerusalem. In the year 70, the Romans would destroy the temple, and though it was a tragedy for the Jews, it was no loss to the Christians, who had come to understand Stephen's words about the unimportance of temples.

FOREIGN AFFAIRS

When the crowds heard Philip and saw the miraculous signs he did, they all paid close attention to what he said. (Acts 8:6)

When they came up out of the water, the Spirit of the Lord suddenly took Philip away, and the eunuch did not see him again, but went on his way rejoicing. (Acts 8:39)

Among the seven men appointed leaders of the Greek-speaking Christians was Philip, who is often called Philip the deacon or Philip the evangelist to distinguish him from the Philip who was one of the twelve apostles. Philip was among the "scattered ones" who spread the gospel after Stephen's martyrdom. Philip took the gospel to Samaria, the province north of Jerusalem. Recall that the Jews and Samaritans detested each other, but Jesus set a new standard by visiting Samaria—remember the story of the woman at the well—and by telling his parable of the good Samaritan. Most Jews hated Samaritans, but God did not. Like the Jews, the Samaritans were awaiting the Messiah, the one they called the *ta'eb*, "the restorer." Philip preached that the *ta'eb* had come. Like Stephen, Philip performed miracles, including exorcisms and healings. There was

Ethiopia

Ethiopia in that time was not the same region as modern Ethiopia. It referred to a kingdom south of Egypt, in what today would be the nation of Sudan. Ethiopia's king was regarded as the child of the sun, and being divine, he did not busy himself with affairs of state but gave the governing of the country over to his mother, who had the title Candace.

The Ethiopians of that time were famously dark-skinned. In fact, the name Ethiopia is from the Greek *Aithiops*, meaning "burnt-faced."

"great joy" among his converts—not the first or last time in Acts that joy is associated with coming to faith.

Through Philip, joy would come to an interesting individual, a eunuch and a servant of the queen of Ethiopia. The eunuch had been to Jerusalem to worship, which tells us he was a God-fearer, a Gentile who practiced the Jewish religion but was not a full convert. In fact, he could not be, given that he was a eunuch.

Appropriately, after leaving the holy city, the eunuch was reading the Jewish Scriptures. Probably he was reading it in the Greek translation, and definitely he was reading aloud, as all reading was done in ancient times. People in those days believed words on a page were "dead" and had to be spoken in order to be real. Most ancient languages had no separation between words, so reading aloud was essential to get the feel of where one word ended and another began.

Acts makes it clear that Philip did not simply bump into this foreigner on the road. The Spirit led Philip to him. And it was surely not coincidence that the eunuch was reading this passage of Scripture: "He was led like a sheep to the slaughter, and as a lamb before the shearer is silent, so he did not open his mouth. In his humiliation he was deprived of justice. Who can speak of his descendants? For his life was taken from the earth" (Isaiah 56:3–5). The eunuch asked Philip: Was the prophet referring to himself, or someone else? "Then Philip began with that very passage of Scripture and told him the good news about Jesus" (Acts 8:35).

The Isaiah passage is part of one of the "Servant Songs," which speak of a "Suffering Servant" of God. The Jews interpreted these passages as applying to Israel, the holy nation persecuted by the pagans around them. The first Christians saw it differently: The Servant was Jesus, the Messiah and Savior of the world.

We aren't told how long the two men talked, only that they were riding in the eunuch's chariot. At some point Philip must have sensed the man had come to faith. On the desert road they spotted some water, and the eunuch asked to be baptized. Again, not luck but the hand of God, for in that land that was desert, or nearly so, finding water deep enough for baptism was not a common thing.

The Ethiopian went "on his way rejoicing." Again, there is the theme of joy among the new believers. An old tradition says that the Ethiopian became a missionary among his people. Considering the joy he felt, he certainly did not keep the faith to himself.

By Jewish law, the eunuch could never have become a full member of the faith community. For the Christians, his physical condition was not an obstacle. What mattered was faith.

After his encounter with the eunuch, Philip continued his missionary work in Azotus, one of the old cities held by the Philistines in the Old Testament period. So by this point the gospel has spread not only to the Samaritans but also to people who were probably the descendants of the hated Philistines.

PAUL'S SPONSOR

He [Barnabas] was a good man, full of the Holy Spirit and faith, and a great number of people were brought to the Lord. (Acts 11:24)

While they were worshiping the Lord and fasting, the Holy Spirit said, "Set apart for me Barnabas and Saul for the work to which I have called them." (Acts 13:2)

Stephen and Philip both had a connection with Paul. At the stoning of Stephen, Paul (still called Saul at that point) gave approval to the lynching and then set about persecuting Christians wherever he could find them. Several years later, he would meet Philip in the city of Caesarea, where Philip's four unmarried daughters were all prophets.

In this section we will look at a man who had a much closer relationship to Paul, the great Barnabas. We first encounter him in Acts 4, where we learn his name was Joseph, and he was from the island of Cyprus in the Mediterranean. Being of generous nature, he sold some land and gave the proceeds to the Christians in Jerusalem. He made such a deep impression on the other believers that they nicknamed him Barnabas, meaning "son of encouragement"—or, as we might put it, "the Encourager." We aren't told what became of Barnabas during the "scattering" that occurred after the stoning of Stephen. Presumably, wherever he was, he was witnessing to his faith.

Saul was on his way to Damascus, with a commission from the Jewish high priest to arrest Jewish Christians and take them back to Jerusalem. On the road to Damascus he had his blinding vision of Jesus, asking, "Saul, Saul, why do you persecute me?" Saul had to be led by the hand into the city.

A neglected figure in this story is Ananias, a Christian of Damascus. While praying, Ananias had his own vision: The Lord told him to go to a certain house and find Saul and restore his sight. The message frightened Ananias, for he had heard of this fanatical Saul and what he intended to do to the believers in Damascus. Going to Saul might, Ananias thought, result in his being taken back in chains to Jerusalem. But God assured Ananias

that he had great plans for Saul, who was "chosen" to do great things for God. In speaking to Ananias, the Lord said Saul would bear the gospel to the Gentiles and to kings. The Lord also told Ananias that Saul would "suffer many things." Saul had already inflicted suffering on Christians and had planned to do even more. God's plan is much different: The one who inflicted suffering will become a fellow sufferer with the believers.

Ananias must have been a man of deep trust in God, for he approached the notorious persecutor and addressed him as "Brother Saul." Saul's sight was restored, he was filled with the Spirit, and he was baptized. Ananias is not mentioned again in Acts, but we can safely assume he was Saul's first Christian friend, and the one who introduced him to the other believers in Damascus. Naturally they were suspicious of him at first, but in time he became a dynamic spokesman for the faith he had once persecuted. His conversion pleased the Christians but outraged the Jews, who plotted to kill him, so that Paul had to be smuggled out of the city in a basket lowered over the city wall.

Back in Jerusalem, Saul found himself friendless. The Christians knew him as a persecutor, the Jewish authorities now saw him as a turncoat—the Christian-hater turned Christian.

We don't know exactly how he and Barnabas met, only that it was Barnabas who vouched for him, assuring the Christians in Jerusalem that the ex-persecutor was now a brother in the faith. Had it not been for Barnabas seeing the hand of God on Saul, Saul

CULTURAL INSIGHTS

Roman Names

In both the Old and New Testaments, a person was typically known as "X, son [or daughter] of Y," as in "Isaac, son of Abraham." There were no family names, no last names in our sense. For the Romans, the situation was different. A Roman citizen would have three names—the *praenomen*, *nomen gentile* and *cognomen*. Typically a man would be known by the second and third names—for example, Gaius Julius Caesar was generally called simply Julius Caesar. Paul, a Roman citizen, had the cognomen Paulus. It is curious that Luke, a friend of Paul, did not tell us his other two names, but clearly he did not consider them important. From this point on in Acts, however, the apostle is called Paul instead of by his Jewish name Saul. Probably Paul, in speaking to the official Sergius Paulus, could not resist pointing out that they had the same cognomen, Paulus.

might have remained forever under a cloud, with the Christians wondering when he might revert to his "real" self, the Christian-hater. But Barnabas saw not only a brother but also a man on fire for the faith, so much so that the Jews of Jerusalem began plotting against him, so for a time he went to live in his hometown, Tarsus.

The two men were destined to meet again. Christians had begun preaching to the Gentiles in the great city of Antioch. The Christian leaders in Jerusalem naturally wanted to investigate what was happening there. They sent the wise and tactful Barnabas, who was a native of Cyprus, as were some of those who were witnessing to Gentiles. When he reached Antioch, he was glad to see that the Gentile conversions were real. Apparently he did much more than simply observe and admire, for this "good man, full of the Holy Spirit and of faith" brought many others to faith. He was being true to his name, which means "son of encouragement." More than just giving the Jerusalem fellowship's stamp of approval to what happened, he encouraged it and participated in it.

At some point he realized the work there was so important he needed a friend and colleague, and he thought of his old friend Saul, who had gone back to his home in Tarsus. Instead of sending word to Saul, he went in person to Tarsus. The fact that he had to seek Saul out raises some questions. Was Saul not at his family home? There is a hint here that Saul's devout Jewish family may have disowned and disinherited him, for there were numerous cases of such behavior. Years later, when he wrote the Letter to the Philippians, Saul (Paul) stated that for the sake of Jesus, "I have lost all things" (Philippians 3:8). If indeed Saul had been turned away by his own family, this would have been a terrible burden to bear, especially for people as family-oriented as the Jews were. At any rate, Barnabas did find him in Tarsus and took him back to Antioch, the city that was quickly becoming the vibrant heart of Christianity.

Acts 13 states that there were several "prophets and teachers" in Antioch, including Barnabas and Saul. "The Holy Spirit said, 'Set apart for me Barnabas and Saul for the work

---

CULTURAL INSIGHTS

Preaching "The Lord Jesus"

Acts 11 says the evangelists spoke to the Gentiles about the "Lord Jesus." Some of these Gentiles would have had little or no knowledge of the Jewish religion, so talk about a Messiah and Old Testament prophecies would have been meaningless to such people. However, many of them would have been prepared to hear about a divine Savior and Lord, for there were numerous religions and cults in the empire focusing on a god or demigod who could give his worshippers salvation. The key difference was that these divine figures existed only in the realm of legend, while the Lord the Christians proclaimed was a real person, walking the earth only a few years earlier.

Yoked Together

Our word *conjugal*, which means "relating to marriage," is from the Latin *conjugium*—"yoked together." A yoke is a piece of wood used to harness two or more farm animals together so they can pull a plow or wagon. If two beings are yoked together, they have a common purpose, which ideally a married couple should have. In Roman marriage ceremonies, a literal yoke was used to symbolize that husband and wife were being united in a common purpose, and a Roman might refer to his or her spouse as *conjux*, "yokefellow."

As mentioned earlier in the chapter, Paul referred to a man named Syzugus, a Greek word meaning "yokefellow," and Greek writers often used the term to refer to spouses, close friends or teammates. Paul, who was single, did not have a spouse as his yokefellow, yet he saw all his fellow workers for the faith as his yokefellows, people with a common task on earth.

to which I have called them'" (Acts 13:2). We don't know how the Holy Spirit said that Barnabas and Saul were to be set apart for service. Perhaps the believers in Antioch sensed inwardly that the two men were specially qualified for the enormous task ahead of them.

And so Barnabas and Saul began what was called the first missionary journey. Appropriately, their first stop was Barnabas' homeland, the island of Cyprus. A pattern was set: Barnabas and Saul were Jews, so they took their message of Jesus, the Jewish Messiah, to the synagogues. Both men had gladly accepted that the Gentiles too were included in God's plan of salvation, yet they felt the compulsion to first proclaim the message to their fellow Jews. This was not an either/or situation, because most synagogues would have had some God-fearers in attendance, and in time these would prove much more receptive to the message than the Jews were.

Among the God-fearers was, surprisingly, a local Roman official, "an intelligent man," Sergius Paulus, who summoned the two missionaries to hear what they had to say. He held the title proconsul, meaning he administered a Roman province on behalf of the Senate.

Barnabas and Saul were fortunate to already have a friend—or at least a receptive listener—in a high position. Unfortunately, they also had an enemy, a local magician named Elymas, apparently the name being a Semitic word meaning "sorcerer." He went by the name Bar-Jesus, meaning "son of Jesus," but this doesn't mean he had any connection with the Christians or even knew about Jesus Christ. Jesus was a common name in those days, so Elymas may have simply been son of a man named Jesus. He was a Jew but clearly not a faithful one, for Jews were prohibited from dabbling in magic. He must have had the ear of Sergius Paulus, and resented Barnabas and Saul as intruders on his turf. Saul confronted this charlatan, saying he was not "son of Jesus" but "son of the devil." The troublesome man was smitten with blindness, a physical manifestation of his spiritual blindness. The miracle deeply impressed Sergius Paulus. He "believed"—though we aren't sure if this means he fully converted to the faith or simply believed intellectually that Saul and Barnabas definitely possessed some spiritual power.

The two missionaries left Cyprus and continued on the mainland. Departing from them was John Mark, a cousin of Barnabas who apparently had aided them in their work but was now returning to Jerusalem. We aren't told why John Mark departed. He may not have felt up to the challenge of continuing missionary work. It is also possible that he resented the way his cousin Barnabas seemed to be playing second fiddle to Paul. At any rate, his departure from them would have serious repercussions later on.

PAUL'S SHADOW

Paul and Barnabas answered them boldly: "We had to speak the word of God to you first. Since you reject it and do not consider yourselves worthy of eternal life, we now turn to the Gentiles." (Acts 13:46)

Barnabas they called Zeus, and Paul they called Hermes because he was the chief speaker. (Acts 14:12)

At this point in the story, "Barnabas and Saul" gives way to "Paul and Barnabas," with Saul/Paul clearly being the dominant personality. Yet the two were still very much a team. In the city called Pisidian Antioch, they encountered great opposition from many Jews. "The whole city" came to hear the men speak at the synagogue, and many Jews were irked that these outsiders could draw such a crowd. In theory, the Jews should have been pleased that "the whole city"—which would have included many Gentiles— would turn up at the synagogue. But on this occasion, the "regulars" would have been outnumbered by the "intruders," and this made the Jews uncomfortable.

This is a critical moment in Acts, and in the history of Christianity. A pattern was set: The Jews heard the gospel and most of them rejected it, so the missionaries turned to a more receptive audience, the Gentiles. The Jews were ingrates—they rejected God's Messiah, and then were upset that others accepted him.

If the missionaries' words irked the Jews, they were received joyfully by the Gentiles. And so "the word of the Lord spread through the whole region." But the good news was followed by its sequel: The Jews with influence stirred up such opposition that Paul and Barnabas had to leave.

Paul and Barnabas stuck to their game plan, taking the gospel to the synagogue, this time in Iconium. As before, they made converts, but, also as before, the Jews as a whole rejected them. This time something new was added: The Jews were in cahoots with the city's leaders, and they planned something more drastic than just driving the missionaries from the city; they plotted to stone them. The two wisely moved on. They had escaped stoning—for the moment.

In the town of Lystra, Paul performed a miracle: A man who had been lame from birth was listening to Paul preach, and Paul sensed the man had faith. Paul commanded him, "Stand up on your feet!" The man did; in fact, he jumped up. The local pagans reacted by shouting, "The gods have come down to us in human form!" They believed Barnabas was Zeus and Paul was Hermes. The people wished to offer sacrifices to the men, and the local priest of Zeus had bulls brought in. Having been brought up as devout Jews, Paul and Barnabas were horrified at this idolatry. They assured the people they were only men, not gods. In fact, Paul insisted that the time had come for all people to put aside such "worthless things" as idols and temples and worship the true God.

Pagans had a violent streak in them, as any reader of mythology knows. The same people who were willing to offer sacrifices to Paul and Barnabas were swayed by some Jews to turn on the two men. It is also possible that the Jews took advantage of some anti-

---

CULTURAL INSIGHTS

Immoral Gods

Consider the pagan world that Paul and Barnabas were preaching to. What a people bows before tells us a lot about those people. Put another way, "I like that" means "I am like that." Zeus was the chief god, the one with the most power—and yet the myths present him as an unfaithful husband, a serial philanderer who impregnates goddesses and mortal women at will, and he kills Asklepios, the god of healing, for daring to bring a man back from the dead. Hermes was a god much beloved by merchants but also by thieves—which tells us a lot about merchants in ancient times!—and was also a god of cunning and deceit. While they and the other gods were depicted in statues as having fine physiques, morally they were at rock bottom, and while they might on occasion benefit mankind (which explains why the people of Lystra attributed the healing of the lame man to them), the average pagan was lucky if his contact with the gods was kept to a bare minimum. No wonder so many of the pagans turned from their violent, erotic myths to the moral religion of the Jews—and, as Acts shows, to Christianity.

Jewish feeling among the pagans by portraying Paul as a Jewish troublemaker trying to turn them away from the worship of their native gods. The locals stoned Paul, dragged him outside the city, and left him for dead. We aren't told why they did not stone Barnabas, although probably they directed their ire at Paul because he did most of the speaking.

The region where this took place had a long reputation for being wild and lawless. The travesty of justice meted out to Paul tells us its reputation was deserved. Though technically part of the Roman empire, there is no sense in this episode that any imperial official had a say in what took place.

We can only imagine what went through Paul's mind while they were stoning him. Surely he had to think of the stoning of Stephen, which at the time he had approved of. But Paul was not down yet. He revived, and then the next day he and Barnabas departed. For the remainder of the journey they retraced their steps, stopping in the cities they had evangelized to build up the new communities of faith. Not being able to stay with each group permanently, the two appointed elders to lead each community. When they told the believers that "we must go through many hardships to enter the kingdom of God," they were speaking from experience.

Despite much adversity—and nearly the loss of Paul's life—the first missionary journey had been a great success. The two men reported back to Antioch how the word of God was spreading among the Gentiles.

Paul and Barnabas would do further work as missionaries but not together. Paul proposed making another journey, revisiting and strengthening the communities they

---

CULTURAL INSIGHTS

"Women of High Standing"

The story of Paul and Barnabas in Pisidian Antioch says that the influential ones in the synagogue included "women of high standing." The synagogues were obviously not totally dominated by men. Some of these women were God-fearing Gentiles who sometimes expressed interest in the Jews' religion but did not take it too seriously. Upper-class women in the Roman Empire (who, like the wealthy in all ages, had too much time on their hands) often dabbled in various religions and cults, a classic example being the empress Poppaea, wife of the vile emperor Nero. Poppaea, a woman so immoral that her behavior scandalized even the cynical Romans, was interested in the Jews' religion, but certainly she had no intention of abiding by its moral standards. Wherever Paul and his fellow missionaries traveled, they would encounter women like these, women whose social status gave them more clout than they deserved. The combination of high rank and low principles was lethal.

had established. Barnabas was willing, but he wanted to take along John Mark, who had left them right after their first journey had begun. "They had such a sharp disagreement that they parted company" (Acts 15:39).

Why did such a close and effective missionary team split up? The reason given is that they disagreed over taking along John Mark, who had left them for reasons Acts does not tell us. Paul may have seen Mark as unstable or insufficiently committed. Certainly the missionary life was demanding, to say the least, and the mission field was no place for someone who was halfhearted. Then again, there is much about Mark we do not know. Did he have health problems? Whatever the case, Paul did not see him as a suitable fellow traveler while Barnabas, who, after all, was a relative, did.

Acts does not assign blame here—there is no bad guy in the story, not Paul, nor Barnabas, nor Mark. The "sharp disagreement" had a pleasant outcome—instead of one missionary team of Paul, Barnabas and Mark, there were now two—Paul and Silas, and Barnabas and Mark.

We should be glad Luke included this detail in Acts. He has been accused of sugarcoating the story of the early Christians, but if that were the case he could have simply omitted this detail and simply said that Paul and Barnabas chose different mission partners and went on their way amicably. Instead, he told the truth.

Remember that it was Barnabas who vouched for Paul and was his "sponsor" for Paul's acceptance by the Jerusalem Christians. Paul would never have forgotten this kindness, of course, and it must have made the parting more bitter for him.

If there was any bitterness or antipathy, it vanished in time, for Paul refers to Barnabas (and Mark also) affectionately in some of his letters.

DID YOU KNOW?

The New Testament name James is actually the same as Jacob—in the Greek the name is *Iakobos*. Over the years the name evolved into Jacobus, then Jacomus, then James.

POINT MAN IN JERUSALEM

James, Peter and John, those reputed to be pillars, gave me and Barnabas the right hand of fellowship. (Galatians 2:9)

Paul and Barnabas' activity includes their involvement in the so-called Council of Jerusalem, recorded in Acts 15. The two men had been spreading the faith among Gentiles, and with great success. However, back in Antioch they encountered some Jewish Christians from Jerusalem, who insisted that in order to be saved, Gentile Christians would have to be circumcised. Some of these Jewish Christians were former Pharisees—as was Paul himself. But Paul and Barnabas both spoke boldly about seeing the power of God at work among the Gentiles, and they were backed up by Peter, who had led the Roman centurion Cornelius, to faith (Acts 10).

Interestingly, the person presiding over this important debate was not Paul or Barnabas or Peter, but James—not the apostle James, but James "the brother of the Lord." The designation "brother" has caused much controversy among Christians. For some, he was the son of Joseph and Mary, while others take "brother" in a general way to mean "relative," meaning he might have been a cousin of Jesus. Obviously he was in some way a member of Jesus' extended family, but Acts tells us nothing about how and why he came to be an important figure among the Jerusalem Christians. The Gospels make it clear that none of Jesus' brothers put their faith in him during his ministry, and yet, clearly, James did so afterward. Paul, in 1 Corinthians 15:7, states that James was privileged to see the risen Jesus, and Paul also refers to James as an "apostle," meaning one commissioned by Jesus himself. In Galatians 2:9, Paul refers to the "pillars" of the Jerusalem church as James, Peter and John—in that order. It was they who gave him and Barnabas the "right hand of fellowship," taking them into the community there.

It is unfortunate that we do not know more about James's history, but clearly he is a respected and unignorable presence among the first Christians. Having heard Peter, Paul and Barnabas report so favorably about the conversion of the Gentiles, James renders the judgment that Gentile Christians need not be circumcised. He issued a letter to that effect, not in his own name but in the name of "the brothers, both the apostles and the elders." The conclusion of the Council of Jerusalem was that, in effect, Gentiles did not have to become Jews in order to become Christians.

CHARACTERS AT LARGE ## The James Box

A very controversial "find" came to public notice in 2002: a stone box that supposedly had once contained the bones of James. The stone box was an ossuary, meaning "bone box," the custom being that, after a person had been in the tomb for several years, his bones were collected and put into a box (the goal being to free up space for more tombs). The ossuary that made news in 2002 had this Aramaic inscription: *Ya'akov bar Yosef achui d'Yeshua*—"James, son of Joseph, brother of Jesus." The inscription got attention because such inscriptions commonly mentioned a father's name, but not a brother's. Ossuaries were in use by Jerusalem Jews for only a brief period, from about 20 BC to AD 70, which would include the date of death of James.

Much excitement attended the finding of this box. If it was indeed James's ossuary, it would have once held the bones of the brother of Jesus. To the deep regret of many, the Antiquities Authority of Israel declared the box a forgery.

James is mentioned again in Acts 21, where Paul, having concluded his third missionary journey, visits Jerusalem and reports to "James and all the elders." James must have been present when Paul was arrested after being falsely accused of trying to take a Gentile into the temple.

Acts shows persecution of Christians, with the martyrdom of Stephen, the beating and imprisonment of Peter and John, and the many calamities Paul endured. We have to wonder: Why was James, so prominent among the Jerusalem Christians, not persecuted? The answer to that lies not in the Bible, but in the writings of the Jewish historian Josephus, who claimed that James continued to live according to the Jewish laws and customs, while Paul did not. James gave his wholehearted approval to the missions to the Gentiles, but he himself lived as he had been brought up, observing the Sabbath, the kosher food laws, etc. Outwardly, he was a faithful Jew, but he did not insist that Gentiles abide by the same rules.

But eventually James, the Christian, did run afoul of the Jews. According to Josephus, he was stoned to death in AD 62, at the instigation of the high priest and the Sanhedrin. Like Jesus, he was condemned as a blasphemer and false teacher.

It is interesting that Acts shows James and Paul as being on cordial terms during their lifetimes, for that has not been the case with the commentators on their epistles. Paul in his many letters insisted that salvation comes through faith, not by works, whereas the Letter of James stresses that "faith without works is dead." The great Martin Luther saw James as contradicting Paul, and hesitated to include James in his German translation of the Bible, since he called James "an epistle of straw."

But in fact there is no contradiction. Paul insisted that we do good works not to obtain salvation but because we are grateful to God for our salvation. He heartily agreed that "faith without works is dead." In his letters, Paul was dealing with the issue of legalism—the common human belief that we earn our way to heaven. He had to fight legalism by insisting that faith was what brings salvation. James, in his letter, was not writing to people who were flirting with legalism; in fact, the recipients of his letter were flirting not with legalism but laziness. The message of his letter is: So you are a saved person, a person of faith—then act like it! Paul would not have disagreed.

PUTTING THE WORD TO WORK

1. Reflect on the verse that says Stephen's face was "like an angel." What would people have seen in the face? Authority? Power? Goodness?

2. Philip, a Greek-speaking Jewish Christian, had a life-changing encounter with a dark-skinned foreigner, the Ethiopian eunuch. Can you think of times in your own life when faith enabled you to bridge a culture gap and reach out to someone else?

3. Ananias and Barnabas have to be admired for being willing to accept Paul, the notorious persecutor, as a brother in the faith. Have you known of people who had the courage to stand with someone of suspect reputation?

4. As Acts progresses, Barnabas seems to take a back seat to Paul, the more forceful personality, yet he shows no bitterness or envy. Keep Barnabas in mind the next time you feel slighted or offended when someone else seems to take precedence over you.

5. Paul and Barnabas came to a parting of the ways, yet Paul's letters indicate there was no bitterness or ill will later on. If you have had some serious disagreement with a fellow believer, make an effort today to reach out to that person.

Aaron and Sons

Throughout this book, we look at various members of Israel's clergy, the priests, and for the most part they are an unimpressive lot, men whose behavior is no better than the laity's—in fact, often much worse. But in this chapter we'll look at the original Hebrew clergyman Aaron, brother of Moses, and also consider the whole idea of what priesthood meant. Along the way we'll take a look at the priest tribe the Levites, and their amazingly violent beginnings. We'll also look at the last-mentioned priest in the Bible, who was one of the worst.

KEY TERM FOR TODAY

Priesthood

While the Old Testament mandates a holy priesthood for Israel, most of the priests are unworthy characters, but a key theme in the Bible is that all God's people are to be holy.

MOSES' SHADOW

Have Aaron your brother brought to you from among the Israelites, along with his sons Nadab and Abihu, Eleazar and Ithamar, so they may serve me as priests. Make sacred garments for your brother Aaron, to give him dignity and honor. (Exodus 28:1–2)

For thousands of years, religions have had clergy in the role of middlemen, men (and sometimes women) who acted as go-betweens, the idea being that a god could not be approached by just anybody but needed the priest to "introduce" the layperson and present his requests and sacrifices. But in the early chapters of the Book of Genesis, there were no priests. Cain and Abel offered up sacrifices to God, and no priest was involved, and later Noah, Abraham and the other patriarchs offered sacrifices and spoke directly with the Lord, no middleman needed. The only priests in Genesis were foreigners—Melchizedek, the priest-king of Salem and the priests of Egypt.

The change came in Exodus where, after freeing the Israelites from slavery in Egypt and taking them to Mount Sinai to receive the Law, God instituted a priesthood, with Moses' own brother Aaron as Israel's first high priest. Certainly Aaron had proved himself a worthy man. He was at Moses' side during the confrontations with the stubborn Pharaoh, and he proved himself loyal—a notable exception being the incident of the golden calf (see Day 11), when he caved in to the Israelites' pressure to make them an idol to worship while Moses was away on Sinai with God. Aaron was human—and, despite his failings, a far better man that most of the high priests who would follow after him.

The great man Moses is, amazingly, described as very "meek." Perhaps this isn't too surprising, since the man who encountered God in the burning bush—and who witnessed the plagues on Egypt, the parting of the Red Sea, and was "up close" with God on Mount Sinai—was indeed aware of his own smallness compared to the greatness of God. Perhaps the greatest sign of Moses' meekness was his willingness to share authority with his brother. Logically, the leader Moses could have been the Israelites' king, military chieftain and high priest, and certainly he played the role of intercessor for Israel many times, asking God to show mercy to the chronically ungrateful Israelites. But in the wisdom of God, authority in Israel was shared—a situation that political scientists might call a separation of powers, a situation that prevents an overly ambitious leader who loves power from taking total control. In some nations, the king, who was its military commander, was also its high priest—meaning he was not only the political and military head but the spiritual head as well. God did not intend this situation to exist in Israel, and the Old Testament contains several incidents where kings overstepped their bounds and tried to play the role of priests—and were punished for doing so.

CULTURAL INSIGHTS

Scented Oil

The oil used in anointing priests was extremely fragrant, and the recipe, which included myrrh, is given in Exodus 30. In a world much more accustomed to bodily odors and other natural smells that we seldom encounter in our sanitized world, perfume of any kind was truly special. To say the oil smelled "heavenly" is to catch the whole meaning of the anointing oil. The high priest of Israel was being marked for a distinctive purpose. He was not better than other Israelites, but his office was special. He was God's minister, offering sacrifices to God on behalf of the people, acting as mediator between God and man, which is why he wore distinctive and very attractive garb, and why he was even given a distinctive and pleasing scent at his commissioning. In fact, the fragrant oil was also used on the other sacred furnishings in the Tent of Meeting.

Throughout the Bible, Moses is regarded as a prophet—not one who foretells the future but rather one who speaks for God, directly communicating God's words to man. In many religions, there was no distinction between prophets and priests. In Israel there definitely was, for a true prophet had to be called by God, whereas the priesthood was hereditary—a big difference. One did not inherit the office of prophet, and though Moses had sons, they did not inherit his office or his power. (His successor as Israel's leader was Joshua, a man chosen by God.) Throughout Israel's history, prophets were the men God chose, in his own time and at his own pleasure, to speak to the people. The priesthood was another matter: Aaron's descendants would minister continuously, so the priesthood was a stable institution, something people could always rely on, with the priests and the rituals being constant signs of God's presence among the people—even if the priests themselves were not always decent men.

Days 28 and 29 describe the institution of the priesthood, with Aaron and his four sons as the first priests. The robes and accessories they were to wear are described in detail, and it is made clear that the garments are for "beauty" and "glory"—not to enhance the men themselves but to remind the people of the majesty of the invisible God they serve. The Israelites had recently departed, as ex-slaves, from Egypt, so we can assume the people were not dressed luxuriously, but even so, no expense was to be spared in dressing the priests in splendor. These vestments were not the everyday garb of the priests, of course; they were the robes to be worn as they ministered in the Tent of Meeting, the ornate tent that served as Israel's worship center during their years in the wilderness.

> **DID YOU KNOW?**
>
> Mount Hor, the place where Aaron died (Numbers 33:38) has long been identified as Jabal Harun, near Petra in Jordan. A shrine at the summit covers the supposed grave of Aaron, and Muslims in the region make pilgrimages there. *Harun* is the Arabic form of the name Aaron.

When officiating in the rituals, Israel's high priest wore a breastpiece, a linen square worn over the chest, held in place by gold cords. In it were mounted twelve gems, each one engraved with the name of one of the twelve tribes of Israel, so that the priest literally had the names of the tribes over his heart while he ministered. The breastpiece is described in Exodus 28:15–29. The Hebrew names of the twelve stones give translators fits, since no one is absolutely sure how to translate them. For example, the Hebrew word rendered "sapphire" in many translations is "lapis lazuli" in others. In the past, some very imaginative commentators liked to read deep meanings into the gems and tried to link each to a particular tribe. This is to miss the main point of the breastplate, which was to symbolize that the tribes of Israel were, even with all their failings, God's "jewels." All were very precious to him.

The high priest's turban had a solid gold plate attached to it, engraved with the words "Holy to the Lord." Considering what rogues some of the high priests turned out

DID YOU KNOW?

An old Jewish legend explains why Aaron and not Moses was Israel's first high priest; it was due to Moses' initial reluctance when God called him from the burning bush.

to be, the plate hardly applied to the men who wore it. But "Holy to the Lord" was a designation not just of the priests but of the whole nation. All Israel, God's chosen people, was supposed to be holy.

One of the duties of Israel's high priest was to burn incense morning and evening on a gold altar in the Tent of Meeting. The recipe, which included gum resin and frankincense, is found in Exodus 30:34–38, and this sacred incense could not be used for any other purpose besides worship. In the Tent of Meeting—and, later, in the temple—animals were being sacrificed on a regular basis, so one purpose the incense served was to fumigate an atmosphere that stank of blood. But the Old Testament saw incense more as offering up something beautifully fragrant to the Lord, and as it wafted upward it symbolized the prayer of the priests and of all the people of Israel. When a priest burned the incense, people in the temple area were expected to observe a profound and reverent silence. Once a year, on the Day of Atonement, the high priest would burn incense in the innermost sanctuary, the Holy of Holies, so that the ark of the covenant, the gold-covered chest that symbolized God's presence, would be surrounded by fragrant smoke.

The biblical world was, to put it mildly, less fragrant than ours, and if we were transported back in time, our noses would certainly notice the difference, since

CULTURAL INSIGHTS

"Open" Priesthood vs. Mumbo Jumbo

Israel's priesthood and rituals were extremely public, and the regulations recorded in Exodus and Leviticus were spoken to all the people, not just the priests. With all the people being familiar with the regulations for sacrifices, the priests were prevented from having the people at their mercy. The people were told what portion of the sacrifices were for the priests' use, so the priests could not hog everything for themselves. The priests could not use their office to threaten or intimidate people, because God had revealed his laws to all the people.

This definitely set Israel apart from the other priesthoods of ancient times, in which the rituals and "magic words" were closely guarded secrets known only to the priests. As Israel's God was radically different from the other gods, so Israel's priests were different from the manipulative priests of other gods. In fact, the priests of the pagan nations that surrounded Israel were what we might call witch doctors, called upon to cast spells and cure the sick, even though they had the power to do neither. In Israel the focus was on God, not on the supposed magical powers of priests.

The Phinehas Episode

Aaron had two unworthy sons, Nadab and Abihu, but his son Eleazar was a worthy man, and when Aaron died, Moses took the high priestly garments and put them on Eleazar. He carried out his duties faithfully, but his story is less interesting than that of his son Phinehas. Numbers 25 tells the story of the Israelites encamped in the wilderness at a place where the local women enticed the Israelite men into both sexual immorality and worship of the local gods, including Baal—the first but definitely not the last time the Israelites would worship this false god. Moses told Israel's leaders to put to death all the men who had worshipped the pagans' gods, and many of the people went to the Tent of Meeting to weep over this lapse into paganism.

While they wept, one Israelite man had the nerve to bring his pagan paramour into his own tent. Deeply offended by this was Eleazar's son, Phinehas. He followed the man and woman into the man's tent and ran a spear through both of them. Horrible as it sounds, the act was commended by the Lord, who promised that Phinehas "and his descendants will have a covenant of a lasting priesthood, because he was zealous for the honor of his God and made atonement for the Israelites" (Numbers 25:13). Phinehas seems like a bloodthirsty brute, but his bold act is a warning to others: just because your friends and neighbors see what you are doing—and condone it—does not mean you are in the clear.

people learned to live with bodily odors (both human and animal), and there were few odor-free zones anywhere. The incense used in Israel's worship helped make worship a pleasant experience, and in a world that literally stank, the sweet scent was a reminder of God's holiness, his being distinct from his creation.

As Israel's high priest, Aaron's routines would have been a peculiar mix of prettiness and gore: He would have dressed splendidly and breathed in incense, but he would also have slaughtered rams, cattle, lambs and other beasts. Our minds revolt against the picture, but remember that in ancient times, animal sacrifice was taken for granted, and the sight and smell of animal blood would not have affected the Israelites as it would us. The point of all the priestly dress and rituals was holiness: people acknowledging their sins, offering sacrifices to atone for them, and recognizing the priests' elaborate garb as a sign of holiness.

Sadly, two of Aaron's sons did not seem to take their duties as seriously as they should have. The Book of Leviticus, which most people fail to read because it consists mostly of laws, does contain one interesting bit of narrative: "Aaron's sons Nadab and Abihu took their censers, put fire in them and added incense; and they offered unauthorized fire before the Lord, contrary to his command. So fire came out from the presence of the Lord and consumed them, and they died before the Lord" (Leviticus 10:1–2). This incident is puzzling. The familiar King James Version refers to the "strange fire," while most modern versions have "unauthorized fire." In either case, we aren't sure precisely what Nadab and Abihu did wrong, except that it displeased God. The censers and other ritual utensils were to be used only in the worship of God, and the two brothers were apparently playing priest for their own amusement. Their punishment sounds cruel, but the rest of Leviticus 10 explains it: The priesthood is serious business, and priests had to perform their duties conscientiously. In fact, God specifically tells Aaron that the priests are not to drink while on duty (Leviticus 10:8–9), which has made some readers suspect that is what Nadab and Abihu were guilty of. The point of the episode is that Israel is to be a holy nation, and its priests are to be holy men.

BLOODY MINISTERS

[Moses] stood at the entrance to the camp and said, "Whoever is for the Lord, come to me." And all the Levites rallied to him. (Exodus 32:26)

You are to set the Levites apart from the other Israelites, and the Levites will be mine. (Numbers 8:14)

Moses and Aaron were Levites, descendants of Levi, one of the twelve sons of Jacob. From Exodus on, the Levites are the priestly tribe of the Israelites, given the duties of caring for the Tent of Meeting and its furnishings—and, centuries later, of being in charge of the music in the temple.

Were they given this privilege because Moses and Aaron were Levites? Not at all—as already noted, Aaron's own sons Nadab and Abihu were killed for being unworthy. Being a blood relation to Moses and Aaron was not important but loyalty to the Lord was. In Exodus 32, the famous episode of the Israelites worshipping the golden-calf idol, Moses calls upon the people who are still loyal to God to gather around him—and the Levites "rallied to him." Moses had asked, in the King James Version, "Who is on the Lord's side?"—and the Levites were. What followed is not pleasant to relate: They took their swords in hand and killed three thousand of their fellow Israelites, those who had worshipped the idol. Moses praised them: "You have been set apart to the Lord today, for you were against your own sons and brothers, and he has blessed you this day." This strikes us as horrible and un-Christian, though it might be more precise to call it pre-Christian. It appears that in the context of the story, the extreme violence was needed to get the point across that worship of idols was a grave sin—especially since Moses had been on the mountain receiving the Ten Commandments, one of which prohibited bowing down to idols.

We think of the ministers of religion as being spiritual people, less prone to violence than most people. This is a very modern view, and certainly not a view found in the Bible. The Levites had a violent streak a mile wide—not surprising, for their ancestor Levi was a violent man. In the Genesis stories of Jacob and his twelve sons, Levi gave no hint that he or his descendants were likely to be mild-mannered clergymen. On the contrary, Levi and his brother Simeon perpetrated the brutal slaughter of the Shechemites, the tribe members of the Canaanite man who raped and then offered to marry their sister, Dinah (Genesis 34). Jacob was horrified at this, and he chastised the two brothers for possibly igniting a blood feud that might continue indefinitely. The brothers justified their behavior by claiming that no man had the right to treat their sister like a harlot. Their violence did have a positive effect: Jacob was compelled to move his large family elsewhere, away from the morally lax Shechemites.

At the end of Genesis, the dying Jacob pronounced blessings—and prophecies—over the twelve sons. He had not forgotten the slaughter: "Simeon and Levi are brothers—their swords are weapons of violence. Let me not enter their council, let me not join their assembly, for they have killed men in their anger . . . Cursed be their anger, so fierce, and their fury, so cruel! I will scatter them in Jacob and disperse them in Israel" (Genesis 49:5–7). The prophecy came true for the Levites when, in the Book of Joshua, Canaan was divided among the twelve tribes, with Levi not receiving a block of land as the other tribes did but instead receiving some cities scattered among the other tribes—and being given the task of ministering as priests and assistants. This decision on God's part was wise: Who knows what might have happened if this ferocious tribe had its men all concentrated in one region? Better to scatter them throughout Israel.

We might say that the ministry of the Levites was a case of God turning a lemon into lemonade. Here was a tribe that clearly had a violent streak going all the way back to the violent Levi himself. In the Exodus 32 story, the Levites showed a willingness—horrible to us, but necessary at the time—to forgo family ties and take the sword to all idol-worshippers, even their own sons and brothers. Later, in the Book of Judges, we see Levites roaming from tribe to tribe—something that, in those violent days, might have been safe only for those who had a well-deserved reputation for ferocity. Happily, over time, the Levites became much less violent and settled into their peaceful roles as priests and temple attendants, and we owe much of the Book of Psalms to those Levites who had ability with music and poetry—as well as the willingness to preserve the poems of men like David and Asaph.

DID YOU KNOW?

The Levites are mentioned so often in 1 and 2 Chronicles that Bible scholars assume the author must have been a Levite.

> David left Asaph and his associates before the ark of the covenant of the Lord to minister there regularly, according to each day's requirements. (1 Chronicles 16:37)

It would not be quite accurate to call Asaph an unsung hero of the Bible, for in fact his words are sung—and read and recited—worldwide. Asaph is said to be the author of twelve of the Psalms: 50, and 73 through 83.

Who was he? Asaph was a Levite, appointed to direct the services of praise in the time of David and Solomon. Long after he lived, the Levites who were in charge of singing and playing instruments in the temple were still referred to as the "sons of Asaph," which suggests he might have founded a kind of music school—or at least that he had a reputation as a gifted musician and poet. And although David was the most prolific of psalm-composers, Asaph's contribution was not forgotten: "King Hezekiah and his officials ordered the Levites to praise the Lord with the words of David and of Asaph the seer" (2 Chronicles 29:30). Obviously Asaph was regarded as more than just a temple musician and songwriter. He was also a seer, which is equivalent to calling him a prophet. Beyond having a skill with words, he saw deeply into the nature of God and faith.

In spite of Asaph's devotion to the temple and it services, the psalms he wrote recognize that rituals themselves are not enough to please God: "To the wicked, God says: 'What right have you to recite my laws or take my covenant on your lips?'" (Psalm 50:16). In fact, Asaph seems to question the worth of animal sacrifices, and certainly he questions whether God needs the sacrifices at all: "Every animal of the forest is mine, and the cattle on a thousand hills. . . . If I were hungry I would not tell you, for the world is mine, and all that is in it" (Psalm 50:10–12). Having seen (and smelled) many animals being sacrificed, Asaph must have looked forward to a time when true religion consisted more of the heart being committed to God.

CULTURAL INSIGHTS

Samaritan vs. Religious Professionals

One of the great stories in the Bible is Jesus' parable of the good Samaritan, found in Luke 10:25–37. Modern readers respond so warmly to the story that we forget how jarring it was to the original hearers. In the story of a man who is robbed, stripped, beaten and left for dead by the roadside, the two passersby who do nothing to help him are a priest and a Levite—in other words, religious "professionals" whom the parable's first hearers would have respected. Putting the story in modern terms, it is as if Jesus had spoken of a pastor and a teacher in a Christian school passing the man by.

Asaph's frequent presence in the temple must have made him conscious of how those who were rich but wicked would hypocritically participate in the worship, leading him to a crisis of faith: Why do the wicked and proud prosper? "This is what the wicked are like— always carefree, they increase in wealth. Surely in vain have I kept my heart pure; in vain have I washed my hands in innocence" (Psalm 73:12–13). This awareness leads to anger and resentment: "When my heart was grieved and my spirit embittered, I was senseless and ignorant; I was a brute beast before you" (Psalm 73:21–22). But from this, faith emerges: "Whom have I in heaven but you? And earth has nothing I desire besides you. My flesh and my heart may fail, but God is the strength of my heart and my portion forever" (Psalm 73:25–26).

God as the righteous Judge is the theme of several Asaph Psalms, notably 75: "To the arrogant I say, 'Boast no more,' and to the wicked, 'Do not lift up your horns. Do not lift your horns against heaven; do not speak with outstretched neck.' . . . it is God who judges: He brings one down, he exalts another" (Psalm 75:4–5, 7).

At times Asaph could sound like the prophet Amos, chiding the people for their injustice and neglect of the poor: "How long will you defend the unjust and show partiality to the wicked? Defend the cause of the weak and fatherless; maintain the rights of the poor and oppressed. Rescue the weak and needy; deliver them from the hand of the wicked" (Psalm 82:2–4).

Asaph's psalms prove that not all the priests and Levites in Israel were merely doing a job. Some were decent men like himself, spiritually sensitive to the point that they had doubts about the whole system of sacrifices. What a pity there were not more clergy like him.

JEREMIAH, IN STOCK

When the priest Pashhur son of Immer, the chief officer in the temple of the Lord, heard Jeremiah prophesying these things, he had Jeremiah the prophet beaten and put in the stocks at the Upper Gate of Benjamin at the Lord's temple. (Jeremiah 20:1–2)

Here we focus on the episode of Jeremiah's confrontation with the wicked priest Pashhur, a classic case of prophet versus priest. Remember from the early part of this chapter that a priest held his office for life, by virtue of his being descended from Israel's first high priest, Aaron. A prophet, on the other hand, was called by God, so he was truly "God's man," while priests were often not. Jeremiah's case is particularly interesting because he himself was a priest, but clearly one of better material than the corrupt Pashhur.

It is notable that the priest is referred to as "the chief officer in the house of the Lord" instead of "high priest" or "chief priest." In Jeremiah's view, Pashhur is just an "officer," a man doing a job, not a man who has any real concern for holiness or spirituality. While he ministers in "the house of the Lord"—the temple—he is far from being a man of God, as he proves by having poor Jeremiah put in the stocks.

What had Jeremiah done? He had preached an unwelcome message: The people had forsaken God, worshipped many false gods and shed innocent blood. Their punishment would be conquest by a foreign power, Babylon. To illustrate his point, Jeremiah broke an earthenware flask in the sight of the people. As he had broken the flask, so God would "break" Jerusalem and its faithless people.

But there was more to Pashhur's ire than this one sermon. Jeremiah had said many, many harsh things about the priests. "The prophets prophesy lies, the priests rule by their own authority, and my people love it this way. But what will you do in the end?" (Jeremiah 5:31). "From the least to the greatest, all are greedy for gain; prophets and priests alike, all practice deceit" (Jeremiah 6:13). Note that Jeremiah did not condemn only the priests but also the many false prophets. One of the difficulties in being a true prophet of the Lord was that there were so many false ones about, telling people what they wished to hear instead of what God said. But what would have rankled Pashhur was what Jeremiah said about the priests. And the priests had an advantage over the prophets: Priests held official positions no matter how they behaved.

So the priest had him put in stocks for a day—perhaps on the assumption that if Jeremiah used his flask as a visual aid, the sight of the prophet in stocks would also be a powerful visual aid. But Jeremiah was not cowed by his experience. When he was released, his anger burst loose on the priest: No longer would his name be Pashhur, but rather Terror on Every Side, for Pashhur would witness the conquest and looting of Jerusalem, and he would be taken as a captive to Babylon.

"Prophecy never had its origin in the will of man, but men spoke from God as they were carried along by the Holy Spirit" (2 Peter 1:21). Jeremiah was "carried along" by the Lord, and he got into trouble—often. Pashhur, as a priest, should have been deeply concerned for the fate of the nation, God's people, and as one who performed the rituals in the temple, he, of all people, should have been concerned that the people were also bowing down to pagan gods. But, as so often happened in the Old Testament, the divine message, the warning to repent, came not from the priests but from the prophets.

Jeremiah's prophecy came true, for Jerusalem was indeed conquered by the Babylonians, with many of the people carried off into exile. Presumably Pashhur was among them. Perhaps in exile, when he no longer had a temple to minister in, he had time to reflect on the words of Jeremiah.

THE LAST—AND GOOD RIDDANCE!

The high priest Ananias ordered those standing near Paul to strike him on the mouth. (Acts 23:2)

The high priest Ananias went down to Caesarea with some of the elders and a lawyer named Tertullus, and they brought their charges against Paul before the governor. (Acts 24:1)

We began this chapter by looking at Israel's first high priest Aaron, brother of Moses. We will end the chapter by looking at the last high priest mentioned in the Bible, Ananias, an utterly unworthy man very different from Aaron.

In other chapters we look at the shameful high priest Caiaphas, the man who condemned Jesus as a blasphemer and handed him over to Pontius Pilate. Later, in Acts, the same man persecuted Jesus' apostles for spreading the gospel. Caiaphas was deposed in AD 36, but the priests who came afterward were no better. One who is just as unspiritual and corrupt appears later in Acts, in the violent story of Paul's arrest in Jerusalem.

Having undertaken three missionary journeys, Paul had spread the faith to thousands of Gentiles (non-Jews). This pleased the Jews who were Christians but horrified the Jews who were not, so Paul had many enemies in Jerusalem, and when it was rumored that he had taken a Gentile into the temple—a capital crime—his enemies believed it. Had the Roman soldiers not intervened to prevent a riot, Paul would have been lynched by the mob. Hoping to get at the truth, the Roman commander had the Sanhedrin assemble, giving Paul a chance to state his case calmly before them.

The episode did not begin well. "Paul looked straight at the Sanhedrin and said, 'My brothers, I have fulfilled my duty to God in all good conscience to this day'" (Acts 23:1). This sounds innocent enough, but the high priest, Ananias, ordered his attendants to strike Paul on the mouth. Unlike Jesus, Paul did not endure this calmly: "Paul said to him, 'God will strike you, you whitewashed wall!'" Those standing close to Paul were horrified: How dare he speak that way to the high priest! "Paul replied, 'Brothers, I did not realize that he was the high priest.'" This episode puzzles readers: Did Paul have vision problems, and was he not able to recognize the priest? Or did he mean that he could not imagine that a man like Ananias could be high priest? The more likely meaning is that this meeting of the Sanhedrin had been called hurriedly, and the priest may not have had on his official garb, and so Paul would have assumed that the man ordering him to be hit could not have been the high priest.

But why did Ananias order that Paul be struck? Probably Paul's curt introduction—"my brothers"—was not considered servile enough. Note that when Peter had to defend himself before the Sanhedrin, he began "Rulers of the people, and elders" (Acts 4:8), and Stephen before the Sanhedrin began, "Brothers and fathers" (Acts 7:2). Ananias, with a high opinion of himself, would not have considered himself to be included in Paul's "my brothers."

History records that Ananias was one of the most corrupt men ever to hold the office, making himself rich by the Jewish people's tithes. He frequently had his enemies assassinated, and most of the Jews detested him for being openly pro-Roman. He was high priest from AD 47 to AD 59. He came to a bad end when the Jewish revolt broke out in AD 66; the anti-Roman Jews killed him after finding him hiding in an aqueduct. (How appropriate, a Roman puppet hiding out in a Roman-built aqueduct!) When Paul said, "God will strike you, you whitewashed wall!" he was unconsciously uttering a prophecy. And Paul may have been thinking of Jesus' reference to hypocrites as "whitewashed

CHARACTER CLOSE-UP ## Felix

The Roman historian Tacitus wrote that Antonius Felix carried out his duties "with all sorts of cruelty and lust," and that Felix "exercised the power of a king with the mind of a slave." He was in fact a freedman, meaning a former slave, but he had connections with the emperor Claudius that enabled him to rise to high office. While Felix was governor of Judea (from AD 52 to 59) there was frequent anti-Roman activity in the province, including the emergence of the sicarii, the "dagger men" who assassinated both Romans and pro-Roman Jews. Felix put down this activity with great ruthlessness, crucifying hundreds of rebels, which led to even more anti-Roman feeling.

A man of bad character, Felix had married into a family full of bad characters: the Herods. His wife was Drusilla, the daughter of Herod Agrippa I, the ruler who had executed the apostle James and jailed Peter. When she was sixteen, Felix, aided by a magician, stole her away from her husband and married her.

Poor Paul, falling into the hands of a greedy, corrupt priest (Ananias) *and* a greedy, immoral Roman official (Felix)!

tombs." Perhaps Paul was also aware that during his interrogation by the priest Annas, Caiaphas' father-in-law, Jesus had also been struck on the face (John 18:22).

Paul knew his rights: He was innocent until proven guilty, and this kind of physical abuse was not proper. Even so, he must have been aware that when the Sanhedrin had condemned Jesus, they had struck him and spit in his face.

This physical interruption gave Paul a chance to change tactics. Defending his honor might not sway this group. But he knew the group was not united. It had both Pharisees and Sadducees, who disagreed on many points. He turned this to his advantage. "My brothers, I am a Pharisee, the son of a Pharisee. I stand on trial because of my hope in the resurrection of the dead." This led to a ruckus, for whatever the Pharisees may have thought of him up to this point, they felt the need to side with one of their own. The Sadducees, which would have included the high priest and his minions, did not believe in a resurrection from the dead, and for the Pharisees—and Christians—it was one of the core beliefs. Paul had turned his enemies against each other.

The Sanhedrin, divided, became just as unruly as the Jerusalem mob in the temple courts. The Roman soldiers again feared for Paul's safety. So again, Paul had to be escorted out by soldiers and taken into the barracks.

Paul was not out of danger. Forty Jews swore an oath not to eat or drink until they had killed him. The high priest gave his approval to the plot. But Paul's nephew learned of the conspiracy and reported it to the Roman soldiers who were guarding Paul. The Romans realized Paul's presence in Jerusalem was leading to nothing but trouble, so they sent Paul off—under a heavily armed escort of four hundred seventy men—to the Roman governor Felix, in the port city of Caesarea. How ironic that Paul, raised as a devout Jew, must have felt relieved at leaving behind the holy city of Jerusalem—and as a Roman prisoner!

Though he was out of the reach of the lynch mob, Paul was not beyond the reach of the high priest. Ananias and his cronies traveled to Caesarea, bringing with them a trained *rhetor*, an eloquent lawyer named Tertullus, who began his accusations against Paul with disgustingly lavish praise of Felix. According to Tertullus, Felix had brought peace and reforms to Judea—words which must have provoked smirks among some of the Jews, who knew that "peace" often meant "killing Jews." Having lubricated the wheels, Tertullus identified Paul as a troublemaker, not just in Jerusalem but all over "the world" (meaning the Roman empire). This Paul was a leader in the "Nazarene sect," the name used by the Jews then and later to refer to the Christians. Worse, Paul had supposedly committed the unthinkable crime of trying to take a Gentile into the temple. The Jews who accompanied the orator then chimed in.

In response, Paul defended himself ably, making it clear he was no troublemaker. Since his story and the story spun by Tertullus were clearly in conflict, Felix had to wait for more information. Felix could have released Paul, for certainly Paul had committed no crime. But he kept him in custody, probably to pacify the Sanhedrin, since his actions as governor had earned their hostility.

Poor Paul was essentially a pawn in a political game played between Rome (Felix) and the Jewish priests. And yet, ironically, Felix was removed from his post anyway. The Jews and Gentiles in Caesarea had quarreled, and Felix's troops killed many of the Jewish leaders. Felix was replaced by the much more conscientious governor Festus, whom we meet in another chapter (Day 18).

Acts notes that Felix kept Paul in custody for two years, during which he hoped Paul or his friends would offer him a bribe—standard procedure for Roman officials hoping to line their pockets. Felix was as big a hypocrite as the priests, for he was posing as a fine example of Roman justice, a man who supposedly was looking out for the best interests of his subjects.

While Paul languished in prison, Judea had a dress rehearsal for the great Jewish revolt that would break out in AD 66. Felix had countless Jewish freedom fighters—Zealots—crucified, but in making martyrs, he further inflamed anti-Roman feeling. In a sense, Paul was the victim of Jewish Zealotry, because the hatred so many Jews felt for Rome was sometimes unleashed not just on the Romans but on any Jew who seemed remotely unpatriotic. As the apostle to the Gentiles, naturally Paul was hated.

And what about Ananias? As noted already, he was deposed from his office and killed when the Jewish revolt broke out—killed not by the Romans, with whom he had been an eager collaborator, but by Zealots who saw him not only as a Roman puppet but also as a corrupt, unspiritual man with no scruples. We can only imagine what the history of the Jews and Christians would have been like if the high priests of this period had been decent men of God instead of self-seeking rogues.

The high priesthood ended when the Romans destroyed the Jerusalem temple in AD 70. It was a tragedy for the Jews but not a loss for the Christians, who had come to view Jesus as the "heavenly high priest," a theme we will take up in the next chapter. Christians had also come to emphasize what theologians call "the priesthood of all believers," an idea stated beautifully in 1 Peter 2:6: "you are a chosen people, a royal priesthood, a holy nation, a people belonging to God." Peter was harking back to Exodus 19:6, where God told Moses, "you will be for me a kingdom of priests and a holy nation," words spoken before the office of priest had been created in Israel. The ideal—in Exodus and throughout the Bible—was that all God's people, not just its clergy, would be holy, committed to God, bringing blessings to the entire world.

PUTTING THE WORD TO WORK

1. Having read this chapter dealing with Israel's clergy, take a moment to pray for clergy that you know.

2. What do you think of Israel's hereditary priesthood? While the Bible makes it clear that there were many unworthy priests, would there have been disadvantages to having priests elected by the people—or appointed by the king?

3. This chapter has looked at some people, such as Jeremiah and Paul, who suffered at the hands of religious officials. Try to think of others—from elsewhere in this book, from the Bible, from history—who have suffered in this way. Try to imagine what it would be like, as a person of faith, to be persecuted by those who claim to share that faith.

4. Take a moment to reflect on what it means for you, personally, to be part of "a royal priesthood, a holy nation, a people belonging to God."

5. Given what you've read in this chapter, and elsewhere in the book, about Israel's priests, how do you respond now to the New Testament idea of Jesus as the "heavenly high priest" who mediates between us and God?

What If God Was One of Us?

THE HUMAN JESUS

The Bible often calls Jesus such lofty titles as "Lord" and "Christ" and "Son of God." His followers understood that he was a divine being, that he was "God with us." Yet he was also a human being, one who endured suffering and temptation as all humans do. In this chapter we will focus on the humanity of Jesus, taking a look at the term he used for himself (Son of Man) and two titles for him that are often neglected (servant of God and high priest). Along the way we will see the importance of having a Lord who has walked where we walked, someone able to sympathize with human weakness, a Lord who is not only Son of God but also a friend.

> **MEMORY VERSE**
>
> **The Son of Man did not come to be served, but to serve, and to give his life as a ransom for many.—Matthew 20:28**

KEY TERM FOR TODAY

Servant

Jesus was the "Suffering Servant" prophesied in the Old Testament, and he set his disciples an example: The road to glory is through service and humility. As servant, he set a new pattern for what "human" really means.

"HERE IS MY SERVANT"

Whoever wants to become great among you must be your servant . . . just as the Son of Man did not come to be served, but to serve, and to give his life as a ransom for many." (Matthew 20:26, 28)

Many followed him, and he healed all their sick, warning them not to tell who he was. This was to fulfill what was spoken through the prophet Isaiah: "Here is my servant whom I have chosen, the one I love, in whom I delight; I will put my Spirit on him, and he will proclaim justice to the nations." (Matthew 12:15–18)

The important word in this passage is "servant." Matthew 12 is quoting Isaiah 42:1–4, one of four passages in Isaiah known as the Servant Songs because they speak of a Suffering

Servant of God. The Gospels show that the first Christians took the Servant Songs to be prophecies of Jesus.

Before the time of Jesus, most Jews interpreted the Servant Songs as applying to Israel. A tiny nation surrounded by expansive empires, Israel often seemed to have no friend but God, for more often than not it suffered at the hands of some foreign power. Jews saw their land as a humble servant of God, enduring great sorrows while the mighty pagan empires around them seemed to grow and prosper.

But the New Testament does not give the impression that Israel—the Jews collectively—was God's servant. On the contrary, the lion's share of Israelites seemed mired in their legalism and rituals. The leaders, the corrupt priests in Jerusalem, were hardly suffering—they lived quite well, in fact, and they were hardly the models of righteousness that Isaiah spoke of. The idea persisted of a "righteous remnant" among the Jews, people who were still faithful to God. But the first Christians narrowed the focus: The Servant was one righteous person, Jesus.

The apostles perceived Jesus as a servant after the fact—that is, prior to his crucifixion and resurrection, they did not see him as the Suffering Servant, and almost certainly they would not have followed him if they had known all the tribulations that lay ahead. Yet constantly he was teaching, both by word and example, that the way of humility and servanthood was the path to God. John 13 tells the story of him washing his own disciples' feet, doing a task that was normally the duty of the lowliest household servant. Peter protests, and understandably: A master did not normally lower himself in this way. But Jesus insists. "You call me 'Teacher' and 'Lord,' and rightly so, for that is what I am. Now that I, your Lord and Teacher, have washed your feet, you also should wash one another's feet. I have set you an example that you should do as I have done for you" (John 13:13–15). Within a few hours of this, the disciples would learn that being God's servant involved more than footwashing: For Jesus it would mean mockery, flogging and crucifixion. He had prophesied that he would die in Jerusalem—and Peter had protested loudly. But the resurrection proved that what Jesus had told them was true, that the way of suffering and degradation was also the way to glory and exaltation.

In one sense, the Bible comes full circle, from the beginning with a single man (Adam), to the fulfillment through another single man (Jesus). From Adam springs the entire human race, but Adam, who is made in God's image, falls into sin. The original man is a failure, but then the focus widens to a one tribe-nation (Israel), which also proves to be a moral failure. So the focus narrows from Israel to a righteous remnant of Israelites, and then from the remnant to one righteous individual, Christ.

"Here is my servant, whom I uphold, my chosen one in whom I delight; I will put my Spirit on him and he will bring justice to the nations" (Isaiah 42:1). Compare this to the words God spoke at Jesus' baptism: "This is my Son, whom I love; with him I am well pleased" (Matthew 3:17). The Gospels record that the Spirit descended upon Jesus at that time—a fulfillment of "I will put my Spirit on him." It may well be that, at the baptism, Jesus himself became conscious of his being God's servant.

Matthew, who quoted the Old Testament constantly, saw other occurrences in Jesus' life as fulfillments of the Servant Songs: "When evening came, many who were demon-possessed were brought to him, and he drove out the spirits with a word and healed all the sick. This was to fulfill what was spoken through the prophet Isaiah: 'He took up our infirmities and carried our diseases'" (Matthew 8:16–17, quoting Isaiah 53:4). The

---

CULTURAL INSIGHTS

Isaiah and Handel

The Isaiah passages about the Suffering Servant of God are often called the Servant Songs. Some of them are indeed songs, for they were set to some memorable and frequently performed music. One of the world's musical masterpieces, George Frideric Handel's choral work *Messiah*, is a selection of Bible passages set to music, and among them are verses from the Servant Songs, prophecies of the humiliation the servant endures. Although *Messiah* is usually presented around Christmastime, the Isaiah passages allude to the crucifixion, so parts of *Messiah* are in fact appropriate for Holy Week.

The quotations here are from the King James Version, which is used in *Messiah*.

He is despised and rejected of men; a man of sorrows, and acquainted with grief. (Isaiah 53:3)

I gave my back to the smiters, and my cheeks to them that plucked off the hair: I hid not my face from shame and spitting. (Isaiah 50:6)

Surely he hath borne our griefs, and carried our sorrows: yet we did esteem him stricken, smitten of God, and afflicted. (Isaiah 53:4)

He was wounded for our transgressions, he was bruised for our iniquities: the chastisement of our peace was upon him; and with his stripes we are healed. (Isaiah 53:5)

All we like sheep have gone astray; we have turned every one to his own way; and the Lord hath laid on him the iniquity of us all. (Isaiah 53:6)

He was cut off out of the land of the living: for the transgression of my people was he stricken. (Isaiah 53:8)

The Servant Songs and Missions

Were the Jews active as missionaries? Some were, because they saw their faith as being the one true religion, and though they believed the Jews were God's chosen people, they also believed that he had chosen them to bless the entire world. This is reflected in one of Isaiah's Servant Songs: "It is too small a thing for you to be my servant to restore the tribes of Jacob and bring back those of Israel I have kept. I will also make you a light for the Gentiles, that you may bring my salvation to the ends of the earth" (Isaiah 49:6). Most Jews believed the "servant" Isaiah spoke of was Israel—all Jews, collectively.

The first Christians, of course, believed the "servant" was Jesus, and that it was their mission to be a "light for the Gentiles" by spreading the gospel. Acts 13 tells the story of missionary companions Paul and Barnabas in the city of Antioch. Following their usual pattern, the two men, both Jews, attempt to preach in the local synagogue and make Christians of the Jews there. As usual, they were met with hostility by most of the Jews, which provoked Paul to quote from Isaiah: "This is what the Lord has commanded us: `I have made you a light for the Gentiles, that you may bring salvation to the ends of the earth'" (Acts 13:47). This angered the Jews even more, but "when the Gentiles heard this, they were glad and honored the word of the Lord; and all who were appointed for eternal life believed. . . . And the disciples were filled with joy and with the Holy Spirit" (Acts 13:48, 52).

other Gospels also quoted the Servant Songs: "They crucified two robbers with him, one on his right and one on his left. And the Scripture was fulfilled, which says, 'He was counted with the lawless ones'" (Mark 15:27–28, quoting Isaiah 53:12).

One person who knew the Servant intimately was Peter. Despite his frequent failings as a disciple, Peter became a major figure in the early church, and like his fellow believers, he saw his Master as the Servant prophesied by Isaiah. We see this in a passage from his first epistle: "If you suffer for doing good and you endure it, this is commendable before God. To this you were called, because Christ suffered for you, leaving you an example, that you should follow in his steps. 'He committed no sin, and no deceit was found in his mouth.' When they hurled their insults at him, he did not retaliate; when he suffered, he made no threats. Instead, he entrusted himself to him who judges justly. He himself bore our sins in his body on the tree, so that we might die to sins and live for righteousness; 'by his wounds you have been healed.' For you were like sheep going astray, but now you have returned to the Shepherd and Overseer of your souls" (1 Peter 2:20–25). Here Peter quotes Isaiah 53 more than once. Bear in mind that this is the same Peter who protested when his Master came in the role of servant to wash his feet. Clearly Peter had grown in his spiritual perception.

In other parts of the New Testament, Isaiah is not quoted directly but was clearly in the writer's mind, as in Hebrews 9:28: "Christ was sacrificed once to take away the sins of many people." There is no doubt the author had in mind Isaiah 53:12: "For he bore the sin of many, and made intercession for the transgressors."

As the apostles spread the gospel in Acts, they preach that the Suffering Servant has now been glorified. "The God of Abraham, Isaac and Jacob, the God of our fathers, has glorified his servant Jesus. . . . When God raised up his servant, he sent him first to you to bless you by turning each of you from your wicked ways" (Acts 3:13, 26). "Herod and Pontius Pilate met together with the Gentiles and the people of Israel in this city to conspire against [God's] holy servant Jesus" (Acts 4:27)—the people with power conspired to destroy the humble servant of God, but God had the last word, for he exalted the one who had humbled himself utterly. Jesus' life was an illustration of his own words: "Whoever humbles himself will be exalted" (Matthew 23:12). Paul commended the servant mentality: "Your attitude should be the same as that of Christ Jesus: Who, being in very nature God, did not consider equality with God something to be grasped, but made himself nothing, taking the very nature of a servant, being made in human likeness" (Philippians 2:5–7).

"GET SOME REST, FRIENDS"

The apostles gathered around Jesus and reported to him all they had done and taught. Then, because so many people were coming and going that they did not even have a chance to eat, he said to them, "Come with me by yourselves to a quiet place and get some rest." So they went away by themselves in a boat to a solitary place. (Mark 6:30–32)

I no longer call you servants, because a servant does not know his master's business. Instead, I have called you friends, for everything that I learned from my Father I have made known to you. (John 15:15)

While I was with them, I protected them and kept them safe by that name you gave me. None has been lost except the one doomed to destruction so that Scripture would be fulfilled. (John 17:12)

We saw in the previous section that the first Christians saw Jesus as the Suffering Servant prophesied in the Old Testament. In this section we will look at how he was servant to his own followers, the men who called him "Master" and "Rabbi."

While the Gospels show almost ceaseless activity on the part of Jesus, the passage from Mark 6 shows that there were times of needed rest. In this case, however, the rest could not be had, so insistent were the people, who chose to walk ahead of him, and the disciples, who were crossing the lake in a boat. Jesus orders a brief retreat from the world, to a "solitary place."

Note that there is a certain tension in the Gospels: Following Jesus does not mean life on a featherbed. He demands total commitment. "If anyone would come after me, he must deny himself and take up his cross and follow me" (Matthew 16:24). But at the same time, Jesus is not some sadistic drill sergeant, oblivious to the disciples' needs. He loves them, and on this occasion (and, we can only assume, on other occasions as well) he orders a break in the constant activity. They are human. Jesus understands this.

The two verses from John's Gospel are from the very long passage, running from John 14–17, that is Jesus' last address to the disciples, just before his arrest. Jesus understands the men's weakness. He knows one of them has already arranged to betray him to the authorities. He also knows that at the time he is arrested, the other disciples will flee in panic. He even knows that the most devoted of them, Peter, the one so sure of his own steadfastness, will three times deny even knowing Jesus. Most of us might be inclined to feel disgust in such a situation, thinking of what a bunch of disloyal ingrates these men were. Indeed, as the Gospels show, the disciples griped and complained constantly—and they misunderstood Jesus' teachings much more often than they understood them.

Their fickleness makes this long passage in John even more touching. For all their faults, Jesus loves his disciples. In their three years together, he has played the role of master, they of disciples and also servants. But before he addresses them he has washed their feet, putting himself in the role of servant. This shocked them. Now he says something else that is jarring: They are no longer servants but "friends." In Jesus' day, disciples did not think of themselves as "friends" of their master, since that would imply equality. When he calls the men "friends," Jesus is giving them a social "promotion"—even though within a matter of hours they will prove to be frightened and disloyal friends. (A friend "up to a point" is no friend at all.) But Jesus is thinking ahead, to the time after his resurrection, when the men will prove to have backbones will be willing to spread the gospel far and wide, speaking out boldly even when it entails persecution.

The disciples at this point are not fully aware of who Jesus is. At one point Peter professed that Jesus was the "Christ, the Son of the living God." But the group doesn't know Jesus as a divine being, not fully able to grasp his words, "I and the Father are one." When Jesus calls them "friends," they are becoming "friends of God." The Old Testament mentions only two men who were considered "friends" of God: the patriarch Abraham and the great lawgiver Moses (Exodus 33:11, Isaiah 41:8). In fact, "the Lord would speak to Moses face to face, as a man speaks with his friend." The disciples are truly privileged characters, daily speaking face-to-face with the Holy One, though they are slow to realize it.

John 17 is known as the "high priestly prayer" of Jesus because Jesus puts himself in the role of a priest, praying for his people—not just the disciples who are present then but future generations of believers as well. "My prayer is not for them alone. I pray also for those who will believe in me through their message, that all of them may be one, Father, just as you are in me and I am in you. May they also be in us so that the world may believe that you have sent me" (John 17:20–21). Jesus knows that within a matter of hours he will be nailed to a cross, serving as the ultimate sacrifice for humankind. Here he is the priest, praying to God before making the sacrifice.

We can well imagine the priests of the New Testament going through the motions of offering prayers and sacrifices in the temple, while all the time looking down on the people, referring to them as a "mob" that is "cursed" (John 7:49). But Jesus is the true high priest, the one chosen by God, and he genuinely cares for his followers. Jesus says to his Father, "I have made you known to them, and will continue to make you known in order that the love you have for me may be in them and that I myself may be in them" (John 17:26). This is what being "friends" of Jesus is all about: sharing in the deep love that Jesus and the Father shared.

As always, Jesus' words matched his actions. He had called the disciples "friends" and would shortly prove himself. "Greater love has no one than this, that he lay down his life for his friends" (John 15:13).

"THE MAN"—AND SOMETHING MORE

In my vision at night I looked, and there before me was one like a son of man, coming with the clouds of heaven. He approached the Ancient of Days and was led into his presence. (Daniel 7:13)

Foxes have holes and birds of the air have nests, but the Son of Man has no place to lay his head. (Matthew 8:20)

The Son of Man is going to come in his Father's glory with his angels, and then he will reward each person according to what he has done. (Matthew 16:27)

Based on the New Testament, Christians believe that Jesus of Nazareth was, in some indefinable way, both divine and human. Pastors often explain to the congregations that the title "Son of God" speaks of Jesus' divine nature, while "Son of Man" speaks of his human nature. This is an interesting and neat way of explaining the New Testament—but, unfortunately, it's not quite accurate.

To begin this section, consider how the Bible uses "son of." To the Jewish mind, in biblical times, "son of the lie" meant "liar," "son of wealth" meant "wealthy man," "son of sin" meant "sinner," and so on. "Son of man" (*ben-adam* in Hebrew, *bar-nasha* in Aramaic) meant simply "man." To call oneself *ben-adam*—"son of man" and also "son of Adam"—was to say "man" or "human being." Jesus, speaking his native tongue of Aramaic, called himself *bar-nasha* many, many times. It is clearly the name and title he uses for himself—and, curiously, no one else ever uses it to refer to him. No one ever asks him to explain what he means by "Son of Man," so we can assume people knew (or thought they knew) what he meant.[1]

Did his listeners think that he was just calling himself a man? Or did they connect him with the vision of the future in Daniel 7:13–14: "In my vision at night I looked, and there before me was one like a son of man, coming with the clouds of heaven. He approached the Ancient of Days and was led into his presence. He was given authority, glory and sovereign power; all peoples, nations and men of every language worshiped him. His dominion is an everlasting dominion that will not pass away, and his kingdom is one that will never be destroyed"? In this passage, the "Ancient of Days" is, of course, God. This sounds like a prophecy of the Messiah, and many Jews of Jesus' time interpreted it that way. The "son of man" in Daniel is obviously more than just a man—he is God's Chosen One.

It is clear that when Jesus referred to himself as "Son of Man" that he did not just mean a man. Consider his words in John 3:13: "No one has ever gone into heaven except the one who came from heaven—the Son of Man." Also consider his prophecy of the end times: "At that time the sign of the Son of Man will appear in the sky, and all the nations of the earth will mourn. They will see the Son of Man coming on the clouds of the sky, with power and great glory" (Matthew 24:30).

Jesus may have intended a double meaning. He would not call himself Christ or Messiah, of course, since that title had political connotations. The Messiah was expected to be a powerful political figure, but "Son of Man" is another way of saying "average guy" or "John Doe" or even "nobody." By calling himself Son of Man, it was a way of saying he was just a man while also giving a hint of the meaning of the cosmic figure of Daniel 7. In his face-off with the high priest Caiaphas in Matthew 26:64, obviously he let the cat out of the bag: he wasn't just a man anymore but the end-time figure of Daniel's vision—which led to his being condemned as a blasphemer. "In the future you will see the Son of Man sitting at the right hand of the Mighty One and coming on the clouds of heaven."

---

[1] Most Bible translations capitalize "Son of Man" when spoken by Jesus, the idea being that all titles of Jesus (such as Son of God, Christ, Savior) should be capped. When "son of man" occurs in the Old Testament, and means simply "a man," it is not capped.

So it is written: "The first man Adam became a living being"; the last Adam, a life-giving spirit. . . . And just as we have borne the likeness of the earthly man, so shall we bear the likeness of the man from heaven. (1 Corinthians 15:45, 49)

As already stated, "Son of Man" was Jesus' self-designation. His disciples did not call him that, nor is he referred to by that name in the New Testament epistles. The one occasion on which the title was used by someone else was by the martyr Stephen, just before he was stoned: "I see the heavens opened and the Son of Man standing at the right hand of God" (Acts 7:56).

Though the title "Son of Man" is missing from the epistles, a related idea is there: Jesus as the second Adam. The first Adam, made in the image of God, sinned through pride and arrogance. He was not content to be what God made him—the "image" and "likeness" of God; instead, he wanted to be a god himself. Jesus as the "second Adam" reversed what Adam did. Satan tempted both Adam and Jesus. Adam failed the test; Jesus did not. Instead of showing arrogance, Jesus the Son of God humbled himself, living and suffering as a human being. Paul commends this humility in a famous passage: "Your attitude should be the same as that of Christ Jesus: Who, being in very nature God, did not consider equality with God something to be grasped, but made himself nothing, taking the very nature of a servant, being made in human likeness. And being found in appearance as a man, he humbled himself and became obedient to death—even death on a cross! Therefore God exalted him to the highest place and gave him the name that is above every name" (Philippians 2:5–9). In other words, the original Adam tried to exalt himself and ended up humiliated, while the second Adam humbled himself and ended up exalted—a key idea among the first Christians. Jesus himself taught this—and followed his own teaching: "Whoever exalts himself will be humbled, and whoever humbles himself will be exalted" (Matthew 23:12).

Paul urged Christians to model themselves on the new Adam, not the old one: "You have taken off your old self with its practices and have put on the new self, which is being renewed in knowledge in the image of its Creator" (Colossians 3:9–10). The word here is literally "man," not "self."

Jesus, the Son of man, the second Adam, is man as he *ought* to be. One of the aims of God living as a

> **DID YOU KNOW?**
>
> Luke's genealogy of Jesus traces his ancestry backward all the way to Adam. The genealogy ends with "the son of Seth, the son of Adam, the son of God." Luke must have intended his readers to notice the connection: Jesus and Adam are both "sons of God," but Adam sinned while Jesus did not.

Jesus and (Part of) Adam in Art

An old legend says that Jesus was crucified on the same spot on which Adam fell into sin—or, in another version of the legend, on Adam's grave. The idea is that the first Adam disobeyed God and brought sin and death into the world, while the second Adam, Jesus, obeyed God fully and brought salvation. When you see a painting of the crucifixion and notice a skull at the bottom of the cross, be aware that the artist intended this to be the skull of Adam, a reminder that the second Adam was undoing the work of the first. (And remember that the name of the site of the crucifixion, Golgotha, means "skull.") Also be aware that in the New Testament, Jesus' cross is often referred to as a "tree." The writers may have intended us to make this connection: Adam sinned when he ate the fruit of the forbidden tree, and Jesus saves us from sin through his death on the "tree."

human being on earth is that, through Jesus, he goes beyond the boundaries of what we normally mean by "human," and in Jesus showed what it really means. When people talk about Jesus' human nature, they refer to him sleeping, eating, feeling physical pain, feeling anger—all these are human, of course, but they are also part of animals' nature. "Jesus wept" is often held up as an example of Jesus' humanity, which it is. But Jesus forgiving his enemies from the cross is a better example. How did God intend human beings to live? Like animals—eating, sleeping, reproducing, fighting? Or were there higher possibilities that God had in mind when he created Adam? Jesus showed us that human nature could involve doing things animals cannot do, such as forgiving—and loving—one's enemies. Adam was created in the image of God but fell into sin. Jesus did not: He is the true "image of God," so his life shows what God intended human life to be.

THE RIGHT JUDGE

We must all appear before the judgment seat of Christ, that each one may receive what is due him for the things done while in the body, whether good or bad. (2 Corinthians 5:10).

My judgment is just, for I seek not to please myself but him who sent me. (John 5:30)

"Judgmental" is a nasty word in our day. Jesus was, as we see clearly in the Gospels, a man of infinite love and compassion—and yet, amazingly, judgmental also. He spoke often about God's love for man—and the coming Last Judgment. Some people see this as inconsistent, or they think the New Testament passages dealing with divine judgment were put there by the writers and were not the words of Jesus himself. But we have to take the New Testament as is and believe that when the Gospels report Jesus speaking of judgment, they are just as accurate as when he speaks of God's love.

One of the oldest Christian creeds, the Apostles' Creed, contains the statement: "He shall come to judge the living and the dead." Paul refers to the "judgment seat of Christ" (2 Corinthians 5:10) and calls Jesus the "righteous judge" (2 Timothy 4:8). Acts 10:42 refers to him as "Judge of the living and the dead," and the same phrase is used in 1 Peter 4:5. In John 5:27 Jesus himself states that he has been given authority by God to judge because he is the Son of Man. Jesus said bluntly that "men will have to give account on the day of judgment for every careless word they have spoken" (Matthew 12:36). And one of Jesus' greatest parables, the sheep and the goats, opens with these words: "When the Son of Man comes in his glory, and all the angels with him, he will sit on his throne in heavenly glory. All the nations will be gathered before him, and he will separate the people one from another as a shepherd separates the sheep from the goats" (Matthew 25:31–32).

Was Jesus being inconsistent? Didn't he say, in the Sermon on the Mount, "Do not judge, or you too will be judged"? (Matthew 7:1). Indeed. And this is where the "Son of Man" title seems to apply so well. Jesus lived as human beings do, he immersed himself in the real world of work and everyday life. Jesus has been where we are. So who better to judge people fairly? A poor man having his case tried in court might wonder if the judge had lived a sheltered life, gone to elite schools, married well, lived in a fine house; could that judge possibly sympathize with a defendant from the wrong side of the tracks? Possibly. But the defendant might feel better knowing the judge *did* know what it was like on the other side of the tracks.

Jesus did. He faced temptation as all human beings do, but he did not give in to it. He is, according to Hebrews 4:15, "one who has been tempted in every way, just as we are—yet was without sin." The human race faces a Judge who has been in our shoes. Jesus has the divine, God's-eye view of our lives—but also the human view. There could be no fairer judge. When he told his listeners, "Do not judge," he knew how biased people can be, especially in favor of themselves. He himself is competent to judge.

In spite of the inevitability of divine judgment, the New Testament is full not of gloom but of joy. Jesus, the Son of Man, the second Adam, is the path to salvation. The one who judges is the one who saves from judgment.

He had to be made like his brothers in every way, in order that he might become a merciful and faithful high priest in service to God, and that he might make atonement for the sins of the people. (Hebrews 2:17)

He has become a high priest forever, in the order of Melchizedek. (Hebrews 6:20)

Such a high priest meets our need—one who is holy, blameless, pure, set apart from sinners, exalted above the heavens. (Hebrews 7:26)

The Letter to the Hebrews is unique in many respects, one being that it presents Jesus as the "heavenly high priest." We see in the Gospels and Acts that the Jews' high priests in the New Testament period were a sorry lot. Caiaphas condemned Jesus to death, and his father-in-law Annas, a former high priest, concurred. In Acts the priests persecute the apostles and send off Saul to harass Christians. The New Testament doesn't distort the picture, for Jewish writers agree that the Jerusalem priesthood was utterly corrupt in Jesus' day, the priests being wealthy and unspiritual.

They probably had no clue that their days were numbered, although Jesus certainly did, for he prophesied the destruction of Jerusalem, including the temple. The prophecy was fulfilled in AD 70, when a Jewish revolt against Rome led to the Romans destroying the magnificent temple. With the temple gone, the priesthood went too. Spiritually, this was a case of "Good riddance!"

We don't know if the Letter to the Hebrews was written before or after the temple was destroyed, but it does not refer to the priest serving in the temple. Rather, it refers to the tabernacle, the large tent that was the Israelites' worship center until the temple was built. Of course, the tabernacle no longer existed either, but Hebrews is not speaking of a material structure. Rather, it imagines the tabernacle as heaven, where Jesus, as high priest, offers up a perfect sacrifice—himself.

Remember that a priest was thought of as a kind of middleman between man and God. He represented the people to God, and God to the people. He offered up sacrifices to atone for the people's sins—and for his own, because priests were human and committed sins. But the New Testament sees Jesus as being sinless, as perfect. As high priest in heaven, he can offer up a sacrifice for man's sins, but not for any sins of his own. He is, as the letter says, "blameless, pure, set apart from sinners, exalted above the heavens."

But he is not out of touch with human weakness—far from it. He is, according to Hebrews 4:15, "one who has been tempted in every way, just as we are—yet was without sin." And "he had to be made like his brothers in every way, in order that he might become a merciful and faithful high priest." Jesus is one of us, yet also greater.

Growing Jesus

One of the early heresies among Christians was Docetism, the belief that Jesus only appeared to be human but was really a phantom. When he appeared to show emotion or suffer, this was a matter of the phantom going through the motions. Docetism had its roots in Greek and Roman philosophy and the notion that gods were so far removed from humanity that no divine being could genuinely suffer.

Obviously this is not the teaching of the New Testament. Jesus is depicted as the Son of God—but also fully human. The Letter to the Hebrews emphasizes this strongly, observing that Jesus experienced temptation and suffered as all humans do. Thus he is not some aloof, distant deity who cannot sympathize with human weakness. Hebrews also observes that Jesus "learned obedience from what he suffered" (Hebrews 5:8). This is in keeping with Luke 2:52: "Jesus grew in wisdom and stature, and in favor with God and men." In other words, Jesus wasn't born an adult. We often think of the infant Jesus in the manger and the adult Jesus on the cross and forget all the years in between. Jesus, being human, had to grow—physically, mentally, morally. The fact that he "learned obedience from what he suffered" tells us that his education was not even complete when he reached adulthood: The persecution he endured as he ministered was part of his learning.

In the garden of Gethsemane, knowing he was about to be arrested and killed, "being in anguish, he prayed more earnestly, and his sweat was like drops of blood falling to the ground" (Luke 22:44). No man wants to die an agonizing death by crucifixion. He was not some phantom going through the motions of anguish, nor was he facing the ordeal like some philosopher who accepts death as a natural part of life. This was a young man who had, like all humans, grown from fetus to child to youth to adult, constantly changing physically and mentally. This was Jesus the human being.

Did Jesus, in his days on earth, see himself as a high priest? We can be fairly certain that he did. In his fateful encounter with the high priest Caiaphas, he said, "In the future you will see the Son of Man sitting at the right hand of the Mighty One and coming on the clouds of heaven" (Matthew 26:64). Caiaphas was an unspiritual man, but he knew Jesus was referring to Psalm 110: "The Lord says to my Lord: 'Sit at my right hand until I make your enemies a footstool for your feet.' . . . The Lord has sworn and will not change his mind: 'You are a priest forever, in the order of Melchizedek.'" Jesus saw himself as the one at the right hand of God, a priest forever. Melchizedek was the priest in Genesis who blessed Abraham. The Letter to the Hebrews contrasts Melchizedek—"a priest forever"—with the earthly priesthood, the descendants of Moses' brother Aaron. That priesthood ceased to function when the temple was destroyed. The heavenly priesthood "in the order of Melchizedek" endures forever because the one perfect priest and perfect sacrifice, Jesus, is in heaven.

Back to Jesus and Caiaphas: In his statement about sitting at the right hand of God, Jesus was in effect telling Caiaphas that his own priesthood was heavenly, not earthly—just as he had told Pilate that his "kingdom" was not of this world. Neither of these two power figures could have comprehended his meaning, of course. For Pilate, the only kind of kingdom was "of this world," and Caiaphas could not have imagined a heavenly priesthood.

The earthly priesthood of the Jews would come to a dramatic end shortly after this meeting, when the temple was destroyed. But for Christians there was no need to be concerned about the absence of priests and sacrifices. In fact, they would never again need to give a thought to purchasing an animal to sacrifice, for the old system was at an end. "Unlike the other high priests, he does not need to offer sacrifices day after day, first for his own sins, and then for the sins of the people. He sacrificed for their sins once for all when he offered himself… we have been made holy through the sacrifice of the body of Jesus Christ once for all" (Hebrews 7:27, 10:10).

Think back to the dramatic story of Jesus' crucifixion. One of the details, too often overlooked, is this: "At that moment the curtain of the temple was torn in two from top to bottom" (Matthew 27:51). This refers to the enormous, heavy curtain that closed off the section known as the Holy of Holies, the place where only the Jews' high priest could enter. It is obviously God who tears the curtain in two, signaling that the old priesthood—typified by the villainous Caiaphas, who condemned God's Son to death—is ended. Humankind's access to God is not through a priest or temple but through Jesus, God's man, who lived on earth as a fully human being and sympathizes with frail human beings.

PUTTING THE WORD TO WORK

1. Today, and in the days ahead, take to heart the Bible's image of Jesus as a servant, and try to be a servant to those you meet.

2. The first Christians thought of Jesus as both "Lord" and "servant." Do you see this as a contradiction? How can you put the two ideas together?

3. How does it affect you to read the verse in which Jesus calls his disciples "friends"? In what ways can being a friend of Jesus affect your thoughts and actions?

4. "Son of Man" was the title Jesus used for himself constantly. It simply means "human being," yet Jesus clearly meant more by it. How do you respond to Paul's teaching that Jesus was the second Adam, showing us what it truly means to be a human being?

5. The Letter to the Hebrews shows Jesus as a heavenly priest who has experienced human weakness and can sympathize with us. The next time you experience temptation or face any difficult situation, think of Jesus' humanness.

Rebels from the First

As the Bible sees human beings, they are never indifferent to God. They are either actively obedient to him or, more often, actively disobedient. God reveals his will—and his love—to people, and they make a choice: obey or resist. This is not a matter of a tyrannical master wanting people to be groveling slaves. Rather, God is a compassionate Father, whose guidance leads to the best kind of life, while rebellion only leads to trouble. The pattern of rebellion is set all the way back in Eden.

KEY TERM FOR TODAY

Rebel

In revealing God as a loving Father, the Bible presents human sin and suffering as the result of foolish and selfish rebellion against divine authority.

THE "BE LIKE GODS" PROPOSAL

The man and his wife heard the sound of the Lord God as he was walking in the garden in the cool of the day, and they hid from the Lord God among the trees of the garden. (Genesis 3:8)

Your first father sinned. (Isaiah 43:27)

We are well into the twenty-first century, and yet the old debate—God or evolution?—continues. The debate will never be settled for the obvious reason that people of faith will continue to believe that the universe did not just happen. Even if evolution were true, God would be behind it all, and God intended mankind to be distinctive from other living things, "in the image of God."

And man is most definitely distinct from everything else in creation. In Genesis 1, God brings things into being with a mere statement: "Let there be . . ." But a change occurs with the creation of man: "Let us make man." Man isn't like the sun, moon, stars, earth, plants and animals. Three times, for emphasis, Genesis says man is "in the image of God." And though man is taken from the earth, God breathes into man the breath of life, which is not true for the animals. Being made from the ground, man is linked with the rest of creation, but the breath from God also sets him apart from it.

Like all the rest of creation, man is called "good" by God. This sets the Old Testament religion apart from all other ancient religions, which gave very little thought to creation. Most of the religions had some colorful (usually sexual and violent) stories about how the earth came into being, but such stories were for amusement more than for belief. In some of those religions, there is no beginning at all, just an earth that always existed.

But in Genesis there is a sense of purpose: God made the universe, called it "good," and gave his distinctive creature—man—dominion over all of it. He gives the man a task: name the animals, with naming being a sign that the man is superior to them. But among the animals there is none that is a suitable companion for man. So, according to Genesis, the man falls into a deep sleep, and God makes from man's own flesh a suitable companion, the woman. The Hebrew word translated "rib" in Genesis is almost always translated "side" elsewhere. The meaning is that woman is not taken from man's head, which would suggest superiority, or his legs or feet, which would suggest inferiority. And although, later in the Old Testament, some of the men had more than one wife, it is clear in Genesis that God's intention for the human race was monogamy—one man and one woman.

The two were given a task: tend the garden, which had the name Eden, "pleasure." The Hebrew word translated "tend" actually means "guard." Guard from what? Genesis doesn't tell us, but the impression is that there is some danger outside the garden. The garden of Eden is not the entire world but a sheltered part of it—presumably there is jungle or wilderness beyond. The ancient Israelites did not think of wilderness the way we do, as an unspoiled environment to admire. A wilderness was a desolate, threatening region, whereas a garden was a place planted—by God, in this case—for man's benefit

CHARACTERS AT LARGE   ## Adam and Eve in Literature

It does no credit to the human imagination that a very serious story—man's rebellion against God—has usually been treated comically in books and on stage. One grand exception to this is *Paradise Lost*, John Milton's epic poem, which covers not only the Eden story but also the rebellion of Satan and the demons against God. But the story of Adam and Eve has more often been treated comedically, such as in Mark Twain's wry *Diary of Adam and Eve*, which served as the basis of a Broadway musical, *The Apple Tree*. Playwright Arthur Miller, famous for his glum *Death of a Salesman*, wrote the comedy *The Creation of the World and Other Business*—which was not a success. Stephen Schwartz, who wrote the popular play *Godspell*, also wrote *Children of Eden*, a musical comedy based on Genesis.

and pleasure. God saw that the garden was irrigated by four rivers. Presumably the world outside the garden was not so lush.

The man and woman were not idling away their time like a permanent vacation. They had to tend and guard the garden, but it was pleasant labor, not backbreaking, sweaty toil. That would change.

It is interesting that there is no religion in Eden. Man is not told to do anything, religiously speaking—not offer up sacrifices, not bow or pray to God, not tithe. He is simply told to "tend" the garden—and avoid the tree of knowledge. The man and woman lived under a minimum of rules. They should have been perfectly content.

In one sense, the creation of man and his time in Eden is a period of probation. Will Adam exist in a state of happy and loving obedience to God and of harmony with his wife—or not?

Enter the serpent, or snake. In Genesis 3, he is not represented as evil, although people later understood that the snake was merely a disguise for Satan. What is forgotten when people read the story today is that Adam and Eve were told to have dominion over the animals, and giving heed to one of them—even a clever one that could talk— was a matter of a superior giving undue attention to an inferior.

The snake spoke to Eve while she was alone. God had made man and woman to be helpmates to each other, and presumably the two together might have resisted the snake. But the snake found her alone, and raised the question: "Did God really say, 'You must not eat from any tree in the garden'?" The form of the question is revealing:

CULTURAL INSIGHTS

"Image of God" in the New Testament

Human sin is referred to again and again in the Bible, but the Bible authors never completely forgot that man was made, as Genesis 1:26–27 says, "in God's image." God gave life to all other living things, but man was special, made to be "like" God. This image was not physical, since God is an invisible spirit, but a matter of mind, will, emotion—what we normally call a "soul" as opposed to existing only to eat, sleep and reproduce. Man, unlike animals, has a spiritual and moral nature. He can sin—which is exactly what happens in Genesis 3. Sin touches all of human life, but never is the image of God completely erased.

Part of the New Testament message is that the relationship with God can be restored and we can be more like God—the whole meaning of "image." Paul urged Christians to "put on the new man which was created according to God, in righteousness and true holiness" (Ephesians 4:24). In Colossians 3:10 he refers to "the new man who is renewed in knowledge according to the image of Him who created him."

the snake implies that God is holding something back. God is not really good at all, but a killjoy. "The woman said to the serpent, 'We may eat fruit from the trees in the garden, but God did say, 'You must not eat fruit from the tree that is in the middle of the garden, and you must not touch it, or you will die.'" The snake has already misrepresented God—and so has Eve, for God never told her not to *touch* the fruit, only to avoid eating it. Eve is thinking as the snake thinks: God must be holding back some pleasure from his creatures.

The snake goes further: Not only is God withholding some good thing, but God is also a liar: "You will not surely die… For God knows that when you eat of it your eyes will be opened, and you will be like God, knowing good and evil" (Genesis 3:5).

The key words here are "like God." God is the Authority, the one in charge. Adam and Eve are his creations, living happily in a place whose name means "pleasure"—but they want more. Being subordinate to God is not good enough, nor is being "in God's image." They want to be "like God." God, according to the snake, has told them a lie in order to keep them in their lowly status.

Doubt is a key factor here. Once Eve doubts what God has clearly told them, she has stepped onto the slippery slope to disobedience and rebellion. Why on earth should she doubt God, who has provided for them so richly, and pay heed to a lowly snake?

"Knowing good and evil" means "deciding for ourselves what is right and wrong"— that is, relying on ourselves, rather than on God, for moral guidance. Some people misread this verse and assume that before Adam and Eve ate the fruit, they had no conception of right and wrong. Not true. They knew that obeying God was right, and disobeying was wrong.

Also, "knowing evil" is another way of saying "rejecting God." Man already knew good, for he experienced it every day in Eden. What did he have to gain from knowing evil?

Let's pause to reflect on what the Bible consistently reveals about God: He is good, righteous, holy. The gods the pagans worshipped hardly seemed moral—in fact, their sexual shenanigans and other acts often showed contempt for moral order. The pagan gods had moral freedom—that is, they did what most human beings want to do, and got away with it. This was the prospect the serpent dangled before Adam and Eve: Become like gods and be above good and evil. The words translated "be like God" in some versions can also be rendered "be like gods"—and it is possible that the writer of Genesis intended both meanings. Being like the promiscuous, violent, temperamental gods the pagans worshipped would not have been a moral step forward but rather several steps backward.

According to Genesis, the fruit of the tree of knowledge had three temptations: (1) "good for food"; (2) "pleasant to the eyes"; and (3) having the power to "make one wise." It was, from a marketing standpoint, well packaged—it looked good, but also possessed a psychological payoff. A product has to be attractive but also promise the buyer something—it will make you stronger, smarter, sexier, more sophisticated.

So Eve, hoping to be "like God," ate the fruit—and gave it to her husband. Note that there is no dialogue between Adam and the snake. The snake has made his sales pitch only to the woman, and she caves in. And then Adam caves in to her. Of course, Adam may have already contemplated eating the fruit himself before she made the suggestion. If he chose to share her fate, it is the pattern for many a later marriage where a man, out of his love (or lust) for the woman, chooses to follow where she leads, for good or ill. We might commend Adam for choosing to share his wife's fate, yet morally it would have been far more commendable to try to set her straight, to avoid the same sin and beg her to seek God's forgiveness.

But both disobeyed. And what was the immediate payoff? "Then the eyes of both of them were opened, and they realized they were naked; so they sewed fig leaves together and made coverings for themselves" (Genesis 3:7). We have read the story so often that we miss the ironic humor. Man and woman sought "knowledge," but what they learn is merely an embarrassment: They are naked. Knowledge has resulted not in power and happiness but in a sense of shame. The snake was correct about one thing: "their eyes were opened," but this led to shame, not power or pleasure.

In the next verse, God is described as "walking in the garden" in the cool of the day. This is recounted as something ordinary, suggesting God and Adam and Eve regularly

---

CULTURAL INSIGHTS

Sex in Eden?

One old and persistent misinterpretation of the Eden story is that the fall of man was the discovery of sex. This is nonsense, for Genesis makes it clear that man's fall was his disobedience of God, eating the fruit of the tree of knowledge. Originally, before the fall, God had told man to "be fruitful and multiply." Presumably, had they not sinned, children would have been born in Eden. Now, despite their sin and punishment, human life will still continue, though not as God originally planned. Given that they had been "naked and unashamed" and that they had been urged to "multiply," their stay in Eden could not have been long or else children would have been born.

met socially. Their hiding from him is the sign that this intimate fellowship is broken. The child has disobeyed and, typical of a child, his first instinct is to hide. Adam and Eve are no longer two adults, with dominion over God's creation but two foolish, frightened children, hiding away. Later in the story, God will expel Adam and Eve from Eden, but already they are uncomfortable there. Home is not a pleasant place to be when the children are avoiding the Father.

In a sense, the real test is when God asks, "Have you eaten of the tree?" The two have the chance to say, "Yes, we did—and we are so sorry!" Instead, they make excuses and pass the blame. Eve blames the tempting words of the snake. Adam blames the woman—the woman God gave him, as if it were ultimately God himself who was to blame for what happened. Instead of becoming like gods, they become like irresponsible children. Adults admit they have done wrong; children dodge.

The two had only one rule hanging over them—and they broke it. They had been warned that the punishment was death. But here, at the very beginning of the long, sad story of man's disobedience, we also see the beginning of the long story of God's mercy. Adam and Eve will indeed die—but not yet. In fact, we learn later in Genesis that Adam lives to the ripe age of nine hundred thirty. But though death is delayed, other punishments follow immediately. The pleasurable state of matrimony is broken— which is already obvious when Adam places the blame on Eve for what happened. God informs Eve that from now on, she will be dominated by her husband. This curse on Eve makes it clear this was not part of the original divine plan. Genesis is unique in ancient writings in that it shows man and woman as being equal at the beginning.

Adam is punished also: Originally he had dominion over all living things, but now he will have to sweat and toil to gain his food. Creation is "good" as God made it. Due to man's disobedience, it is "unmade," becomes unruly, with thorns and other obstacles to man's comfort.

The religions of Egypt, Babylon and other neighboring nations took the curses on man and woman for granted. Humans lived in a state of unhappiness and strife because the gods willed it, no explanation needed. In Genesis, man's tribulations in this world are of his own making. Man's sweaty labor, the struggle to bring forth crops, difficulties in the home, and finally death—these were not part of the divine plan.

Then God "drove" man from Eden—but as we have already noted, the pleasant fellowship they had enjoyed with God in Eden was already broken.

In reading the Eden story, we might well ask: How long were Adam and Eve in the garden? Years? Months? We aren't told. The story in Genesis moves immediately from the creation of Eve to the temptation of Eve. For all we know, it was only a matter of days before man disobeyed God. Most ancient religions taught that there was a golden age of many centuries, when mankind lived in bliss. Genesis does not tell us how long man lived in Eden, only that the rebellion against God happened very soon and led to nothing but trouble.

In concluding this section, we ought to focus not on the details of the story—the garden, the snake, the tree, Adam and Eve's nakedness—but on God, who is consistently described in the Bible as "slow to anger." This is especially significant because nowhere in the story is there the slightest hint that Adam and Eve were sorry for what they did—and yet God delayed the punishment, death, for centuries. Genesis 3 sets the pattern for the entire Bible: rebellious man, compassionate God. This is summed up rather beautifully in Numbers 14:18: "The Lord is slow to anger, abounding in love and forgiving sin and rebellion."

MURDER THEY BORE

The Lord said to Cain, "Where is your brother Abel?" "I don't know," he replied. "Am I my brother's keeper?" (Genesis 4:9)

By faith Abel offered God a better sacrifice than Cain did. (Hebrews 11:4)

Genesis 4:1 has the Bible's first use of "know" in the sense of "have sexual relations with." Adam "knew" Eve, and she gave birth to their first son Cain—who would prove to be a sign of the path the human race would take. The story unfolds quickly: Adam and Eve produced a second son Abel, and Abel was a keeper of flocks while Cain was a farmer. The two sons made offerings—sacrifices—to God, the Bible's first mention of what we would call a religious act. We are not told why, but Abel's offering pleased God, while Cain's did not. The Hebrew word translated "offering" here is *minhah*, which is literally "gift." It is the word used to refer to a gift brought by a subject to a ruler. Cain and Abel were acknowledging that God was in charge—a good thing in itself. In fact, all ancient religions took it for granted that people had to make offerings to their gods.

But there is something distinctive about the religion of the Bible: God, unlike the pagan gods, can see into man's heart. If the person's heart is not right, the sacrifices make no difference. Our attitudes and motivations matter more than the outward rituals. So although Genesis does not state why Cain's offering was not acceptable, it does tell us that Cain was not quite right on the inside. Cain grew angry at his sacrifice not being accepted, and God said to him, "If you do what is right, will you not be accepted?" (Genesis 4:7).

God has more to say: "But if you do not do what is right, sin is crouching at your door; it desires to have you, but you must master it." Sin is depicted like some ravenous beast lurking outside. Man has to master the beast, just like Adam was told to have dominion over the animals.

But we see quickly that Cain is not going to master the beast—quite the contrary. He deceives his brother with an innocent request: "Let's go out into the field." While there, away from the sight of Adam and Eve but not out of sight of God, Cain kills his brother. The first child born into the world is a killer. Cain, the sign that God is allowing life to continue, is one who takes life. This was murder done not in a moment of anger but in a premeditated fashion: "Let's go out into the field."

In an odd way, there is humor in the episode: it is sibling rivalry run amok, a jealous brother killing the other. Why didn't Cain just hit Abel or kill some of his sheep? Cain is a prototype: Bad people really do hate good people. From the very beginning, the violent kill the innocent, a theme found throughout the Bible: "Do not be like Cain, who belonged to the evil one and murdered his brother. And why did he murder him? Because his own actions were evil and his brother's were righteous (1 John 3:12). Adam and Eve had rebelled against God, but their son Abel was showing hopeful signs, making an offering that was acceptable to God—was the human race back on the right track? Cain took care of that: He murdered the one-fourth of the human race that seemed to be in fellowship with God.

In relating this horror, Genesis also relates something comforting: God does not ignore sin. Abel's blood "cries" from the ground. This is the Bible's first mention of blood, and, appropriately, it occurs in the context of violence. A pattern is established for the whole Bible: The shedding of innocent blood does not go unnoticed by God. For God, there are no unsolved crimes. Immediately after the murder, God asks Cain, "Where is Abel, your brother?" Cain's infamous reply is in the pattern of his parents, an evasive non-answer: "Am I my brother's keeper?" This reply is insolent. Instead of being repentant—or at least horrified at having been caught—Cain reacts like a smart aleck: "Am I my brother's keeper?" What right does God have to even question him?

Cain takes after his parents—he evades moral responsibility. When confronted by God, Adam blames Eve, Eve blames the serpent. Cain responds with "Am I my brother's keeper?" From the very beginning, human beings think God is deaf and blind to sin. From the beginning, mankind illustrates the words of the psalm: "The fool says in his heart, There is no God."

But there is a God, and he punishes the guilty. Adam was cursed with having to till the ground. Cain's punishment goes further: The ground will not produce food for him, and he is condemned to wander. The farmer, tied to the soil, is condemned to live in the wilderness, the region of beasts and outlaws and even demons, with meager vegetation. Consider the decline: Adam and Eve were given the light task of tending the garden, but then because they disobeyed, Adam had to work "by the sweat of his brow" to bring forth food from the earth. Cain was presumably doing the same, but he is punished with exile into a land that can barely sustain life at all.

When Adam and Eve were punished, there is no mention of their response. Cain, on the other hand, reacts like a brat: "My punishment is more than I can bear" (Genesis 4:13). Having murdered his own brother and been caught, he is now whining about the punishment being too severe.

In fact, Cain's punishment was light—after all, in the rest of the Old Testament, the penalty for murder is death. Take a life, and you give up your own life. Cain is allowed to live, another example of God's mercy. Yet being a "fugitive and wanderer on the earth" is by no means a light punishment. But it is an appropriate one: A man who murdered his own innocent brother is not a fit companion for anyone. Cain "went out from the presence of the Lord," the ultimate rebel and antisocial character, isolated from both God and man.

Cain recognizes that he is an outlaw, "and whoever finds me will kill me" (Genesis 4:14). Whom did he fear, given that the only other people on earth were his parents? This is one of several mysteries in the Cain story, and the most likely answer is that Cain had no way of knowing if there were other people on the earth. And while he had not repented of murdering his own brother, he understood that he had done wrong, and that anyone else he encountered might feel free to kill him. To prevent this from happening,

CHARACTERS AT LARGE Cain in Legend

Genesis 4 leaves many questions unanswered: Why was Cain's sacrifice to God not accepted? Where did Cain get a wife? Where the Bible is silent, the imagination has taken over and produced many legends. In some Jewish legends, Cain was not the son of Adam but of Satan, or the serpent. These same legends say that Cain, a child of demons himself, was the ancestor of all demons. In some legends, Cain rejected the wife God had chosen for him, and God's rejection of his offering was the punishment for this. According to the ancient Book of Jubilees, Cain's wife was Awan, a daughter of Adam and Eve.

Josephus, the Jewish historian, told of one explanation for why Abel's offering was accepted while Cain's was not: God preferred Abel's offering (sheep) over Cain's (crops) because he preferred what grew according to nature over what man forced from nature.

In Muslim legend, Cain and Abel each had twin sisters, and it was God's intention that Cain marry Abel's twin. Cain would not, but instead married his own twin. Muslims say this is why God rejected his sacrifice.

"the Lord put a mark on Cain so that no one who found him would kill him." Just what this mark was, and why God chose to protect Cain from being murdered, is one of several mysteries in the story.

Genesis presents us with one of the great puzzles of the Bible: Cain, the antisocial fugitive, married and fathered children. Where did he get his wife? We have to assume Adam and Eve had daughters, and that the wife had to be one of his own sisters—incest that, under the circumstances, was allowable in order to populate the earth. But then we are told that Cain built a "city," which seems to contradict the earlier verses about his living in the "land of wandering." "City" here does not refer to permanent buildings but probably to a tent encampment of several families who, being nomads, would not settle in any one area for any length of time. Even so, it is interesting that the Bible's first mention of a "city" is connected with the first murderer Cain, and the next time cities are mentioned is in connection with the first tyrant, Nimrod (see Day 21). The Bible has a distinct anticity bias, which is not surprising, given what notoriously immoral places ancient cities were. Cain, who had foolishly thought he could hide his sin from God, in a sense typifies the person who, in the thick of the city, believes his sins will go unnoticed.

In the story of Cain we encounter a familiar theme in the Bible—the firstborn son, of whom so much is expected, is a disappointment. Birth order is not destiny. Or, looked at another way, Cain is the fitting first son for Adam and Eve, for like them he rebels against God.

The end of Genesis 4 tells of the descendants of Cain, and, not surprisingly, what we learn of them is not good. One of his descendants, Lamech, has two wives—the Bible's first case of polygamy. Although the Bible condones polygamy as practiced by some of its better characters—such as David—Genesis connects the beginning of polygamy with a thoroughly rotten man, Lamech. Like his ancestor Cain, Lamech is a murderer. But while Cain tried to hide his crime from God and man, Lamech boasts to his two wives: "I have killed a man for wounding me, a young man for injuring me. If Cain is avenged seven times, then Lamech seventy-seven times" (Genesis 4:23–24). Lamech is proud of himself: Someone struck him, but instead of just striking back, he murdered the man. Lamech is a symbol of man's further decline into evil. He kills a man for injuring him and then brags about it. Lamech's boast about his vengefulness is probably what lies behind the words of Jesus about forgiveness: "Peter

DID YOU KNOW?

Around AD 200, a religious sect called the Cainites arose, hailing Cain as a hero and honoring other biblical villains such as Judas.

came to Jesus and asked, 'Lord, how many times shall I forgive my brother when he sins against me? Up to seven times?' Jesus answered, 'I tell you, not seven times, but seventy-seven times'" (Matthew 18:21–22). Jesus was telling Peter that good people have to be as dedicated to mercy as bad people are dedicated to vengeance.

Missing from this story of Lamech the murderer is God. This doesn't mean that God took no notice of what Lamech did. Rather, at this point in time, God and the wicked descendants of Cain no longer even communicated.

It is notable that Cain's genealogy breaks off after Lamech. Cain was the "bad seed," and Genesis shifts its attention to a better son, Seth, who will be the ancestor of righteous Noah. Presumably Cain's evil descendants were all wiped out by the flood. Sadly, the desire to rebel against God was not wiped out.

BACK TO THE ORIGIN

I will put enmity between you and the woman, and between your offspring and hers; he will crush your head, and you will strike his heel. (Genesis 3:15)

Be self-controlled and alert. Your enemy the devil prowls around like a roaring lion looking for someone to devour. (1 Peter 5:8)

In dealing with the sad story of human rebellion against God, it seems appropriate to deal with the person—or *being*—whose rebellion preceded humankind's. This is Satan, the Hebrew word meaning "adversary." Curiously, he is not mentioned at all in Genesis, where the temptation of Adam and Eve is attributed merely to the snake. Even so, readers of Genesis understood that this was no mere snake but rather a guise for God's great adversary, who had a stake in corrupting God's creation. Although Satan is mentioned only a few times in the Old Testament, the New Testament has a lot to say about him, calling him the devil (the Greek word is *diabolos*, meaning "slanderer"), the evil one, the prince of this world and several other titles. He is often depicted as the great tempter of mankind, including Jesus himself, with the key difference being that while Adam and Eve gave in to the temptation, Jesus did not.

How did Satan become the great adversary of God? The Bible gives us a few hints. In Luke's Gospel, Jesus sends out a large group of disciples known as the Seventy, and after awhile they return and joyfully report that, working in the name of Jesus, they have power over demons. Jesus replies by saying, "I saw Satan fall like lightning from heaven" (Luke 10:18). One clear meaning is that Jesus is witnessing the diminishing of Satan's power in the world. But another meaning is that he is warning against the pride the Seventy disciples take in their ministry. They can become too proud and fall, just as Satan, full of pride, fell from heaven. Like most Jews of his day, Jesus probably believed that Satan had at one time been one of God's angels; in his pride he and some other angels rebelled against God and were cast out of heaven. These rebel angels became the demons that made up the forces of Satan, and they were dedicated to thwarting God in any way possible, including the corruption of mankind. In the guise of the snake, Satan

Professor Lewis' Demons

Perhaps the most insightful book ever written on the power of demons in human life is *The Screwtape Letters*, written by the shy literature professor C. S. Lewis, who understood that the spiritual warfare that goes on in the human soul consists of the hourly temptations to selfishness and pettiness that collectively distance us from God and each other. The book is presented as a series of letters from an experienced senior tempter, named Screwtape, to a novice, Wormwood. Evil as he is, Screwtape has a thorough grasp of the human mind and all its weaknesses. Throughout the book, Screwtape refers to God as "the Enemy."

It is noteworthy that the book was published in 1941. While so many people focused on the global evils unleashed by World War II, Lewis chose to think about the spiritual battles going on within an individual soul.

tempted Adam and Eve to do what he himself had done: rebel against the authority of God, try to be like God himself, achieve independence.

Speaking further to the Seventy, Jesus said, "I have given you authority to trample on snakes and scorpions and to overcome all the power of the enemy; nothing will harm you" (Luke 10:19). It is surely not a coincidence that Jesus refers to snakes here. His works hark back to Genesis 3, where the snake is punished for its tempting of Adam and Eve by having to crawl on its belly. Further, God tells the snake, "I will put enmity between you and the woman, and between your offspring and hers; he will crush your head, and you will strike his heel" (Genesis 3:15). Taken on the literal level, this is a prophecy that snakes will bite human beings' feet, while humans will strike a snake's head. But for centuries the Jews also took it as a prophecy that the power of Satan would strike at human beings, while in time the Messiah would deal Satan a mortal blow—a "head wound." In using the power of Jesus to cast out demons, the Seventy disciples were figuratively "trampling on snakes."

In our secular age we tend to be skeptical about the reality of Satan and demons. This was surely not the case in Jesus' time, and the first Christians were convinced that "the reason the Son of God appeared was to destroy the devil's work" (1 John 3:8). Satan had been the enemy of mankind from the very beginning, and his power on earth was so immense that Jesus more than once referred to him as "the prince of this world" (John 12:31, 14:30, 16:11). In speaking of "this world," Jesus meant the world where evil and suffering so often seem to have the upper hand. Satan's "kingdom," based on selfishness and rebellion against God, is a powerful one, but Jesus came to usher in the kingdom of God, based on love and obedience.

Jesus and the first Christians understood that Satan's power over human beings was rooted in something that is evident in the tempting of Eve: deceit. The snake misrepresented God, making him appear to be a killjoy who wanted to withhold something good—the fruit of the tree of knowledge—from human beings. God had said man would die if he ate the fruit, but the snake claimed this was a lie, that eating the fruit would lead to "being like gods." The snake was lying, of course. According to Jesus, "When he lies, he speaks his native language, for he is a liar and the father of lies" (John 8:44). The "prince of this world" maintains his kingdom through lies, while the kingdom of God is rooted in the truth.

The Apostle Paul understood Satan's deceitful nature: "Satan himself masquerades as an angel of light" (2 Corinthians 11:14). Paul had in mind the fact that Satan had once been one of God's angels, and even after rebelling against God he is able to disguise himself as mankind's benefactor, which is evident in the Eden story, where the snake convinces Eve that he, not God, has her best interests at heart. In fact, Paul's epistles are full of warnings to the early Christians to be on their guard against false teachers and prophets who seem to be on God's side but who are actually on the side of Satan.

"The God of peace will soon crush Satan under your feet" (Romans 16:20). So ends Paul's great Letter to the Romans. But the key word here is "soon." The defeat of Satan is not yet a "done deal." Satan's power is great, but God's is greater, and believers can rest in the confidence that they are ultimately on the winning side. But in the meantime the life of faith is the life of constant vigilance, for Satan looks out for any opportunity to corrupt and mislead God's people. Peter counseled believers to "be self-controlled and alert. Your enemy the devil prowls around like a roaring lion looking for someone to devour" (1 Peter 5:8). Paul warned the Ephesians, "Do not give the devil a foothold" (Ephesians 4:27). Later in the same letter he counseled them to "put on the full armor of God so that you can take your stand against the devil's schemes" (Ephesians 6:11). Christians, though people of peace, are engaged in never-ending spiritual warfare, and they have to use all the spiritual weapons God puts at their disposal, including "the shield of faith, with which you can extinguish all the flaming arrows of the evil one" (Ephesians 6:16).

In reading passages such as this, it is helpful to think back to Genesis 3. If Adam and Eve engaged in any inward struggle after hearing the snake's words, Genesis does not tell us so. The impression is that Eve caved in quickly—easy prey for the snake's lies. But Christians have to be made of sterner stuff. Thankfully, they are relying not only on their own inner resources but also on God. Note the words of James 4:7: "Submit yourselves, then, to God. Resist the devil, and he will flee from you." Submitting

> **DID YOU KNOW?**
>
> John Bunyan, author of the classic book *Pilgrim's Progress*, also wrote *The Holy War*, the story of how the devil, named Diabolus, tries to capture the city of Mansoul.

to God is precisely what Adam and Eve did *not* do, and so they did not resist the devil. Submitting to God and resisting the devil amount to the same thing.

Satan in the guise of a snake appears at both the beginning and end of the Bible. In Genesis he is a mere snake, but in Revelation a snake of a more formidable kind, depicted as a fearsome red dragon with seven heads (Revelation 12:3). "And there was war in heaven. Michael and his angels fought against the dragon, and the dragon and his angels fought back" (Revelation 12:7). The dragon Satan gives amazing power to a human figure known as the "beast," the 666 figure that has had readers puzzling for centuries (see Day 6 for more about the "beast"). Whoever he is, his doom is certain, for at last he and the dragon will be thrown into the "lake of burning sulfur" (Revelation 20:10). So ends, finally, the rebellion against the Lord. The people of God—those who find their happiness in acknowledging his love and authority instead of rebelling against him—are in Paradise. The Bible comes full circle, from the original Paradise, Eden, which Adam and Eve lost through their rebellion, to the final Paradise, the home of those who submit to the loving Father.

PUTTING THE WORD TO WORK

1. One of the great lessons of the Eden story is that much of human suffering is caused by willful disobedience of God. See if you can develop the habit, when troubles arise, of asking, "Is this the result of my own choices?" instead of, "Why is this happening to me?"

2. When they realize what they have done, Adam and Eve hide from God. Make a resolution to "be an adult" with God, admitting when you've done wrong, asking forgiveness and accepting God's discipline.

3. God tells Cain he must "master" sin, meaning that there is effort required in keeping pettiness and selfishness in check. Make an effort today, as you deal with stress and frustrations, to see yourself in the role of "mastering" bad impulses—and don't be afraid to call on God for help.

4. Reflect on Paul's statement that Satan "masquerades as an angel of light." Have there been times in your life when someone you trusted and whose opinion you valued ended up leading you away from God?

5. As you go through the day, try to practice James's admonition to "submit to God," recognizing God as a loving Father who desires your happiness.

Righteous Roots

One of the great mysteries of the Bible is that Jesus of Nazareth was "God with us"—the divine Son of God and yet also a genuine human being. Although he was God's Son, he also grew up in a working-class home, subject to a human father and mother. God obviously did not choose just any home at random

MEMORY VERSE

The righteous will shine like the sun in the kingdom of their Father.—Matthew 13:43

as the place where his Son would grow up, and the Gospels make clear that the human family was righteous. This included not only Mary and Joseph but also Mary's elderly relative Elizabeth and her husband Zechariah—and the son they had in their old age, who would grow up to be the amazing wilderness prophet John the Baptist, the preacher of righteousness who would pave the way for an even greater prophet, his kinsman Jesus.

KEY TERM FOR TODAY ## Righteous

In the Bible, a righteous person is one who fulfills his obligation to God and to his neighbor. Jesus, called the "Righteous One" several times in Acts, not only was the Son of God but also grew up among good stock—righteous people.

AMAManation CONCEPTION

AMAZING CONCEPTION

> The angel said to him: "Do not be afraid, Zechariah; your prayer has been heard. Your wife Elizabeth will bear you a son, and you are to give him the name John... Many of the people of Israel will he bring back to the Lord their God." (Luke 1:13, 16)

Luke opens his Gospel with the story of a priest named Zechariah, ministering in the temple in Jerusalem. He was married to a woman named Elizabeth, and both of them were "righteous before God, walking blamelessly in all the statutes and command-ments of the Lord (Luke 1:6, ESV). These two good and decent people had never had children; theirs was a righteous home, but they had no children to be brought up in it. The two were past the age of producing children, but that is an obstacle that God had overcome in Israel's past, and he would do so again.

People often recall that the Jews' chief priests were instrumental in bringing about the death of Jesus. These belonged to the corrupt, materialistic family of Caiaphas, the high priest, and they were a decidedly unrighteous bunch. But there were many other priests in Israel, many of them like Zechariah, good and decent people. These priests did not minister full-time in the temple or even live in Jerusalem. Each priest would minister in the temple for one week, twice per year. The choice of which priest would offer up incense was done by casting lots, and a priest would do so only once in his lifetime. So the episode in Luke 1 was the high point of Zechariah's priestly career. For some of the priests this might have been a matter of going through the motions; for a devout man like him, it was full of meaning.

His moment in the temple took an unexpected turn, for at the right side of the incense altar stood an angel. The angel told him, "Fear not." (Angels in the Bible are not the soft and adorable angels of popular art but are intimidating at first.) The angel told Zechariah his prayer has been heard. Possibly this refers to his prayer for a child, though by this age, probably not. A devout man like Zechariah would have more likely prayed for the Messiah. If so, that prayer would also be answered.

Zechariah and Elizabeth would have a son, whom they would name John, meaning "the Lord is gracious." This would be a cause of great rejoicing—and not just for the parents but for many, for he would in time bring many people back to the Lord. This son would be one to "prepare" the people. The angel did not say for what, but a man like Zechariah could only have assumed he meant preparing Israel for its Messiah.

Zechariah doubted—understandably, considering his age. Then the angel identified himself as Gabriel, "who stands in the presence of God." Zechariah would be truly blessed in having a son in his old age. But because he had doubted God's angel, he would be punished by being mute until the child was born.

The old man was alone in an inner part of the temple, and incense offering took only a short time, so the people in the temple court wondered what delayed him. When he

CULTURAL INSIGHTS

Greeks and Jews and Justice

The Greek word *dike* (it has two syllables—DYE-key) is literally "justice," but in practice it means "doing what is proper." The Greeks thought of Dike as a goddess. A person who is *dikaios*, "righteous," is correct and proper. For the Jews, the righteous person was one who fulfilled his obligation to God and neighbor. It could also mean innocent, for Pilate's wife calls Jesus *dikaios*, and so does the centurion who sees Jesus die on the cross. Jesus is called the Righteous One several times in Acts. The Jews expected the Messiah to be utterly righteous, meaning his whole life would conform to God's will. That is exactly what Jesus was.

DID YOU KNOW?

Zechariah is the only priest depicted favorably in the Gospels.

came out, he could not speak but could only make signs. The people assumed correctly that he had seen a vision in the temple.

Back at his home, the old man's doubts were soon put to rest, for Elizabeth did indeed conceive. Elizabeth was a saintly woman, but she lived in a culture that saw childlessness as a curse. After she conceived, she "hid herself for five months"—not out of shame, but perhaps she wanted her pregnancy to be obvious when she came out of her seclusion. Her visible condition would finally end people's reproaches of her.

AND A MORE AMAZING CONCEPTION

An angel of the Lord appeared to him in a dream and said, "Joseph son of David, do not be afraid to take Mary home as your wife, because what is conceived in her is from the Holy Spirit." (Matthew 1:20)

In Elizabeth's sixth month of pregnancy, another angelic visitation took place. The angel Gabriel went to the town of Nazareth, approaching a virgin named Mary with the words, "Greetings, you who are highly favored! The Lord is with you." (Luke 1:28) Like Zechariah, Mary was "troubled" at the angel's words. The angel told her she would give birth to a son, who would be named Jesus, and "he will be great and will be called the Son of the Most High" (Luke 1:32). Mary raised an obvious question: How could she conceive a child, since she was still a virgin? The angel answered, "The Holy Spirit will come upon you, and the power of the Most High will overshadow you. So the holy one to be born will be called the Son of God" (Luke 1:35). As a sign that miracles were already being done, the angel told Mary that her elderly relative Elizabeth was already six months pregnant—"for nothing is impossible with God" (Luke 1:38).

Soon Mary paid a visit to Elizabeth. The unborn John "leaped" in Elizabeth's womb, and Elizabeth was filled with joy at greeting Mary, who was to be "mother of my Lord." Both women—one elderly, the other a virgin—had each been supremely blessed by the Lord. Mary burst forth in a hymn of praise that Christian tradition has called the Magnificat, found in Luke 1:46–56. Mary realizes that she, a humble girl from a small town, has been truly privileged, for God has "been mindful of the humble state of his servant. From now on all generations will call me blessed, for the Mighty One has done great things for me." The end of her praise song mentions Abraham, the

DID YOU KNOW?

The visit of the angel Gabriel to Mary is known in Christian tradition as the Annunciation, and many denominations celebrate it on March 25—exactly nine months before Christmas.

patriarch who, in his old age, finally fathered a son with his aged wife Sarah. God had done miracles in the past, and was doing them now.

We should be thankful that there is more than one Gospel in the New Testament, for Luke's, fascinating though it is, leaves some questions unanswered, such as: What about Mary's fiancé Joseph? Matthew's Gospel fills in some gaps. Both Gospels agree that Mary had conceived through the workings of the Holy Spirit. "Because Joseph her husband was a righteous man and did not want to expose her to public disgrace, he had in mind to divorce her quietly" (Matthew 1:19). Early on, Joseph must have had some doubts about Mary's pregnancy—as most any man, even a righteous one, would. Was his innocent fiancée as innocent as everyone believed? In those days engagement was legally binding, so even though Mary and Joseph had not married, breaking the engagement entailed a kind of divorce, and Joseph planned to do it as quietly as possible. But the angel of God communicated with him in a dream: He should go ahead and marry the girl, for the child she carried was indeed conceived by the Spirit. The child would be named Jesus—a form of the old Hebrew name *Yehoshua*, "the Lord saves," and indeed Jesus would save people from their sins.

As a righteous man, Joseph would have been familiar with the Hebrew Scriptures, certainly with the much-read and much-loved Book of Isaiah, in which verse 7:14 speaks of a virgin conceiving a son, whose name will be called Immanuel, meaning, "God with us." Perhaps he was the first person to sense what Christians have proclaimed for two thousand years, that the words of Isaiah were "fulfilled" in the conception and birth of Jesus.

And so, under the Lord's guidance, Joseph married Mary. Two decent, God-fearing people of working-class background had, in the strange workings of providence, been called to bring up Israel's Messiah and the world's Savior.

In the meantime, Mary had spent a long time with Elizabeth but finally returned to Nazareth. Soon after, Elizabeth gave birth to a son. Let's pause here to consider that, quite unlike today, when we can determine an unborn child's sex very early, there was no way to do this in ancient times. Biologically speaking, there was as much chance of having a daughter as a son. But the angel had foretold a son, and so it came to pass. On the eighth day, when it was Jewish custom to circumcise

the child and give it a name, the mute Zechariah wrote on a tablet, "His name is John." After nine months of being mute, Zechariah was able to speak again, and appropriately, he burst forth in praise to his God. He not only praised but prophesied as well: "You, my child, will be called a prophet of the Most High; for you will go on before the Lord to prepare the way for him, to give his people the knowledge of salvation through the forgiveness of their sins" (Luke 1:76–77). Alert readers notice that Zechariah regains his own voice and immediately announces that Israel will once again have a prophet, a human voice speaking the word of God.

The name Zechariah means "the Lord remembers." It is the most common personal name in the Bible, with thirty-three men bearing that name. In the case of the aged priest in Luke 1, the name was appropriate, for here was a righteous man who, after many years of being childless, was remembered by God, a sign that God does things in his own good time. Not only did Zechariah and Elizabeth have a son, but that son would also be a great prophet who would prepare people to meet God. The Jews had gone for centuries with no prophets at all, but God had not forgotten them, and the son of the aged couple would be a prophet, one who would remind people of the mighty prophet Elijah of the past.

The Bible, alas, tells us nothing—or almost nothing—about John's childhood and youth. He "grew and became strong in spirit; and he lived in the desert until he appeared publicly to Israel" (Luke 1:80). Living in the "desert" may mean he grew up among the Essenes, a Jewish sect whose people separated themselves from the sinful world and lived a simple life in the wilderness. We will return to John shortly.

AT HOME IN NAZARETH

The child grew and became strong; he was filled with wisdom, and the grace of God was upon him. . . . Jesus grew in wisdom and stature, and in favor with God and men. (Luke 2:40, 52)

Elsewhere in this book I look at two important political figures who played major roles in the birth of Jesus: the Roman emperor Augustus and the Jewish king Herod the Great (see Days 6 and 18). I also look at the wise men, or Magi, who came to honor the newborn Jesus. These were the big names in the story of Christmas, but thankfully Luke's Gospel gives us some information on the lesser names—or, in the case of the shepherds who visited Jesus, no names at all. It is hard to imagine the Christmas story without the angel appearing to the simple shepherds, who afterward were "glorifying and praising God."

Mary and Joseph had, in a brief span of time, been visited by angels, shepherds and Magi bearing expensive gifts from faraway lands, and had heard prophecies that Jesus would in time do amazing things. We may well wonder what everyday life would have

Gray Joseph and Young Mary

Mary, Joseph and the infant Jesus are often depicted in art, a familiar title being *The Holy Family*. More often than not, Joseph is shown as much older than Mary, old enough to be her father. Why so? The Bible tells us nothing about their ages. If they were a typical couple of their time, they would have both been very young when they married, probably both in their teens. However, a popular writing called the Protevangelium of James, written around AD 200, depicted Joseph as a widower with children who married the much younger Mary but had no children with her. The image of Joseph as much older than Mary has persisted, but the popular 1977 TV miniseries *Jesus of Nazareth* jarred some audiences by showing Joseph and Mary to be the same age, which was also true of the 2006 movie *The Nativity Story*.

been like for the family. How could things be normal in a home where the husband and wife knew the son they saw at play was the Son of God?

The Bible tells us little about the childhood of Jesus, except that Luke includes the charming story of the family visiting the temple when Jesus was twelve years old. Wanting to fill the gaps in Jesus' history, various fanciful "infancy gospels" were written, showing Jesus performing amazing feats as a child. Whether these have any basis in reality is questionable. In fact, life in Nazareth was probably normal enough for the family, but given the two-thousand-year gap that separates us, let's consider just what normal life would have been for them.

The typical house in Galilee was square and flat-roofed, made of mud bricks that were often whitewashed on the outside but left natural inside. There was usually just one door, opening onto the street, and during the day it was open. Windows were simply openings in the walls. The floor was hard-packed clay, with some straw and leather mats for sitting on, though there were probably some wooden stools and a low table. A wooden ladder would have led to the flat roof, made of soil, straw and lime packed together over the ceiling beams. In the hot months people often slept on the roofs, and at other times might eat there or do laundry and other chores.

The day began at sunrise for both husband and wife, starting with a simple breakfast of bread and cheese curds. Mary would have carried her earthenware jug to the village well, and then purchased needed items in the village marketplace, where merchants and farmers sold things. The wife's main task of the day was baking barley bread, using not yeast but day-old dough that had fermented. Bread was usually plain but for special days spices or herbs might be added. Kneading was done in a large wooden or clay bowl, the kneading trough. The dough would have been shaped into large flat disks.

Other chores included spinning and weaving flax or wool, and making cheese from goat's milk. There was relatively little meat, but salted fish from the Sea of Galilee was often part of the meal, and at times a chicken from a farm might be purchased, but the lamb, kid goat and veal favored by the rich were rarities for the working class. There were sufficient vegetables, including leeks, onions, cucumbers and a variety of beans, and dessert was usually nuts or fruits, such as dates, melons, figs, grapes or pomegranates. Sweetening was done not with sugar but with honey or syrup made from figs or grapes. There were no utensils; all eating was done by hand, using the bread as scoops.

In a devout home, every meal was preceded by a hand-washing and a blessing. While the well-to-do had low couches to recline on while dining, most people sat or reclined on mats, which were also used as beds. The husband but not the wife would have gone to each evening's service at the synagogue.

Each Friday evening, when the first star was visible, three blasts on the shofar (ram's horn) from the roof of the synagogue announced the start of the Sabbath, the day of rest. The wives would have already prepared the Sabbath meal beforehand, since no cooking could be done on the Sabbath. People did not bathe all over, but they washed their hands and faces and put on scented olive oil and clean clothing for the service. The overall Sabbath mood was joyful, not solemn.

The same hall used for worship services was a schoolroom for the village boys, who at age six began studying under the rabbi. The boys would sit in a semicircle on the floor, and the rabbi would take a scroll of the Law from the ark, the curtained chest containing the five scrolls of the Law. The scrolls were wrapped in linen and treated with great reverence. These were the only textbooks. In devout homes, both mother and father reinforced the learning of the Scriptures by frequent repetition. The boys would have learned to write also, using wooden tablets covered in wax, the "pen" being a stylus made of metal, bone or wood. Copying out passages of Scripture on parchment was a common exercise.

Luke 2 tells of the family going to Jerusalem every year for the Passover celebration. Typically only the men in the family would do this, but the more devout women did also, and we know Mary did. We also get some indications elsewhere in the Gospels that Jesus' family went as often as possible to the other Jewish holy-day celebrations in Jerusalem. Since they lived in Galilee, this involved a certain amount of travel, either on donkeys or most likely on foot.

Jesus' devout home might have been a sheltered environment but only up to a point, for the pagan culture was not far away, and Joseph would have probably done business with Greek-speaking Gentiles whose religions and morals were far different from his own.

The Gospels refer to Joseph as a *tekton*, usually translated "carpenter," though "builder" might be more accurate, and a *tekton* might work in stone and metal as well as wood. A *tekton* would have worn a chip of wood behind one ear to let people know his trade. He would have made plows, yokes, tables, stools, cabinets, kneading troughs, and door and window frames. At times he might have built an entire house, cutting and installing the main beams. His tools were axes, saws, planes, mallets, adzes and a compass. (When sawing a board, the carpenter usually sat on it and sawed away from himself.) Joseph might have worked at home, or possibly had a shop in the marketplace, alongside a potter, smith, weaver and dyer. Like most Jewish boys, Jesus would have begun learning the family trade at a young age.

Jesus must have learned much more than carpentry at the side of Joseph. As a righteous man, Joseph would have charged people a fair price for his goods and services, and would have taught the boy that there is no separation between the business world and the world of the synagogue. Each moment of each day was an opportunity to honor God, to live as moral beings in an immoral world. Mary would have instilled the same teachings in her son.

"Jesus grew in wisdom and stature, and in favor with God and men." He did not do so unaided, for he grew up under the loving guidance of two decent people and, no doubt, other relatives and family friends nearby. One lesson of the Gospels that we should never forget is that even though Jesus was the Son of God, he "grew," just as all human children must grow.

Joseph is not mentioned as being alive once Jesus reached adulthood, so in all likelihood he must have died. Several times in the Gospels people refer to Jesus as "Joseph's son" or "son of the carpenter." While Jesus' greater vocation was as the Son of God, it was no insult to be considered the son of as good a man as Joseph.

MAN IN THE WILDERNESS

The word of God came to John son of Zechariah in the desert. He went into all the country around the Jordan, preaching a baptism of repentance for the forgiveness of sins. (Luke 3:2–3)

Israel had gone for centuries with no prophet, but at long last, "the word of God came to John." God was speaking to his people again.

All four Gospels quote Isaiah 40:3: "A voice of one calling in the desert, 'Prepare the way for the Lord, make straight paths for him.'" But Luke adds more from Isaiah: "And all mankind will see God's salvation." Salvation is to be universal—not just for Israel but also for the world.

John practiced baptism as a sign of repentance, a change of life. Jews had always believed that Gentiles wishing to join the Jewish community had to be baptized. John said *all* people needed to repent, Jews included. This message did not sit well with some Jews, who said, "We have Abraham as our father." They believed that all Jews would be saved simply because of descent from Abraham. There was a popular belief that Abraham stood at the gate of Gehenna—hell—to save any Jew who was inadvertently headed there. John said this wasn't so. Every individual needed to repent, give his life over to God, and show it outwardly through baptism. Notice what is happening: The focus is on the individual's salvation, not the collective salvation of Israel. John's message is that God will save people one at a time—and Jesus will repeat that message.

But this wasn't all. Repentance must bear "fruit." John was intensely practical. To people in general, John told them to share charitably. To tax collectors and soldiers, he said to do their jobs honorably. The Gospel writers were painfully aware that in ancient times, soldiers were notorious looters and shakedown artists, using their position and power to steal—legally. Obviously the soldiers who came to John would have been among the better sort. John did not tell either group of men to leave their jobs but to do them justly. On the one hand, John's message was harsh—everyone needed cleansing. But on the other hand, anyone—even disreputable people like tax collectors and soldiers—could be saved. John was indeed a forerunner of Jesus in his openness to such people.

John, the son of the righteous Zechariah and Elizabeth, was righteous himself, and righteousness was his message. He lived in the desert—presumably he had no wife, children or permanent home—wore a simple hair tunic and lived on locusts and honey. He was, to put it mildly, a character, and some of the people who came out to hear him must have been merely curious. But many responded to his preaching, and some began to wonder: Was this the Messiah that Israel had prayed for? John said no. Someone greater than he was coming soon—in fact, so great that John did not feel worthy to untie his sandals. Rabbis received great deference from their pupils, but there was a saying that the pupil should not have to stoop to do the menial task of untying his master's sandals. John was more humble: He was not even worthy to perform that menial task for the one who is coming after him. This coming one would baptize not in water but with the Holy Spirit and with fire. Baptism by fire means both testing and judgment.

The one to come was his kinsman, Jesus. The Gospels, alas, don't tell us just how well the two men knew each other during their younger days—if indeed they even did.

Certainly their mothers were on close terms. At any rate, when Jesus came to John to be baptized, John recognized that this was the man, the Messiah, the one he had prepared the way for. John hesitated; wasn't it more appropriate that he be baptized by Jesus than vice versa? The sinless Jesus did not need to be washed for his sins. But Jesus insisted—doing so would "fulfill all righteousness." Jesus was no sinner, but he identified with the rest of mankind. In being baptized, he showed other men that this was the route they must follow.

JOHN'S "WHO ARE YOU?"

When John heard in prison what Christ was doing, he sent his disciples to ask him, "Are you the one who was to come, or should we expect someone else?" (Matthew 11:2)

After his baptism, Jesus withdrew in the wilderness, where he endured tempting by the devil. Then, "When Jesus heard that John had been put in prison, he returned to Galilee" (Matthew 4:12). Jesus' ministry of preaching and healing did not begin until John's ended. There was no competition between the two. John's work of turning the people's thoughts to God had been accomplished.

The righteous John, the man lauded as a prophet, ran afoul of the decidedly unrighteous Jewish ruler, Herod Antipas, who threw John in prison. Later in the chapter we will look at the sad ending to that story.

Though held in prison, John still had followers. And he still thought of Jesus as the Messiah—yet as the quotation above indicates, he or perhaps his followers had doubts. After all, the Jews had been expecting their Messiah to be a political and military leader, someone who would drive out the Romans and establish Jewish self-rule. Jesus had done none of those things. Had John been mistaken—or had Jesus perhaps taken the wrong turn?

So John, in prison, asked if Jesus is "the one who was to come," clearly referring to the Messiah. To John's disciples who posed the question, Jesus replied, "Go back and report to John what you hear and see: The blind receive sight, the lame walk, those who have leprosy are cured, the deaf hear, the dead are raised, and the good news is preached to the poor" (Matthew 11:2–6). Jesus' answer was that he was not behaving in quite the way John expected, yet his actions showed clearly that he was doing God's work, and what more could be hoped for? The Messiah was not a conqueror but a healer.

John may have been asking the question not because he had doubts himself but in order to satisfy his doubtful disciples. The Gospels give the impression that Jesus and John understood each other quite well, but their disciples were often clueless. Great men are often misunderstood not only by the public at large but even by their closest followers. In

John in John

Of the four Gospels, the one that devotes the most attention to John the Baptist is the Gospel of John—a matter of coincidence that the Baptist had the same name as the disciple who wrote the Gospel. Apparently when the Gospel was written there were still numerous disciples of John the Baptist around (this is also evident in Acts), and so the Gospel emphasizes that John was not the Messiah himself but the Messiah's forerunner. "He himself was not the light; he came only as a witness to the light" (John 1:8). John's Gospel is the one in which the Baptist identifies Jesus as the "Lamb of God, who takes away the sins of the world" (John 1:29). Also, it says that Andrew, Peter's brother, had been first a disciple of John, and there is a suspicion that another disciple of John who later follows Jesus is John, brother of James, who throughout the Gospel never names himself, possibly because he wanted to avoid confusion with his former teacher, John the Baptist.

fact, John, coming before the Messiah, had prepared people not for political triumph but for judgment. Neither John nor Jesus shared the people's view of the Messiah.

At the end of this passage, Jesus says, "Blessed is the man who is not scandalized by me." A *skandalon* was a stumbling block, anything that caused one to trip. Jesus' whole ministry was a *skandalon*, even to his own disciples, who were slow to see what the real nature of the Messiah was. To the eyes of faith, Jesus' deeds were signs that God was walking on earth.

MORE THAN A PROPHET

> As John's disciples were leaving, Jesus began to speak to the crowd about John: . . . "I tell you the truth: Among those born of women there has not risen anyone greater than John the Baptist." (Matthew 11:7, 11)

The Gospels regard John the Baptist as the fulfillment of the prophecy of Malachi 4:5: "See, I will send you the prophet Elijah before that great and dreadful day of the Lord comes." But at the time John's disciples had come to question Jesus, there were still doubts among many people: Was John the Messiah? Was Jesus the Messiah?

In speaking to the confused crowds, Jesus asked them, "What did you go out into the desert to see? A reed swayed by the wind? If not, what did you go out to see? A man dressed in fine clothes? No, those who wear fine clothes are in kings' palaces. Then what did you go out to see? A prophet? Yes, I tell you, and more than a prophet."

"A reed swayed by the wind" referred to the rushes that grew on lakesides and riverbanks. No one could make a special trip to the desert to see something so commonplace, but they would—and did—go out to see the great prophet John. "Shaken by the wind" can also refer to something weak that bends with the wind, which was definitely not a description of John. In a world of men with weathervane minds and weathervane morals, he stood for what was right. John was not a man dressed in fine clothes either. He dressed in the roughest of clothing, and rather than living in a palace, he spoke out against the immorality of one who did live in a palace, the depraved Herod Antipas.

John was indeed a prophet, as the people understood, but as Jesus said, he was more than that—he was the forerunner of the Messiah, the Elijah figure that the Jews had awaited for centuries. No man was, according to Jesus, a greater figure than John—and yet, jarringly, Jesus says, "Yet he who is least in the kingdom of heaven is greater than he." How so? For all of his greatness, John was of the old order, as his question to Jesus indicated. He was the forerunner of the Messiah, yet he himself did not fully grasp what the Messiah would be like. Although he appears in the New Testament, John is in a sense a part of the Old Testament age, the age of expectation of the Messiah; Jesus' followers are part of the new age, with the awareness of the Messiah—not as a conqueror but as the suffering man on the cross. Trapped in the dungeon of Herod's fortress, John would never live to see what the apostles of the risen Jesus would accomplish.

John was in prison, a situation that would make many men bitter toward God. Had John been an entirely different man, he might have also been bitter toward Jesus, who was traveling about Galilee, performing miracles and drawing crowds, including many people who had followed John himself. In short, Jesus was being the "greater one" that John had foretold. It takes a great-souled person to be what John was, content to be the opening act for the mighty works of God that Jesus did. Jesus understood what a truly righteous and humble man John was, which is why he praised him so highly.

AXING THE RIGHTEOUS

> Herod feared John and protected him, knowing him to be a righteous and holy man.... [Herod] immediately sent an executioner with orders to bring John's head. The man went, beheaded John in the prison, and brought back his head on a platter. (Mark 6:20, 27–28)

In another chapter we look at the corrupt and immoral Herod family that is so prominent in the New Testament. One member of the vile family not covered in that chapter is Herod the Great's son, Herod Antipas. At the time of John's and Jesus' ministry, he ruled over Galilee, not as king but as tetrarch, a title meaning "ruler of a fourth." He was half-Samaritan—his mother was Samaritan—and certainly the Jews knew this and held it against him. He was as decadent and unscrupulous as the other members of his family, and he had scandalized many people by running off with his brother Philip's wife Herodias, who despised John for openly condemning the marriage. The kinship was not the only issue, for the real scandal was the open adultery that had preceded the marriage. Also, Herod had divorced his wife, a Nabataean princess, to marry Herodias. John's criticism of the second marriage had political ramifications, since he could have been seen as whipping up support for the Nabataean king to take retributive action. But Luke adds the detail that John rebuked Herod not just because of his marriage but also for "all the other evil things he had done."

So Herod shut up John in Machaerus, one of many fortress-palaces built by his paranoid father. It was situated on an isolated peak on the shore of the Dead Sea. Yet, curiously, "Herod feared John and protected him, knowing him to be a righteous and holy man. When Herod heard John, he was greatly puzzled; yet he liked to listen to him." What does this mean? Did John's righteous preaching in some way touch Herod's heart—or was this a case of an utterly corrupt, worldly man being amused by someone who was his polar opposite? Whatever the case, he knew of John's popularity with the people, so, despite his wife's urgings, he kept John in prison but would not execute him.

Then came one of the most gruesome incidents in the Bible: Herod had a birthday party, inviting the leading men of Galilee. His wife's daughter danced for them, and Herod—no doubt quite drunk at this point—was so enchanted he promised her anything she wished, even half his kingdom. This was a priceless opportunity. She went to ask her mother what she should request, and the wicked woman said, "The head of John, on a platter."

Herod was in an awkward situation: He had sworn an oath to give her what she asked, and the leading men of the province were all watching him. So he sent for an executioner and had John beheaded, his head brought in on a platter. The important people were witness to—and probably approved of—an act of utter barbarity. Herod, so fond of the "civilized" lifestyle of the pagans, had the heart of a savage.

Like his father, Herod lived in constant fear of the Jews rebelling against his authority. He was hated, but John was popular. Yet if he expected some violent reaction on the part of John's disciples, he was wrong; nothing of the kind happened. The disciples quietly came, took John's body and buried him. Their peaceful reaction made it clear they were not violent revolutionaries. Men like John—prophets, social critics—could speak out boldly without being violent or advocating violence.

Jesus certainly would have been aware of what this all boded for himself in the days ahead. If they killed John with impunity, the same fate awaited him. A righteous man of God who spoke the truth was bound to get into trouble. John was indeed the forerunner of the Messiah.

If this seems a sad way to end a chapter on righteous characters, consider this: People of faith believe that John received an eternal reward far different than Herod's. And even during their lifetimes, John lived with the satisfaction of doing the will of God, while Herod lived in constant fear of the people he ruled over, and was so mired in his vanity and worldliness that even the secular historians wrote disapprovingly of him. Perhaps Jesus had John—and people like him—in mind when he concluded one of his parables of the Last Judgment with these words: "The righteous will shine like the sun in the kingdom of their Father" (Matthew 13:43).

CHARACTERS AT LARGE | Herodias' Daughter

The daughter of Herodias, whose enchanting dance proved fatal to John the Baptist, is not named in the Gospels, but history tells us her name was Salome, and she was probably in her early teens when the incident occurred. The grisly incident has fascinated artists and authors for centuries, and rightly so, thanks to the dramatic contrast between the righteous John in his rough garment and the well-dressed, decadent party of Herod.

The author Oscar Wilde, most famous for his witty comedies, also wrote a very grim drama, *Salome,* in which, at the end, the perverse girl kisses the mouth of John, which so outrages Herod that he orders her execution. The play was made into an opera by Richard Strauss. In a 1953 movie, the sultry Rita Hayworth played Salome, but in a typical Hollywood distortion of the Bible, Salome attempts to save John, not have him executed. Interestingly, a 1902 German movie titled *Salome* is probably the oldest biblical film in which the main character is not Jesus.

PUTTING THE WORD TO WORK

1. Make a list of people you know who fit the Bible's definition of "righteous." Then thank God for those people.

2. Put yourself in Joseph's place and ask: How would I respond to learning my fiancée is pregnant—and claiming the baby has no human father? How would this test your righteousness?

3. How do you react to the description of home life in Nazareth? What does it mean to you, that the Son of God actually matured as a human child in a humble environment?

4. John is an amazing example of humility, willing to acknowledge that he was only preparing the way for someone greater than himself. Take a moment to reflect on the very rare virtue of discerning greatness in others.

5. Although you may have been familiar with the story of John's execution already, how do you respond to it now? Does it remind you of other stories—from history, the news, your own experience—where a righteous person suffered at the hands of an evil one?

Steady, Sisters

The focus in this chapter is a quality that is emphasized throughout the Bible: steadfastness, a feature attributed constantly to God and less constantly to human beings. In a world of change and decay, God is a fixture, and so are people of deep faith who put their trust in him.

While there are many examples of steadfast men in the Bible, here we will be focusing on women from both the Old and New Testaments, women who were models of steadfastness—or, in the case of the first woman we'll look at, a model of fickleness and inconstancy, who had the good fortune to have a steadfast and forgiving husband.

KEY TERM FOR TODAY ## Steadfast

One of the qualities of God that people are called to imitate is steadfastness, the quality of being reliable and immovable in one's faith.

HEAVENLY HUSBAND

When the Lord began to speak through Hosea, the Lord said to him, "Go, take to yourself an adulterous wife and children of unfaithfulness, because the land is guilty of the vilest adultery in departing from the Lord." So he married Gomer daughter of Diblaim, and she conceived and bore him a son. (Hosea 1:2–3)

Your Maker is your husband—the Lord Almighty is his name—the Holy One of Israel is your Redeemer; he is called the God of all the earth. (Isaiah 54:5)

"Like a woman unfaithful to her husband, so you have been unfaithful to me, O house of Israel," declares the Lord. (Jeremiah 3:20)

We are so accustomed to referring to God as "Father" that it surprises many readers that God is almost never referred to by that title in the Old Testament. This is understandable, for most of the pagan religions were filled with stories of gods mating with human

DID YOU KNOW?

When the Romans destroyed the Jews' temple in AD 70, many Jews wondered how they could continue to offer sacrifices. One of the Jewish leaders, Rabbi Yohanan ben-Zakkai, found the solution in Hosea, where God says, "I desire mercy, not sacrifice." Henceforth the Jews would focus on acts of mercy and kindness instead of the sacrifices in the temple.

women, and these promiscuous gods were hardly models of morality. Typically a king was considered a son of a god—for example, the Egyptian Pharaoh was thought to be the child of the sun god, Ra. Israel's religion was different, for the Israelites were prohibited from depicting God in human form, and Israel's righteous God did not go around seducing mortal women.

Interestingly enough, the Old Testament often depicts God figuratively as the husband of Israel. The image is found often in the writings of the prophets, and the first to use the image was Hosea, whose book is the longest of the twelve Minor Prophets. Hosea is often called the "prophet of love," but to be more precise we might call him "prophet of love that suffers and forgives constantly," for Hosea's own life story is a love story only in the sense that it was a very one-sided love that involved more suffering than pleasure.

At the Lord's command, Hosea married a woman named Gomer. The Bible version quoted here refers to her as "an adulterous wife," while other versions have "wife of whoredom" or even "whore." But Gomer was not a prostitute in the sense of a woman who made her living through sex. She was a loose woman, who simply wasn't satisfied with one man. She was a woman with a past, and poor Hosea would learn one of the basic lessons of human behavior: You can usually tell a person's future based on past actions.

Hosea was, on God's orders, put in the awkward position of being what past ages called a cuckold, a man whose wife cheated on him. A cuckold was usually considered a figure of fun, a pathetic creature. But in fact there is nothing remotely funny about a decent man married to a faithless woman.

Some things remain constant throughout human history, and one is the double standard of sexual morality. People have assumed that husbands would stray, and it was the wife's duty to accept or ignore his philandering. On the other hand, women were expected to be completely faithful to their husbands. Lucky was the woman whose husband never strayed—and very unlucky was a man with a wayward wife.

Why did God command the prophet to marry such a woman? So that Hosea's own personal life would teach him an object lesson about divine love. God understood the mind of the human male: A man was hurt more deeply by his wife's adultery than a woman by a husband's adultery. In a sense, Hosea is a man's book, for it looks at adultery from the husband's viewpoint, and what it sees is terrible.

Throughout the Old Testament, idolatry is referred to as "adultery." God had been infinitely kind to Israel, leading the slaves out of Egypt, giving the divine law through

Moses, leading the Israelites to settle Canaan, sending prophets to lead the people when they strayed. And how had faithless Israel repaid such kindness? By constantly whoring after other gods, mere idols, gods that didn't even exist. Faithless Gomer was a symbol of faithless Israel.

Gomer gave birth to children, including a daughter named Lo-Ruhamah, Hebrew for "not loved." She also had a son named Lo-Ammi, "not my people"—truly an appropriate name since, given Gomer's infidelity, Hosea had no way of knowing if the children were actually his. The names also represented the emotional distance that had been created by Israel's straying from God. And yet, amazingly, God's love and forgiveness continued, and there was a promise of reconciliation: "In the place where it was said to them, 'You are not my people,' they will be called 'sons of the living God'" (Hosea 1:10). Despite telling the sad story of a mismatched marriage, the book overflows with promise: "I will remove the names of the Baals from her lips; no longer will their names be invoked. I will betroth you to me forever; I will betroth you in righteousness and justice, in love and compassion. I will betroth you in faithfulness, and you will acknowledge the Lord" (Hosea 2:17–20). The Baals were the fertility gods of the region, and the worship of a Baal resembled a sexual orgy more than a religious service. Israel was always whoring after the Baals and other false gods, and though this spiritual infidelity grieved God deeply, he held out the hope of restoration.

In our age of tolerance and diversity it is hard for us to understand the Bible's obsession with idolatry. Hosea and the other prophets understood the nature of idol worship: "They consecrated themselves to that shameful idol and became as vile as the thing they loved" (Hosea 9:10). In a sense we become what we worship. "I like that" leads to

CULTURAL INSIGHTS

Hesed

Like many other books of the Old Testament, Hosea uses the Hebrew word *hesed*, which in the King James Version was translated "lovingkindness." It is one of the qualities of God, a steadfast love, deep devotion that endures in spite of human beings' ingratitude and infidelity. God's *hesed* is unchanging and human beings are urged to imitate God by practicing this same kind of steadfast love.

Prophets and the Song of Solomon

The Song of Solomon is one of two books of the Bible that never mentions the name of God. (Esther is the other.) In fact, the book doesn't seem even remotely religious, since it consists of a series of poems, with a man and woman who are infatuated with one another heaping praise on the other—mostly praise of the other's physical charms. Why, some readers wonder, was this unreligious and very "earthy" book included in the Bible? The answer is that the book has for centuries been interpreted spiritually— that is, the man and woman in the Song symbolize God and the community of faith and their deep love for each other. In a sense the Song of Solomon is a companion piece to the Book of Hosea, and to the passages in Isaiah, Jeremiah and Ezekiel that refer to God as Israel's "husband." The image is found at the end of the Bible, where the community of saints is referred to as the "Bride" (Revelation 19:7, 21:9).

"I am like that." To worship the fertility god Baal was to honor and model oneself after a promiscuous force of nature with no moral center. The references to Hosea's wife as an "adulterous woman" or "wife of whoredom" may mean she was one of the many women who engaged in the orgiastic worship of these pagan gods.

Another problem with idolatry is that it seems like a relationship but really isn't. An idol isn't a living thing and cannot love. Worshipping anything besides God is not only immoral but also foolish, for the idol—Baal, Zeus, a house, a car—cannot give love. Worshipping and pursuing things is a waste of time, for true satisfaction is found in relationships, not things. And ultimately the greatest satisfaction is found only in God. Deep relations, such as marriage, require work and commitment, but in the end they bring greater rewards than the shallow relations of adultery and promiscuity.

In a sense idolatry is like the original sin of Adam: wanting to decide for ourselves what is good and evil instead of following God's way. In fact, Hosea is the only prophet in the Old Testament to refer to Adam as the "prototype" of human infidelity: "Like Adam, they have broken the covenant" (Hosea 6:7). The covenant, the binding agreement, between God and man has been broken—not by God but by man. Yet God's love endures.

Like other prophets, Hosea saw the mockery of "going through the motions," people who practiced the correct religious rituals in Israel but strayed from God anyway. God says that "I desire mercy, not sacrifice, and acknowledgment of God rather than burnt offerings" (Hosea 6:6). The Israelites who were unfaithful to God on a daily basis foolishly thought that they could make things right by offering up the required sacrifices in the temple. In effect, they were like a wayward spouse making a big fuss over an anniversary or birthday and giving lavish presents. But all the pretty rituals in a marriage can't compensate for frequent infidelity, and religious rituals can't compensate for behavior that shows the person is not truly committed to God.

To fully appreciate Hosea's situation, remember that the punishment for a wife committing adultery was death by stoning. Whether this was commonly done is unknown, but certainly most people of the time considered it a just punishment. Hosea could have divorced his cheating wife or had her put to death, and no one would have thought the less of him. Instead, he chose to love and forgive, and in doing so he was behaving like God.

Hosea prophesied in the reign of Jeroboam II of Israel, who ruled 783–743 BC. Outwardly, things seemed to be going well for Israel, for Jeroboam's reign was peaceful and prosperous. Inwardly, at its heart, Israel was at a low point, far from God. As in a marriage, things can appear pleasant enough on the surface even though the two people are emotionally and spiritually distant.

> ### DID YOU KNOW?
> Although God in the Book of Hosea is presented as the "husband" of Israel, Hosea also presented God as father: "When Israel was a child, I loved him, and out of Egypt I called my son" (Hosea 11:1). If the verse sounds familiar, it is because it is quoted in Matthew's Gospel and connected to the story of Joseph and Mary fleeing with the infant Jesus to safety in Egypt.

"Whoever is wise, let him understand these things; whoever is discerning, let him know them; for the ways of the Lord are right, and the upright walk in them, but transgressors stumble in them" (Hosea 14:9). So ends the Book of Hosea. Marriage to the faithless Gomer had taught Hosea a great deal about heartache, making him aware of how deeply it grieves God when human beings distance themselves from him. Through his disastrous marriage Hosea had become a sadder but wiser man. His hope that the people of his own time would learn from his hard lessons went unfulfilled, for Israel continued in its idolatry and infidelity and was conquered by the cruel Assyrians in 722 BC. Thankfully, though the people of his own time did not listen to him, many generations have profited from the story of Hosea and Gomer, the relationship between the steadfast and forgiving (God) and the fickle and faithless (Israel, and all humankind).

THE REAL MAGDALENE

The Twelve were with him, and also some women who had been cured of evil spirits and diseases: Mary (called Magdalene) from whom seven demons had come out... and many others. These women were helping to support them out of their own means. (Luke 8:1–2)

Early on the first day of the week, while it was still dark, Mary Magdalene went to the tomb and saw that the stone had been removed from the entrance. (John 20:1)

Skeptics and Gnostics

The pagan critic Celsus, writing sometime around AD 170, claimed Mary Magdalene was an unreliable witness to the Resurrection, since she was clearly insane. The Gospels tell us she had been demon-possessed, and two of the Gospels (Mark and Luke) report that the disciples themselves did not believe her at first. Some pagan critics may have noticed that Mary is not listed among the witnesses of the risen Jesus in 1 Corinthians 15:5–7. Celsus referred to her as a "hysterical female" and could not believe anyone would follow a religion with such shaky foundations. He and other pagans observed there were more female than male Christians, so they wrote off Christianity as a ridiculous religion for women and simpleminded men.

On the other hand, the Gnostics, who combined some elements of Christianity with aspects of pagan myths and philosophies, took the opposite view, that Mary was not only a reliable witness but also had received secret teaching from Jesus after his resurrection. These teachings were incorporated into the Gnostic Gospel of Mary, the Gospel of Philip and Pistis Sophia. These old writings, mostly ignored for centuries, have gotten a new lease on life in recent years, at the core of a conspiracy theory that Christians, motivated by antiwoman feeling, suppressed the mystical revelations Jesus gave to Mary.

Mary Magdalene is one of the best-known people of the Bible. Unfortunately, what most people know about her is simply wrong, and what the Bible does tell us about her has mostly been forgotten.

The above quotation from Luke 8 is all that the Bible tells us about Mary's life—except for her being present at Jesus' crucifixion and, later, her encounter with the risen Jesus. It is appropriate that this information is in Luke's Gospel, since Luke seems to have had great sympathy for women, and his is sometimes called the Women's Gospel. From what he tells us in Luke 8, Mary had been cured of her demon possession by Jesus and afterward showed her gratitude by contributing to the support of him and his disciples.

The mention of her having had seven demons mystifies many people. It shouldn't, since the Gospels contain the story of the extremely violent man who was possessed by a whole legion of demons (Mark 5:9, Luke 8:30). In other healings of possessed people, only one demon is mentioned. Judging from Luke's mention of seven demons, we can assume Mary's possession showed itself in bizarre ways, though probably less extreme than the man possessed by a legion.

Then Luke tells us that "many" women contributed their own money to support Jesus and his disciples, and Mary Magdalene is mentioned first on the list. Luke might have mentioned her first because she held some kind of leadership position among the women or, more likely, because she was the first person to see the risen Jesus. Some readers have assumed that Mary and these other women were wealthy and could afford to contribute to the disciples' support, but that isn't necessarily the case at all, for often people with very limited resources have given generously to support ministry. Whether she was rich or poor, certainly Mary was grateful to Jesus for curing her of her demons.

Along with several other women, Mary Magdalene was present at the crucifixion—something remarkable when we remember that Jesus' disciples, with the exception of John, were not, having fled from the garden of Gethsemane when Jesus was arrested. Some of these women must have been known as Jesus' followers, so they were taking a certain risk by drawing near to the cross. Their devotion to Jesus makes quite a contrast to the disciples, who at that point were interested mainly in saving their own skins.

Mary endured the tragedy of seeing the man she honored and admired dying in the most humiliating way imaginable. Happily, on the following Sunday morning, she received one of the greatest privileges ever granted to any human being. Mary had seen where Jesus was buried: a crucial detail in the story, for if she had not known where he was buried, she could not have returned later and found the tomb empty. The Gospels differ in their reports of what happened that first Easter: Matthew, Mark and Luke speak of Mary going with other women to the tomb, while John mentions only Mary. The important detail is that Mary knew where Jesus had been laid and later found it empty. Reporting this news to the disciples, she was not believed: "They did not believe the women, because their words seemed to them like nonsense" (Luke 24:11). Later, as John reports, Mary went back to

CHARACTERS AT LARGE Mary the Bad Girl in Movies

The old tradition (not based on the Bible) of Mary Magdalene as a former prostitute has certainly found its way into popular culture, especially movies, perhaps because audiences are drawn to the character of a bad girl who repents. In Cecil B. DeMille's 1927 movie *The King of Kings*, Mary is no ordinary streetwalking prostitute but a high-class courtesan, living in luxury until she decides to follow Jesus. The stage and movie versions of *Jesus Christ Superstar* made Mary an important character—and, of course, a former prostitute. In the controversial 1998 movie *The Last Temptation of Christ*, Mary is a common whore who had once been in love with Jesus, turning to prostitution after he refused to marry her.

The popular 2004 movie *The Passion of the Christ* depicted Mary not as a former prostitute but, oddly, as the woman caught in adultery (from John 8:3–12). *The Da Vinci Code*, based on a best-selling novel, claimed that Jesus and Mary married and had children who were the ancestors of the kings of France.

In the New Testament period, Mary was the Greek form of the Old Testament name Miriam, the sister of Moses. It was the most common women's name among Jews of this time.

the tomb and encountered the risen Jesus, whom she at first did not recognize. Mary went back to the disciples with the world-changing news: "I have seen the Lord!" (John 20:18).

At this point Mary vanishes from the story. She is not mentioned in Acts or in the New Testament letters. The Eastern Orthodox churches stuck close to the Bible by honoring Mary as the "myrrh-bearer" who came to Jesus' tomb with myrrh and spices on Easter morning and encountered the risen Jesus. But around AD 600, Pope Gregory the Great claimed that Mary was the immoral woman who anoints Jesus' feet (Luke 7:36–50), apparently because this episode is immediately followed by 8:1–3, in which Mary is mentioned first among the women followers of Jesus. Thanks to Gregory's clout, she became a popular saint and continued to be identified with the repentant sinner of Luke 7. It was assumed this woman was a sexual sinner, so eventually people came to think of Mary Magdalene as a reformed prostitute. What a pity that the real Mary, a model of steadfast devotion to Jesus, is so seldom remembered for what the Bible actually tells us about her.

MRS. AND MR.

Greet Priscilla and Aquila, my fellow workers in Christ Jesus, who risked their necks for my life, to whom not only I give thanks but all the churches of the Gentiles give thanks as well. (Romans 16:3–4, ESV)

The churches in the province of Asia send you greetings. Aquila and Priscilla greet you warmly in the Lord, and so does the church that meets at their house. (1 Corinthians 16:19)

In Acts 18, Paul meets "a Jew named Aquila . . . with his wife Priscilla." This married couple, both Christians, were destined to play a key role in the life of Paul and the early church, and it is interesting that once they have been introduced, they are usually referred to as "Priscilla and Aquila," which is contrary to ancient custom, where the husband's name was almost always mentioned first. This tells us that of the two, Priscilla was the dominant personality—or, put another way, that she was more of a spiritual force than her husband was. Aquila wasn't necessarily a henpecked husband, merely one whose wife was more of an influence on those around her.

Paul met the couple in the Greek city of Corinth. They were living in Rome but had left when the Roman emperor Claudius expelled all the Jews from the city—an act that, though Claudius would never know it, had the effect of bringing Paul into contact with two of the most important people in his life and minis-try. Aquila, according to Acts, was a native of Pontus, a region of what is today Turkey. Over the course of his life he had lived there, in Rome, in Corinth and later in Ephesus—in short, he was a man with no permanent home, a man like Paul, a man not averse to travel and thus the perfect type to be a missionary, since he saw his true home as being in heaven.

Priscilla and Aquila shared Paul's trade of tent-making, but more importantly they shared his faith. In a notoriously depraved city like Corinth, they must have been immensely pleased to meet another fellow believer, someone who managed to lead a moral life in immoral surroundings, and their home became Paul's base during his long stay in the city. When he left Corinth, they accompanied him to Ephesus, where they encountered one of the most fervent evangelists among the early Christians, a Jew named Apollos. Like many of the early Christians, he had been a disciple of John the Baptist. Apollos was deeply familiar with the Old Testament, a trait he shared with Paul, and like Paul he was in the habit of presenting the gospel in the synagogues to his fellow Jews. Acts says he "spoke with great fervor"—the Greek literally means he was "boiling with the Spirit." Despite his zeal and wisdom, however, his knowledge of the gospel was inadequate, and so "when Priscilla and Aquila heard him, they invited him to their home and explained to him the way of God more adequately" (Acts 18:26). Very wisely they chose not to embarrass or humiliate this very zealous man in public. Considering him a Christian brother, not a competitor, Priscilla

CHARACTER CLOSE-UP Lydia

In Acts 16, Paul takes the Gospel to the Greek city of Philippi. Most large cities in the Roman Empire had synagogues, but Philippi had only a small community of Jews that met for prayer by a riverside instead of in a synagogue. Among them was a business-woman named Lydia, a dealer in purple dye. Lydia was a God-fearing non-Jew who was drawn to the Jewish religion and converted to Christianity after hearing the gospel preached by Paul. Philippi was Paul's first stop on the continent of Europe, and Lydia held the distinction of being his first Christian convert in Europe. "The Lord opened her heart to respond to Paul's message," and afterward she invited Paul and his missionary companions to stay in her home, which they did (Acts 16:14–15).

The purple dye Lydia dealt was made from the shells of a sea snail and was very expensive, so Lydia would have sought out a very wealthy clientele. No doubt this opened up opportunities for her to present the Gospel to some among the upper class.

House Churches

"Aquila and Priscilla greet you warmly in the Lord, and so does the church that meets at their house" (1 Corinthians 16:19). When the New Testament uses the word *church*, it never refers to a building but to the assembling of the people of faith. Among the first Christians, the custom was to gather for worship and teachings in the homes of members, and a couple of centuries past before actual church buildings existed. When William Tyndale first translated the New Testament from Greek into English in the 1520s, he hesitated to use the word *church*, since he knew the word made people think of buildings, and no church buildings existed in the New Testament period.

Throughout the history of Christianity, house churches have often existed in situations where persecution made it impractical for Christians to meet in designated church buildings. Certainly the New Testament proves that Christianity can exist and even grow without church buildings.

and Aquila were more interested in setting Apollos on the right path than on challenging him in a public debate—a commendable example of more mature Christians gently guiding an enthusiastic newcomer.

It is interesting that Priscilla and Aquila were friends of both Paul and Apollos, for we see in 1 Corinthians 3 that factions had sprung up in the church of Corinth, with some Christians claiming to be followers of Paul, others followers of Apollos. Paul hated this kind of divisiveness and constantly warned against it, emphasizing that there was no place for egotism or party spirit among Christians, for all Christians had one Master, Christ. Later in the same letter, Paul speaks warmly of "our brother Apollos" (1 Corinthians 16:12). Paul and Apollos both had important roles to play in the unfolding of God's plans, and Priscilla and Aquila had the privilege of being involved with the ministry of both these dynamic men of faith.

Paul, as discussed elsewhere in this book (see Day 10), was a single man who commended the celibate life for Christian workers who were able to commit themselves wholly to the Lord. This was not an option for most believers, and Priscilla and Aquila provide the classic example of a married couple who, though they both had full-time jobs, also were zealous workers for the gospel.

We wish the New Testament told us more about this missionary couple, particularly in light of the last

DID YOU KNOW?

In Acts, Luke is more colloquial in regard to personal names than Paul is in his letters. Luke refers to Priscilla, Silas and Sopatros, while Paul uses the formal names Prisca, Silvanus and Sosipatros. Since Acts was written later than most of Paul's letters, Luke may have been using the names that had become most familiar in the Christian world. Most modern translations aim for consistency and use the name Priscilla throughout.

Alexandria, Home of Apollos

Alexandria in Egypt was the Roman Empire's second-largest city, founded centuries earlier by Alexander the Great, who immodestly named numerous cities after himself. It is appropriate that Apollos was a learned man, for Alexandria was an intellectual center. It had a huge Jewish community that traced its origins back to the fall of Jerusalem in 587 BC, when numerous Jews, including the prophet Jeremiah, left Judea and settled in Egypt. Far from being some outpost of Judaism, Alexandria was in some ways the center of it, certainly for the many Jews who spoke Greek. It was in Alexandria that the Septuagint, the Old Testament in Greek, was produced.

Consider how diverse and multicultural the early church was: Apollos was a Jew who spoke Greek, was a native of a city in Egypt, and who spread the gospel through the multilingual, multiethnic Roman Empire.

---

chapter of Romans, where Paul praises Priscilla and Aquila, who "risked their necks" for him (Romans 16:3). In his tireless preaching of the gospel, Paul had made numerous enemies among both Jews and pagans, and on more than one occasion he came close to death. Acts 19 records the story of the pagans in Ephesus engaging in an anti-Paul riot, and possibly it was at this point that the couple took steps to ensure Paul's safety. We know from the ending of Paul's final letter, 2 Timothy, that not all of Paul's fellow Christians were reliable (see Day 20), but Priscilla and Aquila were models of steadfastness. In risking their lives for Paul they displayed the self-giving love that was to draw so many people to the faith.

ANONYMOUS BUT FAITHFUL

I commend to you our sister Phoebe, a servant of the church in Cenchrea. I ask you to receive her in the Lord in a way worthy of the saints and to give her any help she may need from you, for she has been a great help to many people, including me. (Romans 16:1–2)

I plead with Euodia and I plead with Syntyche to agree with each other in the Lord. Yes, and I ask you, loyal yokefellow, help these women who have contended at my side in the cause of the gospel, along with Clement and the rest of my fellow workers, whose names are in the book of life. (Philippians 4:2–3)

Give my greetings to the brothers at Laodicea, and to Nympha and the church in her house. (Colossians 4:15)

Junia or Junias?

Were there women apostles? Consider Romans 16:7: "Greet Andronicus and Junias, my relatives who have been in prison with me. They are outstanding among the apostles, and they were in Christ before I was." Translators disagree on whether the original Greek text here refers to Junias, which is a man's name, or Junia, a woman's name. Since the New Testament makes no reference to women as apostles, tradition says the apostle here was probably a man named Junias. Still, translators admit that it's possible the name is Junia, which would mean there were indeed women apostles, and this one happened to also be a relative of Paul—a double honor. There is no way of knowing for certain, and perhaps it is a moot point, since the New Testament—not to mention two thousand years of Christian history—abounds with examples of devoted and selfless women who witnessed to the gospel, whether they were referred to as apostles or not.

The quote from Philippians 4 mentions those "whose names are in the book of life." Paul is referring to those who are fellow believers, people who are destined for heaven and are already doing God's work on earth. Paul was well aware that his preaching and teaching had made many converts—far more women than men. Then, as now, there were more women in church than men. In fact, historically and globally, women have been and continue to be more religious than men. In the Roman empire during the New Testament period, most of the religious sects attracted far more women than men. One notable exception was the cult of the Persian god Mithra, with no women members at all; Roman soldiers formed the bulk of the membership.

Why are women more drawn to religion than men? The Bible does not answer that question, nor does it try. It simply accepts as a fact that women have an inclination to religion—which, in the case of worshipping false gods is a terrible thing but a good thing in cases where a husband or son comes under the woman's influence and turns to God.

In this chapter we've looked at the quality of steadfastness—a quality notably lacking in the wayward Gomer, wife of Hosea, but present in saintly women like Mary Magdalene and Priscilla. Here we pay tribute to the many women—some of them mentioned by name in the Bible but most of them anonymous—who helped the faith to grow and spread. These are the steady, decent lives that history tends to overlook. In the endings of his letters, Paul often included shout-outs to people he knew, and so his letters preserve the names of several women of faith. One of these is Phoebe, whose name, appropriately, means "shining" or "radiant." "She has been a great help to many people" (Romans 16:12). This certainly must have been true of many other unsung heroines of this period. In the closing of his letter to the Colossians, Paul greets a woman named Nympha "and the church in her house," meaning she was one of many faithful people of this period who let her house be used as a place of worship and fellowship.

These women were human, of course, which is evident in the quote from Philippians 4, where Paul tells Euodia and Syntyche to patch up their quarrel. After all, they were sisters in the faith, and Paul recalls fondly that they had "contended at my side." Clearly these women—and many other nameless ones like them—were not mere spectators in the churches but were actively promoting and modeling the faith.

Not all the women among the early Christians were steadfast in the faith, of course. Acts 5 contains the disturbing story of Ananias and Sapphira, a married couple who sold some land and gave the proceeds to the Christian community in Jerusalem. But, hoping to appear more generous than they actually were, they lied and told the apostles they were donating the full amount, when in fact they were only contributing part of it. Peter, head of the apostles, was irate at this deceit, and when he confronted Ananias, the man fell down dead. Not knowing what had happened to her husband, Sapphira later repeated the lie of Ananias, claiming they had donated the full amount to the church. She too fell down dead. The story makes many readers uncomfortable, since it puts Peter in a bad light, but the story's point is that in this community of faith, there was no place for self-serving deceit.

There were worse women than Sapphira among the early Christians. Revelation 2 contains a message from Jesus to the church in the city of Thyatira, which happened to be the home of Paul's convert Lydia. In contrast to the faithful Lydia was a woman

---

CULTURAL INSIGHTS

Passing on the Faith

"I have been reminded of your sincere faith, which first lived in your grandmother Lois and in your mother Eunice and, I am persuaded, now lives in you also" (2 Timothy 1:5). This quote, from the hand of Paul, presents a unique situation in the New Testament: the Christian faith shared by three generations of one family—Timothy; his mother Eunice; and his grandmother Lois. At the time Paul wrote this, Christianity had existed long enough that there were people like Timothy who had been brought up as Christians, seeing the faith in practice at an early age. The fact that Timothy managed to mature in the faith is all the more remarkable when we remember that though his mother was a Jewish Christian, his father was a pagan (Acts 16:1). We don't know what influence, good or bad, Timothy's Greek father had on his upbringing, but clearly the faith of his mother and grandmother played a role in his own deep faith, and resulted in a devoted young man whom Paul thought of fondly as his spiritual son.

Widows among the First Christians

"Religion that God our Father accepts as pure and faultless is this: to look after orphans and widows in their distress and to keep oneself from being polluted by the world" (James 1:27). The early Christians took James's words to heart, for widows had an honored place among them, and most churches maintained a charitable fund to aid poor widows. As a rule, a widow would live with one of her adult children, but a widow without children was often at the mercy of the world. Among the Christians, widows found not only financial assistance but the warm welcome of a spiritual family as well.

Paul, giving pastoral advice to young Timothy, warned that some widows with too much time on their hands became troublemakers, and yet many others were shining examples of compassion, renowned for "bringing up children, showing hospitality, washing the feet of the saints, helping those in trouble and devoting herself to all kinds of good deeds" (1 Timothy 5:10). Instead of pining away in loneliness and poverty, or wasting time in gossip and idleness, widows could lead lives of service and devotion.

referred to as Jezebel, which was probably not her real name but a reference to the evil Old Testament queen and wife of Ahab. This Jezebel of Thyatira called herself a prophetess and was leading Christians there into all sorts of wickedness, just as the Jezebel of the Old Testament had led her husband into all manner of evil.

But for every Sapphira and Jezebel among the first Christians, there were many saintly women, women like "Tryphena and Tryphosa, those women who work hard in the Lord" (Romans 16:12). Such women were like Tabitha, whom we look at in another chapter (pages 25–26) and "who was always doing good and helping the poor" (Acts 9:36). Such women take up little space in the Bible, and some of their names are unknown to us, but certainly they occupied a great space in the lives they touched. Historians, including the author of Acts, tend to focus on the big names, the movers and shakers, and neglect the little people, who are not so little in God's eyes.

While it is true that men held the leadership positions among the first Christians, there would have been no communities of faith without women like these. If power could be defined not as being in charge but as accomplishing things, then certainly women had great power in the community of faith.

PUTTING THE WORD TO WORK

1. Reflect on Hosea's view of God as a "husband" who is hurt by humans being unfaithful. Does it enrich your understanding of God to think of him not only as Father but also as a faithful and forgiving husband?

2. Take a moment and reread the Cultural Insights box on *hesed*. Make it a point today to try to practice this kind of steadfast love with people close to you.

3. Mary Magdalene was a faithful follower of Jesus, not only helping to support his ministry but also following him to the cross and even to the tomb. Can you think of people you have known who showed such devotion to God?

4. Reflect on Paul's statement that Priscilla and Aquila "risked their necks" for his sake. Take a moment to thank God for people who have gone the extra mile to help you during a crisis.

5. Spend a few moments calling to mind the names—or maybe the faces, if you've forgotten the names—of caring women who have played a positive role in your own life.

Four Profiles in Courage

The fighting men of the Bible are a mixed lot—some good, some bad. At their best they were men who put their confidence more in the power of God than in their own abilities. On many occasions this courage, rooted in faith, proved stronger than many formidable foes. The person who trusts God can act as if an army stands behind him rather than in front of him.

> **MEMORY VERSE**
>
> They who wait upon the Lord shall renew their strength; they shall mount up with wings like eagles; they shall run and not be weary; they shall walk and not faint.
> —Isaiah 40:31 (ESV)

KEY TERM FOR TODAY

Courage

Those who put their confidence in God can face any obstacle, as exemplified in the careers of valiant men recounted in Joshua and Judges.

FOLLOWING THE MOSES ACT

No one will be able to stand up against you all the days of your life. As I was with Moses, so I will be with you; I will never leave you nor forsake you. (Joshua 1:5)

If serving the Lord seems undesirable to you, then choose for yourselves this day whom you will serve, whether the gods your forefathers served beyond the River, or the gods of the Amorites, in whose land you are living. But as for me and my household, we will serve the Lord. (Joshua 24:15)

The great leader Moses married and had sons, and yet he did not establish any kind of dynasty, for there is never a hint in the Bible that he intended to pass on his leadership to his sons. On the contrary, he left the choice of successor to God, and God chose the amazing man Joshua.

The first mention of Joshua is in Exodus 17, where the Israelite slaves, having left Egypt, face their first battle, against the nomad Amalekites—a ragtag mob of ex-slaves facing nomads experienced in desert warfare. Numerically, the Israelites had the advantage, but experience-wise and weapon-wise, the Amalekites were almost certain to win, with their bronze-tipped arrows and spears. To give the Israelites courage, Moses stood on a hilltop with his arms outstretched, and when his arms tired, they were supported by two men. The Israelites took heart from the sight of Moses—and also from the fighting skill of Joshua. The victory in this first battle was important, for had the Israelites lost, they might well have given up hope of ever reaching the promised land, Canaan.

The next mention of Joshua is in Exodus 24. Moses has gone up to Mount Sinai to commune with God, and Joshua, now referred to as Moses' aide, stays on the lower slopes of the mountain to keep watch. While they are on Sinai, the faithless Israelites lose heart and make the infamous golden-calf idol. Moses, with the Ten Commandments in his hands, comes down from the mountain and, like Joshua, hears the commotion in the camp. Joshua notes that it is "the sound of war"—and in a sense he is right, for the Israelites have rebelled against God and are engaged in a pagan orgy at the foot of the mountain. Joshua shares in Moses' disgust at these faithless people.

Later, in Numbers 11, Joshua shows himself to be protective of Moses' honor. Moses has lamented to God that the burden of leading Israel has become too heavy for him to bear. God tells Moses to appoint seventy elders among the Israelites, and these seventy will receive the Spirit of God, just as Moses has been endowed with the Spirit. Hearing two of these men prophesying—speaking under the influence of the Spirit—Joshua calls out, "Moses, my lord, stop them!" Moses replied, "Are you jealous for my sake? I wish that all the Lord's people were prophets and that the Lord would put his Spirit on them!" (Numbers 11:29). Joshua's devotion to the great man is commendable.

Even more commendable is his behavior on the important mission of spying in the land of Canaan. Numbers 13 tells of Moses sending several Israelite men into the land to find out about its people and its productivity. Joshua was among this group. At one locale they found a cluster of grapes so enormous that it had to be brought back on a

---

CULTURAL INSIGHTS ## Pomegranates

When the Israelite spies brought back the enormous cluster of grapes from Canaan, they also brought with them some figs as well as a favorite food of the Israelites, pomegranates. Combining sweetness and tartness, the juicy red pomegranate was and still is one of the most popular fruits of the Middle East, and one of the complaints of the Israelites was that in their slave days in Egypt, they had pomegranates to eat. Moses assured them there were plenty of pomegranates in Canaan also.

Pomegranates were not only pleasant to eat but a beautiful shape as well, and the hem of Israel's high priest's robe was embroidered with pomegranate figures. Later, pomegranate likenesses were carved into the temple in Jerusalem.

pole carried by two men—solid evidence that Canaan was indeed a fertile place, a "land flowing with milk and honey," as God had promised.

Despite this promising sign, most of the Israelite spies were pessimistic: They informed the Israelites that Canaan was full of fortified cities, and the men of the region were huge. Only Joshua and another spy, Caleb, were convinced that Israel could enter the land and subdue it. But the cowardly Israelites harkened to the pessimistic report and ignored Joshua and Caleb. Despite all the miracles God had worked on their behalf, they still had no faith in him.

The punishment for the Israelites was severe: The group that had left Egypt would never enter Canaan—the exceptions being Joshua and Caleb. Because of their courage, grounded in their faith in God, they would enter the promised land.

Later, in Numbers 27, Moses lays his hands on Joshua, a sign of his commissioning as Moses' successor. At the end of Deuteronomy, the great Moses dies, and the Lord speaks these spine-stiffening words to Joshua: "Be strong and courageous, for you will bring the Israelites into the land I promised them on oath, and I myself will be with you" (Deuteronomy 31:23).

Joshua had one key advantage over Moses: During the forty years in the wilderness, the generation of slaves that had left Egypt had all died off. Those people—constantly witnessing miracles from God, yet constantly complaining and losing faith—were no more. The Israelites whom Joshua led into Canaan had all been born free men, with no memory of Egypt or slavery. They were tough people, raised in rough conditions, and they were also disciplined, having been brought up under the Law that God gave to Moses. They were eager to leave the dry wilderness and take possession of the fertile land God promised their parents.

The Book of Joshua opens with heartening words from God, who tells Joshua that "no one will be able to stand up against you all the days of your life. As I was with Moses, so I will be with you; I will never leave you nor forsake you" (Joshua 1:5). Israel's success is conditional; the people must stay faithful to the Law that Moses gave them: "Do not let this Book of the Law depart from your mouth; meditate on it day and night, so that you may be careful to do everything written in it. Then you will be prosperous and successful" (Joshua 1:8).

Right away the Lord gave a sign that he was with Joshua: As the Red Sea had parted to let the Israelites pass over, so now the Jordan River also parted (Joshua 3:14–17). If the Israelites feared that the passing of Moses had left them miracle-less, they were

DID YOU KNOW?

In Jewish tradition, the "commander of the army of the Lord" that Joshua encounters is said to be the archangel Michael, who is usually shown in art bearing a drawn sword.

wrong. As a memorial of this great miracle, Joshua had the people set up twelve large stones, symbolizing the twelve tribes of Israel. Word of the miracle at the Jordan went out to the Canaanites, who feared these new people who had God on their side.

As a sign that he intended to keep the people devoted to God, Joshua had the Israelites celebrate the Passover, commemorating their deliverance from Egypt. From that point on, the Israelites fed not on the miraculous manna that God had supplied them in the wilderness but on the produce of their new home, Canaan.

Conquering this land, with its stone-walled cities, would not be easy—but Joshua did not lose heart. Like Moses, he had a fateful encounter with the Lord. Near the city of Jericho, Joshua meets a "man"—an angel, in fact—with a drawn sword in his hand, who identifies himself as "commander of the army of the Lord." Knowing he is in the presence of a divine being, Joshua falls facedown on the ground. He is given instructions: Instead of storming the walled city, he is to march around it for six days, carrying the ark of the covenant, the gilded chest symbolizing God's presence. On the seventh day, when the priests blew rams' horns, the walls of the city of Jericho fell down flat. Skeptics might attribute the fall of the walls to an earthquake. The person of faith would ask: How did it "just happen" that an earthquake occurred when the Israelites blew their trumpets?

The Israelites had their first victory. "So the Lord was with Joshua, and his fame spread throughout the land" (Joshua 6:27). To his credit, Joshua did not let the fame go to his head. He knew the Israelites' victories were the work of God, and he built an altar to the Lord and read the entire Law aloud to the people to remind them they belonged to the Lord (Joshua 8:30–35).

In the midst of this serious story of the conquest of Canaan, a little humor intrudes. The Canaanites in the town of Gibeon heard of Israel's victories and decided to meet the threat with deceit instead of force. Dressing in ragged clothes and looking like riff-raff, men from Gibeon visited the Israelites, claimed to be from a far country, and offered to make a peace treaty. The Israelites agreed—and once the ruse was revealed, they could not go back on the treaty, meaning they could not attack and conquer Gibeon. But as punishment for their deception, the Gibeonites were forced to be menial laborers for the Israelites (Joshua 9).

Chapter 10 is one of the great battle episodes in the Bible, with Joshua and the Israelites facing a great Canaanite army near Gibeon. Aiding the Israelites

DID YOU KNOW?

The Hebrew name Caleb means "dog," and although the Israelites did not have a high opinion of dogs, Caleb is an admirable character.

Amalekites

According to Genesis 36, the Amalekites were descendants of Esau, the brother of Jacob. Technically, then, the Israelites and Amalekites were kin, but there was no love between the groups, and the Amalekites were a thorn in Israel's side beginning with their attack on Israel in Exodus 17. Though the Israelites won that battle, the Amalekites continued to be a threat, infamous for their swift attacks using their camels. Judges 7 refers to their camels as being "thick as locusts," like the "sand on the seashore."

Since they were nomads, the Amalekites had no permanent home. They controlled —and patrolled—the trade routes between Arabia and Egypt, making a profit either by imposing tolls or by plundering any travelers.

was a shower of great hailstones, sent by God—in fact, more of the Canaanites were felled by the hail than by the Israelites' swords. This was the second time that hail had miraculously aided Israel, the first time being the plague of hail that God sent on Egypt in the days of Moses.

In the midst of the fighting at Gibeon, Joshua prayed for the sun to stand still: "So the sun stood still, and the moon stopped, till the nation avenged itself on its enemies . . . The sun stopped in the middle of the sky and delayed going down about a full day. There has never been a day like it before or since, a day when the Lord listened to a man. Surely the Lord was fighting for Israel" (Joshua 10:13–14). Modern readers, more familiar with astronomy than people in ancient times were, have difficulty with this verse—after all, we know the sun itself isn't literally moving across the sky. What did happen? In his book *Worlds in Collision*, author Immanuel Velikovsky proposed this theory: The sun seemed to stand still because a near-collision between the earth and a comet caused a temporary halt in the earth's rotation. Whatever happened, Joshua and the Israelites had no doubt that the power of God was at work. God had led them out of Egypt and sustained them in an arid wilderness for many years, and now he was with them in Canaan.

The Book of Joshua ends with the inspiring farewell address of Joshua to the people. At this point the land of Canaan has been divided up among the twelve tribes of Israel, and Joshua knows he will die soon. The great man reminds the people that it was not their own military prowess that gave them the land but rather the power of the Almighty. In gratitude to God they should "fear the Lord and serve him with all faithfulness," worshipping only him and not the gods of Canaan. Joshua presents them with a choice: God or idols. "If serving the Lord seems undesirable to you, then choose for yourselves this day whom you will serve, whether the gods your forefathers served beyond the River, or the gods of the Amorites, in whose land you are living. But as for me and my household, we will serve the Lord" (Joshua 24:15). Heeding these words of their honored leader, the Israelites insist that they too will serve only God and continue to obey him. And so "Israel served the Lord throughout the lifetime of Joshua and of the elders who outlived him and who had experienced everything the Lord had done for Israel" (Joshua 24:31). What a pity that the next generations did not persist in this dedication to the Lord.

THE ANTI-BAAL MAN

The Lord turned to him and said, "Go in the strength you have and save Israel out of Midian's hand. Am I not sending you?" (Judges 6:14)

The Book of Joshua is admittedly very violent, but it is a triumphant and optimistic book, ending on a happy note, with the Israelites settled in Canaan and swearing to be faithful to God, as Moses and Joshua had commanded. The Book of Judges is a disappointing sequel. It becomes clear that the Israelites had not done a thorough job in driving out the immoral pagan inhabitants and, as God foresaw, the Israelites had adopted the habits of their pagan neighbors, worshipping local fertility gods such as Baal and Ashtaroth. In his farewell speech, Joshua had given the Israelites a choice: Serve God or serve the idols. Put another way, the choice was to conform to the world around you or to live as God commanded. There was no middle ground. In Judges we see that most had chosen the route of conforming to the pagan world. The punishment for this was the constant harassment of the violent nations on Israel's borders.

But God had not abandoned Israel. He raised up military leaders—the "judges"—to fight off Israel's many enemies. Among these were Barak and the amazing woman Deborah, whose story is told in another chapter (Day 7). For forty years—an entire generation—after Deborah, Israel was at peace. Then, according to Judges 6, Israel began to suffer at the hands of the desert marauders, their old enemies the Amalekites, and also of the Midianites, notorious for their swift raids on their camels. "Midian so impoverished the Israelites that they cried out to the Lord for help" (Judges 6:6). In answer to their cry, the Lord sent a prophet, reminding them of the good things he had done for them in times past—and how they had flagrantly disobeyed him.

But in spite of their disobedience, God was not abandoning them. He sent an angel to a man named

> **DID YOU KNOW?**
>
> Founded in 1899, the Gideons International is famous for placing Bibles in hotel rooms. The jug that is the Gideons' logo is based on the account in Judges 7 of the clever device Gideon and his men use to startle the Midianites.

Gideon, who was busy threshing wheat—not out in the open but hidden away in a winepress, in the hope that the Midianites would not see him. No doubt he was hoping that if the raiders arrived suddenly, at least they would not make off with the wheat in the winepress. The angel greeted Gideon in a surprising way: "The Lord is with you, mighty warrior." Gideon was taken aback: If the Lord was with him, why was Israel suffering at the hands of the Midianites? Like many people in Israel, Gideon was convinced God had abandoned the people. But the Lord's angel was insistent: "Go in the strength you have and save Israel out of Midian's hand. Am I not sending you?" If Gideon was truly a mighty warrior, he did not regard himself as one—yet. He protested to the angel that he was an unimportant man in one of the most unimportant families in Israel. But the angel would not be put off: "I will be with you, and you will strike the Midianites as one man" (Judges 6:16, ESV).

Gideon had doubts about himself—and the visitor as well. To test whether this mysterious visitor was indeed sent from God, Gideon brought out some meat and bread and placed them on a rock. The visitor touched the food with his staff and fire sprang forth from the rock. Then the visitor vanished suddenly, but Gideon was convinced he had heard the voice of the Lord.

Gideon had been summoned to do God's work, but Gideon's own family worshipped idols. Gideon's father had dedicated an altar to Baal and set up a pole symbolizing the fertility goddess Asherah. At the command of God, Gideon tore these down and set up an altar to God—but he did so at night, fearing the wrath of his idol-worshipping neighbors. The next morning the locals were furious. They sought out Gideon's father and insisted Gideon be put to death. Apparently Gideon's father had more loyalty to his family than to Baal, for he told the locals that if Gideon had dishonored Baal, then Baal

---

CULTURAL INSIGHTS

"The Lord" or an Angel?

Gideon's encounter with the angel in Judges 6 is one of several episodes in the Bible where a divine messenger is sometimes referred to as "the angel of the Lord" and sometimes simply as "the Lord." Was the narrator confused? Not at all. The narrator believed that the angel was a messenger sent from God, so whatever the angel said was like the voice of the Lord himself speaking.

The Bible is insistent that God himself is an invisible spirit, which is why the Israelites were prohibited from making any image of God. But the stories of angelic visitations show that God can, when he wishes, assume a visible form.

Farming in Canaan

An Israelite farmer's life centered on three products: grain, wine and olives. His agricultural year began in September with the olive harvest. In late October, at the time of the winter rains, he planted wheat and barley. Flax for making linen was cut down in March and April. Barley was harvested in April, wheat in May. Summer was the season for fruits and vegetables, such as lentils, chickpeas, cucumbers, pomegranates, figs, dates and melons. In the heat of summer, vineyards were pruned and tended, and the grape harvest was in late August.

Egypt had its Nile waters to irrigate with, but Canaan was weather-dependent, and the weather was not always kind, for there were sometimes drought and sometimes floods, plus the constant threat of insect pests such as locusts. In the time of Gideon, the worst problem was the "human locusts," the feared Midianite raiders on their camels.

should avenge himself. Because of this incident, Gideon was given the name Jerub–Baal, meaning "let Baal contend." Needless to say, the nonexistent god Baal did nothing.

Gideon's gumption was up. Facing a fearsome coalition of Midianites and Amalekites, Gideon sounded the trumpet and summoned more Israelites to join him. "The Spirit of the Lord clothed Gideon" (Judges 6:34, ESV). The man who had feared to thresh his wheat in the open, the man who regarded himself as an unimportant man from an unimportant family, was about to lead the army of the Lord.

As God saw it, Gideon's army was too large. He was going to make them victorious over the Midianites—but their victory would be due to him, not to their great numbers. So he had Gideon pare down the band from thirty-two thousand to ten thousand, sending home those who were fearful. Then, to Gideon's astonishment, the force was pared down even further—to a mere three hundred. By human standards, this was folly. Three hundred men could not possibly defeat the Midianite forces—unless, of course, God was on their side.

Dividing the men into three companies, Gideon staged a midnight raid on the Midianites. Raising a ruckus by blowing trumpets and breaking jars, they sent the Midianites into wild panic, so that some of them even killed each other. The Israelites' cry—"A sword for the Lord and for Gideon!"—rallied other Israelites into the field.

Gideon's defeat of the dreaded Midianites was so total that it was remembered thereafter as a sign of God's power. He had so impressed the Israelites that they made him an offer: Rule over Israel as its king and establish a dynasty. A lesser man would eagerly have accepted—and, in fact, the situation Gideon faced is the situation that has established kingships throughout history. But Gideon was not only a valiant warrior but a man of character and humility as well. "I will not rule over you, nor will my son rule over you," he said. "The Lord will rule over you" (Judges 8:23). In another chapter (Day 21) we will look at Gideon's ambitious, selfish son Abimelech, a man of very different caliber from his father, who did indeed try to make himself king over Israel.

Gideon, the stouthearted man of honor, gave Israel forty years of peace from foreign enemies. Regrettably, he did not give them forty years of freedom from idolatry. Gideon took the gold earrings and camel neck-chains that had been plundered from the Midianites and made them into an ephod—probably a large medal or trophy that was intended to commemorate victory. But eventually the Israelites began to worship it as an idol—ironic, considering that it was God who had given them victory over the Midianites.

CASTOFF SON

Jephthah the Gileadite was a mighty warrior. His father was Gilead; his mother was a prostitute. (Judges 11:1)

Jephthah made a vow to the Lord: "If you give the Ammonites into my hands, whatever comes out of the door of my house to meet me when I return in triumph from the Ammonites will be the Lord's, and I will sacrifice it as a burnt offering." (Judges 11:30–31)

In the Book of Joshua, one of its most appealing characters is the prostitute Rahab, who hides the Israelite spies when they come to Jericho. In Judges, one of its most appealing characters is the son of a prostitute. In the Old Testament, God sometimes uses people of doubtful reputation to accomplish his purposes.

Jephthah, a "mighty warrior," had many brothers, or rather half-brothers, but they drove him away from their home and made it clear he would have no share in the family inheritance. In a locale called Tob, Jephthah gathered around him a band of thugs. As it turned out, at this period in its history Israel did not fear this band of thugs so much as they feared the neighbor nation of Ammonites. So Israel sent word to Jephthah: Lead them in battle against the Ammonites. Jephthah was put off by this, and reminded them that they had driven him away. What business did they have asking him for aid now? Nevertheless, they were in dire straits and pressed him to come to their aid. And considering how they had treated him in the past, better to have him on their side than—horrors!—possibly joining forces with the Ammonites. So Jephthah agreed to aid them, sealing the deal at Mizpah, which was an appropriate location, the site where, centuries earlier, Jacob and his scheming father-in-law Laban had made an agreement with each other. Mizpah seemed a perfect place for sealing agreements between parties who didn't entirely trust each other.

Ammonites

According to Genesis 19, Ammon was the son of Lot, Abraham's nephew. In this sordid story, Lot's family has been allowed to escape from sinful Sodom before it is destroyed. Lot's wife disobeys God, looks back on the city, and is turned into a pillar of salt. In the wilderness, Lot's two unmarried daughters get their father drunk, sleep with him, and conceive. One daughter gives birth to Moab, the other to Ammon. The two sons become the ancestors of two pagan nations that were a constant menace to Israel. The first mention of Ammon as a threat is in Judges, especially in the story of Jephthah. He defeats them, but they are periodically a threat to Israel for many centuries.

The Ammonites worshipped a god name Molech—the name means "king." Huge metal images of the god were actually designed as furnaces, in which people sacrificed infants. It is ironic that Jephthah, the man who defeated the Ammonites, ended up sacrificing his own daughter. It is also ironic that Solomon, who built the Lord's temple in Jerusalem, also married Ammonite women and built a shrine to Molech. Some of the later kings in Jerusalem would sacrifice their own children to Molech.

The name lives on in Amman, the capital of the present-day nation of Jordan. Amman is on the site of the old Ammonite capital, Rabbath Ammon.

Surprisingly and commendably, Jephthah's first act was to try to use diplomacy, not force. He sent a messenger to Ammon with an obvious question: Why are you attacking us? As is always the case in international disputes, the Ammonites had an excuse: When the Israelites settled in Canaan, they took away some of Ammon's land. At this point, Israel had held the area for three hundred years, so it seemed a bit absurd for the Ammonites to claim it was their land. Jephthah put the situation in religious terms: the Israelites held what God had given them, and the Ammonites held what their god Chemosh had given them. "The king of Ammon, however, paid no attention to the message Jephthah sent him" (Judges 11:28). Jephthah's attempt at diplomacy and nonviolence had failed.

So Jephthah stepped into the role he had been drafted for—that of the military leader. "The Spirit of the Lord was upon Jephthah" (Judges 11:29). Although the Spirit endowed him with great courage at this time, it does not seem to have endowed him with wisdom, for Jephthah made a very foolish vow: If God would give him victory over the Ammonites, he would offer as a sacrifice whatever came from the door of his house to meet him afterward.

The Lord was with Jephthah, and he and his men defeated the Ammonites. "When Jephthah returned to his home in Mizpah, who should come out to meet him but his daughter, dancing to the sound of tambourines! She was an only child. Except for her he had neither son nor daughter" (Judges 11:34). When Jephthah had made his vow to the Lord, it may not have occurred to him that "whatever" came out to meet him when he returned home might not be a calf or a sheep but his own flesh and blood—or had it? Living among a gang of hoodlums, perhaps Jephthah had imbibed some of their contempt for human life, even to the point of accepting the gruesome custom of human sacrifice.

Realizing what a terrible thing he had done, he tore his clothes in agony. A vow to God was a binding thing, as Jephthah well knew, and he could not go back on it. The poor daughter, too, was aware of the nature of the vow: "My father . . . you have given your word to the Lord. Do to me just as you promised, now that the Lord has avenged you of your enemies, the Ammonites." But the daughter made a request: Before killing her as a sacrifice, give her two months to go away with her friends to the mountains. Having never known a man nor had children, she was "mourning her virginity."

Child sacrifice was taken for granted among the nations that bordered Israel. It horrified the Israelites, and it is tragic that the story of Jephthah's triumph over the Ammonites ends so sadly. Clearly a man of great courage does not always possess wisdom.

HOTBLOODED HEBREW

> The Philistines seized him, gouged out his eyes and took him down to Gaza. Binding him with bronze shackles, they set him to grinding in the prison. But the hair on his head began to grow again after it had been shaved. (Judges 16:21–22)

In the last section we looked at a man of gumption, Jephthah, who made a rash vow. Here we will look at a man who set the gold standard for rash behavior as well as the gold standard for valor and strength: the amazing Samson.

The judges Gideon and Jephthah were already adults when God called them to his service. Not so Samson, who from his very conception was destined to do great things for God. Samson's mother, of the tribe of Dan, was childless, but an angel from God appeared to her and announced she would bear a son, whom she was to dedicate to God from his birth. He would be a Nazirite, meaning he would never touch alcohol, cut his hair or have contact with any dead thing. Most importantly, this son would in time "begin the deliverance of Israel from the hands of the Philistines." These were the people who had settled on the coast west of Israel and were steadily moving inland, the latest and most threatening of the many foreign enemies that Israel had faced. Israel was at a very low point, yet things were about to change, for an angel of God had promised a long-barren woman that she would conceive, a sign that God was doing marvelous things again.

The son was named Samson, and at some point "the Spirit of the Lord began to stir in him," though we aren't told how this was evident. It soon became obvious that even

Samson in Art

Artists have long been attracted to the Samson story, and museums are filled with paintings of the vivid scenes from Judges: Samson forcing apart the pillars of the Dagon temple, being shorn of his locks, slaying the Philistines with the jawbones of a donkey, wrestling with a lion, toiling sightless at the mill in Gaza. Pictures of Samson asleep in the lap of Delilah are common, providing artists an excuse to depict a bare-chested, muscular man with a sensuously clad, often bare-breasted woman. (Some of these Delilah images are correct in showing the Philistines, not her, giving Samson his haircut.) In a sense the Samson story is all visual, as artists have learned. Probably another reason Samson has attracted artists is that he is one of the few biblical characters who is presumed to have a muscular physique, much like the gods and heroes of Greek mythology, such as Hercules.

though his mother had dedicated him to the Lord, Samson had a rash streak in him, for he decided to take a wife from, of all people, the Philistines. Naturally his parents were horrified—not just a foreign woman, but a woman from the violent Philistines, who oppressed Israel! But in his rashness Samson would accomplish God's purpose, for his close contact with the Philistines made him "the enemy within."

Going to visit his future wife, Samson was attacked by a young lion. Charged with the Spirit of God, Samson tore the lion into pieces with his bare hands. Some time later, passing by the scene of the attack, Samson found that bees had made a hive in the lion's skeleton, and Samson took some of the honey with him. At a wedding feast hosted for the Philistines, Samson posed his famous riddle: "Out of the eater, something to eat; out of the strong, something sweet." If they could explain what this meant, he would give them thirty changes of clothes; if not, they would have to give him thirty changes of clothes.

The Philistines were stumped, so they talked his wife into wheedling the answer out of him. He finally caved in, and naturally she told the Philistines, who revealed the answer: "What is sweeter than honey? What is stronger than a lion?" Samson was furious. He knew they had learned the answer from his wife. So he kept his side of the bet—in a violent way. He went to the Philistine city of Ashkelon and killed thirty men, taking their clothes and giving them to the wedding party. Instead of taking up residence with his wife, he went back home, while his wife married his best man. Later, when Samson decided he wanted her back and found she was with another man, he took vengeance on the Philistines by tying torches to the tails of three hundred foxes and turning them loose in the Philistines' grain fields.

In vengeance, the Philistines conducted raids on the Israelite tribe of Judah. Samson agreed to let the men of Judah bind him and hand him over to the Philistines. But when they handed him over, he snapped the ropes as if they were mere threads. Using the jawbone of a donkey, he struck down a thousand of the Philistines.

Samson was lustful as well as violent. He went to visit a prostitute in the Philistine city of Gaza. Ancient cities had gates that were shut at night, and the Philistines were certain they had Samson in their clutches. Samson arose at midnight and, finding the city gates locked, lifted them off their posts and went on his way.

Lust would get him into deeper trouble. He was infatuated with the Philistine woman Delilah. Knowing this, the Philistine lords made her an offer: they would give her eleven hundred pieces of silver if she could discover the secret of Samson's incredible strength. Samson would reveal the secret to her—but not immediately. Instead he toyed with her awhile. First he told her that if he were bound with seven bowstrings, he would be as weak as other men—but when she roused him up by shouting, "The Philistines are upon you, Samson!" he snapped the bowstrings as if they were threads. The same thing happened when he was bound with ropes. Then he told her that if the seven locks of his long hair were woven into a loom he would become weak, but again this was a joke on Delilah. She did her feminine best to find the true secret, and finally he gave in: If his long hair—the sign of his dedication to God since his birth—were ever cut, he would lose his strength. Falling asleep on her lap, the mighty man awoke to find his hair had been cut—not by Delilah herself but by one of the Philistine men.

Worse things followed: The Philistines gouged out his eyes and bound him with iron chains. They took him to a prison in Gaza, where they put him to work turning the huge wheel of a mill, a task usually done by an animal.

CULTURAL INSIGHTS

Gaza

The city of Gaza, near the Mediterranean shore, existed as early as 2000 BC. Sometime in the 1100s BC the Philistines occupied the area and made it the chief of their five cities. In the Samson story, the city was where the Philistines attempted to ambush Samson after the city gates had been shut at night—but Samson carried off the city gates. Later, it was in Gaza that the blinded Samson was made to work like an animal at a millstone, and where he brought down the temple of the god Dagon.

The prophet Amos condemned the busy commercial city for trafficking slaves. When Christianity spread through the region, Gaza resisted it strongly, holding on to the old paganism for many centuries.

Many cities mentioned in the Bible long ago ceased to exist, but Gaza is still very much on the map, partly because it sits within the Gaza Strip, a narrow belt of land that has been in the news often, being contested by Israel and Egypt.

"But the hair on his head began to grow again after it had been shaved" (Judges 16:22). This is perhaps the most dramatic "but" in the Old Testament, setting the stage for the violent climax to this very violent story. The Philistines had decided to hold a festival to honor Dagon, one of their gods. They believed Dagon had delivered Samson into their hands, and so they decided to celebrate the humiliation of Samson in an appropriate place, the huge temple of Dagon. Drunk with wine, they watched as the blind Samson was led into the temple by a boy. Samson was supposed to be the "entertainment" of the day. Samson's hands were on the temple's two main pillars. The man with a violent and lust-filled past behind him prayed: "O Sovereign Lord, remember me. O God, please strengthen me just once more, and let me with one blow get revenge on the Philistines for my two eyes" (Judges 16:28). Finding his strength returned, he pushed apart the two pillars, bringing down the temple of Dagon on the three thousand Philistines. "Thus he killed many more when he died than while he lived."

Samson's last words were, "Let me die with the Philistines!" Despite his rashness and lustful nature, no one could accuse this amazing man of lacking courage. While he could hardly be called a role model of saintliness, he was fully aware that his strength and courage were gifts from the Lord. And in the workings of God, Samson, a rather selfish and carnal character, is used by God to strike a blow at Israel's enemies.

Samson is in a sense the climax of Judges because he is battling the worst enemy Israel had faced, the Philistines. He accomplishes less than some of the other judges, such as Deborah and Gideon, but we cannot help but admire him for singlehandedly taking on the greatest threat in the book. Of such men we need reminding.

In closing this chapter, it's helpful to remember that most of us never face situations such as those that Joshua, Gideon, Jephthah and Samson faced, yet all of us, like them, at times need the unshakable courage that comes only from God, spoken of so vividly by Isaiah: "They who wait upon the Lord shall renew their strength; they shall mount up with wings like eagles; they shall run and not be weary; they shall walk and not faint" (Isaiah 40:31, ESV).

PUTTING THE WORD TO WORK

1. Meditate for a few moments on God's words to Joshua: "I will be with you." Consider that Joshua was leading the conquest and settlement of an entire country, yet his courage arose from his full confidence that God was with him.

2. Joshua's words "as for me and my house, we will serve the Lord" have been quoted often, but pause to reflect on what those words really mean for your life. How can you serve the Lord at this moment?

3. Gideon, a timid farmer, had his life changed by his encouraging encounter with the angel. Make a special point today to say a word of encouragement to someone who needs it.

4. Before fighting the Ammonites, the warrior Jephthah made an attempt at diplomacy. In your prayers today, pray for world leaders, asking God to give them the special courage to try to settle disputes peacefully instead of through violence.

5. Though you were probably familiar with the Samson story already, what did you learn about him from this chapter that you can apply to your own life?

Men in Awe

Today we focus on some of the great prophets of the Old Testament, particularly Isaiah, whose life was never the same after his amazing vision of God in his glory. Like other prophets, his awareness of God's majesty made him aware of the limitations of human power, and of the necessity to pursue justice in the world.

KEY TERM FOR TODAY ## Awe

The great prophets of the Bible were filled with awe when they experienced God. They knew him as the Almighty One who rules over all things, yet also as the One who draws near to those who practice humble faith.

THE DIVINE PRESSURE

The Lord reached out his hand and touched my mouth and said to me, "Now, I have put my words in your mouth." (Jeremiah 1:9)

Prophecy never had its origin in the will of man, but men spoke from God as they were carried along by the Holy Spirit. (2 Peter 1:21)

In an earlier chapter we looked at Israel's priests—on the whole, a sorry lot, though a few were saints. Who can forget that the high priest condemned Jesus as a blasphemer and handed him over to Pilate for execution? Far more admirable than the priests were the prophets, and we have already looked at some of the great ones, such as Elijah and Elisha. In this chapter we will look at some other great prophets, but first let's consider just what prophecy meant in ancient Israel.

In the Bible, a prophet was one who spoke for God, one who often began his speeches with, "Thus says the Lord . . ." He was God's spokesman, God's mouthpiece. The Hebrew word we translate as "prophet" is *nabi*, which is connected with a root word meaning "to call" and "to proclaim." The *nabi*, the prophet, is both called by God and told to proclaim God's word. "Then the Lord reached out his hand and touched my mouth and said to me, 'Now, I have put my words in your mouth'" (Jeremiah 1:9). "The Sovereign Lord has spoken—who can but prophesy?" (Amos 3:8). "The Lord took me from tending the flock and said to me, 'Go, prophesy to my people Israel'" (Amos 7:15). The prophet may, like Jeremiah, be aware that being God's proclaimer may bring him insult, even physical harm, but he feels the compulsion to express it: "I am weary of holding it in; indeed, I cannot" (Jeremiah 20:8–9). The true prophets feel a kind of divine pressure to speak.

According to 2 Peter 1:21, "Prophecy never had its origin in the will of man, but men spoke from God as they were carried along by the Holy Spirit." In other words, prophecy is "Spirit-driven." The prophet speaks not on his own initiative but on God's.

A prophet was at times a predictor of the future but more often brought a warning of a future that was still in doubt—a future that might be promising or woeful, depending on whether the people were living in accordance with God's will. A prophet felt a certain compulsion from God to interpret the events of the day, sometimes to show the deeper spiritual meaning behind world events that might, on the surface, seem hopeful. In a sense, the prophet took God's view of things—the eternal view—and could look at the past, present and future from God's point of view. Thus he could see a looming catastrophe when others did not—or see a hopeful outcome when others expected disaster.

There were two sides of the prophetic message: threat and consolation. For God's people, pardon and punishment are complementary. "See, today I appoint you over nations and kingdoms to uproot and tear down, to destroy and overthrow, to build and to plant" (Jeremiah 1:10). It would be a mistake to think of the prophets strictly as "prophets of doom," because in all their messages is an undertone of love, of divine compassion wanting to spare people from catastrophe. The prophet attempts to lead the idol worshipper back to the true God, lead kings from oppression to justice, lead the proud to humility, lead the corrupt to purity.

In many ancient cultures, prophet and priest were the same person. Not in Israel. In fact, from the very beginning some of the priests were corrupt men, hardly fit to speak for God. The sons of Israel's first priest Aaron were bad men, and the Gospels make it clear how corrupt the priests of Jesus' day were. The priesthood was hereditary, passed on from father to son, but one became a prophet by being called by God. We see in many books of the Old Testament that the priests were often the worst enemies of the prophets, since the prophets spoke out boldly against priests who were corrupt and immoral. The prophets saw the people and priests going through the motions of religious rituals but behaving immorally the rest of the time, and they knew God was not pleased. The prophets spoke of this kind of hypocrisy as being "adulterous." For prophets, the adultery of Israel was something like a spouse who showed up every year with expensive anniversary presents and then cheated the rest of the time. The rituals might be right, but the behavior did not match, meaning the rituals were mere mockery. When there was religious reform in Israel, it was initiated by the prophets and kings, not by the priests.

Prophets could call kings on the carpet as well. Nathan called David on the carpet for his adultery and murder, while Elijah did the same to Ahab for his murder of Naboth and the seizing of his land. The prophet is the interpreter and the delegate of God, and thus superior to the king who does not obey God, superior to the priest who does not understand God, superior to the people who have deserted God to run after idols. From the very beginning of the monarchy in Israel, the prophets played the role of reminding the people that human monarchy was bound to have its oppressive side, and God was the true king of Israel. You might say that "the kingdom of God" was the theme of every prophet. Small wonder that Israel's kings often persecuted prophets.

FROM "WOE IS ME!" TO "SEND ME!"

> In the year that King Uzziah died, I saw the Lord seated on a throne, high and exalted, and the train of his robe filled the temple. . . . "Woe to me!" I cried. "I am ruined! For I am a man of unclean lips, and I live among a people of unclean lips, and my eyes have seen the King, the Lord Almighty." (Isaiah 6:1, 5)
>
> Ah, sinful nation, a people loaded with guilt, a brood of evildoers, children given to corruption! They have forsaken the Lord; they have spurned the Holy One of Israel and turned their backs on him. (Isaiah 1:4)

"God is awesome!" is one of the key themes of the whole Bible, and certainly of one of its most-read Old Testament books, Isaiah. The theme could also be stated as "God is holy!"—a quality that the God of the Bible did not share with the gods the pagans worshipped, gods who were perceived to have great power but were not particularly good or righteous. In fact, in the pagans' myths their gods were often more violent, temperamental, deceitful and promiscuous than the average human being. Not so the God of the Bible, who is not just the Almighty One but also the Holy One. What sets him apart from human beings is not just his overwhelming power but his moral nature.

Isaiah's famous commissioning as a prophet occurred "in the year that King Uzziah died," which was about 740 BC. Uzziah had reigned over Judah for almost forty years and was a good king. So was his son Jotham, who reigned from about AD 740 to AD 736. A great change would come in AD 736, when Jotham's son Ahaz would prove to be one of the nation's most wicked kings. However, his long and inglorious reign still lay in the future when Isaiah had his life-changing vision in the temple, related in Isaiah 6. Two things stood out in the vision: the awesomeness of God and the pettiness and sinfulness of human beings. Even under good kings like Uzziah and Jotham, the people had not been fully faithful to God. Isaiah saw in his vision the throne of God, with six-winged angels—the seraphs, or "burning ones"—calling to one another: "Holy, holy, holy is the Lord Almighty; the whole earth is full of his glory." With these sights and sounds burning his mind, Isaiah experienced a sort of spiritual panic attack: "Woe is me! For I am a man of unclean lips, and I live among a people of unclean lips, and my eyes have seen the King, the Lord Almighty." What right did an unclean man have to be in the presence of this holy God?

Then, in the vision, one of the seraphs took a live coal from the altar and touched Isaiah's lips, a sign of purging away his sin. Then he heard the Lord's own voice: "Whom shall I send? And who will go for us?" And Isaiah responded, "Here am I. Send me!" The Mighty and Holy One, who had filled Isaiah with such dread and awe, cared about these "people of unclean lips." As always in the Bible, he did not wish to destroy the sinners or distance himself from them but to draw near to them. But doing so would require their spiritual transformation. In effect, they would have to experience what Isaiah had experienced: comprehending the awesomeness of God, comprehending their own failings and inadequacies, and dedicating themselves to being holy, as God himself is holy.

In other words, what was required was *conversion*. The prophets often use the Hebrew word *shub*, literally meaning "to turn." In modern times, we might say the person "does a spiritual 180." The idea is that the person seeks the Lord, humbles before him, directs

---

CULTURAL INSIGHTS

Grass

Though you will find the word *grass* in the Bible, it never refers to neatly mown turf grass, and people in ancient times had no conception of a lawn. The "grass" in the Bible was any low-growing wild plant. Because it was common and insignificant and did not live long, grass symbolized the brevity of life, and many Bible verses (such as Psalms 37:2, 90:5, 92:7, 102:11 and 103:15) use grass in this symbolic way.

No doubt the most familiar quote regarding grass is found in Isaiah: "A voice says, 'Cry out.' And I said, 'What shall I cry?' 'All men are like grass, and all their glory is like the flowers of the field. . . . . The grass withers and the flowers fall, but the word of our God stands forever" (Isaiah 40:6–8). Later in the same book, God reminds his faithful ones not to "fear mortal men, the sons of men, who are but grass" (Isaiah 51:12).

"Almighty" and "of Hosts"

One Hebrew phrase that has been translated in very diverse ways is *Yahweh Sabaoth*. *Yahweh*, the name of God, is almost always translated "Lord," but *Sabaoth* has been rendered in many ways, notably the King James Version's "Lord of Hosts," using "hosts" in the old sense of "hordes" or "armies." Although the usual interpretation is that the "hosts" referred to Israel's armies or to heaven's armies of angels, *Yahweh Sabaoth* probably means "Yahweh over all things," God as both Creator and Ruler. The pagans thought of the planets and stars as divine beings, the "hosts" of heaven, but for Israel, God ruled all things, even these "hosts."

Contemporary readers are often puzzled by "Lord of Hosts," so most modern versions do not use the phrase. The New International Version, quoted in this book, translates *Yahweh Sabaoth* as "Lord Almighty." The Message, a popular paraphrase, has "God-of-the-Angel-Armies," the New Life Bible has "Lord of All," and the New Century Version has "Lord-All-Powerful."

Isaiah uses *Yahweh Sabaoth* sixty-one times, notably in his vision passage in chapter 6. The similar "holy, holy, holy" verse in Revelation 4:8 refers to God as *Kurios Pantokrator*, Greek for "Lord of all things." With faith in the "Lord of Hosts," Isaiah did not fear the armies of Assyria or any nation.

his heart to him, learns to obey God and to do good to other men. This turning, this conversion, is a change on the inside but it inevitably results in change in behavior. When this soul-turning occurs, the Lord is always willing, even eager, to forgive.

In his long ministry, which probably lasted more than forty years, Isaiah lived in Jerusalem and had easy access to the court, even during the reigns of wicked kings like Ahaz. Despite changes of kings and changes in the political climate, Isaiah never ceased to dwell on the theme of God as the awesome Holy One. In fact, the Book of Isaiah uses the phrase "the Holy One of Israel" twenty-six times, much more than the other prophets. While the people of his nation were in awe of the military power of the neighboring empires, notably Assyria, Isaiah was much more in awe of the eternal power of God. And while he never forgot God's awesomeness, he also never forgot the moral failings of human beings, which is announced at the very beginning of the book: "Ah, sinful nation, a people loaded with guilt, a brood of evildoers, children given to corruption! They have forsaken the Lord; they have spurned the Holy One of Israel and turned their backs on him" (Isaiah 1:4).

Happily, Isaiah was active during the reign of one king who most definitely did not turn his back on God, the saintly Hezekiah.

A CROWN ON A DESERVING HEAD

Hezekiah trusted in the Lord, the God of Israel. There was no one like him among all the kings of Judah, either before him or after him. He held fast to the Lord and did not cease to follow him; he kept the commands the Lord had given Moses. And the Lord was with him; he was successful in whatever he undertook. (2 Kings 18:5–7)

Rotten kings often were succeeded by rotten sons. Not so in the case of Hezekiah, who was radically different from his wicked father Ahaz. The fact that Hezekiah reigned at all may have been due to Ahaz committing the horrible crime of sacrificing his own son—and it was usually the first-born son—to the god Molech. Growing up at the court, Hezekiah would have been painfully aware of his father's pagan practices, not to mention the corruption and exploitation of the poor that Isaiah and other prophets condemned.

Hezekiah was aware of something else: the fall of the northern kingdom Israel, to the Assyrians in 721 BC. This fall was due to Israel's moral and spiritual decline, despite all the warnings from great prophets like Elijah and Elisha. If Judah had continued on the immoral course pursued by Ahaz, it would likely have suffered the same fate as Israel. With his eyes on God, Hezekiah determined that this would not occur. He kept Judah's worship pure, throwing out all the pagan idols that his father had condoned.

Even so, the same empire that conquered Israel would vex Judah as well. The king of Assyria captured the fort cities in Judah, and Hezekiah felt compelled to pay tribute—that is, pay the conqueror not to complete his conquest. This involved stripping the temple of its gold and silver. Treacherously, the Assyrians did not take their loot and leave—their goal was total conquest. One of the high Assyrian officials went to Jerusalem and made a very public speech, assuring the people that Hezekiah was foolish to resist the powerful Assyrians, for nothing could help him, not even God. Hezekiah's court was aware of the effect these words were having on the people, so they begged the official to address them not in Hebrew, the people's language, but in Aramaic, at that time the second language of the upper classes. But the Assyrian knew exactly what he was doing with this very public address: tearing down the people's confidence in Hezekiah—and in God. The official assured the people that if the Assyrians chose to attack, not only the king would suffer but the whole population—who, in a time of siege, "will have to eat their own filth and drink their own urine" (2 Kings 18:27).

Terrified, Hezekiah tore his clothes, the familiar sign of distress and grief. And he prayed. Then his officials went to Isaiah, hoping for a word from the Lord. They got one, one that took them completely off guard. The Lord, Isaiah said, was well aware of the boastfulness and violence of Assyria. Indeed, the aggressive empire had conquered many

Hezekiah's Tunnel

The king was not only a man of deep faith but a community-minded builder as well. When he became king, Jerusalem had an aqueduct for bringing water to the city, but in times of war it could serve as an entry point for attack. Hezekiah ordered the digging of an underground tunnel, which would ensure a steady water supply even if the city endured a long siege. The tunnel was 1,750 feet long, cut through solid limestone. Two teams of workers started from opposite ends of Jerusalem and met in the middle, tunneling toward each other when they could hear voices. The height of the tunnel, which is today open to tourists, varies from four to twenty feet.

nations and shown their gods to be helpless idols. But Hezekiah did not need to fear: Sennacherib, the Assyrian king, would never enter Jerusalem or besiege it. "That night the angel of the Lord went out and put to death a hundred and eighty-five thousand men in the Assyrian camp. When the people got up the next morning—there were all the dead bodies!" (2 Kings 19:35).

And what of the boastful Sennacherib himself? When he returned to the Assyrian capital Nineveh, he was murdered—by two of his own sons. As so often recorded in the Bible, the violent were dispatched by other violent men.

Hezekiah's faith in God had been rewarded. It would not be the last time. Some years later, Hezekiah became ill, and Isaiah sent him a divine message: Set your house in order, for you will die. "Hezekiah turned his face to the wall and prayed to the Lord, 'Remember, O Lord, how I have walked before you faithfully and with wholehearted devotion and have done what is good in your eyes.' And Hezekiah wept bitterly" (2 Kings 20:2–3).

Israel's God was not some cold abstraction but a living personality. Through Isaiah he had warned of the king's impending death, but seeing the king's reaction, he changed his plan. Isaiah sent a message to the king: The Lord had heard his prayer and seen his tears. He would not die. In three days he would be up and worshipping again in the temple. And he would rule fifteen more years.

How fortunate were both the king and prophet, both of them devoted to the Lord. Sadly, the last episode involving both of them was ominous. Hezekiah had received ambassadors from Babylon and showed them all his royal treasures. Isaiah was disturbed to hear this. In fact, he prophesied that Hezekiah's descendants would not be on such cordial terms with the Babylonians—in fact, they would be conquered and deported to Babylon, along with thousands of others. Sad as this news was, Hezekiah was at least grateful to God that his kingdom would be at peace during his own lifetime.

> "My thoughts are not your thoughts, neither are your ways my ways," declares the Lord. "As the heavens are higher than the earth, so are my ways higher than your ways and my thoughts than your thoughts." (Isaiah 55:8–9)

> This is what the high and lofty One says—he who lives forever, whose name is holy: "I live in a high and holy place, but also with him who is contrite and lowly in spirit, to revive the spirit of the lowly and to revive the heart of the contrite." (Isaiah 57:15)

We wish the Bible told us more about the relationship between Isaiah and Hezekiah. Since Isaiah's ministry had begun under Hezekiah's grandfather and continued under his wicked father Ahaz, the prophet may well have been a spiritual mentor for the king. Certainly the king shared Isaiah's concept of God's power. And at moments of crisis, Hezekiah proved himself to be one who was "contrite and lowly in spirit," one who leaned on God instead of his own resources or on shaky political alliances.

Isaiah's famous vision had occurred in the temple in Jerusalem, and clearly he had affection for the place. But like all the Bible's heroes—including, notably, Jesus

---

CULTURAL INSIGHTS

Water in Isaiah

Israel was and still is a fairly dry country, subject to frequent droughts, and the people of the Bible appreciated rain, wells and rivers in a way that we do not. Water is mentioned frequently in Isaiah, sometimes in passages in which God rescues his people from the flood waters, but more often water is used to symbolize God's care for his people.

"With joy you will draw water from the wells of salvation." (Isaiah 12:3)

"The burning sand will become a pool, the thirsty ground bubbling springs. In the haunts where jackals once lay, grass and reeds and papyrus will grow." (Isaiah 35:7)

"The poor and needy search for water, but there is none; their tongues are parched with thirst. But I the Lord will answer them; I, the God of Israel, will not forsake them." (Isaiah 41:17)

"Come, all you who are thirsty, come to the waters; and you who have no money, come, buy and eat! Come, buy wine and milk without money and without cost." (Isaiah 55:1)

"The Lord will guide you always; he will satisfy your needs in a sun-scorched land and will strengthen your frame. You will be like a well-watered garden, like a spring whose waters never fail." (Isaiah 58:11)

"I will extend peace to her like a river, and the wealth of nations like a flooding stream; you will nurse and be carried on her arm and dandled on her knees." (Isaiah 66:12)

---

himself—Isaiah understood that no building, not even the beautiful temple, could contain God, who dwells "in a high and holy place"—meaning heaven, not the temple. But while no building, not even a temple, can contain God, he draws near to the humble, to the people Jesus would call "the poor in spirit."

God says, "My thoughts are not your thoughts." Man and God see things differently, and part of spiritual growth is learning to see things as God sees them. The human eye would have looked at Hezekiah's situation—facing the seemingly invincible army of Assyria—and concluded that surrender was the only option. But Isaiah and Hezekiah were able to see as God sees, so they could trust in the Lord's word that the foreign army would not attack. The Assyrians relied on the "arm of flesh," but the faithful king in Jerusalem understood that "with us is the Lord our God to help us and to fight our battles" (2 Chronicles 32:8).

"Do not call conspiracy everything that these people call conspiracy; do not fear what they fear, and do not dread it. The Lord Almighty is the one you are to regard as holy, he is the one you are to fear, he is the one you are to dread" (Isaiah 8:13). People live in dread and fear of many things: The only thing that ought to inspire awe or fear is God himself. God is holy and awesome. With him on our side, what can our enemies do?

> **DID YOU KNOW?**
>
> The prophets Isaiah and Micah were both active during the reign of Hezekiah, but there is no indication that they worked as a team or even knew each other. Taking on the role of prophet usually meant working alone—with God at his side, of course.

> **DID YOU KNOW?**
>
> Though the Bible does not tell us how or when Isaiah died, an old tradition says he was martyred by being sawn in two during the reign of the wicked king Manasseh. The tradition may be rooted in 2 Kings 21:16, which speaks of all the "innocent blood" that Manasseh shed. An old writing known as the Ascension of Isaiah tells the story of his martyrdom.

LET JUSTICE ROLL!

"What do you mean by crushing my people and grinding the faces of the poor?" declares the Lord, the Lord Almighty. (Isaiah 3:15)

They covet fields and seize them, and houses, and take them. They defraud a man of his home, a fellow man of his inheritance. Therefore, the Lord says: "I am planning disaster against this people." (Micah 2:2–3)

This is what the Lord says: "For three sins of Israel, even for four, I will not turn back my wrath. They sell the righteous for silver, and the needy for a pair of sandals. They trample on the heads of the poor as upon the dust of the ground and deny justice to the oppressed. (Amos 4:6–7)

Amos is often called the "Prophet of Justice," and the name surely fits, but it fits just as well with most of the other prophets, because almost all of them spoke out against greed and materialism, against those who exploit the most vulnerable members of society, the poor. As we see in the quote from Isaiah, that great prophet, awed by his vision of God in the temple, was very much aware of social injustice. Indeed, one who understands the might and holiness of God could not help but speak out against the oppression of God's creatures.

Like Isaiah, the prophet Micah preached during the reign of the wicked king Ahaz of Judah. Not only was Ahaz an avid pagan, but corruption and exploitation were also rampant during his reign. Although Judah got a better king when Ahaz died and was succeeded by Hezekiah, the injustice did not end overnight, and Micah continued preaching against the people's sins. "Woe to those who plan iniquity, to those who plot evil on their beds! At morning's light they carry it out because it is in their power to do it" (Micah 2:1). Happily, this is the rare case of a prophet's words being heeded, for the Book of Jeremiah records that, under Hezekiah, needed reforms took place in response to the words of Micah (Jeremiah 26:18). Jeremiah was pointing out to a very bad king, Jehoiakim, that in the past a good king, Hezekiah, had heeded a prophet's words.

Micah was fortunate in having his words reach the ears of a decent ruler. Such was not the case for Amos, whose words went utterly unheeded, as we shall see shortly.

Amos comes third in the group of the twelve Minor Prophets, but chronologically he is the earliest of them, ministering around 755 BC, during the reigns of Uzziah of Judah and Jeroboam II of Israel. This was a time of relative peace and prosperity, and the two kingdoms together were roughly the same large area ruled over by David and Solomon, meaning that, for the time being, they weren't being harassed and oppressed by neighbor nations. But it is clear in the book that material prosperity can be cover for spiritual poverty.

Speaking the words of the Lord, Amos lashed out against the injustices of the time. "I know how many are your offenses and how great your sins. You oppress the righteous

---

CULTURAL INSIGHTS

Ivory

Ivory was and still is a luxury item, and the great prophet Amos spoke out harshly against the idle and corrupt rich who reclined on beds of ivory (Amos 3:15, 6:4). One of Israel's worst kings, the wicked Ahab, had an ivory house; it was not made completely of ivory, of course, but richly ornamented with it. The wealthy used ivory for utensils, boxes, game pieces, beds and couches.

The Hebrew word translated "ivory" is *shen*—literally "tooth." Whether it means tooth or ivory depends on the context. Ivory is in fact the tusk of an elephant, and the Greek word for ivory is *elephantinos*.

International Prophecy

"Babylon, the jewel of kingdoms, the glory of the Babylonians' pride, will be overthrown by God like Sodom and Gomorrah" (Isaiah 13:19). "This is what the Lord says: 'For three sins of Tyre, even for four, I will not turn back my wrath'" (Amos 1:9). "'In that day,' declares the Lord, 'will I not destroy the wise men of Edom, men of understanding in the mountains of Esau?'" (Obadiah 8). Babylon, Tyre and Edom were foreign nations—so why were the prophets of Israel speaking—and writing—words for people that would never hear them? Although the main aim of the prophets was the repentance of God's people, most of the prophets also directed their words against enemy nations. The real audience for these was God's people, who might take a word of warning from hearing their prophets denounce the evils of other nations. And of course, people who read the prophets' words centuries later can still take warning from what the prophets had to say about corrupt and oppressive nations. The Babylonians and Edomites of biblical time may not have heard the prophets' words, but certainly millions afterward have read them and profited from them.

---

and take bribes and you deprive the poor of justice in the courts. . . . . Seek good, not evil, that you may live. Hate evil, love good; maintain justice in the courts. Perhaps the Lord God Almighty will have mercy on the remnant" (Amos 5:12–14).

Amos was a simple man, one who herded sheep and gathered figs. Like many simple folk, he saw through the hypocrisy of those more sophisticated than himself. Israel had plenty of people who tithed and observed the religious feasts faithfully—all the while thinking of how they could increase their wealth through exploitation of others. The holy days were observed with music and great solemnity—but God was not deceived: "Away with the noise of your songs! I will not listen to the music of your harps. But let justice roll on like a river, righteousness like a never-failing stream!" (Amos 4:23–24). He was especially harsh against the rich, reclining on their ivory beds, drinking wine and listening to music, living large off their ill-gotten gains.

The verses from Amos quoted here are probably familiar to you, since they have been the subjects of countless sermons. What is often overlooked is that, like Isaiah, Amos had an awesome view of God. "The Lord roars from Zion and thunders from Jerusalem; the pastures of the shepherds dry up, and the top of Carmel withers" (Amos 1:2). "He who made the Pleiades and Orion, who turns blackness into dawn and darkens day into night, who calls for the waters of the sea and pours them out over the face of the land—the Lord is his name" (Amos 5:8). "He who forms the mountains, creates the wind, and reveals his thoughts to man, he who turns dawn to darkness, and treads the high places of the earth—the Lord God Almighty is his name" (Amos 4:13). As a farmer, living close to the created world, Amos saw the Lord as the Almighty Ruler of nature—and also the One who sees into human hearts, who is not deceived by hypocrisy, and who is mightily displeased at human beings exploiting one another.

Like other prophets, Amos felt the irresistible pull of God: "The lion has roared—who will not fear? The Sovereign Lord has spoken—who can but prophesy?" (Amos 3:8). "The Lord took me from tending the flock and said to me, 'Go, prophesy to my people Israel'" (Amos 7:15). And like other prophets, Amos met with hostility. He journeyed to Bethel, one of two worship centers in the northern kingdom, Israel. There he found himself nose to nose with a very hostile priest, Amaziah, who had no use for a prophet full of dire warnings. He reminded Amos that his own country was Judah, not Israel, and he should return there and prophesy there. He also told Amos that Bethel was "the king's sanctuary"—as if it were the king's private chapel instead of the house of God and a place of worship for the entire nation. Not satisfied with sneering at Amos to his face, Amaziah lied to the king Jeroboam, and told him Amos had prophesied the king's death, something Amos never said. Amaziah, at that time the highest religious official in Israel, completely rejected Amos' words and tossed him out. It was a classic case of a prophet of the Lord being despised by an unspiritual priest. What a pity that Amaziah did not, like Amos, revere the God who "forms the mountains, creates the wind, and reveals his thoughts to man."

SERIOUS AWE DEFICIT

Now the word of the Lord came to Jonah the son of Amittai, saying, "Arise, go to Nineveh, that great city, and call out against it; for their evil has come up before me." But Jonah rose up to flee to Tarshish from the presence of the Lord. He went down to Joppa and found a ship going to Tarshish. . . . But the Lord hurled a great wind upon the sea, and there was a mighty tempest on the sea, so that the ship threatened to break up. (Jonah 1:1–4, ESV)

Earlier in the chapter we looked at the invasion of Judah by the terrifying army of Assyria. It is hard to overemphasize just how feared these people were in those days, for they were not only notoriously cruel but also proud of it, as shown by their artworks in which they mutilated and tortured those they defeated.

And yet, curiously, Assyria was an advanced culture in many ways. In terms of their art, technology and military prowess, they were far ahead of Israel and Judah—but morally and spiritually they were barbarians, using their technology and military might to conquer and oppress. An ancient Israelite would be filled with loathing and disgust at the mention of the name Assyria or its sprawling capital, Nineveh.

All this has to be understood to appreciate one of the most discussed but least understood books of the Bible, Jonah. Thus far we have looked at some of the prophets and their awe of God. Jonah, by contrast, suffered an awe deficit.

Let us admit that Jonah was given a task no prophet could have relished: The Lord told him to go to Nineveh and preach repentance. Other prophets in the Bible were initially reluctant to take on the prophetic role, but Jonah went beyond reluctance to panic and flight. Instead of being the missionary, Jonah became the anti-missionary. He tried to flee "from the presence of the Lord"—as if that were possible. Nonetheless he set sail for Tarshish, probably the area later known as Spain, and regarded then as being the end of the earth—and also in the opposite direction from Nineveh.

Did Jonah really think that he would be beyond God's reach? The Israelites were not a maritime people and had an aversion to ocean travel. Jonah was willing to override this aversion to get away from God. Was he foolish enough to think that the God of Israel only had power in the land of Israel itself? He was quite mistaken. The Lord sent a storm, and the ship was in danger of sinking. The mariners were all praying to their gods for aid. Jonah was wise enough to know that his presence was the cause of the storm. He identified himself as a "Hebrew, one who fears the Lord, the God of heaven"—although

CHARACTERS AT LARGE Jonah in Art and Literature

Brief as the Book of Jonah is, and despite the fact that the prophet was hardly a role model of faith, Jonah was honored highly by the early Christians. He was often depicted in the earliest art, mostly because the Christians saw his time in the belly of the whale as a kind of preview of the Resurrection of Jesus, who himself said, "as Jonah was three days and three nights in the belly of the great fish, so the Son of Man will be three days and three nights in the heart of the earth" (Matthew 12:39–40).

Writers have tended to treat Jonah's story in a comic way, as in *A Masque of Mercy*, by the great American poet Robert Frost. In it, the "Fugitive" is the prophet Jonah, running away from God. Playwright Wolf Mankowitz also treated the story humorously in his play *It Should Happen to a Dog*. English writer Laurence Housman gave the story a more reverent treatment in his play *The Burden of Nineveh*. An interesting mix of humor and seriousness is found in the animated film for children, *Jonah: A Veggie Tales Movie*, using the popular Veggie Tales cartoon characters.

his behavior had not shown him to be one who feared God. (Surely the storm changed his attitude!) He had the sailors cast him overboard, and the storm ended, making such a deep impression on them that they offered sacrifices to Jonah's God—the God he was running from.

We all know where Jonah ended up, of course. Despite all the skepticism about whether a person could be swallowed by a whale and survive, we know of one documented case. The point of the biblical story is not the creature that swallowed Jonah but the fact that he finally understood that his vision of God had been far too small. God was present not just in Israel but everywhere. And so God had the whale vomit Jonah onto dry land, and he pressed on to Nineveh, preaching the message God had given him: In forty days the wicked city would be overthrown—unless the people had a change of heart.

To Jonah's immense surprise—and horror—the people of Nineveh did repent, from the king on down. Seeing their repentance, God revoked the sentence of doom. Jonah should have been pleased: A city full of sinful pagans had repented due to his preaching. But instead Jonah was angry. As it turned out, he had fled from his mission not because of fear of the Ninevites, but fear they might actually repent. They had—and so he prayed to God to take his life.

Poor Jonah! In this story so loved by Jews, the Jewish character is the only unsympathetic person, while the pagans are all good and sensible. The fearful and, later, sullen prophet is hardly a saint or role model, although he does prove the familiar biblical theme: God accomplishes his will through deeply flawed people.

The story of Jonah in fact illustrates the theme stated at the beginning of this chapter: God is awesome. He controls all things, everywhere, and though he is Israel's God, his love and compassion extend everywhere, even to the cruel barbarians of Nineveh. Jonah, like so many others in his country, had forgotten that centuries earlier God had promised the patriarch Abraham that through his descendants, all the earth would be blessed. Indeed, Isaiah foretold a blissful future when "the Lord Almighty will bless them, saying, 'Blessed be Egypt my people, Assyria my handiwork, and Israel my inheritance'" (Isaiah 19:25). In time, people in every corner of the globe would worship the awesome, righteous and loving God of the Bible.

PUTTING THE WORD TO WORK

1. Reflect on the Bible's view of prophets as people who felt a divine pressure to speak out for God. How do you think they sensed this pressure? When have you felt this pressure in your own life?

2. Isaiah experienced his life-changing vision during a temple service. What were occasions in your own life when you felt the awesomeness of the Lord?

3. Hezekiah was that rare thing, a saintly political leader. What political figures have you known, either during your own lifetime or from reading history, who have exhibited strong faith?

4. For Isaiah and Amos, their awe of God meant they were aware of how God views human exploitation and injustice. Take a moment to pray for the victims of economic and social injustice.

5. Jonah began with a limited view of God's power, but events changed him. What events in your own life enlarged your awareness of God?

Jesus' Word, and Jesus Is Word

When the apostles began to spread the gospel of Jesus, they encountered persecution and harassment—but also a warm reception by many people. Part of the success of Christianity is that it began in a time when most of the old pagan oracles—places where the gods supposedly expressed their will—were mute,

MEMORY VERSE

The Word became flesh and made his dwelling among us.
—John 1:14

and people were longing for sources of certainty. Likewise the Jews had gone for centuries without any new prophet speaking to them, and though they had their Scriptures—the Old Testament—as a guide to life, many of them were open to a new word from the Lord.

In this chapter we will look at Jesus as the teacher of eternally valid words—and Jesus as the Word of God in the flesh. We will take a close look at an important title of Jesus that is often neglected: Prophet.

KEY TERM FOR TODAY Word

This is Word with a capital W, and it translates the Greek term *Logos*, with a richer meaner than just "word." It can also mean "saying" or "message," and John's Gospel applies it to Jesus and uses it to mean the ultimate revelation of God.

WORDS UNSHAKABLE

Heaven and earth will pass away, but my words will never pass away. (Matthew 24:35)

Everyone who hears these words of mine and puts them into practice is like a wise man who built his house on the rock. The rain came down, the streams rose, and the winds blew and beat against that house; yet it did not fall, because it had its foundation on the rock.

But everyone who hears these words of mine and does not put them into practice is like a foolish man who built his house on sand. The rain came down, the streams rose, and the winds blew and beat against that house, and it fell with a great crash. (Matthew 7:24–27)

Strictly speaking, Matthew 24:35 was applied by Jesus to what he had told his disciples about the end times—that is, he was emphasizing that his prophecies about the end of the world were true and would stand. But generations of readers have rightly applied these words to all of his sayings. The words are particularly important for the apocalypse because Jesus has just described horrible things—wars, earthquakes, persecution. But instead of being terrified, the disciples can take courage: They are following one who will endure and whose words will endure.

Jesus' Jewish listeners would have heard these words and thought of the permanence of the written words of the Scripture—permanent because the rabbis insisted on the Torah being copied only with ink made from soot or lampblack, so permanent that they are still readable today. Jesus' words would live on as well, not just as ink on paper but also carried in people's hearts and minds. "The grass withers and the flowers fall, but the word of our God stands forever" (Isaiah 40:8). "Your word, O Lord, is eternal; it stands firm in the heavens" (Psalm 119:89).

"My words will never pass away"—this promise has certainly proved true over the centuries. Despite the hostility of a world that seems to scorn religion more and more, Jesus' words continue to be pored over and discussed—and sometimes even put into action! Even some of the severest critics of religion find much to admire in the words of Jesus.

In reading the parable of the two houses in Matthew 7, we need to remember that Jesus was himself a builder. Most English translations refer to him as "carpenter," but the Greek word *tekton* usually meant something more, a craftsman of some skill, like a contractor. Presumably in his work he had helped to build houses on solid foundations. He knew that for a house to endure in Galilee, the builders had to dig deep into the soil to make sure there was solid rock underneath. Otherwise a house, no matter how beautiful and well-made, could not endure when the storms came. In Palestine at that time, sudden rains could literally wash away houses not built on the foundation of bedrock lying deep under the soil.

The key words here are "hears these words of mine and puts them into practice." Faith that consists of mere words is no faith at all. The words are a challenge, and failing to rise to the challenge is serious: "It fell with a great crash." What good is faith if it collapses under calamity?

Jesus' teaching reflected the Old Testament. Like Jesus, the Book of Proverbs praises the wise and the righteous and saw them as worthy to endure: "When the storm has swept by, the wicked are gone, but the righteous stand firm forever." (Proverbs 10:25). "Wicked men are overthrown and are no more, but the house of the righteous stands firm" (Proverbs 12:7).

The apostles must have had Jesus' parable in mind when they spoke of the foundation of faith: "No one can lay any foundation other than the one already laid, which is Jesus Christ" (1 Corinthians 3:11). The community of faith is "built on the foundation of the apostles and prophets, with Christ Jesus himself as the chief cornerstone" (Ephesians 2:20). "The world and its desires pass away, but the man who does the will of God lives forever" (1 John 2:17).

KEEP THEM AND LIVE—FOREVER

I know you are Abraham's descendants. Yet you are ready to kill me, because you have no room for my word. (John 8:37)

I tell you the truth, if anyone keeps my word, he will never see death. (John 8:51)

As for the person who hears my words but does not keep them, I do not judge him. For I did not come to judge the world, but to save it. (John 12:47)

In John 8:39–59, Jesus is facing criticism from "the Jews," which in John's Gospel refers not to all Jews but to the priests and other Jewish authorities in Jerusalem. These people take comfort in the fact that the patriarch Abraham is their ancestor. Jesus assures them that if they are truly Abraham's children, they will be people of faith, as Abraham was. Remember that in the Bible's view of things, "child of" means "obedient to" and "imitators of." Biological descent is not what saves people.

The Jewish leaders press Jesus further and insist that God is their Father, but Jesus states that, on the contrary, they act like children of the devil. As we see in John 8:37, he is well aware that they are already plotting to destroy him. If they were really God's children they would welcome him and heed what he said.

"I tell you the truth, if anyone keeps my word, he will never see death." The Jewish leaders are aghast. Who does this man think he is? They are so offended that they pick up stones and prepare to kill him, but he leaves the temple precincts. His time has not yet come. He will die at the hands of these same people, but will be raised to life again. He promises this eternal life to his followers.

Note that Jesus says that anyone who "keeps" his word will never see death. Merely hearing it is not enough. Many people of Jesus' day heard him speak, but not all were saved.

"As for the person who hears my words but does not keep them, I do not judge him. For I did not come to judge the world, but to save it." These words remind us that the whole aim of the Bible is salvation. God's spokesmen—Jesus and all the prophets and apostles of the Bible—were not sent by God to be scolds and killjoys. On the contrary, the motivation behind their preaching and teachings was divine love for mankind.

When Jesus tells his listeners, "I tell you the truth, if anyone keeps my word, he will never see death," the word translated "word" is the Greek *logos*, which has a richer meaning than we usually associate with "word." We will take a closer look at the richness of *logos* later in this chapter.

"LORD, TO WHOM SHALL WE GO?"

"The words I have spoken to you are spirit and they are life. Yet there are some of you who do not believe." For Jesus had known from the beginning which of them did not believe and who would betray him. . . . From this time many of his disciples turned back and no longer followed him.

"You do not want to leave too, do you?" Jesus asked the Twelve.

Simon Peter answered him, "Lord, to whom shall we go? You have the words of eternal life. We believe and know that you are the Holy One of God." (John 6:63–64, 66–69)

We need to read this passage more often, because it reminds us that Jesus' message was rejected not just by the snobbish priests and Pharisees but also by the majority of his listeners. Jesus' words were so detested by the Jewish authorities that they were willing to have him arrested and put to death. For most people their response was less drastic: Rather than conspiring against Jesus, they simply ceased to follow him.

"Disciples" in this passage does not refer to the Twelve but to a much larger group—larger but not nearly as committed as the Twelve, who had left their homes and vocations to follow Jesus on the dusty roads of Palestine. Many of these turned back and no longer followed Jesus. His words had interested them but only for a time. It is easy for a speaker to attract fans for a while, but few of them were willing to go the distance with Jesus.

The Twelve—or at least Peter, who so often served as spokesman for the band—were not willing to turn away. Peter sensed that Jesus was no ordinary Jewish rabbi who was respected for his wisdom. His words had a substance, a weight, that the words of other teachers did not possess. They were "the words of eternal life"—and where else could the Twelve go to receive such words? Through the eye of faith, Peter could see that the man they followed—both literally and figuratively—was the "Holy One of God."

DID YOU KNOW?

Peter's words to Jesus in John 6:68 were the inspiration for the beloved old hymn "Wonderful Words of Life," by Philip P. Bliss.

DISCRETION IN JEWELRY

> Do not give dogs what is sacred; do not throw your pearls to pigs. If you do, they may trample them under their feet, and then turn and tear you to pieces. (Matthew 7:6)

In the last section we witnessed the falling away of some of Jesus' halfhearted followers. Here we look at a verse that speaks of a more contentious reaction to his words—not just rejection but aggressive hostility. This verse from the wonderful Sermon on the Mount raises an important question: Did Jesus intend his words, his preaching, to be for everyone—or were there some people who were not worth the effort? And since he directs these words to his disciples, did he intend they, too, should be selective about whom they preached to?

To understand this verse, we need to grasp that the people who heard the Sermon on the Mount detested both dogs and pigs. In that time and place, dogs were rarely kept as pets but were more often scavenging and sometimes dangerous street dogs, running around in packs and generally being a nuisance. The Jews regarded them as unclean animals, which was also true of pigs.

Jesus reached out to tax collectors, prostitutes, lepers and others regarded as unclean by his contemporaries, and the Bible praises him for it. Was there anyone he himself regarded as beyond the pale? The only person in the Gospels whom Jesus is shown as refusing to speak to is the corrupt and immoral Herod, after Jesus is sent to him by Pilate. Was Herod a "dog" and "swine" to whom Jesus did not wish to speak the truth? Such questions are hard to answer, and this verse has never failed to generate controversy.

As harsh as the words sound, it is a simple fact that some people are not only not receptive to the message of faith but also blatantly hostile to it. This raises the question: Are we to decide on our own that person X is not worth our trouble, not worth presenting the truth to? This might be a matter of praying that even if we cannot talk about the truths of the faith, our lives may—and should be—a witness of another kind. Peter counseled believers to "live such good lives among the pagans that, though they accuse you of doing wrong, they may see your good deeds and glorify God" (1 Peter 2:12).

Jesus' words seem to echo Proverbs 23:9—"Do not speak to a fool, for he will scorn the wisdom of your words"—and Proverbs 9:7—"Whoever corrects a mocker invites insult; whoever rebukes a wicked man incurs abuse." There are some people so hostile and scornful that it seems pointless to speak of spiritual things to them: "The god of this age has blinded the minds of unbelievers, so that they cannot see the light of the gospel of the glory of Christ, who is the image of God" (2 Corinthians 4:4). While we would be wrong to shut ourselves off from the world and give up serving as witnesses to our faith, there is a limit to our association with the mockers: "Do not be yoked together with unbelievers. For what do righteousness and wickedness have in common? Or what fellowship can light have with darkness? . . . What does a believer have in common with an unbeliever?" (2 Corinthians 6:14–15).

In 1 Corinthians, Paul definitely applies the pearls-before-swine teaching to the controversial issue of speaking in tongues. Though Paul himself spoke in tongues and approved of the practice, he was wise enough about the world to see how it could be misunderstood by the unspiritual: "So if the whole church comes together and everyone speaks in tongues, and some who do not understand or some unbelievers come in, will they not say that you are out of your mind?" (1 Corinthians 14:23).

In summary, the New Testament makes it clear that the words of Jesus and the apostles will not only not be accepted by many people but will also be met with scorn and contempt. We are counseled to love all people and to pray for their salvation, yet we are also counseled to be prepared to face what Jesus himself faced—harassment and persecution by those who, spiritually speaking, are "dogs" and "swine" with no concern for spiritual things, the "pearls" that are valued by people of faith.

A PROPHET LIKE MOSES

> After the people saw the miraculous sign that Jesus did, they began to say, "Surely this is the Prophet who is to come into the world." (John 6:14)
>
> When Jesus came to the region of Caesarea Philippi, he asked his disciples, "Who do people say the Son of Man is?" They replied, "Some say John the Baptist; others say Elijah; and still others, Jeremiah or one of the prophets." (Matthew 16:13–14)
>
> When the chief priests and the Pharisees heard Jesus' parables, they knew he was talking about them. They looked for a way to arrest him, but they were afraid of the crowd because the people held that he was a prophet. (Matthew 21:45–46)

In the previous chapter we looked at the nature of prophecy in Israel and observed that the prophet was seen as one who was God's spokesman, one who spoke not on his own initiative but because he felt the "divine pressure" to speak the word of the Lord. We rarely refer to Jesus as a "prophet" for the obvious reason that there are better and higher titles for him: Christ, Lord, Son of God, Savior, etc. But to really understand the Gospels, we have to look at the concept of prophet, for the impression Jesus made on many of his contemporaries was that he was a prophet sent from God.

By Jesus' day, the "profession" of prophet no longer existed, at least not in the sense of people believing that a certain man had received a special calling from God to deliver a message. The Jews possessed the writings of the Old Testament prophets, but no new prophets arose. What the Jews hoped for was not just a prophet but *the* prophet of the age of the Messiah, the prophet of the end time. They believed in the prophecy of Deuteronomy 18:15: "The Lord your God will raise up for you a prophet like me from among your own brothers. You must listen to him." In a sense, every prophet of God had been a fulfillment of that prophecy, but in Jesus' day the Jews were expecting *the* prophet, one who would, like the great Moses, know God's will fully: "Since then, no prophet has risen in Israel like Moses, whom the Lord knew face to face" (Deuteronomy 34:10).

The longer the Jews went without prophets, the deeper their yearning was for *the* prophet. Joel, one of the last of the Old Testament prophets, foretold an age when the Spirit of prophecy might pour out on not just one person but many: "I will pour out my Spirit on all people. Your sons and daughters will prophesy, your old men will dream dreams, your young men will see visions. Even on my servants, both men and women, I will pour out my Spirit in those days" (Joel 2:28–29). This mass outpouring did not negate the belief that the power of prophecy would focus on one individual. The Jews believed the great prophet would be like Moses in the sense of not just proclaiming God's will but also the working of miracles. Some called this Moses-to-come the *Ta'eb*, meaning "the Returning One" or "the Restorer." Also, this prophet would announce the end of the age and would present God's final offer to repent. (In Acts 3:22 and 7:37, we see that the early Christians taught that this prophecy had been fulfilled in Jesus.)

The idea of this prophet of the end time existed alongside the Jews' hope for the Messiah. Most of the people saw the Prophet as a kind of forerunner of the Messiah, though he was also seen as the forerunner of the kingdom of God, the full reign of God on earth. It was possible to combine both Prophet and Messiah in the same person, an idea that was slow to take hold among the people of Jesus' time.

According to the Gospel, a new prophet did arise: John the Baptist. Luke's Gospel opens with the announcement to the aged and childless priest Zechariah that he and his wife Elizabeth, will at long last become parents. The angel Gabriel informs Zechariah that his son will do great things: "Many of the people of Israel will he bring back to the Lord their God. And he will go on before the Lord, in the spirit and power of Elijah, to turn the hearts of the fathers to their children and the disobedient to the wisdom of the righteous—to make ready a people prepared for the Lord" (Luke 1:16–17). At their age, this is nothing short of a miracle, and after the birth of the child, whom they name John, Zechariah breaks forth in his own dazzling prophecy of his new son: "You, my child, will be called a prophet of the Most High; for you will go on before the Lord to prepare the way for him" (Luke 1:76).

When the adult John the Baptist began preaching and baptizing in the wilderness, he was widely believed to be a prophet, and perhaps *the* Prophet, the entry point of the end time. "The word of God came to John son of Zechariah in the desert" (Luke 3:2).

Ear-centered People

One reason non-Jews mocked Jews in biblical times was the prohibition against making images of God. This, of course, was in obedience to the second of the Ten Commandments: "You shall not make for yourself an idol in the form of anything in heaven above or on the earth beneath or in the waters below. You shall not bow down to them or worship them; for I, the Lord your God, am a jealous God" (Exodus 20:4–5). This set Israel's religion apart from every other: it had no pictures or statues of the one it worshipped. The human desire to worship something visually is powerful, and so the Israelites constantly lapsed into idolatry, bowing down to idols of the gods of other nations. But although they disobeyed the part about bowing down to idols, they did take seriously the part about making images of their own God. The hundreds of idols found by archaeologists in Israel are images of other gods, but never Israel's God, Yahweh.

The religion of the Bible is aural, not visual. The Bible speaks of God's "hands" and "face," and it speaks of God with male pronouns, but the Israelites never depicted their God as a human male nor as any animal, nor the human-animal combinations that Egypt was famous for. God was too big, too powerful to be represented by anything people could see—or bow down to. The focus in the Old and New Testaments is the word of God, not visual images of God. In the view of the Bible's writers, we bow down to God's word by obeying it.

Note Luke's use of the Old Testament phrase "the word of the Lord." After a gap of centuries, God was speaking through a prophet once again. It was to be expected that people would ask John, "Are you the Prophet?" (John 1:21). He flatly replied that he was not; though he was *a* prophet, he was not *the* Prophet they were speaking of. He was, in his own words, "the voice of one calling in the desert, 'Make straight the way for the Lord'" (John 1:23). The real Prophet foretold by Moses was Jesus.

We see clearly in the Gospels that people were referring to Jesus as a prophet long before anyone spoke of him as Christ or Son of God: "Jesus' name had become well known. Some were saying, 'John the Baptist has been raised from the dead, and that is why miraculous powers are at work in him.' Others said, 'He is Elijah.' And still others claimed, 'He is a prophet, like one of the prophets of long ago'" (Mark 6:14–15). "The dead man sat up and began to talk, and Jesus gave him back to his mother. They were all filled with awe and praised God. 'A great prophet has appeared among us,' they said. 'God has come to help his people'" (Luke 7:15–16). "After the people saw the miraculous sign that Jesus did, they began to say, 'Surely this is the Prophet who is to come into the world'" (John 6:13–14). When the Pharisees assured the blind man whom Jesus had healed that Jesus was not sent by God, the man did not agree: "He is a prophet" (John 9:16–17). Jesus' miracles reminded the people of the great miracles of such prophets as Elijah and Elisha. Of course, the Old Testament recognized that a false prophet might perform miracles also, and a false prophet was to be killed (Deuteronomy 13:2–6 and 18:20–22). But the people saw clearly that Jesus was a true prophet from God, not a false one.

People expected prophets to be seers, those who discern things that ordinary people cannot. We see this in the story of the immoral woman who anoints Jesus' feet with expensive perfume in the house of a Pharisee. "When the Pharisee who had invited him saw this, he said to himself, 'If this man were a prophet, he would know who is touching him and what kind of woman she is—that she is a sinner'" (Luke 7:37–39). Of course, Jesus *does* see what kind of woman she is—a repentant sinner. He sees her present state while the Pharisee only knows of her past. Jesus really is a seer and prophet.

Jesus did not object to being identified as a prophet, as we see in his rejection in his hometown of Nazareth: "And they took offense at him. But Jesus said to them, 'Only in his hometown and in his own house is a prophet without honor'" (Matthew 13:57). Although he consistently played down his role as Messiah, and urged people not to refer to him as such, he had no objection to being identified as a prophet sent from God. However, it was inevitable that some people would make the connection: this great prophet sent by God was also the Messiah.

In John's Gospel, the first person to identify Jesus as a prophet is the Samaritan woman at the well, whom Jesus asks for a drink of water. When Jesus says to her, "Go, call your husband," the woman replies, "I have no husband"—and Jesus says that, indeed, she has had five husbands in the past, and the man she now lives with is not her husband. In a bit of uncomfortable moral evasion, she replies, "'Sir,' the woman said, 'I can see that you are a prophet'" (John 4:19). She is eager to change the subject from her living arrangement to religious matters, and she was certainly right in seeing that the man she was speaking with was gifted with supernatural insight. In fact, despite all their differences and hostility, the Jews and Samaritans both expected the coming of "the Prophet" who would be like Moses. The Samaritan woman, thinking Jesus is a prophet, says to him, "I know that Messiah is coming. When he comes, he will explain everything to us." Then Jesus tells her, "I who speak to you am he" (John 4:25–26). This is the only occasion where Jesus clearly identifies himself to someone as the Messiah—and it appears his words were spoken partly to correct the woman's identifying him as a prophet.

> **DID YOU KNOW?**
>
> The Pharisees claimed that Jesus could not be a prophet because "no prophet arises from Galilee." (John 7:52) They apparently did not know their own Scriptures well, because the prophet Jonah came from Galilee. Their statement reflects the snobbery that people of Jerusalem typically felt toward the bumpkins from Galilee.

Not everyone was pleased at this idea of a great prophet roaming around. The corrupt and immoral Herod had executed the prophet John the Baptist (see Day 26). He had gotten rid of one prophet and there was no reason he could not do to Jesus what he had done to John. "At that time some Pharisees came to Jesus and said to him, 'Leave this place and go somewhere else. Herod wants to kill you.' He replied, 'Go tell that fox, "I will drive out demons and heal people today and tomorrow, and on the third day I will reach my goal." In any case, I must keep going today and tomorrow and the next day—for surely no prophet can die outside Jerusalem!'" (Luke 13:31–33). This is one of the few places where Jesus identified himself as a prophet, and he places himself firmly in the tradition of being persecuted as the prophets of old were.

And indeed he was persecuted. At his trial, the cruel members of the Council mock his reputation as a prophet. "They spit in his face and struck him with their fists. Others slapped him and said, 'Prophesy to us, Christ. Who hit you?'" (Matthew 26:67–68). Clearly they regard him as a false prophet, so they could take some solace in the fact that they were, as they saw it, obeying the commandment in Deuteronomy to execute a false prophet. Yet, ironically, Jesus' last predictions—the disciples all fall away, Peter denies him—have just come true.

After Jesus' crucifixion and resurrection, we read in Luke's Gospel of two dejected disciples who, without knowing it, encounter the risen Jesus on the road: "He asked them, 'What are you discussing together as you walk along?' They stood still, their faces downcast. One of them, named Cleopas, asked him, 'Are you only a visitor to Jerusalem and do not know the things that have happened there in these days?' 'What things?' he asked. 'About Jesus of Nazareth,' they replied. 'He was a prophet, powerful in word and deed before God and all the people'" (Luke 24:17–19). At this point, still believing Jesus lies in his tomb, the disciples can only see him as a prophet, "powerful in word and deed"—but dead and buried nonetheless. Soon they would see that Jesus had claim to be much more than a prophet.

THE WORD, LIVE AND IN PERSON

In the beginning was the Word, and the Word was with God, and the Word was God.... The Word became flesh and made his dwelling among us. (John 1:1, 14)

In the past God spoke to our forefathers through the prophets at many times and in various ways, but in these last days he has spoken to us by his Son, whom he appointed heir of all things, and through whom he made the universe. (Hebrews 1:1–2)

For the Jews of biblical times, the "word" was never a dead letter. It accomplished things. The word of God was not just an utterance or ink marks on a page. It was active, living. Though they valued the words written down in ink in their Scriptures,

In the first sentence of Acts, Luke refers to his Gospel as his first *logos*, which in this context is usually translated as "book" or "treatise" or "account." The basic meaning here is "message." His Gospel is his first message; Acts is his second.

they regarded them as just a transcript of the spoken word, which was most important. Like most people in ancient times, Jews never read silently, not even when alone. The word was not really alive unless spoken. We see this concept of "living word" in Hebrews 4:12: "The word of God is living and active. Sharper than any double-edged sword, it penetrates even to dividing soul and spirit, joints and marrow; it judges the thoughts and attitudes of the heart."

The Jews believed the word of the Lord had been expressed through God's prophets. But for hundreds of years, no prophet spoke any new word from the Lord. They had, of course, the scriptures to turn to for guidance and consolation. But for centuries the Jews had been prophetless—until John the Baptist and Jesus, both of whom were seen by many people as prophets. But Jesus, to the early Christians, was much more than a prophet.

As noted earlier, Jesus did not object to people referring to him as a prophet. But one thing that set Jesus clearly apart from the great prophets of Israel's past is that he never prefaced his statements with "Thus says the Lord . . ." Rather, he could speak on his own authority with, "I say to you . . ." It is appropriate that in John's Gospel, in which several people express their belief in Jesus as a prophet or *the* Prophet, Jesus is referred to as the *Logos*—the Word—of God. Jesus does not, like the prophets of old, speak the word of God; he is himself the Word. This idea is present not only in John's Gospel but also in the opening words of the Letter to the Hebrews. Hebrews and John share a belief about Jesus that certainly does not apply to any other prophets: He existed from before the creation of the world: "He was with God in the beginning. Through him all things were made; without him nothing was made that has been made" (John 1:2–3). "The Son is the radiance of God's glory and the exact representation of his being, sustaining all things by his powerful word" (Hebrews 1:2–3). Clearly the first Christians saw that though Jesus was a prophet, he was something infinitely greater— so much greater that John and the author of Hebrews are stretching language to its limits to describe what Jesus is.

Although the other New Testament writings do not use *Logos* as a title for Christ, they share with John the concept of "the Word" as God's revelation to man, his message, the proclamation of salvation. When Paul and others refer to "the word," they mean the gospel message. Whereas the Old Testament speaks often of "the word of the Lord" being revealed to the prophets, the New Testament has the idea that the word of the Lord is finally revealed in its ultimate form, the Word in human form, Jesus Christ.

John 1 and Hebrews 1 both speak of the Son being present at the creation and active in it. Without using the word *Logos*, Hebrews presents Christ as pre-existent and as the final, ultimate revelation of God to man. Like John, Hebrews places emphasis on both the divinity of Christ and also his humanity. "In the past God spoke to our forefathers through the prophets at many times and in various ways, but in these last days he has spoken to us by his Son, whom he appointed heir of all things, and through whom he made the universe. The Son is the radiance of God's glory and the exact representation of his being" (Hebrews 1:1–3). Both John and Hebrews speak of the Son as existing before the beginning of the world. In this they made a connection with the expectation of the Messiah, for all Jews believed that in some mysterious way, the Messiah had existed before the world began.

Why did John use the Greek word *Logos* in his Gospel? Possibly as a hook to get the attention of people who had been seeking the truth through pagan philosophies. Among the Greek and Roman philosophers, the Platonists and Stoics taught that the Logos was a sort of impersonal world soul, the cosmic law that rules the universe and is also present in the human mind. But the philosophers could never conceive that "the Logos became flesh," as in John's Gospel.

The Gnostics, who combined some Christian teachings with pagan myths and philosophies, thought of the Logos as an intermediary between God and man. It was both revealer and redeemer. So far, this sounds like the teaching of the New Testament. In fact, the Gnostics believed that the Logos appeared to become man—but only *appeared* to. Like the pagan philosophers, the Gnostics could not stomach the notion of the Divine actually walking the earth as a human being, much less suffering and dying on a cross.

CULTURAL INSIGHTS

Creation by Word

Except for the Israelites, people in ancient times almost always thought of creation and nature as the result of divine sex, which explains why pagan worship often resembled an orgy. (This also explains why the Old Testament prophets so heartily condemned worshipping pagan gods.) Although God was conceived of by the Israelites as male, the prohibition of images of God meant that people did not see him as a human male, and thus the Israelite religion did not think of God or gods participating in sex in order to create things or bring fertility. The Genesis creation story differs from pagan myths in countless ways, but the most obvious is that God strictly speaking "does" nothing—he brings the whole cosmos into being with his word: "God said, 'Let there be light,' and there was light." The idea is reflected elsewhere: "By the word of the Lord the heavens were made" (Psalm 33:6). While pagan creation myths had the heavenly god impregnating some goddess or mother earth, or some brutal cosmic battle taking place, Genesis gives us a God who brings it all into being with his word. Clearly the Old Testament sees the word of God not as mere letters on a page but as something alive, active.

John's Gospel owes nothing to these pagan beliefs, of course. In fact, what lies behind John's use of Logos is the entire Old Testament, with the idea of God revealing himself to man. He was not the first Jewish author to connect the Old Testament with the term *Logos*. The Jewish philosopher Philo identified the divine Logos with the Wisdom in the Old Testament, particularly in the Book of Proverbs: "I, wisdom, dwell together with prudence; I possess knowledge and discretion" (Proverbs 8:12). "The Lord brought me forth as the first of his works, before his deeds of old; I was appointed from eternity, from the beginning, before the world began" (Proverbs 8:22–23). Many other Jews followed Philo in identifying the Logos with divine Wisdom, but most of the rabbis thought that Wisdom and the Logos were in fact the Law of Moses. No doubt John was aware of this when he wrote his Gospel, which revealed Jesus as being greater than the Law. John must have also been aware that many of the rabbis taught that the Law existed—in heaven—long before God created the world. But Jesus, so John teaches, is older than the Law: He was always "with God" and in fact "was God." Philo and John started from different places: Philo started from Greek philosophy and its abstract concepts, while John started with the life of Jesus and saw in him the Word of God personified. Instead of an abstract or mythological Logos, John gives us a human who weeps at the death of a friend. Outside of Christianity, no one could imagine such a Logos.

According to John, "the Word was with God." This brings us back to the old prophecy of Moses that God would raise up a prophet like him. Remember that the Old Testament says Moses had the rare privilege of closeness to God, for "the Lord would speak to Moses face to face, as a man speaks with his friend" (Exodus 33:11). Jesus, the Logos, the Word, was with God in a way surpassing God's closeness to Moses, for the Word and God were together for all eternity.

When John says, "the Word was God," he really means it. The Gospel in fact connects its beginning—"the Word was God"—to its end—Thomas' exclamation "My Lord and my God!" (John 20:28). Those who know Christ, the Word of God, know God.

There is an obvious puzzle here: John 1 says both that "the Word was with God, and the Word was God"—which sounds like a contradiction. It is a mystery we have to be willing to accept, just as in the Gospel Jesus says both "I and the Father are one" (John 10:30). and "the Father is greater than I" (John 14:28). The eye of faith sees that both statements are true.

The book you have been reading has looked at the most fascinating people in the Bible. Clearly, Jesus is the most fascinating person, and yet, in wrapping up our study, pause to consider this: God, in the Bible, is a Person, not some vague force or abstraction. So, in a sense, the most fascinating person in the Bible is God himself. While he does not possess a body, he does have a personality, and though he is higher and greater than any of the people we have looked at in this book, these people, at their best, bear the image of God, in some way reflecting his greatness and goodness. In the case of Jesus of Nazareth, we see the ultimate revelation of God's personality in human form. We have to agree with the writers of the New Testament: when we see Jesus, we see God.

PUTTING THE WORD TO WORK

1. How do you respond to Jesus' statement that his words will never pass away? Have there been times in your life when you found comfort in his words, believing they would endure longer than your present difficulties?

2. Reflect on the New Testament image of Jesus and his words being a foundation for life. What are ways your life can show that you are built on a solid foundation?

3. As you study the Bible and listen to sermons, try to keep in mind John 8:51: "If anyone keeps my word, he will never see death." Remind yourself that not just hearing the word of God but keeping it, is what matters.

4. The passage from John 6 shows many of Jesus' disciples falling away, while the faithful ones like Peter knew that only Jesus spoke the words of eternal life. Think of times in the past when your own faith wavered. What restored your belief that Jesus, the Holy One of God, was worth following?

5. John 1 and Hebrews 1 make the bold statement that Son of God, the Word, existed from all eternity. How does this affect your view of Jesus? How do you react to the idea that the Son was present and active in the world's creation?

Who Decided What Went into the Bible?

The traditional answer to this question is: God did. But how? That question leads us to two important and elusive concepts: *inspiration* and *canon.*

What does "inspired" mean? We can read a book, view a painting, hear a symphony and say it is an inspired work or that the author was inspired. We might also say that the book/painting/symphony inspires us. Meaning what? That it is a cut above the ordinary? That there is some hard-to-define spiritual quality about it? That it moves or touches us?

The Bible, so Christians believe, is definitely above the ordinary. It definitely has a spiritual quality. And over the centuries it has moved and touched millions of lives. When we say the Bible is "divinely inspired," we mean that God—in some mysterious way—moved the authors to write what they wrote. They were not just taking dictation, because it is obvious in different parts of the Bible that the authors' very different personalities shine through the writing. God was speaking his words through theirs. You might say he was the unseen co-author. In one of Paul's letters, he refers to the holy writings with the Greek word *theopneustos*—literally "God-breathed." Paul stated that the "God-breathed" writings were given so that believers "may be competent, equipped for every good work" (2 Timothy 3:16). Another letter, 2 Peter, states that the holy writings were not mere human products, "but men spoke from God as they were carried along by the Holy Spirit" (2 Peter 1:21).

People sometimes say that the Bible is inerrant—no errors in it at all. This makes sense. After all, God would not make mistakes, would he? No, but human beings would. And so we encounter places in, for example, the Gospels, where Matthew, Mark and Luke tell of the same event, but the details differ slightly. Is one correct, with the other two in error? A better explanation is this: Human beings made tiny errors or the difference in details was not a huge concern for God. He is more concerned about the big picture. And the big picture is this: The Bible is a book revealing God's will to humankind.

He created human beings and wants them in a close personal relationship with him. The Bible is intended to build and nurture that relationship. It is not intended to be a textbook on science or history—even though archaeologists continue to find that the Bible got most of its historical details correct. As noted in the last paragraph, the Bible is given so people may be "equipped for every good work."

The sixty-six books that make up our Bible were studied over the centuries and found to have a spiritual depth that other books do not possess. Christians believe it is no accident that, over the course of time, these books came together in one volume. They were inspired, and they continue to inspire.

Yes, some parts of the Bible seem supremely skippable. Most of Leviticus is dry reading; ditto for the endless genealogies in the Old Testament. The books of Esther and the Song of Solomon do not even mention God. But in spite of all the variety within it, the Bible is a unit, since the same God reveals himself through it. We do the Bible—and ourselves—a disservice when we focus on our favorite parts and neglect the rest, for the Bible as a whole will give us the deepest knowledge of God. The whole Bible, from Genesis to Revelation, is what God intended us to have—no more, no less.

WHAT ABOUT THE "HIDDEN" GOSPELS?

The belief that the Bible we have is just what God intended us to have has been seriously questioned in recent years. There is a huge interest in the "hidden Gospels," writings that lay buried in the dust for centuries but are now translated and selling, sometimes selling very well, in bookstores. The editors and translators of these ancient writings would have us believe that the early Christians were in on a vast conspiracy. They deliberately suppressed some fine writings which contained the "real" or "deeper" truth of what Jesus taught. The fans of the hidden Gospels accuse the early Christians of cultural imperialism, spreading a narrow Christianity that was far from what Jesus intended. To mention one notable example, the phenomenally popular novel *The Da Vinci Code* spread the centuries-old idea that Mary Magdalene, a minor character in the Bible, was really one of Jesus' closest followers and the recipient of his deepest teachings—which the Christians wrongly suppressed. *The Jesus Papers* and *The Gospel of Judas* are other popular books that offer readers revisionist views of Jesus, catering to an age-old urge to prove that the Bible itself misrepresents the "real" Christ.

Any truth to this "conspiracy theory" at all? (One of the best books on this subject is Philip Jenkins' *Hidden Gospels: How the Search for Jesus Lost Its Way*.)

The fans of the nonbiblical Gospels are correct about one thing: the writings in the New Testament were definitely not the only writings of the first Christians. There were dozens of other Gospels and epistles, most of them claiming to be written by some of the apostles, and many claiming to contain "secret" and "higher" teachings that were not given to most of Jesus' followers. One of the best-known of these is called the Gospel of Thomas, and it was included (along with the four New Testament Gospels) in a recent book titled *The Five Gospels*. The editors of this book take the interesting position of judging the truth of the four New Testament Gospels by comparing them to the Gospel of Thomas.

What happened among the early Christians was just the opposite: They used Matthew, Mark, Luke and John to judge the numerous Gospels that did not make it into the Bible. Some of those Gospels mingled sayings from the four Gospels with teachings that sound radically different from the Jesus of Matthew, Mark, Luke and John. In a sense the nonbiblical Gospels were "parasitic"—that is, they could not have existed if the four Gospels of the New Testament weren't already in circulation.

And how do we know for certain that Matthew, Mark, Luke and John were the Gospels that God intended us to have? We don't, actually—not if you demand scientific proof. There is an element of faith here—you can believe that those four Gospels give us a pretty accurate view of what Jesus said and did. Or you can take a leap of faith in the other direction: believing that the hidden Gospels give us the "real" Jesus. The fans of the hidden Gospels have no way of proving they were suppressed, and that Christians have been duped by the wrong writings for all these centuries.

The simple fact is that most of the writings that are finding their way to bookstore shelves today were written much later than the writings of the New Testament—more than a century later, in most cases. The Gospels and epistles of the New Testament were all written down by AD 100, perhaps even by AD 70. They were all written within the lifetimes of Jesus' first followers, meaning there were plenty of people around who could vouch for the accuracy of the writings. The Gospel of Thomas—which is definitely *not* by the Apostle Thomas—came much later. What do you think would be more accurate—a biography written within fifty years of the life of its subject, or one written two hundred years later?

The early Christians produced hundreds of writings—some based on the memories of Jesus' apostles, some not. Over time, some of the writings continued to inspire people, so they were preserved and duplicated. The false writings had their fans, of course, but mostly they ended up on the ash heap of history.

As time passed, Christians debated among themselves which of the writings were uniquely inspired by God. They already accepted the Jews' sacred books—what they came to call the Old Testament—as inspired. What was taking shape was the New Testament, which eventually included twenty-seven writings—the four Gospels (telling the story of Jesus), Acts (telling of the activities of the earliest Christians), the Epistles (early Christian leaders giving instruction about beliefs and morals), and Revelation (a vision of the end of time). There was no precise date when it was decided, once and for all, that these books were the God-inspired New Testament. But we have writings from the mid-300s that show that Christians spread out over a wide area had pretty much agreed about these twenty-seven books. There were a few "almosts," such as some popular epistles—one was called the Epistle of Barnabas—that continued to be widely read. But one thing was certain: By the mid-300s, the hidden Gospels had been definitely, finally rejected by the vast majority of Christians. There was no conspiracy, no sinister group trying to suppress deep spiritual writings. There was just a powerful sense, existing over a long period of time, that certain writings were rooted in what really happened to Jesus and his apostles—and some writings that clearly were not.

In fact, the early Christians were very suspicious of writings that seemed to be mere fiction, even if those writings were produced for a good purpose. A bishop wrote the Acts of Paul, which contained some inspiring and miraculous stories. His intentions were good, but when it was revealed that the work was pure fiction, he was removed from his post as bishop around AD 190. The Christians were equally dead set against the many fictional Gospels circulating, many of which replaced the historical Jesus of Nazareth with a mythical Jesus who sounds more like a guru attached to no particular time and place.

So why are these old documents being published now? One obvious answer: They sell. And they sell because people enjoy a good conspiracy theory. Also, after two thousand years of Christianity, people can point to a lot of bad things done in the name of Christ—which might lead people to believe that maybe the real teaching of Jesus got lost along the way and deserves a hearing. You might say the hidden Gospels have the attraction of being both really old (which they are) and really new (since for centuries no one read them). Pop culture makes a big fuss over these writings, with people never bothering to ask the most obvious question: Might there be a good reason why these writings were rejected by most Christians—like, maybe, the fact that they weren't regarded as true?

Most of the Gospels that were not accepted into the Bible were produced by people loosely known as Gnostics. There isn't space enough here to fully explain Gnosticism, but in general the Gnostics, some of whom considered themselves Christians, saw themselves as spiritually higher people, believing in secret teachings that were not intended for the great mass of Christians—or for mankind in general. There were numerous Gnostic Gospels floating around, most of them mixing parts of the four biblical Gospels—a nice hook to get Christians' attention—with the secret teachings that the risen Jesus supposedly passed on to Thomas, Mary Magdalene, Judas or others. (Tacking on the name of one of Jesus' actual followers was another hook, obviously.) In general, the Gnostic Gospels emphasize these teachings at the expense of the moral teaching that is so important in the four Gospels found in our Bible. The Gnostics saw themselves as being saved not by faith nor by righteous living but by the "knowledge" that only special people knew. (*Gnosis* is the Greek word for "knowledge.") Gnosticism was, you may say, "spirituality from the neck up." In other words, Gnosticism spread via the age-old appeal of intellectual snobbery. As proof that some things never change, the same appeal can be found today among those who read the "suppressed" Gospels and find Gnosticism more to their taste than the Christianity of the New Testament. Add intellectual snobbery to the belief in a conspiracy theory, and the current vogue for these old writings is understandable.

But again, we come back to the basic question: *Are they true?* Or are the four Gospels in our Bible—which almost certainly are the oldest Gospels of all—what God intended us to have for living the life of faith? The consensus, after two thousand years, is that the four Gospels in our Bible are there because God inspired them, and because they present an accurate picture of Jesus.

WHAT ABOUT THE APOCRYPHA?

One key question in discussing the Bible: Just which writings does the Bible include? Jews, Catholics and Protestants do not agree on which books are included in the Bible. Jews, of course, don't regard the Christian writings known as the New Testament as part of their Bible. They only accept the books that Christians know as the Old Testament. But Christians themselves disagree about just which books to include in the Old Testament.

Here is the standard list of the books that Jews and Protestant Christians regard as part of the Bible:

Genesis	Nehemiah	Hosea
Exodus	Esther	Joel
Leviticus	Job	Amos
Numbers	Psalms	Obadiah
Deuteronomy	Proverbs	Jonah
Joshua	Ecclesiastes	Micah
Judges	Song of Solomon	Nahum
Ruth	Isaiah	Habakkuk
1 and 2 Samuel	Jeremiah	Zephaniah
1 and 2 Kings	Lamentations	Haggai
1 and 2 Chronicles	Ezekiel	Zechariah
Ezra	Daniel	Malachi

These books are found in *all* Bibles—Jewish, Protestant and Catholic. However, Roman Catholic Bibles include these other books in the Old Testament:

Tobit	Wisdom	Baruch
Judith	Ecclesiasticus (*not* the	Additions to Esther
1 and 2 Maccabees	same as Ecclesiastes)	Additions to Daniel

Confused? This last group of books, known as the Apocrypha, has been the subject of controversy for many centuries. *Apocrypha* is a Greek word meaning "hidden things." But these books never were, strictly speaking, hidden. They were widely read, just like the other books of the Old Testament. But the Jews did not hold them in quite as high regard as the other Old Testament books, partly because they were written later—in the period between the Old and New Testaments—and so they hadn't been read and cherished as some of the other books had.

Keep something in mind: For many centuries, there was no standard list of books of the Bible. The individual "books" were actually written on scrolls, meaning that people in ancient times didn't have the luxury we have of having all the writings together under one cover or on one scroll. Over time, though, both Jews and Christians thought it was important to lay down a canon—a rule or standard—that is, to make it clear that certain books were definitely inspired by God and were to be used as the basis for morals and belief. Books that were not included were outside the canon. They might still be read but were not as important as the writings within the canon.

Sometime around AD 100, a council of rabbis met in the town of Jamnia in Palestine to debate the matter of which books the Jews included in their canon. The Jews read a popular Greek translation of the Old Testament known as the Septuagint, and it included all the writings that we now call the Apocrypha. However, the council at Jamnia chose not to include those books in the Jewish canon.

The early Christians were mostly Jews, and they knew the Old Testament through the Septuagint translation. However, the books of the Apocrypha are never quoted or even referred to in the New Testament, which gives us the impression that the early Christians did not regard them as divinely inspired. The books of the Apocrypha did continue to be read, even though many Christians followed the lead of the Jewish council of Jamnia and questioned whether the books of the Apocrypha ought to be considered sacred.

In AD 382, a Christian scholar named Jerome was commissioned by the pope to prepare a standard Latin version of the Bible. Jerome learned Hebrew so he could translate the Old Testament from the original language. In discussing the Old Testament with rabbis in Palestine, Jerome became convinced that the Apocrypha should not be included in the Old Testament. However, the pope ordered him to include them in the new Latin Bible, so for centuries they were, even though many Christian scholars had doubts about whether they truly belonged there. From the time Jerome completed his

Latin Bible in about AD 404 until the early 1500s, it was the only Bible available in Europe, so for more than a millennium most Bibles contained the disputed books.

In the 1500s, Martin Luther began the Protestant Reformation in Germany. Luther translated the Old Testament from Hebrew into German, and he had the same doubts about the Apocrypha that Jerome had. Luther made an important change: While the Latin Bible had the books of the Apocrypha scattered through various places in the Old Testament, Luther put them in a separate section, bestowing the name "Apocrypha" on them. He said they deserved to be read but were not on a par with the other parts of the Bible. The other Protestants leaders agreed, and the first complete English Bible, published in 1535, placed the Apocrypha after the New Testament. The Protestants agreed that quotations from the Apocrypha could not be used as the foundation for Christian beliefs—one reason being that the Catholic belief in purgatory is based solely on a single verse in 2 Maccabees. By affirming that the Apocrypha could not be used as a foundation for Christian beliefs, the Reformers demolished all the ideas and practices connected with the Catholics' belief in purgatory.

Catholics reacted to this: At the 1546 session of the Council of Trent, they made it clear that the books of the Apocrypha *were* part of the divinely inspired Bible—although they were given the name *deutero-canonical*, meaning "of the second canon." To this day, Catholics do not refer to "the Apocrypha" but to "the deutero-canonical writings." For Catholics, Judith and 1 Maccabees are as much a part of the Old Testament as Genesis and Psalms are.

Let's throw in another complication: The Eastern Orthodox churches (Russian, Greek, Romanian, etc.) have a canon that differs from both the Catholic and Protestant canons. In 1672 an Orthodox council meeting in Jerusalem chose to include Tobit, Judith, Wisdom and Ecclesiasticus in their Old Testament but omitted Baruch and 1 and 2 Maccabees.

Since the Protestants had pushed the books of the Apocrypha into a separate section of the Bible and made it clear that they were second-class at best, it was only a matter of time before Protestants dropped the Apocrypha entirely. Protestant scholars weren't writing commentaries on the books, and Protestant preachers rarely quoted the Apocrypha or preached on it, so by the 1800s, most Protestant Bibles did not include the Apocrypha.

What about today? Some Protestant Bibles today do include the Apocrypha, partly for historical purposes, since 1 and 2 Maccabees contain some important history about the period between the Old and New Testaments. Also, many people find the books of Wisdom and Ecclesiasticus useful to read, containing some of the same kind of wisdom found in Proverbs. However, Protestants have serious doubts about the historical value of Tobit and Judith, even though the stories are inspiring. And the simple fact is that the Apocrypha as a whole has never inspired people in the same way that the other books of the Bible have done.

Should you read the Apocrypha? Instead of answering that with a simple yes or no, here is our answer: First get familiar with the sixty-six books that *all* Christians agree are part of the divinely inspired Bible. That is what the book you are now holding was intended to help you do.

APPENDIX B
Approaching the Bible: How Not to Do It

1. APPROACH IT AS A "CHURCH BOOK."

Many people grew up hearing the Bible read only in church. Not hearing it read at home, they associate the Bible with the stuffiness of a worship service. They may associate the Bible with a pompous, reverent tone of voice. This made the Bible seem like a Sunday thing—something sacred, stuffy and separate from the other six days and from "real life." In fact, the original Hebrew and Greek in the Bible are very much written in everyday language, not a special holy language. The original Bible was written in ordinary language to communicate with as many people as possible. Just as everyone today understands the language of TV shows and radio talk-show hosts, so the Bible's words were the common ground of their day.

2. APPROACH IT AS A BOOK OF RULES.

Well, it *does* have rules. All religions do. So do all schools, employers, sports teams and any other kind of human grouping. No one joins a baseball team and gripes, "I don't like this 'three strikes and you're out' rule." That's just baseball. Well, the Bible's assumption is that life, like baseball, has rules. They're not there to stifle and repress. They're just there. This is the way things are. And the rules are there for a good reason. Any married person who's ever been suspicious of his spouse understands the wisdom of the "Do not commit adultery" rule. And anyone who owns any type of property understands "Do not steal." The rules aren't all bad, are they?

But it is wrong to see the Bible as a book of "do nots." It has so much more: images of loving fellowship with God and with other people. The "do nots" are balanced with a lot of very positive "dos."

3. APPROACH IT AS A BOOK OF MYSTERIES.

Parts of the Bible puzzle people. The Book of Revelation, for example, has been interpreted in many, many ways. The same goes for parts of the Book of Daniel. But generally the Bible is rather straightforward. If you're reading a good modern translation, you'll find the Bible is rather easy to understand. Books like Acts and Mark's Gospel are easy enough for most children to grasp. We say the Bible is holy and sacred, but its writers didn't intend it to be mysterious or cryptic. In its original Hebrew and Greek its language is amazingly ordinary—the language of everyday thought.

4. APPROACH IT TO PROVE A POINT.

People love to do this: use the Bible to prove something they already believe. (Some people have used the verse "You must be born again" to support their belief in reincarnation—definitely *not* what the verse really means.) This is an abuse of the Bible. Instead of really studying the Bible and reading it to find out its main themes, people scrounge around to find particular verses to support their own ideas. (The classic example is the "Peanuts" cartoon in which Lucy goes running to her brother Linus, pointing out that she found the word "sister" in the Bible. Then she says, "That proves you have to give me a Christmas present.")

5. APPROACH IT AS IT IF WAS DULL.

It isn't—not by any means. The problem is, people approach it assuming that since it is holy, it is boring. People in cultures that have no prior knowledge of the Bible or its religion often take it, read it and find it fascinating. It would be interesting to see what people would do if they could clear their minds of everything they'd ever heard about the Bible. If they could approach it as they would any other book, what might happen? "The Bible? Wonder what this is? Let's read this and find out . . ."

Oddly, some of the same people who claim the Bible is dull will gladly tell you about some fascinating book on Buddhism or New Age beliefs.

6. APPROACH IT AS IF IT WERE HOLY.

Well, isn't it? Yes, in the sense that many intelligent people really do believe that it contains God's revelation to mankind. But it—the paper and ink that make up the physical Bible—isn't holy. The revelation is. There is nothing magical about the book itself—even though people have done silly things like place a Bible on the chest of a dying person, hoping it will help him recover. It is not a lucky charm, like a rabbit's foot or horseshoe.

For centuries people have believed that the Bible's words can change human lives—assuming that the reader actually puts them into practice. Having a cookbook does not make you a cook, nor does it fill your stomach. Likewise, having a Bible does not change a human life. It doesn't fill your spiritual hunger unless you act on what's there. You could starve to death with a cookbook in your hand even if you'd memorized every recipe in it, and you could feel spiritual emptiness even if you had memorized every verse in the Bible. The ink and paper—and even the words themselves—make no difference in human life unless the reader acts on them. There is a classic French novel, *The Red and the Black*, which tells the story of a brilliant clergyman who has memorized the entire New Testament in its original Greek. This impresses everyone, and many people think he must be a very spiritual person. In fact, he is a totally immoral character, selfish and cruel. Another character in the novel tells him, "I fear for your salvation."

Putting Your Heads Together:
Organizing a Bible Study Group

The Old and New Testaments present a community faith, not a private faith. You can and should study the Bible on your own. But you can gain a lot—and so can other people—by studying the Bible in a group setting. Keep a key motive in mind: There is safety in numbers. An individual can—and often has—come up with some pretty kooky interpretations of the Bible. A group could do this also, but it's more likely that someone in the group will say, tactfully, of course, "That's a kooky idea." On the positive side, in the group setting you can share insights. Someone in the group will perceive some aspect of a Bible passage that you didn't see. This may have happened in high school and college when you engaged in group study.

1. GET IN TOUCH WITH PEOPLE YOU THINK WOULD BE INTERESTED.

You might do this through your church, but it can be done with fellow workers, neighbors, etc. You might even post a notice on your supermarket's bulletin board, stating your name, phone number and what you're trying to organize. Churches should, of course, have regular Bible-study groups. But there is something to be gained from groups outside the church. For one thing, such a group could be interdenominational—which makes for an interesting mix of viewpoints. It also allows members to shoot for the meat of the Bible, not for things that only confirm people's denominational biases. It also allows you to include seekers who are more interested in the Bible than in attaching themselves to a church.

2. AIM FOR A GROUP OF BETWEEN SIX AND TWELVE PEOPLE.

As Jesus was aware, twelve was a good number for a group. (It's a commonly used number in the Bible.) Anything more than twelve allows shyer members to fade into the wallpaper. A group smaller than six or seven has the danger of too much agreement, not enough creative discussion.

3. SET UP THE STUDY AS A REAL STUDY TIME, NOT A SOCIAL HOUR.

People have come to expect food and drink in any kind of human encounter, and eating does seem to mellow people out. But if you want the group to focus on the Bible, keep the munching to a minimum. Coffee and tea are pretty standard, but see if you can do without edibles. (People don't eat during church services, a system that seems to work pretty well.) A rule of thumb: If food is to be a normal part of the group meeting, count on adding a half-hour to the time you actually expect to spend in study.

4. SET UP THE MEETINGS FOR A DEFINITE TIME.

A weekly meeting usually works best. Generally, an hour is too cramping, but two hours is more than some people want to commit. So compromise with ninety minutes, and try to begin and end the meetings on time. This is particularly important for parents who need to get home to their children and babysitters.

5. PICK A PLACE.

Private homes are cozy and relaxing, but there's the danger of group members getting too interested in the host's home and furnishings. There may be a problem with adequate parking in some residential areas. Some other possibilities: a room in a church (not necessarily your own church), a public room available for use in a library or community center or the club room in your apartment complex (only make sure you can shut the door and have quiet). Rooms like these can seem chilly compared to someone's den, but public rooms do seem more serious than private homes.

For many reasons, men's study groups often choose to meet over breakfast. If a local restaurant is open to this, why not schedule a weekly meeting over a breakfast? The only flaw with breakfast meetings: If a lively discussion gets started, it can't continue too long, since most of the people have to leave. Then again, this limitation could be a blessing.

Note: If you expect the group to include people very unfamiliar with the Bible—maybe even people who don't consider themselves believers yet—you should definitely not hold the meetings in a church. Many people have had unpleasant experiences with churches. It's possible for people to be interested in the Bible but not the least bit interested in attending a church. Holding a meeting in a church suggests to many people that you intend to get them involved in church—that church and its denomination, to be specific. So if you're casting a wide net, hoping to include seekers who may not yet be pro-church, choose your place carefully.

6. CHOOSE THE BOOK OR PASSAGE OR TOPIC THE GROUP WILL STUDY.

Go for the obvious: one of the four Gospels, one of Paul's great letters (Romans, Galatians, Ephesians), Acts, Psalms, Proverbs, Isaiah. In the case of a long book like Psalms or Isaiah, you might opt for only part of the book, not the whole. A warning: If this is your first venture with the group, avoid any book that is surrounded by controversy—like Revelation, Daniel or Genesis.

7. DURING YOUR FIRST MEETING, DECIDE ON THE FORMAT THE MEETINGS WILL FOLLOW.

One logical method: Assign for the coming week a portion of the book to be read ahead of time and discussed at the meeting. For example, if you're studying John's Gospel, assign chapter 1. The group members will (you hope) read that chapter before the next meeting and be prepared to discuss it then. Discussing the passage involves members telling what they've gotten from the reading, what problems they encountered and how they might apply the text to their lives.

8. DESIGNATE A LEADER.

This doesn't necessarily mean a lecturer or teacher. It means an organizer, a monitor, one who will arrange the meetings, keep in touch with members and guide the discussion. The leader will always come to the group prepared, having read the text even if no one else did and jotted down some discussion questions and suggestions on how the text applies to human life, etc. One necessary role of the group leader: keeping very talkative members from dominating the discussion. The flip side of this: drawing out comments and questions from the quieter members. The leader needs to be a people person. But the leader should not be an egomaniac who likes to be the center of attention constantly.

The leader does not need to be a certified Bible scholar or someone with a degree in religion. Christianity is most healthy when laymen, not scholars and clergy, are willing to interact with the Bible. We don't have to be spoon-fed by religious professionals. But the leader of a Bible study does need to come to class prepared. This means not just reading through the assigned passage but also consulting at least one good commentary or Bible dictionary to help explain problem areas. Your pastor or religious bookstore can recommend some good Bible commentaries and other helpful aids.

9. KEEP THE GROUP FOCUSED ON WHAT THEY'RE STUDYING. THIS INVOLVES TWO THINGS.

One, keep them from going off on tangents concerning events in the news or in their own lives. True, applying the Bible to our lives and to world events is fine. It should be a goal of all Bible study, in fact. But if you have only an hour or so for study, try to stay focused on the Bible itself. Anyone who has worked with a Bible-study group knows how easily the members can get derailed off the track of actually discussing the Bible. Another matter: If you sense that a particular group member wants to discuss a personal problem that may or may not relate to the Bible passage you're studying, you might just want to call that person at home at another time. The group might not be the ideal setting.

Two, keep them from focusing too much on minute details so that they won't miss the big picture of what they're studying. In every group you'll find an academic type who likes to discuss little historical or theological details. This person can be helpful—or a real hindrance if he dominates the group discussions. You may also get a person who simply likes to argue. Example: The group is studying John's Gospel, and you're focusing on chapter 20, the story of the resurrected Jesus. You may have a group member who likes to quibble over Jesus' resurrected body. How could it have wounds in it? How was Jesus able to walk through doors? Legitimate questions, but not if they dominate the entire meeting. The big picture you should focus on is the fact that Jesus was clearly raised from the dead, and that his resurrected body was like—but also different from—his original body. The group leader needs tact and a gentle but firm hand in steering the group back to the material.

A LITTLE HISTORICAL REMINDER HERE: Until the printing press in the 1400s, mass production of Bibles wasn't possible. Before then, and for a long time afterward, Bible reading and study was usually a group thing, not a private thing. It was possible for an individual to read the book (or scrolls, in the preprinting press era), but most people were exposed to the Bible in a group setting—in worship, in a family study, in church classes. Much of people's exposure to the Bible came from hearing it read aloud and then being discussed or preached on.

So group study of the Bible is an old and respectable custom. When your group meets together, it is carrying on a tradition as old as the Bible itself. The Apostle Paul wrote to one of his assistants, "Until I come, devote yourself to the public reading of Scripture, to preaching and to teaching" (1 Timothy 4:13).

Why You Don't Need an Expert to Study the Bible

Throughout this book I've mentioned ways you can get help from Bible scholars, the "experts." You probably can't meet them personally, but you'll find their work available in Bible dictionaries, commentaries and thousands of other books on the market. This is comforting—knowing you aren't getting in over your head when you start to read the Bible. The scholars have studied the Bible closely. Some of them make their living this way. They are pleased to make their knowledge available to you—and it helps them sell books, incidentally.

But you don't need to become expert-dependent. Millions of people over the centuries have read the Bible—and understood it—with little or no aid from experts. God is present when a commentary or Bible dictionary helps to enlighten a Bible reader. But God can also work without such books.

One problem with the scholars: They swim in the world of the Bible, easily as a fish swims in water. It is their element. But for most readers, this isn't so. The fish says to the man, "Just jump on in, use your gills and you can breathe underwater." Easier said than done! Most of us are trying to live our lives, doing jobs that have little or nothing to do with the world of the Bible. At the end of a workday, we approach the Bible, not as if we belong in it but hoping to get some good out of it. We want to use it. This isn't selfishness—it's just being practical. Unlike the Bible scholars, we can't spend an entire day speculating about Babylonian emperors and the exact date that one of them invaded Israel. "That's nice for them," we say, "but please, let's get back to reality. I have a job, a family, hobbies, retirement plans. I also have problems. What I *don't* have is a huge amount of time to decipher the Bible."

Well, happily, we don't need huge amounts. But we do need the dedication to read the Bible with some sense of purpose. It does take some commitment. And why not? Dieting does, and so does exercise—and people gladly fling themselves into weight loss and workout programs.

But again, you can do this with little help from the Bible pros, although you do need some help. For many people, what they need is a study partner, a fellow seeker. Think of times in your school days when you benefited from studying with a group. Maybe your teacher was excellent, but when you asked him for help he a) explained things you understood already, b) gave you a lot of information you didn't need, or c) failed to address the thing that really puzzled you. The teacher often forgets what it was like to be a learner, a beginner. A fellow student knows less than the teacher—but maybe he understands your needs and questions better than the teacher does. Maybe he has gotten snagged at the same places you have. He may have untangled some of those—and you may have untangled some that he is still struggling with.

So don't underestimate the power of a fellow seeker. Two people beginning from the same point can aid each other. Also helpful: someone who is, say, just a few steps ahead of you in what he has learned. Think of it as the high school junior telling the sophomore, "What, you're hung up on geometry? Hey, I had that just last year. Here, let me help you out here . . ."

Here's a simple, everyday example: A neighbor and I were discussing talk radio. I raised a question that had puzzled me: "Why are so many of the callers calling from their car phones?" My neighbor replied, with no hesitation, "Because those call-in shows put them on hold for such a long time. If they're sitting in their cars, they have the phone at hand. If they were at home and they stay on hold for a long time, they get antsy and start wanting to move around." A simple and no doubt correct answer. I hadn't thought of it, but once he said it, it seemed so obvious. Sometimes two heads really are better than one.

A little historical note: Martin Luther, the great Christian leader of the 1500s, wrote and preached a great deal about the Bible. Yet he went on record as saying, "O that God would grant that my commentaries and those of all other teachers were destroyed. For every Christian should take the Bible in his own hands and read God's word for himself. He would then see that there is a vast difference between the word of God and the words of man."

Why You Shouldn't Fly Solo

The Bible has no conception of a solitary faith. In the Old Testament, the faith community is Israel. In the New Testament, it is the Christian community. An individual can interact with God, and an individual can read and grasp the Bible— sometimes. But not always. An individual can experience the revelation of God. But the Bible pictures people experiencing that revelation in a community.

When you read the Bible, you are reading the words of more than forty authors. In the course of time, their words have been studied and interpreted by thousands of people. Some of these interpretations have been weird, misguided and often just plain wrong. But with the passage of time, some agreement develops too. Century after century, readers find some of the same meanings in the words of the Bible—not in every verse but in many, especially the most important ones.

If you read the Bible on your own, never bothering to find out how other people have interpreted it, you can still gain a lot of insight. But you would be depriving your-self of a lot of other people's insights. For two thousand years people have been making some intelligent observations on the Bible. Doesn't it make sense to know what their comments were?

You may find that your own insights into the Bible were the same as theirs. If so, wonderful. You can feel some satisfaction that your own mind and heart are part of the mainstream. You'll find many times that your own fresh discovery may be two thousand years old. But it's still valid. It just means your own mind works in ways similar to other readers' minds.

Occasionally you'll find that your own interpretations are radically different from what the commentators thought. Does that mean they were right and you're wrong? Not necessarily. But it doesn't mean they're wrong and you're right either. Over the years a lot of weird religious groups have begun because someone had a "new insight" into the Bible. An example: The Adamites, a group that read Genesis 2:25 and had a "new insight." The verse reads "The man and his wife were both naked, and they felt no shame." The Adamites concluded that if God made Adam and Eve naked, then that was the normal human state, so let's be naked. So, a group calling itself Christian concluded from the Bible that nudity was the norm. Needless to say, most readers have *not* drawn that conclusion.

As part of the human family, we owe it to each other to share insights and ideas. ("Sharing" is not the same as forcing them down people's throats, by the way.) If you find that reading the Bible gives you insights into how to handle stress, find purpose in life and deal with problems, others can benefit from your sharing those insights. Other people might not agree with all of them—just as you might not agree with their insights. But there's a lot to be gained by sharing. This is why Christians have, for two thousand years, chosen to worship and study together, not just in isolation.

What's a Family to Do?

Charity begins at home, and so does biblical literacy. Attending Sunday school and weekly worship are essential to a knowledge of the scriptures, but can we really expect two or three hours of church activity each week to give us enough exposure to the Bible? Relying on those few hours communicates a message to children: The Bible is just a church thing, something reserved for Sunday mornings, largely separate from the rest of the week and from real life. Here are some modest proposals for families wanting to become more biblically literate.

1. STUDY THE BIBLE TOGETHER, AND USE A PLAN.

Yes, the contemporary family is supremely busy, but every family ought to set aside a time daily for systematic study of the Bible. Many parents have found that immediately after dinner—assuming all members can be assembled together for one meal a day—is a good time.

2. READ.

The decline of biblical literacy is connected with the general decline in literacy. For many people, books—especially older books—do not seem user-friendly. How much easier to turn on the TV or stereo! Yet consider how many centuries passed without video or audio, which meant that families entertained themselves by reading, playing games together or making their own music. If you are out of the habit of reading, it may take some nudging to force yourself. Consider it a worthwhile personal investment—like dieting or exercising. Communicate this message to the children: Reading is a pleasant way to pass the time. More importantly, make it clear that private reading of the Bible is a normal part of everyday life.

3. PLAY WITH THE BIBLE.

There is no reason parents can't combine education with play, and nearly all Christian bookstores—and many secular stores as well—sell Bible board games and quiz books for all age levels. While we should never lose sight of the fact that the Bible's teachings are to be taken with the utmost seriousness, Bible trivia games can be a delightful way for a family to spend time together.

4. ENCOURAGE MEMORIZATION.

Memorizing is a good thing. Why should Sunday school be the only place where memorization takes place? As a modest beginning, have the entire family aim to memorize one Bible verse per month—an important verse (John 3:16, for example, or any one of the Beatitudes in Matthew 5) that is fairly short. From one new verse per month you might increase it to one every two weeks, and so on. Use such a plan as a way of memorizing longer passages—for example, memorizing two of the Ten Commandments per month, so that in five months the family can recite all ten.

Do you think the human memory is limited? Listen closely to the man who can rattle off sports statistics from the last fifty years. Listen to the aging baby boomer who knows the words to a limitless number of rock-and-roll oldies. Most educational experts agree that human beings underuse their memories even more than they underuse their bodies' muscles.

See pages 474–484 for tips on memorizing the Bible.

5. DISCUSS THE DAY'S EVENTS IN THE LIGHT OF THE BIBLE.

This can occur during the family's daily Bible study, or at any time parent and child are interacting. Where a healthy parent-child situation exists, the child will probably feel comfortable discussing events of the school day. On a broader level, if the family watches the evening TV news together, discuss world, national and local news in the light of the Bible's view of God's will for mankind. You can also discuss any TV show—a sitcom, a talk show, a drama, even a sports event—in the light of what the Bible teaches about God and human beings.

The Bible, like anything written hundreds of years ago, helps us put things in perspective by reminding us that human nature never really changes. The evening news will assure you that human beings are often greedy, immoral, militaristic, cruel, hypocritical—in short, just plain selfish. The Bible will assure you that nothing of this is new. There were saints and heroes in Bible times, as there are today. There were also lying politicians, unjust laws, religious persecution, oppression of the weak, wars, broken homes, alcohol dependence—does the world really change much?

The Bare Minimum to Know:
Just What Is "Bible Literacy"?

Several years ago I interviewed several Christian leaders, asking them about biblical literacy. What, I asked them, were the key things—the basics—that a person should know about the Bible?

THE TEN COMMANDMENTS

This is the core of the Old Testament moral law, given by God to Israel. Survey after survey shows Americans' ignorance of this crucial Old Testament passage. There are only ten, and could they be that difficult to memorize? (*Living Bible* author Kenneth Taylor, father of ten and author of several books for children, mentioned that children, properly taught at an early age, have no trouble memorizing the ten.)

No, most of us don't like to memorize things—especially rules. On the other hand, we do so when we feel the need. We're glad to learn rules of the road so we can get our driver's license. Rather than viewing the Ten Commandments as an outdated series of rules irrelevant to a high-tech world, we can look at them as the basic rules God intended for us to follow—for our own best interests.

THE NAMES OF BOOKS OF THE BIBLE, AND THEIR SEQUENCE

Bible drills in which children are taught to locate particular verses as quickly as possible have fallen into disuse. Gone also is the standard memorization—again, by children—of the order of the books of the Bible. Still, we do need to know where to find the passage referred to in the pastor's sermon or in the book we are reading.

AN OVERVIEW OF SALVATION HISTORY

No one has to know the names of all the kings of Israel, but all the Christian leaders I interviewed mentioned the necessity of knowing the high points of salvation history— creation and man's fall; Noah and the flood; Abraham, Isaac and Jacob; Moses and

Israel's exodus from Egypt; the kingdom under Samuel, Saul, David and Solomon; Israel's spiritual decline and exile; the messages of the prophets, particularly Elijah, Isaiah, Jeremiah and Ezekiel; Jesus' life, death, Resurrection and teachings; the growth of the church in Acts and the Epistles, especially the work of Paul; and the final judgment.

THE SERMON ON THE MOUNT

Matthew 5–7 contains the essence of Christian ethical teaching. Memorization of such a long passage may be too much to hope for, but every Christian should have at least a familiarity with the Beatitudes, the Lord's Prayer, the words on salt and light, etc.

KEY ETHICAL PASSAGES

Besides the Ten Commandments and the Sermon on the Mount, a familiarity with Proverbs is useful. Matthew 19, on divorce, is perhaps crucial in the modern church, as are Paul's teachings on marriage and family, particularly Ephesians 5–6 and Colossians 3–4.

THE APOSTLES' CREED

A creed is a basic summary of Christian beliefs. Not all churches use a creed, but many do, and knowing—and even better, understanding—the points of this ancient formula are essential. Kenneth Taylor adds one disclaimer: "The Creed is sparse in regard to the Holy Spirit, and this needs expansion regarding the gifts and fruit of the Spirit. We need to know that help is available from the Spirit in crippling the sin nature and helping us in good works and thoughts."

Pastors have preached sermon series on the Apostles Creed. It could be called a "Bible creed," since all parts of it are drawn from the Bible. And in case you're not familiar with the creed, here it is:

> I believe in God the Father Almighty, maker of heaven and earth;
> And in Jesus Christ his only Son our Lord; who was conceived by the Holy Spirit, born of the virgin Mary, suffered under Pontius Pilate, was crucified, dead, and buried; the third day he rose from the dead; he ascended into heaven, and sits at the right hand of God the Father Almighty; from thence he shall come to judge the living and the dead.
> I believe in the Holy Spirit, the holy universal Church, the communion of saints, the forgiveness, the Resurrection of the body, and the life everlasting.

You may know this creed already, or it may surprise you to know that for many years, people recited it by heart, not by reading, in churches all over the world. It's a good summary of the Bible's teaching about God and Christ.

BASIC DOCTRINES

The Apostles' Creed is a good summary of doctrine, but it leaves out some critical points—sin and our need of redemption, for example. A more complete summary was given by pastor Brett Griffith, whose congregation studies the Westminster Confession of Faith: "Creation, the nature of God, the Trinity, Christ as true man and true God, the nature of sin (Genesis 3 and Romans 5), the atonement, salvation through faith, sanctification ('made holy by union with Christ'), the last things (particularly the implications of Judgment for our walk with God)."

Thanks for the Memory: Why We Should Memorize the Bible, and How We Can

When I was in high school, my church's pastor introduced something new into our Sunday-evening worship: memory time. Shortly before his sermon, the congregation would stand and recite, if they could, a Bible verse that he had given them the previous week. He didn't select the verse at random; he chose a verse that related to his sermon on that Sunday.

Most of us liked doing this. We had an entire week to roll the verse around in our minds, and there was the good feeling of doing something as a congregation. Sometimes peer pressure can be a good thing.

Do I now remember what all those verses were? No. I doubt if even the pastor remembers them all. Yet I don't think they've left my mind completely. I'm sure they're in my brain somewhere, probably more accessible than hundreds of things I learned in college but have had no reason to recall since then.

Memorizing passages from the Bible is an old practice. For centuries, any educated person in Europe and America was expected to know the Bible very well. Even if you weren't a college graduate, it was assumed you would know certain verses, or at least phrases, from the Bible, which, until recently, always meant the King James Version of 1611. This was something that united people of all social classes and backgrounds. The bank president, the college professor, the housewife and the farmhand would all share a basic knowledge of the Bible. Until the last fifty years or so, we were a "people of the Book."

There was more to this than just learning the materials you were taught in church and home. Most people assumed that the Bible was a moral guide for life. You remembered it, not just to be smart but to help yourself and others in all seasons of life.

An example: It was not unusual to call to mind, when someone close to you died, a verse like John 11:25: "I am the Resurrection, and the life." These words of Jesus brought a lot of comfort to grieving people over the years, and still do. But of course, most of us don't walk around with a Bible in our hands all the time. In times of stress or anxiety we may not have a Bible nearby, and even if we do, we may not feel like reading it, searching through it for some word of comfort. This is the advantage of having a biblical memory bank.

Take an obvious example: A married man away on a business trip strikes up a conversation with a woman he just met. If he's had any exposure to the Bible at all, the words "You shall not commit adultery" may cross his mind. If the precise words do not, at least the basic thought will. And if he's lucky—and if his wife is lucky—his remembering those words will affect his behavior.

I'll use another example from my own life. My grandmother frequently repeats a verse that was a favorite of her own mother, Hebrews 10:25: "Not forsaking the assembling of ourselves together." In context, the verse refers to the need Christians have to meet together for worship. In fact, Hebrews presents this as a command, and so my grandmother and her mother interpreted it. Whenever I get the urge to skip church, I can practically hear my grandmother's voice saying those words. Amazing what repetition can do, isn't it? She did her work well, and apparently so did her own mother. Good. That verse from Hebrews is important. I'm happy to say it isn't the only Bible verse that has been part of my grandmother's memory bank.

Two friends of mine, a married couple, went through some marital strife a few years ago. They're on the mend now, and the husband mentioned to me that one thing that pulled them through was the verse that says that love "beareth all things, believeth all things, hopeth all things, endureth all things." He couldn't remember exactly where that verse is—it's 1 Corinthians 13:7—but he said the "love endureth all things" part stuck in his mind through twelve years of marriage.

In case you were wondering, this practice of tucking away Bible verses in our minds is urged by the Bible itself. Consider a few of these verses:

"In your hearts set apart Christ as Lord. Always be prepared to give an answer to everyone who asks you to give the reason for the hope that you have" (1 Peter 3:15).

"Your commands make me wiser than my enemies, for they are ever with me. I have more insight than all my teachers, for I meditate on your statutes. I have more understanding than the elders, for I obey your precepts" (Psalm 119:98–100).

"I have hidden your word in my heart that I might not sin against you" (Psalm 119:11).

"Let the word of Christ dwell in you richly as you teach and admonish one another with all wisdom, and as you sing psalms, hymns and spiritual songs with gratitude in your hearts to God" (Colossians 3:16).

These are just a few of the Bible's words concerning memorizing and meditating on God's word. Keep in mind that for hundreds of years most people did not have their own copies of the Bible. Bibles were rare and fairly expensive, so people had to share. A person's exposure to the Bible may have happened only in church, or around the family Bible. In such a situation, if a person wanted access to the Bible—and many people did—they had to store it in their minds.

The situation has changed. Most people can afford a Bible, and if you can't, organizations like the American Bible Society and the Gideons give them away. But the human need to "hide the word in our heart" hasn't changed. Having the words in the printed book is fine, but there's nothing quite like having them engraved on the mind.

PACKAGING A MEMORY

Religious publishers work on the same principle as all publishers: find a need and fill it. At least one, NavPress, has found a need (an aid to Bible memorization) and filled it (with their *Topical Memory System*). The NavPress system is wonderful. It uses cards about the size of a business card that you take with you in a plastic pocket pack. Carrying them with your wherever you go, you can look at the verses when you have spare moments and brush up on ones you memorized previously. The system uses verses on key topics of the Bible (temptation, for example), so you usually memorize several verses on the same topic. The verses are usually the most important verses on a particular topic, and also the easiest to memorize. The system also comes with the memory verses printed in several different Bible versions—the King James Version, the New International Version and most other popular versions.

But of course, a homemade version of this system is easy to make. Using small file cards, which are more durable than slips of paper, you can write a favorite verse on one side, then the reference—book, chapter and verse—on the other side. You can write on one side of a card, "God was reconciling the world to himself in Christ." On the other side of the card you can write "2 Corinthians 5:19" and maybe the topic ("salvation" or "Jesus Christ"). As you begin to memorize verses, you can test your memory by looking at the back side with the reference and trying to recite the verse. And, by the way, writing out a verse is a helpful part of memorizing. (It's a lot more fun and rewarding than in your younger days when you had to write "I will not talk in class" five hundred times.)

As with the Topical Memory System, you can carry your cards with you to work, to the gym, anywhere. Modern life is full of frustrating spare moments—often waiting in line, for instance, or waiting on the phone while you're on hold. Instead of doing what most people do—fuming or grumbling—you can put these useless minutes to good use, rereading your memory verses. Or give your brain something to do while you're working your muscles on a Stairmaster or a treadmill.

If you're new at this, try one verse, a short one. Try 1 John 4:8: "Whoever does not love does not know God, because God is love." (If you feel intimidated by this, try the short form, "God is love.") Read the verse, and then write it on a slip of paper or a card. Read it aloud. Then put the paper face down and see if you can say the verse from memory. Check the paper. If you missed a word or two, don't be frustrated.

When you've chosen a verse you want to memorize, try paraphrasing it—that is, restating it in your own words and then writing those down. Understand that restating it in your own words doesn't mean rewording it in a way that suits you. Take one of the Ten Commandments: "You shall not commit adultery" (Exodus 20:14). Although that's a pretty straightforward, easy-to-remember verse, you could write it down this way: "I must not be unfaithful to my spouse." That's a pretty accurate paraphrase. It would *not* be accurate to paraphrase it, "I should not be unfaithful to my wife, except that the last few weeks she's really getting on my nerves and we don't love each other like we used to anyway, so . . ." Putting your own spin on the Bible is something all human beings do—but in doing so, we're missing out on what the Bible really says.

Anyway, you'll find paraphrasing a great aid in memorizing a verse. But make up your mind to memorize the verse as it is in the Bible, whatever translation you may be using. Your own paraphrase is just an aid, helping you connect the words on the page to your own mind.

Besides paraphrasing, you can aid your memorizing by visualizing whenever possible. In our video-saturated age, we are probably more visual than people ever were. We've already said that it helps your memory by writing a verse down, actually seeing it on the page. But even words in ink and paper are less stimulating to us than actual pictures. Take a favorite verse, a saying of Jesus: "Come to me, all you who are weary and burdened, and I will give you rest" (Matthew 11:28). This isn't a very visual verse. But notice the word *burden*. Can you visualize a person—yourself, maybe?—carrying a huge load on your back? Picture yourself with an enormous bundle strapped on you. You are bending low, maybe sweating, your face pained. Up ahead on the path is someone—Jesus, however you picture him—saying, "I will give you rest." Perhaps he has his arms extended, indicating he is ready to take the burden you're carrying—or maybe catching you just before you fall down from fatigue. Does visualizing the verse this way help you? It seems to aid most people. Even if you are no Rembrandt, you might want to make a quick sketch of how you visualize the verse, even using just stick figures. (If you have a copy of the Good News Bible version, also called Today's English Version, it has some excellent drawings showing how Bible verses can be illustrated very simply but dramatically.)

Another example could be Jesus' words on worry: "Who of you by worrying can add a single hour to his life?" (Matthew 6:27). You could sketch a stick figure of a person, a worried expression on his face, staring at a large clock. Or try this verse: "All a man's ways seem right to him, but the Lord weighs the heart" (Proverbs 21:2). Here the most visual words are *heart* and *weigh*. Try sketching a heart, in the usual shape, sitting on a scale—maybe the old-fashioned balance-type scales, not your bathroom scale.

A little mental effort is required to do this sort of thing, of course. You have to do it yourself—whereas MTV producers are happy to put the latest song in visual images, while advertisers package their newest ad slogans with dynamic images. Don't let it be said that you're completely lacking in imagination. And remember, you don't have to show your artworks to anybody. They're for your own use.

Incidentally, make a habit of memorizing the book, chapter and verse of what you've memorized. The actual words of the verse are more important, of course, but it helps you to memorize its location as well. You may want to turn back to the Bible to refer to it again, show it to a friend, etc. Remember how in your grade-school spelling bees you were supposed to say the word, spell it and then say it again? Do that with your chapter and verse references. Let's say you've memorized Psalm 19:1, an easy verse to remember. Repeat it to yourself in this way: "Psalm 19:1. 'The heavens declare the glory of God; the skies proclaim the work of his hands.' Psalm 19:1."

Most of us are soft in the memory, just as a couch potato feels during a first workout at a gym. But a couch potato can, with determination, change as muscles gradually come into use again. So it is with the human memory. The capability for incredible memorization is there—if we put it to use.

FIRST STEPS: SOME SUGGESTED MEMORY VERSES FOR BEGINNERS

There is no official list of Bible verses worth memorizing. Still, over the centuries, certain verses have become favorites of many people. Probably one of the most-loved and most-quoted passages in the Bible is Matthew 5:3–12, a part of Jesus' teaching known as the Beatitudes. (The word is from the Latin *beatus*, meaning "blessed.") The Beatitudes are a list of "blessed are," with Jesus describing the sorts of people who are the people of God's kingdom. The whole passage is worth memorizing, and some of its parts are in the list of verses below. If you're feeling ambitious someday, try memorizing the whole passage of the Beatitudes. It's shorter than the lyrics to your average pop song—but without the rhymes, unfortunately.

This list here is arbitrary—which means any author of a book like this is bound to pick some of his own personal favorites. However, I selected these on the bases of:

- brevity
- popularity with several generations of Bible-readers
- coverage of several basic themes of the Bible

The verses as they are quoted on the next page are from the New International Version of the Bible, a popular contemporary translation published in 1978. Many people, including this author, grew up with the King James Version of 1611, a version that is old-fashioned in its language but also, perhaps for that reason, very quotable. Some people still find the older version easier to memorize—maybe because its language seems dignified and different from everyday speech. Our recommendation if you're interested in memorizing some Bible verses: Memorize from the version(s) that you're most comfortable with. You might find the King James Version very memorizable—over the centuries, millions of people have—or you may prefer a newer translation like the New International Version (NIV). One advantage of the NIV is that in many cases it retains the wording of the King James or uses very similar wording. This is also true of the English Standard Version and the New King James Version, while versions such as the New Living Translation have an even more contemporary feel.

One command of memorizing verses: Don't just pick a verse, including the verses below, without reading it in context. That is, read the paragraph of chapter surrounding it so you'll understand the verse in relation to what precedes and follows it. (Consider that in Shakespeare's *Hamlet*, Prince Hamlet makes his famous "to be or not to be" speech in which he considers committing suicide. The speech is famous and readable all by itself. But it helps your understanding of the speech if you've read the rest of the play and understand *why* this young man is considering suicide.)

As you study the Bible and become more familiar with it, you'll probably become an underliner or highlighter, marking verses that you find especially meaningful. Thanks to the human mind's underused capacities, you may find yourself memorizing these special verses without even trying, just as you probably memorize pop song lyrics without meaning to. This is fine—memorizing without trying to. But it's also kind of fun and challenging to push yourself a little bit to memorize verses on the Bible's key teachings. That is what the verses below are all about.

ABOUT THE BIBLE ITSELF:

"All Scripture is God-breathed and is useful for teaching, rebuking, correcting and training in righteousness." (2 Timothy 3:16)

"Your word is a lamp to my feet and a light for my path." (Psalm 119:105)

ABOUT NATURE:

"The heavens declare the glory of God; the skies proclaim the work of his hands." (Psalm 19:1)

ABOUT GOD'S LOVE:

"God so loved the world that he gave his one and only Son, that whoever believes in him shall not perish but have eternal life." (John 3:16)

"Whoever does not love does not know God, because God is love." (1 John 4:8)

"God does not judge by external appearance." (Galatians 2:6)

"God demonstrates his own love for us in this: While we were still sinners, Christ died for us." (Romans 5:8)

"We know that in all things God works for the good of those who love him, who have been called according to his purpose." (Romans 8:28)

ABOUT GOD'S GUIDANCE:

"Trust in the Lord with all your heart and lean not on your own understanding." (Proverbs 3:5)

"The ways of the Lord are right; the righteous walk in them, but the rebellious stumble in them." (Hosea 14:9)

"It is better to take refuge in the Lord than to trust in man." (Psalm 118:8)

"The Lord disciplines those he loves." (Proverbs 3:12)

ABOUT OUR LOVE FOR GOD:

" 'Love the Lord your God with all your heart and with all your soul and with all your strength and with all your mind'; and, 'Love your neighbor as yourself.' " (Luke 10:27)

"Whom have I in heaven but you? And earth has nothing I desire besides you." (Psalm 73:24)

"The fear of the Lord is the beginning of knowledge." (Proverbs 1:7)

"This is love for God: to obey his commands." (1 John 5:3)

"May the words of my mouth and the meditation of my heart be pleasing in your sight, O Lord, my Rock and my Redeemer." (Psalm 19:14)

ABOUT LOVE FOR OTHER HUMAN BEINGS:

"These three remain: faith, hope and love. But the greatest of these is love." (1 Corinthians 13:13)

"Do to others what you would have them do to you, for this sums up the Law and the Prophets." (Matthew 7:12)

"Love your enemies and pray for those who persecute you, that you may be sons of your Father in heaven." (Matthew 5:44–45)

"The only thing that counts is faith expressing itself through love." (Galatians 5:6)

"He has showed you, O man, what is good. And what does the Lord require of you? To act justly and to love mercy and to walk humbly with your God." (Micah 6:8)

"He who refreshes others will himself be refreshed." (Proverbs 11:25)

"Rejoice with those who rejoice; mourn with those who mourn." (Romans 12:15)

ABOUT HUMAN FAILINGS:

"He who conceals his sins does not prosper, but whoever confesses and renounces them finds mercy." (Proverbs 28:13)

"All have sinned and fall short of the glory of God." (Romans 3:23)

"All a man's ways seem right to him, but the Lord weighs the heart." (Proverbs 21:2)

"There is a way that seems right to a man, but in the end it leads to death." (Proverbs 16:25)

"The wages of sin is death, but the gift of God is eternal life in Christ Jesus our Lord." (Romans 6:23)

"Blessed is he whose transgressions are forgiven, whose sins are covered." (Psalm 32:1)

"The heart is deceitful above all things and beyond cure. Who can understand it?" (Jeremiah 17:9)

"Man looks at the outward appearance, but the Lord looks at the heart." (1 Samuel 16:7)

ABOUT WEARINESS IN LIVING:

"Come to me, all you who are weary and burdened, and I will give you rest." (Matthew 11:28)

"In this world you will have trouble. But take heart! I have overcome the world." (John 16:33)

"I can do everything through him who gives me strength." (Philippians 4:13)

"If God is for us, who can be against us?" (Romans 8:31)

"Blessed is the man who perseveres under trial." (James 1:12)

"The eyes of the Lord are on those who fear him, on those whose hope is in his unfailing love." (Psalm 33:18)

ABOUT PRIORITIES AND WORLDLY SUCCESS:

"What good will it be for a man if he gains the whole world, yet forfeits his soul?" (Matthew 16:26)

"Whoever wants to become great among you must be your servant." (Mark 10:43)

"Where your treasure is, there your heart will be also." (Luke 12:34)

"Everyone who exalts himself will be humbled, and he who humbles himself will be exalted." (Luke 14:11)

"The love of money is a root of all kinds of evil." (1 Timothy 6:10)

ABOUT SALVATION:

"God was reconciling the world to himself in Christ." (2 Corinthians 5:19)

"God did not send his Son into the world to condemn the world, but to save the world through him." (John 3:17)

"Jesus answered, 'I am the way and the truth and the life. No one comes to the Father except through me.'" (John 14:6)

"Here is a trustworthy saying that deserves full acceptance: Christ Jesus came into the world to save sinners." (1 Timothy 1:15)

"In repentance and rest is your salvation, in quietness and trust is your strength." (Isaiah 30:15)

ABOUT ETERNAL LIFE:

"Surely goodness and love will follow me all the days of my life, and I will dwell in the house of the Lord forever." (Psalm 23:6)

"Jesus said to her, 'I am the Resurrection and the life. He who believes in me will live, even though he dies.'" (John 11:25)

"As in Adam all die, so in Christ all will be made alive." (1 Corinthians 15:22)

"Our citizenship is in heaven." (Philippians 3:20)

"The world and its desires pass away, but the man who does the will of God lives forever." (1 John 2:17)

"Blessed are the dead who die in the Lord." (Revelation 14:13)

ABOUT PERSONAL RENEWAL:

"If anyone is in Christ, he is a new creation; the old has gone, the new has come!" (2 Corinthians 5:17)

"Do not conform any longer to the pattern of this world, but be transformed by the renewing of your mind." (Romans 12:2)

"Whatever you do, whether in word or deed, do it all in the name of the Lord Jesus." (Colossians 3:17)

"A broken and contrite heart, O God, you will not despise." (Psalm 51:17)

"Those who hope in the Lord will renew their strength. They will soar on wings like eagles." (Isaiah 40:31)

"Blessed are those who hunger and thirst for righteousness, for they will be filled." (Matthew 5:6)

ABOUT FREEDOM:

"Where the Spirit of the Lord is, there is freedom." (2 Corinthians 3:17)

"If the Son [Jesus] sets you free, you will be free indeed." (John 8:36)

ABOUT TEMPTATION:

"Resist the devil, and he will flee from you." (James 4:7)

"God is faithful; he will not let you be tempted beyond what you can bear." (1 Corinthians 10:13).

ABOUT LOVING PEOPLE WE DON'T LIKE:

"Do not be overcome by evil, but overcome evil with good." (Romans 12:21)

"Above all, love each other deeply, because love covers over a multitude of sins." (1 Peter 4:8)

"Let us not love with words or tongue but with actions and in truth." (1 John 3:18)

"Blessed are the merciful, for they will be shown mercy." (Matthew 5:7)

ABOUT FORGIVENESS:

"Do not judge, and you will not be judged. Do not condemn, and you will not be condemned. Forgive, and you will be forgiven." (Luke 6:37)

"Be kind and compassionate to one another, forgiving each other, just as in Christ God forgave you." (Ephesians 4:32)

"Forgive as the Lord forgave you." (Colossians 3:13)

ABOUT JOY IN LIVING:

"The cheerful heart has a continual feast." (Proverbs 15:15)

"[Jesus:] 'I have come that they may have life, and have it to the full.'" (John 10:10)

"Light is shed upon the righteous and joy on the upright in heart." (Psalm 97:11)

"The peace of God, which transcends all understanding, will guard your hearts and your minds in Christ Jesus." (Philippians 4:7)

BOOK 2 ALSO INCLUDED:

Old Testament Passages Quoted by Jesus

Old Testament Passages That the New Testament Applied to Jesus

Psalm Passages Echoed in Jesus' Passion

Old Testament Passages That the Jews of Jesus' Time Saw as Prophecies of the Messiah

Chronology of the Time of Jesus

From Adam to the Apostles:
A Concise Chronology of Bible Times

You can read and enjoy the Bible without knowing when events in the Bible took place. Learning valuable life lessons by reading about King David is more important than knowing that David reigned in Israel around 1000 BC. Still, it helps to see the sequence of Bible events. It also helps us to remember that events in the Bible actually took place—they weren't just visions or legends.

This chapter presents the actual historical dates when key events in the Bible took place. More importantly, this is a "quickie" tour of the Bible from beginning to end, giving you a concise overview of major people and movements.

Chronology of the Old Testament

THE BEGINNINGS

We do not know the precise dates for the events in the early chapters of Genesis. However, long, long ago, God created the universe, including man and woman, out of nothing and called all his creation "good." Man and woman (Adam and Eve, that is) chose to disobey God (this is called "the Fall of man" or "man's fall into sin") and were punished by being expelled from the beautiful garden God had given them and forced to work hard for a living. Their firstborn son Cain, became the first murderer by killing his younger brother, Abel. Human wickedness escalated, and God resolved to punish mankind with a universal flood. God spared one righteous man, Noah, along with Noah's family, who also survived—along with specimens from the animal kingdom—in an enormous boat, the ark. After the flood subsided, Noah's sons populated the world again. Human evil continued, however, and arrogant people tried to "reach heaven" by building the tower of Babel. God punished their arrogance by changing one universal language into hundreds of incomprehensible tongues.

- Creation *(Genesis 1–2)*
- Adam and Eve in the garden of Eden *(Genesis 3)*
- Cain and Abel *(Genesis 4)*
- Noah and the great flood *(Genesis 6–9)*
- The tower of Babel *(Genesis 11)*

THE PATRIARCHS

The nation of Israel had its beginnings with Abraham, whom God calls to be the "father of a great nation." Abraham moved from Ur, a pagan country, to the land of Canaan. Abraham and his nephew Lot witnessed the destruction of the immoral cities of Sodom and Gomorrah. In old age Abraham fathered his longed-for son Isaac. Strangely, God then asked him to sacrifice Isaac. Abraham, a man of faith, obeyed, but an angel intervened at the last minute, commending Abraham for his faithfulness. Isaac fathered the crafty trickster Jacob, later nicknamed Israel. (Collectively, Abraham, Isaac and Jacob are known as the patriarchs.) By his wives and concubines, Jacob/Israel fathered twelve sons, ancestors of the twelve tribes of Israel. His favorite son Joseph, provoked his brothers' jealousy and ended up sold into slavery in Egypt. With wisdom and God's oversight, Joseph became the pharaoh's right-hand man. Later this worked out to save Jacob's family, who suffered a famine in their homeland. The brothers were reunited, Jacob found the long-lost Joseph and the families settled happily in Egypt.

- Abraham leaves Ur and settles in Canaan. c. 1900 BC *(Genesis 12–20)*
- Isaac, son of Abraham, is born. *(Genesis 21–22)*
- Jacob, son of Isaac, is born. *(Genesis 25)*
- Jacob (also named Israel) has twelve sons, the ancestors of the twelve tribes of Israel.

One son, Joseph, becomes chief advisor to Egypt's pharaoh. *(Genesis 27–50)*

ISRAEL IN EGYPT

A new ruling family in Egypt decided the numerous Israelites there were a threat. They were enslaved by the Egyptians. Through a curious turn of events, an Israelite child, Moses, was raised in the Egyptian court. Later, identified as an Israelite, he was forced into exile in the wilderness, where God called him to lead the Israelite slaves to freedom in their homeland of Canaan. Aided by his brother Aaron, ancestor of Israel's high priests, Moses confronted the Egyptian pharaoh (probably Rameses II), demanding that he release the slaves. Pharaoh finally did—after God sent several horrible plagues on the Egyptians. The Israelites departed, and when Pharaoh, after a quick change of mind, sent his armies after the Israelites, the soldiers were drowned miraculously in the Red Sea.

Following God's deliverance of the Israelites, he delivered his divine Law, including the Ten Commandments, to Moses. The liberated Israelites proved ungrateful to both God and Moses. As they made their way slowly from Egypt to Canaan, Moses and God put up with rebellions and attacks from the nations Israel passed through. After forty years in the wilderness, poor Moses died before the nation finally entered the land God had promised them.

Moses is the great hero of the Old Testament, Israel's lawgiver and liberator. He had his faults—the Old Testament shows him warts and all—but he was highly moral and one of the great leaders in world history. He is considered the author of the first five books of the Old Testament, and is mentioned in the Old Testament more than any other person.

The exit—exodus—from Egypt is the key event in the Old Testament. For the Israelites/Jews, it was the great thing that God did to show that Israel was his chosen people. The feast known as Passover, still celebrated by Jews today, commemorates the liberation from Egypt.

- The Israelites (Jacob's sons' descendants) are enslaved in Egypt. c. 1700 BC–c.1250 BC (*Exodus 1*)
- Moses, an Israelite reared in the Egyptian court, leads the Israelites out of Egypt, preceded by miraculous plagues on the Egyptians. c. 1250 BC (*Exodus 2-15*)
- The Israelites wander in the desert for forty years before entering the land of Canaan. In this period Moses receives the Law at Mount Sinai and passes on divinely given laws to the Israelites. c. 1250 BC–c. 1210 BC (*Exodus 16-Deuteronomy 34*)

CONQUERING AND SETTLING THE LAND OF CANAAN

Moses' successor Joshua led the Israelites as they settled in Canaan, their homeland promised by God. The conquest/settlement was extremely violent, since the native inhabitants resisted the invasion. God often intervened miraculously to aid the Israelites in defeating the idol-worshipping Canaanites. (The famous story of the walls of Jericho falling down is from this period.)

In the Book of Judges, the Israelites were more or less settled in Canaan, but they still faced attacks from neighboring tribes. Worse yet, the idol-worshipping tribes threatened to lead the Israelites away from worshipping the true God, the one who delivered them from Egypt. Charismatic leaders, the "judges," arose to lead the Israelites from time to time. With no unified government, though, the Israelites suffered numerous political and spiritual setbacks.

- Joshua leads the first wave of the invasion of Canaan. c. 1210 BC (*The Book of Joshua*)
- Israel in Canaan is a loose confederation of tribes, still often at war with the resident idol-worshipping Canaanite tribes. Occasional leadership is exercised by the "judges"— Gideon, Samson and others. c. 1200 BC–1025 BC (*Judges, Ruth*)

- While under the leadership of Samuel, the Israelites demand a king. c. 1030 BC (*1 Samuel 1–8*)

THE UNITED KINGDOM OF ISRAEL

Israel's last judge was the beloved Samuel. The people pressured him to give them a king to unite the country. He reluctantly agreed, and he anointed Saul as the first king. Saul was handsome and a good leader, but he also proved temperamental and unstable. God rejected him as king and chose David as Saul's successor. Saul and David were sometimes friends, sometimes enemies, though David was always forgiving and respectful. Saul was killed in battle with the Philistines, and David officially became king and made Jerusalem his capital. Despite his numerous character flaws and sins, David was essentially a good king, one who loved God dearly. With many wives and children he endured revolts and all sorts of domestic squabbles. With the exception of Moses, he is probably the best-loved figure in the Old Testament.

David's peace-loving son Solomon succeeded him as king. As often happened in peacetime, Solomon pursued a tax-and-spend policy, building lavishly, including a splendid temple for God in Jerusalem. Solomon gained a reputation for both wealth and wisdom. His many pagan wives, however, led him away from God.

- Reign of Israel's first king, Saul c. 1030 BC–c.1010 BC (*1 Samuel 9-31*)
- Reign of David, noted not only as a military leader but also as a poet. He makes Jerusalem the nation's capital. His numerous wives and children lead to major crises in his own home and in the nation. c. 1010 BC–970 BC (*1 Samuel 16-1 Kings 2*)
- Reign of Solomon, David's son, who builds lavishly, including the first temple of God in Jerusalem. Solomon's wealth and wisdom become legendary, as do his marriages to numerous idol-worshipping women. c. 970 BC–931 BC (*1 Kings 2-11*)

THE TWO KINGDOMS, ISRAEL AND JUDAH

Restless under Solomon's government, part of the kingdom of Israel revolted after his death. The breakaway kingdom in the north kept the name Israel, while Solomon's son Rehoboam ruled the smaller southern kingdom, called Judah, (which contained Jerusalem). For years the two kingdoms existed side by side, sometimes friendly, sometimes hostile. Israel's kings were, for the most part, immoral and corrupt rulers who had no interest in the true God. Judah's rulers were a mixed bag. Some (Asa, Hezekiah, Josiah) were godly men who tried to bring the people back to God. Others (Ahaz, Manasseh) allowed and encouraged worship of other gods, including rituals of child sacrifice.

Prophets arose to confront the kings and preached a message of repentance. The most famous were Elijah and Elisha, working in Israel. Elijah confronted wicked King Ahab and his wife, Jezebel. In a contest with the prophets of the pagan god Baal,

Elijah, God's man, triumphed. Later, Elisha anointed a somewhat good king, Jehu, who wiped out the entire family of the wicked Ahab. Still, the northern kingdom's unstable government and immorality led to decline, and in 721 BC the nation fell to the brutal Assyrian empire led by Sargon II.

Judah, the southern kingdom, hung on longer. Prophets like Isaiah and Micah preached messages of spiritual purity and social justice, and a few good kings like Josiah led spiritual renewals. (Immorality, by the way, was never just a matter of sexual shenanigans. The prophets condemned greed, dishonest dealing, oppressing the poor, materialism, etc. All of this followed when people neglected Israel's true God.) But in 586 BC Judah fell to the Babylonian Empire under the famous king Nebuchadnezzar. Much of the population of Judah was deported to Babylon, leaving only the lower-class people. The prophet Jeremiah, who had predicted the nation's political and spiritual ruin, painfully watched it take place. The people of Judah—now called Jews—lived in Babylon many years. One of them, the prophet Ezekiel, wrote most of his prophecies in Babylon.

Keep in mind that this period of the Old Testament involved constant interaction with foreign empires. The history here is real, not fiction, and 1 and 2 Kings frequently referred to the invasions and conquests of historical figures like the Babylonian king Nebuchadnezzar, the Assyrian kings Sennacherib and Tiglath-Pileser, and the Egyptian pharaohs Shishak and Necho.

JUDAH (SOUTHERN KINGDOM)	PROPHETS	ISRAEL (NORTHERN KINGDOM)
KINGS		KINGS
Rehoboam 931–913 (1 Kings 12:1–24, 14:21–31)	Elijah [reigns of Ahab, Ahaziah]	Jeroboam 931–910 (1 Kings 12:25–14:20)
Abijah 913–911 (1 Kings 15:1–8)		Nadab 910–909 (1 Kings 15:25–32)
Asa 911–870 (1 Kings 15:9–24)	Elisha [reigns of Jehoram, Jehu]	Baasha 909–886 (1 Kings 15:33–16:7)
Jehoshaphat 870–848 (1 Kings 22:41–50)		Elah 886–885 (1 Kings 16:8–14)
Jehoram 848–841 (2 Kings 8:16–24)	Amos [reign of Jeroboam II]	Zimri 885 (1 Kings 16:15–20)

KINGS	PROPHETS	KINGS
Omri 885–874 *(1 Kings 16:21–28)*	Hosea [reign of Jeroboam II]	Ahab 874–853 *(1 Kings 16:29–22:40)*
Ahaziah 841 *(2 Kings 8:25–29)*	Micah [reign of Jotham]	Ahaziah 853–852 *(1 Kings 22:51– 2 Kings 1:18)*
Queen Athaliah 841–835 *(2 Kings 11)*	Isaiah [reign of Hezekiah]	Joram 852–841 *(2 Kings 9:14–26)*
Joash 835–796 *(2 Kings 12)*		Jehu 841–814 *(2 Kings 9–10)*
Amaziah 796–781 *(2 Kings 14:1–22)*		Jehoahaz 814–798 *(2 Kings 13:1–9)*
Uzziah 781–740 *(2 Kings 15:1–7)*		Jehoash 798–783 *(2 Kings 13:10–13)*
Jotham 740–736 *(2 Kings 15:32–38)*		Jeroboam II 783–743 *(2 Kings 14:23–29)*
Ahaz 736–716 *(2 Kings 16)*		Zechariah 743 *(2 Kings 15:8–13)*
Hezekiah 716–687 *(2 Kings 18–20)*		Shallum 743 *(2 Kings 15:13–16)*
		Menahem 743–738 *(2 Kings 15:17–22)*
		Pekahiah 738–737 *(2 Kings 15:23–26)*
		Pekah 737–732 *(2 Kings 15:27–31)*
		Hoshea 732–723 *(2 Kings 17:1–4)*
		Fall of northern kingdom to Assyria 721 *(2 Kings 17:5–41)*

THE LAST YEARS OF THE KINGDOM OF JUDAH

KINGS	PROPHETS
Manasseh 687–642 (*2 Kings 21:1–18*)	Zephaniah [reign of Josiah]
Amon 642–640 (*2 Kings 21:19–25*)	Nahum [reign of Josiah]
Josiah 640–609 (*2 Kings 22, 23:1–30*)	Jeremiah [reigns of Josiah, Jehoiachin, Zedekiah]
Joahaz 609 (*2 Kings 23:31–34*)	Habakkuk [reign of Josiah]
Jehoakim 609–598 (*2 Kings 23:35–24:7*)	Ezekiel [c. 586]
Jehoiachin 598 (*2 Kings 24:8–17*)	Obadiah [c. 586]
Zedekiah 598–587 (*2 Kings 24:18–25:7*)	
Fall of Jerusalem to Babylonians 587 or 586 (*2 Kings 25:1–17*)	

BABYLONIAN EXILE AND RETURN

Empires come and go, and the Babylonians lost ground to the Persians. (Persia is modern-day Iran.) The Persians were more tolerant than the Babylonians, and the Persian emperor Cyrus decreed that the Jews could return to their homeland to resettle and rebuild. Under leaders like Nehemiah and Ezra, the city of Jerusalem was rebuilt (sort of), and an attempt was made to practice a pure faith, with faithful attention to the Old Testament laws. Prophets like Haggai, Zechariah and Malachi arose to encourage the people in rebuilding their faith and their homeland.

KINGS

Jews taken into exile in Babylon
after the fall of Jerusalem 586
(*2 Kings 25:18–21*)

Persians conquer Babylon. 539
(*Daniel 5:24–31*)

Decree of Persian king Cyrus
allows Jews to return home 538
(*Ezra 1*)

Foundations of new Jerusalem
temple laid 520 (*Ezra 3–6*)

Completion of the temple 515
(*Ezra 6:13–18*)

Esther made queen of Persian
king Xerxes c. 473 (*Esther*)

Restoration of Jerusalem's walls
445–443 (*Nehemiah 2–6*)

PROPHETS

Daniel [c 539]
Haggai [520]
Zechariah [c. 520]
Malachi [c. 760]
Joel? [c. 400]

THE PERIOD BETWEEN THE TWO TESTAMENTS

The Bible doesn't say much about this period, but through other writings we've learned a lot about it. The Greek conqueror Alexander the Great expanded his empire all the way to India, conquering the area of Israel in the process. Alexander then died at an early age, with his vast empire divvied up among his generals. Several of them and their descendants ruled over the Jews, sometimes peacefully, sometimes not. Then, under a Jewish family called the Maccabees, the Jews achieved political and religious freedom, although their alliance with a rising power called Rome would come to haunt them later. The dramatic story of these times is told in 1 and 2 Maccabees in the Apocrypha.

During this period, Greek—the language of Alexander and his empire—became widely spoken among the Jews. In fact, a Greek translation of the Old Testament known as the Septuagint was done to serve the many Greek-speaking Jews across the vast empire Alexander left behind. Many Jews, especially the upper classes, became thoroughly Hellenized—that is, devoted to Greek culture.

Along came an even more powerful empire, the Romans. The Jews' territory was divided into three Roman provinces—Judea, Samaria and Galilee. In the New Testament period, Galilee and Judea, with Jerusalem as its chief city, were the sites of most of Jesus' activity—he was born in the Judean town of Bethlehem but reared in the Galilean town of Nazareth.

More important than this period's politics was its spirituality. Between the two Testaments, the Jews came gradually to believe in an afterlife, which was barely hinted at in the Old Testament. Most Jews came to believe that faithful people would live in heaven, while a sad fate awaited bad people. Also, after they were conquered by Rome and their own monarchy was abolished, many Jews believed in a Messiah, a political deliverer who would oust the Roman rulers and establish a saintly Jewish nation that would endure forever. As time passed and the Romans still ruled, some Jews began to wonder if the real Messiah might be a spiritual liberator, not a political or military leader.

During this period, two noted Jewish religious parties arose. One group, the Pharisees, emphasized being faithful in every detail to the Old Testament laws given to Moses. Since Israel had failed in a political sense, the Pharisees believed it could succeed in a spiritual sense. At their best, the Pharisees were good, idealistic, moral people who tried to honor God by obeying his laws. At their worst, they were self-righteous and legalistic, more concerned with petty rules than with really loving God and other people. In the New Testament, Jesus sometimes praised the Pharisees, but often he spoke harshly against their legalism.

The other important religious group was the Sadducees. This was the religious upper crust of the Jews, mostly high-class Jerusalem families that controlled the very important priesthood. They hobnobbed with their Roman overlords and looked down their noses at the common folk and sometimes at the Pharisees. Unlike the Pharisees and the common people, they did not believe in an afterlife. Comfortable in this world, their religion was mainly a ritual matter centered on animal sacrifices at the temple in Jerusalem. Theirs was a religion with little emotional appeal and no hope for eternity. They had a lot of clout but weren't very important spiritually.

Note: From now on in the timeline, the name *Israel* refers to a geographical area, since Israel as a political unit no longer exists.

- Alexander the Great establishes Greek rule over Israel. 333 BC
- Israel ruled by the Egyptian Ptolemies 323 BC–200 BC
- Israel ruled by the Syrian Seleucids 200 BC–166 BC
- Sacrilege of Seleucid ruler Antiochus IV provokes Jewish revolt led by Judas Maccabeus and his brothers 167 BC
- The Maccabee brothers reestablish Jewish independence. Israel ruled by their descendants, known as the Hasmoneans 165 BC–63 BC
- Hasmoneans make alliance with Rome 160 BC

- Emergence of the Pharisees and Sadducees among the Jews c. 145 BC
- Jews destroy Samaritans' temple 128 BC
- Israel conquered by Roman general Pompey and made part of the Roman empire 63 BC

CHRONOLOGY OF THE NEW TESTAMENT PERIOD

When Jesus was born, the Jews were still under Roman rule. Most people accepted it, but there were always agitators around wanting to overthrow and throw out the Romans. One of Jesus' disciples was a Zealot, an anti-Roman activists.

Before Jesus began his public life, his kinsman John the Baptist, was already preaching and gathering followers. John was a sort of "nature boy" prophet, living a simple life and urging people to repent of their sins and turn to God. He baptized Jesus—though he believed Jesus had no sins to repent of—and this marked the beginning of Jesus' public career. Jesus gathered around him numerous followers, in particular twelve known as the Apostles. They followed him around the towns of Judea and Galilee, while Jesus cured people of illnesses, exorcised demons, and preached his message of repentance and turning to God, a loving and forgiving Father. Unlike many Jews, Jesus showed deep compassion for the poor, for outcasts and for foreigners. Jesus criticized the religious establishment—the Pharisees in particular—for caring more for the rules than for genuine kindness and mercy. Like most rebels, his words got him into trouble. The Jewish authorities looked for some excuse to arrest him, and with the aid of a turncoat disciple, the notorious Judas, they succeeded in arresting Jesus and bringing him to trial before Pilate, the Roman governor. On flimsy charges of being a political subversive, Jesus was executed by the cruel method known as crucifixion. His disheartened disciples fled in dismay. But shortly afterwards Jesus' tomb was found empty. Numerous followers claimed he had appeared to them in the flesh and later ascended into heaven. He ordered them to preach his method of salvation to the ends of the earth.

The Book of Acts tells how they did that. Gathered in Jerusalem, the Apostles received an amazing surge of spiritual power when the Holy Spirit came to them, as Jesus had promised. They boldly preached that Jesus was the Messiah—Christ—the Jews had been expecting. Like Jesus, they also performed numerous miracles of healing. Also like Jesus, they were persecuted by the Jewish authorities—one, the Apostle James, was executed. Still, their message spread, not only to the Jews but to the Gentiles—the non-Jews—as well. One eloquent preacher, Stephen, was stoned to death by an angry Jewish mob, thus becoming the first Christian martyr. Aiding in the persecution of Christians was a devout Pharisee, Paul. Miraculously, Paul later became the best-known Christian preacher, the Apostle to the Gentiles who traveled over the Roman empire to spread the new faith. The tireless Paul suffered imprisonment, shipwrecks and other adventures. At the end of the Book of Acts, Paul was in prison, awaiting his trial before the Roman emperor.

Paul not only helped start Christian communities wherever he traveled, but he also maintained contact with them via his many letters, some of which are now in the New Testament. Like Acts, these letters tell us much about the new faith and how the first Christians believed the faithful person should live.

Jesus' other disciples were also busy as missionaries and authors. Two of the Gospels were written by the disciples Matthew and John, and two letters were written by Peter. John may also be the author of Revelation, the New Testament's last book, which describes the persecutions Christians must endure and how God will finally bring about an end to all sorrow with a new heaven and new earth.

Politically, the Roman empire was in control during the entire New Testament period. The international language of the Roman empire, though, was Greek. Because this one language was so widely spoken, the Gospels and Letters in our New Testament were all written in Greek and could be widely circulated throughout the empire. This, along with the Romans' excellent roads and communication systems, made it easy for any new faith to spread. Many of the Jews scattered across the empire believed that God would send a Messiah, and many—but definitely not the majority—of these Jews listened readily to the message of the early Christians.

- Herod the Great begins rebuilding the temple. 20–19 BC
- Birth of Jesus 6–4 *(Matthew 2, Luke 2)*
- Death of Herod the Great 4 AD *(Matthew 2:19–20)*
- Herod Antipas begins rule as tetrarch of Galilee AD 4
- Annas is Jewish high priest AD 6–AD 15
- Caiaphas becomes Jewish high priest AD 18
- Pontius Pilate becomes prefect of Judea AD 26
- Ministry of John the Baptist; baptism of Jesus and beginning of his ministry c. AD 27 *(Matthew 3, Mark 1, Luke 3, John 1:6–35)*
- Execution of John the Baptist AD 29 *(Matthew 14:3)*
- Death and resurrection of Jesus AD 30 *(Matthew 27–28, Mark 15–16, Luke 23–24, John 18–21)*
- Outpouring of the Spirit at Pentecost AD 30 *(Acts 2)*
- Caiaphas replaced as high priest spring AD 36
- Pilate recalled to Rome fall AD 36
- Stoning of Stephen c. AD 36 *(Acts 6–7)*
- Conversion of Saul, later called Paul c. AD 36 *(Acts 9:1–31)*
- Execution of the Apostle James c. AD 43 *(Acts 12)*
- Paul's first missionary journey c. AD 45–AD 49 *(Acts 13–14)*
- Apostles' council in Jerusalem c. AD 48 *(Acts 15, Galatians 2)*
- Paul's second missionary journey c. AD 49–AD 51 *(Acts 16:1–18:22)*

- Paul's third missionary journey c. AD 52–AD 57 *(Acts 18:24–20:38)*
- Paul's arrest in Jerusalem AD 58 *(Acts 21–23)*
- Paul in prison in Caesarea AD 58–AD 60 *(Acts 24)*
- Paul's trial before Festus and Agrippa AD 60 *(Acts 25–26)*
- Paul's journey to Rome and shipwreck AD 60–AD 61 *(Acts 27:1–28:15)*
- Paul under house arrest in Rome AD 61–AD 63 *(Acts 28:16–31)*
- Completion of the temple in Jerusalem c. AD 63
- Great fire in Rome is blamed on Christians, who are persecuted by order of Emperor Nero 64
- Beginning of Jewish revolt against Rome AD 66
- Romans destroy Jerusalem temple AD 70

ROMAN EMPERORS

Augustus 27 BC–AD 14
Tiberius AD 14–37
Caligula AD 37–41
Claudius AD 41–54
Nero AD 54–68

RULERS OF JUDEA

King Herod the Great 37–4 BC
Archelaus 4 BC–AD 6
Coponius AD 6–9
Marcus Ambivius AD 9–AD 12
Annius Rufus AD 12–AD 15
Valerius Gratus AD 15–AD26
Pontius Pilate AD 26–AD36
Marcellus AD 37
Marullus AD 37–AD41
King Herod Agrippa AD 41–AD 44
Cuspius Fadus AD 44–AD 46
Tiberius Julius Alexander AD 46–AD 48
Ventidius Cumanus AD 48–AD 52
Antonius *Felix* AD 52–AD 59
Porcius *Festus* AD 59–AD 62

In these lists of rulers, those whose names are in *italics* are mentioned in the New Testament. The New Testament sometimes refers to the Roman emperor as "Caesar" without mentioning his actual name. (They used "Caesar" generically, just as we might use "the

President" instead of "President Smith.") Luke 2:1 does mention that when Jesus was born, the Caesar named Augustus was ruling. In Jesus' adult life, when he referred to Caesar (as in Matthew 22:21), he was referring to Tiberius. When the Apostle Paul requested a trial before Caesar (Acts 25:11), the Caesar (emperor) at that time was Nero, who later became notorious for persecuting Christians. According to tradition, Nero had both the Apostles Paul and Peter executed.

APPROXIMATE DATES OF THE NEW TESTAMENT WRITINGS

James c. AD 49 (or AD 58)

1 Thessalonians AD 51

2 Thessalonians AD 51–AD 52

Galatians AD 55–AD 57

1 Corinthians AD 55–AD 56

2 Corinthians AD 56–AD 57

Philippians AD 56–AD 57

Romans AD 57–AD 58

Ephesians AD 61–AD 63

Colossians AD 61–AD 63

Philemon AD 61–AD 63

Mark early AD 60s

1 Peter c. AD 64

1 Timothy AD 64–AD 65

Titus AD 64–AD 65

Matthew AD 60s

Luke AD 60s

Acts AD 60s

Hebrews AD 65–AD 69

2 Timothy AD 66–AD 67

2 Peter c. AD 67

Jude 70–AD 80

John AD 80–AD 90

1, 2, 3 John AD 90s

Revelation c. AD 95

CORRESPONDING EVENTS ON THE WORLD STAGE

Rule by pharaohs begins in Egypt c. 3000 BC

Great Sphinx and Pyramids of Egypt constructed c. 2600 BC

Hammurabi, king of Babylon, develops oldest existing law code c. 1700 BC

Pharaoh Akhenaten imposes monotheistic religion on Egypt c. 1375 BC

Greeks destroy Troy c. 1190 BC

The Greek poet Homer composes the *Iliad* and *Odyssey* c. AD 800

First Olympics held in Greece AD 776

Founding of Rome AD 753

Solon, Greek lawgiver AD 640–560

Zoroaster, Persian religious founder c. AD 628–c. AD 551

Assyrian empire conquered by Babylonia AD 606

Minting of coins begins in Lydia c. AD 600

Lao-tzu, Chinese philosopher, born c. AD 600

Pythagoras, Greek philosopher and mathematician c. AD 582–c. AD 507

Buddha, Indian religious founder c. AD 563–c. AD 483

Confucius, Chinese philosopher AD 551–AD 479
Aeschylus, Greek dramatist AD 525–AD 465
Persian wars against Greek states AD 499–AD 479
Flowering of Greek culture under Pericles AD 450–AD 400
Hippocrates, father of medicine c. AD 450–c. AD 377
Death of Greek philosopher Socrates AD 399
Plato, Greek philosopher c. AD 427–AD 348
Aristotle, Greek philosopher AD 384–AD 322
Archimedes, Greek mathematician AD 287–AD 212
Construction begins on the Great Wall of China c. AD 215
Romans defeat Carthage in Third Punic War AD 146
Julius Caesar, Roman general and ruler AD 100–AD 44
Spartacus leads slave revolt against Rome AD 71
Cleopatra rules Egypt AD 51–31
Chinese develop use of paper c. AD 100
Virgil, Roman poet AD 70–19
Assassination of Julius Caesar AD 44
Ovid, Roman poet 43 BC–AD 18
The Pax Romana, years of relative peace in the Roman empire 27 BC–AD 180

Chronology of the Bible in English

Prior to the translation done by John Wycliffe's followers in the 1380s, England had the same Bible that all of Europe had, the Latin version called the Vulgate, dating from about AD 400. Latin was the scholars' language, so most English-speaking people had no access to the Bible in their own language. Church authorities outlawed translations, fearing that common people would get "revolutionary" ideas if they could read and interpret the Bible on their own. Wycliffe's followers risked persecution for making their translation, and William Tyndale was executed as a heretic.

1383 Wycliffite translation, based on the Latin Vulgate version

1408 The Council of Oxford rules that the Bible is not to be translated into English. Violators are to be prosecuted as heretics.

1476 England's first printing press set up in London. After this, Bibles in England were printed, not hand-copied.

1522 Martin Luther's German New Testament translated from the original Greek is published, stimulating other translations into the people's languages.

1525–1530 William Tyndale's New Testament and parts of the Old (Genesis through Chronicles), the first English Bible based on the original Greek and Hebrew. In 1536 Tyndale was executed as a heretic.

1535 Miles Coverdale's completion of Tyndale's version

1539 The Great Bible, commissioned by King Henry VIII and based on Tyndale's and Coverdale's versions

1560 The Geneva Bible, the most popular English version until the King James Version. The first Bible divided into verses, and the first printed in regular (Roman) typeface

1568 The Bishops' Bible, a revision of the Great Bible. Though it was the official Bible of the English church, most people preferred the Geneva Bible.

1610 Rheims-Douai version, a Catholic translation from the Latin Vulgate. For centuries this was *the* Bible for English and American Catholics, although revised considerably by Richard Challoner in a 1750 edition.

1611 Authorized, or King James, Version (KJV), commissioned by King James I. Based on the 1568 Bishops' Bible but used wording from other versions. The most popular English version until the late 1900s

1826 The British and Foreign Bible Society drops the Apocrypha from its Bibles. Thereafter, most Protestant Bibles exclude the Apocrypha, while Catholic Bibles include it.

1881–1885 The English Revised Version, revision of the King James Version. Popular among scholars but never came close to replacing the King James Version

1901 American Standard Version, a U.S. version of the English Revised Version of 1881

1927 The Complete Bible: An American Translation, a readable version by J. M. P. Smith and Edgar Goodspeed

1952 Revised Standard Version (RSV), sponsored by the National Council of Churches. It is a revision of the 1901 American Standard Version. It was widely used but not accepted by many conservative readers. A revision in 1989 replaced the RSV.

1958 The New Testament in Modern English, translated by J. B. Phillips, a lively and popular translation. It was revised in 1972.

1959 The Holy Bible, the Berkeley Version in Modern English. Revised in 1969 as The Modern Language Bible

1966 The Jerusalem Bible (JB), the first Catholic Bible in English to be based on the original Greek and Hebrew. Includes the Apocrypha. The revised "gender-inclusive" New Jerusalem Bible (NJB) was published in 1985.

1970 New English Bible (NEB), sponsored by Bible societies and churches in Britain. More popular in Britain than the U.S. Includes the Apocrypha. An updated "gender-inclusive" version was published in 1989 and is known as the Revised English Bible (REB).

1970 New American Bible (NAB), an American Catholic version. It has become the standard modern translation for Catholics in the U.S. and is often marketed as The Catholic Bible.

1971 New American Standard Bible (NAS), an evangelical revision of the American Standard Version of 1901. Popular among conservative scholars as the best "literal" translation but not considered highly readable.

1971 The Living Bible (LB), a phenomenally popular paraphrase (not an actual translation) by Kenneth N. Taylor. It was the best-selling nonfiction book in the U.S. for both 1972 and 1973. It is a rare example of a one-man Bible version becoming a tremendous success.

1976 Good News Bible (also known as Today's English Version, or TEV), an easy-to-read version sponsored by the American Bible Society. Popular among people who were new to the English language because it uses a fairly simple vocabulary. A revised "gender-inclusive" version was published in 1992.

1978 New International Version (NIV), a popular evangelical translation. Among many evangelicals it has replaced the once-popular King James Version. It is the translation usually quoted in the book you are now reading. An inclusive-language edition was published in 1995 and revised in 2005.

1982 New King James Version (NKJV), an update of the KJV. It has been popular with evangelicals but not as popular as the New International Version.

1989 New Revised Standard Version (NRSV), a revision of the Revised Standard Version of 1952. Aimed to eliminate "sexist" language and make the wording "gender-inclusive." It has become the accepted version in many mainline churches but has not been popular with evangelicals.

1993 The Message: The New Testament in Contemporary English, a popular contemporary paraphrase (not a translation) by Eugene H. Peterson. The complete Bible was published in 2002.

1996 New Living Translation, an evangelical version.

2001 English Standard Version, an evangelical version based on the King James and Revised Standard versions.

2004 Christian Standard Bible, an evangelical translation.

Subjects Index

census, Roman, 77–79
child sacrifice, 134, 213, 276
childhood of Jesus, 360
Christian, coining of the term, 29
cisterns, 40
Claudius, 84–86
coat of many colors, 39
cock's-crow, 21
concubines, 36, 64, 132
contentment, 288–295
Corinth, immorality of, 146–147
Cornelius, 269
crucifixion of Jesus, 80–81, 110
cupbearer, 192–193
Cyrus, 192

Dagon, 245–246, 418–419
Damascus Road, 289, 322
dancing, 4–6, 217
Daniel, 183–188
David, 1–15, 72–75, 103–105,
    250–256, 308–314
day of the Lord, 201, 221, 358,
    386
deacons, 318
Deborah, 99–101, 411
Delilah, 417–418
demons, casting out, 19, 49–52,
    86, 108
devil, 372–375
Diaspora, 196
Docetism, 360
Domitian, 120
dreams, 34, 39–43

Eden, 122, 363–368
Edom, 33
Eli, 244–246
Elijah, 86, 123, 212–223
Eliphaz, 70–71
Elisha, 219, 222–226
Elizabeth, 376–379
Elkanah, 243
Elymas, 325
Enoch, 122–124

Epicureans, 144
Esau, 31–34, 36–38
Esther, 188–191
Ethiopia, 321
Ethiopian eunuch, 205, 321–322
Eunice, 403
eunuchs, 41, 193, 225, 321
Euodia and Synteche, 142
Eve, 363–368
Ezekiel, 230, 355
Ezra, 192–193, 195

Fall of man, 366
family life in the time of Jesus,
    380–383
famine, 43, 101–102, 130
farming in Canaan, 102, 413
Felix, 270, 344–346
fertility religions, 161, 214–218,
    278, 393–394, 411–413
Festus, 86, 269–271, 346
fishers of men, 16–17
flax, 97
Flood, the, 124–129
friends of Caesar, 80, 83
friends of God, 83, 311, 319, 353
friendship, pagan conception
    of, 83

Gabriel, 208, 377–378, 442
Galilee, Sea of, 18, 111, 228,
    382
Gaza, 416–418
Gehazi, 28, 224–225, 382
genealogy of Jesus, 92–93,
    238–239, 356
Gethsemane, 20, 108, 173–174,
    235, 360, 397
giants, 124–125
Gibeon, 409–410
Gideon, 411–414
gleaning, 102–103
Gnostics, 447, 453–454
gods, Greek, 146–147, 327
goel, 74

golden calf, 161–162, 338
Goliath, 2–3, 251
Gomer, 391–395
Gospels
    authors of, 115–117, 227–239
    "hidden," 451–454
government, Christian view of,
    89–91
grass, symbolism of, 424

Habakkuk, 71
Hagar, 132–133
Ham, 128
Haman, 189–191
Hannah, 243–244
harems, 64–65, 73
Hebron, 310–311
Herod Agrippa I, 26, 81, 114,
    267–268
Herod Agrippa II, 86, 269–271
Herod Antipas, 385, 388–389
Herod the Great, 79, 228,
    258–264
Herodias, 388–389
Hezekiah, 426–428
High Priest (title of Jesus),
    353–354, 359–361
high priestly prayer of Jesus,
    353–354
Hilkiah, 285
Holy of Holies (or Most Holy
    Place), 180, 336, 361
Holy One, 50, 353, 391,
    423–425
Hor, Mount, 335
horns of the altar, 315
Hosea, 391–395
house churches, 400
Huldah, 285
humanity of Jesus, 354–361
hunting, 303–304
Hushai, 73

Ichabod, 246
IHS, 210

Scripture Reference Index